YALE LAW SCHOOL STUDIES, 3

Publication of this book was assisted by

the Fund established in memory of

Louis S. Weiss

PREVIOUSLY PUBLISHED:

1. E. M. BORCHARD AND W. H. WYNNE,
   State Insolvency and Foreign Bond Holders

2. H. LASSWELL AND A. KAPLAN,
   Power and Society

LOYALTY and SECURITY

Employment Tests in the United States

by RALPH S. BROWN, JR.

New Haven

YALE UNIVERSITY PRESS, 1958

To My Parents

Preface

THE ISSUES and events surrounding loyalty and security tests for employment are very much in flux. Supreme Court decisions and Congressional or executive action may make parts of this book obsolete in a short time—even before it appears. Change, rapid and often unplanned, has been characteristic of the programs of the last decade. Created in response to acute and natural anxieties, they show the impact of many stresses and conflicting ideas. But the main outlines and the main problems are not ephemeral. They are part of the conflict between the open society and the closed society, part of the cost of survival for a society that aspires to remain free.

Barring a cataclysm or the millennium, these problems will be with us for a long time, like the related issues of which Dean Acheson spoke in 1946:

> Our name for problems is significant. We call them headaches. You take a powder and they are gone. These pains . . . are not like that. They are like the pain of earning a living. They will stay with us until death. We have got to understand that all our lives the danger, the uncertainty, the need for alertness, for effort, for discipline will be upon us.[1]

Of equal weight with the need for alertness and discipline, as Mr. Acheson would be the first to remind us, is the need to cherish respect for human dignity and individual freedom. These are values which tend to be subordinated in a global struggle for power and survival. Nowhere is this more evident than in the policies and practices of our loyalty and security programs. The central problem of employment tests, then, is part of the larger problem of reconciling the needs of national security with the claims of individual freedom.

The purpose of this book is first to explore and synthesize our disorderly growth of loyalty and security measures, and then to suggest ways of correcting or eliminating their apparent excesses. To provide focus and to hold the work within bounds, I have kept close to the sub-

1. Address of June 4, 1946, quoted from *The Pattern of Responsibility,* ed. Bundy (Boston, Houghton Mifflin, 1952), p. 18.

ject of employment tests, and therefore have little to say about other internal security techniques, such as passport restrictions and political deportations. I have also had to resist the lure of the far-flung and sometimes far-fetched trivia of anticommunism. For example, New York City requires a loyalty oath of those applying for permits to fish in its reservoirs.[2] Is this a useful security measure, or just another way of penalizing Communists?

Within the prescribed boundaries, the scheme of the book is comprehensive. It surveys every kind of employment test of any consequence. Still, it is not encyclopedic. It was not possible to record every episode that I knew about, and there have surely been many that have escaped me. Details of regulations and procedures are also subordinated in the interest of comprehensiveness.

Since the inquiry is directed to the situation of the United States, it might be well to keep in mind that other countries, even our allies, may take a far different approach to questions of political loyalty. For example, Professor Otto Kahn-Freund recently called my attention to an important decision of the French Conseil d'Etat. Five candidates who were excluded from examinations for entry to the National School of Administration, and thus barred from the higher ranks of the civil service, asserted that their membership in the Communist party was the reason, and that it was not a proper one. The Conseil agreed and reversed the exclusion. Even the "Commissaire du Gouvernement" urged this result, in emphatic terms: "Is the ruling by which a candidate is excluded from the examination by reason of his political opinions or by reason of his membership in a political party based upon a legally valid motive? For a Frenchman, to ask the question is to answer it." [3]

For us, to ask such a question—when the subject is communism—is to start an argument.

The argument as presented here is not put in technical legal terms, nor are the recommendations and the proposals confined to technical legal remedies. To realize the rule of law in this field will require, as it always does, examination of the subject from many sides. Some aspects are illuminated by fairly precise data, and are controlled by settled principles. Others require us to look beyond existing rules and to raise questions of conscience, of fair dealing between man and man. Layman and lawyer, in this kind of inquiry, stand on the same ground.

2. *New York Times,* May 7, 1957.
3. Case of *Barel et autres,* Conseil d'Etat May 28, 1954, *Revue du Droit Public* (1954), *60:*526, 535.

This book was made possible by a generous grant to Yale University from the Louis S. Weiss Fund, Inc. The Fund was established by his friends to honor the memory of a leader of the bar who, in spite of the demands of a busy practice, devoted his talents with unceasing energy, imagination, and courage to the cause of civil rights and human freedom, to the advancement of adult education, and to the sympathetic guidance and assistance of all who came to him with their personal problems or for help and advice in social undertakings. The directors of the Fund, and particularly Lloyd K. Garrison its president, initially stimulated my interest in the field through their informed concern with it and through their sponsorship of the study by Professors Jahoda and Cook described in Chapter 7. They have subsequently been models of encouragement, detachment, and forbearance as the years lengthened since the work was first undertaken at the end of 1951.

The Yale Law School, besides providing a hospitable environment, has been a source of indispensable assistance. Special thanks are owed to Dean Wesley A. Sturges, under whose benign guidance the Weiss Fund grant was arranged, and to Dean Eugene V. Rostow, without whose helping hand on critical occasions the whole project might have aborted.

The Weiss Fund grant, augmented by research funds of the Law School, enabled me to have the assistance of several able students. John D. Fassett, '53L, now of the Connecticut bar, collaborated in the articles on "Loyalty Tests for Admission to the Bar" and "The Port Security Program," which form the foundation for the relevant sections of the book; he was also the author of the *Yale Law Journal* Comment on "Loyalty and Private Employment," on which I relied in Chapter 18. William M. Bradner, '54L, now of the New York bar, helped particularly with Chapters 8 and 9. Ellen Ash Peters, '54L, now my colleague, worked mainly on Chapters 4 and 13. Burton M. Weinstein, '56L, and Samuel L. Highleyman, Jr., '57L, cheerfully immersed themselves in footnotes. The diligence of these people, and of others whose contributions were briefer, is not fully evident in the finished work. This is so partly because of space limitations, and partly because publications recently sponsored by the Fund for the Republic have made available statutes, regulations, and other material (which my helpers had laboriously collected), and thus obviated many elaborate references. Through the Yale College bursary program, Lawrence T. Zimmerman, '55, and George A. Hoopes, '60, rendered faithful clerical service. The former also returned, while a member of the Law School class of 1958, to help with the last stages of preparation for the press.

Still another use of the Weiss grant was to support research for two studies by Harold W. Horowitz of the University of Southern California Law School: "Report on the Los Angeles City and County Loyalty Programs," and "Loyalty Tests for Employment in the Motion Picture Industry," more fully described and cited in Chapters 4 and 5, respectively. Through the interest of James L. McCamy of the University of Wisconsin, Donald Habbe was assisted in the preparation of an M.A. thesis, "The Role of the Security Officer in Federal Administration," which was useful in Chapter 2.

From the staff of the Yale University Press, I should like to mention especially David H. Horne, a sympathetic and tireless editor. He also made the index.

It is a pleasure to record a long list of those who were helpful, in more than a routine way, with criticism, information, or interviews. Three groups are not named individually. First, my colleagues, past and present, at the Law School, though some of them did far more than academic neighborliness would call for. Second, government officials; again, there were several who took pains beyond the normal helpfulness of public servants, but I will omit all of them, on the ground that mistaken attributions of facts or opinions to them might prove embarrassing. Third, people who were the subjects of cases. Here the hazard of unwarranted embarrassment applies with even greater force. After excepting all these people, to whom I am none the less grateful, I have to thank the following:

Dean Acheson, R. Maxil Ballinger, Edward L. Barrett, Jr., William J. Barron, Carl W. Berueffy, Eleanor Bontecou, Dorothy Borg, Joseph Borkin, Bennett Boskey, Lemuel R. Boulware, Robert Braucher, Clark Byse, Montague Casper, Harold W. Chase, Elliott E. Cheatham, Mitchell J. Cooper, W. H. Corrigan, Harold A. Cranefield, Lloyd N. Cutler, Nathan H. David, Gabriel DeAngelis, Sidney Dickstein, Alex Elson, Joseph Fanelli, Arthur J. Freund, Joseph Forer, Clifford Forster, Milton V. Freeman, Warner W. Gardner, Walter Gellhorn, Sylvia B. Gottlieb, Richard G. Green, Eugene Gressman, James H. Heller, Oren Herwitz, William Holland, Everett L. Hollis, Charles Horsky, James S. Jackson, Sandra Weinstein Jacobson, George Jacoby, Marie Jahoda, Gerard P. Kavanaugh, Laurence A. Knapp, Fletcher Knebel, William A. Krebs, Jr., A. Harry Levitan, Herbert M. Levy, Edwin McElwain, Arthur MacMahon, Mrs. James Malone, Henry Mayer, John P. McGoorty, Charles R. Miller, Walter Millis, John Lord O'Brian, Alice F. Orans, Benjamin C. O'Sullivan, John G. Palfrey, Irving Panzer, James C. Paradise, Leon M. Pearson, Daniel Pollitt, H. W. Poulton, Joseph L. Rauh, Jr., Charles E. Rhetts,

Jacob S. Richman, James H. Rowe, Jr., Edward Sage, Wallace Sayre, Byron N. Scott, Philip W. Shay, Anthony W. Smith, Blackwell Smith, John R. Starrs, Harold Stein, Walter Sterling Surrey, Philip Taft, Arvo Van Alstyne, Gerhard P. Van Arkel, Rowland Watts, Jerre Williams, William J. Woolston.

Most of my talks with lawyers and officials took place in the first years of this inquiry. As a result, I have conferred with scarcely any of the new people who came in during the present national administration. This I should have had to remedy, were it not for the great interest taken in the federal programs by Congressional committees in the last three years. The hearings of the subcommittees chaired by Senators Hennings, Humphrey, and Johnston (more fully identified in the short-title list following the Table of Contents) have adduced a wealth of information in the testimony of many officials who understandably told the committees a great deal they would not have told me. Also, a considerable volume of information about individual cases has become available in the last few years, through the work of the same committees and, notably, through the publication of Yarmolinsky's *Case Studies in Personnel Security,* 1955; so I did not find it necessary to continue interviewing lawyers with experience in loyalty–security cases, because the results, I decided, would only be cumulative.

Of equal importance with the sources already mentioned have been the writings of other scholars, lawyers, and journalists who have worked in this field. I fear the footnote references inadequately indicate my debt to them, for I have got useful impressions from studies that it was not feasible to cite, and their great variety makes a complete bibliography impractical.

I have reserved for final grateful mention the friends who read and criticized all or most of the completed manuscript: Thomas Emerson, Leon Lipson, Herbert Packer, Howard Sacks, Alan Westin, Adam Yarmolinsky, and for most perceptive editing, my wife Elizabeth Mills Brown.

R. S. B.

New Haven, Connecticut
December 31, 1957

Contents

Short Titles

ACLU	American Civil Liberties Union.
ANNALS	*The Annals of the American Academy of Political and Social Science.*
ASS'N OF THE BAR, REPORT	*Report of the Special Committee on the Federal Loyalty-Security Program of the Association of the Bar of the City of New York,* 1956.
BAS	*Bulletin of the Atomic Scientists.*
BNA MANUAL	Bureau of National Affairs, Inc., *Government Security and Loyalty: A Manual of Laws, Regulations and Procedures,* 1955– .
BONTECOU	Eleanor Bontecou, *The Federal Loyalty-Security Program,* Cornell University Press, 1953.
FUND DIGEST	The Fund for the Republic, Inc., *Digest of the Public Record of Communism in the United States,* 1955.
HENNINGS HEARINGS	Senate Committee on the Judiciary, Subcommittee on Constitutional Rights, Hearings, *Security and Constitutional Rights,* Nov. 1955 (printed 1956).
HUAC	House of Representatives, Committee on Un-American Activities.
HUMPHREY HEARINGS	Senate Committee on Government Operations, Subcommittee on Reorganization, Hearings, *Commission on Government Security,* March 1955.
ISC	Senate Committee on the Judiciary, Subcommittee to Investigate the Administration of the Internal Security Act and Other Internal Security Laws.
JOHNSTON HEARINGS	Senate Committee on Post Office and Civil Service, subcommittee Hearings, *Administration of the Federal Employees' Security Program,* May 1955–Jan. 1956 (printed 1956).
JOHNSTON REPORT	*Report* of the above subcommittee, printed 1956 for the use of the Committee.
NYT	*New York Times.*

PART I

The Operation and Effects of Employment Tests

1. Introduction and Definitions

LOYALTY and security tests for employment have now been a notable phenomenon in American life for more than a decade. They have roots, to be sure, going deeper than 1947, the date of President Truman's loyalty order for federal employees that is usually taken as the starting-point of large-scale programs. The federal government began to bar Communists and Nazis from public employment at the outbreak of World War II in 1939. Some of the states have prohibitions, especially against disloyal teachers, that stem from the red scare following World War I, or even more remotely from the stresses of the Reconstruction era. In the three great wars of the last century—the Civil War, World War I, and World War II—special measures were taken to remove people of suspect loyalty from government service and from critical private posts. But none of these earlier episodes approached the experience of the last decade in intensity, in sweep, or in the degree of public concern to which they gave rise.

The background of the recent experience with employment tests has of course been the cold war with communist Russia. There was also the limited but protracted shooting war in Korea. The beginning of hostilities was the signal for tightened security measures; but the truce was followed by no relaxation. It seems fair to say that, in the continuing crisis of world politics, Korea was only one bitter episode.

So long as chronic cold war is likely to be our normal state of existence, cold-war practices need examination. We have to maintain a security system that brings us close to the severities of a garrison state; at the same time, we desire to maintain our prized constitutional freedoms, and those human decencies that we prize beyond the Constitution. Perhaps the garrison state demands sterner measures of internal security than we have yet pursued. On the other hand, a long-run equilibrium of security and freedom may be attainable, less rigorous in its operation than the employment practices we will examine. The conclusions that I reach do tend toward substantial modifications of those practices; but these recommendations for change will be postponed until the loyalty and security tests of the last decade have been fully described.

EMPLOYMENT, TESTS, AND PROGRAMS

Definitions are necessary; and the easy definitions may as well come first. "Employment," as used here, includes all means of earning a livelihood and gathers in professional people, who may be self-employed, managers, and others who are not usually thought of as "employees." All these people may be affected by one type of employment test or another. A lawyer may be disbarred; the owner of a business may be declared ineligible for certain government contracts, or subjected to a private boycott. "Employment" thus means any way of earning an income; "employee" includes any recipient of an earned income. I shall also use "employee," for convenience, to refer to those former employees whose employment has been cut off by a loyalty or security test.

"Test" is a generic term for any qualification for employment based on the loyalty or security considerations about to be explored. A "test oath" is one historic and familiar form. As the requirements grow more complex, the test becomes a "program." Mention of a "loyalty program" or a "security program" usually calls to mind the administrative arrangements of the federal government for dealing with its employees, with military personnel, with defense contractors' employees, and other groups. We shall also see, however, that there are state programs, and that some tests imposed by private employers are sufficiently systematized to be called "programs."

LOYALTY AND DISLOYALTY

"Loyalty" is a word of many interpretations,[1] and, not surprisingly, there have been objections to its use as a justifying label for employment tests. Loyalty to a government or a country originally had etymological associations of lawful obligation; in this sense it is akin to allegiance, which in earlier times meant fealty to the monarch or other overlord. A citizen still owes allegiance to the United States; reciprocal rights and

1. The meanings of loyalty in philosophy and political theory are reviewed in John Schaar, *Loyalty in America* (1957). See also Morton Grodzins, *The Loyal and the Disloyal* (1956), for a sociological treatment broader than the current communist problem. In addition to those cited hereafter, other useful discussions of the concept of loyalty, in a variety of contexts, include: Henry Commager, *Freedom, Loyalty, Dissent* (1954), pp. 135–55; Merle Curti, *The Roots of American Loyalty* (1946); W. H. Dunham, Jr., "Doctrines of Allegiance in Late Medieval English Law," *New York Univ. Law Rev.* (1951), 26:41–75.

duties flow between him and the government. He must obey its lawful commands; government must give him its protection.

But for most people loyalty has no such narrow legal bounds. It is something one *feels,* a generous emotion, personal and free. To make such an emotion the subject of tests and sanctions deeply offends some people. Alan Barth and Francis Biddle are good spokesmen for this point of view. In *The Loyalty of Free Men,* Barth reminds us that loyalty is like love; it must be freely given, it cannot be coerced. Biddle emphasizes the personal, moral, and undefinable character of loyalty. And Zechariah Chafee adds that the way for a government to achieve loyalty is to deserve it and win it.[2]

If loyalty is to be tested, it has to be defined, which means that some set of officials has to decide what it is. That, I suspect, is what Biddle and Barth fear more than the debasement of an ideal. For loyalty, when freely given, takes many forms. It is evoked by a shared experience, a common history, an acceptance of common values. As a bundle of sentiments toward one's country, it is closely related to patriotism, but it does not necessarily have the associations of patriotism with ritual and quasimilitary observances. For each of us the focus may be different. The man who is indifferent to Flag Day may be deeply moved by the Bill of Rights. Others may derive their loyalty from the simple familiar features of life that we consider especially our own—baseball, apple pie, the face of the land. With such diversity, how can a test of loyalty be devised that will not stultify a source of national vitality and strength?

This difficulty can be avoided, at least at the start. Examination of the operation of loyalty tests will show that they are not concerned with the wide range of loyalty. They are concerned with disloyalty, and essentially with one form of disloyalty: a preference for communism. The statutes and regulations express this in varying ways. Though much of the language refers to "overthrow of the government by force and violence," in our era this phrase refers almost entirely to communism and Communists. The terms "loyalty test" or "loyalty program" can be defined meaningfully as referring to the disloyalty of those who reject our form of government and society and would supplant it, by violence if need be, with communism. Perhaps it would be more accurate if we talked of "disloyalty tests." But ever since the Truman program of 1947, "loyalty" in this

2. Alan Barth, *The Loyalty of Free Men* (1951), p. 231; Francis Biddle, *The Fear of Freedom* (1951), pp. 185–96; Zechariah Chafee, Jr., *Free Speech in the United States* (1941), pp. 564–5.

special sense has been a household word, so we may as well continue to use it.

However, to say that disloyalty means communism oversimplifies a complex issue. Loyalty tests are not confined to readily identifiable Communists. Major programs do not even attempt such a limitation. The federal employees' program, for example, came to include cases where there was a "reasonable doubt" as to the employee's loyalty. In our eagerness to search out cold-war enemies, we have in many cases undertaken to remove from employment people who *may be* Communists. This pursuit immediately breaks the bounds of any narrow definition.

Moreover, there has not been full agreement on the elements that constitute disloyalty. An acceptable rationale for punishing the disloyal, or for withholding from them the respect and protection afforded other members of our society, requires more than the epithet "Communist." Accordingly, it may be said that disloyalty is a denial of one or more of the basic premises on which the society rests. The disloyal are those who attack the foundations of our society, and thus literally seek to subvert it.[3] For practically all of us a basic political premise is the survival of the United States free of any domination by Communists. Our criminal sanctions against disloyalty reflect this premise. Since the conversion of the United States to communism would mean the end of the present form of government, laws against disloyalty denounce either acts or speech directed at the overthrow of the government.

But when we go further in equating disloyalty, subversion, and denial of fundamental premises, differences of opinion arise. The objects and intensities of loyalty in a society like ours are so diverse that there may not be agreement on what all the major premises are. For example, nationalism—a high regard for the political separateness and sovereignty of the United States—is a badge of loyalty that communism rejects, because of its international character and its domination by the Russian party élite. If Communists are said to be internationalists, anti-Communists must be nationalists. The simple premise that we don't want domestic communism, whatever its global implications may be, also tends to magnify nationalist sentiments. We see other nations weakened by their domestic Communists, and the United Nations hopelessly divided; so we turn to a strong national government for salvation. Now for many

3. See Learned Hand, "A Plea for the Freedom of Dissent," NYT, *Magazine* (Feb. 6, 1955), p. 33, for penetrating criticism of "our constant recourse to the word 'subversive,' as a touchstone of impermissible deviation from accepted canons." Since subversion is such a loose concept, varying with the values of every speaker, I will use the word and its variants as little as possible.

people nationalism is not a basic premise. They see it as a precursor of imperialism and a cause of wars. Such people may favor some sort of world order, to be peacefully achieved. For their pains they find themselves attacked as disloyal, not because they deny the basic premise of national survival, but because they do not admire its exuberant nationalistic offshoots.

Others believe that a major premise of our society is the maintenance of representative government democratically chosen, with freedom of belief, inquiry, and expression as its prime requisite. If they feel strongly enough about the preservation of freedom of political belief and discussion, they will not concede punishable disloyalty even in a Communist so long as he *acts* lawfully. This tolerance may make them suspect. But still others, starting from the same premise, will note that communism denies freedom and attempts to destroy it. Therefore, they say, there is no place for Communists in a free community. Some Socialists take this position, and are then dismayed to find that for other Americans, who take capitalism as a basic premise, socialism is as bad as communism. So it goes. To some religious people, Soviet irreligion is the denial of a major premise; is irreligion then disloyal?

The result is that, though the attack on disloyalty may have started in good faith, and on a narrow front, it has widened to include people who share with Communists any preference that to some influential group seems disloyal.

A final consideration that makes an elementary definition of disloyalty hard to manage is that it depends to a large extent on an examination of beliefs. If disloyalty, as we shall see is the case, is at bottom a state of mind, tests for disloyalty are not confined to analysis of overt acts; they must explore beliefs, which must pass through the imperfections of communication to be known at all.

The consequence of failing to pass a loyalty test is more severe than the denial of employment; it also carries with it a substantial stigma. Barth makes the penetrating observation that "The term 'disloyalty' as it is commonly used today is nothing more or less than a circumlocution for treason." Adhering to the enemies of the United States, giving them aid and comfort, is the constitutional definition of the crime of treason that closely resembles the current disloyalty of preference for Soviet communism. But a conviction for treason, the Constitution goes on to say, cannot be had "unless on the testimony of two witnesses to the same overt act, or on confession in open court." [4] A loyalty pro-

4. Barth, *The Loyalty of Free Men*, p. 8; U. S. Constitution, Art. III, § 3.

ceeding is bargain-counter treason, an accusation of a treasonable state of mind that may lead to a treasonable act. The punishment flowing from an employment test, to be sure, is not the same as that following a trial for treason; their relative seriousness is something that has to be explored.

This tentative comparison with treason serves to emphasize that, though one may try to confine loyalty programs to a limitable area of disloyalty, it is hard to stay within those limits, partly because disloyalty (unlike treason) is not confined to "overt acts."

SECURITY

Since the same questions of loyalty may arise in either kind of test, the chief difference between a loyalty test and a security test is a difference in emphasis and purpose. In those employment tests where loyalty, as I have defined it, is at once the basic standard and the justification for the test, the major emphasis rests on the employee's freedom from disloyalty. The relevance of loyalty to fitness for the particular employment, though not ignored, is of subordinate importance. A security test is—or should be—primarily concerned with the risk to national security created by having a particular person *in a particular job*. When the nature of the job is such that its holder could substantially injure national security, the employment is called "sensitive."

What do we mean by "national security"? For present purposes, an official definition will suffice, one that has had considerable currency because it is used in all the departmental regulations under the Eisenhower security program: "The term 'national security' relates to the protection and preservation of the military, economic and productive strength of the United States, including the security of the Government in domestic and foreign affairs, against or from espionage, sabotage, and subversion and any and all other illegal acts designed to weaken or destroy the United States."

A similar definition goes on to make it clear that ". . . the term national security does not include questions of policy or judgment with respect to other Government matters relating to the general welfare, health and happiness of our people in their economic and political life, not requiring security classification." [5]

5. National Security Council Interdepartmental Comm. on Internal Security, *Report . . . on the Government Employee Security Program* (April 29, 1952; released Aug. 8, 1952; mimeo.), p. 27. This distinction was also drawn in Cole v. Young, 351 U. S. 536 (1956); see Ch. 2 below, p. 24.

Protection against domestic breaches of national security, as distinguished from external attacks either by armed warfare, political and economic warfare, or propaganda, is the province of internal security; and the branch of internal security that we are concerned with is called personnel security.

It is often said that "security" is a more precise standard for an employment test than "loyalty." Against the proposition that loyalty is a state of mind, difficult to ascertain, is posed the inviting premise that security requirements are facts. Certainly some statements about security can be made in fact-forms that will command general agreement. It is universally accepted that successful espionage or sabotage injures the national security. But, as we move away from the simple facts of selling secrets or blowing up bridges, consensus eventually turns into controversy. There are people who sincerely believe that open debate about touchy issues of foreign policy injures national security. Criticism of Chiang Kai-shek, for example, destroys national unity and invites a Communist attack on Formosa.[6] Contrariwise, others fear for the security of the country unless there is the fullest possible debate on such matters. This is an extreme instance of lack of consensus; but, in the range of issues between sabotage and Formosa, there are many other points on which only the most dogmatic can say with assurance what the national security requires.

Another major uncertainty in an employment test based on security needs is that it involves predictions of human behavior, and this rapidly takes us away from the realm of fact into that of prophecy. A security risk is a person who *may*—with some more-than-average probability—injure the nation. We have nothing resembling scientific knowledge about the way Americans with certain political involvements in the 1930's and 1940's will behave in the 1950's and 1960's. Since our ignorance is great, and the danger that we face is of unknown vastness, there is a temptation to say that *any* element of risk is unacceptable. "You can't be too careful." "Take no chances." These are likely to be the slogans.

6. "In Houston, Texas, Walter Ankerbrand and his wife were eating in a Chinese restaurant. They were discussing a radio program with the owner. A man in a nearby booth overheard one of them say that Generalissimo Chiang Kai-shek was on the skids. The man telephoned the police, reporting, 'Some people here are talking communism.' Two policemen descended on the restaurant and arrested the husband and wife. They were questioned and kept in jail for 14½ hours. Then it was decided that a comment on Chiang Kai-shek represented no dire threat to the security of the United States." Leo Rosten, "Is Fear Destroying Our Freedom?" *Look,* Sept. 7, 1954.

Finally, it should not be thought that the search for security risks lets us out of the unpleasant work of appraising disloyalty. Most security cases are cut from the same cloth as loyalty cases, and involve the same elements of beliefs and associations.

There are two other types of security risks, which may be found either separately from or in conjunction with loyalty cases. One will be called "reliability risks." This refers to traits of character and stability that may be especially pertinent to sensitive employment, that is, to positions that have a close relationship to national security. The other class is composed of "pressure risks"; this group, summarily, consists of people whose habits or histories make them especially vulnerable to blackmail by which, it is thought, they may be led to betray their trust. But the essential point in distinguishing security from loyalty tests is that the search for security risks requires first of all an identification of the sensitive areas where risks have to be minimized. Why some existing programs have a security label, and others a loyalty label, is something that will have to be explained.

By emphasizing the open ends of the security problem, I do not intend to put the reader in the frame of mind of a veteran Civil Service official who said to me, "We should never have abandoned the loyalty program for a security program. A man is either loyal or he isn't. But who knows who is a security risk?" The purpose is only to suggest that "security" is not a password to assurance. There is a security danger; there are security risks to be found; detecting them gets one into judging loyalties. A major purpose of this study is to suggest some reasonable limits to these pursuits.

THE POLITICAL CHARACTER OF EMPLOYMENT TESTS

These preliminary definitions, while open to debate and revision, are not strikingly controversial. The next proposition is rather more controversial. It is this: the strongest common bond between loyalty tests and security tests is their political character. Some people do not see it in this light. I have asserted that the tests are essentially anticommunist, and for many people communism is not part of politics. Politics is the orderly process of gaining and keeping control of the government, typified by elections, lobbying, and the like. It is Republicans against Democrats, liberals against conservatives. In this view, politics stops well before revolution begins. Communism, on the other hand, is one side of a life-and-death struggle for power and survival.

But in another sense politics is the whole theory and practice of power.[7] The political goal of Communists is to gain power, by consent if possible, by fraud or force if need be, because it is through the organs of power, notably the national state, that they can impose their ideas and ideals about the good society. One of our political aims is to prevent the Communists from seizing power. We want to foster our own ideas and ideals, which for most of us are embodied in such concepts as democracy, individual dignity, free inquiry, and free enterprise. So long as the struggle for power does not break out into violence, it is part of politics. Employment tests, as one weapon in this struggle, are also part of politics.

They are political for another reason. Even if one accepts the popular definition of politics as excluding communism, the observed operation of the tests puts them into everyday politics. I do not mean the partisan recriminations about the extent of infiltration of the federal government. That is still a third political aspect of these programs, though a relatively trivial one. The second and important political aspect arises from the observation that the tests inquire into, and may penalize, political beliefs, expressions, and activities that are not solely communistic. The search for people who may be, or may become, Communists spreads out in many directions. Since few people openly proclaim that they are Communists, far-reaching inquiries are directed at millions who are not. Elaborate webs of inference and circumstance seek to connect lawful beliefs and associations with unlawful ones. That these tendencies are characteristic of the tests the following chapters will demonstrate.

Though the tests are dominantly political, they are not entirely so. Where loyalty is at issue, social and even religious views may be called into question. Security tests, as has been said, probe for weaknesses of character or of conduct. Also, the political issues are not entirely communist. Now and then the tests pick up a member of the Ku Klux Klan, which the Attorney General has listed as subversive, or of the Puerto Rican Nationalist party, a clearly violent revolutionary group. But such cases are infrequent. The main body of the cases is concerned with the mainstream of world politics—the power and influence and contacts of communism. And in their course the cases reach a far wider range of political belief, expression, and activity.

The significance for present purposes of this political character of the tests is threefold. First, it emphasizes the seriousness of employment

7. For a thorough analysis of the theory of power in a political context, see Harold D. Lasswell and Abraham Kaplan, *Power and Society* (1950), pp. 74–102.

tests. As part of our great conflict with communism, they need to be correctly appraised and realistically adapted to the necessities of that conflict. Second, it requires us to take account of the special safeguards which the Constitution attaches to political belief, expression, and activity. Third, and related to the other two, the social consequences of using denials of employment as a weapon of politics need to be examined.

The first point needs little elaboration. It is in contradiction to the contention sometimes advanced that loyalty and security tests are irrational and unnecessary.[8] Those who take this position say that the forces of orthodoxy and conformity have created tests as an instrument for repressing any kind of radicalism or dissent. But, though the tests readily lend themselves to repressive ends, their primary purposes, I would insist, are the political, anticommunist ones already defined.

The second point rules out an easy escape from responsibility. Confronted with a rival system of politics and morals that is abhorrent, we are tempted to declare it and its adherents entirely out of bounds, and liable to suppression by any means available. Our history includes a number of episodes in which hated and feared minorities were treated in this way; we are not proud of those episodes now. Most of us prefer the dominant tradition expressed in the Bill of Rights, which holds that all human beings have rights, and that political rights include the right to hold, voice, and act on a great range of political views. Free from *any* reprisal? Not necessarily; the kind and degree of permissible reprisal are a central concern of this book.

The third point invites an appraisal of the severity of employment tests. What sort of injury do they inflict on those who cannot pass them, or on all who must undergo them? Are those injuries, whether to income or status, deserved? In legal terms, do the tests invade any legally protected interests?

THE NEW IMPORTANCE OF EMPLOYMENT TESTS

There is no clear answer to these questions, not even the last one. Some very general propositions assert that employers have a basic right to hire and fire at will, and that no one has a right to a particular job, or to any job. But these propositions are qualified in law; and they are at odds with strong policies designed to stabilize employment relationships, notably through collective bargaining. The first of many paradoxes

8. This interpretation is eloquently advanced by Carey McWilliams, *Witch Hunt: The Revival of Heresy* (1950).

we will encounter is that national security policies seem to encroach on another kind of security that our generation has been pursuing—job security. In an era in which we have been striving to lessen the economic hazards of employment, we have intensified the political hazards. The strength of the cross-current is indicated by the fact that political tests sometimes lead to ineligibility for unemployment insurance,[9] the last and latest protection against the risk of losing a job.

The lessons of history, like those of law, are disappointing as a guide to appraisal. It is a common assumption that political tests have markedly extended their reach, not just in comparison with 1940 or 1930, but in comparison with 1920, another time of tension and repression. The observations of two expert witnesses whose experience spanned both eras— Zechariah Chafee and John Lord O'Brian—tend to confirm this impression.[10] Direct comparisons between still earlier periods of political crisis and the present are hard to make. One reads very little about employment tests in standard accounts of the events of 1798–1800 (the span of the Alien and Sedition Acts), or of the nativist, anti-Catholic movements of the 1830's and 1840's (though they gave us a discriminatory phrase, "No Irish need apply"), or in the annals of the Abolitionists, the Mormons, the anarchists, and other persecuted minorities.[11] But we should be naive indeed to assume, when our forebears would tar-and-feather an Abolitionist or shoot a Mormon without much compunction, that they would have any more scruples about destroying his livelihood. It may be that the Civil Service Act of 1883 is the first significant recognition that employment should be divorced from politics.[12] The history

9. *The States and Subversion,* ed. Walter Gellhorn (1952), p. 363. Former employees of the Communist party have had special difficulties with Social Security benefits and unemployment compensation. See NYT, June 23, 1956; ACLU, *37th Annual Report* (1957), p. 18. See also Ch. 13 below, n. 27.

10. Zechariah Chafee, Jr., *The Blessings of Liberty* (1956), ch. 3; John Lord O'Brian, "Changing Attitudes toward Freedom," *Washington and Lee Law Rev.* (1952), 9:157–72.

11. See, for examples of this negative finding: John C. Miller, *Crisis in Freedom: The Alien and Sedition Acts* (1951); Ray A. Billington, *The Protestant Crusade* (1938); C. C. Eaton, *Freedom of Thought in the Old South* (1940); Leon Whipple, *The Story of Civil Liberty in the United States* (1927). There was a going federal loyalty program in the Civil War, pushed by a House Select Committee on the Loyalty of Clerks. See Harold M. Hyman, *Era of the Oath: Northern Loyalty Tests during the Civil War and Reconstruction* (1954), pp. 7–11.

12. Civil Service Rule I, issued in 1884, required that "No question in any form of application or in any examination shall be so framed as to elicit information concerning the political or religious opinions or affiliations of any applicant, nor shall any inquiry be made concerning such opinions or affiliations, and all disclosures thereof shall be discountenanced." For background of the Rule see Thomas

of political employment tests may be hard to write because it is the history of something that was taken for granted.

Let us return to 1919–20 as a baseline. The favored techniques of that period for suppressing Communists and other revolutionaries were criminal prosecutions and deportations.[13] There is no question that on the evidence of recorded government or private action our own era has given far more scope to employment tests than did its predecessor. This has been the decade of investigative committees and of loyalty tests; they have nourished each other.

ALTERNATIVES

When we try to appraise loyalty tests as a device for controlling persons suspected of communist preferences, or security tests as a device for protecting ourselves against Soviet machinations, their merits and demerits should be compared with those of the available alternatives. This is best done with respect to a particular program and a specified objective; but a catalog of the main possibilities should be suggested. They are (1) doing nothing, (2) censorship, (3) exposure, (4) security police countermeasures against severe security breaches like espionage, and (5) criminal sanctions.

(1) Doing nothing has a good deal in its favor as a practical solution, when a manifestation of disloyalty is so eccentric or isolated that it can have no substantial consequences. It may also be the only permissible course, depending on the extent to which the Constitution still forbids interference with disloyal belief and speech, no matter how offensive.

(2) Censorship is a traditional device for curbing dangerous speech. It is worthy of mention chiefly because, in the political sphere, the times have passed it by.[14] But the decline of conventional censorship has been more than offset by a new development, censorship of the speaker rather

---

I. Emerson and David Helfeld, "Loyalty among Government Employees," *Yale Law Jour.* (1948), 58:5, n. 13. See *Code Fed. Regs.* 5:§ 04.2 (present form of rule).

13. Robert K. Murray, *Red Scare, a Study in National Hysteria, 1919–1920* (1954), pp. 231–5 (prosecutions), 210–13, 247 (deportations). Employment tests are mentioned in Zechariah Chafee, Jr., *Free Speech in the United States* (1941), p. 554, n. 61 (disbarments of lawyers); Bessie L. Pierce, *Public Opinion and the Teaching of History in the United States* (1926), p. 128 (teachers).

14. But cf. Comment, "School Boards, Schoolbooks, and the Freedom to Learn," *Yale Law Jour.* (1950), 59:928; Note, "Government Exclusion of Foreign Political Propaganda," *Harvard Law Rev.* (1955), 68:1393. Compare the revival of literary censorship based on obscenity laws, and aimed particularly at comic books and paperback reprints.

than the speech. This is vividly illustrated in the textbook field by recent statutes that require a loyalty oath from the author, or if he be dead, from the publisher on his behalf.[15] These laws, foolish as they are, reflect a widespread preoccupation with the source of what is said rather than with the substance. Conventional employment tests can effectively exclude the author of a book or the producer of a movie from the channels of mass distribution. In view of the fact that official censorship of any medium is likely to crumple under legal attack, it seems rather remarkable that employment tests can fill the gap so easily. For the present, it appears that in the communications industries, as far as results are concerned, censorship and employment tests are almost interchangeable.

EXPOSURE

(3) Exposure is the reverse of censorship. Censorship curbs dissent by forbidding its expression. Mass communications, reaching tremendous publics almost instantaneously, have given new weight to the opposite pressures of publicity. Theoretically a good case can be made for publicity as a democratic and humane way of giving vent to disfavor with dissenters. Unlike censorship, it lets everybody talk—at least for a while. Unlike criminal proceedings, it involves no formal coercion. Unlike employment tests, it involves no direct economic deprivation. Senator Taft once took the position (though he soon modified it) that he would not disqualify an avowed Communist from college teaching. But, he added, "I know of no civil rights infringed by . . . publicity, particularly in

15. Code of Alabama (1954), Tit. 52, § 433(6a), required that all textbooks or written instructional material, in order to be approved for use in the schools, must carry a statement by the author or publisher indicating whether or not the author is, or ever was, (1) a member of the Communist party, (2) an advocate of communism or Marxist socialism, or (3) a member of any communist-front organization listed by the Attorney General of the United States or Congress or any committee or subcommittee of Congress. The statement must also cover the same information with regard to the author of any book or writing cited in the work under scrutiny as parallel or additional reading. § 433(6b) provided that any taxpayer may, by injunction, halt the use of such material as the act forbids. The Texas Revised Civil Statutes (1953), Tit. 110A, Art. 6252–(7), approach the problem in a different manner, by limiting membership statements, for other than the Communist party, to the previous five years; and by allowing a former member of other than the Communist party to purge himself by stating the reason for joining, and swearing he did not know (1) that the purpose of the organizations was as designated by the Attorney General, i.e. "to further goals of the Communist party" or (2) "that it was controlled by the Communist party." The Alabama statute has been declared unconstitutional by the Circuit Court of Montgomery County (no opinion reported); see ACLU, *34th Annual Report* (1954), p. 11.

fields infiltrated for the purpose of affecting public opinion, like the teaching profession, the movie and television field, the publishing field. . . . Certainly, the people of this country have a right to criticize Communists, and even criticize them to an extent which might drive them from the positions where they are able to influence people." [16]

There has been, nevertheless, much outcry against the weapon of exposure. Most of it arises from the fact that legislative investigating committees (at least until they were curbed by the Supreme Court in the *Watkins* case) have been the most successful exposure device of our era. It is hard to say which has been more denounced, the committees or their targets. The charges against the antisubversive committees challenge their purposes as well as their tactics. The committees have sometimes turned the "spotlight of public opinion" on persons who were truly private citizens, entitled to have their privacy respected. Others who might be accountable for their public speech and actions have had their private beliefs examined. Though the investigators, when they had no immediate legislative purpose in mind, have professed to be seeking only public enlightenment, the tenor of questioning has often foreshadowed loss of jobs by "unfriendly" witnesses. As to tactics, complaints include misleading reports of proceedings in executive session, claims with respect to impending hearings that were not fulfilled, and other tricks of press-agentry. There are also the familiar legal objections that notice, confrontation, rebuttal, participation of counsel, and other procedural advantages are improperly denied or restricted. Finally, there are the intangibles of behavior. At some point sternness becomes browbeating.[17]

The shortcomings of legislative committees as sources of publicity are

16. Robert A. Taft, address to 46th annual Convention of the National Canners' Association, Chicago, Ill., "Freedom, the Key to Progress," Feb. 21, 1953. In a news conference after his address Senator Taft told newsmen that his statement that he would not disqualify an avowed Communist from college teaching referred only to those in fields not connected with communism, such as astronomy. *New Haven Register,* Feb. 22, 1953. Sometime later, Taft expressed the view that he had concentrated too much on the astronomer case. *Yale Daily News,* April 8, 1953.

17. Recent material on Congressional investigating committees is virtually inexhaustible. Specifically, see Robert Carr, *The House Committee on Un-American Activities* (1952), esp. pp. 290–311 (browbeating of witnesses); Alan Barth, *Government by Investigation* (1955) (Senate Internal Security subcommittee); James Rorty and Moshe Decter, *McCarthy and the Communists* (1954) (McCarthy Committee on Government Operations). For more general comment, see Symposium in *Univ. of Chicago Law Rev.* (1951), *18:*425–661; Telford Taylor, *Grand Inquest* (1955). Contrast William Buckley, Jr., and Brent Bozell, *McCarthy and His Enemies* (1954); and John T. Flynn, *The Lattimore Story* (1953).

said to be mirrored in the irresponsibility of the press and of the public. The channels of mass communication transmit whatever the investigators emit, without sifting or correcting it. The public swallows the result un-critically, and fails to reprove the authors, either at the polls or through the channels of opinion.

There are of course familiar rejoinders to practically all of these criti-cisms. In their broadest form, the rejoinders brush off the objections to committee purposes and procedures on the grounds that the critics, at best, don't understand the committees' mission to expose subversive forces and, at worst, are actually hostile to it. The press and the public also escape criticism in this view, because both are believed to be making a generally correct appraisal of the work of the committees and of the obstacles that the committees face. These obstacles are said to include the conspiratorial organization of the enemy, apathy on the part of opinion leaders to the gravity of the danger, misuse of the Fifth Amend-ment, and a widespread reluctance to cooperate on the part of those who presumably have broken with communism, but who refuse to come forward, confess their own past wrongdoing and name names.

From this review of the controversy surrounding the pursuit of ex-posure by legislative investigation, we gain only an awareness that exposure, *as it has been practiced,* is a slippery subject. The controversy over methods and powers of the legislative committees has so occupied the field that we have lost hold of their purposes.

The Supreme Court in the *Watkins* case was fairly explicit in its dec-laration that exposure for the sake of exposure alone is not permissible. What the Court held in that case was that pertinence to a proper subject of legislative action must be clearly established before a witness could be punished for contempt in refusing to answer questions. There is little doubt that the decision will have a restrictive effect on the hitherto wide-ranging inquiries of the House Committee on Un-American Activities, and the Senate Internal Security subcommittee. These are the two com-mittees whose work has pre-eminently contributed to exposure in the loyalty and security field, and which have had the most direct impact on employment tests by bringing to light possible cases. It is too early to say how much their influence will be diminished. Legislative pertinency has considerable breadth; but the difficulty of making it clear to reluctant witnesses may dampen if it does not quench the investigators' ardor.[18]

18. Watkins v. U. S., 354 U.S. 178 (1957). In the companion case of Sweezy v. New Hampshire, 354 U.S. 234 (1957), a concurring opinion by Justice Frank-furter, in which Justice Harlan joined, found that state legislative inquiries about

I have digressed at some length about legislative exposure, because, though not my subject, it has been a conspicuous companion of employment tests. I will have much to say about the direct relation of the committees' work to employment tests; here it seemed desirable to bring the larger issues into view.

(4) Security police countermeasures against espionage and sabotage are specific remedies against the most feared breaches of internal security. Their effectiveness will be considered in Part II.

CRIMINAL SANCTIONS

(5) Criminal sanctions are the last of the major alternatives to employment tests. They are available either to repress disloyalty or to punish breaches of security, and are thus of general application, whereas the other alternatives have only limited utility. Criminal sanctions include the trial itself, with its expense and suspense, the penalties of fine and imprisonment (and possibly capital punishment), certain attendant civil disabilities, such as disqualification from voting and office-holding, and whatever social stigma the community attaches to either accusation or conviction. Criminal proceedings are traditionally the most formal kind of official coercion. Their long history and their gravity have led to careful procedures and safeguards for the accused. Whatever the shortcomings of criminal trials, they are a model of fairness, in comparison to most other forms of official deprivation.

However, the effectiveness of punishing crimes already committed in order to prevent future crimes is one of the perennially disputed issues of criminology. The deterrent effect of punishing offenses against national security may not be considered a strong enough preventive against espionage, for example. Of course, a long jail sentence effectively prevents any further wrongdoing by a person who is caught.

The punishment of disloyalty as a crime runs into another kind of obstacle. Disloyalty is a matter of attitude and preference. One can be disloyal enough to turn the whole community into stone, just by uttering "Damn the United States! I wish I may never hear of the United States again!" That was the disloyalty of "The Man without a Country." In this fictional case a fictional punishment of banishment plus ostracism

---

a university lecture and the Progressive party invaded rights protected by the First Amendment. Such a position, if adopted by the Court, would put a more effective curb on political inquiries. See Comment, *Yale Law Jour.* (1956), 65:1159.

was decreed. Ordinarily there are constitutional limitations on punishing people as criminals for what they believe or say rather than for what they do. Of this more later, in Part III.

Despite these limitations, our society has relied heavily on criminal sanctions, even against speech, in times of crisis like the period following World War I, and the present. Criminal sanctions are both an independent form of pressure, and a backstop for the other principal alternatives we have outlined. Thus, acceptance of government employment by a Communist, a breach of censorship regulations, and obduracy under investigation may all be made criminally punishable. In turn, criminal punishment will be followed by further denials of employment.

The range of criminal sanctions has another relevance to this study. By and large, it represents settled community standards of what is allowable and what is not. This substratum of legislation is about the closest we come to a solid footing of policy. But one cannot build uncritically on the criminal law. Some of it is obsolete and unregarded; some of it, conceived in times of crisis, is impulsive and ephemeral.

The appropriateness of these several courses of action varies with the particular internal security problems to be considered. At some points, employment tests will seem best suited to a particular goal; at others one of the alternatives will be; often a combination of devices will be desirable; more often an accumulation of them will be found to exist, whether desirably or not. The purpose is to inquire which one (or which combination) may help to achieve a valid loyalty or security goal desired by the community, and at the same time cause the minimum deprivation of other values. These other values include freedom of thought and expression, mutual respect, economic security, and efficient use of human resources.

This approach is the familiar one of trying to strike a balance when social and individual claims, each with some validity, seem to conflict. Unfortunately, all the elements in this complex relationship are variable. Any solutions will be more intuitive than algebraic. But I assume that the lack of precise analytical tools is no excuse for abandoning a serious issue of national policy. Similarly, the available data are seriously incomplete, as will be frequently emphasized. But while we wait for more facts, new problems erupt; and the old ones remain obstinately unresolved.

In the remainder of Part I, the standards, procedures, and effects of all current employment tests of any significance are described and synthesized. Part II examines the justification for employment tests on security grounds, considers the alternatives in the security context, and makes recommendations about the effective operation of a legitimate security program. Part III makes the same examination of loyalty tests and their alternatives, drawing as sharp a distinction as is permissible between loyalty and security tests; as has already been said, they are not entirely separable. These two parts go beyond description to make prescriptions of the limited circumstances in which political employment tests are necessary and defensible. Part III also accepts a considerable range of loyalty programs as accomplished facts, whether or not they are desirable. It then considers how, within this situation, standards and procedures may be improved to everyone's advantage, and harsh effects mitigated. Part IV is a concluding summary of the whole.

2. Programs for Federal Civil Servants

THE SUCCESSIVE PROGRAMS that have attempted to ensure the loyalty and reliability of civilian employees of the national government have been foremost among systematic screening arrangements in point of duration, thoroughness, and the degree of public attention which they have attracted. They have set the pattern for other federally operated programs that have received far less notice, though these other programs reach the armed forces, contractors' employees, maritime workers, and other extensive areas of employment.

The attention lavished on the programs for civil servants is in part a reflection of the Washington sounding-board, echoing every exchange between a resurgent Congress and an embattled executive branch. Congress took the first modern statutory step toward a loyalty program in 1939. Section 9-A of the Hatch Act forbade federal employment to members of a party or an organization "which advocates the overthrow of our constitutional form of government in the United States." An appropriations rider of 1941, which was regularly re-enacted and then permanently codified in 1955, extended the ban to personal advocacy of violent overthrow, and made the acceptance of employment by such an advocate or party member a felony. Under this authority the Civil Service Commission attempted to check communist or fascist affiliations among the flood of World War II employees. The military departments, under wartime legislation, had the power of "immediate removal" of civilian employees, when "warranted by the demands of national security." The administration of these measures has been succinctly described elsewhere.[1] For present purposes it is enough to observe that the machinery ran down at the end of the war.

1. BONTECOU, ch. 1. See also Thomas I. Emerson and David Helfeld, "Loyalty among Government Employees," *Yale Law Jour.* (1948), 58:14–20, and Gladys Kammerer, *Impact of War on Federal Personnel Administration, 1939–1945* (1951), ch. 6. P.L. 330, 69 Stat. 624 (1955), 5 U.S.C. § 118 (p–r), codifies the Hatch Act and the appropriations riders which, having appeared with only ten omissions in every money bill from 1941 to 1956, became unnecessary. See Senate Report No. 1256 (July 29, 1955). The 1955 Act adds, with respect to membership, "knowing that such organization so advocates." An affidavit is required that "acceptance or holding" of the "office or employment does not . . .

As the cold war with Russia succeeded the shooting war with the Axis, concern about the internal security problem revived. In 1945 a hoard of classified documents had been found in the offices of the magazine *Amerasia,* some of whose editors had strong communist ties. In June 1946 a Royal Commission published its report on the Canadian spy ring, the existence of which had come to light through the dramatic defection of Igor Gouzenko. The penetration of Canadian government agencies disclosed by this report probably gave more impetus to demands for strong measures than any other single event. As time passed, the impact of the Canadian report was strengthened by charges that our own government service had been compromised; these charges reached a climax in the testimony of Elizabeth Bentley and Whittaker Chambers in 1948.

During this same period, though there was widespread skepticism about the reality of these threats to internal security, there were few to question the gravity of the international situation. Here the President and the State Department had taken the lead in awakening the country. Early in 1947 the Truman Doctrine of resistance to further communist aggression, with particular regard to Greece and Turkey, was announced. Soon the Marshall Plan of economic aid to Europe was formulated, just as the term "the cold war" was gaining currency. When the Marshall Plan was before Congress early in 1948, the communist coup in Czechoslovakia had just occurred, and a crucial Italian election, in which the Communists were believed to have a fair chance of success, was impending. The Soviet blockade of Berlin, countered by the airlift, began on April 1. The Chinese Communists were resurgent; Chiang Kai-shek's armies were retreating in Manchuria.

This, briefly, was the setting in which the employment tests of the last decade came into being. There was an atmosphere of emergency, while policies were first improvised and then reoriented in recognition of the fact that the World War II coalition with Russia had collapsed. Wartime tolerance for Communists and communism evaporated. While Congress called for action to clean out the Civil Service, department heads faced the more immediate problem of disseminating and executing new and sensitive policies without the safeguards of wartime discipline and circumspection. It was necessary to reach a new equilibrium between claims

---

constitute a violation of . . . this Act." Such affidavits have been a regular practice at least since 1949; see n. 4 below. The criminal penalties are retained. As of 1955 there had been no prosecutions under the appropriations riders. JOHNSTON HEARINGS, p. 896.

of security and individual freedoms. The first hasty attempts at postwar security programs—in the military departments, and the State Department—had been harsh on the employees, and of doubtful effectiveness. A systematic program was called for.[2]

The immediate result was Executive Order 9835 of March 21, 1947, establishing the Employees Loyalty Program, the first thorough, all-inclusive screening of federal employees. This program lasted for six years. Giving effect to a lengthy period of recruitment and preparation, it had five years of full-scale operation before it was supplanted in May 1953 by the then new administration's Executive Order 10450.[3]

Executive Order 10450 derived partly from the loyalty program, partly from security programs already in existence. A statute of 1950 (Public Law 733) had preserved part of the wartime powers of the military departments. In the interest of national security, the heads of these departments, and (by the 1950 Act) of State, Justice, Commerce, the Atomic Energy Commission, the National Security Resources Board (since abolished), and the National Advisory Committee for Aeronautics, could summarily suspend any employee. If the employee had a permanent appointment within the Civil Service, he was entitled to charges, a hearing, and review before dismissal. The machinery required by this legislation was articulated with that of the loyalty program. Since civilian employees of the Defense Department alone account for at least half of all federal employment, more than half of the federal establishment already had to meet both loyalty and security standards.[4]

2. On the *Amerasia* episode see House Comm. on the Judiciary, Report No. 2732 (Oct. 23, 1946), summarized in FUND DIGEST, pp. 571–2; see also Nathaniel Weyl, *The Battle against Disloyalty* (1951), ch. 14. On the Canadian spy ring, consult the *Report of the [Canadian] Royal Commission* (June 27, 1946). On later exposures of espionage, see references in Ch. 9 below, nn. 8–9. The atmosphere of 1947–48 is recalled in Eric Goldman, *The Crucial Decade* (1956), pp. 57–81. Some of the observations on the problems of the executive were helpfully suggested by an anonymous reader of the manuscript. The earliest postwar employment tests are discussed in Bert Andrews, *Washington Witch Hunt* (1948), and Walter Gellhorn, *Security, Loyalty, and Science* (1950), pp. 92–103.

3. E.O. 9835, *Fed. Reg.* (1947), *12*:1935; E.O. 10450, *Fed. Reg.* (1953), *18*:2489. On the time lag before the 9835 program became fully effective, see Emerson and Helfeld (n. 1 above), pp. 32–3.

4. P.L. 733, 64 Stat. 476 (1950), 5 U.S.C. § 22–1. The Treasury is included, but only with respect to the Coast Guard. There were also special statutory requirements for persons in the various foreign-aid programs; for examples see BONTECOU, pp. 293–9. On the administration of combined loyalty–security programs on the eve of E.O. 10450, see unpublished M.S. thesis (Univ. of Wisconsin) by Donald Habbe, *The Role of the Security Officer in Federal Administration* (1954), pp. 23–36, research for which was assisted by the Weiss Fund, Inc., grant to Yale Uni-

E.O. 10450 attempted to replace this dual system with a comprehensive security program. But regardless of labels, the common elements in the loyalty and security programs are substantial, and the pattern established by the loyalty program is still pervasive. The 1956 decision of the Supreme Court in *Cole v. Young* again ended, at least for a time, any single program covering all federal civil servants. The Court held that P.L. 733, on which E.O. 10450 was based, was intended to apply only to sensitive positions, and that the executive order could have no wider scope. The immediate consequences of *Cole v. Young* were not far-reaching. The screening of incumbent federal employees was substantially complete. Those in nonsensitive positions remained subject to the Hatch Act and the appropriations riders. New employees still had to satisfy a Civil Service Commission regulation which, by barring persons of doubtful loyalty, preserved the substance of the loyalty standard.[5]

This recent diffusion of authority did not alter the essential characteristics of the federal programs. What follows will accordingly describe more or less simultaneously the main elements of the loyalty program, of the overlapping security programs that also existed during the Truman administration, and of the Eisenhower security program.

INVESTIGATION

A distinctive characteristic of the federal program is its routine resort to investigation—a laborious and expensive process—and its correspond-

---

versity. The legislative branch has never had a systematic loyalty or security program for Congressional employees; but the General Accounting Office, Government Printing Office, and Library of Congress, technically part of the legislative branch, followed both the 9835 and 10450 programs; see HUMPHREY HEARINGS, p. 109. On congressional employees, see also Ch. 15, below. New employees of the federal courts make an affidavit which states "I am not a Communist or a Fascist. I do not advocate . . . the overthrow . . . I will not so advocate . . ." etc. This oath with minor variations is taken by all federal appointees (Civil Service Form 61). It seems to extend beyond the statutory requirements; see n. 2 above.

5. See *Code Fed. Regs. 5:* § 2.106(a)(7) (Supp. 1957). For a review of some questions left open by Cole v. Young, 315 U.S. 536 (1956), see Notes, *Harvard Law Rev.* (1956), *70:*165–8; *Northwestern Univ. Law Rev.* (1957), *51:*788. Reinstatements following the decision are tabulated in Commission on Government Security, *Report* (1957), p. 38. A ruling by the Attorney General that reinstatement and back pay would be denied those who did not seek relief within 18 months of their improper dismissal (regardless of the interval between dismissal and the decision in Cole v. Young) was upset as unreasonable by the D.C. Court of Appeals, Dec. 31, 1957. See NYT, Jan. 2, 1958.

ingly slight reliance on oaths and other declarations by the employee or
his superiors. Of course the employee supplies a detailed personal history
when he first applies for a position (the Truman program also called
for an examination of all incumbents; each employee had to fill out a
new questionnaire and be fingerprinted). But the information that the
employee supplies is used chiefly as a starting-point for investigation.

The first step is a "national-agency name check," which means an
examination chiefly of the files of the FBI, the Civil Service Commission, the military intelligence branches, and the House Committee on
Un-American Activities.[6] The purpose of this file check is to see if any
"derogatory information" turns up. What is "derogatory information"?
Anything, it may be said, that bears directly or indirectly on the ultimate
question to be resolved: is there a reasonable doubt as to loyalty (under
the old program)?

Is the employment consistent with the national security (under the
new)? And what has a bearing on these standards? This question raises
intricate problems of relevance. It is fair to say that such problems are
not faced at the name-check stage. The process seems to have become
quite mechanical, with some safeguards against mistakes in identity.
Affiliations with suspect organizations, associations with suspect persons, reports of behavior, expression and opinions that have been filed
because they suggest sympathy with communism—all are extracted. As
the files grow more voluminous, and the kinds of information that are
considered relevant grow more extensive, the chances increase that derogatory information will be found. These untested data may lead to
the summary rejection of an aspirant for employment; but routinely their
discovery leads to a "full field investigation."

Even without the appearance of adverse material in the file check,
the 10450 program requires a full field investigation for every sensitive
position, a category that has been generously defined. For example, all
State Department employment is considered sensitive. In such an investigation, "Friends, neighbors, fellow students, fellow employees, former
teachers and colleagues, even one's grocer or one's hairdresser may be
interviewed." [7] Another round of file-checking must also occur; for as

6. Civil Service Commission Standard Form 57, "Application for Federal Employment," Standard Form 85, "Security Investigation Data for Nonsensitive Position," are reproduced in BNA MANUAL, pp. 15/701–12. Incumbents were specifically
included in E.O. 9835 by Part VI, § 1. For the content of a national agency name
check, see E.O. 9835, Part I, § 3; E.O. 10450, § 3(a); Civil Service Commission
regulations under E.O. 10450, § 4(b) (in BNA MANUAL, pp. 11/10–11).
7. BONTECOU, pp. 83–4. A "background investigation" is the same as a full field

the names of more of the employee's associates come to be known, it is considered necessary to establish whether there is derogatory information about *them*. The result of all this industry is a report popularly known as an "FBI report," though the FBI is responsible for only a small part of the investigative reports that are assembled.[8]

The composition of these reports is one of the most controversial aspects of the process. The FBI, the agency chiefly criticized (however erroneously), stoutly maintains that it is not an evaluating agency; it simply collects facts, opinions, and rumors—whatever people tell its agents—and reduces the mass to some degree of coherency. It is the job of the recipients to assess significance.

Four factors militate against this picture of detached, impersonal transmission of information. First is the imperfection of the interviewer, which of course varies with the capacity and predilections of each individual. Investigators take only sketchy notes, if any, during an interview; there are many instances of interviewees who claim to have been misrepresented. Second is the fallibility inherent when the "raw" files are edited to produce the finished report. Third (related to both the foregoing stages) is an almost unavoidable stress on unfavorable information. The primary object of the investigation, after all, is to discover if there is evidence of disloyalty or of security risk.

The fourth factor involves a policy that overshadows the entire process, the concealment of the identity of many of the investigators' sources. This is not the point at which to discuss the justification and ramifications of this policy. It is enough to say now that concealment of the source is widely practiced, whether the source is an undercover agent whom it would be hazardous to expose, a wiretap that is *sub rosa,* or simply a casual informant who does not wish his role to be known. The system protects everything, and, in spite of disclaimers, *does* undertake to evaluate the reliability of the informant. If it did not, the anonymous

---

investigation, and is a frequently used synonym, e.g. Air Force Reg. 40–12 (Civilian Personnel), § III(10)(c) (June 22, 1954).

8. The military departments have their own investigative staffs; so have the State Department and the Post Office Department and a few other agencies. Initial investigations in most cases are undertaken by the Civil Service Commission, which took over this burden from the FBI in 1952. See HUMPHREY HEARINGS, pp. 182, 190, 504; BONTECOU, pp. 75–76. The FBI investigates initially for certain especially sensitive positions, and any cases of "questionable loyalty," or of pressure risk, are turned over to it. 66 Stat. 43 (1952), 5 U.S.C. § 655; E.O. 10450, § 8(d). See J. E. Hoover, "Role of the F.B.I. in the Federal Employment Security Program," *Northwestern Univ. Law Rev.* (1954), *49*:333.

information could be given scarcely any independent weight. So the report will state whether the unidentified informant is believed to be of known reliability, of probable reliability, or of unknown reliability. It certainly makes a great difference whether the source of a report that the employee is a Communist is labeled reliable or unreliable by the FBI. These judgments must also have some degree of fallibility.

"How Good Is an FBI Report?" Alan Barth asked in a magazine article. Not very, he concluded, on the basis of the scraps of information available to the public. Officials who have used the reports have expressed to the present writer a remarkable range of over-all opinions on their usefulness. They were, of course, not free to give examples, so that an outsider's judgment has to be rather speculative.[9]

EVALUATION OF REPORTS BY SECURITY OFFICERS

Some of the concern over the nature of investigative reports might be allayed if it could be said that the reports are used cautiously and skeptically. But the judgments that are introduced into the reports may not be so important as the judgments that the security officers of the employing agency bring to bear on them.

The security officer was not, until recently, a familiar species of civil servant. Though personnel security officials had necessarily functioned under one guise or another in connection with the World War II programs, E.O. 9835 marked the beginning of the requirement that "each department and agency of the executive branch should develop and maintain, for the collection and analysis of information relating to the loyalty of its employees and prospective employees, a staff specially trained in security techniques" (Section IV. 3). In minor agencies with modest problems, these responsibilities may occupy only one-third of a security officer's time.[10] In the Department of State, with only 11,000 citizen em-

9. For the FBI's position, see J. E. Hoover, "A Comment on the Article 'Loyalty among Government Employees,'" *Yale Law Jour.* (1949), *58*:401–11. The mechanics of evaluation are described in Commission on Government Security, *Report* (1957), pp. 658–9. Barth's article is in *Harper's* (March 1954), p. 25; see also Barth, *The Loyalty of Free Men* (1951), ch. 7. FBI or other reports are of course to be distinguished from the "raw files" and the original investigator's reports, which are never circulated outside the agency. See J. E. Hoover, "The Confidential Nature of FBI Reports," *Syracuse Law Rev.* (1956), *8*:2. Some production of these reports in criminal proceedings may be required as a result of Jencks v. U.S., 353 U.S. 657 (1957).

10. Chairman Philip Young of the Civil Service Commission has testified that 43 out of 67 agency security officers have other functions. JOHNSTON HEARINGS, p.

ployees but more than its share of loyalty–security troubles, the Division of Security had a staff of 322 in 1953. But almost half of the State Department security force consisted of investigators; a much smaller Evaluations Branch had the critical role of assessing the reports of these and other investigators.[11]

Not much is known about these new men. Senior security officers who have made headlines, like Scott McLeod of the State Department, are exceptional. The person bearing the title "Director of Security" or its equivalent in a federal agency will normally be found in the administrative and personnel branch of the agency, reporting to the Assistant Secretary or equivalent ranking official in charge of administration. In small agencies, or those with light security responsibilities, he will still have other personnel duties. Where a separate security office has been established, its chief has in some instances been drawn from personnel work, in others from a career in military intelligence, in others from service as an investigator, especially in the FBI. We know even less about the intermediate people—the evaluators, the attorney-advisors who present cases to hearing boards, the security officers in charge of offices and installations outside Washington. Probably the one element of personal history common to all ranking security officers is that, in the jargon of security, their own records must be "lily-white," which means entirely devoid of derogatory information.[12]

---

388. An example of an agency with only a part-time security officer is the Bureau of the Budget (as of 1953), Habbe (n. 4 above), pp. 61–4.

11. The State Department also has approximately 9000 foreign employees overseas; see Civil Service Commission, *1954 Annual Report* (1955), p. 86. Security safeguards in their cases are on a different footing from the domestic programs; see statement by Scott McLeod, HUMPHREY HEARINGS, pp. 302–5. The figure of 322 for Division of Security staff is from Habbe (n. 4 above), p. 119, n. 125; in 1952 there were 186 investigators, State Dept. Pamphlet 4530, *Loyalty and Security Program* (March 1952), p. 8. The number of evaluators was only 12 in 1954; Charlotte Knight, "What Price Security," *Collier's* (July 9, 1954), p. 64.

12. Much of the information in this paragraph is drawn from Habbe (n. 4 above), chs. 2, 3. There are civil service classifications for investigators; on the difficulty of recruiting competent investigators see HUMPHREY HEARINGS, pp. 502–9 (statements by Philip Young that 50 per cent fail the written examination, and that of the 50 per cent remaining, 50 per cent fail the oral examination). Qualifications for personnel security officers, in grades GS 11–GS 13, have also been established, and are set forth in HUMPHREY HEARINGS, pp. 736–9. The qualifications state that "substantial" derogatory information will create ineligibility.

Scott McLeod came into the public eye because of his role in specific cases—e.g. the Bohlen confirmation; see *Time* (March 30, 1953), p. 14—and because of his lofty position in the State Department hierarchy as Administrator of the Bureau of Security and Consular Affairs with "rank and compensation equal to that of an

The immediate result of the security investigation, then, is a decision by security officers as to what action is warranted. These courses are open:

(1) The derogatory information may be appraised as insubstantial, and nothing done. Doing nothing requires a modest degree of bureaucratic fortitude, for the employee's retention may be later criticized and that criticism deflected onto the security officer. The terms of the Eisenhower and related security programs appear to discourage this course by requiring an affirmative finding that keeping the employee is consistent with the national security.

(2) At the other extreme, the choice is to disqualify a prospective employee on the strength of the investigative report, without inquiring any further. Security officers can and do summarily reject applicants; only the Atomic Energy Commission habitually gives a person applying for employment an opportunity for a hearing.[13] Under the Truman loyalty program, summary rejection was ordinarily not possible. A person first received an appointment and was then investigated; if derogatory information appeared, he was entitled to a hearing. But investigations prior to appointment were made in the Department of Defense and other agencies with security problems; and the Eisenhower program requires pre-appointment investigations in the broad category of sensitive positions.

(3) A third technique permits the employee to thresh out his problems with the security staff, under varying degrees of informality. It has been said that this common-sense approach has been neglected, that much technically derogatory information can easily be explained away, and that the subject of the investigation is uniquely qualified to make the

---

Assistant Secretary of State"; see Immigration and Nationality Act of 1952, 66 Stat. 174, 8 U.S.C. § 1104. McLeod for a time had control of both personnel and security within the State Department, but, after various episodes embarrassing to the Administration, he was relieved of his authority over State Department personnel by Secretary Dulles and left in charge of security and consular matters. See NYT, March 2, 1954; W. H. Hale, "Big Brother in Foggy Bottom," *The Reporter* (Aug. 17, 1954), pp. 10–17; R. Harris, "Reply" (to Hale), *The Reporter* (Sept. 14, 1954), p. 6; and Knight (n. 11 above), pp. 64–66.

13. E.O. 9835 provided for hearings as a matter of right in Part II(2)(a)(b), and Part II(4). E.O. 10450 makes no provision for hearings, giving considerable discretion to the agency and department heads (subject to the requirements of P.L. 733). The AEC provision for hearings for applicants is contained in *Code Fed. Regs. 10:* § 4.22. Air Force Reg. 40–12, §§ 18(d)(e), 19, also give liberal hearing opportunities. For indications that these opportunities are not always available, see HUMPHREY HEARINGS, p. 233 (testimony that Air Force applicants are often denied hearings).

explanations. There is, as usual, another side of the coin. Direct contact between security officer and employee permits pressure, either subtle or crude, to be brought on the employee to resign. This may or may not be the best solution to his difficulties. The employee may also be informally urged to "cooperate" with the security staff by submitting to prolonged questioning, lie detector tests, or other indignities from which an impersonal procedure shields him. In the State Department, where the security officers have had frequent contacts with the employees under investigation, informal pressures seem to have been much employed.[14] On the other hand, I am aware of no complaint about the AEC's practice of arranging an interview between employee and security officer before charges are filed.

(4) A more common step is the presentation of the derogatory information to the employee for written comment. These interrogatories are often effective to clear up mistakes and misconstructions derived from the investigative reports. About one-half of all the cases decided by the loyalty boards went in favor of the employee at this stage without further proceedings. Under P.L. 733 the submission of statements and affidavits is, for temporary and probationary employees, their single opportunity to challenge the information against them.[15]

FORMAL STANDARDS

It is only when the employee begins to participate in the process of evaluation, by responding to interrogatories or defending himself in a

14. The case of Theodore Kaghan presents a prime example of the use of pressure to resign. He had incurred the wrath of Senator McCarthy by characterizing Roy Cohn and David Schine as "junketeering gumshoes" during their European investigation of the Voice of America for McCarthy. While his hearing before McCarthy's committee in Washington was in progress, he was informed that Scott McLeod (the State Department personnel security officer) expected his resignation, with the alternative that security charges would be pressed. He resigned. See T. Kaghan, "The McCarthyization of Theodore Kaghan," *The Reporter* (July 21, 1953), pp. 17–25; James Rorty and Moshe Decter, *McCarthy and the Communists* (1954), pp. 35–7, 91–4. The State Department, during the period May 28, 1953– June 30, 1955 reported 10 dismissals under § 8(a) of 10450, and 273 resignations. The ratio was even higher for the U. S. Information Agency, another target for McCarthy pressures, with only 2 dismissals under 8(a), but with 74 resignations. Civil Service Commission, "Fourth Consolidated Report," JOHNSTON HEARINGS, p. 732.

15. See Haynes v. Thomas, 232 F. 2d 688 (D.C. Cir. 1956). The ratio of cases decided by the Loyalty Boards on the basis of interrogatories is drawn from the Terminal Report on the 9835 program, in Civil Service Commission, *Annual Report, 1953* (1954), p. 32.

hearing, that the effective standards of the program come into view, however obscurely. At this point the security officers or other officials (e.g. the "screening boards" that in some agencies make the preliminary evaluations) must make their doubts manifest, if the employee is to allay them.

The formal standards are of course set down in statutes and executive orders. We have already referred to the Hatch Act and the appropriation riders, forbidding federal employment to believers in revolution, or to members of revolutionary organizations. The basic standard of the loyalty program was initially "reasonable grounds . . . for belief that the person involved is disloyal to the Government of the United States." This was changed in 1951 to "a reasonable doubt as to the loyalty of the person involved to the Government of the United States." [16] P.L. 733 authorized termination of employment by the heads of eleven sensitive agencies when they found it "necessary or advisable in the interest of the national security of the United States." Executive Order 10450, extending the principles of P.L. 733 to the entire executive establishment, reiterates that the employment must be "clearly consistent with the interests of the national security." These general expressions tell us that the emphasis was on "loyalty" in one program and "security" in another. And it is significant to note that the shifts in wording in each instance represented a hardening of the standard: from reasonable grounds for belief of disloyalty, to reasonable doubts as to loyalty; from discharge if advisable in the interest of national security, to retention only if clearly consistent with national security. The later standard, both in the loyalty and security cases, puts more of a burden on the employee to clear him-

16. E.O. 9835, Part V(1) provided, "The standard for the refusal of employment or the removal from employment in an executive department or agency on grounds relating to loyalty shall be that, on all the evidence, reasonable grounds exist for belief that the person involved is disloyal to the Government of the United States." E.O. 10241 of April 28, 1951, *Fed. Reg., 16:*3690, amended Part V(1) after the phrase "on all the evidence" to read: "There is a reasonable doubt as to the loyalty of the person involved to the Government of the United States." This shift in wording has been attributed to the desire to reopen a number of proceedings against employees previously cleared under the old standards; the Loyalty Review Board ordered all agencies to readjudicate, under the new standard, several categories of cases, including all those in which an initial decision adverse to the employee had been reversed on appeal. The Board also authorized the reopening of any other case at the "discretion" of the head of an agency. Another reason for the shift, apparently, was the supposed reluctance of hearing boards to brand anyone as disloyal; it seemed easier to make the less specific finding that there was "reasonable doubt." See in general on E.O. 10241, BONTECOU, pp. 70–1, 150–1, 243; the change caused the State Department to announce that it would reopen "every one" of its loyalty cases. Ibid., p. 150.

self, and a heavier onus on the administrator who clears him. But the standards alone do not and cannot tell us what raises a doubt about loyalty, or when employment is inconsistent with the national security.

The standards are given some content by the "criteria" included in the two executive orders; and these criteria are further expanded in some departmental regulations. The criteria of the loyalty program, in E.O. 9835, are succinct enough to be set out in full:

> 2. Activities and associations of an applicant or employee which may be considered in connection with the determination of disloyalty may include one or more of the following:
>
> a. Sabotage, espionage, or attempts or preparations therefor, or knowingly associating with spies or saboteurs;
>
> b. Treason or sedition or advocacy thereof;
>
> c. Advocacy of revolution or force or violence to alter the constitutional form of government of the United States;
>
> d. Intentional, unauthorized disclosure to any person, under circumstances which may indicate disloyalty to the United States, of documents or information of a confidential or non-public character obtained by the person making the disclosure as a result of his employment by the Government of the United States;
>
> e. Performing or attempting to perform his duties, or otherwise acting so as to serve the interests of another government in preference to the interests of the United States;
>
> f. Membership in, affiliation with or sympathetic association with any foreign or domestic organization, association, movement, group or combination of persons, designated by the Attorney General as totalitarian, fascist, communist, or subversive, or as having adopted a policy of advocating or approving the commission of acts of force or violence to deny other persons their rights under the Constitution of the United States, or as seeking to alter the form of government of the United States by unconstitutional means.

Executive Order 10450 added a sweeping paragraph that caught up a variety of disqualifying circumstances mostly unrelated to loyalty:

> (1) Depending on the relation of the Government employment to the national security:
>
> (i) Any behavior, activities, or associations which tend to show that the individual is not reliable or trustworthy.
>
> (ii) Any deliberate misrepresentations, falsifications, or omission of material facts.

(iii) Any criminal, infamous, dishonest, immoral, or notoriously disgraceful conduct, habitual use of intoxicants to excess, drug addiction, or sexual perversion.

(iv) Any illness, including any mental condition, of a nature which in the opinion of competent medical authority may cause significant defect in the judgment or reliability of the employee, with due regard to the transient or continuing effect of the illness and the medical findings in such case.

(v) Any facts which furnish reason to believe that the individual may be subjected to coercion, influence, or pressure which may cause him to act contrary to the best interests of the national security.

The remaining criteria of E.O. 10450 cover the same ground as those of 9835, with more words. They extend the earlier criteria in three respects. First, "sympathetic association" is included, not only with spies and saboteurs but with any advocate of violent overthrow. This extension formalizes what had in any case become the practice in the loyalty program. Second, disfavored membership in organizations is not confined to those "designated by the Attorney General," as in 9835. This limitation to organizations on the Attorney General's list was, I believe, generally adhered to in the loyalty program; but it did not apply to the concurrent security programs. Each agency is presumably free to make its own list. Third, an amendment to 10450, of Oct. 13, 1953, added a new criterion: reliance on the privilege against self-incrimination before a congressional committee.[17]

The application of these standards has to be deduced from the charges

17. E.O. 10491 of April 27, 1953, *Fed. Reg., 18*:6583, adds to § 8(a) of E.O. 10450 subsec. (8) as follows: "Refusal by the individual, upon the ground of constitutional privilege against self-incrimination, to testify before a congressional committee regarding charges of his alleged disloyalty or other misconduct." The wording of subsec. (iv) in the text follows an amendment by E.O. 10548 of Aug. 2, 1954, *Fed. Reg., 19*:4871.

Loyalty Review Board Directive II (Aug. 15, 1951) stated that "insofar as an individual's membership in, affiliation with, or sympathetic association with organizations is concerned, all Loyalty Boards shall confine their consideration to organizations on the Attorney General's list," but went on to say that if disloyal activities were alleged, then an organization not on the list could be cited, since, "Disloyal activities on the part of an individual are not privileged because they have occurred in connection with an organization not on the Attorney General's list." Thus Dr. John P. Peters (of Peters v. Hobby, 349 U.S. 331 [1955], in n. 38 below) was charged under the loyalty program with membership in organizations not on the Attorney General's list; but the membership allegations were coupled with alleged subversive activities, and were thus presumably consistent with the Directive.

that are made and from the questions that are asked at hearings. There is of course no systematic published collection of these materials; the government normally keeps them private, for the protection of the employee, and of others who may figure in them. However, enough case histories have been disclosed to journalists and scholars to permit rough generalizations.[18] Conclusions might be more assured if one had access to the memoranda of grounds for decision that some hearing and review boards prepare. Even if they were perfunctory, the memoranda would tell us what charges, when proved, require dismissal. But the grounds for decision are never published except in cases of great notoriety. One can readily list the important ones. Terse Loyalty Review Board decisions were released in the well-known cases of three State Department officers: Service, Vincent, and Davies. The later decision recommending Davies' dismissal on security grounds was also released. The Atomic Energy Commission disclosed the basis for action on three of its advisors: Condon, Graham, and Oppenheimer. We have little more, for grounds for decisions are not even disclosed to the employee, except by a rare indulgence or by inadvertence.[19]

18. The chief sources of case histories, or of appraisals based on study of groups of cases, are BONTECOU, esp. ch. 4; and *Case Studies in Personnel Security,* ed. Adam Yarmolinsky (1955). Many other published accounts of cases are cited herein; see esp. Ch. 3 below, n. 7 (Dept. of Defense *Report*), and n. 36 (Watts study). Through interviews with lawyers and an occasional employee, I have had the benefit of their summaries of perhaps 100 cases in the various federal programs. I have also had the opportunity to examine fifteen or twenty transcripts of hearings and other records.

19. Atomic Energy Commission, *In the Matter of J. Robert Oppenheimer, Texts of Principal Documents and Letters* (1954), is the primary source for the Oppenheimer decisions. For the AEC action clearing E. U. Condon see NYT, July 16, 1948. On the clearance of Frank P. Graham, see NYT, Dec. 21, 1948; Walter Gellhorn, *Security, Loyalty, and Science* (1950), pp. 90–1. On the State Department cases, see Ch. 15 below, pp. 366–9.

The Loyalty Review Board, quite inexplicably, discouraged even the preparation of reasoned decisions by hearing boards; BONTECOU, pp. 59–60. In security programs, both before and since E.O. 10450, memoranda of the grounds for decision are generally required for the guidance of the agency head. The "memorandum of reasons" for the decision of the hearing board in the Chasanow case was apparently given to the employee through a misunderstanding of the regulations. The Navy Civilian Personnel Security Regulations, NCPI 29, as amended to Feb. 4, 1955, explicitly provide that "Under no circumstance will a copy of the Security Hearing Board's decision or memorandum of reasons therefor be made available to the employee, his counsel or his representative"; §§ 2–9f(4), 4–14a(6), 4–14c(9). Cf. the novel Air Force release to the employee of a "Tentative Decision," with reasons, in the case of Sidney Hatkin, BNA MANUAL, p. 19/535. Most of the other administrative decisions referred to in this note are reprinted ibid. following p. 19/501.

CHARGES

After describing the nature of charges and hearings, I will attempt to characterize the effective standards of the programs, to the extent that they differ from the formal ones. The reader should have some idea of the form and style of a set of charges. These are from the Navy case of Abraham Chasanow:

"This is notice of proposed adverse action against you. The action contemplated is that of removal from duty in the Hydrographic Office based upon information available which reflects upon your suitability as an employee from the viewpoint of security. Accordingly, it is proposed to remove you under the provisions of Executive Order 10450 and Public Law 733 of the 81st Congress in the interest of National Security, based on the following charges:

a. You have associated for a considerable time with persons who are known Communists. Among others, this association applies to (Mr. and Mrs. *A*), and (Mr. and Mrs. *B*).

b. You have been an associate of one (*C*), who has been described as an individual having Communistic tendencies, and it is of record that his wife signed Communist nominating petitions during 1939. (*C*) was formerly employed at the Hydrographic Office and resigned while under investigation relative to his status as a security risk.

c. There is record of your attending a meeting at which donations were required from everyone present. It is recorded that the donations made were for the benefit of the United American Spanish Aid Committee, which is on the Attorney General's list of subversive organizations. It is believed your interest in this meeting was more than just personal since it is of record that you solicited and requested other individuals to attend the meeting.

d. It is known that you were at one time a subscriber to the Communist newsletter "In Fact," and you were a subscriber after this publication had been exposed by the press as expressing the view of the Communist party.

e. It is also of record that you at one time were a member of the National Lawyers Guild, an organization cited by the House Committee on Un-American Activities as a Communist organization.

f. One (*D*) is known to have been a regular associate of yours and it is of record that he was the editor of the "Cooperator" (Greenbelt newspaper) at a time when you and Mrs. Chasanow were listed as members of the staff of this newspaper as of May 1940. The "Cooperator" was listed as a member of the Washington Bookshop Association.

g. It has been reported that a list of names found on your desk at the Hydrographic Office during October 1952 contained the following, who either are known Communists or suspected of having Communistic tendencies:

(1) (*E*), who was a member of the National Lawyers Guild. It is also of record further that (*E*) was a Chief Defense Attorney in the Amerasia case.

(2) (*F*), a known Communist and subscriber to the "Morning Freiheit."

h. Several reliable informants have described you as a leader and very active in a radical group in Greenbelt, Maryland. Many of this group are thought to be of questionable character concerning loyalty to the United States. Included in this group are those described as ever willing to defend Communism in any discussion of ideology which may occur." [20]

As in the Chasanow case, the overwhelming preponderance of charges in both loyalty and security cases relate to associations with politically suspect persons and affiliation with allegedly left-wing organizations. These associations and affiliations are often linked to communism only remotely or by elaborate inference. Charges that relate to more serious criteria—e.g. attempts at espionage—are rarely encountered.[21] Nor does

20. The documents in the Chasanow case, including the charges here reproduced, were released by Chasanow and his counsel April 15, 1954. For accounts of the Chasanow case see Arnold Forster and Benjamin Epstein, *Cross Currents* (1956), ch. 3; *Time* (May 10, 1954), p. 22; NYT, Sept. 2, 1954. A 20th Century-Fox film of 1956, "Three Brave Men," was based in part on the case.

21. Indeed, taking espionage as the offense most feared from government employees, we find no responsible claims that the loyalty-security programs have caught a single known spy. See BONTECOU, p. 105. Of course, the programs are designed not to catch the guilty but to exclude the potentially guilty. Nevertheless, some doubt is raised about their efficacy when it appears that actual spies slip through the net. The case of Judith Coplon comes first to mind because, though her convictions were reversed, "her guilt is clear," U.S. v. Coplon, 185 F. 2d 629 (2d Cir. 1950). She was in a sensitive position, but it appears that her loyalty investigation had not proceeded very far when a suspicion of espionage activities developed, apparently independently. See Don Whitehead, *The FBI Story: A Report to the People* (1956), p. 353, n. 9. The claim is made, by authors who were

one encounter many charges having anything to do with treason, sabotage, compromise of classified information, or performance of duties so as to serve the interests of a foreign power.

In the mainstream of charges, those relating to questionable associations and affiliations, two polar situations can be distinguished. The first is a history that leads to a reasonable conclusion of present Communist party membership, or of communist sympathies practically indistinguishable from membership. Here dismissal would be obligatory. At the other extreme is a single episode in the relatively remote past. The Loyalty Review Board was on record as excusing such a deviation in an employee's student days.[22] It is also clear that the *prima facie* case created by a longer list of charges can be overcome. The employee has often, it is apparent from the number of clearances after hearings, been able to show that the association was in fact innocent or misguided, and that his present outlook and maturity are such as to dispel any doubts about his loyalty or reliability in security matters.

Closely related to charges of communist affiliations and associations are charges of communist sympathies as expressed in conversation or writings, or as inferred from the employee's reading or other intellectual interests. In the seventy-five case histories analyzed by Miss Bontecou, charges with respect to sympathetic expressions occurred in fourteen cases; with respect to reading communist literature in ten.[23] The number of such charges, however, understates the significance of opinions and attitudes in the resolution of a case. Whether or not there are direct

---

close to official sources, that the apprehension of Joseph Peterson, an employee of the National Security Agency who divulged cryptanalytic material—to friendly governments, not to the Russians—was facilitated by the security program. R. and G. Harkness, "How about Those Security Cases?" *Reader's Digest* (Sept. 1955), 67:202. Peterson's employment was said to be under review because of personal instability marked especially by prolonged absence from work. When documents were found to be missing from NSA, attention was directed to Peterson. Regular police interrogations then led him to confess. Note that, according to the Harkness article, it was the known loss of documents that led to Peterson, not the security doubts about Peterson that led to an unknown loss of documents. See also HUMPHREY HEARINGS, p. 66; JOHNSTON HEARINGS, p. 707. See Ch. 11 below for a fuller discussion of the prevalence of different types of charges.

22. "No one has been branded as disloyal or rated ineligible for Government employment simply because when he was in college he joined a radical organization or expressed radical opinion in debate . . ." Hiram Bingham, Chairman, Loyalty Review Board, address delivered before the General Session of the Section on Criminal Law of the American Bar Association, New York City (Sept. 18, 1951), p. 7 (mimeo.).

23. BONTECOU, p. 109.

charges about the employee's beliefs, if the case goes on to a hearing such matters are very likely to be explored.

I now turn from substance to form. Do the charges, as drafted, adequately inform the employee of the derogatory information he has to meet? Practice on this score has varied widely. Some agencies have in effect denied that this is their function; the employee, they say, will get this information from questions at the hearing, and his reaction to the element of surprise helps to test his veracity. Most have operated on the more familiar assumption that clarification of the issues in advance of the hearing helps the pursuit of truth.

Under some spur from court rulings, administrators have conceded the unfairness to the employee of blanket allegations. The trend has been away from charges like "You have shown sympathy with the Communist party aims and ideology," toward some specification of place, time, and content of the alleged exhibitions of sympathy. This trend is repeatedly checked, however, by the policy against revealing sources of information. A typical regulation directs that the statement of charges "shall be as specific and detailed as security considerations, including the need for protection of confidential sources of information, permit." [24]

Under the authority of this caveat, a security officer may easily persuade himself that a particularization of the occasion when the employee showed communist sympathies will, if it was in conversation, necessarily identify the other party to the conversation. If that person wishes to remain anonymous, the wish is usually respected, and the employee will get no details about the alleged expression of sympathy. There is little the employee can do to upset such a determination. In a flagrant case he can seek judicial relief, though with slim chance of success. He can beseech. He can guess; sometimes a lucky cast will bring up a witness who was in fact the source of the derogatory information, and who at the hearing either contradicts his alleged charges or discredits himself. [25]

---

24. Department of the Interior Security Reg., Order No. 2738, § 15(a). The quoted charge is from BONTECOU, p. 109. The cases, of limited effect, are Deak v. Pace, 185 F. 2d 997 (D.C. Cir. 1950) (the predecessor statute to P.L. 733 required that the employee be "fully informed" as to the reasons for security removal); Kutcher v. Higley, 235 F. 2d 505 (D.C. Cir. 1956) (Veterans' Preference Act requirement of "reasons, specifically and in detail," held applicable to loyalty proceeding under E.O. 9835).

25. See BONTECOU, pp. 127–31. The following exchange from a hearing was supplied by counsel for an employee charged with making statements sympathetic to Russian communism. The witness was the original source of the charge.

It should be said that there appear to be few cases in which ignorance of the source of withheld evidence is fatal to the employee's cause; but there are many in which he is hindered by his inability to be confronted with the witnesses against him. The legality and the merits of the policy against confrontation will be discussed later; here I only note its pervasive influence.

A last observation about charges combines form and substance. The multitude of charges based on associations—"You knew *B*," "You joined *X*"—require some characterization of *B* and *X*. *B* may be described as "a known Communist" when he is in fact not a Communist at all. But the files contain an informant's statement that he knew *B* as a Communist, so down goes *B* as "a known Communist." Sometimes boards take these thumbnail descriptions as gospel,[26] so that the em-

---

Chairman: Can you state for the Board what you previously stated to the FBI agent regarding this matter?

Witness: There were several occasions where there was a comparison made between communism and our government and which more or less favored—

Chairman: Could you recall as best you can the substance of just what was said?

Witness: I can't really recall any definite statements.

Chairman: Will you try to give us the substance of anything which you heard Mrs. *O* say?

Witness: Exactly what do you mean by that, sir?

Chairman: On the subject of communism, her beliefs about it, or any observations which she may have made with respect to Russia, communism, or any similar subject.

Witness: Well, I won't say that it was a definite statement, but I do think there was an intimation of some substance. She had said on several occasions she was from Russia.

Chairman: All right. But what we are trying to find out is what did you ever hear Mrs. *O* say either about Russia, about Communists, or any such subject. For example, what did you ever hear, if anything, Mrs. *O* say about Russia?

Witness: There was an occasion. I think it was near the big coal strike in 1948— and I made some comments merely in passing about the Communists being behind it, and someone—I don't know who said that—someone said that Communists weren't bad people at all.

Chairman: Who said that?

Witness: I don't know.

Chairman: Did Mrs. *O* say it?

Witness: I couldn't say.

Chairman: What we are trying to find out is what you have heard Mrs. *O* say about Russia.

Witness: Yes. Well, on one occasion there was a statement made by Mrs. *O*. I don't know how it was built up to or what the circumstances were. This is not a definite statement—I think she had said something about a return there. I don't know . . ."

26. "In the hearing of a case where the employee was charged with association with certain 'known Communists,' there was an extensive colloquy between the

ployee can only dissociate himself as best he can from unclean *B;* usually he will be permitted the laborious task of rehabilitating *B* (who will nevertheless go right on turning up in future cases as *"B,* a known Communist").

As for the *X* organization that the employee once belonged to, it may be described as "reliably reported to have been infiltrated by Communists." We will not stop here to consider the tangle of implications that the employee must break loose from in such an instance. The loyalty program, as has been said, attempted to avoid some of the difficulty by restricting chargeable affiliations with organizations to those on the Attorney General's list of subversive organizations. The Attorney General's procedures in compiling the list were challenged in the courts; the accuracy of his determinations was criticized; nevertheless, the Loyalty Review Board directed that an employee charged with membership in a listed organization should be precluded from attacking the damaging characterization of the organization. But at least the employee did not have to establish the respectability of Consumers' Union, which was never on the list, or his own economical motives in subscribing to its reports. Such affiliations have been freely charged in other programs, because only the loyalty program was bound to the list.[27]

The framing of charges that seem far-fetched or trivial suggests more than the loose use of words, or the uncritical acceptance of everything in the investigative report. It is another clue, I believe, to the effective standards of the programs. Infrequently, the position has been advanced that it is desirable to throw in everything derogatory without prejudgment, for the sake of letting the employee "clear the record." The official position, in the Eisenhower security program and some of its antecedents,

board's counsel and the employee's counsel as to the meaning of 'known Communists,' and board counsel stated that 'known Communists' meant 'known to the government.' At the conclusion of this colloquy, the Chairman suggested that once it had been disclosed to an employee that a particular individual was a 'known Communist,' then 'the only safe thing for a person to do for his own protection, is to assume that the government knows what it is talking about.'" Yarmolinsky (n. 18 above), p. 7.

27. On the genesis and history of the Attorney General's list, see BONTECOU, ch. 5; FUND DIGEST, pp. 67–78. Consumers' Union, the publisher of *Consumer Reports,* was cited by the HUAC in 1944, having previously been called a "red" organization by Rep. Martin Dies; in 1951, with some 500,000 subscribers, it issued a "Letter to Readers" that said: "We have not had and will not have any truck with communism . . ." See also *Business Week* (March 20, 1954), p. 144. HUAC, *Annual Report 1953* (1954), p. 127, states that the Union has been removed from its list, since there was "no present justification for continuing this organization as one that is cited."

is that charges as presented to the employee on their face warrant dismissal.[28] It is the totality of the charges, to be sure, that leads to the tentative determination of unfitness. But the whole is the sum of its parts; none of the parts can be taken lightly. Consequently the employee must somehow defend himself against every charge of the kind that we see in the Chasanow case. Consider, for example, association with *C,* "described as an individual having communistic tendencies, and it is of record that his wife signed communist nominating petitions during 1939." Note first that this charge involves a technique that we may call *remote association:* "You associate with *C,* who associated with Mrs. *C,* who . . ." No direct connection between the employee and Mrs. *C* is charged. Second, *C* is "described as . . . having Communistic tendencies." Described by whom? What does this mean? It may be a cautious description of *C*'s political orientation; it may simply mean that he has leanings toward his wife, who, it is stated, signed "communist nominating petitions in 1939." Third, consider the relevance of signing communist nominating petitions in 1939. If it had been the employee who did so, it would have some bearing on his politics in 1939. He might have signed as a Communist; he might have signed as a non-Communist who thought that the communist position should be put to the test of the polls. What is charged here is that *C*'s wife, not even an acquaintance of the employee, signed the petitions.

That such tidbits are unearthed is a tribute to the mechanical perfection of the FBI files. Their inclusion in a set of charges, however, is the result of human judgment. The association with *C* in the Chasanow case, it should be added, took place at board meetings of a community organization. The inclusion of this casual relationship, and the further injection of the remote history of *C*'s wife, as elements in a tentative decision that Chasanow was a poor security risk, help us to sense the security officers' idea of a security risk.

HEARINGS

The primary purpose of hearings, for the government, is to give the board a good look at the employee. He is usually the principal witness —sometimes the only one. If he brings on witnesses, their chief function is to corroborate the employee's image of himself. He cannot compel the production of unfriendly witnesses. If he knows who they might be,

28. See, e.g., the opening paragraph of the letter of charges in the Chasanow case, p. 35 above.

he can ask to have them invited to attend; but they may decline the invitation. The government infrequently produces witnesses in support of the charges.[29] It does not need to, unless the employee has contradicted important elements in the charges that testimony would reinstate. Even then the policy against disclosing sources may inhibit calling witnesses, especially since the witness, if exposed to cross-examination, might be discredited. The security staff may do better to stand on the investigative report, which the hearing board sees, though the employee does not.

The primary purpose of the hearing, for the employee, is the climactic opportunity it gives him to rebut the charges, and, in a revealing phrase, to *clear himself*. In presenting himself for examination, the employee hopes to strengthen the affirmative case that, if well-advised, he has already advanced in writing. He will try to show that he is anticommunist, prospectively (if not retrospectively) free of bad associations, and a good citizen. In making these claims, he invites challenges to explain his beliefs and attitudes. Questions from the board and its counsel are likely to be more sweeping than anything provoked by the charges. There seems to be little effort to confine hearings to narrow issues. Posers, like the following, result (from an AEC hearing of a biologist): "Q. Do you think it would be possible for a person to be a deeply religious person and also to be a 'dyed-in-the-wool' Communist? A. Gee, there you got me. I really don't know." Political riddles are popular. Recognition of communist China, relations with Franco Spain—any current problem may be thrown at the employee to draw out his opinions. Thus a Navy Yard artisan was asked, around 1948, "Do you feel that Jacques

29. See Appendix B, Table 29, below. Civil Service Commission Handbook IN-203, *Guides for Members of Security Hearing Boards under E.O. 10450* (July 1953), Part V(D); reprinted HUMPHREY HEARINGS, p. 769, also BNA MANUAL, p. 15/575, states that witnesses may be invited to testify by the personnel security officer or at the discretion of the board concerned. Most departments provide that invitations will be transmitted to all witnesses who are accessible i.e. nonconfidential witnesses. The Civil Service Handbook, Part VI(G), in recognition that even those nonconfidential witnesses invited may not appear, provides that "If a person who has made charges against the employee and who is not a confidential informant is called as a witness but does not appear, his failure to appear shall be considered by the board in evaluating such charges, as well as the fact that there can be no payment by the Government for travel of witnesses." This has been incorporated into virtually all Departmental regulations. Even if a witness appears, he can elect to be heard without the employee or his counsel present; e.g. Naval Civilian Personnel Security Regulations (Feb. 4, 1955), § 4–13(d)(3); and see sample "Letter Inviting Witnesses," Army Security Reg., Appendix II, in BNA MANUAL, p. 15/161.

Duclos or DeGaulle would offer France a greater opportunity for recuperation?"

This free-for-all discussion puts at a disadvantage an employee who does not have an articulate and informed political philosophy. Furthermore, such questioning, unless it is conducted with great caution, can hardly fail to convey to the employee an impression that some beliefs are officially frowned on. A vivid example is a question put to Dorothy Bailey which Judge Edgerton cited disapprovingly: "Did you ever write a letter to the Red Cross about the segregation of [white and Negro] blood?" The board member who asked the question later explained that "Objection to blood segregation is a recognized 'party line' technic," and that he was simply exploring Miss Bailey's adherence to party lines as distinct from her personal convictions.

Occasionally the questioning slips over the line from suggestion to direct admonition. In one of Yarmolinsky's cases, a "noted civic leader" was in effect reproved for making contributions to certain causes, and urged to be "a lot more cautious in the future." [30]

While hearings extensively probe the employee's beliefs, they also of course deal with the specific episodes in his personal history brought up by the charges. Indeed, the matching of the employee's version of events with the investigative reports opens the way to a new standard for judgment. That is, simply, whether the employee is truthful. Sometimes the employee will be forced to concede an earlier falsehood—for example in his application for employment. More likely there will be contradictions between the information furnished by the FBI and the testimony of the employee. In either case the Board, if it comes to doubt the employee's honesty, can avoid difficult issues of loyalty, and come quickly to rest on what appears to be the firm rock of credibility. A material misrepresentation may either cast doubt on the whole of the employee's defense, or, under a security program, it may lead directly to a finding that the man can't be trusted, whatever his political sympathies.

There is no way even to guess at the number of cases in which the

30. Yarmolinsky (n. 18 above), p. 255. For the Bailey question see Bailey v. Richardson, 182 F. 2d 46, 73 (D.C. Cir. 1950); BONTECOU, p. 139. The DeGaulle example is from O. J. Rogge, *Our Vanishing Civil Liberties* (1949), pp. 146–7. The AEC quotation is from a transcript that I have seen. For other specimens of political quizzing see Emerson and Helfeld, "Loyalty Among Government Employees," *Yale Law Jour.* (1948), *58*:73–4. Even if the hearing board does not take the initiative with such questions, the employee's counsel, if he is well-prepared, will volunteer this sort of information. See Yarmolinsky, "How a Lawyer Conducts a Security Case," *The Reporter* (March 2, 1954), p. 18.

issue is transmuted from loyalty to honesty. From discussions with administrators and lawyers, I am convinced that this is an important element in the federal programs, one that weighs heavily in the burden of persuasion that the employee carries.[31]

The mechanics of the hearing stage may be briefly summarized. Under the Truman program, incumbents were heard by a three-man board selected from the staffs of their own agencies, applicants by regional panels recruited by the Civil Service Commission from private citizens. The Eisenhower program, as has been pointed out, does not provide hearings for applicants. The agency boards for incumbents may *not* be selected from their own staffs. Each agency contributes staff members to panels maintained by the Civil Service Commission, and draws from those panels employees of other agencies for its own needs. The purpose of this change was to increase the objectivity of the board members; of course it also decreased their familiarity with the security requirements of the agency in which they might be sitting. But the using agency makes its own selections from the panel; and a practice soon developed whereby the military departments draw only on each other for board members.[32]

There is no way for an outsider to judge what difference in adjudication, if any, results from the use of extra-agency boards. Nor can one estimate what differences may have resulted from the fact that in the Eisenhower program security officers appear to have more control than formerly over the selection of hearing boards. The most dangerous threat to the integrity of the hearing process that has yet arisen came from the persistent efforts of Senator McCarthy to question board members about their decisions.[33] The executive branch resisted the Senator's demands in this instance. Whether the mere possibility of Congressional intervention has colored decisions is another matter.

Hearings are conducted privately. The employee is entitled to counsel. A practice in some agencies of providing government counsel to repre-

31. This problem is further developed in Ch. 17 below.

32. On hearing boards in the Truman program see BONTECOU, ch. 2, esp. pp. 35–48. For description of the composition of hearing boards in the Eisenhower program see BNA MANUAL, pp. 11/45–7; for a typical military department regulation see Army SR 620-220-1, § IV (19), BNA MANUAL, p. 15/141.

33. After one of his repeated rebuffs, based upon former President Truman's directive of 1948 banning such disclosure, Senator McCarthy said: "I still feel strongly that we should get the names of persons who gave loyalty clearance to Communists employed by the Army. It is more important to get those who cleared Communists than to get a Communist himself. I am convinced there is a definite tie-in in Red infiltration in every government department. It is all part of the conspiracy." NYT, Sept. 17, 1953.

sent the employee was soon checked by the Loyalty Review Board, so that the expense of retaining private counsel has remained one of the obstacles to making a successful defense.[34] Similarly, the employee gets no assistance, either by way of subpoena power or travel expenses, in procuring witnesses. One result of this handicap has been a heavy reliance on affidavits, which the boards may discount because of their very profusion and because the affiants (like the government's informants) are not subject to cross-examination.

REVIEW AND COORDINATION

The loyalty program afforded an employee who lost out at the hearing level an appeal to the Loyalty Review Board. This was a group of about twenty-five private citizens, mostly lawyers and educators of considerable standing, who sat usually in panels of three. The Civil Service Commission selected it, and provided it with a full-time staff, including examiners who "post-audited" all cases, whether favorable or unfavorable to the employee, and summarized them for the Board.[35] The Board had a general rule-making and coordinating power under Executive Order 9835, but its power to review cases was by the Order confined to mak-

34. For general regulations on the conduct of hearings see Civil Service Commission Handbook, n. 29 above. On the Loyalty Review Board's disapproval of providing government counsel see BONTECOU, p. 60. On the fees charged by private attorneys see below, Appendix B, Table 17. The American Bar Association has established a special committee to give free legal assistance to government employees who become involved in security cases. NYT, Jan. 13, 1955. In the federal civilian programs as a whole (that is, those surveyed both in this chapter and in Ch. 3), it has been estimated that one-half to two-thirds of the employees do not have counsel. See ASS'N OF THE BAR, REPORT, p. 99.

35. The personnel and operation of the Board are described in BONTECOU, pp. 44–8. A spirited defense of its performance is made by Murray Seasongood and R. L. Strecker, "The Loyalty Review Board," *Univ. of Cincinnati Law Rev.* (1956), 25:1. Seasongood was a member of the Board. An example of an examiner's summary (ordinarily unavailable) may be found in HUAC, Hearings, *Communist Methods of Infiltration* (1953), pp. 3045–6. The formal record of the Board's administrative decisions (as distinct from decided cases) is in regulations and directives which were published in *Fed. Reg.*, and in Memoranda 1–78, Mar. 9, 1948–May 7, 1953 (mimeo.).

A rare indication of the character of the policy deliberations of the Board became available when Senator McCarthy revealed minutes of a Board meeting which had been leaked to him by an employee of the Board. See McCarthy's Senate speech on this subject in *Cong. Rec.* (1952), 98:191–3. *U.S. News and World Report* (Feb. 8, 1952), pp. 18–20, contains material not in McCarthy's speech. For the later dismissal of the Board employee, see NYT, Nov. 3, 1952.

ing "advisory recommendations" to the agency head where dismissal had been recommended below. The Review Board soon extended its jurisdiction, and, whether the departmental hearing recommended dismissal or clearance, would in its discretion remand cases for a new hearing, or hear them itself with new evidence. For example, in the case of John P. Davies, Jr., the Review Board noted that it heard "highly confidential testimony" from General Walter Bedell Smith, then director of the Central Intelligence Agency, and Ambassador George Kennan on a pivotal issue in the case, Davies' motives in suggesting "utilization by the C.I.A. of the services of persons alleged to be Communists." In only one known case was the Review Board's recommendation not accepted. That was when Secretary of State Acheson found himself unable to follow the Board's reasoning in the case of John Carter Vincent.[36]

Acheson, though rejecting the Board's finding of doubtful loyalty, did not then challenge the Board's jurisdiction; nor did any executive department openly challenge the penetrating control that the Review Board assumed over every aspect of the program. One element that perhaps forestalled attack was the forceful character of the two men (both Republicans, though appointed by President Truman) who presided over the Board. Chairman Seth Richardson, an attorney, seemed chiefly interested in procedural regularity. His successor in 1950, former Senator Hiram Bingham, was apparently dissatisfied with the rate of dismissals, and took responsibility for lowering the basic loyalty standard from "reasonable grounds" to "reasonable doubt." [37]

In 1955, long after the Loyalty Review Board had been dissolved, the Supreme Court held in the *Peters* case that E.O. 9835 did not give the

36. In the Vincent case, a five-man panel of the L.R.B., by a vote of 3–2, held that "Mr. Vincent's whole course of conduct in connection with Chinese affairs" raised a reasonable doubt as to his loyalty. Secretary Acheson, with presidential approval, referred the case to an *ad hoc* board headed by Judge Learned Hand. After the change of administration, Secretary Dulles decided that the *ad hoc* board would not be helpful, cleared Vincent on both loyalty and security grounds, said that he could exercise his summary dismissal powers because Vincent's reporting and advice had been inadequate, and accepted his resignation. NYT, Feb. 18, 1952; Dec. 12, 1952; Jan. 4, 1953; Jan. 25, 1953; and March 5, 1953. The Review Board decision in the Davies case is also in NYT, Dec. 12, 1952. On both cases see also Ch. 15 below.

37. Seth Richardson had a successful career in the legal profession, as Assistant U. S. Attorney General under President Hoover, and later as a member of a leading Washington law firm. Hiram Bingham was an explorer, author, and professor at Yale before entering politics as Governor of Connecticut; he later became a U. S. Senator. Obituary notices on Richardson, NYT, Mar. 18, 1953; on Bingham, NYT, June 7, 1956.

Board power to reverse agency decisions favorable to the employee. This it had done in 19 cases besides Dr. Peters'.[38]

The Eisenhower program has had no interdepartmental review or coordinating agency comparable to the Loyalty Review Board. The principle of departmental responsibility, though subordinated in the loyalty program, has always dominated the security programs. The military departments especially have insisted that, since the Secretary is responsible for the integrity of his department, his authority should be equal to his responsibility. Within a department, the practice under the Eisenhower program looks toward some further consideration of a hearing-board decision by the agency head or a person designated by him. This may consist simply of a review of the record as an automatic prelude to any final decision, favorable or unfavorable, with no participation by the employee. Sometimes the regulations permit the submission of further evidence or argument to the reviewing official.[39] The Departments of the Army, Navy, and Air Force have appeal boards in Washington which make recommendation to the Secretary on all hearing-board decisions. This means that the employee has his case considered by a central board, which serves the further purpose of coordinating the activities of far-flung hearing boards.

As a medium for coordination, E.O. 10450 directs the Civil Service Commission to make a "continuing study" of all the departments' and agencies' operations, and to report to the National Security Council. Six persons constituted the entire staff carrying out this task in 1954. The National Security Council staff, though it can sponsor amendments to the Executive Order, has not emitted directives and frequent memoranda to all agencies, as the Loyalty Review Board did.[40]

38. Peters v. Hobby, 349 U.S. 331 (1955). The record of the dismissal on loyalty grounds was ordered expunged in the Peters case, and in a proceeding that John S. Service had commenced immediately after his dismissal. See Service v. Dulles, 235 F. 2d 215 (D.C. Cir. 1956), reversed on other grounds (see n. 55 below), 354 U.S. 363.

39. The principle of Secretarial responsibility is evident in P.L. 733, which embodied the preferences chiefly of the military departments. See House Comm. on Post Office and Civil Service, Hearings, *To Protect the National Security . . .* (March 1950), esp. pp. 57–63. On the distinction between review and appeal in these cases see ASS'N OF THE BAR, REPORT, pp. 102–3.

40. See E.O. 10450, § 14. Philip Young, Chairman of the Civil Service Commission, gave a description of the Commission's role under 10450 in HUMPHREY HEARINGS, p. 501. The "six persons" figure is from a 1954 interview with a Commission staff member. Other coordinating bodies are described in HUMPHREY HEARINGS, pp. 10–14, 54–5; JOHNSTON HEARINGS, p. 872; Commission on Government Security, *Report* (1957), p. 81.

An increase in the number of stages through which a case must pass before final decision, whatever equities it may introduce, certainly introduces opportunities for delay. One of the most persistent criticisms of both the loyalty and the security programs has been directed to the way the proceedings are often dragged out. From published chronologies, and others supplied to me by employees and their attorneys, it appears that intervals of a year, eighteen months, or even two years are not uncommon between the initiation of charges and the final decision.[41] If the employee were at work all this time, the chief cost would be in efficiency and peace of mind. But suspension without pay has been a routine first step in the security programs. Faced with the gamble that a long period of suspension may end either in clearance and an award of back pay or in dismissal, employees must often feel constrained to abandon their defense and resign.

For convenience, we have been referring to "final" decisions. Lack of finality, however, has been an outstanding characteristic of the federal programs taken as a whole. There are probably several hundred persons who, as the result of suspect histories and stubbornness in remaining in federal service, have gone through proceedings of varying complexity and thoroughness, as follows:

(1) the World War II programs;

(2) the loyalty program, under the "reasonable grounds" standard;

(3) the loyalty program again, under the "reasonable doubt" standard;

(4) the Eisenhower security program, which ordered re-adjudication of all cases where, following a full field investigation, the previous adjudication had not been "under a security standard commensurate with that established under this order."

This array can be extended. The appearance of new derogatory information reopens a case. A transfer to an agency that considers its standards more exacting than those of the prior place of employment reopens a case. A change in the security personnel, or in the agency head, or in congressional pressures, may reopen a case. It is reported that John S. Service had been cleared seven times by the Department Loyalty-Security Board before the Loyalty Review Board finally ordered his dismissal (this does not mean that he had seven hearings).[42]

---

41. See below, App. B, Table 15. According to ASS'N OF THE BAR, REPORT, p. 108, the "average elapsed time for the processing of a contested security case from beginning to end in the Federal Employees Program is probably around five months."

42. On readjudications under the "reasonable doubt" standard see n. 18 above.

EFFECTIVE STANDARDS

In cases where the employee has some opportunity for defense, the effective standards of the federal programs, it appears, have reached this sort of resolution. More or less specific charges are brought, related to the detailed criteria of the regulations. Most charges will refer to associations and affiliations of varying proximity to communism. Even if the connection is remote, it must be denied or explained. If a complete point-by-point refutation is not possible, the employee may still clear himself by meeting four overriding conditions for clearance. Indeed, he must meet these conditions in every case; they are, I believe, of the essence in avoiding a decision either of doubtful loyalty or of security risk.

(1) He must persuade the hearing board and the reviewing authorities that he shares prevailing anticommunist sentiments. It is not enough to dispel an appearance of communist sympathies. How anticommunist must the civil servant appear to be? The answer varies with the times and with the judges.

(2) He must forswear the associations and affiliations that got him into trouble. This obligation has reached the point where employees have sometimes felt constrained to promise to cut off any connection with blood relatives. Hearing boards have urged this on the employee, not vindictively, but because it appeared that was what the employee would have to do.[43]

(3) He must exhibit a willing disposition to acquiesce in the demands of the security system. The Atomic Energy Commission made this requirement clear in the Oppenheimer case. The necessity for assent apparently extends to the very process from which the employee is trying

---

See also E.O. 10450, § 4. On the seven clearances of Service see NYT, Dec. 14, 1951; Ch. 15 below, n. 10. Numerous examples of repeated adjudications are reported in Yarmolinsky, n. 18 above. It is also possible for a person to undergo repeated adjudications in different capacities under various programs. For example, a clearance for a "sensitive position" in Civil Service under the Truman program was received by an individual in 1950; in 1954 he received a security clearance from the Western Industrial Personnel Security Board in connection with his employment by a private employer holding a defense contract requiring access to classified military information; and in 1955 he was cleared of security charges by the Army, which had proposed to withdraw his reserve commission. The same charges were aired in each adjudication: a brother and sister-in-law alleged to be Communists. ACLU [Northern Calif.] *News* (Dec. 1955), p. 4.

43. Cf. Yarmolinsky (n. 18 above), p. 109; Anthony Lewis, in *Democratic Digest* (March 1954), p. 86.

to extricate himself, for employees are sometimes asked in hearings whether they think the program is fairly administered.[44]

(4) He must appear to be wholly truthful. Inconsistencies in his own record, and conflicts between his testimony and the investigative report must be dispelled.

These four conditions for clearance are nowhere, so far as I know, explicity and authoritatively laid down. They are my own conclusions from the materials available: charges, transcripts of hearings, outcome of cases, and the handful of reasoned decisions.

The content of these effective standards has naturally altered somewhat through time. The wording of the formal standard, in each major revision up till now, has shifted toward greater strictness. Effective standards, with some variations, have followed a similar evolution.

There was a flurry of protest at cases of vague and indiscriminate charges tried by summary procedures, from 1946 to 1948. These cases occurred in the first wave of alarm at the resurgent Red menace. The period from 1948 to 1950 was one of consolidation and of procedural reform. A degree of standardization between the criteria of the loyalty program and of the agencies with security responsibilities, notably the Defense Department, the State Department, and the Atomic Energy Commission, was achieved. Despite these apparent improvements over the primitive initial measures, effective standards were hardening. This period, I would say, marks the legitimization of reliance on asociations and affiliations, with all that this implies in the way of inferences and imputations of unworthiness. Still, it was a time when ex-Communists could be and were cleared, on the theory that they were currently loyal.[45] The change of terminology in the loyalty standard in 1951 to "reasonable doubt" marked another hardening. With Senators McCarthy and

44. See Yarmolinsky (n. 18 above), p. 126; AEC, *In the Matter of J. Robert Oppenheimer* (n. 19 above), p. 15 (Commission opinion): "There remains an aspect of the security system which perhaps has had insufficient public attention. This is the protection and support of the entire system itself. . . . It must include active cooperation with all agencies of government properly and reasonably concerned with the security of our country. It must involve a subordination of personal judgment as to the security status of an individual . . . the question arises whether an individual who does not accept and abide by the security system should be a part of it."

Commissioner Murray, in a concurring opinion, ibid., pp. 60–3, puts this idea even more strongly. He argued at length that "security regulations . . . are the special test of the *loyalty* of the American citizen who serves his government in the sensitive area of the atomic energy program." Ibid., p. 63 (emphasis supplied).

45. BONTECOU, p. 108. Seasongood (n. 35 above), pp. 30–1, says that the Loyalty Review Board would not excuse membership occurring later than 1945–46.

McCarran and other figures denouncing inadequate security measures, especially in the State Department, the position of the ex-Communist in government, to use him as a yardstick, became everywhere more precarious. At some time before 1953, I should guess, his position became untenable, except as a paid "consultant" to the Department of Justice. Under the Eisenhower program, it was unthinkable. The necessity of finding that the employee's retention was "clearly consistent with the national security" ruled out much indulgence.[46]

This trend paralleled the increasing influence and authority of security officers throughout the federal establishment. But I would hesitate to suggest more than a parallel. During this whole period the international situation worsened, from Czechoslovakia and the Berlin blockade to Korea and Indo-China. The short-lived sunshine of the Geneva meeting in 1955 was followed by the new crises of Hungary and the Middle East. Public feeling against any suggestion of communist influence in government became ever more hostile. It was reflected not only in the strictures of Senator McCarthy and his associates but also in the attitude of responsible department heads. An example is the blunt pre-judgment of the Oppenheimer case by Secretary of Defense Wilson, in a press conference while the hearing was still going on.[47] Though the tensions of

46. Yarmolinsky (n. 18 above), p. 60, has an example of an ex-Communist who was twice cleared under the loyalty program, but was dismissed after proceedings under E.O. 10450. At least one exception to the general rule that an ex-Communist could not be cleared under 10450 was the case of Clarence Smith, a backwoods Negro who moved to the city during the war and who was duped into joining a "club." As he put it in a compelling letter to the board, "It was a lot of pretty girls at the party they ask me to join there club I join to be friend with the girls, I didn't no it was against the U.S." The letter at first failed to convince the board, but after Smith got legal assistance he was cleared and returned to his job. See ACLU, Greater Philadelphia Branch, *The Federal Security Program: Some Philadelphia Episodes* (1956), p. 13.

47. Secretary Wilson's press conference of April 14, 1954, is quoted in part in AEC, *In the Matter of J. Robert Oppenheimer,* Transcript of Hearing (1954), pp. 501–3. Wilson said: "I have great sympathy for people that have made a mistake and have reformed, but we don't think we ought to reform them in the military establishment. They ought to have a chance somewhere else" (p. 502). He also offered this homely parable to illustrate the nature of a security risk: "It is a little bit like selecting a teller in a bank. . . . If the man frequents gambling joints and has contacts with the underworld you ordinarily don't hire him. Or if you found out after you did hire him that at one time he had been convicted of theft or something like that, maybe he is reformed and all, but still you don't expose him again. You don't wait until he has stolen money from the bank and then try to do something about it" (p. 501). Wilson's method of removing Oppenheimer from his position as consultant to the Research and Development Board he explained as follows: "We dropped the whole Board. That was a real smooth way of doing that one" (p. 502).

that period have diminished, it is doubtful that the effective standards have significantly relaxed.

POWERS OF SECURITY OFFICERS

Most of the preceding section has referred to the effective standards in cases where the employee had an opportunity to clear himself. There are important situations where he has no such opportunity, and where the decisions are almost entirely those of the security officers, based on their concept of a risk.

Under E.O. 10450 the authority of the security staff was especially enhanced by three procedural characteristics of the security program. These are: (1) Denial of hearings to applicants and probationary employees. The Atomic Energy Commission alone has followed a contrary course.[48] (2) Routine suspension without pay of any employee against whom charges are brought. This practice was modified somewhat in 1955.[49] (3) Denial of access to classified material, without charges or hearing. This is a device that has not been mentioned before. It puts the employee in a sort of limbo if his normal occupation requires the full use of confidential information. He is kept on the payroll, but the work that is found for him is probably unimportant. His incentive and opportunities for advancement are both curtailed. It is a form of pressure that seems to have been extensively used.[50]

48. See n. 13 above; see also AEC, *Fourteenth Semiannual Report* (1953), p. 71.

49. Attorney General Brownell's letter of March 4, 1955, reprinted in HUMPHREY HEARINGS, pp. 135–6, recommended that the final decision to suspend should not be delegated below the Assistant Secretary level. Later in 1955 Brownell said he would recommend to Congress that P.L. 733 be amended and that suspension be left to the discretion of agency heads. See NYT, Nov. 16, 1955; BNA MANUAL, Newsletter (November 25, 1955), p. 3. Congress did not act on this proposal. The idea that P.L. 733 makes suspension mandatory, though it is widely acted upon, is not a necessary conclusion from its language. Still less so is a theory, which I am advised has been seriously put forward by government attorneys, that the employee has a "right" to be suspended. Whether suspension is a "right" or a disability, if neither the department nor the employee insists upon suspension before hearing, no one can complain—except the Congress.

50. On the use of this practice in one installation see Scientists' Committee on Loyalty and Security, *The Fort Monmouth Security Investigations, August 1953– April 1954* (1954) (mimeo.), pp. 5/6, 5/11 and 6/5. For later developments, see John Phelps and Ernest Pollard, "Fort Monmouth," *Scientific American* (June 1954), p. 29; and NYT ("Monmouth Hearings: Balance Sheet to Date"), Nov. 21, 1954. No comprehensive material on the practice is available; regulations with respect to revocation of clearance are apparently themselves classified.

Each of the three developments just listed leaves the security officer free to evaluate derogatory information out of context. The applicant for employment is rejected by the security office without intimation or explanation of the difficulty. The temporary employee may get a limited opportunity to defend himself, perhaps by a submission in writing, perhaps in an interview; but the usual machinery puts the decision right back in the channels from which the charges came. The decision to suspend is usually the security officer's; so also is the decision to withdraw clearance for access to classified materials. I do not mean that a single individual makes these decisions. In the larger agencies the security routines are as involved as any familiar bureaucratic procedure: Washington tries to confine the discretion of the field; the agency head deputizes someone to see that actions taken in his name are not foolish; the Office of General Counsel infiltrates the process in the classic manner of government lawyers. But the security office, and its officers, stand at the center of the web. Even when there is a hearing, the boards are usually selected by security officers. If the hearing is favorable to the employee, the security office is free to comment critically to the Secretary's reviewing assistant.

If the security officers effectively control the disposition of many cases, as they surely do, it would be useful to know what their collective image of a security risk is like. Does it differ from the consensus of hearing boards? We have already suggested that the kinds of charges that come to light are an important clue to the security office outlook, and that this clue points to a much tougher attitude than one would infer from the frequently favorable outcome of hearings. If the employee cannot clear himself, the derogatory information in his file probably disqualifies him. It may be unverified; it may, when illuminated, be preposterous; it may, put in perspective, be insignificant. But security officers, who within the regulations have to decide what kind of information is derogatory, naturally take their own concepts seriously. There is a plausible belief among lawyers who have been close to the program than any substantial item of derogatory information will normally cause the security office to veto an applicant for employment, even if the rest of the available data repels the implications of the derogatory information.[51]

With the security officers intervening at every stage of the proceeding,

51. Cf. the discussion between Scott McLeod and the Humphrey subcommittee. HUMPHREY HEARINGS, pp. 330, 335–8. See generally, on the subject of this section, the perceptive remarks of S. A. Goudsmit, "The Task of the Security Officer," BAS (1955), *11*:145.

it is not surprising to hear that later stages can be bypassed through the exertion of only modest pressure by them. It is reported that in the State Department, where the new administration thought drastic action was necessary and put Scott McLeod in charge of effecting it, there was a practice of advising employees informally that charges would be brought against them in forty-eight hours, but that they were free to resign in the interim. There is no way of knowing how many resignations have occurred out of alarm, or under pressure, nor of estimating whether the people concerned could have met the standards of the programs at any particular time. We know that security officers do exert informal pressures, and that some people resign without exercising the rights that the program gives them. Some observers that I have talked to take this to be the main thrust of the program, behind the façade of regulations and hearings. I think this position is exaggerated; but it would be an unrealistic picture that did not give considerable prominence to behind-the-scenes activities.

Finally, the influence of the new bureaucracy of security officers is also evident in another trend that we have already noted. That is the "mechanization" of the program. You put a name in the investigative machinery. Along the way it may pick up derogatory information, mechanically defined. If there are two or three derogatory items on the processed product, it is stamped "security risk" and discarded. In comparison, a process that emphasizes hearings before persons who are not professional worriers about security is more likely to bring out the offsetting factors in the case.

However, one should not rush to conclude that the first causes of these trends are to be found only in the predilections of security officers. They may simply be the faithful executors of a dominant public policy. That policy, which in turn has a multiple origin in our fear and alarms about security, boils down to the cautious phrase: take no chances.

RESULTS OF THE FEDERAL EMPLOYEES' PROGRAMS

It will be convenient to distinguish between the results (by which I mean the simple tabulation of numbers of cases) of the various programs, and their effects, which are complex and speculative.

The Civil Service Commission published periodic surveys of the loyalty program. Here is the last one:

"In the course of the program, 4,756,705 loyalty forms on individuals were checked with the files of the Federal Bureau of Investigation and with other records and sources as appropriate. Of the total, 1,787,188 forms related to "incumbent" employees, i.e. persons on the rolls October 1, 1947, and 2,969,517 forms related to persons subsequently appointed or considered for appointment.

Whenever a question of loyalty was revealed by these checks, an investigation was scheduled. In all, the reports of investigation on 26,236 persons were referred to appropriate boards for consideration—the cases of 101 persons under investigation when the program began and 26,135 investigated thereafter by the Federal Bureau of Investigation. During the consideration of these cases, loyalty boards issued 12,859 interrogatories and letters of charges and held 4,119 hearings.

The results of action by agencies, by regional boards of the Commission, and by the Loyalty Review Board on the cases of the 26,236 employees, new appointees, and applicants were as follows: 16,503 persons were cleared by favorable decisions on loyalty, including 252 on appeal; 560 persons were removed or denied federal employment on grounds relating to loyalty; proceedings were discontinued in 6,828 cases because these persons left the service or withdrew their applications; 1,192 after they had been sent interrogatories or charges; and the cases of 569 persons were considered by the Department of the Army solely under security laws. Loyalty proceedings involving the remaining 1,776 persons were incomplete when the program was terminated; these cases were therefore to be decided under the provisions of the President's security order.[52]

The significant rough ratios are these: derogatory information was discovered (thereby making a case) about one employee out of 180. Final decisions were made in two-thirds of those cases (the rest resigned or the process was incomplete when the program ended). Hearings were required in one completed case out of four (the other three were cleared on written interrogatories, or on the file). One hearing out of seven resulted unfavorably to the employee.

If one wanted to know the total number who (as the standard of the program was applied) were of doubtful loyalty, one would have to add some unknown portion of those who resigned while their cases were undecided. There is no warrant whatever for including all those who resigned. The rate of turnover in federal employment was as much as one-

52. Civil Service Commission, *1953 Annual Report* (1954), p. 32.

third annually during the loyalty program's life.[53] A person who was planning to leave the federal service in any event did not often stay on for the sake of carrying through a loyalty case. The effect of resignation was to leave the case unresolved; no further steps were taken.

Information about the security programs is incomplete and disorderly. The Defense Department reported in March 1950 that under the statutory dismissal power bestowed on the military departments in 1942, 375 employees had been removed. Since 216 cases were pending at the time of the report, there had apparently been considerable activity in the postwar period.[54]

The Department has not released any figures on its security operations under P.L. 733 from 1950 to the beginning of the Eisenhower program in the spring of 1953. This omission may conceal the largest block of security dismissals up to 1953.

Most Atomic Energy Commission cases involved employees of its contractors, who do not belong in this listing.

The State Department, before its inclusion in P.L. 733, was the holder of remarkable summary dismissal powers bestowed on it annually in appropriations bills since 1946. It had accordingly set up a security program, under which apparently only two or three dismissals occurred through 1949. Thereafter the pace accelerated: 12 in 1950, 35 in 1951, 70 in 1952. At the same time the State Department was dismissing homosexuals at twice this rate, on security grounds but without using security channels.[55]

The Department of Commerce, as we have seen, was included in P.L.

53. BONTECOU, pp. 152–4.

54. 141 employees had been cleared, and 106 had transferred or resigned. House Hearings (n. 39 above), p. 30.

55. The summary dismissal provision (generally called the "McCarran Rider") provided that "the Secretary of State may, in his absolute discretion, during the current fiscal year, terminate the employment of any officer or employee of the Department of State or of the Foreign Service of the United States whenever he shall deem such termination necessary or advisable in the interests of the United States." See 63 Stat. 456, § 104, July 20, 1949. The figures on dismissals after 1949 are from Scott McLeod's letter to the Government Operations Committee released July 2, 1953; see NYT, July 3, 1953. McLeod has testified that the State Department summary dismissal power was used "exclusively" in only two cases from 1947 to 1953. JOHNSTON HEARINGS, p. 676. See also BONTECOU, p. 290; William Buckley, Jr., and Brent Bozell, *McCarthy and His Enemies* (1954), pp. 14, 15. Service v. Dulles, 354 U.S. 363 (1957) held that, in effecting removals under the McCarran rider, the Secretary was obliged to follow procedural regulations he had made which limited his discretion. On homosexual removals see Ch. 11 below, n. 4.

733 in 1950. The next year, when questioned by a House Appropriations subcommittee about 31 employees regarded as security risks, Secretary Sawyer said, "They are all gone." Many of them, he added, had resigned. Despite (or perhaps because of) Secretary Sawyer's assurance that he had made a clean sweep, he was in 1951 given the same summary dismissal power held by the Secretary of State. In 1953 the House of Representatives refused to renew the summary dismissal power of the Secretaries of State and Commerce, largely because they had sufficient authority under the over-all security program. Furthermore, this power completely undercut civil service rights, especially veteran's preference.[56]

Security dismissals were probably few from the remaining agencies named in P.L. 733, and from other agencies like the Office of Defense Mobilization which (on its own initiative) required all its employees to meet security standards for access to classified information.[57]

As a very rough guess, there may have been twice as many dismissals from the federal service on security grounds during the life of the loyalty program (1948–53) as there were loyalty dismissals.

The official collections of figures on the Eisenhower program through 1954 were injected into partisan controversy, and suffered from it. The tabulations as collected and published by the Civil Service Commission permitted administration spokesmen to make misleading claims about the vigor with which the security program was being pursued. These boasts back-fired; and the welter of claims and recriminations came to be known as the "numbers game." The last figures released before the form was revised in some respects (they covered the period May 1953–Oct. 1954) came out with a grand total of 8008, which permitted wags to point out that this was indeed a significant number, because it was the same forward or backward, right-side up or upside down.

More serious observations that could be made about this reporting, either from the face of the tabulations themselves or from the background provided by Congressional inquiries, are these:

56. Secretary Sawyer's statement is in House Comm. on Appropriations, Hearings, *Department of Commerce Appropriations for 1952* (1951), p. 30. The extension of the summary dismissal power to the Department of Commerce first appeared as a rider to the Dept. of Commerce Appropriation Act for 1952, 66 Stat. 567, § 304 (1952). On the termination of the summary dismissal power of the Secretaries of State and Commerce see *Cong. Rec.* (May 5, 1953), 99:4511–4537; NYT, May 6, 1953. See Scher v. Weeks, 231 F. 2d 494 (D.C. Cir. 1956) (constitutionality of summary dismissal legislation upheld on authority of Bailey v. Richardson, in a case further described in JOHNSTON HEARINGS, pp. 531–42).

57. See Habbe (n. 4 above), pp. 129–33 (ODM program).

(1) A little less than 40 per cent of the total had been "terminated"; the rest had resigned from federal service with some derogatory information in their records. But it did not follow that those who had resigned knew that they might become subject to charges. So the figures told nothing about derogatory information as a motive for resigning.

(2) The tabulation by major categories of derogatory information showed that in only about 25 per cent of the "cases" was there material bearing on disloyalty. All the rest fell into the broad areas of unreliability that had been swept into the security program by the first paragraph of section 8(a) of E.O. 10450 (quoted above, p. 32). With the exception of the sex perversion cases (8 per cent), none of these instances of criminal records, mental instability, etc., necessarily had any special security-risk significance. They could have been handled as ordinary suitability cases.

(3) Most of the terminations had in fact been made under regulations and procedures *other than* E.O. 10450. Chairman Young of the Civil Service Commission belatedly made this clear. That is, the reporting agencies ascribed a certain number of the federal employees dismissed for cause during the period to "Termination for information under 8(a)," even though neither 8(a) nor any other part of the security risk program played any part in the removal proceeding. Indeed, it appeared that the earlier reports included some separations that had been brought about by death.[58]

Ultimately, as the result of an extensive search of personnel records stimulated by the Johnston Subcommittee, the numbers were deflated. The committee staff announced in December 1955 that, through June 30, 1955, only 343 persons had actually been dismissed "pursuant to

58. On this point see NYT, March 24, 1954. The "numbers" controversy began in October 1953 with the first reports purporting to give experience with the 10450 program. Republican spokesmen promptly seized on the figures as an illustration of the purging of "spies and traitors" by the administration. The Democrats used appropriations hearings early in 1954 as a means of extracting information from the various departments about the actual scope and significance of the reported figures. The resulting confusion defies disentangling. An analysis is attempted in Sandra Weinstein, *Personnel Security Programs of the Federal Government* (1954), pp. 85–95 (mimeo., not published in this form; in Yale Law Library).

The "numbers" continued to be an issue in the 1954 Congressional campaigns. When further investigations were made in 1955 by committees under Democratic control, the significance (or insignificance) of the summaries issued by the Civil Service Commission was at last established. Chairman Young's extended testimony, and other material bearing on this subject, is in HUMPHREY HEARINGS, pp. 530–4, 547–50; JOHNSTON HEARINGS, pp. 400–2, 407–8, 682–3, 726–32, and Part 2, passim; JOHNSTON REPORT, pp. 364–86 (pp. 376–86 on partisan use of the numbers).

Executive Order 10450." Of this shrunken group, the cases of 315 did involve the "loyalty" paragraphs, 2 through 8 of section 8 of E.O. 10450, in marked contrast to the predominance of suitability defects in the total of reported cases. Of the 3243 who were terminated by civil-service procedures—not by E.O. 10450—2089 were probationary employees, who had worked less than a year. Only 32 of the cases processed under E.O. 10450 fell into the probationary group. The fact that so many of those included in the large numbers were recent employees—Chairman Young conceded that 40 per cent of the entire collection had been employed by the Eisenhower administration—finally demolished any partisan utility that those numbers might have had, and they were heard no more.[59]

In addition to the profound ambiguities in the reports of terminations, there were remarkable variations between the agencies in the reported ratios of dismissals to resignations. For the period May 28, 1953–Oct. 31, 1954 the military departments reported a total of 1311 dismissals and 1877 resignations "with security information" under the Civil Service Commission rubric. Ignoring rather marked differences between the services, this gave a ratio of resignations to reported dismissals of roughly 3–2. The Post Office, with 526 cases, had the same proportion. On the other hand, the next largest agency, the Veterans' Administration, reported 353 dismissals and 1112 resignations. The State Department reported only 5 dismissals (which, atypically, all apparently followed hearings under 10450), and 228 resignations. The reported practice in the State Department of pressing for resignations before charges or hearing seems to be strikingly confirmed by these figures. To wind up this catalog of inconsistencies, the Foreign Operations Administration reported 184 terminations, which included only 26 resignations.[60]

Some of these varying ratios, as in the case of the State Department, reflect differences in practice. Others emphasize the unreliable character of the reporting for 1953 and 1954. The notorious numbers included

---

59. JOHNSTON HEARINGS, Part 2, esp. pp. 1050, 1331; REPORT, pp. 371–5.

60. See HUMPHREY HEARINGS, pp. 318–20, 342–3, on the State Department's five dismissals. The figures on resignations are taken from the "Third Consolidated Report," following which there were some changes in the form used for collecting data. The "Fourth Consolidated Report," covering operations through June 30, 1955, though not strictly comparable with the earlier reports, is of interest because the program by that time was, according to Chairman Philip Young, substantially on a current basis. JOHNSTON HEARINGS, pp. 682–4, 728–32. There is no significant difference in the ratios of dismissals to resignations between the Third and Fourth Report.

too many cases that were not processed under E.O. 10450, and could not have been part of the program except by a loose interpretation of its reliability provisions.

We noted that an overwhelming proportion of hearings went in favor of the employee under the loyalty program. I will not stop to assemble the odd bits and pieces of information for the security programs. The 1953–54 experience of the Department of Defense—clearance in one-half to two-thirds of the cases that went to hearing—is probably close to the over-all recent experience.

On turning from employees separated to the equally important question of applicants excluded on loyalty or security grounds, one finds little meaningful information. It appears that pre-appointment investigations, which turn up information bearing on general suitability more than on security issues, may rule out one applicant in ten because of criminal records and other disqualifications.[61] There are some valuable figures from the State Department for the eight-year period beginning Jan. 1, 1947, about the same time-span that this book is concerned with. The Office of Security conducted 42,795 investigations of applicants during that time, and rejected 554 for "purely security reasons." The percentage of rejections (1.3 per cent) was the same for the five-year period 1947–51 as for the three-year period 1952–54. This is of interest because the Department was severely criticized for alleged laxity in security in the earlier period; and indeed the two periods are separated in the report we are citing, because of uncertainty about the extent of some investigations before 1952; all since then had been full field.[62] Of course, the identical rate of rejections in the two periods is consistent with a hypothesis that the standards had been lax and got tighter; as they did so, ineligible persons did not even bother to apply. This leads into an area beyond arithmetic: the deterrent effect of the programs on people who could not qualify, on those who could qualify but thought they could not, and on those who were unwilling to have anything to do with the process. There must be such effects, but it would be idle to speculate about their numerical extent.

61. See Hoover (n. 8 above), p. 337.
62. See HUMPHREY HEARINGS, pp. 350–1.

3. More Federal Programs

GOVERNMENT CONTRACTORS AND THEIR EMPLOYEES

FAMILY resemblances among the other programs administered by the federal government are so marked that one can identify the differences without explaining the similarities in detail. The security programs that are closest to those for civil servants are those for government contractors and their employees.

The security dangers are about the same whether the Navy builds an atomic-powered submarine in the Brooklyn Navy Yard or has it built by the General Dynamics Corp. But the installation of employment tests must proceed through different channels in the two instances. Though General Dynamics may subsist largely on government contracts, it is a private enterprise, and its employees are not government workers. Employment tests have therefore not been imposed directly, but instead have been stipulated in the contracts between the government and the individual, corporation, or institution with which it was dealing.

The Atomic Energy Commission and the Department of Defense have had almost all of the contractual relationships in which classified information or material had to be safeguarded. Their techniques have not been the same; so the main elements of each will be noted.

ATOMIC ENERGY COMMISSION

The basis of the AEC's program is a prohibition in the Atomic Energy Act against giving anyone access to "restricted data" unless his "character, associations, and loyalty" have been investigated and the Commission has cleared him. "Restricted data" is a statutory coinage to encompass any information about atomic weapons and fissionable material, except what the Commission decides can be safely published.

The AEC has relied to a remarkable extent on private contractors to carry on both its operations and its research. Consequently the manpower used by contractors on AEC projects may, depending on the volume of construction, run from 75 to 150,000, while the Commission's employees stay at around 7500 or fewer. Not all of the contractor

61

employees have to be cleared, especially in the early stages of construction work; but even if an employee does not have access to "Restricted data," clearance may still be required if he is going to work inside a restricted area—a concept which seems to be generously defined.[1]

The tremendous volume of full field investigations which the original Atomic Energy Act was believed to require was mitigated by a 1954 amendment which gave the Commission power to prescribe the scope of investigation (§ 145 f.). The Commission then created what is called an "L" clearance, for contractor employees who do not require access to material classified higher than Confidential. The existing "Q" clearance is retained for Commission employees and for higher access. The initial investigation for "L" clearance consists only of the national-agency name check, with full investigation reserved for cases where the name check reveals derogatory information.[2]

The procedures after investigation are practically identical for Commission employees and for contractor employees, and follow the standard pattern of evaluation, hearing and review. The criteria also are similar to those of other agencies with well-developed security programs, like the Air Force. The present regulations were adopted in 1949 and 1950, with some modifications in 1956. From the employee's standpoint, they represented a great improvement over the rather rough-and-ready methods the Commission had inherited from the Manhattan Engineer District; and they also include some refinements not found elsewhere. Foremost of these is the extension of hearing and review procedures to applicants for employment. The Commission has stated that most cases where derogatory information has appeared have occurred at this stage; but it has found that the administrative burden of providing hearings for applicants, which seems to alarm other agencies, has not been diffi-

1. E.g. Confidential clearance suffices for access to a classified area if the employee can only *see* Secret buildings. AEC Manual, § 2302.041, HUMPHREY HEARINGS, p. 1301. Private atomic power development has created new necessities for clearance. Employees of business firms who want access to Restricted data may seek clearance for "Access Permits," which are apparently readily available for Confidential material, and are available on a "need to know" basis for Secret. This new set of controls, which draws into the circle of clearance people who are employees neither of the AEC nor of its contractors, is ably explored by Harold Green, "Information Control and Atomic Power Development," *Law and Contemp. Prob.* (1956), *21:*91.

2. Responsibility for investigations is divided between FBI and CSC as described in Ch. 2 above, n. 8. The shift to two types of clearance is discussed by Herbert Marks and George Trowbridge, "Control of Information under the Atomic Energy Act of 1956," BAS (1955), *11:*128.

cult to carry. One reason may be that the Commission has made extensive use of informal interviews, which have often served, in its words, to "eliminate doubt." There is no indication that these interviews have been used as a form of pressure to withdraw. The Commission has also maintained an appeals board composed of distinguished citizens not on its staff. The initial hearing boards draw both on contractor employees and on private citizens.[3]

The Commission reported that in the five-year period ending Dec. 31, 1952, about 400,000 investigations were made. Derogatory information had appeared in 4000.

> Slightly more than one-half of these cases were not processed to conclusion for one reason or another, such as a decision by the employer not to use the services of the individual concerned in a place involving access to restricted data, as had been originally contemplated, or the resignation or dismissal of the individual before a clearance determination could be made. In somewhat more than 25 per cent of the 4000 cases, security clearance was granted following informal interviews or formal hearings. Security clearance had been denied or revoked in about 450 cases, as of December 31, 1952. Some of these denials occurred before the AEC adopted the formal hearing and appeal procedures.

The 1955 figures brought the total number of investigations to 504,000 and of denials to 494; other ratios also held steady.[4]

The AEC program, if one puts to one side the Wagnerian splendors and tragedy of the Oppenheimer case, has been remarkably stable. Though the Commission recognizes a formal submission to E.O. 10450,

3. The early development of the AEC's security policies is presented in Walter Gellhorn, *Security, Loyalty, and Science* (1950), esp. pp. 79–91; AEC, *Oppenheimer . . . Hearing* (1954) is revealing on Manhattan District practices, esp. testimony of General Leslie Groves (pp. 163–80) and John Lansdale (pp. 259–80). On the usefulness of extending procedures to applicants, and of making wide use of interviews, see AEC source in n. 4 below. The composition of hearing boards is described in ASS'N OF THE BAR, REPORT, p. 96.

The May 1956 amendments to the 1949–50 regulations are in *Fed. Reg.* (1956), *21*:3103. The basic regulations are in *Code Fed. Regs. 10: Part 4.* The amendments emphasize the necessity of correctly evaluating remote affiliations or associations, and the desirability of hearing adverse witnesses. The AEC's subpoena power, which is unique among the federal programs, may be invoked, and confidential witnesses, if at all accessible, are to be questioned by the hearing board. See AEC mimeo. statement for release May 10, 1956.

4. AEC, *Fourteenth Semiannual Report* (1953), pp. 70–1; HUMPHREY HEARINGS, p. 294.

it has pretty much pursued its own course, and in some respects has set an example for other agencies.[5]

DEPARTMENT OF DEFENSE

The Department of Defense has screened contractors and their employees, through channels different from those used for its own employees, without specific statutory authority. As authority for elaborate security provisions in its contracts it has relied chiefly on the general legal duty of the department heads to safeguard classified information. These contract provisions, and the regulations that stand behind them, oblige the contractor to meet both physical and personnel security requirements minutely prescribed by the government. Before he can enter into a contract, his facilities and his key officers and employees must be cleared. Then he must solicit clearance for any employees who are to work on Top Secret or Secret material. But in the case of the much larger numbers handling only Confidential data, the initial clearance is rather vaguely left to the employer. This hole in the fence may be a tacit recognition that the "Confidential" stamp is not significant enough to justify the expense of a name-check. The contract does reserve to the government the power to require the removal of an employee from any classified work if something derogatory turns up. Employers have been troubled by their responsibilities in the "Confidential" areas. Lacking access to official records, some of them have resorted to private investigative agencies, which are not well-equipped for this kind of work.[6]

Where the Department undertakes the screening, the investigative routines are about the same as those for its own employees. An initial

5. See ASS'N OF THE BAR, REPORT, p. 84, on the AEC and E.O. 10450. For overall evaluations of the program cf. Brown, "Personnel Security," ANNALS (1953), 290:100, with John Palfrey, "The AEC Security Program: Past and Present," BAS (1955), 11:131.

6. See Ch. 5 below, n. 33. The basic Armed Forces Industrial Security Regulation (see BNA MANUAL, p. 21/1, §§ 1–101), makes only a reference to the National Security Act of 1947 as its authority. 5 U.S.C. § 22, directing the heads of departments to safeguard records, is another source. The implied power to include conditions in contracts, in support of the prohibitions of the Espionage Act and similar statutes, is probably the soundest basis. See Comment, "Loyalty and Private Employment," Yale Law Jour. (1953), 62:973, n. 95. Standard contract clauses refer to the Industrial Security Manual for Safeguarding Classified Security Information, which is a handbook for the contractor. This, along with other documents, is reproduced in BNA MANUAL, Part 25.

evaluation and recommendation is made by the contracting military department and forwarded to a central Screening Board in the Pentagon. This Board, after further investigation if it wishes, either clears or issues a tentative denial of clearance, with a "Statement of Reasons" which is sent to the employee (or contractor, if his own clearance is in doubt). The Screening Board also controls suspensions. The employee can make a written reply to the charges, and request a hearing before one of three regional boards. The pattern of the hearing is the conventional one already described for government employees, and the criteria by which both the screening and hearing boards are guided are conventional security criteria. The basic standard is whether access to classified information is "consistent with the interests of national security." The recommended decision of the Hearing Board goes back to the central Office of Industrial Personnel Security Review. The record will be brought before a Review Board, if the decision of the hearing board was not unanimous, or if the Director of the Office (or some higher official) so recommends. This is not an appeal board to which the employee has access.[7]

The preceding paragraph is a thumbnail description of the 1955 reorganization of the program, the third such since its obscure beginnings, which were entirely under military control and marked by rather arbitrary methods. In 1949 a single Industrial Employment Review Board was set up, responsible to the three service Secretaries and with a civilian chairman. Under his direction there appeared to be a marked liberalization in the effective standards of the program. In its first months of operation, the IERB is reported to have reversed about half of the

7. A significant difference in investigative routine between this program and the civil servants' is that a file check suffices initially for Secret clearance, and a full field investigation is routinely made only for Top Secret. AFISR (n. 6 above), §§ 2–203. There are special provisions for aliens, and a statute of 1926 imposes further disabilities on aliens working on aircraft contracts: 44 Stat. 787, 10 U.S.C. § 310(j). As the result of a requirement in the May 1955 version of AFISR, §§ 2–203, that aliens will not be cleared unless they have declared their intention to become U.S. citizens, Dr. Fritz Zwicky of the California Institute of Technology, a Swiss citizen resident in the U.S. since 1927, and an eminent authority on jet propulsion, was removed from classified projects with which he had long been connected. *Time* (July 11, 1955), p. 67.

The Industrial Personnel Security Review Regulation of Feb. 2, 1955, *Fed. Reg. 20*:1553, 5079, is reprinted in Dep't of Defense, Industrial Personnel Security Review Program, *First Annual Report* (1956), p. 174. The Report is a valuable discussion of the operation of the current program. Two recent attacks on the program were unsuccessful; appeals are pending. Greene v. Wilson, 150 F. Supp. 958 (D.D.C. 1957); Webb v. U.S. (E.D. Pa. 1957), BNA MANUAL, p. 29/142.

denials of clearance appealed to it from the Screening Board. This ratio apparently continued until 1955. Screening panels could be (and in the past have been) composed entirely of military officers.

The next reorganization, in 1953, met objections to the inconvenience of having only one appeal board in Washington. Three regional boards were established. At the same time the screening division was also decentralized, with one military service responsible for each region (Eastern, Army; Central, Air Force; Western, Navy). The result was apparently lack of coordination, divergence of effective standards, and a somewhat trigger-happy practice of suspension. With the 1955 reorganization, control was again centralized in Washington, both at the beginning and at the end of the process.

Until 1955, the hearing was treated as an appeal from a decision already reached at the screening level. However, the screening board permitted written replies by the employee, and occasionally reversed its own initial decision.[8] Until rather recently its charging practice seems to have been stereotyped and uninformative. One set of charges that I have seen said, in essence: "(1) You are a Communist. (2) You have been a Communist. (3) You have associated with Communists." The

8. The early history of the program was explored by Gellhorn (n. 3 above), esp. pp. 100–10. See *Fortune* (Sept. 1950), p. 47, on the performance of the reformed IERB. The screening board was called the Army-Navy-Air Force Personnel Security Board, and had its own "Charter" and Procedures of June 19, 1950 (mimeo.). The criteria of the IERB "Charter" of Nov. 7, 1949, revised Nov. 10, 1950, are printed in HUMPHREY HEARINGS, p. 204; they resemble E.O. 9835, with the addition of a reliability requirement.

The 1953 revision, called the Industrial Personnel and Facility Security Clearance program, was established early in the new administration by a directive of May 4, 1953, mimeo. Apparently not in *Fed. Reg.*; see *Stanford Law Rev.* (n. 10 below), p. 243, n. 71. The standard was essentially that of E.O. 10450. Indications that suspensions were considered excessive under this program are found in testimony of Secretary Wilber Brucker, HUMPHREY HEARINGS, p. 217, and in *First Annual Report* (n. 7 above), p. 5 (60 per cent of cases considered by the screening board now result in clearance, compared to 37 per cent under the preceding program). Until the 1955 changes, the appeals board had continued to overrule the screening board in more than half of the cases carried to it. Ibid.

The Secretary of Defense, or the three service Secretaries jointly, can reverse a Review Board decision. IPSR Reg. § 22. The Secretary of any military department can require reconsideration by the Review Board. In 1954 Secretary of the Navy Charles Thomas directed a reconsideration of the case of Dr. Edward U. Condon, who then decided not to go through the process again. This had been his fourth clearance. Condon resigned as Director of Research of Corning Glass Co., retaining a connection as a consultant. NYT, Oct. 22, Dec. 14, 1954. He has since become Chairman of the Department of Physics at Washington University, St. Louis. See his informative speech of Nov. 1957 in BAS (1958), *14*:80.

first two counts, in view of the facts, could not have been seriously intended, and the third was hopelessly unspecific. Recent charges ("Statement of Reasons," as they are called) conform to the usual practice, which, however, includes withholding anything that might compromise investigative sources.[9]

Over all, there is not much deviation between the AEC and Defense Department contractor employee programs on the one hand and the civil service security programs on the other. They are alike in their essentials, with these two significant points of difference. First, in the industrial security programs the government is dealing not with its own employees—public servants—but with private citizens. Yet it still puts the burden on the employee to clear himself with inadequate knowledge of the evidence against him. Second, the result is not ostensibly the same. The contractor is not ordered to dismiss the employee, only to remove him from classified work. The final result depends on the availability of another job for the particular employee.

Here it is difficult to generalize, partly because the term "industrial" gives a wrong impression of the scope of these programs. Numerically, their impact is undoubtedly heaviest on industrial workers. But the government has been spending hundreds of millions a year on research contracts of which some large but unknown part is for classified work. Both in industry and in nonprofit institutions many scientists and other professional people are subject to these programs because they are working under classified contracts with the AEC or the Defense Department.

In the case of the industrial worker, his chances of successful relocation after a denial of clearance will often depend on the strength and diligence of his union. The employer, even if he has unclassified work for which the employee is suited, may consider him rather a liability, and there is evidence that dismissals often follow routinely on denial of clearance. The union may be indifferent to this result, if the security risk derives from unpopular political views. But a few unions have found it worth while to fight for the avowed policy of the program, which is to avoid outright dismissals.[10]

9. See *First Annual Report,* pp. 5–6, and App. C and D on recent charging practice. Examples of inadequate charges before 1955 are in *Case Studies in Personnel Security,* ed. Yarmolinsky (1955), pp. 226, 240, 244, 268. In some of these cases the employee was able to get further specification of the charges.

10. On government research outlays see Ch. 5 below, n. 16. On employers' disposition to dismiss employees who are denied clearance see Comment, "The Role of Employer Practices in the Federal Industrial Personnel Security Program—A Field Study," *Stanford Law Rev.* (1956), 8:234, esp. pp. 245, 252, 257. This

Union support has developed when employers have attempted to suspend employees pending the resolution of their clearance troubles. Several arbitration cases have been brought, protesting suspenion as a breach of the collective bargaining agreement, with varying results. Finally, if a suspension has occurred, there is the question of back pay if the employee is ultimately cleared. The apparent policy of the Defense Department industrial security programs, at least since 1950, has been to recommend the payment of lost earnings by the employer. But there appeared to be no official machinery to enforce such payments; so again the issue, when it was contested, turned on the requirements of collective bargaining agreements. Regulations since 1953 provide for reimbursement by the contracting Department.[11]

The professional man caught up in clearance difficulties is not likely to have the support of a union. And if his field is, for example, nuclear physics, denial of clearance may make him almost unemployable. The absence of union support, however, is somewhat counterbalanced by the superior opportunities of the scientist to organize and present a coherent, successful defense. Most of the kind words that I have heard about the performance of the Industrial Employment Review Board came from scientists or their counsel.[12]

UNCLASSIFIED RESEARCH

The scientist as the recipient of government grants is also exposed to political tests in certain situations where the security context is slight at most. After a Congressional *cause célèbre* involving a communist graduate student, fellowships awarded by the Atomic Energy Commission were made subject to an FBI investigation. The work to be done was unclassified, but there was strong Congressional sentiment that any research in the atomic field might produce results of military usefulness. A distinction was made in the case of recipients of National Science

Comment also contains a helpful description of the current regulation and procedures. Labor union attitudes are mentioned by some of the speakers in Industrial Rel. Res. Ass'n., *Personnel Security Programs in U. S. Industry* (1955), pp. 36, 59, 88.

11. See IPSR Reg. (n. 7 above), § 26. A similar provision was in the preceding regulation. Back pay from the employer was denied in Bell Aircraft Corp., 16 Lab. Arb. 234 (1951). The cases on suspension are in Ch. 5 below, n. 26.

12. See Anonymous, "Cleared for Top Secret," *Scientific Monthly* (1952), *74:* 145, for a remarkably docile account of a complex clearance case, written by the subject.

Foundation fellowships for research and training in basic science. They are required only to execute a loyalty affidavit. Both of these instances, and the research grants made by the Public Health Service, may be thought of as conditions on government bounty rather than restrictions on employment. Whatever effect this distinction might have, it is of dubious accuracy. The government can carry on medical research, for example, either through the National Institutes of Health and other government agencies or through contracts with private investigators and institutions. It in fact does both, and both channels are important for the execution of national policy with respect to research.[13]

In 1954 it came to light that the Department of Health, Education, and Welfare was making decisions, based on doubts about loyalty, to withhold certain research grants. These decisions appeared to be completely unilateral, without charges, hearings, or review. After a while, considerable opposition developed within the scientific community to the arbitrary and unpredictable character of these measures. The White House asked the National Academy of Sciences for recommendations. When a committee appointed by President Detlev Bronk of the NAS brought in its report, it unqualifiedly condemned the application of loyalty tests to unclassified research grants. "The idea persists," the report said, "that the government in granting funds for research confers a favor upon scientists as individuals. We consider this contrary to the fact. In appropriating funds for the support of research, we believe the Congress to have been motivated by an urgent national need. . . . A fundamental contribution leading ultimately to the cure of cancer, providing it were made generally available, would be no less beneficial to all humanity for having been made by a Communist. Authentic scientific progress carries with it no ideological flavor from its source." After a period of apparently stunned silence, the administration accepted the recommendations, thus ending a major intrusion of political tests into a nonsensitive sphere.[14]

13. On the AEC fellowship controversy see Carey McWilliams, *Witch Hunt* (1950), pp. 82–96; John Palfrey, "The Problem of Secrecy," ANNALS (1953), *290*:94. The National Science Foundation affidavit is required by its basic statute of 1950, 64 Stat. 156 (1950), 42 U.S.C. § 1874(d). In its *Fifth Annual Report, 1955* (1955), p. 20, the Foundation stated the following policy: "The Foundation . . . will not knowingly support anyone who is, by admission or conviction, disloyal to this country. In the interest of science, however, it will not pass judgment on the loyalty of an individual on the basis of unsupported charges but will rely on the judgment of those who best know the individual and his qualifications."
14. See Scientists' Committee on Loyalty and Security, "Loyalty and U.S.

However, the screening of private employees in classified work continued as a major undertaking of both the Defense Department and the AEC, especially the former. An accurate census of Defense contractor employees required to have clearance has been difficult, perhaps because of the contractor's own power to grant access to Confidential material. But as Congressional committees developed an interest in the program, successive departmental estimates, each larger than the one before, resulted in an apparently authoritative estimate late in 1955 that the current coverage of the programs was close to 3,000,000.

The Department has not been satisfied with its control over the access to classified materials even of so many people. Its desire to obtain statutory authority for controls over other defense-related employment will be discussed in Chapter 10; and apparently it has collaborated with employers in screening employees who were not in fact engaged in classified operations.

On the other hand, the latest reorganization seems to have been followed by an earnest attempt to minimize unnecessary initial denials of clearance, to cut down unwarranted delays, and to apply the given standards and criteria carefully.[15]

Public Health Service Grants," BAS (1955), *11:*196 (quoting and commenting on a statement by Secretary Oveta Hobby of April 28, 1954); J. T. Edsall, "Government and the Freedom of Science," *Science* (1955), *121:*615. The Public Health Service permitted some circumvention of its test by reinstating grants in the name of a principal assistant to the ineligible researcher. BAS, *11:*197. The report of the NAS committee, of March 13, 1956 (mimeo.; reprinted in part in BAS (1956), *12:*227), has attached to it the letter of Jan. 11, 1955, requesting the formation of the committee, in which Assistant to the President Sherman Adams had said, "No one will question the fundamental principle that only those who are loyal to our government should be beneficiaries of government grants-in-aid or contracts." Adams advised the NAS in a letter released Aug. 14, 1956 (NYT, Aug. 15, 1956), that government agencies would "follow practices consistent with the recommendations" of the report. At about the time the report was made, the Public Health Service had announced a modification of its policies so as to make them substantially in accord with those of the National Science Foundation, n. 13 above. NYT, April 2, 1956. Cf. Commission on Government Security, *Report* (1957), p. 318.

15. See Ch. 6 below, n. 16, on the number covered; Ch. 5 below, n. 27, on cooperation with employers who want to screen beyond classified jobs. It appears from other cases reported to me in interviews that this problem is of long standing. On performance under the 1955 program see *First Annual Report,* n. 7 above. Another program involving contractors and their employees is administered by the International Cooperation Administration. Apparently the necessity for clearance is not contingent on access to classified information. The effective regulations are those of the predecessor agency, the Foreign Operations Administration. See F.O.A. Manual, Orders 610.2 (Feb. 24, 1955) and 610.4 (Sept. 22, 1954).

THE PORT SECURITY PROGRAM

Unlike the evolution of the Defense and AEC contractor programs, which from crude origins achieved considerable sophistication, the Port Security program never really advanced much from its flurried beginnings early in the Korean War. Perhaps because of wretched conditions of employment, the maritime trades had been especially vulnerable to communist influence in the 1930's. In 1950 there were still two communist-dominated unions on the Pacific Coast, Harry Bridges' longshoremen, and the Marine Cooks and Stewards, a smaller seagoing group led by Hugh Bryson. Fears of political strikes and of sabotage encouraged a revival of World War II security measures in July 1950. For a few months there was a voluntary program, to which the ship operators and the anticommunist unions both subscribed. Although the Coast Guard, which licenses seamen, was actively engaged in designating unacceptable security risks, this program had no legal foundation. However, a statute was passed in August 1950 (known as the Magnuson Act), which authorized the president to take measures "to safeguard against destruction, loss, or injury from sabotage or other subversive acts . . . vessels, harbors, ports, and waterfront facilities . . ." On the strength of this broad grant, an Executive Order was issued, soon followed by a detailed regulation. By the beginning of 1951 a settled program was in operation, under which the government undertook to bar any person from seagoing employment or from access to restricted areas of the waterfront "unless the Commandant (of the Coast Guard) is satisfied that the character and habits of life of the applicant are such as to authorize the belief that the presence of such individual on board a vessel or within a waterfront facility would not be inimical to the security of the United States." The nonpolitical habits of seamen were already scrutinized in the licensing process. The regulations therefore inquired only of waterfront employees whether they were narcotics addicts, illegally in the United States, etc.

The political criteria of the regulations were taken in substance from those of the loyalty program; but the procedures were rather different.

The initial step was a decision by the Coast Guard, based on file-check reports only, that the seaman should be denied clearance. His first intimation of this was the suspension of his license, accompanied by a stereotyped assertion that he was a Communist. He was then allowed to "appeal" to a three-man board, made up of one representative each of the Coast Guard, of management, and of labor. These hearings followed the pattern of loyalty hearings, and were marked by extensive questioning unrelated to any specific charges. The Coast Guard produced no evidence or witnesses, so that the issue of confrontation was entirely foreclosed. From an adverse recommendation, the employee, if he could get to Washington, could appear before a National Appeals Board, also tripartite. The final decision, however, was the Commandant's. Even if the outcome was favorable, the employee got no compensation for a period of enforced idleness of perhaps a year or more.

The execution wrought by this program was considerable. In two years the Coast Guard screened practically all the maritime labor force— roughly 600,000—and denied clearance to about 2500. By the end of 1955 the number denied clearance had risen to 3783, half of them seamen, who were thus completely prevented from following their calling on American ships. Some of the others, longshoremen and other dock workers excluded from waterfront facilities, may have been able to follow their trades in unrestricted areas. After the Korean War access to waterfront facilities was relaxed.[16]

The proportion of denials of clearance in the Port Security program has not been approached in any other screening operation on which we have figures. Four explanations may be suggested. First, there may have been more Communists and near-Communists in these trades than in any other group yet subjected to employment tests. Second, most of the victims were men of small means and little education; the majority did not have counsel and were ill-equipped to extricate themselves. Third, no other major program maintained such shoddy procedures throughout a large-scale screening. The Coast Guard, it should be said, was poorly staffed for such an undertaking, and was forced to make haste in an atmosphere of claimed (but never verified) emergency. Fourth, some of the major unions, which might have been expected to protest such a drastic invasion of private employment by the government, were themselves immersed in anticommunist vendettas and were insensitive to the issues of due process involved.[17]

16. This section, except for more recent events, is based on Brown and Fassett, "Security Tests for Maritime Workers: Due Process under the Port Security Program," *Yale Law Jour.* (1953), 62:1163. ASS'N OF THE BAR, REPORT, has the Dec. 1955 figures (p. 221) and the information on the cutback of the waterfront programs (p. 117). The government's attempts to deport or to denaturalize Harry Bridges, all of which have failed, are summarized in U.S. v. Bridges, 133 F. Supp. 638 (N.D. Cal. 1955); but Hugh Bryson's conviction for perjury in a Taft-Hartley oath case was affirmed in Bryson v. U.S., 238 F. 2d 657 (9th Cir. 1956), rehearing denied 243 F. 2d 837 (1957).

17. Further information on the politics of the National Maritime Union, in

Legal challenges sponsored by the Marine Cooks and Stewards were, after long litigation, successful in one respect: in *Parker v. Lester* the Coast Guard was ordered to give adequate notice of specific charges. It cautiously amended its regulations in April 1956, carefully reserving the disclosure of investigative sources. More litigation followed, in which the challengers won a resounding victory. Without even deciding whether the new regulations satisfied the degree of due process which the Ninth Circuit felt was required, the court held that, since the old procedures were clearly inadequate, the licenses must be restored, at least pending new decisions under new procedures. At the beginning of 1957, the Coast Guard began to comply with the decree by issuing credentials stamped "Order of U. S. District Court." How helpful these documents were to men who had been away from the sea for five years or more was uncertain, as was the future of the entire program.[18]

POLITICAL TESTS FOR LABOR UNIONS

The problem of the communist-dominated labor union stands at the borderline of the present study, though it is much entwined with the programs just discussed. The various control measures that have so far been taken by the federal government raise a host of controversial issues, but they have not had much direct effect upon the employment of any individual union member. They do, however, affect the careers of union officials.

---

addition to sources cited in Brown and Fassett, is in Murray Kempton, *Part of Our Time* (1955), ch. 3; Philip Taft, *The Structure and Government of Labor Unions* (1954), pp. 176, 198. President William Bradley of the racket-ridden International Longshoremen's Association said in 1956 that it was expelling members who did not have clearance; NYT, Feb. 24, 1956.

18. The main stages of Parker v. Lester were: 227 F. 2d 708 (1955), regulations held invalid, reversing 112 F. Supp. 433 (1953); government decided not to appeal to Supreme Court, NYT, March 25, 1956; 235 F. 2d 787 (1956), rehearing denied BNA MANUAL, p. 52/245, injunction upheld forbidding Coast Guard to interfere with plaintiffs' employment. The first opinion of the Court of Appeals contained some strong language in opposition to denial of confrontation, but did not in terms require full due process.

The regulations, which are in *Code Fed. Regs. 33:* Parts 121, 125, were amended effective May 1, 1956. *Fed. Reg. 21:*2814, 2940. The description of the 1957 papers is from BNA MANUAL, Newsletter, Jan. 31, 1957. A suit against the government in the Court of Claims for back pay by a ship master denied clearance under the invalid regulations was dismissed. Dupree v. U.S., 141 F. Supp. 773 (1956). So was a suit by the same plantiff under the Federal Tort Claims Act, 247 F. 2d 819 (3rd Cir. 1957).

There has been no serious contention that the rank-and-file of any significant union has been permeated with Communists. It is possible that, as rival unions draw members away from the left-wing unions expelled from the CIO, the residue will contain an increasing proportion of members who are in sympathy with their leadership on political as well as economic issues. But such persons, if their employment in maritime or defense industries raises any security problem, can be plucked out one by one under the security programs just described. The problem has always been one of inhibiting any subversive activities of those Communists who had achieved positions of union leadership.

The first attempt of this sort was § 9(h) of the Taft-Hartley Act of 1947. It effectively bars from resort to the National Labor Relations Board any union unless each of its officers has filed an affidavit that "he is not a member of the Communist party or affiliated with such party, and that he does not believe in, and is not a member of or supports any organization that believes in or teaches the overthrow of the United States government by force or by any illegal or unconstitutional methods." For five years this oath seemed to have had slight effect on the position of suspected labor leaders. Some who were open party members purported to resign. In other cases, union offices were reshuffled so that the vulnerable leaders took posts that were not technically offices. Not until late 1952 did the Department of Justice take Senator Taft's advice that "They ought to prosecute more of these fellows. They may not be able to pin it on them all, but they can catch some of them with a jury." The Department then obtained a series of perjury indictments, and was indeed able to convince juries in 1953 and 1954 that, for example, Ben Gold, longtime national president of the Fur and Leather Workers Union and longtime Communist, had not in fact resigned from the party when he took the Taft-Hartley oath in 1950.

The Gold case went to the Supreme Court, which turned it off on a point about FBI interrogation of jurors, without reaching controversial issues of proof that abound in these cases. A number of other appealed cases were thus left unresolved, while in still others the defendants apparently began serving their sentences. Meanwhile, the Court declined to extend the effect of noncompliance on the part of the union beyond the literal reach of the statute—that is, exclusion from the services of the NLRB. The legal status of such unions, achieved without NLRB intervention, was declared to be unimpaired. Furthermore, the NLRB was forbidden to inquire into the validity of questionable oaths in administrative proceedings. The only remedy for the filing of a false affidavit is the criminal penalty.[19]

Another official measure to hasten the decline in influence of left-wing unions had no apparent consequences for employment. In 1948 the Atomic Energy Commission directed one of its contractors, General Electric, not to recognize the United Electrical Workers (later expelled from the CIO) as representative of employees at atomic energy installations. At that time the union could not protest the nonrecognition to the National Labor Relations Board, because its officers had not taken the Taft-Hartley oath. A suit for an injunction against the Commission was unsuccessful; the court held that the Atomic Energy Act authorized the directive.

The Department of Defense, which was equally alert to the asserted dangers of Communist leaders in defense plant unions, sought similar statutory powers. Several years of debate followed. The role of the National Labor Relations Board was in issue, as well as the increasingly impressive claim of the principal labor organizations that they could clean house themselves.[20]

The long discussion bore strange fruit in 1954 amendments to the Internal Security Act of 1950. These were passed at the very end of the 83d Congress as part of the burst of election-year bipartisan zeal to outlaw the Communist party. The 1950 Act had already created "commu-

19. The statute is 61 Stat. 146 (1947), 29 U.S.C. § 159(h). Senator Taft's advice is from NYT, Feb. 16, 1952. In the Gold case, remanded by the Supreme Court, 352 U.S. 819 (1957), the Circuit Court was evenly divided. The only opinion printed is Judge Bazelon's dissent, 237 F. 2d 764 (D.C. Cir. 1956). See Justice Clark's dissent listing the issues left open in the case. The Gold indictment was dismissed. NYT, May 10, 1957. See also Jencks v. U.S., 353 U.S. 657 (1957). The status of other Taft-Hartley perjury cases is reviewed in National Lawyers Guild, *Civil Liberties Docket* (1955–   ), *1:* § 240, *2:* § 290.

The right of a noncomplying union to picket for representation was upheld in United Mine Workers v. Arkansas Oak Flooring Co., 351 U.S. 62 (1956). Note that the union in this case is strongly anti-communist. Its officers have refused to take the oath as a matter of principle. The decisions excluding the NLRB from consideration of the validity of the oaths are Leedom v. Int'l Union of Mine Mill and Smelter Workers, 352 U.S. 145 (1956); Amalgamated Meat Cutters v. NLRB, 352 U.S. 153 (1956). Periodical material on the oath is profuse. See, e.g., Walter Daykin, "The Operation of the Taft-Hartley Act's Non-Communist Provisions," *Iowa Law Rev.* (1951), *36:*607; *Columbia* and *Northwestern* references, n. 21 below. The constitutionality of the oath is discussed in Ch. 13 below, p. 321.

20. See Alfred Scanlan, "The Communist-Dominated Union Problem," *Notre Dame Lawyer* (1953), *28:*458; UEW-CIO v. Lilienthal, 84 F. Supp. 640 (D.D.C. 1949).

nist-action" and "communist-front" organizations as legally operative concepts. Members of such organizations are forbidden nonelective government employment. They are required to reveal their membership in seeking or holding employment in defense facilities. They may not, without special authorization, receive classified information. Members of "communist-action" organizations may not be employed in a defense facility at all. There are other deprivations—such as ineligibility to have a passport—not pertinent here.

The machinery of the 1950 Act, involving hearings before the Subversive Activities Control Board with an appeal to the courts, had not been invoked against a labor union, partly because the machinery had been grinding slowly—the status of the Communist party itself is still in litigation—partly because it would have been difficult to prove that any labor union was *"primarily* operated for the purpose of giving aid and support" to communism.

The 1954 legislation removed the latter difficulty by directing sanctions at "communist-infiltrated organizations." Summarily, the new concept dropped the limiting term "primarily" from its definition.

The chief reason for seeking to identify "communist-infiltrated organizations" is to diminish their influence, and to withhold the benefits of the National Labor Relations Act, a sanction that was added to those already in the Internal Security Act. The legislation, however, encourages the ousting of Communist leaders by providing that an organization may petition to have the "communist-infiltrated" label expunged. More directly, it speeds the flight of members from a "communist-infiltrated" union by permitting 20 per cent of them to ask for an NLRB-sponsored election to choose a new bargaining representative. The Communist Control Act further includes a direct prohibition on union staff employment, by forbidding members of "communist-action" or "communist-front" organizations "to hold office or employment with any labor organization, as that term is defined in § 2(5) of the National Labor Relations Act or to represent any employer in any matter arising or pending under that act." Finally, any member of a "communist-infiltrated organization" is apparently subject to one (but a critical one) of the restrictions on employment mentioned above: denial of access to classified information. This of course excludes a considerable area of government and private employment. In 1955 the Attorney General commenced proceedings to have the United Electrical and the Mine Mill and Smelters unions declared "communist-infiltrated." [21]

21. The Communist Control Act, of which these provisions form §§ 6–11, is

EMPLOYMENT IN INTERNATIONAL ORGANIZATIONS

The next federal program to be considered turns in the opposite direction from private employment and disturbs a most delicate area of public employment: the staff of the United Nations and of its affiliated specialized agencies, such as UNESCO and the World Health Organization. From the League of Nations the UN inherited the principle, embodied in Section 100 of the Charter, of the "exclusively international character" of the Secretariat. Every UN employee takes an oath "to exercise in all loyalty, discretion and conscience the functions entrusted to me as an international servant." The spirit of this obligation requires the employee to detach himself from nationalistic or partisan ties. He retains allegiance to his national government, but that government must recognize his supranational obligations. The first operational step in securing the independence of the staff from national influences was to give the Secretary-General freedom in recruiting it; this principle is also embedded in the Charter. It has been assumed, however, that the Secretary-General would welcome information and advice from member states (and indeed Trygve Lie, the first Secretary-General, recognized that he would be ill-informed without such assistance); but he does not have to act on it. Dismissal is similarly in the control of the Secretary-General, subject to regulations of the General Assembly with respect to cause, tenure, etc.

So much, very briefly, for the theory of employment in international organizations.[22] Not surprisingly, this theory has come into conflict with the practice of employment tests as they have developed in this country.

The first open conflict came in 1952, when a grand jury, sitting in New York, and the Senate Internal Security Subcommittee, both engaged in a hunt for Communists in government, found that a number of former government employees with alleged communist sympathies had

---

68 Stat. 775. The Internal Security Act which it amends is 50 U.S.C. § 781. See Comment, "The Communist Control Act of 1954," *Yale Law Jour.* (1955), *64*:752–64, esp. pp. 753, 759, 762; Note, "Federal Anti-Subversive Legislation of 1954," *Columbia Law Rev.* (1955), *55*:674–701; Comment, "Control of Communist Unions," *Northwestern Univ. Law Rev.* (1955), *50*:396. The institution of the two proceedings is reported in NYT, July 29 (Mine Mill) and Dec. 21, 1955 (UE).

22. The foregoing relies chiefly on the careful study by S. M. Schwebel, "The International Character of the Secretariat of the United Nations," *British Yearbook of International Law* (1953), p. 71, which also reviews UN policies with respect to the American loyalty problem through 1953.

got jobs in the United Nations. The grand jury issued an angry presentment (but no indictments); the Committee promptly exposed to public
gaze twenty-two employees of the UN and related agencies who, when
questioned in executive session, had invoked the privilege against self-
incrimination.[23] The familiar enigma of the significance of the Fifth
Amendment plea tended to obscure the underlying issue: to what extent
should the Secretary-General defer to American measures against Communists and persons who might be Communists? What about those who
refused to clarify their position? Lie, after taking the opinion of three
eminent jurists, decided to dismiss all those who had invoked the privilege against self-incrimination, and indicated also that he would not retain a staff member against whom he had "tangible and convincing evidence" that the employee "had been, was, or was likely to be engaged
in activities directed toward the overthrow of a government by force."

The employees dismissed for invoking the privilege against self-incrimination appealed to the Administrative Tribunal constituted by the
General Assembly. Nine dismissals of temporary appointees were sustained, one such was reversed, and dismissals of eleven permanent appointees were reversed. Since the Secretary-General declined to reinstate
any of the staff members in question, the Tribunal awarded them compensation. In the face of objections, chiefly from the United States, to
voting an appropriation for such compensation, the General Assembly
requested an advisory opinion from the International Court of Justice.
The Court ruled that the Assembly was bound to give effect to the Tribunal's awards.[24]

Meanwhile the United States government, by E.O. 10422 (Jan. 1953,
as amended by E.O. 10459, June 1953) had established an International
Organizations Employees Loyalty Board in the Civil Service Commission. The Board transmits derogatory information to the Secretary-
General, "in as much detail as the Board determines that security considerations will permit." It also conducts a hearing, and, with criteria and
procedures similar to those of the employees' security program, makes
an "advisory determination" whether there is "reasonable doubt as to

23. ISC, Hearings, *Activities of United States Citizens Employed by the United
Nations* (1952–54), Parts 1–6; Reports, Jan. 2, 1953, and March 22, 1954. The
grand jury presentment is in NYT, Dec. 3, 1952, and ISC, Hearings, p. 407.

24. Schwebel (n. 22 above), pp. 83–98, cites the UN documents. The decisions of the Administrative Tribunal are in ISC, Hearings (n. 23 above), pp.
501–79. The decision of the International Court of Justice is in its *Reports* (1954),
p. 47. The United States, after many objections (see Hearings, p. 495), acceded
to the indemnity payments. NYT, Dec. 4, 1954.

the loyalty of the person involved to the government of the United States."

Note that the standard of reasonable doubt as to loyalty, taken from the discarded loyalty program, is used. There had been some expressions of alarm that subversives on the UN staff constituted a security risk to the United States. Lie pointed out that "the secretariat of the United Nations works in a glass house not only physically, but in every respect," and that opportunities for espionage and sabotage were practically nil. Eventually Ambassador Lodge conceded that staff members had no opportunity, by reason of their position, to jeopardize American security. A security standard would therefore have no logical basis.

The procedures of the Executive Order were, with respect to the transmission of information, doubtless a great improvement over a clandestine arrangement between the State Department and the Secretary-General, made in 1949 and revealed during the investigations of 1952. The Department had been supplying merely its conclusion whether a staff member would be a "poor risk" without giving any supporting evidence.[25] But suppose the new Loyalty Board found a reasonable doubt of loyalty? Would this finding, conveyed to the Secretary-General as an "advisory determination," satisfy his standards of due process and substantial evidence? Suppose he felt it his duty to reach a contrary conclusion, or to assert that a "doubt" as to loyalty did not justify dismissal? In either event, what political repercussions would follow? [26]

The last loyalty board went about its business with such circumspection that for some time no conflict arose. Patterned on the Loyalty Review Board, it was composed (except for the Chairman, Pierce Gerety, General Counsel of the Commission) of a panel of private citizens, who sat in groups of three. Attorneys who appeared before it report that the Board was aware of the limitations of anonymous accusations, and understanding of the changes in the political climate since the 1930's.

25. The State Department explained the 1949 arrangement in ISC, Hearings (n. 23 above), p. 415; cf. the comments of the UN Secretariat, p. 418. E.O. 10422, amended by E.O. 10459, is in *Fed. Reg. 18*:239, 3183. The order applies to forty-odd other international organizations in addition to the UN itself. Lie's statement is quoted from Schwebel (n. 22 above), p. 90; Lodge's is from NYT, Feb. 3, 1954.

26. Lie's successor, Dag Hammarskjold, modified Lie's position so that invocation of the privilege would be open to explanation, and not constitute an automatic ground for dismissal. He also emphasized that the basic standard was one of "integrity." The divergences between these standards and those implied by the Executive Order are explored by Schwebel, pp. 106–12. See also, for a succinct account of UN procedures and standards, BNA MANUAL, p. 41/4.

The Board disposed of almost 4,000 UN cases without giving them any notoriety. It was impossible to keep from the press the fact that the prominent Negro, Ralph Bunche, was the subject of a hearing. He was promptly cleared, and was soon promoted by Secretary-General Hammarskjold to the post of Under Secretary-General. Two of the Department of Justice's professional informers are said to have testified against Bunche.[27]

After dealing with the backlog of UN cases, the Board went to Europe in the summer of 1954 to hold hearings for American employees of the specialized agencies with European headquarters. Thirty-nine Americans abroad had received interrogatories; eight of them refused to appear for hearings, of whom seven were employees of UNESCO. Director-General Luther Evans announced that he would not renew the contracts of four whose contracts would terminate at the end of 1954. The other three cases, of employees with indefinite appointments, he referred to the next general conference of UNESCO with a recommendation that they be dismissed. The conference agreed. All the cases were then taken to the appropriate Administrative Tribunal, with results identical to the UN cases: denial of the propriety of the removals, followed by indemnity awards.

An unfavorable determination was made by the Board on one UNESCO employee, after a hearing. This was one of a total of only seventeen adverse determinations made by the Board through 1956. Director-General Evans said that the employee was responsive at the hearing, that he, Evans, was convinced of his reliability and would re-

27. The fact of the Bunche hearing is reported in NYT, May 26, 1954. The work of the Board through 1954 is reviewed in a letter of Dec. 10, 1954, by Gerety on his resignation from the Board; see NYT, Dec. 20, 1954. One case, a near-miscarriage of justice, came to public attention in 1955 when the advisory opinion was released to the employee and by him to the press. This was the case of William Henry Taylor, an employee of the International Monetary Fund, who had been a Treasury official under Harry White. The Board reached the searing conclusion that Taylor "has engaged in espionage and subversive activity against the United States . . . and that he was and possibly still is an adherent to the communist ideology." But Taylor and his counsel, Byron Scott, pressed new evidence on the Board, discrediting particularly Elizabeth Bentley's accusations against Taylor. The Board reversed itself and wrote Taylor on Jan. 5, 1956, "It has now been determined that, on all the evidence, there is not a reasonable doubt as to your loyalty to the government of the United States." Both opinions are reprinted in BNA MANUAL, p. 41/76; see also NYT, July 22, 1955; Jan. 7, 1956; Byron Scott, "The Letter Nobody Wrote," *The Nation* (Jan. 5, 1957), p. 5; Senate Comm. on Gov't Operations, Permanent Subcomm. on Investigations, Hearings, *William Henry Taylor–Treasury Department* (Nov. 1953, released 1955).

tain him.[28] I do not know that any other such cases have occurred. The one UNESCO case attracted no attention, and leaves unanswered the questions raised on page 79.

MILITARY PERSONNEL

I have left until the last the most baffling of the federal programs. The security regulations that cover the 3,000,000 members of the armed forces of the United States have had an obscure evolution. As recently as 1953 the Army regulations were withheld from the public, even though an open court-martial of some notoriety was then in process, in which nondisclosure of Communist party membership was the issue.[29] Since that time all three military departments have slowly brought their programs into view and into a degree of harmony, not only with each other but with the programs for civilian employees. The soldier—if we may so term all military men and women of all ranks and all branches of service—is in about the same position as his civil-service counterpart when his membership in the armed forces is voluntary, either as enlisted man or as officer. The volunteer soldier, like other government employees, gets whatever protections the programs afford once he has

28. See NYT, July 5, Aug. 25, Oct. 17, Nov. 14, 1954; Jan. 6, April 27, June 23, Oct. 30, Nov. 19, Nov. 26, 1955. The awards of the Tribunal were upheld by the International Court of Justice, *Reports* (1956), p. 77. The Swiss government refused to permit hearings to be held in Switzerland. NYT, July 13, July 26, 1954. Four more hearings were held in Italy in 1956 as the whole program was winding up (except for applicants). *Washington Post,* July 28, 1956. The number of adverse determinations (16 incumbents, 1 applicant) is from Commission on Government Security, *Report* (1957), pp. 427, 435.

There have been persistent but so far unsuccessful proposals to provide a statutory basis for the program, which might include penal sanctions for unauthorized acceptance of UN employment. See Schwebel, p. 86; NYT, Dec. 18, 1956.

29. This was the case of Lt. Sheppard Thierman, a doctor, who was charged with fraudulently concealing past Communist party membership in applying for a commission, and with failure to cooperate with an investigating committee. He was acquitted. NYT, May 1, 2, Aug. 6, 1953. The Army regulation, SR 620–220–1, was declassified in Jan. 1954. The Navy regulations were also initially restricted. See Navy Dep't *Bulletin* (Jan.–June 1949), pp. 6, 109. However, the Air Force regulations were not. AF Reg. 35–62, Dec. 21, 1951. The programs began in 1948. See Sandra Weinstein, *Personnel Security Programs of the Federal Government* (1954), p. 45.

An officer may be dismissed from the service only following a court-martial, 10A U.S.C. § 1161. But administrative separations of varying types are available, so courts-martial have been rarely used in the area under discussion. On the distinction between "dismissal" and "discharge" of an officer, see Robert Pasley, "Sentence First—Verdict Afterwards," *Cornell Law Quar.* (1956), *41:*568–72.

achieved status as a member of the armed forces. A would-be recruit, like an applicant for employment in civil service, can be summarily turned away; however, current regulations provide for a hearing.

The situation of conscripts, however, is unique. Without any voluntary act on his part, the young man called to the Army, or the doctor drafted for special medical duty, finds himself exposed to a political test. The Department of Defense, on its side, has the national security to worry about. At the same time it has to worry about draft-dodgers, and possible evasion of military service through a pretended espousal of subversive causes. One may be skeptical about the prevalence of this device; but it makes defense officials hesitant to erect very high security barriers against conscripts.[30]

Adjusting reasonable security needs to a constant stream of somewhat reluctant "employees" would have been difficult enough at best. Since the Air Force and the Navy have been able to rely on volunteers, and to insist that they be politically spotless, most of the hard problems fell to the Army. Right at the time when some stability in the program had been achieved, Senator McCarthy, then in his ascendancy, brought the Army's security policies under heavy fire. The Army retreated, embarrassed by the case of Dr. Irving Peress, a supposed Communist who was routinely given a promotion and then hastily awarded an honorable discharge just when the Senator was close on his heels. Public statements in 1954 confirmed that the Army had breached a fundamental policy. The character of a discharge from military service, Army spokesmen conceded, had always been supposed to reflect the quality of the service rendered, and nothing more. Now the discharge was openly and formally linked to the outcome of security proceedings which took account of acts and associations before induction. This was no different from what all three services had in fact been doing for some time,[31] but the avowal

30. See statements by Secretary Charles Wilson and Admiral Arthur Radford, Senate Comm. on Armed Services, Hearings, *Doctor Draft Act Amendments* (March–April 1954), pp. 6, 67.

31. The Air Force and the Navy have taken some drafted doctors, but no other conscripts. Hearings (n. 30 above), pp. 15, 37. The Peress case was copiously reported at the end of January and the beginning of February 1954. In essence, Peress, a dentist commissioned under the Doctor Draft Law, had been under investigation for alleged Communist party membership; he had invoked the Fifth Amendment on his loyalty form. Army officials decided they would prefer to give him an honorable discharge rather than go through the complexities of a forced separation. McCarthy, who had got wind of the presence of the suspect Communist at Camp Kilmer, N.J., demanded that the Army delay the discharge. Department of the Army counsel John Adams refused. McCarthy's resulting

that conventional derogatory information from civilian life would lead to less-than-honorable military discharges brought on public distaste and Congressional inquiry. The Army retreated to new positions. In 1957, after years of turmoil, there was no certainty that any equilibrium had been reached. The screening of conscripts and the regulation of discharges were still uncertain in their actual operation. These are, however, the unique and controversial aspects of the military programs that must be examined.

SCREENING CONSCRIPTS

The armed forces security program gets under way when the prospective soldier, before induction, enlistment, or appointment, fills out Department of Defense Form 98, a searching loyalty questionnaire covering both individual conduct and affiliations with subversive organizations. A failure satisfactorily to complete the form automatically bars a volunteer; but the conscript goes through full investigation and hearings if any derogatory information, including a plea of the Fifth Amendment, is disclosed by the sworn questionnaire. Investigatory branches of the armed services may independently turn up derogatory evidence sufficient to initiate action under the security program; but it seems likely that in the vast majority of cases a satisfactory response to DD 98 is tantamount to clearance. Secretary of Defense Wilson has stated that not all military personnel go through a comprehensive check on their loyalty.[32]

DD 98, until its recent revision, was a formidable combination of military and security jargon. At large induction centers it was doubtless perfunctorily executed, with little comprehension of its import. A conscript

broil with Adams, Secretary Robert Stevens, and Brig. Gen. Ralph Zwicker, commander of Kilmer, was one of the major causes of the great controversy between McCarthy and the Army. There is a good review of the case in NYT, Jan. 23, 1955, § E, on the eve of a Congressional investigation of the affair held after the tumult had somewhat diminished. This inquiry was Senate Comm. on Gov't Operations, Perm. Subcomm. on Investigations, Hearings, *Personnel Actions Relating to Irving Peress* (March 15–31, 1955); Senate Report No. 856, July 14, 1955. The Report (from the subcommittee of which McCarthy had been chairman in the preceding Congress) said the Army had been afflicted with bad judgment and bad procedures in the case.

The Doctor Draft Hearings, n. 30 above (which are far broader than their title suggests), have figures on security discharges through March 1954; for types of discharges see pp. 65, 91, 100.

32. Doctor Draft Hearings (n. 30 above), p. 50. The regulations, issued subject to Dep't of Defense Directive 5210.9, April 7, 1954, amended June 19, 1956, are in BNA MANUAL, Part 31. They have been frequently amended.

who took it seriously, however, was first advised that "The Department of Defense has the authority to establish procedures implementing the national policy relating to loyalty of persons entering on duty with the Armed Forces." He then waded through a set of criteria, the Attorney General's list (in very small type), a paragraph combining admonition against falsehoods and acknowledgment of the right to invoke the privilege, until at last he came to a six-point certification. The clarity of the document did not improve as he went along. Indeed, it steadily deteriorated, as is indicated by the third item of the certification: "I have entered under Remarks below, the name(s) of the organization(s) from the above list of which I am or have been a member, or by which I am or have been employed, or which I have attended or been present at, or engaged in, organizational or social activities or activities which they sponsored, or for which I have sold, given away, or distributed written, printed, or otherwise recorded matter published by them, or with which I have been identified or associated in some other manner." The sixth item was itself an invitation to false swearing: "I understand the meaning of the statements made in the certification above."

The new form asks the same questions but in a much more comprehensible manner.[33]

If a conscript, either from his own unlikely declaration or other information, is considered a "known Communist," he will not be inducted. But until a recent change in Army policy, anyone who invoked the Fifth Amendment, acknowledged substantial derogatory information, or otherwise fell under suspicion was nevertheless inducted and put into "specially controlled duties." This is a euphemism for retention at the lowest pay grade, usually in a quite humble capacity. The status is not supposed to last beyond the resolution of the case, but this can take a long time, in the Army as in other programs. Furthermore, the outcome of the case was sometimes a decision to retain the soldier with no improvement in status.

The most recent Army policy postpones induction in cases that require investigation. Furthermore, a Defense Department directive requires that any conscript whose rejection is proposed on security grounds may have a hearing before a board of officers. Thus the conscript can have his acceptability determined before he is inducted.[34]

33. For accounts of casual exposure to DD 98, see HENNINGS HEARINGS, pp. 382, 410; cf. pp. 522–4. The revised form of July 12, 1956, is in BNA MANUAL, p. 31/195.

34. See Directive 5210.9 (n. 32 above), June 19, 1956 amendment, § IX. F.

Once the disclosure or discovery of derogatory information has started security procedures rolling, their resemblances to civil-service processes are marked. The bureaucratic complexity is, as one might expect, somewhat greater than one would find in the average civilian agency. Each service has in the long chain of reviewing officials an intermediate screening group which has the power to enter a final clearance without sending the case further. This stage precedes the hearing in the field and may involve an interview or interrogatory with the accused soldier prior to the formal hearing. Final decisions emanate from the Department in Washington and are communicated to the appropriate commanding officer through channels. The necessity of maintaining the integrity of military channels may account for the profusion of administrative agencies passing on the soldier's loyalty both before and after he has had a chance to rebut the charges against him.

The soldier may avoid the full administrative procedures by making a tender of separation after he has received charges. However, a tender of separation makes the disposition of the case an act of grace on the part of the soldier's superiors. He must express a willingness to resign or to accept a discharge, either honorable or under conditions less than honorable.[35]

Military standards and criteria are now practically identical to civilian ones. The Army, as might be expected, has had its full share of cases involving remote associations, "guilt by kinship," and the like. Criticism of inept decisions, sparked by the publication of Rowland Watts' study, *The Draftee and Internal Security,* led to an Army directive of October 1955 (not released until April 1956), urging that attention be paid to such factors as the soldier's age at the time of the alleged offenses, the nature of family relationships, and the extent of participation in front organizations. In general, the directive called for greater care, sophistication, and understanding than had previously obtained.[36]

On the previous practice, see Secretary Stevens in Doctor Draft Hearings (n. 30 above), p. 73; HENNINGS HEARINGS, pp. 519–20.

35. The procedures as of 1954 are summarized in Weinstein (n. 29 above), pp. 45–50; see also BNA MANUAL, pp. 31/10–17. Tenders of resignations or requests for discharge have some variations in the different regulations.

36. The Army directive (Adj. Gen. letter of Oct. 17, 1955) is in BNA MANUAL, p. 31/97, and NYT, April 28, 1956. The substance of it was incorporated in revised regulations issued by all three services in 1957, in the form of "Factors" governing the application of the criteria. The Watts study, released by the Workers Defense League in Aug. 1955, included, as its App. C., 49 case histories. A supplement was issued in May 1956. See also Jacob Stein, "The Defense of Army Security Risk Cases," *St. Louis Univ. Law Jour.* (1956), 4:34. One dis-

LESS-THAN-HONORABLE DISCHARGES

Separation from the armed forces is of course a normal step for any-one but a career soldier. The severe difficulties that have arisen are the result of the use in security cases of discharges that are less than honor-able. The worst types of discharge, "Bad Conduct" and "Dishonorable," can be awarded only after a court-martial, and have not been of much significance in the recent troubles. Administrative discharges are of three categories: Undesirable; General, under honorable conditions; and Hon-orable. An Undesirable discharge obviously carries a substantial stigma. The General discharge, which may also be given for various kinds of unsuitability, deprives the veteran of certain benefits. It would not be a serious deprivation were it not for the implications of disloyalty that arise in a security case. The Army has taken pains to convey these im-plications by typing on the discharge "SR 600-220-1 [or AR 604-10] applies"—a reference to the security regulation.[37]

The great problem has been the extent to which the Army (and the other services) could properly take into account pre-induction activities and associations in determining the character of a discharge. The formal decision to do this was made, as I have said, under the political pressures of 1954. A rationalization of this policy was attempted by Secretary Stevens in February 1955, when he wrote: "It is my considered opinion that any person who *limits his usefulness* to the United States Army by acts or affiliations, past or present, *over which he had complete control* and whose performance of service would otherwise warrant characteriza-tion as honorable, should, except under the most exceptional circum-stances, upon the expiration of his term of service, have such service

---

tinctive feature of the military programs is that the soldier may request to have military counsel assigned to him.

37. The law on discharges as it applies to the Army is illustrated by a chart facing p. 28 of Doctor Draft Hearings, n. 30 above. Few if any federal veterans' benefits are affected by a General rather than an Honorable discharge. A number of state benefits, however, require an Honorable discharge. See Shustack v. Herren, 234 F. 2d 134 (2d Cir. 1956), n. 2; Comment, "Judicial Review of Army Discharge Procedures," *Stanford Law Rev.* (1956), 9:171, n. 4. On the practice of indicating the origin of a General discharge in security cases see Watts (n. 36 above), p. 80; AR 604–10, § 18d; HENNINGS HEARINGS, pp. 375–6. That the Army itself recognized the unfavorable effect of a General discharge is shown by an official form of the agreement to accept less-than-honorable discharge (n. 35 above), which recited that "I may expect to encounter substantial prejudice." HENNINGS HEARINGS, p. 527.

characterized as under honorable conditions, and, if discharged, be given a general discharge." [38]

This policy did not stand up under attack. The Army made a confusing series of partial withdrawals, until a document of March 1956 stabilized the situation in this way: any conscript completing his term of service will be awarded a discharge "based on the character of service performed." This much was a return to first principles. However, if security cases require discharge before the service is completed, the character of separation will be based upon "all relevant factors, including the gravity of the substantiated derogatory information (regarding matters occurring prior to and during their period of service) which requires their discharge, and upon the character of service performed." In such cases, evaluation of "character of service" may take into account "falsification in connection with security matters," but not "any limitations on performance of duty imposed for security reasons." The upshot of this seems to be that if a decision of security risk is made after hearing and review, the Army remains free to award any of the administrative discharges, but an Honorable one is not precluded, as it was before.[39]

The Army speaks of separation, not of discharge, in the case of those who finish their term of active service. That raises another complicating element, the obligation of any man subject to the draft to remain in the reserves for a period that, combined with his full-time active service, may total eight years, or even longer. Under the present law a ready reserve and a standby reserve are established, with significant differences between them; the length of time spent in each will vary with the length and form of full-time service. The ready reservist has to attend weekly drills and spend two weeks training in the summer. He can be recalled to active duty by presidential order after a declaration of national emergency by the president and a determination by Congress of the numbers necessary to be called up. The standby reservist can be recalled only in time of war or national emergency declared by Congress or (exceptionally) if there is a shortage of ready reservists with his military skills.

38. Memorandum to Chief of Staff, Feb. 3, 1955, HENNINGS HEARINGS, p. 436; see also Watts (n. 36 above), p. 63. Emphasis supplied.

39. The quoted passages are from AR 604–10, § 18, as amended May 15, 1957, BNA MANUAL, p. 31/76. This apparently crystallized (for the time being) a policy adopted during the criticisms of the Army's policy in HENNINGS HEARINGS, pp. 353–441, 465–534. The evolution of this policy is succinctly described in one of Judge Jerome Frank's encyclopedic footnotes. Shustack v. Herren (n. 37 above), n. 4.

The man who has served the normal two-year term of active duty is thus not free. He may have to keep on training for several years; he is subject to recall under certain conditions. But these liabilities are not fixed. The services, for budgetary or other reasons, may not exact the full period of training. Moreover, Congress has changed the pattern before and can change it again. Also, in the event of major emergency or war, the call to active duty would scarcely be confined to those already enrolled in the reserves.

The present practice of the services seems to be to withhold Certificates of Discharge until the total period of obligation has expired. A consequence of this policy is that the services can, or at least do, continue their interest in the political activities and affiliations of persons in this nebulous reserve status; there have been many cases where men in one reserve status or another have been presented with security charges. These proceedings may result in less-than-honorable discharges for enlisted men, based on their activities not only before but *after* their period of active service. It is true that the "guilt-by-kinship" cases among reservists that have come to public attention have mostly involved officers, who are all considered to hold sensitive appointments and whose reserve status may be voluntary. However, these considerations in no way limit the reach of the regulations or of proceedings under them.[40]

A soldier who has been given a less-than-honorable discharge, either after a security hearing or on the completion of his active service, has an administrative channel of appeal to a statutory Discharge Review Board

40. There were 4,000,000 reservists as of Sept. 30, 1956; Commission on Government Security, *Report* (1957), p. 111. The Reserve Forces Act of 1955, which made substantial changes in the character of the obligations following (or, in some cases, preceding) active duty, is codified in the Armed Forces Act of 1956, Stat. Vol. 70A, U.S.C. Title 10A. On the ready and standby Reserves see §§ 269, 273; on their liability to recall, §§ 672–4. Though § 651 sets eight years as the required period of service, recent practice apparently regarded as normal a combination of two years on active duty, three years in the ready reserve, and one year in the standby reserve. This practice, and its variants, are helpfully set forth in a pamphlet published by Yale University, *Military Service: Opportunities and Obligations* (Sept. 1956), to whose anonymous author I am much obliged. Some shortening of the period of service was reported NYT, March 30, 1957.

The distinction between separation and discharge at the end of the eight-year (or shorter) period is explained in the Shustack case (n. 37 above), p. 139, n. 6. Cf. 10A U.S.C. §§ 1001, 1162–3. Watts Supplement (n. 34 above), pp. 20–1, mentions a case based on activities after separation; cf. the "guilt-by-kinship" cases reviewed in Ch. 11 below, n. 19. In Bland v. Hartman, 245 F. 2d 311 (9th Cir. 1957), a Navy reserve officer of World War II vintage unsuccessfully challenged the Navy's power to give him a less-than-honorable discharge after security proceedings.

in each service. The operation of these Boards is probably one of the least understood aspects of this whole murky subject. Their work has assumed new importance, because the retreat from the policies of the last few years almost requires a re-opening of many questionable discharges handed out in those years.[41]

Several attempts, none so far successful, have been made to persuade the courts to consider some of the policies and practices of the military. Though there are judicial observations about the value and dignity of an honorable discharge, the most recent decisions deny any jurisdiction. This abstention is difficult to understand. When the plaintiffs challenge military consideration of pre-induction activities, and the relation of Fifth Amendment pleas to the character of subsequent discharge, questions of constitutional rights are raised.[42]

For the career soldier, separation as a security risk has about the same severe consequences as does exclusion on loyalty or security grounds from other specialized government employment. For the conscript, the situation is a little different. He may not be sorry to leave the service; but if he receives any discharge other than an honorable one, it will clearly have some detriment to his future employability. Aside from the public stigma, unfavorable security findings are communicated to the FBI and become a permanent part of the individual's file. All this, after all, is the result of a status which he did not seek and could not avoid.[43]

41. Something of the work of the Army Board is explained in testimony of its chairman in HENNINGS HEARINGS, p. 425. There are also Boards for the Correction of Military Records, which seem to have a very limited jurisdiction, but are part of the chain of administrative appeals culminating in the Secretary. See Stanford Comment (n. 37 above), p. 174; Watts (n. 36 above), pp. 69–72.

The Army did announce (see NYT Dec. 26, 1957) the near-completion of a survey of all security discharges from 1948 to 1955. It said that 650 cases out of 725 had been reviewed, and changes made in the character of 280 discharges. The number of cases suggests that some 200 less-than-honorable discharges from inactive duty were included. Cf. figures in Hearings (n. 30 above), pp. 99–100, and in App. A below.

42. After this book had gone to press, the Supreme Court on March 3, 1958, reversing Harmon v. Brucker, 243 F. 2d 613 (D.C. Cir. 1957), held that the Secretary had exceeded his statutory powers, and that his action was reviewable.

The whole subject of this section is ably explored by W. K. Jones, "Jurisdiction of the Federal Courts to Review the Character of Military Administrative Discharges," *Columbia Law Rev.* (1957), 57:917.

43. The situation of two other special classes of involuntary soldiers should be mentioned. First is the Reserve Officers Training Corps, participation in which for two years is compulsory in land-grant colleges. There were objections to a Navy loyalty statement in 1949–50 which led to its abandonment. See NYT, Dec. 2, 1949;

SUMMARY OF FEDERAL PROGRAMS

Despite many variations, the basic pattern of the employment tests carried on by the federal government is the same. They all start with investigative reports based either on file checks or field inquiries; from this beginning usually flows the sequence of evaluation, charges, hearing, and review. Sometimes, however, there is no right to a hearing, and in some programs there is no provision for review. Nowadays, the basic standard is the nonexistence of security risk. This opens up consideration of a variety of matters bearing on reliability; but the main lines of inquiry continue to emphasize political reliability—that is, loyalty. Exceptionally, the program for employees of international organizations retains loyalty as the formal standard, because there is no valid security issue present.

The elements that make up or negate a security risk cannot be precisely stated. They are further discussed in Chapter 11, below. The general pattern is that any history of communist sympathies, associations, or affiliations raises a broadly defined presumption of risk. The employee can overcome it by demonstrating his present anticommunist attitude, unless the association is too close—e.g. a communist spouse—or too damning—e.g. past active party membership. There are also some abso-

---

March 16, 1950. But in 1954 completion of DD 98 was required of all ROTC entrants. Among other cases, a sophomore at the University of Wisconsin, who was also a Sunday-school teacher, was excluded from ROTC activities because he "qualified" his DD 98 by admitting that he once knew a man who had been investigated by the FBI. See Madison (Wis.) *Capital Times,* Sept. 29, 1954; ACLU, *Weekly Bulletin* No. 1672, Nov. 15, 1954. In April 1955 the Defense Department dropped the requirement for students in the compulsory two-year program but continued it for voluntary candidates in the advanced courses. NYT, May 1, 1955; AR 604–10, § 37.

Physicians and dentists drafted under the special Doctor Draft Law of 1950, 50 U.S.C. App. § 454(i), which permits drafting up through age 50 (latterly, 45), are normally commissioned. When a number of doctors refused to execute DD 98, or disclosed derogatory information that created security doubts, they were denied commissions but put in more-or-less professional duties as enlisted men. A challenge to this practice failed in the Supreme Court, Orloff v. Willoughby, 345 U.S. 83, 931 (1953). Then a change in the statute was construed to require the commissioning of all doctors, Nelson v. Peckham, 210 F. 2d 574 (5th Cir., 1954); Levin v. Gillespie, 121 F. Supp. 726 (N.D. Cal. 1954). This development led to the Doctor Draft Hearings (n. 30 above) and an explicit amendment to the statute that a doctor not qualifying for a commission "may be utilized in his professional capacity in an enlisted grade or rank," 68 Stat. 254 (1954), 50 U.S.C. App. § 454(a). See Senate Comm. on Armed Service, Hearings, *Armed Services Security Cases* (July 15, 1954), p. 9.

lutely disqualifying criteria, such as participation in espionage activities, and, on the political side, present party membership, or present membership in "communist-front" organizations designated by the Subversive Activities Control Board. But usually the determination requires the exercise of judgment, by hearing boards and security officers. They must weigh miscellaneous derogatory information, the source of which is often concealed, against the protestations of the employee.

Again, there are variations, and some legislative oddities like the Taft-Hartley oath. But the preceding paragraphs give the essence of the federal programs. In comparison with the state, local, and private programs next to be described, they are remarkably consistent in their structure, if not in their application. They rule the careers of civil servants, of the members of the armed forces, of maritime employees, of government contractors and their employees requiring access to classified information (and some who do not), of labor union officials, and of American employees in international organizations.

4. State and Local Employment Tests

LOYALTY TESTS for state and local government employees, as would be suspected, are marked by a greater diversity of form than are their standardized federal counterparts. They are also likely to be accompanied by rather more sound and fury relative to the results achieved. The principal means used can be broadly classified as either test oaths or administrative programs. Combinations of the two are of course frequent. A few American states still carry on their affairs without questioning the loyalty of their civil servants and teachers. But the legislative itch to do something against communism has been contagious; so the number of states free of employment tests has rapidly declined.[1]

LOYALTY OATHS

The predominant technique of state and local employment tests is the loyalty oath. While constitutional oaths have been common for public school teachers since before World War I, the advent of full-blown loyalty oaths has been fairly recent. Today twenty-four states and two U.S. territories impose test oaths on all public employees, including teachers.[2]

1. In general see *The States and Subversion,* ed. Walter Gellhorn (1952); E. Reutter, *The School Administrator and Subversive Activities* (1951); W. Prendergast, "State Legislatures and Communism: The Current Scene," *Am. Pol. Sci. Rev.* (1950), *44:*556; FUND DIGEST, Part II, State Statutes and Decisions.

2. Teachers have often complained about being singled out to attest their loyalty. Most of the special teachers' oaths of the prewar era were constitutional in form and thus seem innocuous in comparison to current test oaths. However, they were discriminatory in the sense that other employees did not have to take them. There are still constitutional oaths for teachers and not for other employees in Colorado, Indiana, Michigan, Nevada, New York, North Dakota, and Vermont. See FUND DIGEST, Part II, § M (teachers' oaths). States and territories imposing test oaths on all public employees include: Alaska, Arkansas, California, Florida, Georgia, Hawaii, Idaho, Illinois, Kansas, Louisiana, Maryland, Massachusetts, Minnesota, Mississippi, Montana, Nebraska, New Hampshire, New Jersey, Ohio, Oklahoma, Oregon, Pennsylvania, South Dakota, Texas, Washington, and West Virginia. See FUND DIGEST, Part II, § G-2; Ill. Stat. ch. 127, § 166b (1955); South Dakota Session Laws of 1955, ch. 271 (S.B. 122). The Washington oath was recently held invalid because it improperly incorporated the Attorney General's list. Savelle v. Univ. of Washington, Superior Court, Dec. 3, 1956 (unrep.).

Test oaths differ from simple constitutional oaths in that they require more than a pledge to uphold the Constitution and the laws. They require the employee to swear that he is not subversive, that he will not be subversive, and, sometimes, that he has not been subversive. Like their historic antecedents, they tend to become ever more elaborate and more sweeping in their compulsory disclaimers.[3]

The legal status of test oaths has not always been free from doubt. Immediately after the Civil War, Reconstruction legislation attempted to make public employees and professional people swear that they had not committed acts of disloyalty. These oaths were invalidated by the Supreme Court because they violated the constitutional prohibitions against *ex post facto* laws and bills of attainder. The Supreme Court at that time was unable to perceive that an oath attesting to past loyalty established, as its defenders argued, merely a reasonable qualification for employment. Since the Confederate veterans at whom the oath was directed could not honestly subscribe to it, the Court said that it was a form of legislative punishment. This difficulty has been overcome. From the *Bailey* and *Garner* cases have emerged a new set of guiding principles applicable to government employment: freedom from disloyalty, established by oaths or administrative regulations, is a reasonable qualification for government employment in today's complex international situation; government employment, furthermore, is a privilege whose denial, at least when it is not arbitrarily effected, does not constitute punishment. Thus the constitutional prohibitions invoked in the Civil War cases were sidestepped; what had been held an unjust punishment became a reasonable qualification.[4]

Another basis for questioning the validity of loyalty oaths has been their conflict with the form of oath prescribed by the state constitution. The reason for spelling out the oath for officeholders in constitutions was to exclude the imposition of such test oaths. The California consti-

3. On test oaths generally see Howard M. Jones, "Do You Know the Nature of an Oath?" *American Scholar* (1951), *20*:457; S. Koenigsberg and M. Stavis, "Test Oaths: Henry VIII to the American Bar Association," *Lawyers Guild Rev.* (1951), *11*:111.

4. Garner v. Board of Public Works of Los Angeles, 341 U.S. 716 (1951); Bailey v. Richardson, 182 F. 2d 46 (D.C. Cir. 1950), affirmed by an equally divided Supreme Court, 341 U.S. 918 (1951). The earlier Supreme Court cases were Cummings v. Missouri, 4 Wall. 277 (1867); and Ex Parte Garland, 4 Wall. 333 (1867). For a full discussion of the Reconstruction legislation see Harold M. Hyman, *Era of the Oath* (1954). The bill of attainder concept is thoroughly surveyed by Comment, "The Constitutional Prohibition of Bills of Attainder: A Waning Guaranty of Judical Trial," *Yale Law Jour.* (1954), *63*:844.

tution tried to make this quite clear by stating that "no other oath, declaration, or test, shall be required as a qualification for any public office
or public trust." But the California Supreme Court circumvented the
proposition that the historic form of oath in the constitution is the only
one that may be used. The California legislature had prescribed for all
public servants an oath that they did not and would not advocate violent
overthrow, that they did not and would not belong to an organization
so advocating, and that they had not belonged to such an organization
within five years. This was held not in conflict with the constitutional
oath; it merely implemented the constitution, the court said. Then, to
make assurance doubly sure, the voters amended the state constitution
to require the same form of oath.[5]

The sanctions behind loyalty oaths are twofold. Failure to execute
the oath or affidavit "satisfactorily" usually means automatic denial or
loss of employment. This result follows whether or not the failure to
complete the required statement can be related to the purposes for which
the oath was originally enacted. Even a conclusive showing of anticommunism will not excuse one who refuses as a matter of conscience
to take the oath.[6] The second sanction, more remote but more severe, is
the possibility of criminal prosecution for false swearing. Many people
concede that false swearing in itself is no deterrent to the communist
conspirator at whom loyalty oaths are aimed, but they argue that the
threat of future criminal prosecution will give him pause. There is some
support for this view in the history of New York investigations into the

5. The Levering Act loyalty oath was held not in conflict with the state constitutional oath in Pockman v. Leonard, 39 Cal. 2d 676, 249 P. 2d 267 (1952),
and applicable to the staff of the University in Fraser v. Regents of Univ. of Calif.,
39 Cal. 2d 717, 249 P. 2d 283 (1952). The oath which the Regents of the University of California demanded from the faculty was invalidated in Tolman v.
Underhill, 39 Cal. 2d 708, 249 P. 2d 280 (1950), because the legislature had
occupied the field. The California constitutional amendment is to Art. XX, § 3. See
FUND DIGEST, p. 349.

The New Jersey oath was declared unconstitutional for candidates in Imbrie v.
Marsh, 3 N.J. 578, 71 A. 2d 352 (1950) (state constitution forbids other than
constitutional oath for elected officials), but constitutional for teachers in Thorp
v. Board of Trustees, 6 N.J. 498, 79 A. 2d 462 (1951).

6. Fitzgerald v. City of Philadelphia, 376 Pa. 379, 102 A. 2d 887 (1954)
(Pechan Act oath required of nurse who was conceded to be "utterly opposed to
communism and in all respects loyal to the principles of our government"). See
Clark Byse, "A Report on the Pennsylvania Loyalty Act," *Univ. of Pa. Law Rev.*
(1953), *101*:480, 482–4; *The Nation* (June 28, 1952), pp. 668–9 (effects of Ober
law in Maryland); Pickus v. Board of Education of the City of Chicago, 9 Ill.
2d 599, 138 N.E. 2d 532 (1956) (no hearing necessary for person refusing test
oath).

loyalty of public school teachers. Some of the witnesses, who in the early 1940's denied communist affiliation before the Rapp-Coudert committee, ten years later found it advisable to plead the Fifth Amendment in response to similar questions from the Senate Internal Security Subcommittee. One proffered explanation for this change in tactics is the availability of sufficient government witnesses in the current investigation to make a criminal prosecution for false swearing stick.[7]

The effect of loyalty oaths is difficult to measure. Their first impact is usually on conscientious objectors, who refuse on principle to take such an oath. This was certainly the case, for example in early protests against the Pechan Act oath in Pennsylvania and the Regents' oath at the University of California. At California, twenty-six faculty members were dismissed; thirty-seven resigned in protest. There is no evidence that any of these was a Communist.[8] If oaths accomplish no other purpose than this, their utility is negative.

The Civil Defense Oath and Its Variants

Loyalty oaths vary considerably in the scope of activities and beliefs which their takers must abjure. The nearest to a type is the civil defense oath propounded by the federal government, which has been adopted by several states. The state statutes back up the national government's requirement of the oath for civil defense workers. By insisting that state employees "volunteer" for civil defense duties, administrators can convert the oath into a test for state employment. This was done in California as an interim measure, pending the amendment of the constitution. *All* state employees, by legislative command, became civil defense workers. In New York, a similar technique was used in an attempt to canvass the loyalty of Welfare Department employees of New York City. In this case the local administrator took it upon himself to enroll all his employees in the state civil defense program. Vigorous protest by a group of employees and interested civic groups brought about clarification of the purely voluntary nature of the state program. The protests

7. See testimony of President Harry D. Gideonse of Brooklyn College, before isc, Hearings, *Subversive Influence in the Educational Process* (1953), pp. 553–4. It should be added that juries are now probably more disposed to convict in such cases than they were in 1940.

8. See Byse, n. 6 above; George Stewart, *The Year of the Oath* (1950), p. 21. Committee on Academic Freedom, *Interim Report to the Academic Senate, Northern Section of the University of California* (Feb. 1, 1951) is the source of the figures; see also nyt, March 11, 1951.

also resulted in a change in the form of the oath from an affidavit of
nonmembership in organizations on the Attorney General's list to the
standard civil defense oath.[9]

The oath runs as follows,

> I, ————, do solemnly swear (or affirm) that I will support
> and defend the Constitution of the United States against all ene-
> mies, foreign and domestic; that I will bear true faith and alle-
> giance to the same; that I take this obligation freely, without any
> mental reservation or purpose of evasion; and that I will well and
> faithfully discharge the duties upon which I am about to enter.
>
> And I do further swear (or affirm) that I do not advocate, nor
> am I a member or an affiliate of any organization, group, or com-
> bination of persons that advocates the overthrow of the govern-
> ment of the United States by force or violence; and that during
> such time as I am a member of the (name of civil defense organiza-
> tion) I will not advocate nor become a member or an affiliate of
> any organization, group, or combination of persons that advocates
> the overthrow of the government of the United States by force or
> violence.[10]

The first part of this oath is a fairly typical constitutional oath; the second paragraph adds the specific disavowals which constitute a test oath.

State variations on the civil defense model have on the whole been
confined to embellishments of the second paragraph dealing with subversion. The proscribed advocacy in many cases includes not only force
and violence but also revolution and "other unlawful means." The Oklahoma oath of 1953 is perhaps an extreme example of clumsy elaboration. It is atypical in a curious limitation: "I do not advocate, *by the
medium of teaching* . . ." But it does exemplify the attempt to plug
every loophole against subversion. After a conventional constitutional
oath it provides:

> I do further swear (or affirm) that I do not advocate by the
> medium of teaching, or justify, directly or indirectly, and am not
> a member of or affiliated with the Communist party or the Comin-
> form or with any party or organization, political or otherwise,

9. See Edward Barrett, "California," in *The States and Subversion*, ed. Gellhorn
(1952), pp. 49–50. The New York episode is summarized from Bruce Steinberg,
Loyalty and the New York City Department of Welfare (1954) (unpublished paper in the Yale Law Library).

10. 64 Stat. 1255 (1951), 50 U.S.C. § 2255(b). States with civil defense oath
statutes are collected in FUND DIGEST, Part II, § G-2.

known to me to advocate by the medium of teaching, or justify, directly or indirectly, revolution, sedition, treason or a program of sabotage, or the overthrow of the government of the United States or of the State of Oklahoma or a change in the form of government thereof by force, violence, or other unlawful means.

Another paragraph then recites that the office-holder will not do any of these things while in office.

Another legislative trend that the Oklahoma oath typifies is that of naming the organizations in which membership is forbidden. Without deleting general proscriptions of subversion, these oaths may explicitly refer to the Communist party or to organizations listed by the Attorney General or the Subversive Activities Control Board as subversive. Under the Maryland Ober law and its imitations in other states, still another class appears in which membership is forbidden—the foreign subversive organization.[11]

On the side of moderation, recent enactments are careful to observe the ruling of the Supreme Court—in upsetting an earlier Oklahoma oath —that only membership *with knowledge* of the subversive aims of the organization can be penalized.[12]

11. The Oklahoma oath is from Title 51, § 2, 1953 Session Laws, and was drafted to overcome the defects of a prior Oklahoma oath overthrown in Wieman v. Updegraff, 344 U.S. 183 (1952). See James A. Robinson, *Anti-Sedition Legislation and Loyalty Investigations in Oklahoma* (1956), ch. 4. For other examples of elaborate oaths see Texas Civil Statutes, Title 110A, § 6252–7 (1953 Supp.), FUND DIGEST, p. 380; and ibid., p. 483 (City of Oakland, Calif.).

The Ober law in Maryland and in other states which have copied the Ober pattern (see n. 29 below) defines a foreign subversive organization as follows: "any organization directed, dominated or controlled directly or indirectly by a foreign government which engages in, or advocates, abets, advises, or teaches, or a purpose of which is to engage in, or to advocate, abet, advise, or teach, activities intended to overthrow, destroy or alter, or to assist in the overthrow, destruction or alteration of the constitutional form of government of the United States or of the State of Maryland, or of any political subdivision of either of them, and to establish in place thereof any form of government the direction and control of which is to be vested in, or exercised by or under, the domination or control of any foreign government, organization or individual; but does not and shall not be construed to mean an organization the bona fide purpose of which is to promote world peace by alliance or unions with other governments or world federations, unions or governments to be effected through constitutional means." Maryland Ann. Code Gen. Laws, Art. 85A, § 1.

12. Weiman v. Updegraff, n. 11 above. The Texas oath of 1953 (n. 11 above) omits the word "knowingly" from its reference to Communist party membership. Cf. Steinmetz v. Calif. State Board of Education, 126 Cal. App. 192, 271 P. 2d 614 (1954), affirmed 44 Cal. 2d 816, 285 P. 2d 617 (1955), holding that a state employee must answer questions about Communist party membership whether or not he was a member with knowledge of the party's illegal purposes, but cau-

All of the variants discussed thus far probably add little to the substance of the civil defense oath. If the record of the oaths so far challenged in court is representative, these oaths will be judicially restricted to the classic formula of advocacy or membership aimed at force or violence. This formula nowadays will readily comprehend membership in the Communist party. Courts have tended to be cavalier in disregarding other clauses as excess verbiage. Thus in a Maryland case the "foreign subversive organization," as distinct from other subversive organizations, was for all practical purposes read out of the Ober Act. It was this narrow reading of the Maryland law which the United States Supreme Court upheld.[13]

A more substantial deviation from the civil defense oath is illustrated by recent enactments like those in California and Texas, which inquire into past associations as well as present and future ones. Both of these oaths limit their demands to a five-year period, except that, so far as Communist party membership is concerned, the Texas oath requires the taker to swear that he has never been a member.

If the legislators intend to put an absolute ban on people who cannot give unqualified assent to an oath denying certain past behavior, this may be an unconstitutional imposition. There is a strong suggestion in the Supreme Court's decision in the *Garner* case that the prohibition on *ex post facto* laws would come into play if the association in question was not punishable at the time it occurred. However, the continuation of associations after the legislature had given notice of their consequences would be another matter; the passage of time would serve to blunt the edge of the *ex post facto* objection.[14]

TEST OATHS AND ADMINISTRATIVE TESTS

The inclusion of past associations may have the practical effect of turning an oath test into an administrative test. To satisfy constitutional

---

tioning that admission of past membership may not furnish grounds for dismissal if the membership was innocent.

13. See Shub v. Simpson, 196 Md. 177, 76 A. 2d 332 (1950); Gerende v. Board of Supervisors, 341 U.S. 56 (1951).

14. Garner v. Board of Public Works of Los Angeles, 341 U.S. 716 (1951). See Brown and Fassett, "Loyalty Tests for Admission to the Bar," *Univ. of Chicago Law Rev.* (1953), 20:486–7. The Schware case (p. 111 below), while dealing with admission to the bar rather than with government employment, holds that past membership in the party, at least when the membership ended in 1940, cannot *per se* be taken as a ground for disqualification. To do so is a denial of due process.

requirements, or as a matter of legislative policy, the employee may be given an opportunity to establish the innocence of his past association, or his withdrawal from it. This has been the practice under the Los Angeles programs for city and county employees. A study of five years' operation of these programs showed that in most cases the employee's explanation of past affiliations was accepted.[15]

Of course, it does not necessarily benefit the employee to have the program become less automatic and more administrative. The result, if the federal program is any guide, may be to divert attention from present loyalty to speculation about the meaning of the past as a guide to the future.

Also, once the oath or any other form of statement is used as the source of information for an administrative test, there is no logical stopping place to the disclosures which may be exacted. Recently Governor Herman Talmadge, pursuant to Georgia's Anti-Subversive Act of 1953, required all state employees (including teachers) to execute a "Security Questionnaire." It called for past and present subversive affiliations not only of the affiant but also of his near relatives. This led to some outcry; and at the last moment employees were advised that they could ignore the question dealing with members of their families.[16]

ADMINISTRATIVE TESTS

Administrative programs, like test oaths, vary a great deal from state to state. Some statutes merely proclaim a general prohibition on the hiring of subversive persons without defining standards and procedures.[17] Although these enactments have remained unenforced to date, they provide no limits for the zealous administrator. It is possible of course that the courts might in such a situation read civil-service procedures into the statute; but the area of discretion would still be very wide.

15. See Harold Horowitz, "Report on the Los Angeles City and County Loyalty Programs," *Stanford Law Rev.* (1953), 5:233. These programs were superseded by the Levering Act, see Bowen v. Los Angeles County, 39 Cal. 2d 714, 249 P. 2d 285 (1952), which also contemplates an opportunity to explain past membership.

16. See NYT, March 21 and 23, 1954; correspondence of the author with Georgia State Board of Education. But the question still appears on the form. According to *Reader's Digest* (Oct. 1954), p. 143, "in response to the question if any member of your immediate family is a present or past member of any organization which advocates the overthrow of our government or approves acts of force or violence to alter the government, a high school teacher in La Grange answered: 'Yes. My father was a member of the Confederate Army.' "

17. E.g. Illinois Stat. Ch. 127, § 166a, and Indiana Stat. § 10–5207. See also FUND DIGEST, § G-2, pp. 347–52, 361–8, 370–6, 382.

The test oath is still the focal point of the more organized administrative programs. In most states the oath is both the beginning and the end of the investigative process. Unless the employee himself discloses unfavorable information in the course of taking or refusing to take the oath, further scrutiny of his loyalty is unlikely. No state has the investigating staff necessary to pursue questions of employee loyalty to the extent that the federal system does. Here and there some investigative agencies exist. Michigan has in its State Police a special secret division to expose subversives; New York State's department of education has its own investigators and detectives; New York (and other cities) have long had special anti-Red squads in their police forces. Recently the New York State government established a unit in the Civil Service Commission to enforce its emergency security legislation.[18] Officially, the FBI does not make its files available to these state and local administrators of loyalty programs.[19]

Experience to date suggests that, beyond the imposition of test oaths, state administrative programs tend to remain quiescent. Two special factors seem to account for such major enforcement campaigns as there are. One of these is the agitation of a legislative investigating committee, either state or federal, which stirs up old hornet's nests and finds new ones. The other is the existence of a militant left-wing union.

In New York, for example, the hearings of the Rapp-Coudert Committee in 1940 and of the Senate Internal Security Subcommittee in 1953 represented both forces at work, and resulted in the dismissal of numerous teachers.[20] Though committee investigators sometimes un-

18. NYT, Nov. 6, 1953. The New York City Bureau of Investigation has also supplied information leading to dismissals under the state security-risk statute (p. 106 below); NYT, Nov. 18 and 19, 1954. The Michigan legislation, Mich. Laws, §§ 4.448(1)–(6), is discussed in R. Mowitz, "State and Local Attack on Subversion," *The States and Subversion,* ed. Gellhorn (1952), pp. 184, 202–3.

19. Letter from J. E. Hoover, Sept. 27, 1954: "Information in the files of the FBI . . . is provided only to those federal government agencies which are entitled by law to receive it." Cf. statements by a New York City Assistant Corporation Counsel in the departmental trial of police Lt. Arthur Miller, NYT, July 24, 1953. The original information about Miller's party membership, he said, came from the FBI, and he had additional information from the FBI to use in cross-examination if necessary. Perhaps a distinction should be drawn between conventional derogatory information, which the FBI makes available only to proper officials in the executive branch, and substantial evidence of criminal conduct (in the Miller case, false swearing). It seems unthinkable that the FBI would ever act otherwise than it did in the Miller case, and that it would fail to warn cooperating metropolitan police officials that they were harboring a Communist. Ten separations from the New York City force, since 1953, for communist affiliations were reported NYT, March 29, 1957.

20. See Lawrence Chamberlain, *Loyalty and Legislative Action* (1951). Ap-

earth new information with which to initiate action against employees, the main impact of an active committee is through publicity. Committees have skillfully used public hearings to magnify their disclosures of subversive activities. The resulting exposés bring pressure to bear on even the reluctant administrator, if such there still be, to oust the discredited employees.

In California, however, the relationship between legislative committee and administrator has become more intimate and less public. The California Un-American Activities Committee entered into an arrangement with the University of California (and other institutions) which obviated the need for committee questioning in public. As described in detail by the Committee's counsel, R. E. Combs, in sworn testimony, it was agreed that all prospective employees of the University would be "cleared" by the committee before being hired; derogatory information on present employees would be passed on to the University authorities for their consideration. In the course of a dispute about these practices between University officials and critics of the arrangement, notably the Northern California American Civil Liberties Union, the detailed facts became enveloped in confusion, and entangled in another matter—the role of the "security officer" on the Berkeley campus. Nothing appeared, however, to challenge the main elements of Mr. Combs' testimony. The same committee made a comprehensive investigation of employees of the Los Angeles school system, including teachers at private schools under the jurisdiction of the Los Angeles City School Board.[21]

---

proximately thirty dismissals under § 903 of the New York City Charter directly followed the ISC hearings of 1953; see n. 32 below.

21. See testimony of R. E. Combs in ISC, Hearings, *Subversive Influence in the Educational Process,* pp. 605–22; ACLU [Northern Calif.] *News* (1954), passim. Combs testified that a voluntary agreement between his committee and a number of college and university presidents (including private institutions as well as the University of California with its 8 campuses) had brought about 100 forced resignations of faculty members in less than a year. The committee especially urged on each college president the appointment of a full-time security officer, who would serve as liaison with the committee. On the basis of information supplied by the committee, at least 200 appointments, Combs estimated, had been prevented. When the controversy about the accuracy and significance of Combs' testimony blew up, University of California officials first said that their security officer's job was only to supervise the protection of classified contract operations. Then, in a statement of July 6, 1954, they pointed out that the security officer had statewide responsibilities, and properly "had relations with" the State Senate Committee on Un-American Activities; but, the statement concluded, "his relationships are *now* confined to matters affecting defense contracts." Univ. of Cal., Northern Section, Representative Assembly, Committee on Academic Freedom, Report quoted in ACLU [Northern Calif.] *News* (Nov. 1954), p. 4; emphasis supplied.

The relationship between union activity and state loyalty investigations is something like that of the horsefly to the horse. Aggressive left-wing unions of public employees are irritants. The classic example is that of the Teachers' Union in New York. It is only a slight exaggeration to describe the Rapp-Coudert investigation of 1940, which cost fifty-odd teachers their jobs, as a feud between the Committee and the Teachers' Union. As the hearings went on, the Committee procedures deteriorated, and the abusiveness of the Union increased. Another instance where a left-wing union was embroiled in a major loyalty purge, also in New York City, involved the United Public Workers and the city Welfare Department. The same union was active among workers in Detroit when a loyalty crisis occurred there.[22] The sectors of local-government employment that Communists colonized at all successfully seem to have been limited to teachers, welfare workers, and clerical or other non-professional employees. Even so, their success in controlling left-wing unions among these employees was based on support from non-Communists whose economic grievances they championed. When the union leadership moved from conventional trade-union activities, always somewhat constricted in public employment, to political agitation, especially political agitation against loyalty measures, they provoked retaliation. The stung horse switched off his tormentors.

As the left-wing unions declined in importance and numbers, so did their ability to goad officials into intemperate activity. The initiative of Congressional committees and their state counterparts is nowadays the force most likely to arouse sluggish loyalty programs.[23]

LEGISLATIVE PATTERNS

The first part of this chapter considered the use of the test oath in public employment. The next section reviewed in general terms the stimuli for state administrative programs: the loyalty questionnaire or oath as a source of charges; the role of legislative exposure and of the

22. See Chamberlain (n. 20 above), ch. 3; Steinberg, n. 9 above; Mowitz (n. 18 above), pp. 184, 222–5; Combs' testimony (n. 21 above), pp. 606, 612. The Welfare Department of the City of New York separated 217 employees after Departmental investigations, from 1948 to 1951, with new investigations continually in process. NYT, Feb. 17, 1953.

23. An example is the dismissal of twenty-seven school teachers in Philadelphia, the outgrowth of hearings conducted there by the HUAC. See ACLU, Greater Phila. Branch, *Academic Freedom: Some Recent Philadelphia Episodes* [1954]; HUAC, Hearings, *Investigation of Communist Activities in the Philadelphia Area* (1953–54).

left-wing union; the minor use of investigators. This section will trace, for important states or groups of states, the over-all pattern of anti-communist legislation in which employment tests are found.

The most nearly standardized statute is the Maryland Ober law, named for its principal author, a Baltimore lawyer. It combines these elements: criminal sanctions against sedition, a test oath (applicable to candidates for elective office as well as employees), a mandate to employing departments to screen applicants to establish if they are subversive, procedures for discharge of incumbents if "reasonable grounds" exist for belief that they are subversive, a special assistant attorney general to enforce the act (with state police assistance), and a requirement that private schools or colleges receiving state financial aid establish procedures for discovering subversive persons on their staffs. Eight other states have copied the Ober Act—in some instances slavishly, in others with variations. The parts of these laws that impose criminal penalties on sedition are ineffective as a result of the 1956 decision of the Supreme Court in *Pennsylvania v. Nelson*. There the Court held that the enactment of the Smith Act, coupled with the Internal Security Act of 1950 and the Communist Control Act of 1954, led to the "inescapable" conclusion "that Congress has intended to occupy the field of sedition"—to the exclusion of all state sedition laws.[24] It does not appear that the status of employment tests for state employees is directly affected by this decision. It is possible, however, that in some instances the employment tests still in force after the supersession of penal sanctions may be so fragmentary as to be meaningless.

Some of the recent state laws that are most extreme in their penal sanctions against communism make only casual provision for removing suspected subversives from employment. Thus the Massachusetts legislation, among the first to denounce the Communist party by name, disqualifies from state employment those who have been convicted of membership or financial support of any subversive organization; but it

24. Commonwealth of Pennsylvania v. Nelson, 350 U.S. 497 (1956). The Ober Act, Md. Anno. Code Gen. Laws, Art. 85A (1951), was followed in Florida, Georgia, Maryland, Mississippi, New Hampshire, Ohio, Pennsylvania, and Washington. The Alabama, Louisiana, Michigan, and Texas laws are a cross between the Ober law and the Massachusetts Anti-Communist law, n. 25 below. See FUND DIGEST, Part II, § G-2. On the enactment of the Ober law in Maryland see W. B. Prendergast, "Maryland; the Ober Anti-Communist Law," *The States and Subversion* (n. 1 above), p. 140. Some of the variations in other states are reviewed in Warren Hill, "A Critique of Recent Ohio Anti-Subversive Legislation," *Ohio State Law Jour.* (1953), *14*:439.

sets up no administrative program. Similarly, the Indiana legislature, after declaring a public policy "to exterminate communism and Communists, and any or all teachings of the same," barred Communists from public office or employment, but with scant indication how they were to be detected.[25]

There are also a number of statutes which attempt to compel Communists or other proponents of revolution to register with a designated state official. Either the fact of registration, or conviction for failure to register, would presumably bar the culprit from state employment, though most registration statutes do not make this point. The lawmakers might as well not have bothered with the registration device at all, except as a memorial to their anticommunist zeal. Not a single instance of voluntary registration has been reported. Nor have there been reported any successful prosecutions for failure to register.[26]

California and New York, the most populous states, have each gone their own way in advancing from criminal sanctions to test oaths to administrative programs. Before 1950 California had only general prohibitions against employing seditious persons. These statutes formed the basis for the Los Angeles County loyalty program; the Los Angeles city program sprang from a local ordinance. From 1950 to 1953 the legislature and the electorate were engaged in embedding in the constitution the test oaths previously mentioned. In 1953 new legislation made all employees liable to dismissal for refusals to answer questions about present and past subversive associations and activities. The statute contemplated that employing boards and agencies should set about asking such questions, and they have done so.[27] Meanwhile the state Senate's

25. 9 Anno. Laws of Mass., Ch. 264, § 20 (1956); Burns Ind. Stat., §§ 10–5202 (1956).

26. See FUND DIGEST, Part II, § H (registration statutes and cases). Perhaps, in accordance with the Nelson Case (n. 24 above) these statutes are superseded by the Internal Security Act of 1950; see Note, *Harvard Law Rev.* (1956), 70:119 (1956).

27. The 1953 legislation, Calif. Government Code §§ 1027.5, 1028.1 for all public employees except teachers, and Education Code §§ 12600–12607 for teachers, was upheld in the Steinmetz case, n. 12 above. But see San Francisco Board of Education v. Mass, 47 Cal. 2d 494, 304 P. 2d 1015 (1956), adapting the statute to the requirement of the Slochower case (n. 32 below) by requiring an opportunity for explanation of a refusal to answer on grounds of possible self-incrimination. See NYT, Jan. 10, 1954; Los Angeles *Times,* Feb. 24 and 26, March 16, 1954, on the application of the 1953 legislation to the Los Angeles school system. Superintendent Stoddard said that the program was aimed at 171 "suspected loyalty doubtfuls" among 27,000 school employees.

Un-American Activities Committee has stimulated local action through public hearings; in addition it has formed the liaison with the state University already described.

Prewar legislation had established in New York a teacher's oath (constitutional in form), and general proscriptions against employing advocates of violent overthrow.[28] Dissatisfaction with school authorities for failure to enforce the employment ban impelled the legislature in 1949 to enact the Feinberg law. This controversial measure, which the Supreme Court of the United States upheld, imported from the federal employees' program the device of assembling a list of subversive organizations, like the Attorney General's list. Indeed, the Board of Regents was authorized to use the Attorney General's list; and it did so while it went about the task of establishing through its own hearing procedure that the Communist party was subversive. The Feinberg law made membership in a listed organization prima facie evidence that the teacher member was himself subversive. The Regents' regulations under the law added the further presumption that membership in such an organization even before it was listed would be deemed to have continued, unless the employee established that he had ended it in good faith. The burden of clearing himself was thus shifted to the employee, in ways reminiscent of the federal program. The other contribution of the Feinberg law and the regulations implementing it was an elaborate system of annual reports on the loyalty of teachers, collected at each level of the educational hierarchy for those subordinate to the reporter.[29]

In states with the Ober law a somewhat similar reporting procedure is imposed on private educational institutions receiving financial assistance from the state. Such institutions have to demonstrate that they are not harboring subversive persons. A series of certificates to this effect from department heads and deans is thought to bolster the ultimate declaration of purity by the head of the institution.[30]

To return to the Feinberg law, its effect has been modest. Predictions

28. Education Law, § 3002; Civil Service Law, § 12a; Public Officers Law, § 35a; see Chamberlain (n. 25 above), ch. 2.

29. The constitutionality of the Feinberg law was upheld in Adler v. Board of Education of the City of New York, 342 U.S. 485 (1952). The Rules promulgated by the Board of Regents pursuant to the Feinberg law are set forth in the Official Compiled New York State Rules, Reg. 205–6. A new teacher must also have his loyalty certified by previous employers or by his college administration. For agitation about this at the City College of New York, see NYT, Feb. 21, 1952.

30. The process is described in Byse, n. 6 above. Cf., for Oklahoma, Carey McWilliams, *Witch Hunt* (1950), p. 229.

that it would be widely copied [31] have been unfounded, perhaps because more effective measures have been discovered. The extensive examination of New York City teachers since 1950 has operated through an entirely different channel. Suspected teachers are summoned before an Assistant Corporation Counsel and questioned. If they refuse to answer any questions, they are dismissed (after a departmental hearing) for insubordination. If they answer questions unconvincingly, they may face either departmental charges or a criminal prosecution. Until the decision of the Supreme Court in the *Slochower* case, which requires a hearing in Fifth Amendment cases, teachers who invoked the Fifth Amendment were automatically dismissed. More than 250 teachers under investigation have resigned, retired, or been dismissed since 1950. The Feinberg law, despite its burden of presumption from membership in listed organizations, provides every other significant procedural safeguard. The procedures that have in fact been used are rather summary.[32]

Another major innovation in New York is the only state security-risk statute. First passed as an emergency measure in 1951, and since then periodically re-enacted, it permits the suspension, transfer, or dismissal of employees in "security positions" or "security agencies" designated by the state Civil Service Commission. Both incumbents and applicants affected by this statute get a hearing in the form of an appeal to the Civil Service Commission; but there is no appeal to the courts, unlike ordinary civil service proceedings in New York.[33] The statute's coverage has been extended far beyond any reasonable definition of sensitive

31. E.g. Brown, Book Review, *Louisiana Law Rev.* (1952), *12*:540.

32. For a description of the technique used to get supposed Communists out of the New York City schools, see testimony of Superintendent William Jansen, ISC, Hearings, *Subversive Influence in the Educational Process* (1953), pp. 645–62; Ch. 17 below, p. 413. Events in the New York City teachers' program have been extensively reported in NYT and other papers and in *The Nation.* A similar program in the City colleges has resulted in about forty separations. On the number of separations see NYT, April 11, Nov. 26, Dec. 1, 1956; June 17, Nov. 11, 1957. § 903 of the New York City Charter, having been interpreted to require summary dismissals after self-incrimination pleas, was held unconstitutional in Slochower v. Board of Higher Education of the City of New York, 350 U.S. 551 (1955), because no hearing process was provided.

33. N. Y. Unconsolidated Laws, §§ 1101–8 (1951 Laws, Ch. 233). In 1953 (Laws, Ch. 26, § 1) the statute was amended to allow the employee to be represented by counsel, and to present evidence on the appeal to the Commission. However, the statute is modeled on P.L. 733, and permits withholding of confidential information (n. 37 below). The constitutionality of the statute, and the propriety of applying it to a subway conductor, were upheld in Lerner v. Casey, 2 N.Y. 2d 335, 141 N.E. 2d 533 (1957), appeal pending in U.S. Supreme Court.

employment. A study committee appointed by Governor Harriman in
1956 reported that

> scientists in the Paleontology Section of the Department of Educa-
> tion have been specified as holding "sensitive positions," on the
> ground that they have knowledge concerning the location of caves
> and their suitability for defense storage purposes. The Department
> of Sanitation of the City of New York has been designated as a
> "security agency," on the theory that disease might spread in the
> event that department did not perform its duty. Even [the] proba-
> tion service of the New York City Domestic Relations Court has
> been designated as a "security position," though it would seem to
> have no relationship to the "security or defense of the nation and
> the state." One might expand at length the list of agencies or posts
> which have been denominated "security" though they have remote,
> if any, connection with matters which that term ordinarily connotes.
> . . . Approximately 81 per cent of all employees of New York
> City are in agencies or positions which have been designated as
> "security." The Committee has been told that in the state govern-
> ment in the neighborhood of 30 per cent of the employees are in
> "security" positions or agencies.

The statute as thus extended has been the basis for a great deal of
investigation of both state and New York City employees; but the number of dismissals attributed to it has been few.[34] The state Civil Service
Commission has also embarked on a screening program that extends to
applicants for any state job as well as to incumbents in sensitive jobs.
There were also some dismissals and resignations reported in 1953 from
nonsensitive areas. Both this activity and the activation of the security
risk law seem to have been touched off by a visit to Albany of the House
Committee on Un-American Activities.[35]

34. By the end of 1956 twelve state employees had been disqualified, and fifty-
three city employees had been dismissed or had resigned following investigations
under the statute. The interim report, here quoted, of the Committee on Public
Employee Procedures appointed by Governor Harriman, was released Jan. 28,
1957. See NYT, Jan. 29, 1957. A year later, the Committee reported that the coverage of the Act had been much constricted. NYT, Jan. 16, 1958.

35. On these New York developments see NYT, July 11, 12, 15, 16, 1953 (dis-
missals and resignations centering on House Committee visit; total about 20).
On the questionnaire used to elicit affiliations with subversive organizations, NYT,
Sept. 22, Oct. 15, Dec. 11, Dec. 15, 1953. See HUAC, Hearings, *Investigation of
Communist Activities in the Albany, N.Y. Area* (1953), Parts 1 and 2, esp. Part
2; Interim Report, n. 34 above.

SUMMARY OF STANDARDS AND PROCEDURES

The most common standard for exclusion from state employment, it appears, is the familiar formula of advocacy of overthrow of the government by force and violence. *A fortiori,* overt acts leading toward revolution would be included. State legislation is generally deficient in spelling out the criteria for establishing the forbidden forms of sedition. Some statutes, as we have seen, go no further than barring those who have been criminally convicted. There is an increasing trend toward specifying membership in the Communist party. From this central position there are the usual radiations in time and space. Past membership in the party and past membership in other organizations that may be subversive are sometimes called into question, though by their terms most of the administrative programs (unlike some of the test oaths) seem to be focused on present loyalty.

The Ober laws (and the New York security-risk law) seem to open the door wider by permitting exclusion if the administrator finds "reasonable grounds" for his belief that the standard is infringed. This is the original language of E.O. 9835, which permitted wide-ranging inquiries. The fact is, there is no adequate body of material to use in making comparisons among the state programs as to their effective standards. There have been a few hundred dismissals or forced resignations, mostly of teachers. The grounds assigned, whether the label is "insubordination" or "conduct unbecoming a teacher," usually come down to this: the authorities try to make their case by questioning the employee; the employee refuses to cooperate, perhaps by invoking the privilege against self-incrimination; his refusal opens the way for his dismissal.

If either side ever reached the merits of a case, the employee would have a reasonable opportunity to defend himself. Where procedures are specified, they are closely assimilated to standard civil service removal processes. These, in the states, usually combine full administrative due process with some judicial review.[36] This means, among other things, that the employee can be dismissed only on the basis of the record made at a hearing, at which he would be confronted by the evidence against him, and have an opportunity to cross-examine. These safeguards, to be sure, may be available only to employees with permanent civil-service status. The applicant (and the probationary employee) can be summarily dealt with. It is worth noting, however, that the New York se-

36. See Comment, *Northwestern Univ. Law Rev.* (1952), 47:660; Ch. 16 below, p. 405. Cf. Appeal of Albert, 372 Pa. 13, 92 A. 2d 663 (1952).

curity-risk statute gives the same hearing to an applicant who has passed his civil-service examination as to an incumbent. On the other hand, the statute permits incomplete confrontation.[37]

Some of the state statutes are no more illuminating about procedures than they are about standards. In these circumstances it seems likely that state courts would read due-process requirements into the legislation. But the opposite possibility should not be overlooked. Other state legislatures besides New York might decide to ape the federal programs, and might borrow from them the one-sided hearings that are thought necessary to protect sources of information. If a security rationalization were advanced, the legislation would probably, under present conditions, be sustained.

EMPLOYMENT TESTS IN STATE-LICENSED PROFESSIONS

State regulation of employment is not limited to the hiring and firing of state and local government employees. A great variety of trades and professions are subject to the licensing power, either as a measure of economic control, or, more frequently, to protect the public by setting qualifications for practice. While licensing is a governmental function, the setting of standards and their administration is often left *de facto* to the organized segment of the trade and professional group under regulation. Thus medical associations, bar associations, master plumbers, and other guilds may have a powerful voice in deciding who may share their privileges.[38] Either the legislature or the interest group, if it is moved to combat subversion, may be able to carry out its desire.

LAWYERS

The urge to exclude Communists and their allies has been most strongly felt, among the licensed professions, by the organized bar. This is a group that has some access to the legislature, and even more to the judiciary, which shares with the legislature the responsibility of regulating the practice of law.[39]

37. The New York security statute entitles the employee to a statement of reasons only "to the extent possible without disclosing confidential sources of information . . ." § 1105.

38. See Walter Gellhorn, *Individual Freedom and Governmental Restraints* (1956), pp. 140–4.

39. This section, unless otherwise indicated, is based on Brown and Fassett, "Loyalty Tests for Admission to the Bar," *Univ. of Chicago Law Rev.* (1953), *20:*

There are accordingly a number of test oaths for lawyers, some the creature of statute, others prescribed by rule of court. These oaths are adjuncts to a traditional lawyers' oath taken at the time of admission to the bar. They are found in five jurisdictions (Alaska, Colorado, Kentucky, Oklahoma, Washington), and are remarkable in that the first three of them require the prospective lawyer to swear that he is not and "never has been" an advocate of overthrow by force and violence. The "never has been" barrier, though frequently criticized in discussion of test oaths, is actually an uncommon requirement.

Perhaps one-third of the states pose what may be called direct loyalty questions in the documents which applicants—again under oath—are required to complete as part of the requirements for satisfying bar examiners that they are of good moral character. The language in these questionnaires varies considerably, going from simple affirmations of present loyalty, through denials of past subversion, to quite searching inquisitions. The Houston (Texas) Bar Association asks: "Do you belong to or have you attended the meetings of any group which advocates any theory or 'Ism' which would prevent you from taking the [constitutional] oath wholeheartedly?" And Hawaiian aspirants face this effort to close any last loophole: "If you were to be listed as a 'Communist' in the records of any federal investigative agency, what past actions or organizational affiliations of yours not already listed by you might be used by such investigative agency to support its conclusion? In answering this question, assume that all of your past actions and organizational affiliations are known to such investigative agency."

The examiners have other means of informing themselves in addition to the candidate's written statements. Character references may be asked to comment on loyalty; state or local police may investigate; the National Conference of Bar Examiners maintains an efficient character investigating service which is used by most bar examiners for applicants who are already attorneys elsewhere, and by a few states for student applicants not long resident in the state.

An interview with the candidate—part of the routine of admission in more than one-third of the states—is the final channel for loyalty testing. A few character committees ask, almost as a matter of course, "Are you a Communist?" Others raise loyalty issues sporadically, or indirectly by way of such catch questions as, "Do you think that Communists are eligible to practice law?" The "right" answer to this question is "no," for

480. Cf. Vern Countryman, "Loyalty Tests for Lawyers," *Lawyers Guild Rev.* (1953), *13*:149.

any other answer may lead to further and more suspicious grilling. Other oral inquiries that have been reported range from an embarrassed "You aren't a Communist or anything are you?" to the following exchange: "Did you vote for Henry Wallace in 1948?" "No, I voted for Harry Truman." "Don't tell me that—we don't have the right to ask you that."

The difference between these questions and the items classified as test oaths is that adverse answers to the questions need not inevitably disqualify. There have been few cases of denials of eligibility. The committees of the bar that pass on character and fitness for practice have broad discretionary powers. Instances have been reported of the admission of ex-Communists. On the other hand, there have been rejections based on less than solid evidence of subversiveness. When the New Mexico bar examiners excluded an applicant (Rudolph Schware) primarily on the ground that he had been a Communist from 1932 to 1940, and were sustained by the state Supreme Court, the case was carried to the United States Supreme Court. In a unanimous decision, the Court held that New Mexico had denied Schware due process of law. The state court had said that the applicant's communist past was sufficient evidence that he was "of questionable character." Justice Black, in the Court's opinion, pointed out that the Communist party was on the ballot in New Mexico at the time of Schware's membership, that his recent career had been exemplary, and that he had discussed freely with the character committee his career as a Communist. "Assuming that some members of the Communist party during the period from 1932 to 1940 had illegal aims and engaged in illegal activities, it cannot automatically be inferred that all members shared their evil purposes or participated in their illegal conduct. . . . There is no evidence in the record which rationally justifies a finding that Schware was morally unfit to practice law." [40]

Inevitably, cases have arisen of applicants who refused to answer political questions. The first one to be carried through the courts was that of a Chicago graduate, George Anastaplo. Anastaplo attracted the attention of an Illinois character committee by expounding the "right of revo-

---

40. Schware v. Board of Bar Examiners, 353 U.S. 232 (1957). The examiners also relied on Schware's use of aliases (which he did to forestall antisemitism), and on certain arrests during his communist days which were not followed by convictions. The Court rejected these matters as evidence of bad moral character. Cf. In Re Patterson, 302 P. 2d 227 (Ore. 1956) (rejected applicant expelled from Communist party in 1949; court disbelieved his testimony that he did not advocate force and violence); remanded by the Supreme Court for further consideration in the light of the Schware and Konigsberg cases, 353 U.S. 952 (1957).

lution" in Jeffersonian terms. This was in the course of a brief essay on
the principles of the Constitution required by the Illinois (and other)
examiners. When a panel and later the full committee sought to inquire
further into his political beliefs, Anastaplo refused on principle to answer
questions about his political associations, reading habits, or anything else
that would disclose any attitudes save those he himself chose to expound
to the committee. After some delay (and also after the decision of the
Supreme Court in the *Dennis* case) he was denied admission in June
1951. After more delay, he completed a petition to the Supreme Court
of Illinois to reverse the action of the committee. In its answer, the committee in effect narrowed the issue to his refusal to state whether he
was a Communist. It suggested, however, that the petitioner's expressed
opinion on other matters, such as the eligibility of Communists to practice law, sharpened the pertinence of the key question.

The Illinois Court supported the Committee, holding that, under
present conditions, "a member of the Communist party may, because of
such membership, be unable truthfully and in good conscience to take
the oath required as a condition for admission to practice" (a simple
constitutional oath) and that "it is relevant to inquire of an applicant
as to his membership in that party." It denied that any forbidden infringement of freedom of speech or belief followed from such questioning. The practice of law, the court argued in familiar terms, is a privilege
that may be reasonably conditioned; proof of loyalty (measured by
nonadherence to communism) is a reasonable test for lawyers, because
of their special role in upholding, making, and interpreting the law.

This case permitted a singularly uncomplicated development of abstract propositions, because there was not a shred of evidence that the
petitioner was a Communist. It seemed to be tacitly conceded on all sides
that he was not. But the decision established that he could not decline
to answer questions on the subject, on pain of exclusion; and the United
States Supreme Court dismissed an appeal on the ground that the case
raised no substantial constitutional issue. The rule is not surprising;
but its application in the particular case seems an exercise in futility.[41]

41. In Re Anastaplo, 3 Ill. 2nd 471, 121 N.E. 2d 826 (1954). See Note, *Northwestern Univ. Law Rev.* (1955), 50:94. In addition to the direct appeal to the
U. S. Supreme Court which failed, an ingenious petition asking that Anastaplo be
admitted directly to the bar of the Supreme Court also failed. See 348 U.S. 946,
and 349 U.S. 903 (1955). After the Schware and Konigsberg decisions, Anastaplo
renewed his application, and was again rejected. Nat'l Lawyers Guild, *Civil Liberties Docket* (1957), 2:71. The Illinois Supreme Court then directed the Committee
to grant a rehearing. Ibid., 3:8.

In a California case that later went to the United States Supreme Court, a man of 42 who had gone to law school after a career in social work also declined to say whether he was or had been a Communist. California has a statute closing the practice of law to advocates of force and violence. The applicant, Raphael Konigsberg, testified that he did not so advocate; but he would go no further in answering questions about his political beliefs. The committee confronted him with an informant who claimed to remember him as a fellow party member in 1941. Other evidence, taken from the applicant's frequent writings on political matters, seemed to plunge the committee into a thicket of radical views from which it would be quite hazardous to make any inferences about disloyalty.

A majority of the Supreme Court agreed that the record was insufficient to justify Konigsberg's exclusion. The Court's opinion by Justice Black, delivered along with the *Schware* decision, is puzzling. It rests on a debatable declaration that California had not made refusal to answer questions in itself a bar to admission, and that therefore it was unnecessary to decide whether Konigsberg was, as he claimed, privileged on First Amendment grounds not to answer questions about his political beliefs or behavior. The Court then made its own evaluation of the record, and found, as in the *Schware* case, no rational basis for exclusion. Justice Harlan, in dissent, said, "it seems to me altogether beyond question that a state may refuse admission to its Bar to an applicant, no matter how sincere, who refuses to answer questions which are reasonably relevant to his qualifications and which do not invade a constitutionally privileged area. The opinion of the Court does not really question this; it solves the problem by denying that it exists." [42]

The *Konigsberg* decision, taken together with the Court's dismissal of Anastaplo's appeal, had this curious result. Apparently bar examiners can now make refusals to answer a complete ground for rejection; but if they make any allowance for an applicant's principled refusals, then the Supreme Court may apply what Justice Harlan called "its own notions of public policy and judgment." Of course, the Court may, if the issue is ever unavoidably raised, set some limits to political inquiries.

In neither of these cases, it should be emphasized, did the applicant rely on the privilege against self-incrimination. This was prudent. Since

42. Konigsberg v. The State Bar of California, 353 U.S. 252 (1957). The California statute mentioned is the Business and Professional Code §§ 6064.1, 6106.1. Maryland, by a 1952 extension of the Ober Act, excludes a "subversive person" from admission. Acts (1952), Ch. 27, p. 243.

the applicant carries the burden of proof of establishing his fitness for admission, use of the privilege to avoid a question material to eligibility would seriously impair his chances. If the two Harvard law students who invoked the privilege before the Internal Security Subcommittee in 1953 [43] ever seek to enter practice, the question may arise in a double-headed way. The first issue will be whether the examiners should give any weight to the students' claim of possible self-incrimination before the investigating committee. The second will depend on the responses they make to the questions of the bar committee, who will doubtless renew the same line of inquiry by demanding to know if they were Communists.

Disbarment is a more severe sanction than refusal of admission; the practicing lawyer has more of a stake in his profession than the neophyte. The burden of proof is usually shifted; it rests on the Grievance Committee or other moving group to show some act of moral turpitude. The American Bar Association has nevertheless urged that the use of the privilege against self-incrimination, with respect to questions of communism, is inconsistent with a lawyer's professional obligations. This position initially prevailed in the Florida case of Leo Scheiner, whose disbarment was ordered by a lower court in 1954. But on appeal the Florida Supreme Court held that a plea of self-incrimination in itself did not justify disbarment. The case was heard again, and the trial court found that evidence of Communist party membership from 1946 to 1952 warranted disbarment. This finding was again remanded because of its reliance on the testimony of an unreliable informer, and the proceeding was then dismissed.[44]

The organized bar was meanwhile pondering other potential disbar-

43. The Lubell brothers. See ISC, Hearings, *Subversive Influences in the Educational Process* (1953), Part 6, pp. 693–704. Other developments in this case included (1) refusal of the Law School faculty to take any action against them, see Erwin Griswold, "The Fifth Amendment Today," *Marquette Law Rev.* (1956), *39*:198–9; (2) refusal of the *Harvard Law Review* to elect one of them to its editorial board, see Editorial, *Harvard Crimson*, Sept. 26, 1953.

44. See NYT, Sept. 4, 1954; Sheiner v. Giblin, 73 So. 2d 851 (Fla. 1954); ACLU, *Weekly Bulletin* No. 1771, Oct. 8, 1956; David Weissman, "The Proceedings to Disbar Leo Sheiner," *Lawyers Guild Rev.* (1956), *16*:137. The second order of disbarment was vacated Jan. 14, 1957; the court then dismissed the proceeding after considering the evidence without the testimony of the informer Mazzei; Nat'l Lawyers Guild, *Civil Liberties Docket* (1957), *2*:37, 54.

A convicted defendant in a Smith Act case was disbarred. Braverman v. Bar Ass'n, 121 A. 2d 473 (Md. 1956). The American Bar Association position on lawyers and the Fifth Amendment is stated and criticized in Brown, "Lawyers and the Fifth Amendment—a Dissent," *A.B.A. Jour.* (1954), *40*:404.

ment cases with caution—more caution, indeed, than some of its spokesmen were exhibiting in generalized attacks on communist lawyers and
Fifth Amendment lawyers. Charges had, however, been filed in Pittsburgh against two lawyers for party membership and advocacy of violent
overthrow. One of the lawyers in question had previously been the object of an unsuccessful attempt by Judge Musmanno to exclude him
from the courtroom, when the lawyer refused to answer questions based
on the Judge's private belief that he was a Communist. The Supreme
Court of Pennsylvania sharply rebuked Judge Musmanno, as it did in
a parallel case when he attempted to bar a supposed Communist from
jury duty.[45]

Another Pittsburgh episode is worth a paragraph. In 1951 Attorney
General Margiotti attempted to hold a hearing, presumably looking to
removal of an Assistant District Attorney in Pittsburgh, Mrs. Marjorie
Matson. Margiotti charged that she had "communist leanings." Mrs.
Matson got an injunction against the proposed hearing. It was upheld
by the Pennsylvania Supreme Court, which characterized the proposed
hearing as "absurd" and "without legal authority." The Pittsburgh Court
of Common Pleas appointed a lawyers' committee to investigate the
substance of Margiotti's charges. All of them were found insubstantial,
including such items as "fraternization" with one of the Pittsburgh
lawyers who later faced disbarment, and the defense of certain cases on
behalf of the American Civil Liberties Union.[46]

Disbarment proceedings were also directed at some of the defense
lawyers in the first Smith Act trial of the communist leaders. It is doubtful that these should be classified as instances of political tests. The attorneys had been held in contempt of court by the trial judge. The contempt punishments were affirmed by majorities of the Court of Appeals
and of the Supreme Court, both of which could muster a degree of dis-
passion that the trial judge could not. Was it appropriate to add the
heavy sanction of disbarment to the fines and jail sentences already imposed on the lawyers? The precedents, recognizing that the line between
excessive zeal and contempt of court is a thin one, suggested that it
was not. This view prevailed in the end, despite the strong popular resent-

45. See *Lawyers Guild Rev.* (1953), *13*:176; Schlesinger v. Musmanno, 367 Pa.
476, 81 A. 2d 316 (1951); Commonwealth ex rel. Roth v. Musmanno, 364 Pa.
359, 72 A. 2d 263 (1950). Judge Musmanno was later elected to membership
on the court.

46. Matson v. Jacobson, 368 Pa. 283, 83 A. 2d 134 (1951); ACLU, *Weekly Bulletin* No. 1522, Dec. 31, 1951. See also Ruttenberg, "Persecution by Assertion,"
New Republic (Feb. 19, 1951), p. 14.

ment against the communist defendants and their lawyers, and the near canonization of the trial judge. None of the lawyers was barred from practice, except Abraham Isserman in the state courts of New Jersey. Isserman and Sacher defeated, in the Supreme Court, attempts to exclude them from federal practice, and proceedings against other counsel were not pressed.[47]

PHYSICIANS

Inquiry into the loyalty of physicians has been less widespread than the investigation which lawyers have had to face. One reason for this relative quiet may be the failure of the American Medical Association, unlike the American Bar Association, to agitate for badges of loyalty.[48] Loyalty tests for doctors have been confined to a series of sporadic and unrelated incidents, important to the individuals involved but only minor outcroppings on the national scene. I have heard of no denials of licenses to practice. But there have been a few exclusions from medical societies —in Baltimore, of a suspected Communist; in New York, of an ex-Nazi. This is a serious matter, because membership in the local association is linked to hospital privileges, etc. Some California hospitals took direct action and dismissed from their staffs a number of doctors against whom accusations of party membership had been made. This is also a serious matter. A doctor obviously cannot treat his patients properly if he is physically barred from a hospital. These are instances of private, not state, action.[49]

47. In Re Isserman, 9 N.J. 316, 88 A. 2d 199 (1952); In Re Isserman, 345 U.S. 286 (1953), disbarment reversed 348 U.S. 1 (1954). Sacher v. Assoc. of the Bar of the City of New York, 347 U.S. 388 (1954). Cf. Gladstein v. McLaughlin, 230 F. 2d 762 (9th Cir., 1955).

48. The American Bar Association has promoted a test oath for lawyers which calls upon them to renounce "Marxism-Leninism." So far as I know, it has not been adopted. Members of the A.B.A., when joining, must state whether they are or have ever been members of the Communist party. Some of the state bar associations make a similar demand, e.g. Illinois. The New York State Medical Society, through its House of Delegates, has actively urged the imposition of a loyalty oath on doctors. See NYT, Jan. 15, 1952. The attempt was defeated. I reported incorrectly in BAS (1955), *11*:115, that the oath had been adopted; I am indebted to Dr. Benjamin Segal of New York City for the correction.

49. Baltimore: Dr. Ruth Bleier. *N. Y. Herald Tribune,* March 22, 1953. New York: Dr. Godfrey Arnold, NYT, April 29, 1953. On the importance of medical society membership see Comment, "The American Medical Association," *Yale Law Jour.* (1954), *63*:938. On the loyalty requirements of Permanente (Calif.) Hospital see Vern Countryman, "The Bigots and the Professionals," *The Nation* (June 28, 1952), p. 641; ACLU [No. Calif.] *News,* Oct. and Dec. 1951. Cedars of

Doctors may become subject to government loyalty requirements through various professional contacts. The doctor engaged in research, like the physicist, often finds some of his funds coming from the federal government with loyalty qualifications attached. Moreover, the hospital with which the doctor is affiliated may be governmentally owned or attached to a university supported by government funds. In either case, again, the doctor must meet the going loyalty requirements. Concern about the continuation of federal and state aid played an important part, it appears, in the arbitrary dismissal of ex-Communist staff members of the Jefferson Medical College in Philadelphia.[50]

A basis for imposing special loyalty tests on doctors could be found, as with lawyers, in the qualification of "good moral character," for the phrase is of undetermined breadth. In New York it is backed up by a statute authorizing disciplinary measures against a physician who "has been convicted . . . either within or without this state, of a crime." Drs. Barsky and Auslander were suspended for six and three months respectively by the New York Board of Regents because of their contempt conviction, in a federal court, after refusal to produce the books of the Joint Anti-Fascist Refugee Committee for a Congressional committee. They argued unsuccessfully that the statute was intended to reach only convictions involving moral turpitude or professional misconduct. The courts, conceding that the statute was stringent and sweeping, said that it was explicit, and gave it a literal enforcement.[51]

This section has briefly canvassed the kinds of tests to which physicians are subject, without sticking closely to licensing tests. The purpose was to indicate how a profession may encounter a variety of employment tests, even in the absence of concerted activity by its leaders. Other professions and trades are equally liable to the random incidence of tests not directly aimed at them. But these hazards are slight compared to

---

Lebanon Hospital, Los Angeles, dismissed seven doctors from its attending staff (perhaps one was an employee of the hospital). Most of those dropped had made "unfriendly" appearances before the House Committee on Un-American Activities. See HUAC, Hearings, *Communist Activities among Professional Groups in the Los Angeles Area* (Sept.–Oct. 1952), Parts 3–4; Hannah Bloom, "Cedars of Lebanon," *The Nation* (May 3, 1952), facing p. 413; and publications of the Committee for Medical Freedom, Los Angeles, 1952 and 1953.

50. ACLU, Greater Phila. Branch (n. 23 above), pp. 17–22; Ch. 5 below, n. 12.

51. Barsky v. Board of Regents, 347 U.S. 442 (1954). See Samuel E. Morrison, *Freedom in Contemporary Society* (1956), pp. 40–1, for critical comment on the Barsky case by an eminent historian. For examples of other "good moral character" statutes, see Calif. Bus. & Prof. Code, § 2168a; Conn. Gen. Stat. § 4353; and Ill. Rev. Stat. Ch. 91, § 4(2)(b).

the risk of direct pressure from licensing authorities.[52] From the position of the lawyers, where at least a debatable case can be made for some sort of loyalty requirement, it is only a short step to caprice and absurdity. This is illustrated by the edict of the Indiana Athletic Commission that boxers and wrestlers, before they can appear in Indiana, must subscribe to a loyalty oath.[53]

52. New York and New Jersey are joint participants in an interstate compact for the licensing of waterfront employees of the port of New York. This program, which is similar to the Coast Guard licensing system described in Ch. 3, has been held constitutional in Linehan v. Waterfront Commission of New York Harbor, 347 U.S. 439 (1954) a *per curiam* affirmance of three-judge district court decisions in Linehan v. Waterfront Commission, 116 F. Supp. 683 (S.D.N.Y. 1953); Staten Island Loaders v. Waterfront Commission, 117 F. Supp. 308 (S.D.N.Y. 1953). The waterfront program, though chiefly directed at excluding racketeers, also contains antisubversive prohibitions. Texas requires a loyalty oath for the licensing of pharmacists; Washington is said to have one for veterinarians. See Gellhorn, *Individual Freedom and Governmental Restraints* (1956), pp. 129–30. For the case of the District of Columbia piano dealer see Ch. 7 below, n. 13. The District of Columbia Insurance Commission asks would-be insurance salesmen if they are or have been Communists or members of organizations on the Attorney General's list, or if they have ever claimed a constitutional privilege in response to questioning. HENNINGS HEARINGS, pp. 311–19. A like proposal in New York was withdrawn. NYT, Oct. 20, 23, 1955. There is no way of knowing whether such requirements are endemic or epidemic.

53. NYT, Oct. 25, 1954; HENNINGS HEARINGS, pp. 348–52. See Ch. 14 below for further discussion of occupational licensing tests.

5. Tests Administered by Private Employers and Labor Unions

PRIVATE employment tests present even more of a hodge-podge than those of state and local governments. However, four types of private action can be identified. This classification permits a rough comparison with the classification of state and local tests used in the preceding chapter:

(1) *General statements of policy,* not backed up by regular enforcement (compare the legislative equivalents in the last chapter).

(2) *Test oaths*—frequently used, but not the mainstay, as they are with state and local governments.

(3) *Sporadic dismissals* (or expulsions from unions) for political or security reasons. This catch-all category has no significant government equivalent.

(4) *Industrywide programs of exclusion by employers or unions.* This category is somewhat comparable to the organized programs of the federal government and some of the states. By "program" I mean a test with administrative machinery backing it up. The private activities here called "programs" are rather more shapeless than, say, the Atomic Energy Commission's program for contractors' employees. But their coverage of most of an industry or trade, and their systematic character relative to the sporadic episodes, earn them the designation of "programs." Included in this category are the practices of the broadcasting and movie industries.

These four types of private action arise from a variety of stimuli, which may also be divided into four classes:

(1) *Self-starters.* I call a test self-starting when an employer (or union) adopts it out of conviction, or for better public relations, in the absence of any unusual outside pressures. A trade-union test may be self-starting also if there is a struggle for power within the union between right- and left-wing groups.

(2) *Pressure groups.* Private organizations by persuasion, threat of exposure, or threat of boycott sometimes induce the adoption of employment tests.

(3) *Investigating committee exposures.* Testimony before legislative

119

committees—federal and state—has been a frequent source of information leading to dismissals. This source may be considerably diminished as a result of the *Watkins* decision, discussed in Chapter 1.

(4) *Government security programs.* These measures, previously described, have a "radiating potency" that extends beyond their formal requirements.

The following sections describe how, in a number of private sectors of our society, these four influences have stimulated the use of the four types of employment tests.

COLLEGES AND UNIVERSITIES

In 1948–49 the cases of three professors at the University of Washington sharply directed public attention to the propriety of dismissing faculty members solely because of their membership in the Communist party. In two of the three Washington cases there was no charge of deception; Professors Herbert Phillips and Joseph Butterworth freely admitted their party membership to a faculty committee. In neither of these cases was there any evidence of improper classroom indoctrination, or of improper public activities. Furthermore, all three of the professors had tenure, so that they could be removed only for good cause. In dismissing the three men, the Washington Regents were the first governing board in an institution of any standing to meet the issue directly.[1]

There has been no dearth of policy statements saying what academic employers would do about Communists. But most of the university cases, before and since the Washington episode, have been obscured by side issues, chiefly those generated by the activities of investigating committees.

In the discussion that raged in 1948 and 1949 there was considerable

1. State colleges and universities are considered in this section if their trustees have a normal degree of autonomy, and if the policies on employment tests emanate from them and not from the legislature. For the general background of the University of Washington situation, see Vern Countryman, *Un-American Activities in the State of Washington* (1951), ch. 6; *The States and Subversion,* ed. Gellhorn (1952), pp. 298–312; Robert MacIver, *Academic Freedom in Our Time* (1955), pp. 179–82, 218–20; "Academic Freedom and Tenure in the Quest for National Security," AAUP BULL. (1956), *42*:61–4. The third University of Washington case involved Prof. Ralph Gundlach, who was charged with leftist bias in the classroom, using the auspices of the University improperly in a survey for a political aspirant, and with evasiveness in answering questions before the Washington State Committee on Un-American Activities. The bases for these charges, and the counter-evidence, are set forth in Countryman, pp. 214–22, 227–33, and evaluated pp. 360–70.

diversity in the statements of policy that university administrators felt obliged to make. The University of Washington administration was feeling the pressure of a state legislative investigating committee, which had just completed a series of exposés of communist influence in the state. The University of California faculty passed a resolution that in principle seemed no different from the Washington position. "Proved members of the Communist party," it read in part, ". . . are not acceptable as members of the faculty." The California faculty was indirectly under pressure from the legislature; but the direct occasion for this policy statement was the attempt of the Board of Regents to exact a loyalty oath from the University staff.

Chancellor Hutchins of Chicago, also under legislative investigation, said: "The University believes that if a man is to be punished he should be punished for what he does and not for what he belonged to or for those with whom he has associated." This was taken to mean that Communist party membership alone would not be a ground for dismissal.

The then presidents of Harvard and Yale were at once more explicit and more cautious. Neither institution, they said in separate statements, would appoint a Communist to its faculty. Neither would engage in special inquiries to determine the politics of its present faculty, which, they were confident, contained no Communists. But both spokesmen refrained from saying what they would do if their confidence turned out to be misplaced.

The self-starting declarations of private institutions were not necessarily less rigorous than those of state universities under heavier legislative pressure. For example, President Baxter of Williams College declared that if an avowed Communist appeared on his faculty, he would recommend his dismissal.[2]

The pertinency of these earlier policy statements is this: by 1953 the shadings between them had disappeared. The change is demonstrated by the statement of the Association of American Universities. The presidents of thirty-seven pre-eminent universities (including Chicago, Harvard, and Yale), said, as part of a general manifesto on the "Rights and

2. In *Civil Liberties under Attack,* ed. Clair Wilcox (1951), p. 144. For data on the legislative "exposés" in Washington State see Countryman, n. 1 above. The California faculty resolution is reported in George Stewart, *Year of the Oath* (1950), pp. 37–8, 148. For the Hutchins statement see Carey McWilliams, *Witch Hunt* (1950), p. 226. The position of Yale in regard to Communist professors was outlined by President Charles Seymour, NYT, June 22, 1949; that of Harvard by President James B. Conant, quoted in Francis Biddle, *The Fear of Freedom* (1951), pp. 156–7.

Responsibilities of Universities and their Faculties" that "Present membership in the Communist party . . . extinguishes the right to a university position."

It is unnecessary to adduce similar declarations from other sources. By the end of 1953 settled policy throughout public and private seats of higher learning held that Communists would not be employed or retained.[3] But there was little to show what, short of "avowed" membership, would be required in the way of proof. Massachusetts Institute of Technology had previously indicated a cautious avenue of approach. In a statement provoked by accusations against Professor Dirk Struik, President Killian defended "unqualified freedom of thought and investigation," but declared that "If a teacher were found to be subject to improper outside control in his teaching, the Institute would regard him as incompetent." If he was convicted of "advocating the violent overthrow of the American government" he would be discharged. When Struik, who describes himself as a "good Marxist" but not a party member, was indicted in 1951 under a state sedition act, he was suspended with pay, and remained in that status until 1956 when the indictment was quashed.[4]

THE FIFTH AMENDMENT OBSCURES THE ISSUES

The chief reason why the limits of these general policies have been little explored is the Fifth Amendment. At the beginning of the 83d

3. See Association of American Universities, *The Rights and Responsibilities of Universities and Their Faculties* (March 24, 1953); Harold Taylor, "The Dismissal of Fifth Amendment Professors," ANNALS (1955), *300:*79. The Association of American Colleges apparently never adopted a formal position; its Committee on Academic Freedom and Academic Tenure for 1953 and 1954 was content with the statement that "colleges should welcome any fair and impartial inquiry." See Association of American Colleges, *Bulletin* (1953), *39:*103, and (1954), *40:*114. Its Committee on Academic Freedom and Tenure made somewhat bolder recommendations in 1955, *Bulletin* (1955), *41:*121. Compare also the Report of the Special Committee of the American Association of University Professors, "Academic Freedom and Tenure in the Quest for National Security," *AAUP Bull.* (1956), *42:*49–107, which adhered to the AAUP prewar position that Communist party membership was not *in itself* ground for dismissal. This report was adopted at the AAUP Annual Meeting; see *AAUP Bull.* (1956), *42:*339–43. See also Ch. 14 below.

4. President James Killian's statement is in Howard M. Jones, *Primer of Intellectual Freedom* (1949), pp. 3–5. Struik is quoted from "Academic Freedom: 4th Annual Crimson Report," *Harvard Crimson* (June 17, 1952), p. M-1. See also "6th . . . Report" (June 17, 1954), p. M-10. The indictment against Struik was dismissed as a result of Pennsylvania v. Nelson, 350 U.S. 497 (1956), which made

Congress, both the House Committee on Un-American Activities and the Senate Internal Security Subcommittee set out to expose Communists in education, at both the school and college level. At least one hundred teachers, under varying circumstances, refused to answer questions about communist associations on the ground that their answers might tend to incriminate them. Professor Barrows Dunham, of Temple University, refused to answer any questions except to give his name and date of birth. Other witnesses claiming the privilege declined to give information either about their own political activities or about those of other persons in whom the committee was interested. Members of a third group testified to their own present or recent nonmembership but invoked the privilege when some date in the past was reached. A few spoke freely of their own past membership in the party but attempted to invoke the privilege when asked to name their communist associates. Still another line was taken by a few hardy witnesses; they refused on grounds of conscience to testify about the involvement of others, and did not invoke the Fifth Amendment at all. Members of both these last two groups were subjected to contempt citations, as was Corliss Lamont, a lecturer at Columbia, who rested his refusal to answer questions about his career and writings on the ground that such inquiries abridged his freedom of speech under the First Amendment.

Not a single one of all the recalcitrant witnesses, nor any of the larger group who answered fully if reluctantly all the questions put to them, admitted current membership in the Communist party.[5]

Thus it was that the great exposures of 1953 produced no one to whom the policy of dismissing known Communists could be easily applied. The resort to the Fifth Amendment required new policies.

state sedition laws inoperative. Struik's suspension was then lifted, but he was censured by the Institute for his use of the Fifth Amendment. See NYT, Oct. 6, 1956.

5. The hearings themselves are ISC, *Subversive Influence in the Educational Process* (1952–55), HUAC, *Communist Methods of Infiltration (Education)* (1953–54), and a number of hearings in different localities, HUAC, *Investigation of Communist Activities in the . . . Area* (1953–55). A complete roster of those who invoked the privilege in 1953 is in *Cong. Rec.* (March 31, 1954), *100*:4280–94. This combined list for the ISC, HUAC, and McCarthy committees listed 89 teachers from 30 institutions; 51 in colleges and universities, 38 in elementary and secondary schools; p. 4295. See also Telford Taylor, *Grand Inquest* (1955), pp. 1–5, 184–6. Contempt proceedings against 17 witnesses who invoked the Fifth Amendment are reviewed in *Cong. Rec.* (July 23, 1954), *100*:11598–652. These proceedings tested the adequacy of the claimed grounds for invoking the privilege. On the consequences of refusals to answer without resort to the Fifth Amendment, see nn. 9, 11, and Ch. 17, below, and Daniel Pollitt, "Pleading the Fifth Amendment before a Congressional Committee," *Notre Dame Lawyer* (1956), *32*:43–58.

They were almost as varied as the patterns of response described above.[6]

Rutgers University had to take the lead because one of its faculty members invoked the privilege early in 1952 before the Internal Security Subcommittee when, under Senator McCarran's chairmanship, it was investigating the Institute of Pacific Relations. A faculty committee heard this man and another who was among the first group of teachers called by the same committee. After the faculty committee recommended that no action be taken against them, the Rutgers trustees decided that failure to answer questions of investigating committees about communist affiliations was and would thereafter be ground for immediate dismissal. Later, this policy was modified slightly in the case of a law professor who, another faculty committee found, had been subjected to unusual harassment by the investigators, including advance publicity suggesting that he had been a spy. The episode which the Un-American Activities Committee sought to exploit in this case involved improper disclosure of official papers in 1937 and 1938. The case had been thoroughly investigated in 1941 by the Department of Justice. There was nothing new in 1953 except an ambiguous connection between the witness and a person named (but not convicted) in the Canadian spy ring. Under these circumstances, the faculty committee found the witness's refusal to discuss the episode understandable, even if it was not excusable. It recommended that, within the policy already laid down, he not be dismissed, but be allowed to resign. The trustees accepted this recommendation. The general policy of 1952 was finally superseded by new university regulations on academic freedom, adopted November 11, 1957, which provided for a hearing on all charges of unfitness.[7] Other institutions may have taken

6. The discussion here excludes those state institutions whose policies were prescribed for them by statutes requiring dismissal of state employees who refused to answer questions. See Ch. 4 above, nn. 27, 32.

7. The first two Rutgers University faculty members invoked the privilege before ISC, Hearings, *Institute of Pacific Relations* (1952), p. 4152 (Moses Finley), and ISC, Hearings, *Subversive Influence in the Educational Process* (1952), p. 187 (Simon Heimlich). The principal Rutgers documents are Special Faculty Comm. of Review, *Report on the Heimlich-Finley Case* (Dec. 3, 1952, mimeo.); Board of Trustees, *Resolution on the Heimlich-Finley Case* (Dec. 12, 1952, mimeo.); and statement of President Lewis W. Jones, *Academic Freedom and Civic Responsibility* (Jan. 24, 1953). See also *AAUP Bull.* (1956), 42:77–8. For the testimony of Glasser, the law professor at Rutgers, see HUAC, Hearings, *Communist Methods of Infiltration (Education)* (1953), pp. 192–6. The Report of the Faculty Committee of Review of the Rutgers Law School, "On the Matter of Abraham Glasser" (August 26, 1953) is reprinted in Association of American Law Schools, *1954 Proceedings* (1955), pp. 121–31. The Faculty Committee recommendation was for resignation "without prejudice," but the acceptance by the Trustees of the resig-

a similar absolute position, but no other conspicuous cases have emerged.

The conventional position that evolved in 1953–54 was a little more elastic. Again in the words of the Association of American Universities, "invocation of the Fifth Amendment places upon a professor a heavy burden of proof of his fitness to hold a teaching position and lays upon his university an obligation to re-examine his qualifications for membership in its society." How has this warning, and others like it, worked out in practice? In the great majority of cases, the faculty member who invoked the privilege has been dismissed, or has resigned, or, if his appointment was for a term of years, the appointment has not been renewed. But note that both resignations and lapses of appointments may be ambiguous in their significance. In two of the Harvard cases, for example, the teachers whom the Corporation declined to dismiss for invoking the privilege were not reappointed. In one of them, that of Dr. Helen D. Markham, an assistant professor in the Medical School, the Corporation announced that she would not be. This action was taken after Dr. Markham, in a second appearance before a Congressional committee, attempted to suggest that Harvard approved of her invocation of the privilege. The Corporation's statement left no doubt that it was dissatisfied with her conduct. But the Corporation made no statement about the future in the case of Leon J. Kamin. He was a Harvard Ph.D. candidate who had a part-time teaching fellowship. The next year (1953–54) he was a full-time research assistant. When this appointment expired, it was explained that he would not have been reappointed or promoted in any event.[8]

Only a few cases were resolved by explicit announcements that the teacher in question would be retained. Of these the most celebrated was that of Dr. Wendell H. Furry, Associate Professor of Physics at

---

nation was unqualified. Ibid., p. 131. See also the Report of the Committee on Academic Freedom and Tenure, Association of American Law Schools, *1955 Proceedings* (1956), pp. 119–50; *1956 Proceedings* (1957), pp. 112–17. Following a reorganization of the Rutgers governing board, a committee recommended modification of the basic position to conform to the Slochower case but recommended against giving Glasser a rehearing on the ground that his acceptance of a year's severance pay on resigning was accompanied by a release of all claims against the University; its report was adopted by the board. See NYT, April 11, 1957.

8. Kamin invoked the privilege before ISC, Hearings, *Subversive Influence in the Educational Process* (1953), p. 677. See *Harvard Crimson* (n. 4 above, 6th Report), p. M-7. Professor Markham's suspension is described in NYT, May 29, July 18, and Sept. 1, 1953; according to the *Crimson* 6th Report, p. M-7, she was advised by Dean G. P. Berry that she would never be re-employed by Harvard. Her testimony is in ISC, Hearings, ibid., pp. 689, 1007.

Harvard and a teacher there since 1934. After he had twice invoked
the privilege before the House Committee on Un-American Activities
with respect to past membership, the Harvard Corporation made its
own investigation. It found that Furry had been a party member from
1938 to 1947, but that he had "at no time permitted his connection with
the party to affect his teaching, nor has he attempted otherwise to influence the political thinking of his students." The Corporation considered his use of the privilege "misconduct," but insufficient to require his
removal. Furry volunteered an account of a 1944 incident when he
falsely told an investigator he had no reason to believe that an applicant
for sensitive government employment was a Communist. Because of
this episode, the Corporation further found him guilty of "grave misconduct" and put him on probation for a three-year period.

This decision was made in May 1953. In November 1953 Senator
McCarthy, who had begun to display a marked antipathy for Harvard's
new President Pusey, called Furry before his committee in executive
session; Furry again invoked the privilege about past communist activities. Finally, in January 1954, Furry (and Kamin) again appeared
before Senator McCarthy. This time both of them, without resorting to
the Fifth Amendment, testified freely about their own activities but refused to tell the Senator and the public the names of others known to
them as party members. Both Kamin and Furry were indicted for contempt; but the court found that the McCarthy committee had exceeded
its jurisdiction.[9]

In two other instances of "clearance," the teachers in question had
the good fortune not to get embroiled with Senator McCarthy. Associate
Professor Abe Gelbart of Syracuse had invoked the privilege before the
House Committee on Un-American Activities; his counsel persuasively
explained that he felt trapped by the testimony of former colleagues,
who had mistakenly testified that they believed Gelbart to have been a
party member with them. Assistant Professor Paul Zilsel of the University of Connecticut, before the same Committee, offered to waive

9. U.S. v. Kamin, 136 F. Supp. 791 (D. Mass. 1956). See Ch. 17 below, n. 1.
For the 1944 episode that resulted in Furry's probation, see NYT, May 21, 1953.
Furry's committee appearances were: HUAC, Hearings, *Communist Methods of
Infiltration (Education)* (1953), pp. 66, 245; Senate Comm. on Gov't Operations,
Permanent Subcomm. on Investigations, Hearings, *Subversion in Industry* (1954),
p. 32 (Kamin, ibid., p. 22). On the first McCarthy committee appearance, and the
conflict between Pusey and McCarthy, which arose because McCarthy resented
Pusey's opposition to him while Pusey was president of Lawrence College in
Appleton, Wis., see NYT, Nov. 10, 1953, also Jan. 16, 1954. See also Livingston
Hall, "The Furry Case," *Harvard Alumni Bulletin* (Nov. 28, 1953), p. 211.

the privilege and testify about his own activities for the period of 1946–48 if the Committee would excuse him from naming fellow members. The Committee declined this offer. The Syracuse Board of Trustees, in voting to retain Gelbart, apparently made no comment; but the University of Connecticut Board "severely censure[d]" Zilsel.[10]

In the absence of special circumstances such as those of the Gelbart and Zilsel cases, most governing boards that have faced the issue have found that refusals to answer, when their legal foundation was the Fifth Amendment, were grounds for dismissal.

It is not feasible to pigeonhole each case; in general, three types of reasons are advanced to justify this result. First, the invocation of the privilege in itself, whatever lies behind it, may be considered a breach of duty to the public and to the university. This rationale is similar to that advanced by the Rutgers trustees. Or the teacher may be found to have "misused" the privilege if his primary motive was to defy the investigators. Third, a desire to shield others may also be branded as an improper reason for resorting to the privilege. However, most of the handful of teachers who testified about themselves but refused on grounds of conscience to name their party associates have retained their posts so far. Successful contempt prosecutions would pose new problems for these witnesses and for their employing institutions, but several such cases were dismissed following the Supreme Court's decision in the *Watkins* case.[11]

Preoccupation with the ethics and legality of the self-incrimination plea has thus effectively obscured the original question. How far will

10. Zilsel's testimony is in HUAC, Hearings (n. 9 above), p. 1036, Gelbart's at p. 1568. See *N. Y. Herald Tribune*, Oct. 26, 1953, letter of Paul S. Andrews, for Gelbart's counsel's position. The Syracuse University Board of Trustees action in upholding the faculty committee recommendation to retain Gelbart is reported NYT, Nov. 14, 1953; the decision of the University of Connecticut board, NYT, July 29, 1953. With respect to two cases that arose at the University of Chicago, William B. Harrell, vice-president of the university, testified that neither person was dismissed, because a faculty committee concluded that neither was concealing anything that would justify dismissal; HUMPHREY HEARINGS, pp. 404–6.

11. Watkins v. U.S., 354 U.S. 178 (1957). Before the main body of cases discussed in this section arose, Professor Lyman Bradley was dismissed by New York University in 1951, as an outgrowth of a contempt conviction for refusing to turn over to the HUAC, in 1946, records of the Joint Anti-Fascist Refugee Committee. See *AAUP Bull.* (1956), *42*:75–6; Bradley v. New York University, 124 N.Y.S. 2d 238 (Sup. Ct. 1953), affirmed 307 N.Y. 620 (1954). Professor Lawrence B. Arguimbau of M.I.T., who refused to name others, resigned. See *Harvard Crimson* (n. 4 above, 6th Report, p. M-7). He was later convicted of contempt and given a suspended sentence, NYT, Nov. 3, 1955. See Ch. 17 below, p. 412, on other contempt cases.

the universities go in terminating or refusing employment for supposedly subversive political activities, when the Fifth Amendment issue is put to one side? The relatively easy case of the "avowed Communist" no longer occurs. An accused faculty member is much more likely to deny membership. How does one then attempt to prove the charges? Some of the problems that arise are suggested by the New York University case of Professor Edwin B. Burgum. It arose as the result of a plea of privilege to questions about communist activities put by the Internal Security Subcommittee. The University administration preferred two charges to a twelve-man faculty committee. The first charge, that Professor Burgum's use of the privilege was conduct unbecoming a teacher, was not sustained, by a vote of 9–3. The second charge was that he used the privilege to avoid disclosing "acts which would reveal the truth concerning the relation of himself and others to the Communist party and subject him to criminal prosecution." This charge was sustained, 9–3; his dismissal followed.

The hearing was reminiscent of proceedings under the federal loyalty–security programs. Manning Johnson, an ex-Communist who was a well-known informer, and Herbert Philbrick, the former FBI undercover agent, testified. Numerous exhibits were introduced to show Professor Burgum's long connection with the Communist party and with communist causes. Questions directed to the same purpose ranged widely over his political opinions. The chief departure from the pattern of federal employees' cases was that the proponents of the charges assumed the burden of proof and confronted Professor Burgum with all their evidence. He did not attempt to counter the record of close communist ties that was developed, but challenged the propriety of the charges. His refusal to affirm or deny that he was a Communist, or to answer any questions pertinent to such an inquiry, was doubtless a factor in the decision. Few teachers are likely to match Professor Burgum's intransigence; but conflicts between the administration's demand for candor and the teacher's claim to privacy are bound to arise.[12]

12. On the Burgum case see the statement by Chancellor Henry T. Heald, of May 4, 1953, reprinted in ISC, Hearings, *Subversive Influence in the Educational Process*, pp. 981–7. Cf. Committee for the Reinstatement of Professor Burgum, *Academic Freedom and New York University* (Feb. 1954). A case at the University of Kansas City resembles the Burgum case. The ousted professor sued. In Davis v. Univ. of Kansas City, 129 F. Supp. 716 (W.D. Mo. 1955), the court held that refusal to answer questions of trustees was good cause for dismissal. See also *AAUP Bull.* (1957), 43:177–95.

Professor Barrows Dunham of Temple University was cleared of a contempt charge (NYT, Oct. 20, 1955), but the Trustees found he misused the privilege. The

A trio of cases at Michigan neatly illustrates the variety of results that may follow when a University holds its own hearings on the heels of a Congressional committee hearing. The three faculty members were called before the House Committee in May 1954 and suspended following their appearances. I do not know whether outside witnesses were called before the University committees that investigated the case, though it appears that the staff of the House Committee was consulted.

H. C. Davis, a young instructor in mathematics, invoked only the First Amendment in refusing to answer questions put by the Un-American Activities Committee. Like Burgum, he refused to answer any of his colleagues' questions either, if they related to Communist party membership. He was dismissed, with apparently no dissenting vote at any stage of the University procedures.

Dr. Mark Nickerson, an associate professor in the medical school, relied on the Fifth Amendment before the Congressional committee. According to President Hatcher, Nickerson had withdrawn from party membership, "primarily because he did not have time to carry on the party's work." He "does not presently disavow the Communist party." This is the closest to the University of Washington cases of any we have seen. The general faculty committees recommended reinstatement with severe reprimand; but the dean and the executive committee of the Medical School recommended dismissal. The president and the Board of Regents voted dismissal.

C. L. Markert, Assistant Professor of Zoology, also invoked the Fifth Amendment, but he was reinstated—with a letter of censure—at least for the remainder of his appointed term. Markert apparently joined the party when he was young (questions by the House Committee suggest that he fought in Spain), but his withdrawal and "present attitude," President Hatcher said, did not justify summary dismissal.

It is apparent in these three cases that the University authorities did not make the refusals to testify the end of the matter; but they were

---

Board of Trustees voted unanimously not to reinstate him. Temple receives state funds, and must comply with the certification provisions of the Pechan Act, Ch. 4 above, n. 30. However, no finding was made that Dunham was a "subversive person," though the proceedings purported to be directed to that question. See NYT, Sept. 24, 1953; ACLU, Greater Philadelphia Branch, *Academic Freedom: Some Recent Philadelphia Episodes* (1954), pp. 3–16. The Jefferson Medical College, also a recipient of state grants, dismissed three faculty members without any explanation other than that it was "in the best interest" of the College. It appeared that the professors would not answer certain questions about past communist associations put to them by the college administration. See ACLU, Greater Philadelphia Branch, ibid., pp. 17–24.

significant, and, in the case of Davis, who persisted in his silence, probably decisive.[13]

Using the classifications set down at the beginning of the chapter, the following summarizes the political employment tests practiced by private colleges and universities, and by those state institutions having a conventional degree of autonomy, that is, those as yet unaffected by direct legislative mandates to carry on employment tests.

(1) General policy statements have been profuse, and mostly self-started. Their common tenor is that Communist party members will not be employed or retained on a faculty. Policy statements about the consequences of invoking the Fifth Amendment appeared chiefly as the result of the Congressional committee activities of 1953. A few of them took the view that invocation of the privilege automatically leads to dismissal. The dominant theme was to warn teachers that they would have to account satisfactorily for their refusals to answer.

(2) Test oaths (or loyalty statements) have not been much used unless the legislature commanded them. A conspicuous exception is the Regents' oath at the University of California, discussed in the last chapter.[14]

(3) Sporadic dismissals, resignations under pressure, and failures to reappoint, attributable to the Fifth Amendment cases exposed by investigating committees, were numerous in 1953 and 1954. In addition to dismissals in New York and California in response to legislative policies described in the last chapter, there have probably been about a hundred cases in the private or autonomous sector. Because of the ubiquity of the Fifth Amendment issue, cases directly inquiring into party membership have been few. On the other hand, there have been some instances of terminations for only mildly deviant views. For example, Emporia State Teachers College in Kansas removed an instructor who signed an amnesty petition for the Smith Act defendants.

The pressure groups active in the field of public education do not seem to have been particularly effective in the private sector.[15]

13. See HUAC, Hearings, *Investigation of Communist Activities in the State of Michigan* (1954), pp. 5331–87; Univ. of Michigan News Services, Release of August 26, 1954 (mimeo.); and *AAUP Bull.* (1956), 42:89–92. A number of other Fifth Amendment cases in universities are reviewed in the AAUP report and by Taylor, both n. 3 above.

14. See also Clark Byse, "A Report on the Pennsylvania Loyalty Act," *Univ. of Pa. Law Rev.* (1953), 101:498, describing an oath and questionnaire used at Pennsylvania State College that went beyond the statutory requirements.

15. The Tandy case at the Emporia State Teachers College is reported in *AAUP*

(4) Organized programs testing loyalty have not appeared. But the security programs of the federal government have reached far into university life.

SECURITY AND UNIVERSITY EMPLOYMENT

The very existence of security measures within universities is paradoxical. Universities exist for the free discovery and diffusion of knowledge; yet the necessary consequence of a security system is to conceal discoveries once made and to confine their diffusion to persons with clearance. Clearance has no relation to scholarly ability, it is a judgment of reliability based chiefly on political grounds. The separation, especially in scientific fields, of the classified world from the nonclassified world means that some significant basic work can be discussed only behind closed doors; what is reported at open meetings of physicists may be quite out of touch with the mainstream of research. The most pointed illustration of the topsy-turvy world where truth is pursued in secret is the fact that dissertations for the degree of Doctor of Philosophy are written in classified fields, read only by cleared professors, and kept under lock and key. This is in fulfillment of a universal requirement that the Ph.D. thesis make an original contribution to knowledge. Whether the digging of graduate students adds more than a few nuggets to the hoard of knowledge has often been questioned; but when truth, patiently mined, is promptly locked up again, we have a strange situation.

However, our concern at this point is with the relation of security measures to the employment policies of universities. Overtly, there is none. In no important university, so far as I know, is eligibility for pro-

Bull. (1956), *42*:70–1, and in *Harvard Crimson* (5th Report, June 10, 1953), p. M-3.

Pressure groups in education include such organizations as the Minute Women and the National Council for American Education, who aspire to correct both educational and political tendencies that they deplore. They have been especially active in public school systems. On the N.C.A.E., organized by Allen A. Zoll, see MacIver (n. 1 above), pp. 59–61. The Minute Women's activities in Houston are the subject of stories in *Time* (Nov. 2, 1953), p. 49, and (April 22, 1957), p. 54. This group is not only anticommunist, but anti-Negro, anti-UN, and anti-Quaker as well. The American Legion disrupted one state teachers college—Fairmont, in West Virginia; but its attack on a private college for women—Sarah Lawrence in New York—had no visible results. The Fairmont story is in *Harvard Crimson* (n. 4 above, 4th Report), p. M-1, and William Manchester, "The Case of Luella Mundel," *Harper's* (May 1952), p. 54. The *Crimson* 4th . . . Report, p. M-9, describes the Sarah Lawrence affair, which was also reported in NYT, e.g. Jan. 23, April 10, 1952.

fessorial or research appointments formally conditioned on security clearance. Nevertheless, there are enough known instances of scientists with security problems who have had unusual difficulty in getting academic employment to warrant an inference that some institutions take the matter into account, quite aside from any concern with disloyalty. The motives are similar to those of industrial contractors. If a physics department has contracts involving classified work, a man's usefulness will be diminished if he cannot participate. Even the possibility of such contracts in the future may operate as a barrier.[16]

The universities, however, have not been willing to undertake security investigations. The Defense Department's industrial contract practice leaves to the employer the initial responsibility of granting clearance for access to classified materials at the lowest level, Confidential. This responsibility the universities refused to assume; so the Industrial Security Regulations recognize that clearance for university contracts will be done by the government.[17]

Even without the investigative burden, the implications of security measures on the campus have led to varying degrees of concern among universities, ranging from withdrawal to disquiet. Harvard has taken a position of aloofness. The University simply will not enter into contracts for classified work except in wartime. Individual professors are free to serve as consultants for classified projects, but it is expected that their work in such capacities will be done off the campus. Presumably, physical safeguards, such as locked files for classified correspondence, are tolerated; after all, President Conant was a member of the General Advisory Board of the Atomic Energy Commission. But beyond this, Harvard has no institutional participation at all in the realms of secrecy.

Chicago takes a middle ground. The birthplace of nuclear fission, it still enters into secret contracts, if faculty members take the initiative in wanting to undertake them; but no classified work is done on the Midway campus; it is relegated to "isolated" facilities.

16. My statement about classified dissertations is based on interviews. On the academic employment difficulties of security risks, see Ch. 7; Gellhorn, *Security, Loyalty, and Science* (1950), pp. 175–202. As an indication of the size of the government's academic research program, 13 per cent of all federal expenditures for research and development, which currently total in excess of $2 billion annually, go to educational institutions. See Nat'l Science Foundation, *Federal Funds for Science* (1956), covering fiscal years 1955–57, pp. 5, 13.

17. Armed Forces Industrial Security Regs. par. 2-207, Feb. 1957. See Don K. Price, *Government and Science* (1954), pp. 82–3, on the genesis of this policy.

For the University of California, also a center of atomic research, I have not been able to find any formal expression of policy with respect to personnel clearance; but the University does maintain a security officer. The conferral on him of liaison duties with the California Un-American Activities Committee, mentioned in the previous chapter, led to considerable concern that mingled loyalty and security measures might come to dominate the campus. A faculty committee reported in May 1955 that the role of the security officer had been modified, and that he would confine himself to matters arising under classified contracts; but the committee went on to regret the existence of such contracts at all, and to acquiesce in them reluctantly as a necessity of national defense.

To mention one other pre-eminent research institution, the Massachusetts Institute of Technology maintains a tremendous volume of government and industrial research contract work, much of it classified. A vice-president of the Institute heads Divisions of Industrial Cooperation and Defense Laboratories which, though functionally independent of the departments of instruction, are physically somewhat intermingled. The wartime Radiation Laboratory was in Cambridge; now the Lincoln Laboratory in suburban Belmont is the center of the Institute's continuing work in radar defense. But this, though the largest, is only one of many projects on which the Institute's staff is engaged.

Formal regulations (confirmed in an interview) make it clear that if a man is hired at M.I.T. for a classified project and then cannot get clearance, he will not be retained. There is no suggestion that a man with a regular academic appointment need be clearable; it is another matter whether, in some departments, his opportunity for research and thus for promotion might not be much curtailed.

On the secret side, M.I.T. enforces security restrictions rigorously; on the open side, its solicitous handling of loyalty cases was noted with approval by the American Association of University Professors.[18]

18. The Harvard policy was stated by Dean McGeorge Bundy, HUMPHREY HEARINGS, pp. 462–74; Chicago's by Vice-President William Harrell, ibid., pp. 385–90. Harrell said, "We wished to avoid a situation where the free interchange of ideas among members of our staff, engaged in open research and teaching, could not be carried out without interference by the security system" (p. 386). On California see Ch. 4 above, n. 21. The Report of the Faculty Committee on Academic Freedom is contained in Univ. of Calif., *Academic Senate Record* (Berkeley, May 16, 1955), pp. i–iv.

The statement on "Employment Policy at M.I.T. Involving Security Clearance," Dec. 1, 1954, also contemplates separation where clearance is "unreasonably delayed (currently 2 months for Confidential, 8 months for Secret)" (par.A.1.b.).

If these examples are representative, there is at least an awareness in major universities of the conflict between security restrictions and the idea of a university; and a variety of measures has been taken to check encroachments of security criteria on regular academic employment. But it does not appear that, aside from Harvard's policy of total abstinence, these measures are altogether effective. The dominance of government contracts and grants in some research budgets may at times have subdued qualms that would otherwise be voiced. For example, there was little evidence of opposition from university administrations when the Public Health Service conditioned research grants on vague loyalty criteria that had no relation either to security needs or to research competence. And only some universities refused in 1953 to continue a contract with the U. S. Armed Forces Institute, which distributes educational material, when this clause was added: "The contractor shall not employ or retain for the performance of service under this contract such persons as are disapproved by the Government." [19]

INDUSTRIES AND INDUSTRIAL TRADE UNIONS

The experience of the General Electric Company, while hardly typical, illustrates several types of employment tests in operation. Also, three of the four springs of action earlier noted have pressed on the Company and its employees. Again a left-wing union is at the center of disturbance—at once a source of alarm and a convenient pretext for employment tests that may in fact have other origins. The first move was made by the Atomic Energy Commission in 1948, when, on security

If a member of the academic staff has clearance troubles, his case is referred to a "Security Review Committee, which shall recommend whether he may continue to be associated with government-sponsored work at the Institute." (par. B.). On M.I.T.'s policy in loyalty cases see *AAUP Bull.* (1956), *42*:94–5. M.I.T. Bulletin, *President's Report Issue* (1954), pp. 238–40, shows that the Division of Defense Laboratories had government contracts of $19,107,100 involving 1694 persons, of whom only 36 were on the M.I.T. staff. The Division of Industrial Cooperation had a similar volume of government work.

19. Fourteen of the forty-six universities which at that time had been helping grade the assignments and prepare the correspondence courses refused to sign the 1954 contracts. The dissident universities, which included Michigan, California, Illinois, North Carolina, Minnesota, Wisconsin, Louisiana, and Kansas, felt that this clause gave the government unwarranted power over teachers. See NYT, Aug. 21, 1953. The Defense Department's position was based on its supposed loyalty and security responsibilities. NYT, Aug. 27, 1953. The contract provision permitting "disapproval" was later modified to confine it to "security reasons." Federation of American Scientists, *Newsletter* (Oct. 12, 1953), p. 3.

grounds, it ordered G.E. not to recognize the United Electrical Workers, then still in the CIO, as bargaining agent on AEC contracts. This episode has already been described in Chapter 3. In 1949 the United Electrical Workers were expelled from the CIO. A new union, the International Union of Electrical Workers, was formed in the CIO, with James Carey as president. It was fairly successful in subtracting locals from the old UE; but General Electric remained one of the strongholds of the UE, so that, as late as 1953, representation of G.E. workers was about evenly divided between UE and IUE. Carey, who of course wanted the Company to choose sides, and to choose his side, repeatedly charged the Company with favoring the left-wing union, for the sake of weakening the bargaining power of the employees by dividing them, and because the vulnerable UE could not bargain as hard as the purified IUE could. These accusations were given some weight by *Fortune* magazine. The Company's reply, in addition to a general denial, was to point out that its position was legally impeccable and unavoidable. It had to deal with whichever union the National Labor Relations Board certified in a plant, and it could not lift a finger to influence its employees' choice in a contest between the unions. To Congressional committees and to the public, the Company urged a legislative solution for its awkward position: let the government take the responsibility for measures to curb the influence of communist-led unions. Similarly for individual security risks. G.E. had cooperated fully with the programs that protected classified Defense Department and AEC contracts. If further measures were to be taken against Communists in industry, the government, with its superior resources and powers, should do the job of identification.[20]

Meanwhile the Company had not been defenseless. A primary fact to be kept in mind is that the government and the Company were diligently safeguarding classified contracts. There was some suggestion that suspect union officials, though excluded from sensitive areas, could piece together significant details of classified work. Perhaps they could, if the screened employees were careless. There were also allegations, from an unreliable source, that G.E. had no secrets from the Com-

20. On the split in the Electrical Workers and its immediate results see NYT, Dec. 10, 1953; "The Thin Red Line," *Fortune* (June 1952), p. 72, and "Carey v. Boulware," ibid. (Oct. 1952), p. 92. On G.E.'s position see Senate Committee on Labor and Public Welfare, Subcomm. on Labor and Labor-Management Relations, Hearings, *Communist Domination of Certain Unions* (1952), pp. 394–402; and ISC, Hearings, *Subversive Influence in Certain Labor Organizations* (1953–54), pp. 287–315.

munists. But no verifiable breaches of security have come to light. In
any event, the bulk of the Company's operations are now unclassified,
even though during World War II 90 per cent of its production had
been for military contracts (not all classified, however).

The possibility of another major shift of machines and men to war
work led the Company, after the Korean War had taken a serious turn,
to institute a loyalty statement for prospective employees. This statement came into general use for all new employees, and required them
to state whether they were or had been Communist party members, advocated or believed in violent overthrow, or had been denied clearance
for classified government contracts.[21]

Late in 1953 Senator McCarthy briefly turned his attention to General Electric; he held closed hearings in Albany and an open hearing
at Boston, at which a number of informants and recalcitrant employees
appeared (two employees who invoked the Fifth Amendment were
members of IUE, the new CIO union). The Company rather precipitately announced in December 1953 a new general policy: it would
discharge any employee who refused to answer questions in committee
hearings. A suspended employee would have ninety days in which to
purge himself by answering the questions or by getting clearance from
the government. The Company did not dissemble the fact that there
was no government agency that would grant such clearance to a person
not engaged in classified work; it simply hoped that one would be
created. Seventeen employees were soon suspended; the Company announced in June 1954 that seven had been dismissed. None of the
seventeen was on classified work; only eight were UE members. During
1954, NLRB elections at Lynn and Schenectady switched 40,000 employees from UE to IUE, reducing UE's representation to 20,000. The
shift at Schenectady resulted from the defection to IUE of Leo Jandreau,
business agent of the huge local there, and formerly an important UE
leader. The rest of the suspected leadership held fast.[22]

21. The charge that security measures were ineffective in G.E. was made by an
alleged undercover operative for the FBI; testimony of William Teto, Senate
Committee on Government Operations, Permanent Subcomm. on Investigations,
Hearings, *Subversion and Espionage in Defense Establishments and Industry*
(1953), p. 1, and NYT, Nov. 20, Nov. 26, 1953. See ACLU, release of July 26, 1954
(mimeo.), on the use of the loyalty statement.

22. The Albany and Boston hearings are in Senate Comm. on Government Operations, n. 21 above (Nov. 19, 1953–Feb. 19, 1954), Parts 1 and 2. On the G.E.
policy and its results see ISC (n. 20 above), p. 290; NYT, Feb. 23 and 27, 1954; and
Time (June 7, 1954), p. 103. On the decline of UE see *Time* (July 12, 1954), p.
81, NYT, Dec. 10, 1953. On Jandreau see *Time* (March 22, 1954), p. 108, and

The sum of the G.E. story is this: partly on its own initiative, partly under pressure from the rival unions, an investigating committee, and security agencies, the company adopted a comprehensive security test for work not at present within the security area. New employees must heed the policy statement of December 1953. The program is not industry-wide, unless other electrical goods manufacturers have adopted it unobtrusively. But G.E.'s own 280,000 employees are more numerous than the total employment in scores of industries one could name.[23]

Other industries, both large and small, also have bargaining relationships with left-wing unions; but (to mention one example) the employers of fur workers, who until recently had a communist leadership, so far as I know have not instituted any loyalty measures. Of course they do not have the security responsibilities of G.E. and its competitors.[24]

NYT, April 10, 1954. UE attacked the G.E. policy on Fifth Amendment cases in the courts, charging that the policy violated the UE–G.E. collective bargaining agreement by creating a new condition of employment, and that the Company had conspired with the Committee to abridge the civil rights of a local union leader. The lower court held that G.E. merely exercised its right to discharge for "obvious cause," that invocation of the privilege caused such hostile public, stockholder, and employee reaction as to constitute cause, and that UE had not sustained the burden of proof on the conspiracy charge. United Electrical Radio & M. Workers v. General Electric Co., 127 F. Supp. 934 (D.D.C. 1954). On appeal, the Court of Appeals held that the complaint should have been dismissed for lack of jurisdiction, 231 F. 2d 259 (1956).

23. G.E. employment figures are from its 1956 Annual Report. The Stewart-Warner Corp., among middle-sized companies, has taken an aggressive stand against employing persons it believes to be Communists. This policy was announced in 1949, after a contract with UE had expired. Certain dismissals were appealed to the NLRB as anti-union in motivation. The Board found that this was true in some instances, but upheld the Company's privilege to dismiss supposed Communists. Stewart-Warner, 94 NLRB 607 (1951). The Company was then charged by the NLRB with illegally supporting the International Brotherhood of Electrical Workers (AFL) against UE in an election. The Court of Appeals found the evidence insufficient and set aside the Board's order. Stewart-Warner v. NLRB, 194 F. 2d 207 (4th Cir. 1952); cf. *Business Week* (March 1, 1952), p. 124, an approving account of vigorous Company activity against UE. Stewart-Warner's present contracts with IBEW and the International Association of Machinists recognize the Company's privilege to discharge Communist party members. ISC (n. 20 above), pp. 184–5.

24. The telegraph and cable companies that employ members of the small American Communications Association (expelled from the CIO) have complained to Congressional committees that these employees could interfere with message traffic; see ISC, Hearings, *Subversive Infiltration in the Telegraph Industry* (1951–52); ISC Hearings (n. 20 above), pp. 188–92; and Industrial Relations Research Association, *Personnel Security Programs in U. S. Industry* (June, 1955),

In the automobile industry a more cautious history unfolds, by comparison with G.E. The United Automobile Workers has been clearly anticommunist under Walter Reuther's leadership; but there are pockets of communist influence; with them, groups opposed to Reuther sometimes make common cause. The outstanding case of this sort is found in the huge Ford Local 600, which embraces the River Rouge plant. The UAW constitution bars Communists from office. An attempt to invoke this provision against five officers of Local 600 failed. After a prolonged intra-union squabble, the anti-Reuther faction returned to power. The union constitution was then amended to give the international board stronger review over local trial boards.

Another source of disturbance in the automobile industry has been the House Committee on Un-American Activities. It made two election-year forays into Michigan, in 1952 and 1954, and publicized a mass of detail about small-scale communist operations; but the Committee's activities did not perceptibly alter the tempo of anticommunist activity in the industry. The most remarkable disclosures described an attempt to "colonize" the Buick plant at Flint with a group of eastern college-trained Communists, who concealed their higher education in their employment applications. One member of this group, however, hotly rebutted the charges of intellectualism. "People approach me and ask me if I read Shakespeare and things of that sort . . . the closest I came to a university was to watch a football game."

The motor manufacturers have remained singularly unmoved, in the face of the twin distractions of union dissension and investigative exposés. The chief reaction to the latter has come from fellow employees, who after both the 1952 and 1954 hearings roughed up, or refused to work beside, unfriendly witnesses. The union, though it has expelled Communists after trial boards had found them guilty of anti-union activity, has taken the position that accusations aired by the House Committee and pleas of the Fifth Amendment do not justify summary ostracism. The employers have cooperated in seeing that some of these unfriendly witnesses were returned to work. On its part, the union did not protest the General Motors' dismissal of two of the Flint intellectuals.[25]

---

pp. 95–100. ACA no longer represents American Cable employees; ibid., p. 96. Radio Corp. of America suspended several A.C.A. members who refused to testify in 1957. NYT, June 27, July 19, Aug. 3, 1957. An arbitrator's decision ordering the reinstatement of two men, who had relied on the First Amendment only, describes the separation of classified from other traffic. RCA Communications, Inc., 29 Labor Arb. 567 (1957).

25. On the UAW and Ford Local 600, see NYT, Oct. 8, 1950, April 15, 1950,

In the aircraft industry, where the UAW is also strong, the long arm of government security measures is felt much more than in automobiles. The motor companies build tanks and aircraft engines; but the volume of classified work is minor compared to their main task of turning out five to six million cars a year. The reverse is of course true in aircraft, where government orders blanket the industry. Perhaps this explains why there seems to be no significant information about wholly private employment tests in the aircraft industry, or in other industries where government security controls are dominant. In such areas one learns through arbitration reports of disputes auxiliary to the industrial security program, dealing with such matters as these: must the employer find another job for a man denied security clearance? Is a discharge under such circumstances even arbitrable under the contract? May the company suspend employees when a denial of clearance is only tentative? [26]

Throughout industry, lack of information about private employment tests is the rule; the industries here discussed are the exceptions. That is, they are exceptional not because they have or don't have employment tests, but because we have some information about them. The same general ignorance prevails about the service trades. Only in the field of mass communications, it will appear, has there been any sustained exposure and discussion. In this field—notably broadcasting and the movies—neither employers nor employees are accustomed to reticence; the pressure for publicity is intense and unremitting. In other occupations the skeleton in the closet is not immediately wired for sound. This seems to be true even where there are differences between employer and union about the propriety of employment tests.

An example of an almost private debate is to be found in the tele-

---

and March 23, 1952. See George Blackwood, "The Battle for Local 600," *New Leader* (Aug. 10, 1953), p. 10. The HUAC hearings were: *Communism in the Detroit Area* (1952), Parts 1–2; *Investigation of Communist Activities in the State of Michigan* (1954), Parts 8–10. The quoted passage is from the 1954 hearings, p. 5715. For instances of hostile reactions by fellow workers see NYT, June 20, 1954, and *Worthington Corp.*, 24 Labor Arb. 1 (1955); of expulsions from the union see NYT, Oct. 30, 1950, and HUAC 1952 Hearings, pp. 3104, 3147, 3150, 3199, 3219. The UAW's statement on Fifth Amendment policy is in Telford Taylor, *Grand Inquest* (1955), pp. 214–15.

26. In order: No, Bell Aircraft Corp., 16 Labor Arb. 234 (1951); No, Sperry Gyroscope Co. v. Engineers' Ass'n, 304 N.Y. 582 (1951); No, Arma Corp. v. Engineers' Ass'n, 22 Labor Arb. 325 (1954); same issue pending in another Sperry case held arbitrable in Fitzgerald v. Sperry, 283 App. Div. 1036, 131 N.Y.S. 2d 873 (1954). Cf. Liquid Carbonic Corp., 22 Labor Arb. 709 (1954).

phone system. The Bell companies and their employees, though they are the sinews of our communications system, do not attract the same public attention as do some of their customers. Consequently, the company's inauguration of a loyalty statement in 1954 passed almost unnoticed. The occasion was created by a revision of a citizenship questionnaire already in use, at least in some Bell companies. This document, in addition to searching questions about the citizenship and residence of the employee and his close relatives, requires a listing of all organizational memberships in the preceding decade (church and labor excepted), and then puts the familiar inquiry about membership in an organization advocating unconstitutional alteration of the form of government. The Communications Workers of America (CIO—not to be confused with the American Communications Association) complained that the questionnaire, taken as a whole, was an unnecessary invasion of privacy and liberty. The Union complained to the A.T. and T. management, to the Department of Justice, and to the Federal Communications Commission. The responses, I am advised, were noncommittal. The questionnaire seems to be currently in use, as is a "Security Declaration" promulgated by A.T. and T's manufacturing subsidiary, Western Electric. This declaration, which appears to have been adopted in March 1954, runs as follows: "I hereby certify that, except as qualified below, I have not been a member and am not now a member of the Communist party, or of any organization, association, movement, group, or combination of persons which advocates the alteration of the form of government of the United States by force or violence, or of any of the organizations on the attached list of organizations designated by the Attorney General as required under Executive Order." Western Electric has a substantial volume of classified contracts. Other operations of the telephone system may not be technically classified; yet many aspects of the system are undoubtedly of critical importance to military communications. But the "citizenship questionnaire" for telephone employees, and the "Security Declaration" for Western Electric employees, are not confined to sensitive jobs.

In the A.T. and T. incident, in spite of the fact that the union and the Company openly disagreed on policy (the Union denounced the questionnaire in a resolution passed at its 1954 convention), no outside interest developed.[27] It is much more likely that there should be no

27. This paragraph is based on material and information supplied by the Research Department of the Communications Workers of America. A representative of A.T. and T. replied to an inquiry about the operation of the program as fol-

publicity at all in cases where the union and the employer cooperate.

The union may go beyond cooperation in an employment test and take the initiative. Such a situation may readily occur when the union is throwing off actual communist elements, when the union leadership is using the communist label to discredit internal opposition, or when the leadership concludes that it would be expedient for the union to take a strong public anticommunist position.

A substantial number of union constitutions bar Communists from membership. A government survey counted forty in 1954; 6,000,000 members were covered. The ban is usually expressed in terms of party membership; sometimes subversive belief or activities is the test; other totalitarian affiliations are frequently included. A much larger number (fifty-nine, covering 10,000,000 members) bars such persons from holding office in the union. When the Steelworkers decided to take a stronger anticommunist position in 1954, they did so by amending their constitution, which (like UAW's) had conventionally excluded Communists, Fascists, and members of other totalitarian and subversive organizations from union office. Now, following the lead of the right-wing electrical workers, they barred these persons from union membership as well, and further extended the prohibition to exclude anyone who is a "consistent supporter of or who actively participates in the activities of" subversive organizations. No urgent reason appeared for

lows: "As you know, the Bell System Companies are engaged in furnishing telephone service to the public and to our government. It is important that such communications be given protection at all times and particularly so during war times and defense periods. It therefore has been the general practice to appraise employees in regard to their loyalty and to be alert at all times for indications to the contrary.

"I understand that most of the telephone companies supplement their personnel data by requesting additional information, in one form or another, which may deal with citizenship, membership in certain organizations, or other information pertinent to security. In some cases, this may include some form of loyalty oath. However, since there is no uniformity and the procedures followed vary considerably among the companies, I am not in a position to supply any samples or statistics for the Bell System." Letter from G. S. Dring, Sept. 9, 1954. The Western Electric Company has apparently made it a practice to require *all* of its employees (whether working on classified matter or not) to be eligible for Confidential or Secret clearances, on the theory that they might be involved in classified activity in the future. See ACLU [No. Calif.] *News,* May 1956, March 1957. The Department of Defense has cooperated by passing on eligibility through the mechanism of the Industrial Security program. This practice has been challenged in lawsuits brought by employees of the Wisconsin Telephone Co. Dressler v. Wilson, 155 F. Supp. 373 (D.D.C. 1957) (preliminary injunction denied); Nat'l Lawyers Guild, *Civil Liberties Docket* (1957), 2:72.

this change. There were no responsible charges of communist (or fascist) influence in the union at the time. To the outsider, it looked like window-dressing.[28]

Window-dressing or not, such provisions can become an effective basis for excluding or expelling unwanted workers from the union, and they are so used. Sometimes appeals are taken to the courts from such action. These requests for judicial intervention do not often succeed; and it would be fair to assume that many cases are never brought to the courts, in view of the slim chance of success in having union action overturned. Whether denial of union membership results in denial of employment depends first on whether union membership is a condition of employment. In at least two-thirds of all unionized employment such conditions obtain.[29] For any particular industry, inquiry would have to be made whether the union enjoys a closed shop or a union shop or a union-security agreement. Even if none of these exclusive arrangements is embodied in a contract, is it embedded in the practices of the industry?

If the employer accedes to a union request to fire a supposed Communist, there is one minor legal roadblock in his way, a limitation in the Taft-Hartley Act on his otherwise broad power to discharge on loyalty grounds. If an employer is party to a union security agreement, he is prohibited from discriminating against an employee for nonmembership in the union, unless membership in the union was denied or terminated for failure to tender dues or fees.

But this limitation, as a commentator has explained, is "more apparent than real." For, "under such a contract, an employer cannot dis-

28. See William Paschell and Rose Theodore, "Anti-Communist Provisions in Union Constitutions," *Monthly Labor Review* (1954), 77:1097–1100. The National Industrial Conference Board, *Handbook of Union Government Structure and Procedures* (1955), pp. 61–2 is in accord. Cf. Clyde Summers, "Admission Policies of Labor Unions," *Quar. Jour. of Econ.* (1947), 61:75, who then found twenty-nine union constitutions barring Communists from membership. For the change in the Steelworkers' constitution see NYT, Sept. 25, 1954.

29. See Rose Theodore, "Union-Security Provisions in Agreements, 1954," *Monthly Labor Review* (1955), 78:649. See Ch. 18 below for discussion of the legality of union exclusion practices. Philip Taft, *The Structure and Government of Labor Unions* (1954), reports a number of instances of expulsions from unions of Communist party members; e.g. Oil Workers (p. 266), and Upholsterers (p. 284). Examples of expulsions of anti-Communists include the Regelson case (Retail Drug Store Employees Union)—see ACLU, *Report on Civil Liberties, January 1951–June 1953* (1953), p. 102, and *35th Annual Report* (1955), p. 102—and the National Maritime Union controversies (ACLU, *1951–53 Report*, pp. 100–2, and Taft, p. 176).

charge an employee merely because that employee was expelled from or denied admission to the union on grounds of disloyalty. But this obstacle is easily avoided if the employer makes an individual investigation and evaluation of loyalty in each case; he can then support the discharge directly on grounds of suspected disloyalty rather than nonmembership in the union." [30]

OBSCURITY OF BASES FOR PRIVATE ACTION

The employer need not always make an independent finding of disloyalty. He may be free simply to exercise his common-law right to dismiss an unwanted servant. Unless the employee has the protection of an individual contract, ordinarily his only other protection against arbitrary dismissal lies in the union contract and its grievance machinery. I am now assuming a situation where the union is either initiating or tacitly supporting the dismissal. In either event, it is not going to lift a finger; and the employee is practically helpless to contest his dismissal if he lacks union backing. Furthermore, there may not be a union—either helpful or hostile or indifferent—in the picture. Millions of private employees, especially white-collar groups, do not belong to a union.

And so we come back to the practices of private employers, and to an unsatisfied curiosity about the frequency of political tests. It is bound to remain unsatisfied, because of one final insurmountable ambiguity. Even if the employer has to give the employee a statement of the cause of dismissal, as he does under some state statutes; and even if there is an interested union, it is not hard to find a nonpolitical ground for discharge. This is the advice of the National Industrial Conference Board, after an extensive survey of its member firms:

> Where the union is cooperative or where there is no union, companies report that the best thing to do is to fire men of questionable loyalty. Communist affiliation is rarely used as the premise since this may be difficult, if not impossible, to prove legally. Instead, an infraction of a company rule, submission of a false employment application, or failure to perform work satisfactorily are generally the bases of dismissal. Some companies report, however, that, "Commies can be awfully good and conscientious workers when the heat is on."

30. Comment, "Loyalty and Private Employment," *Yale Law Jour.* (1953), 62:966–7, discussing Taft-Hartley, § 8(a)(3). Footnotes have been omitted.

Security personnel maintain, however, that in the long run, with vigilance and careful "bookkeeping" of the actions, comings and goings, absences, vacation leaves and any violations of these or of other company rules, management will be able to get rid of some of its security risks. It may not work every time but, as security officers point out, "It only takes one to sabotage a plant and every risk you get rid of is that much to the good." [31]

When a private employer decides to rid his establishment of potential security risks or persons of doubtful loyalty, what does he use for information? He does not have access to FBI files, though some information may trickle from local agents to company security officers, who themselves are often FBI alumni. The Defense Department procedures are supposed to be self-contained and to preclude feeding derogatory information to contractors for them to act on; but there may be an osmotic transfer of hints and suggestions, especially through the military contract representatives on the premises.

The only case where the contracting agency has made derogatory information available to the contractor on anything resembling a systematic basis has been the AEC's "invite procedure." This is a practice, set down in administrative regulations, of turning over to the employer information that is unfavorable but not substantial enough to warrant further proceedings by the AEC. The question immediately arises whether summary dismissal by the employer, or unobtrusive transfer to unclassified work is "invited." We do not know. Later regulations restricted the freedom with which this information was formerly conveyed, but the AEC has never disavowed the practice.[32]

The richest government material that the private employer can tap is of course the hearings and reports of the congressional investigating committees. I have said so much about the activities of these committees as the detonator for employment tests that it is unnecessary to add anything about the dynamite of their records.

Few employers, and in general only those with large security responsibilities under government contracts, have specialists who can throw

31. N.I.C.B., *Industrial Security I, Studies in Business Policy*, No. 60 (1952), p. 63. For state statutes requiring a statement of cause for dismissal see Comment (n. 30 above), p. 983, n. 133.

32. The practices of the "invite" procedure are described in the AEC *Manual*, §§ 2311.032–034, Nov. 3, 1954, reprinted in HUMPHREY HEARINGS, pp. 1312–13, BNA MANUAL, p. 25/233. See also James Newman, "The Atomic Energy Industry: An Experiment in Hybridization," *Yale Law Jour.* (1951), *60*:1385.

together a dossier from the miscellaneous sources of information available to them. An employer who is serious about digging out supposed subversives hires outside specialists. These include some new firms that have sprung up in response to the demand. The best known were the publishers of *Counterattack* and *Red Channels,* of whom more in the following section on broadcasting. Dun and Bradstreet, the well-known credit-rating firm, also offers a Personnel Security Service. From the scanty information available it appears to depend more on field investigation then on combing congressional hearings, newspaper columns, and the like. The latter is the technique of some of the newly arrived "consultants" on loyalty problems.[33]

It is not possible to make any descriptive generalizations about the kinds of information that industrial employers get from private investigations. Practically no facts are available, and there is no basis for extrapolating the practices of employers in radio and movies. It is likely that information privately gathered will, even if it is accurate, lack political perspective and context in evaluation. On the other hand, the employer who is rooted in a single locality can get character appraisals from fellow employees and others that might be withheld from government agents.

The situation in industry is indeed a hodge-podge. There is some use of general policy statements, notably in union constitutional provisions; there is some use of loyalty questionnaires, notably by G.E. and A.T. and T. There are sporadic dismissals, touched off by Congressional committee exposés, by union action against left-wingers, and by management carrying security precautions beyond the necessities of government requirements. This is what appears on the surface in industry. What is underneath? The private employer does not have to publish

33. See Comment, "The Role of Employer Practices in the Federal Industrial Personnel Security Program: A Field Study," *Stanford Law Rev.* (1956), 8:245–9.

For an example of dismissals resulting directly from committee investigations see NYT, Dec. 8, 1954, reporting that two employees of Bethlehem Steel pleaded the Fifth Amendment before the Senate Comm. on Government Operations, Permanent Subcomm. on Investigations, Hearings, *Subversion . . . in . . . Industry* (1954), pp. 185–214, after being named as Communist party members by an FBI undercover agent. Senator Mundt, acting chairman, sent copies of their testimony to Bethlehem with the request that they be dismissed. Bethlehem complied, and was upheld by the arbitrator in Bethlehem Steel, 7 Am. Labor Arb. Awards par. 69,978 (1955). In HUAC, Hearings, *Communism in the Detroit Area* (n. 25 above), the testimony on pp. 2766, 2775, 2800, 2805, 2859, 2863, 2887, 2907, 2945, 3179, and 3182 refers to lost jobs and threats of dismissal; see also NYT, Feb. 27 and 28, 1952.

standards, criteria, and procedures. So long as he does not decimate the available labor force, he can be quite capricious about whom he hires and (subject to union intervention) whom he fires. If he prefers to avoid the acclaim or controversy that would follow an open purge of alleged subversives, he can find other pretexts for dismissals. This freedom of action, however, does not mean that industrial employers have all taken up employment tests. On the contrary, the only evidence available shows that they crop out here and there, and now and then. It is likely, I believe, that there is a hidden reef from which the outcroppings emerge. It does not block entrance to all industrial employment, but its extent, guessed at from the surface, is considerable.

EMPLOYERS AND UNIONS IN THE COMMUNICATIONS INDUSTRIES

The world of film and radio displays the full flowering of private loyalty tests. In the other mass communications media, newspapers and magazines, there have been significant episodes, but nothing resembling an organized program. Most of the newspaper cases have grown out of Fifth Amendment problems. One important arbitration case arose when two editorial staffmen for the *Los Angeles Daily News,* after having been named as Communist party members before the House Committee on Un-American Activities, invoked the privilege. They were dismissed. The American Newspaper Guild pressed the cases before the arbitration board on the ground that political beliefs were not sufficient cause for dismissal. The labor and management representatives on the five-man board divided, leaving the decision to Dean Paul Dodd of the University of California. He gave decisive weight to the publisher's contention that the charges, if unanswered, would have unfavorable business repercussions. The publisher "has the right," he concluded, "to expect the accused to clear themselves of the serious charges made under oath against them, if they are to continue their employment." [34]

Another group of newspaper cases resulted from the activities of the

34. The *Los Angeles Daily News* case is reported in 19 Labor Arb. 39 (1952). Another arbitration case involving a United Press script writer, Theodore Polumbaum, reached a different result. United Press Ass'n, 22 Labor Arb. 679 (1954). The United Press did not accept the award, and dismissed Polumbaum anyway. This later ouster was upheld in court; see NYT, March 6, 1956. In the course of the hearing at which Polumbaum invoked the privilege, it developed that UP requires a non-Communist affidavit from applicants for employment. HUAC, Hearings, *Methods of Communist Infiltration in Education* (1953), p. 1003.

Senate Internal Security Subcommittee. In the summer of 1955 it called as a witness Winston Burdett, Columbia Broadcasting news commentator, who testified to his Communist party membership in the late 1930's as a member of a cell in the now defunct *Brooklyn Eagle;* he also named as members other newspaper people. Some of these were immediately called to testify, and two (one from the *New York Times,* the other from the *New York Daily News*) were dismissed by their employers after they pleaded the Fifth Amendment. Senators Eastland and Jenner saw in Burdett's disclosures a significant effort by the party to penetrate leading American newspapers, while the Committee counsel, J. G. Sourwine, it was said, perceived grounds for vindication of the late Senator McCarran, who had been much beset by the liberal and international press (Sourwine had been appointed Committee counsel by McCarran). Closed hearings, described as an investigation generally into the press and other communications media, were consequently held in New York by the Committee, Dec. 5–7, 1955. Of the thirty-eight witnesses called, however, thirty were past or present members of the *New York Times* staff, which led to the suggestion that the *Times* had been singled out for attack. The *Times,* conceding that the press was not immune from investigation, charged editorially that this investigation was intended to intimidate the paper for its opposition to Senators Jenner and Eastland on numerous issues, e.g. immigration policy and segregation.

The *Times* meanwhile appeared to be acting on this employment policy: it would not knowingly hire a Communist party member for news or editorial work, and a present member would be discharged upon his exposure, since the *Times* could not trust such people to report the news objectively or to comment on it honestly. Although the *Times* would not discharge either because of past membership or pleading the Fifth Amendment, in view of the public nature of the business the employee would have to show his fitness to continue to hold a place of trust on the news or editorial staff of the paper. The *Times* had an obligation to consider whether in view of all the facts, including the position taken before the committee, the employee was still qualified to hold his position.

After the closed hearings in New York had been completed, the Committee followed the usual custom of calling those who had invoked the Fifth Amendment to repeat their pleas in public hearings. These were held in Washington during the first week in January 1956. The *Times* dismissed two editors, who, after they were subpoenaed, indicated their

intention to refuse to answer questions. The *Daily News* fired another
reporter, and the *Daily Mirror* a copy editor, for invoking the privilege.
The immediate total of dismissals connected with this series of hearings
amounted to six, out of the several thousand employees of New York
newspapers (4000 on the *Times* alone). The *Times,* notably, did not
dismiss some noneditorial employees who invoked the privilege, nor
some who declined to testify on First Amendment grounds, nor several
senior editors who admitted past party membership.

Senator Eastland, at the close of the hearings, acknowledged that
there was no evidence that the party members had injected communist
material into any extant New York newspaper of general circulation.[35]

In the magazine world, the most conspicuous case has been the 1953
dismissal by *Collier's* of a fiction editor, Bucklin Moon, apparently
because an unnamed pressure group was circulating charges that Moon
had extensive communist-front connections. Some nonpolitical grounds
for dismissal were suggested to Moon by his superiors, but these, he
said, were of little weight, and easily refuted. The editor of *Collier's*
denied the version advanced by Moon and his indignant colleagues; but
he gave no other explanation for the removal, and made his position
more awkward by saying that he was "eminently satisfied" with Moon's
work. Moon's immediate superior, who protested the dismissal, was
himself later discharged, but without publicity.

There has also been one conspicuous case in book publishing. In
1951, after he had been denounced by Budenz and others as a Communist, Angus Cameron resigned his post as chief editor of Little, Brown,
and Co. At the time there was considerable feeling that Little, Brown

35. Of the six employees dismissed, the *N. Y. Times* accounted for three; the
N. Y. Daily News dismissed two; and the *Daily Mirror* one. The 1955 hearings
are ISC, *Strategy and Tactics of World Communism,* Parts 14–16, pp. 1323–1583;
see NYT, July 1, 6, 14, and 15, Oct. 27, 1955. The January hearings (ISC, ibid.,
Part 17, pp. 1587–1802) are fully covered in NYT, Jan. 5, 6, 7, and 8, 1956. The
Times employment policy was partly disclosed in an exchange of letters between
the ACLU and the publisher of the *Times,* see NYT, July 22, 1955; and see N. Y.
Times, 7 Am. Labor Arb. Awards, par. 70,081 (1956) (upholding one of the
dismissals). The Newspaper Guild's constitution forbids discrimination in membership for political beliefs. (Communists who were in positions of power in the
Guild were replaced following an election in 1948.) The New York City Guild,
although it had tried to have reinstated the *Times* employee fired after the July
hearings (see NYT, July 14 and Oct. 27, 1955), voted during the hearings not to
contest all dismissals of members who invoked Constitutional safeguards on questions about Communist party relations. NYT, Jan. 7, 1956. See U.S. v. Peck, 154
F. Supp. 603 (D.D.C. 1957) (*Times* employee acquitted in contempt case; investigation invaded First Amendment rights).

had acted precipitately. Later, additional identifications of Cameron with Communist groups were made. When questioned, he invoked the Fifth Amendment, and he entered a new publishing venture which seems to be devoted almost entirely to party-line books. Its most notorious author was Harvey Matusow, the informer who repudiated his prolific accusations. Little, Brown also stopped publishing new works of Howard Fast, whose communist sympathies had never been concealed. Fast said that his novel *Spartacus* had been accepted by Little, Brown until Cameron's resignation. After six other publishers had rejected it, he published it himself.[36]

There are indications, gossipy in character, that political tests have been applied in magazines of large circulation more frequently than in the little magazines and in book publishing. This distinction is plausible; the publishers of the mass magazines doubtless share the apprehensions of the radio and movie magnates more keenly than do the relatively insulated book publishers, who reach different and smaller audiences. However, book publishers with textbook departments are fully exposed to the attacks of pressure groups and even to governmental tests. The extreme example of the latter is the Alabama statute, copied in Texas, which requires a noncommunist certificate from the author of a textbook, and, if he is dead, a certificate from the publisher vouching for his loyalty.[37]

The mechanical side of the press has also had its episodes. Two arbitration cases suggest rather stringent standards. In one, the dismissal by the *Long Island Star-Journal* of a linotypist who admitted former membership in the Communist party was upheld. His specific offense

36. The Moon episode is described in NYT, April 18, 1953, and *Time* (April 27, 1953), p. 50. The Cameron affair attracted considerable attention. See Merle Miller, *The Judges and the Judged* (1952), pp. 70–1. After he left Little Brown, Cameron formed the publishing firm of Cameron and Kahn. Its best-known product was Matusow's *False Witness* (1955), which was the focal point of ISC, Hearings, *Strategy and Tactics of World Communism: The Significance of the Matusow Case* (1955), Parts 1–12. Matusow's pertinent testimony of his relationship with Cameron and Kahn is at pp. 35–6, 62–79, 265–77, and 464–70. Albert E. Kahn's relevant statements are at pp. 589–98, 623–30; Angus Cameron's at pp. 691–5, 736–46, 1161–1212. An article in *Counterattack* that led to Cameron's dismissal is reprinted at pp. 697–8. The Committee *Report* (April 6, 1955), pp. 48–73, surveys the entire relationship between the Cameron and Kahn publishing firm and Harvey Matusow.

Fast published an advertisement in *The Nation* (Jan. 19, 1952), with his account of the fate of *Spartacus*. After the publication of the Khrushchev report to the Twentieth Congress, Fast left the party. See Fast, *The Naked God* (1957).

37. See Ch. 1 above, n. 15, on these statutes.

was that, from copy which referred to the "American system of freedom and security" he set the "American system of fascism and security." The arbitrator thought the error was deliberate, and if inadvertent a "subconscious response of his communistic distaste." In the second case, procommunist activities of another linotypist, while on vacation in Europe, were held sufficient grounds for his discharge. Though the International Typographical Union supported the employees in both cases, it is noteworthy that it has tightened its constitution. In this instance the result has been a loyalty oath; printers must swear that they are not members of the Communist party or of any other group "which fails to place loyalty to the government of the United States of America over any other consideration." [38]

MOTION PICTURES

In the brief annals of private loyalty tests, the troubles of the motion picture industry loom large and long. The House Committee on Un-American Activities precipitated a major crisis in 1947, and went on to stir up another one in 1951. Under the stimulus of its exposures, every element within the industry, and a number of outside groups, notably the American Legion, have reacted vigorously.[39]

The famous hearings of 1947 have rarely been surpassed for drama, flamboyance, and telling effect. The testimony of famous figures poured out fears and suspicions of communist influence that were sometimes ludicrous. In rebuttal, industry leaders now defended freedom of expression on the screen, now asserted their complete freedom from dangerous ideas. The climax came with the refusal of ten witnesses, each relying on the First Amendment, to say whether they were Communists.

38. On the printer's oath see NYT, Aug. 22, 1952. The case of the first erring linotypist is reported in 19 Labor Arb. 40 (1952); see NYT, Aug. 15, 1952. The second case is from the *New Haven Register,* Oct. 9, 1952.

39. This account is based chiefly on Harold Horowitz, "Loyalty Tests for Employment in the Motion Picture Industry," *Stanford Law Rev.* (1954), 6:438, a study supported by the Weiss Fund as a part of this project. Citations and other references that may be found in Horowitz are omitted here. It also takes account of the additional material in John Cogley, *Report on Blacklisting: I. Movies* (1956), and of HUAC, Hearings, *Investigations of So-Called "Blacklisting" in Entertainment Industry—Report of the Fund for the Republic, Inc.* (1956), Parts 1–3. Other useful surveys include Elizabeth Poe, "The Hollywood Story," *Frontier* (May 1954), p. 6; Murray Kempton, *Part of Our Time* (1955), ch. 6; and an unpublished paper by Sandra Weinstein, "The Hunting of the Snark," Yale Law School, 1954. On the 1947 hearings see Robert K. Carr, *The House Committee on Un-American Activities* (1952), pp. 55–79.

When contempt citations of the Ten (as they conveniently came to be called) followed promptly, the major producers with equal promptness abandoned their previous defiance of the Committee and produced the Waldorf-Astoria policy statement of November 1947, which announced that the Ten would not be employed until they declared under oath that they were not Communists, and that "We will not knowingly employ a Communist or a member of any party or group which advocates the overthrow of the government of the United States by force or by illegal or unconstitutional methods."

One consequence of the 1947 action was a number of lawsuits. First, the Ten were convicted of contempt, and served one-year prison terms —the maximum period possible under the statute. Second, five of them who had been under contract sued their employers for breach of contract. The producers' defense was that the employees had breached the "morals clause" of their contracts. In three of these cases, juries found that the employees had not brought themselves into public scorn, offended the community, or prejudiced their employers. These findings were made in a case tried as recently as 1952. But there were appeals, with varying results, and inconclusive settlements in most of the cases; one case was dropped when the plaintiff, Edward Dmytryk, a director, recanted after having served his prison sentence. Third, the Ten (thus reduced to nine) brought actions against all the major producers, charging a conspiracy to deprive them of employment. This action was based not so much on the Waldorf statement as on an announcement by Twentieth Century-Fox in 1949 that it had bought a story by Albert Maltz (one of the Ten), quickly followed by another announcement that it would not use the story after all. Some of the defendants settled this case for $107,500; it is presumably still pending against the others.

The fourth category of lawsuit was one brought by the Screen Writers Guild in 1949. It was a frontal attack on the Waldorf agreement, which was characterized as collusive action by the producers to create a political blacklist. In 1953 the Guild members decided to drop the suit. They were assured by Eric Johnston, president of the Motion Pictures Association, that each studio acted independently in hiring.[40]

40. See NYT, Feb. 7, 1953. The Lardner suit against 20th Century-Fox, decided in his favor by the lower court (see Horowitz (n. 39 above), p. 447), was reversed on appeal. The 9th Circuit held that Fox was justified in discharging him under the "good conduct" clause of their contract. 216 F. 2d 844 (9th Cir. 1954). After a motion for a new trial was granted, the parties settled out of court. NYT, Sept. 1, 1955. A similar action by Adrian Scott, another screen writer, against RKO Studios, was dismissed on appeal, 240 F. 2d 87 (9th Cir. 1956). For a legal dis-

By 1953 there was no reason to doubt Johnston's assurances. The studios no longer needed to band together, as at the Waldorf meeting, in order to carry on political tests. The House Committee had returned to Hollywood in 1951, after it appeared that many people named as Communists in 1947 were still working, and that attacks by pressure groups on persons suspected of communist sympathies were not always effective. Opponents of the Committee fought a rear-guard action in 1951. The fate of the Ten drove those who did not want to answer questions, and who did not want to go to jail either, to resort to the Fifth Amendment. Their assertions of possible crimination avoided contempt citations, but they did not arouse much sympathy. Furthermore, the prevalence of such pleas gave the industry what Professor Horowitz characterized as a "clear and seemingly universal test for employment. . . . if a person has been called to testify before the House Committee, was that person a 'friendly' or an 'unfriendly' witness?" [41] Those who by invoking the privilege became "unfriendly" were among some 200 named during the hearings as present or former party members. If a person who was so labeled did not rehabilitate himself by a "friendly" appearance (the chief test of which was his willingness to name all the names he knew), his own employment became precarious and probably ended shortly afterward. It is this group that is commonly referred to as composing the blacklist. Twenty-three of those who were clearly "unfriendly" brought an action joining the Committee and the studios as parties in a supposed conspiracy to deny them employment. The companies argued that even if they had acted in concert with each other and with the Committee, they were only drawing reasonable inferences from the refusals to answer. A lower court agreed with this reasoning and dismissed the complaint. The appellate court stood on the ground that the plaintiffs had no legally protected interest in continued employment. The case is now before the Supreme Court. If the case ever goes to trial, it might be difficult to prove that the studios had prompted each other. The publicity of an unrebutted charge of party membership was by this time probably enough to touch off any one of the studios. As Horowitz points out, the basis for the standard was "primarily that of

---

cussion of blacklisting see Ch. 18 below. For present purposes, I use this term to mean an industry-wide refusal to hire, on grounds other than skill or ability.

41. Horowitz (n. 39 above), p. 441. For some of the reasons behind the 1951 hearings see Weinstein (n. 39 above), p. 10; and J. B. Matthews, "Did the Movies Really Clean House?" *American Legion Magazine* (Dec. 1951), p. 12.

public relations risk. . . . The safest business course of action for the producers was a policy of absolute nonemployment." [42]

The same prudent considerations, in this case reinforced by group pressures rather than those of Congressional exposure, has led each studio to institute screening arrangements of unknown magnitude. Derogatory information, on about the same level as that used in the federal security program, is collected, and must be countered by satisfactory explanations. Those who have failed to meet the test (whatever it is), or who have refused to repudiate radical associations, make up what is known as the "graylist." This "list"—which is not a formal compilation —includes, according to one reporter, more than 100 people who are no longer employed in the industry.

The primary tactic of those who insist that the industry rid itself of every communist stain is still publicity; but the publicity is carried to the theater door by picket lines; and behind it is the threat of organized boycott. The American Legion is the most powerful group overseeing the political lives of movie people. Starting from the rationale that "men and women of the free world have a right to a highly positive assurance, with no maybe's about it, that the money they spend in idle entertainment will not be used in any way to foment their own destruction," [43] the Legion advanced from sporadic picketing and passing resolutions to an explicit role in the screening operations of the major studios. In May 1952 it presented a list of some 300 employees, along with their "communist associations." The studios asked those on the list to write letters of correction or explanation; these letters were then forwarded to the Legion's national offices. The Legion took pains to deny that it was granting clearances. However, after the letter-writing operation was completed (according to trade-paper reports, satisfactorily in all but twenty-five to thirty cases), Legion pressure relaxed, except for two items of unfinished business. One was continued opposition to the showing of Charlie Chaplin's films, especially a current release. The other was a boycott of "Moulin Rouge" in Dec. 1952, because the star, José Ferrer, and the producer, John Huston, were not yet in the Legion's good graces. However, both of them made whatever decla-

---

42. Horowitz (n. 39 above), p. 445. Wilson v. Loew's, 298 P. 2d 152 (1956), dismissed by the Supreme Court March 3, 1958, after this book had gone to press.

43. Robert Pitkin, "The Movies and the American Legion," *American Legion Magazine* (May 1953), p. 43; from Horowitz (n. 39 above), p. 462. Data on the studio "graylist" are from *Frontier* (n. 39 above), pp. 8, 12.

rations were necessary, for the national commander of the Legion was able to declare on Jan. 15, 1953, that their "present attitude . . . toward communism shows satisfactory progress and they are displaying the type of cooperation we have requested in the past." [44]

The charges that gave the Legion concern in Huston's case (Ferrer had a more lengthy record) were said to be these: (1) He was one of 380 signers of a brief *amicus curiae* to the Supreme Court in the contempt case of the Ten (the brief was chiefly concerned with the scope of the First Amendment). (2) He had supported some (unspecified) appeal on behalf of the Russian people. (3) He was a sponsor of a dinner benefit for the Ten. Since other persons were attacked by the Legion solely because they had joined in the *amicus* brief, Horowitz concludes that the Legion's test for directing unfavorable publicity comprehended any people "who have been at any time in any way associated with an activity in which members of the Communist party were in some way also associated." [45] Alarms on the part of an employer would necessarily parallel such a test.

An employee on whom some sort of dossier has been assembled has a hard time communicating his explanations and recantations. It is not enough that they reach the employers. They must also reach the groups to whom the employer defers. The Legion's arrangement with the major studios at least had the merit of permitting clarification—on the Legion's terms. The process was described by participants as one that involved no standards or attempts at judgment; it was simply a rehabilitation process that assisted people to clear themselves. George Sokolsky, the columnist, who was one of the most influential people to assist in this rehabilitation, gave a "rough estimate" of "about 300 men and women who are today working in the motion picture industry who could not work before because of the record they had established of Communist or pseudo-Communist associations." [46] Some employees outside the eight major studios lacked any such opportunity, and had to hire lawyers and other persons who claimed to possess useful influence or lines of communication.

The role of the professional guilds and trade unions has been one of

44. NYT, Jan. 16, 1953. James F. O'Neill, publisher of the *American Legion Magazine,* minimized the number of those who "wrote letters" in his testimony, HUAC (n. 39 above), pp. 5282–3, saying that only 100 had come to his attention.

45. Horowitz (n. 39 above), p. 462.

46. HUAC (n. 39 above), p. 5288. For an example of rehabilitation following a cooperative second appearance before the HUAC see NYT, March 11, 1957 (Columbia announced contract with Carl Foreman, writer and producer).

steady retreat. The Screen Writers first commenced a lawsuit against
the major studios and then abandoned it. One of the Guild's important
bargaining functions is to protect the proper allocation of "credits" to
its members for screen plays. RKO, then controlled by Howard Hughes,
brought an action in 1952 against Paul Jarrico, who had invoked the
Fifth Amendment in 1951. It sought a declaration that Jarrico had
breached the morals clause, that no obligation remained under the contract, and that the studio was therefore free to ignore his authorship of
a picture about to be released. In this case, the trial judge found that
Jarrico's "unfriendly" status made him an object of ill will among the
public, and that the company did not have to associate his name with
its product.[47]

The Guild tried to protect its interests and at the same time to avoid
direct involvement in Jarrico's case. But the next year it acceded to a
change in the basic agreement; this change permits producers to withhold credit from Communist party members or persons who refuse to
deny such membership. The next year (1954) the Screen Writers proposed to amend their constitution to exclude Communists from membership. The amendment failed by a narrow vote, but was later adopted.
The Screen Directors had begun to exact a loyalty oath from new members in 1950, and the Screen Actors followed suit in 1953.[48]

47. The judge had the support of a public opinion poll in which 68 per cent of
those polled thought that those who invoked the privilege were in fact Communists. American Legion officials also testified. See Horowitz (n. 39 above), pp.
448–9. Another maneuver by Howard Hughes was an announcement, while the
Jarrico suit was pending, that RKO would suspend production until a screening
of employees, and especially of writers, was completed. The studio was at a
standstill anyway. NYT, April 7, 1952; Horowitz, p. 467. Jarrico later was the
producer of "Salt of the Earth," p. 156 below.

48. Screen Directors, see NYT, Sept. 7, 1950; Screen Actors, NYT, March 21,
July 1, 1951; July 28, 1953. The Screen Extras Guild amended its bylaws to
authorize expulsion of any member who refuses to testify before committees,
NYT, March 3, 1955.

The Screen Writers Guild concession on credits is reported in NYT, April 24,
1953. This Guild was later merged with the Radio Writers Guild and the Television Writers Group into the Writers Guild of America, East and West. This
larger organization rejected the proposed constitutional amendment (see NYT,
Jan. 2, 1955) which had been previously approved by the old Screen Writers
for the constitution of an interim group called the Writers Guild of America
West, Inc., NYT, Aug. 27, 1954. Maurice Ries, "Seeing Red in Hollywood," in HUAC,
Soviet Total War, H. Doc. 227 (1957), p. 160, has the final version. These unions
are succinctly identified in Hugh Lovell and Tasile Carter, *Collective Bargaining in
the Motion Picture Industry* (1955).

Dalton Trumbo, one of the Ten, describes in "Blacklist = Black Market," *The
Nation* (May 4, 1957), p. 383, some confused episodes that occurred in 1957

Two groups of employees had taken belligerently anticommunist positions from the beginning. One was the leadership of the AFL craft union, IATSE (International Alliance of Theatrical and Stage Employees), which had survived a racketeering regime in the 1930's and a jurisdictional dispute with a rival AFL union in 1945–46, partly by dint of calling its opponents Communists at every opportunity. Roy Brewer, the Hollywood chief of IATSE from 1945 to 1953, is credited by some observers with having been the pivotal figure in the relations between the American Legion, the producers, and those employees who favored the spread of political tests. The latter joined in the Motion Picture Alliance for the Preservation of American Ideals, and Brewer served as its president. The MPA, which has an influential membership, has been exceedingly strict in its interpretation of who constitutes an unfriendly witness. For example, the actor Larry Parks was at first publicly critical of the House Committee. Then in 1951 he reluctantly confessed his own past party membership and named some names to the Committee, in executive session. The MPA leadership apparently considered this insufficient. So in 1953 Parks made a "clarifying statement" to the Committee, which released his 1951 testimony. In another instance, the MPA newsletter attacked Samuel Goldwyn for buying the Broadway hit musical "Guys and Dolls." The author, Abe Burrows, had not been technically unfriendly but had been described as "very vague."

Hollywood, it is clear, is thoroughly encompassed with loyalty tests. Some of those on the blacklist attempted to get outside the circle and continue in their occupations by making films abroad. The Legion and IATSE have been vigilant to this threat. Film-making in Europe, particularly in Italy, has had other attractions, particularly in tax and labor savings; so protests against foreign invasions have mixed protectionist and political motives in some cases. One group of exiles from Hollywood made a film called "Salt of the Earth," in Arizona. Because of the political complexions of the company, the picture was denounced as "un-American propaganda" even before it was finished, by Congressman Jackson of the Committee on Un-American Activities. The *New York Times* critic said it was "simply a strong pro-labor film." There were also disorders on location, provoked by the local inhabitants; and a Mexican actress was deported before the picture was finished. Finally,

---

with respect to writers' credit for award-winning pictures, and declares that he and other blacklisted writers have in fact been selling scripts, though credit is withheld,

exhibition of the picture was effectively blocked by refusals of projec-tionists and theater-owners to handle it.[49]

RADIO AND TELEVISION

With the motion picture industry already racked by loyalty crises, radio and television were obviously susceptible. Here, however, the initial pressures came not from investigating committees but from private groups. There had been some rumblings of discontent from the Ameri-can Legion, newspaper columnists, and others in 1948 and 1949. One publication, and one episode, in 1950, really started the program roll-ing. The publication was *Red Channels,* a pamphlet listing left-wing associations of 151 persons connected with radio, which appeared in June 1950. The episode was the peremptory removal of Jean Muir, a well-known actress, from the cast of a television serial in August of that year.[50]

Jean Muir was listed in *Red Channels;* and when one of its editors heard that General Foods had engaged her for "The Aldrich Family" he called a few active anti-Communists who in turn organized a modest telephone campaign of protest to the sponsor and to the National Broadcasting Company. General Foods hastily announced that Miss Muir would not appear on the program; the only reason it ever gave was that "General Foods advertising . . . avoids the use of materials and personalities which in its judgment are controversial." The test of controversiality presumably avoided any further inquiry. Miss Muir de-nied communist sympathies. Of the nine organizations with which *Red Channels* had connected her, she disclaimed any association with four.

49. On "Salt of the Earth" see *Frontier* (n. 39 above), p. 17; Cogley (n. 39 above), p. 15 n. For Brewer's contributions see NYT, Aug. 27, 1952, and Sept. 14, 1953; Cogley, passim, and Brewer's testimony, HUAC (n. 39 above), p. 5312. On Larry Parks see *Time* (March 3, 1952), pp. 68–9 (in a story on John Wayne, head of MPA); and HUAC, Hearings, *Communist Activity in the Los Angeles Area* (1953), p. 2307. Parks acted in a road company of "Teahouse of the August Moon" in 1955–56. For the "Guys and Dolls" episode see NYT, April 3, 1954; Cogley, p. 168.

50. The chief sources for this section are: (1) Merle Miller, *The Judges and the Judged* (New York, Doubleday and Co., 1952), a report sponsored by the Amer-ican Civil Liberties Union. I have taken into account the criticisms by Merlyn Pitzele, in *New Leader* (May 12, 1952), p. 21, and (June 16, 1952), p. 15; and the report (mimeo.) of the ACLU Committee which investigated Pitzele's charges, July 31, 1952. (2) John Cogley, *Report on Blacklisting: II Radio* (1956), taking into account the HUAC Hearings, n. 39 above.

She readily conceded that she had been a member of the Southern Conference for Human Welfare, that she had sent fiftieth-anniversary congratulations to the Moscow Art Theater, and that, having been briefly a member of the Congress of American Women, "I quit as soon as I found out they were a front group." She did not recall the nature of her connections with the International Workers Order or with a group called Stage for Action, but was sure that they had been transitory. Like many actors and performers, Miss Muir had apparently made public appearances, on behalf of varied political and social causes, before all sorts of audiences.

General Foods later announced that it would not act on complaints of disloyalty unless they were backed up by proof. This new policy applied, for a few months, to the case of Philip Loeb, who was a leading actor in "The Goldbergs" and who, as a conspicuous entrant in *Red Channels,* was the object of pressure on the sponsor, again General Foods. General Foods dropped its sponsorship of the program. When "The Goldbergs" resumed some months later, under different sponsorship, Loeb was not in the cast.

Both the Muir case and, to a lesser extent, the Loeb case, became public issues. In this respect they were exceptional. The employers learned to avoid trouble simply by not hiring people listed in *Red Channels* or otherwise tagged with communist-front associations. Here the distinction between incumbents and applicants is effective. In broadcasting, the employment of actors and performers—and to a considerable extent of writers, directors, and others—is intermittent. It is not necessary to fire people; they are simply not hired. In the words of a radio executive the Muir case could have been easily managed by saying that "she was too young for the part, too old, too fat, too thin." [51]

There seems to be general agreement that there has been a blacklist in radio. It is not absolute in its operation. Speaking of the *Red Channels* group, a well-informed lawyer quoted by Merle Miller sums it up as follows: "Every one of them has been affected. A few don't even know it, but they've *all* lost some shows. A majority have lost a great many jobs, and a good-sized minority just aren't working at their pro-

51. Miller, p. 200. The Jean Muir episode is fully discussed in Miller, pp. 35–46, from which the quoted passages are taken, and in Cogley, passim. Her testimony in 1953 was released in 1955; HUAC Hearings, *Investigations of Communist Activities—New York Area* (1955), p. 1. The Philip Loeb controversy is reported in NYT, Jan. 8, 9, and 15, 1952. He has since died. NYT, Sept. 3, 1955.

fessions any more." The number thus affected was estimated by the American Civil Liberties Union in 1953 as around 250.[52]

The participants in the broadcasting tests should now be identified a little more clearly. First, the employers. The employers for a sponsored program may be either the network, a producer of package shows, or the sponsor. Any of these, along with the advertising agency handling the account, has some veto power over employment, no matter who signs the pay check. This heightens the elusive aspects of the program, and permits anyone who is taxed with unfairness to disclaim responsibility. The networks, the producers, and the advertising agencies have also their own salaried staffs to worry about. The producers and agencies, however, do not have pressure groups firing directly at them; and in any case a communist account executive is a somewhat unlikely occurrence. The networks (and with them independent stations and the individual broadcasters that form the network) are the direct target of pressure groups. Columbia Broadcasting System in December 1950 instituted a loyalty statement the terminology of which was derived from the federal Civil Service Form 57. A few individual stations have likewise required loyalty statements. Their only direct effect has been the dismissal of a few employees who refused on principle to execute the statement.[53]

The main source of charges has been the publishers of *Red Channels* and *Counterattack* (a weekly anticommunist newsletter). This was a firm (the three officers have now gone separate ways) called American Business Consultants. Besides its publications, it offered advice and information to business clients on ridding their enterprises of communist influence. Its activities are thoroughly discussed by Miller. No peculiar importance should be attached, in my opinion, to this particular outfit. If *Red Channels* became a bible for the broadcasting industry, it was because it arrived at an opportune time not because it was an inspired compilation.

In addition to the independent anticommunist experts who sell their services, there have been amateur sources of charges. One was a Syra-

52. ACLU, *Report on Civil Liberties, Jan. 1951–June 1953* (1953), p. 31. The quotation from Miller is at p. 48.

53. See Miller, ch. 8. Tony Kraber, a former executive producer of C.B.S., testified that he was dismissed in 1951 on the eve of an expected subpoena. HUAC, Hearings (n. 51 above), pp. 2438, 2447. It does not appear whether he had executed the loyalty statement. In the 1955 hearings he invoked the privilege with respect to communist affiliations.

cuse grocer named Laurence Johnson. With the assistance of some Syracuse veterans' units, he made a practice of listing performers' left-wing associations and then suggesting a boycott of the sponsor's product. Another was AWARE, Inc., an organization dedicated to combating "the communist conspiracy in entertainment-communications." AWARE appears to have had two main missions. The first was to promote the "rehabilitation" process described in the movie section above; the second to expose procommunist factions in the entertainment unions.[54] To deal with all these pressures, the networks and the major advertising agencies have made certain employees responsible for screening talent. Inevitably though inaccurately, these functionaries came to be known as "security officers."

Congressional committees have not paid concentrated attention to the industry;[55] they have not needed to, for broadcasting has responded not so much to pressure as to the fear of pressure. Though some of the protestants in the Muir case claimed to speak for large veterans' organizations and the like, they had not in fact mobilized their troops (if they had any). Similarly, though the American Legion's anticommunist experts had fired some warning rounds, the Legion did not move into radio in force, as it did into the movie companies. Again it did not need to. The principle of avoiding controversy is not exclusive with General Foods. The short crowded life of radio and television under advertising control has been dominated by it, and by the commandment "Don't antagonize anybody."

Adherence to these principles does not mean that the networks automatically bow to every protest, even though they may try to forestall them. There have been instances where the chains, having decided to use the services of valued entertainers, have rebuffed objectors. This was the good fortune of Gypsy Rose Lee and Lena Horne. Other figures have had limited success in clearing themselves. Frederick March and his wife Florence Eldredge launched a counterattack on *Counterattack* in the form of a libel suit. The suit was settled, and *Counterattack* published a retraction of sorts. Nevertheless, subsequent television appearances of the Marches have been few.[56]

54. See Cogley (n. 50 above), esp. pp. 54–6, 100–42; HUAC, Hearings (n. 39 above), pp. 5327–67 (officers of AWARE).

55. HUAC, Hearings, *Communist Methods of Infiltration, Entertainment* (1953–54), were directed at radio-TV. HUAC, Hearings, *Investigation of Communist Activities, New York Area* (1955), Parts 6–8 (*Entertainment*) were more diffuse. See also ISC, Hearings, n. 58 below.

56. See Miller, p. 144. The Gypsy Rose Lee and Lena Horne incidents are dis-

The role of the unions—there is a union for everyone in the entertainment world except the vice-presidents—has been indecisive. They have protested occasionally, devised elaborate stillborn plans for clearance, and wound up in a measure of conformity. Actors' Equity, though actively opposed to blacklisting, in 1953 announced that it would bar proved Communists from membership. The American Federation of Radio Artists amended its constitution in 1951. The drafters of the amendment attempted to set up some standards for exclusion beyond the usual vague blanket proscription of Communists and advocates of violent overthrow, and came up with this:

> No person shall remain a member of A.F.R.A., or retain employment in A.F.R.A., who has been proven to have maintained membership in, or to have joined, the Communist party, since December 31, 1945, in state or federal court action; Or who has been named as, or identified as, a Communist by the State Department, Justice Department, or by the F.B.I.; Or, who after the adoption of this amendment renders aid and assistance by knowingly lending his name or talents to, or by actively promoting the interests of, or by making financial contributions to, any organization listed by the Attorney General's office, or by any other duly constituted government agency, as subversive.[57]

The Radio Writers Guild—and an offshoot, the Television Writers of America—both had persisting difficulties with right- and left-wing factions. These were about the last visible vestiges of communist influence in the industry.[58] That influence was strong enough some years ago

cussed, ibid., at pp. 158 and 185–6, respectively. A valuable collection of statements by advertisers and agencies on the desirability of avoiding controversial characters is in Cogley (n. 50 above), pp. 192–5, 199–203, 205.

57. Miller, pp. 204–5. The Equity policy is reported in NYT, Sept. 30, 1953; cf. Cogley, pp. 158–62. AFRA has been merged into the American Federation of Television and Radio Artists. AFTRA authorized its local boards to expel or otherwise punish any member who fails to tell a Congressional committee whether he is or was a member of the Communist party. NYT, Aug. 11, 1955. For a critical discussion of this step see Jack Gould in NYT, July 31, 1955. On the other hand, after AWARE, Inc., actively intervened in an AFTRA election, many members of AFTRA supported a vote condemning AWARE. NYT, July 11, 1955. In 1956 a new "middle-of-the-road" AFTRA board took a decisive position against blacklisting. NYT, March 26, 1956. Cf. Cogley, pp. 154–62.

58. The Radio Writers Guild and the Television Writers of America have merged into the Writers Guild of America; see n. 48 above. For their earlier difficulties see ISC, Hearings, *Subversive Infiltration of Radio-Television and the Entertainment Industry* (1951–52) (closed hearings released Aug. 27, 1952); NYT, Aug. 28, 1952; Cogley, pp. 144–54.

to support some sort of blacklist of anti-Communists. Apparently some directors and producers were pro-Communists and were in a position to discriminate against their opponents. Miller and Cogley were both harshly criticized for not making a more thorough investigation of these charges in their studies of the industry. It seems unlikely, however, that any blacklisting of anti-Communists ever approached the pervasiveness of the recent blacklist of pro-Communists.[59]

The timid giants, films and broadcasting, still have two aged and undersized parents—the concert-hall and the theater. Here the pressures have not been so intense, nor the responses so docile. A number of writers, actors, entertainers, and others who are on the combined blacklist of Hollywood and Madison Avenue have returned to Broadway. There have been some political picketing and boycotts on the road, practically none in New York. The most celebrated case was that of Paul Draper, the dancer, and Larry Adler, the outstanding virtuoso of the harmonica. Their combined recital program ran into trouble in Greenwich, Connecticut, in 1949, sparked by a busy housewife, Mrs. Hester McCullough. A decline in their bookings followed Mrs. McCullough's denunciation of their front associations. They brought a libel suit against her, which ended inconclusively in 1950 with a hung jury. The publicity resulting from the libel suit induced both performers to move to England.[60]

Of course, the theater arts do not have the mass audiences of their offspring, and the opportunities for and rewards from employment are correspondingly limited. But the lack of a mass audience carries with it a partial immunity from mass pressures. The contrast is similar to the one already noted, between the freedom and diversity of book publishing, and the relative caution of the mass periodicals. The locations of "live" performance are, however, peculiarly vulnerable to picketing. There is little point in picketing a radio station; but pickets at the entrance to an auditorium can be quite intimidating.[61]

59. On blacklisting of anti-Communists see Miller, ch. 6; Cogley, pp. 42–8; Pitzele, n. 50 above; Vincent Hartnett testimony, HUAC, Hearings (n. 39 above), p. 5298 (discussing the "patronage apparatus" of the Communists for preferring each other).

60. On the Adler-Draper libel suit see NYT, Feb.–May, 1950; on Adler in England, *Time* (Aug. 23, 1954), p. 45. That "There is no organized blacklisting on Broadway" see Cogley, pp. 210–17.

61. A precedent for political picketing was established by anti-Nazi groups who protested the American appearances after World War II of the singer Kirsten Flagstad (NYT, April 21, 23, 1947) and of the pianist Walter Gieseking (NYT, Jan.

To summarize the state of political tests in the mass media of movies and broadcasting: after they reached a sort of stability around 1955, they were directed both at probable Communists and at people with a wide range of past associations and affiliations that might embarrass employers if exploited by the extreme anticommunist pressure groups. However, the intensity of the programs had probably passed its peak, and a considerable number of people have regained employment by clearing themselves—an obligation reminiscent of the government programs. Though the organization and standards of these private programs are far more shadowy than the government's, they have nevertheless become, as Cogley puts it, institutionalized. That is, there are operating procedures, there is a bureaucracy, and there is much less resistance from the employees than when it all began.[62]

22, 1949), who had not entirely cleared themselves of charges of collaboration with the Nazis.

62. Cf. Cogley, pp. 23, 189, 277. See Ch. 15 below, nn. 20, 21, for instances of both public and private political pressures in the fine arts.

6. The Reach of Employment Tests

IN THIS CHAPTER I will describe the sorts of people currently subject to loyalty and security tests of varying intensity, estimate their numbers, and also estimate the numbers of those on whom the tests have imposed dismissals.

EXPOSURE TO EMPLOYMENT TESTS—
A ROUGH CENSUS

The first appraisal to be attempted deals with the extent and intensity of exposure to political tests. This is a problem of numbers and magnitudes at one level; the aim is to come up with estimates of the percentage of the employed populace that has to pass some kind of screening. But a gross figure, though significant, would not measure the relative intensity of exposure in different walks of life. I use "intensity" to refer to the combination of two judgments, one on relative severity of standards, the other on relative diligence used in applying them.

Even though this survey deals with numbers, no claim of statistical precision is made. All of the estimates are subject to a margin of error, the magnitude of which I will try to indicate as I go along. Sometimes I can only guess at the dimensions of a program. Even if data are available, ambiguity arises from the fact that the extent of exposure of the current labor force is in question, whereas some of the data are cummulative. That is, they give the numbers cleared during the life of a program, and thus require us to take account of the rate of turnover. To be sure, the number of people who have had to be cleared in a five- or ten-year period is also relevant. Certainly, the effect of a denial of clearance is not confined to the situation in which it occurred. One of the chronic complaints about the programs is that a person rejected by them has difficulty in finding any kind of employment. The total numbers that have been exposed, if they could be counted, would also be significant with respect to whatever emotional and economic risks are attendant on having once passed through the system, even successfully. But turnover rates are too uncertain to make this estimate worth attempting.

Census categories and census figures are used where they are appropriate, but they are drawn from various tables which were not designed for this purpose.[1] The main source of imprecision in what follows is that we cannot adhere strictly to counting by occupations. The large categories to be examined are: professional; managers and proprietors; government; mining, manufacturing, construction, transport, and public utilities; trade, service, and finance; and agriculture. This classification does not necessarily distinguish white-collar from manual workers, or craft from craft, except as one or more occupations may be concentrated in a given sector of employment. Thus all miners are presumably engaged in mining, but stenographers are everywhere. However, it is possible to identify some skills the use of which has been thoroughly blanketed by employment tests (e.g. sailors), certain areas of employment in which any skill is likely to be covered (notably government), and so on to areas of almost complete immunity (e.g. small shopkeepers).

Another possible source of error is in double counting. The separate classification of professional and managerial types must be considered in almost all the remaining categories. Thus teachers are the largest professional bloc, and also the largest clearly defined bloc of civilian government employees. These overlaps are not hard to account for if the numbers are substantial; and if they are small they can be ignored.

The procedure here cuts across the descriptions of programs and tests in the previous chapters. The approach there was to count off the employers who make use of tests; now I enumerate the employees who have to pass them.

1. *The Statistical Abstract of the United States, 1954,* § 8, esp. tables 224, 231, 236 and 238, and a variety of specialized publications of the Census Bureau and the Department of Labor. The Report of the Office of Defense Mobilization, Committee on Specialized Personnel, *Resources and Requirements of Specialized Personnel* (Sept. 1951), was also useful. Of course, the population and the labor force have been growing steadily since some of the sources appeared, and during my investigations. Most of my estimates were based on a labor force not much above 60 million; it was recently 65 million. But the relationships of the various occupational groups to the whole labor force have not, I believe, changed significantly.

There are remarkable variations between census figures, on the one hand, especially for the professions, and, on the other, the estimates of sources closer to the particular occupation. I have simply averaged the differences if they were compatible; if there are major discrepancies they are noted. Material from an earlier draft of this chapter was included in my "Loyalty–Security Measures and Employment Opportunities," bas (1955), *11*:113–17.

THE PROFESSIONS

The variety of occupations placed under this heading is expanded beyond the inner circle of learned professions to include a number of other occupations. In most cases they require more-than-average academic training; they are relatively intellectual in the capacities needed; and they have something resembling professional discipline. Even these relaxed criteria are stretched to the breaking-point in what I call the "communications professions." There, to avoid inconvenient refinements, one is compelled to throw together pundits and gagmen, virtuosi and crooners. These examples confirm, by the way, that earning power is not an effective criterion of professionalism; indeed income may vary inversely with the degree of professional dignity. The total numbers in all the professions discussed here exceed 3,000,000; they constitute about 5 per cent of the labor force.

The security-ridden professions, the first subgroup to distinguish, clearly include scientists, engineers, and public administrators—a total of about 600,000. The scientists, who are imperfectly separable from professional engineers on the basis that scientists are preoccupied with research and engineers with its applications, have attracted more attention to their security troubles than any other profession. The reasons are not hard to find. Since the eve of World War II, more and more of them have been drawn into classified work, either in direct government employment or in government-supported work in industry and the universities. Spectacular defections have occurred, notably Fuchs, Nunn May, and Pontecorvo—none of them Americans, however. Spectacularly controversial clearance cases have erupted, notably those of J. R. Oppenheimer and E. U. Condon. Unimpeachable spokesmen have come forward to complain that excessive security measures were injuring scientific morale and productivity.

The public has watched all this with a mixture of respect and distrust—respect for the awesome successes and responsibilities claimed by scientists, distrust of what some took to be "intellectual arrogance" and a claim for special privileges. The scientific community has displayed remarkable cohesiveness in its defense of principles, and yet has so far failed to halt the involvement of more and more of its members in political tests.[2] Consider the situation of a scientist who, out of choice

2. For statements concerning the injuries suffered by scientists because of the security programs see House Comm. on Government Operations, Subcomm. on Military Operations, Report, *Organization and Administration of the Military Re-*

or necessity, seeks a university post that is free of security restrictions. He may nevertheless have to take a teacher's oath, and then make another affirmation of loyalty if federal funds come his way. We have already seen how federal grants have had loyalty strings attached, even when they were for unclassified work. These measures, to be sure, fall short of the close scrutiny required for security clearance; but the scientist may find that he is expected to be eligible for clearance anyhow, in order to enhance his department's eligibility for a classified contract, should one come along. If he has already been denied clearance, then employment becomes especially difficult. Quite aside from the doubtful propriety of concealing one's status from an employer in a world where clearance is so important, the scientific subcommunities are small enough so that (it is said) word quickly gets around that *X* cannot get classified work. Recognition that security rejections imposed extraordinary hardship on scientists was one reason for the decision of the Atomic Energy Commission to open its hearing procedures to applicants, so as to lessen the chance of unfairness.

These observations should be qualified by noting that discussion tends to focus on the difficulties of people in nuclear physics and similar sensitive sciences. There are several substantial branches of science, botany for example, with little or no involvement in classified projects.

One would expect most of the problems of scientists to be shared by the engineers. They, too, are used in large numbers for classified work in government and industry. Engineers have been convicted of espionage —Julius Rosenberg, for example. There have been controversial security cases involving engineers—in particular, most of the Fort Monmouth cases stirred up by Senator McCarthy in 1953. Yet, by comparison with the scientists, engineers do not attract much public attention, and apathy seems to envelop the profession. The juxtaposition with the scientists is so close that one cannot fail to be struck by the contrast in attitude, and to speculate about it. One speculation that comes to mind is that engineers in this era are less glamorous figures than scientists. The role of the engineer in our society is ambiguous to the layman,

---

search and Development Programs (Aug. 4, 1954), esp. the testimony of James Killian, President of M.I.T., at pp. 37–8, and of John von Neumann at pp. 38–9. See also Edward Shils, *The Torment of Secrecy* (1956), ch. 7; and Ch. 7 below, n. 14.

An exception to the scientific community's generally critical attitude is the position adopted by the 1956 convention of the American Association of Petroleum Geologists, which endorsed the federal programs and rejected the 1955 stand of the parent A.A.A.S. See NYT, March 29, 1956.

and apparently to the engineers themselves. Consequently, people at large are not concerned about them.

A possible explanation for their own attitude is that though engineers are equally exposed to employment tests, they are much less vulnerable than scientists. That is, they are politically a more conservative group; fewer of them have been touched by the radical associations that make up the grist of security cases. Furthermore there are surely branches of engineering, as there are of science, that are fairly clear of security problems.[3]

The third security-dominated profession is public administration. By this I mean career civil servants in the upper ranks. They are so obviously subject to the whole range of government-administered tests that it is unnecessary to discuss their situation.

If a generous deduction is made for the branches of science and engineering that are removed from security and loyalty problems, and for public administrators in those states that have no loyalty tests, for 300,000 or more persons, half of the total of about 600,000, the opportunity to practice their professions is very much dependent on their ability to meet loyalty–security criteria.

THE SOCIAL PROFESSIONS

The common element connecting the professions reviewed in this section is that they deal primarily with people in social relationships. Teachers, lawyers, clergymen, social workers, librarians, to be sure, have individual students, clients, parishioners, etc.; but much of their professional activity is directed to adjusting or bettering the place in society of their clients (using that term generically). The members of these professions often have to take positions on controversial social issues, and then to act on them. Those who take unpopular positions become vulnerable to loyalty challenges. In some areas (notably teaching) vulnerability has advanced to full exposure. No profession, and no class of government employees, have been singled out for official loyalty tests the way teachers have been. The types of state and local government tests for teachers have already been described; I should

3. The suggestion that engineers are relatively conservative is only a guess based on some local observations. On the left-wing background of some of the Fort Monmouth engineers, most of whom later successfully refuted the security charges against them, see Ch. 11 below. On the ambiguous role of the engineer in our society see the perceptive essay by George Odiorne, "The Trouble with Engineers," *Harper's* (Jan. 1955), p. 41.

only reiterate that oaths designed especially for teachers—some of them simple constitutional pledges, others formidable test oaths—are numerous and antedate even the present crisis. There are at least a million public school teachers. Approximately 80 per cent of them are in states which require a test oath of all government employees, or which single out teachers.

Private schools do not provide much room for employment free of tests. In the first place, an oath requirement may extend to private as well as public schools. This is true in Massachusetts and elsewhere. Second, many of the 100,000-odd teachers in private schools are in parochial schools, which, even in the absence of formal tests, would have little tolerance for anyone who could not pass a stringent loyalty test. Finally, secular private schools, with a few exceptions, are generally conservative. Though few private schools have had occasion to face the problem, if an investigating committee thrust notoriety upon an institution by exposing one of its teachers, his situation would probably be precarious.[4]

For college and university teachers and administrators, whose total number is about 250,000, the incidence of formal tests is a little less severe than for school teachers. Only half of the field is occupied by public institutions. Furthermore, practice among these varies. The state colleges may either set the same standard for their staff members as for public employees generally, or as for teachers generally, or they may be left by the legislature to their own devices. On the other hand, even private institutions, in states with Ober-type laws, have to certify their freedom from "subversive persons" if they are recipients of state aid; and teacher's oaths may extend to private colleges as well as schools. Security clearance intrudes here for scientists on university staffs, in the forms already mentioned. Except for these partial exertions of state control, private colleges have been free to develop their own policies, along the varied lines discussed in the last chapter.

The kinds of tests that lawyers (180,000) have devised for themselves have already been discussed. Several thousand lawyers are in government service and accordingly subject to whatever tests their em-

4. An exception to this prediction should be noted. When a number of Philadelphia teachers invoked the Fifth Amendment before the HUAC, the public school teachers were dismissed, but the three teachers employed in private schools were not. See ACLU, Greater Philadelphia Branch, *Academic Freedom: Some Recent Philadelphia Episodes* [1954], pp. 25, 34. For the Massachusetts, New York, and Oregon statutes requiring constitutional oaths from private-school teachers see FUND DIGEST, pp. 431–3.

ployers provide. The chief pressure that the lawyer in private practice faces may come not from his bar association but from his clients. If a lawyer, whatever his own sympathies, represents politically unpopular clients, his practice is likely to suffer; the public may wrongly identify him with his client's cause. This poor understanding of the right to counsel and of the lawyer's duty to provide it has a double-edged effect: it imposes a severe employment test on lawyers who undertake the defense of people charged with disloyalty; and it increases the obstacles that such people face in making their defense, because lawyers are reluctant to appear for them.

There have been a number of attacks on the Protestant clergy for lending support to left-wing causes. Most of the attacks have been discredited. When Bishop Oxnam was brought under fire by the Un-American Activities Committee, he defended himself effectively; and when J. B. Matthews fired a broadside in 1953 at 700 supposed clerical Communists, public indignation was so intense that Senator McCarthy was forced to end Matthews' brief tenure as director of research for the investigating committee that the Senator then chaired. The only charges of current complicity that seem to have any substance have been directed at a handful of well-known fellow travelers. Ill-founded blanket accusations did not lead the major Protestant denominations to install loyalty programs. Instead they closed ranks and condemned the intemperance of the accusers.[5]

There have been a few reported instances of ministers who fell out with their congregations because of their political sympathies. A particularly long-drawn-out affair was the status of the Melishes, father and son, in an Episcopal parish in Brooklyn. There the majority of the congregation defied the vestry and the bishop, who nevertheless suc-

5. See HUAC, Hearings, *Testimony of Bishop G. Bromley Oxnam* (1954), and Oxnam, *I Protest* (1954). Charges made before the HUAC also backfired in the case of the Rev. John A. Hutchison; see HUAC, Hearings, *Investigation of Communist Activities in the Baltimore Area* (1954), pp. 4055–161; Alan Barth, *Government by Investigation* (1955), pp. 151–3, and Editorial, *Christian Century* (1954), 71:387.

The statements in the Matthews case are reprinted in NYT, July 10, 1953; see also Murray Kempton, *Part of Our Time* (1955), ch. 5.

Episcopal Bishop James de Wolfe, while hostile to the Melishes (n. 6 below) refuted charges that the clergy was riddled with Communists; see NYT, July 15, 1953. The 166th General Assembly of the Presbyterian Church endorsed a controversial "Letter to Presbyterians" which had been attacked by Dr. Daniel Poling as employing "the exact language" of parts of articles in certain communist publications; ibid., May 25, 1954, and *Time* (Dec. 28, 1953), p. 33. For a general discussion of fellow travelers in the Protestant clergy see Ralph Roy, *Apostles of Discord* (1953), ch. 11.

ceeded through legal processes in removing the elder Melish; but his son, whose fellow-traveling activities were the occasion for the controversy, remained as acting rector until 1957. The center of controversy among the Congregationalists and Methodists was not so much in congregations as in seminaries and especially in the Social Action auxiliaries of both these denominations. These auxiliaries were essentially political in the broad sense in which I am using the term. The politics of their staff members could not be a matter of indifference to their sponsors; so it does not represent a significant appearance of political tests if some of the Social Action functionaries cease to function. It is quite remarkable that there have not been more incidents among the Protestant ministry, when one considers the political extremes, both to the right and to the left, that can be found within it. Thus Los Angeles contains both the Rev. James W. Fifield, who is the founder of Spiritual Mobilization, a politically reactionary group, and the Rev. Stephen Fritchman, who has apparently had many Communist associations. Perhaps these accommodations reflect the diversity of urban congregations.[6]

There have been no publicized episodes involving either rabbis or Catholic priests. Over all, I conclude that the clergy (about 200,000) has been fairly free of political employment tests.[7]

Social workers, about 100,000 in number, include welfare case workers, and all those concerned with the administration of relief and rehabilitation programs. Their professional interests unavoidably include controverted issues of welfare legislation, of minority rights, and of the recognition of organizations made up of the unemployed or of those at the bottom of the employment ladder. These are all issues that the Communists have exploited. Social workers, individually and collectively, have thus found themselves caught up in causes and organizations that could be, and were, called communistic. Among the discredited organizations were the Workers Alliance, a "union" of the

6. Roy, n. 5 above, reviews the matters raised in this paragraph; the Melishes (J. Howard and William H.), pp. 269–72, the Social Action groups, pp. 311–25 and 337–43, Fifield, pp. 286–94, and Fritchman, pp. 272–7. See also HUAC, Hearings, *Testimony of Stephen H. Fritchman* (1953). Attempts to effect the removal of the younger Melish were reported NYT, 1956, 1957, esp. Dec. 6, 1957.

7. The number of clergymen one would expect to be known and accurately reported. However, the 1950 Census gives 168,419 as the total (see *Statistical Abstract of the United States, 1954,* table 238, p. 209), while *A Guide to the Religions of America,* ed. Leo Rosten (1955), p. 205, shows 207,618 pastors with congregations, and 338,250 ordained persons. These discrepancies are partially explained by the differing definitions of "clergy," i.e. those denominations requiring divinity degrees, those in which the congregation merely elects one of their number, those in which each adult member is "ordained," etc.

unemployed, the leadership of which the Communists captured in the mid-1930's; the United Public Workers; and the United Office and Professional Workers—both of which had a similar fate in the 1940's. Social workers have been at the center of loyalty programs for public employees in both New York and Los Angeles.[8]

Librarians (55,000) also find themselves in a crossfire of controversy wherever a question of local censorship arises. There have been many scattered incidents in the last few years of attempted political censorship, especially in school libraries, with the impetus coming variously from the responsible authorities or from irresponsible civic groups. One does not get the impression that individual librarians have exposed themselves unnecessarily in these controversies. It may be said that all librarians face an occupational hazard that freedom to read will be challenged in their community, and that the censors may try to control the book-keepers as well as the books. The risk can be avoided by a sacrifice of principle, or it can be met and overcome by a successful defense of principle. It thus differs from the disabilities imposed by government programs, which turn on past actions and associations that cannot be re-lived. But many, perhaps most, librarians are public employees, and are subject to government programs as well as to their special hazard.[9]

8. The testing of welfare and social workers in New York City was discussed in Ch. 4 above; for the Los Angeles situation see Horowitz, "Report on the Los Angeles City and County Loyalty Programs," *Stanford Law Rev.* (1953), 5:233, who notes (p. 240) that there were twelve social workers among sixteen employees who unsuccessfully challenged the county program. The history of the Workers Alliance is in BONTECOU, pp. 194–8. Members of the United Public Workers of America were employed in federal, state, and local governmental agencies. It was expelled from the CIO in 1950. For some of its difficulties in Detroit while still in the CIO see *The States and Subversion,* ed. Gellhorn (1952), pp. 222–5. See also ISC, Hearings, *Subversive Control of the U.P.W.A.* (1952). The UPWA "disbanded in February 1953, following U.S. security investigations. Four locals were taken in by the Teamsters; New York Teachers Union division is now unaffiliated."

The United Office and Professional Workers "collapsed" after being expelled from the CIO in 1950. Remnants of the union merged with two other CIO-expelled unions to form the Distributive, Processing, and Office Workers of America. For a discussion of the objectives and activities of this combined union see ISC, Hearings, *Subversive Control of the D.P.O.W.A.* (1952). Compare this with the arbitrator's discussion of the old UOPWA in National Council of Jewish Women, 2 Am. Labor Arb. Awards par. 67, 772 (1947). "The D.P.O.W. broke from the party line in 1954 and joined the C.I.O. Retail, Wholesale and Department Store Union." The statements quoted here about the recent history of these unions are from *Fortune* (March 1956), p. 206.

9. For accounts of incidents involving librarians and of various communities'

The incidence of political tests in the medical profession was reviewed in Chapter 4. As yet no state appears to have exerted its licensing power to exclude physicians from practice on loyalty grounds, though the *Barsky* case (in which a physician convicted of contempt was suspended) seems to give that power considerable scope. Medical societies and hospital boards are responsible for such political tests as have occurred. The consequences of their disapproval are severe but not crippling. The combination of state action and professional censure have formidable potentialities, but up till now the private practice of medicine has been relatively free of political tests. However, substantial numbers (around 25,000) of the 300,000 doctors and dentists are in civilian or military government employment. Others on medical school staffs have to meet prevailing tests in education.

Before going on to the next class of professional people, it should be noted that there are several professions (e.g. architecture) that do not conveniently fit the classifications used here. However, they can be passed over, both because the numbers engaged in them are small, and because they seem to have had no serious problems. Also, there are some unclassifiable professions that merge rather indistinctly into large nonprofessional occupations. Accounting and nursing are cases in point. It should be mentioned that a California case indicates that at least one large accounting firm requires loyalty statements from all its employees.[10] A rationalization for this practice is that *some* accountants,

efforts to control the contents of libraries see "Censors and the Library," *Saturday Review* (July 2, 1955), p. 10. The most spectacular episode involving a librarian has been the case of Mrs. Mary Knowles, who, after she had invoked the privilege before the ISC, was dismissed from a post in Norwood, Mass., and was then employed by the Jeanes Library of Plymouth Meeting, Pa., which was under the supervision of the Plymouth Society of Friends (Quakers). The Fund for the Republic made an award of $5000 to the Library, and the resulting notoriety apparently intensified divisions in the community and the Society about Mrs. Knowles' employment. Mrs. Knowles, recalled before the ISC, abandoned her reliance on the Fifth Amendment but continued to refuse to answer any questions about past communist affiliations, attacking the jurisdiction of the Committee. She was then convicted for contempt. See ISC, Hearings, *Subversive Influence in the Educational Process* (1953), p. 1001, and (1955), p. 547; Society of Friends, Civil Liberties Committee, Philadelphia Yearly Meeting, *The Plymouth Meeting Controversy* (1957); HUAC, Hearings, *Investigation of the Award by the Fund for the Republic, Inc. (Plymouth Meeting, Pa.)* (1956), pp. 5457–5536; NYT, Jan. 11, 19, 1957.

10. Arthur Anderson and Co., one of the nation's largest public accounting firms, apparently requires all its employees to sign a loyalty statement whether or not they are working on books of firms handling classified contracts. In a unique decision, the California Department of Employment declared that when

like some lawyers, need clearance to deal with classified operations of clients with defense contracts. The screening of all employees, however, is a typical example of excessive zeal.

THE COMMUNICATIONS PROFESSIONS

Authors, editors, and reporters, of whom there are about 100,000, are barred from large areas of journalistic employment if they have any public record of unrepented communist associations or sympathies. Even if they have recanted, a revealed history of party activity may frighten publishers who fear the sniping of rival publishers.[11] In movies and broadcasting the standards, as we have seen, are equally severe. Many writers are found in federal employment as information specialists; they are subject to the usual security regulations.

Actors, entertainers, and musicians have practically no government contacts, except in the combination of public service and publicity known as cheering up the troops. For them radio, television, and movies are the most lucrative sources of employment; so they (along with some technicians) are the occupations hardest hit by the blacklists and graylists of those industries.

As was observed in the last chapter, there are some employment opportunities outside the mass media for almost all of the types we are here discussing. For example, Dorothy Parker, a writer and wit of great fame in the 1930's who is still identified with fellow-traveling causes, probably could not sell a movie script or make a television appearance; but she had a play produced on Broadway in 1953, and two short stories

a man who had been employed by Anderson as a multilith operator refused to sign their loyalty statement and was fired, he was subsequently ineligible for unemployment benefits on the ground that his own conduct made him unavailable for suitable work. This holding was based on the assumption that loyalty statements are now generally required by private employers. On appeal, the referee modified this aspect of the Department's determination and said that there were numerous employers who did not yet require such statements; but he upheld the result on the ground that the refusal to sign the loyalty statement "constituted a deliberate violation of the standards of behavior which the employer has the right to expect . . ." and "constituted misconduct." See ACLU [No. Calif.] *News* (July 1956), p. 3, and (Nov. 1956), p. 1. A court decision is pending.

11. E.g. Stanley Hancock said that he was fired in Dec. 1949 from a position as public relations director for the Erie, Pennsylvania, *Dispatch* when the opposition newspaper, the Erie *Times,* gave prominence to his appearance that month as a witness in the Harry Bridges case and to his former communist activities in general. See his testimony, HUAC, Hearings, *Investigation of Communist Activities in the State of California* (1954), p. 4562.

published in the *New Yorker* in 1955.[12] But the few channels that are open to such persons could not possibly provide a haven for all of them; and if their employers became more hospitable, the pressure groups that have, as they think, purified the big entertainment industries might very well turn their attention to the small ones.

Freedom of international travel is probably of greater importance to the communications professions than to any other occupational group. Newspaper and magazine correspondents, entertainers, and movie people may lose valuable employment opportunities if they cannot go abroad; so may specialists in some fields of law, business, and scholarship. The movements of citizens (except for occasional restrictions which the Defense Department has imposed on entry into combat or occupied areas) are subject to the mandates of the Passport Division of the Department of State. I cannot digress to speculate about the criteria of this program, or to narrate the delays that have occurred in subjecting it to some degree of judicial control. From publicized cases one can infer that the Division has a variety of reasons for wanting to keep certain people at home. At one extreme are those who might be unduly critical of American policy, especially foreign policy; at the other, those who might be likely to make espionage contacts abroad. The hazard of a passport refusal can be especially severe for one who finds his employment opportunities shrinking in this country and has brighter prospects abroad.

Related to the passport problem are the restrictions on entry, administered by the State Department in the case of visitors' visas, and by the Department of Justice in the case of immigration or re-entry of aliens. These measures at least have statutory foundations, but they are so complex, and so tangential to the main theme, that I must ignore them. Charlie Chaplin, a British subject, is the best-known personage whose American employment was ended by his decision not to challenge a threatened revocation of his re-entry permit. He remained abroad, and accepted a Stalin Peace Prize while his films were sporadically picketed in this country.[13]

12. Dorothy Parker's play, "Ladies of the Corridor," was a collaboration with Arnaud d'Usseau. It was reviewed in NYT, Oct. 22, 1953. Her *New Yorker* pieces appeared Jan. 15, 1955, p. 24, and Aug. 27, 1955, p. 32.

13. Former Attorney General McGranery's decision to exclude Chaplin is reported in NYT, Oct. 3, 1952; Chaplin's surrender of his re-entry permit, NYT, April 16, 1953. The Fox Theatre chain was forced to cancel the showing of Chaplin pictures in California as a result of Legion picketing. NYT, Jan. 16, 1953.

PROFESSIONS—SUMMARY

What does this add up to for the three million or more professional people we have now looked at? Nothing uniform, to be sure. At one extreme are scientists and engineers in security areas, whose difficulties are about matched by those of writers and actors who face loyalty blacklists. At the other are clergymen and most physicians, who can go about ministering to souls and bodies without anyone asking whether they are or ever have been Communists. Some of those in between do not have heavy burdens (relatively speaking); they have only to keep clear of charges that they are now party members or close party followers; and they dare not invoke the Fifth Amendment. Over all, probably half of the total group is exposed to some kind of oath, inquiry, supervision, or surveillance.

For two reasons it has been worth reviewing the state of the professions with more care than it will be feasible to give other occupational classes containing greater numbers. First, they are composed of people on whom special training has been lavished for the sake of giving them skills highly valued by society. To exclude such people from the practice of their professons is presumptively a social and economic loss to the community. Second, the professions include a large proportion of the people who are supposed, now and again, to produce new and useful ideas. But the operation of loyalty and security programs is widely said to discourage thinking of the sort that does produce new and useful ideas.

MANAGERS

If the considerations just advanced are important, they should lead next to consideration of the managerial class, within which is another primary source of leadership and ideas. The nearest census equivalent is "managers, officials and proprietors." After officials are subtracted, the census total is still somewhat larger than the professional group; but the exact figures are not meaningful; any uncertainty about the bound-

For surveys of the passport and visa problems see Commission on Government Security, *Report* (1957), pp. 445–95, 565; Comment, "Passport Refusals for Political Reasons: Constitutional Issues and Judicial Review," *Yale Law Jour.* (1952), *61*:171; Note, "The Passport Puzzle," *Univ. of Chicago Law Rev.* (1956), *23*:260; Leonard Boudin, "The Constitutional Right to Travel," *Columbia Law Rev.* (1956), *56*:47; BAS, Oct. 1952 (symposium on visa policies and foreign scientists).

aries of professions is as nothing compared to the difficulty of defining, in exclusive terms, who is a manager or proprietor. The census throws together corporation executives and push-cart owners.

For present purposes the existence of a class of the same size as the professional class, about 3,000,000, may be assumed.[14] It stands in striking contrast to the professions on the question of loyalty and security tests, because their incidence in the managerial class has been negligible. A few of its members have a turn at government service and must pass security tests. The only programs that have any direct application to the managerial group are the screening of contractors by the Defense Department and the Atomic Energy Commission, and the Port Security program. The total number of persons who have clearance under these programs is about 3,000,000. How many of them are managers, in the sense of this inquiry? At a guess (and it is only a guess) I should say between 5 and 10 per cent. Let us say 200,000. Then allow for the exposure to private programs of some unknown additional number, by assuming that the private programs cover about half as many people as the government programs, a guess which is probably too low, certainly not too high. After 100,000 have been added to the 200,000 already estimated, the total is only 10 per cent of the hypothetical managerial class. If the magnitude of the private programs is twice as great as I have assumed, the exposure is still under 15 per cent, strikingly less than the estimated 50 per-cent exposure of the professions. Furthermore, in contrast to the many professional people who have had clearance difficulties, one hears very few accounts of clearance denied to officers and managers of industrial defense contractors. Yet exposure in the industrial security programs is intense, and there is no reason to believe that any sort of double standard exists—one for the boss, another for the hired hands. Of course, the company's resources are more readily available to defend the boss. Corporation lawyers who would otherwise not touch a security case may find themselves immersed in one if the clearance of an officer of the company is called into question. But this does not often happen; for here is a group that, besides being less exposed, is much less vulnerable than the professions. The politics and associations of business managers are generally assumed to cluster on the conservative side of the political spectrum. Under present circumstances this raises no security hazard, except for the extremist who has been a recent member of the Ku Klux Klan or the like.

14. This estimate seems consistent with one in C. Wright Mills, *White Collar* (1951), pp. 87, 91 (1–1.5 million foremen are "about half of all managers").

The result is a low level of involvement on the part of this large and important group with loyalty and security matters. (I digress to suggest that this leads in turn to a low level of concern and understanding about such matters.) Loyalty and security problems will rarely trouble the managerial élite.

PUBLIC EMPLOYMENT

The largest bloc of employees subject to political employment tests is of course civil servants, state and federal. So much has already been said about them that it remains only to count them, making allowance for professional people already counted, especially teachers. There are still left more than two million federal and more than three million state and local nonprofessional public employees. Approximately 25 to 30 per cent of the state and local employees are in states that are free of tests.[15] This still leaves a total of four to four and a half million. We may immediately add the armed forces, all exposed to high-intensity security tests; their numbers fluctuate near three million. Thus there are seven and a quarter to seven and a half million government employees (plus about one million professionals in public employment already counted) exposed to security or loyalty tests generally of high intensity.

PRIVATE EMPLOYMENT

In dealing with the great mass of private employment, it will be useful to adopt something like the economists' distinction between primary (extractive), secondary (manufacturing), and tertiary (distribution and service) industries. Mining and like industries have only about a million employees, and have no conspicuous exposure. There are, by current definitions, no security-sensitive extractive industries except uranium, which is insignificant in terms of manpower. Loyalty tests exist in militantly anticommunist unions, like the United Mine Workers, and may be latent in employer reactions to the Communist-led Mine, Mill, and Smelter Workers; but in general I characterize the primary industries as having low intensity and extent of exposure.

The same thing is true at the other end of the process. Some fifteen

15. I have not made a separate enumeration of civil servants by states. I used the ratios derived for teachers, with an allowance for those states that have tests for teachers only.

million people are engaged in trade and service industries, and two million more in finance. They have no valid security problems, except for special cases, like cafeteria workers in a secret laboratory.

In some of the service trades, as in the extractive industries, attempts at communist infiltration of labor unions have led to anticommunist provisions in union constitutions, and to efforts by government and employers to purge communist leadership where it has got a foothold. The application of political tests to union leaders is not to be lightly regarded, even though the affected numbers are small and even if the avowed aims of the tests are generally approved. Here is another élite group. Originality and independence of thought are presumably to be encouraged within it, along with stability and responsibility. If employment tests adversely affect professional people or managers, the same injuries will be inflicted on labor leaders. From a quantitative standpoint, however, conflicts of power among labor leaders, and occasional government action against them, leave the rank-and-file undisturbed; so for the tertiary industries, as for the primary, my estimate is: low extent, low intensity.

The sectors of private employment where union conflicts, aggressive employers, and security demands sometimes come to a boil are in manufacturing and what may be called its heavy auxiliaries: construction, transportation, and public utilities. These account for almost 40 per cent of all employment; the problem is to find a basis for estimating how many of this 40 per cent are exposed to loyalty or security tests. As a starting point let us take the estimated coverage by the Department of Defense of its contractor program, something close to three million.[16]

In transportation, there is the Port Security program, which has cleared more than 800,000 seamen and waterfront workers. Nowhere

16. Two million was the estimate given in 1955 by Wilber Brucker, the General Counsel of the Department of Defense, of the number of employees of defense contractors having access to Top Secret, Secret, and Confidential matters. See HUMPHREY HEARINGS, pp. 191–2. Joseph Rauh, Jr., U.A.W. counsel, said later in 1955 that there were nearly three million involved in the program, and stated that this was "the estimate also of the Department of Defense." See HENNINGS HEARINGS, p. 544. Rauh estimated that over two million employees were working on Confidential, and the remainder on Secret and Top Secret matters. The total figure was succinctly confirmed by Jerome Fenton, Director of the Office of Industrial Personnel Security of the Defense Department, who testified that the number was "hugging three million"; ibid., p. 606. Ambiguity frequently arises in estimates of the coverage of the various security programs, because it is not clear whether cumulative or current coverage is being put forward. There has been said to be a 25 per cent yearly turnover of the personnel who are covered by the industrial program. HUMPHREY HEARINGS, p. 225.

near this number is employed in the maritime industry at any given time; an unusually high rate of turnover and of part-time employment impairs any estimate based on the number of persons who have been through the mill. Similarly, the AEC has cleared 500,000 people, more than twice as many as have been employed on all its contracts, classified or unclassified, at any one time.[17] To keep the numbers roughly comparable, these two figures should be sharply cut, say to 400,000 combined. This makes the current exposure to government programs about three and a quarter million.

The open end of the whole tabulation is this: how many employees have to pass tests because their employers want to be prepared for any extension of security controls? Or because their employers, for a variety of other motives, have chosen to institute loyalty questionnaires and investigations? Or because their unions have done likewise? A conservative guess would be to extend the government coverage by about one-half. A solid backlog for this one and a half million figure is found in the 280,000 employees of the General Electric Company and the 780,000 in the Bell Telephone system. Both of these enterprises, as we have seen, make preemployment inquiries about affiliations with subversive organizations whether or not classified work is involved.

What determines the industries of high exposure? The government programs aimed at espionage obviously hit electronics, aircraft production, ordnance, and other producers of classified hardware. Beyond that, what are the criteria? If sailors, why not railroad men? If telephone workers, why not electric-power employees? One group seems as essential as the other. A short explanation for the distinction between sea and land transport is that the railway Brotherhoods are conservative unions. Some maritime unions are not, and others (as the result of recent conversions) are more zealous than the Coast Guard to clean out the Communists. As between telephones and power, a possible distinction is that the Bell system has a high degree of national uniformity in employment policy; the power utilities have rather less. Another answer to all these questions may be that the distinctions are less sharp than one might imagine. Private programs, I reiterate, may flourish without publicity, especially if the unions acquiesce, or if there is no union.

With so many unknowns, I will take 4,500,000 as a round num-

17. Port Security, see ASS'N OF THE BAR, REPORT, p. 221; AEC, HUMPHREY HEARINGS, p. 294.

ber for moderate to intense exposure to official security tests, quasi-security tests, and loyalty inquiries in the great core of 24,000,000 manufacturing, construction, transportation, and utility employees. The earlier estimate of 300,000 managers in these fields is not counted in reaching this total.

Agricultural employment (7,000,000) is the last category. I do not know of any loyalty or security problems in agriculture. Farming may be the last refuge of the heretic.

If the estimates of the numbers of employees exposed to some existing loyalty or security test are combined, this is the result:

	(in thousands)
Professions, including teachers	1600
Managers	300
Government and military	7200
Extractive industry	—
Manufacturing, construction, transport, utilities	4500
Trade, service, finance	—
Agriculture	—
Total, round off to	13,500

Taking the total labor force at around 65,000,000, this means that at least one person out of five, as a condition of his current employment, has taken a test oath, or completed a loyalty statement, or achieved official security clearance, or survived some undefined private scrutiny.

CASUALTY RATES IN EMPLOYMENT TESTS

I will now try to summarize the information at hand on the number of people who have failed to pass employment tests in the last decade. Hundreds instead of millions become the unit of measurement. For a few programs exact figures are available. But any attempt to arrive at accurate over-all totals is condemned to failure for five reasons. First, for most programs there is no information on how many people have been rejected as applicants for a job on loyalty and security grounds. Second, there is no way of knowing how many people have resigned, or passed up job opportunities, because they thought they could not be cleared, could not afford the delays of clearance, or simply refused to submit to it. Third, an unknown number of loyalty or security dismissals has doubtless been veiled with other explanations. Fourth, the figures for federal civil servants under E.O. 10450, as we saw in Chapter 2, are almost meaningless. Fifth, for most private programs reports are incomplete, or absent.

Still, impressions of magnitudes are better than nothing. The following summary is an attempt to estimate dismissals, plus denials of clearance or exclusions from a calling that are equivalent to dismissals. For the basis of these very rough totals see Appendix A.

All federal employees, including military	3900
Private employees subject to federal programs	5400
State and local government employees	1000
Self- and privately employed	1200
Total	11,500

As a figure to keep in mind, an even 10,000 is good enough. Anything more refined would convey a false semblance of precision; and I should emphasize again that these totals are a mixture of official tabulations, extrapolations, and guesses. Nevertheless, they give an order of magnitude. The 10,000 is certainly not too high; it is more likely too low, perhaps by one-half. It cannot properly be compared to the 13,500,000 exposed to tests, because that estimate referred to the current labor force, whereas 10,000 is a cumulative total. Take an arbitrary allowance of 100 per cent for turnover in the exposed sectors of the labor force during the last decade. The number of people whom the tests have directly barred appears to be somewhere between one-twentieth and one-thirtieth of one per cent of those who have been exposed— that is, perhaps one out of every 2500.

These variants of the numbers game have, I trust, been cautious ones. Though this chapter contains many guesses, they have been identified as such, and they are reasonably informed guesses. The arithmetic of loyalty and security at least conveys some idea of the total scale of the phenomena we are studying. The next chapter considers what it means for millions of people to be exposed to loyalty and security tests, and for some thousands to be rejected by them.

7. The Impact of Employment Tests

WHATEVER the uncertainties of the preceding chapter, it at least dealt mostly in numbers, so that commensurate quantities could be added or subtracted. In order to consider how employment tests affect those who do not pass them, those who do, and the community at large, we have to juggle a strange variety of elements. They range from hard facts, like the dollar cost of a full field investigation, to such intangibles as the change in the quality of a man's thinking. One thing that most of the issues of this chapter have in common is that they are what doctors call "side effects." For example, a drug might cure mumps but at the same time cause high blood pressure and eczema. The direct effects of loyalty and security programs are measured by their success in repressing disloyalty and promoting security. These are large topics to which we will devote much further attention. The side effects, however, should not be thought of as incidental. They may appear to be of considerable gravity, just as high blood pressure and eczema may be considered a high price to pay for getting rid of mumps.

WHAT HAPPENS TO THOSE DISMISSED

The major casualties, those who are dismissed, surely encounter the most severe hardships. Whether or not they have been justly dealt with, if they have fought their cases through to the end of appeal procedures, the expenses have probably depleted their savings. If they have been suspended, they may already be impoverished when the final severance of employment occurs. What happens to them then? Generalization is difficult, partly because of insufficient information, partly because the human situation varies too broadly. At the time that J. R. Oppenheimer was barred from government employment, his work for the government was not his main livelihood; he was only an occasional consultant. After dismissal he continued, with the unanimous concurrence of the trustees (who included Chairman Strauss of the AEC) to serve as Director of the Institute for Advanced Study. At the other end of the employment ladder, a messman screened off U.S. merchant ships can probably get a job as a waiter ashore. He is no worse off; indeed, landlubbers recalling Dr. Johnson's views on life at sea ("in jail with a chance of being drowned") might think him better off. It is probable that the very eminent and the very humble suffer the least economic hardship. The former (there are only a handful of such cases) have influential friends and defenders. They also have abilities too valuable to be discarded. The latter have never been able to be choosy anyhow. In prosperous times they can probably pick up some other kind of low-paid work with no questions asked.

The middling specialist has a hard time. What is there for a foreign service officer to do outside the foreign service? Perhaps he can teach; perhaps he can write. He would be useful to a business firm with international interests. Neither a university appointment nor (for example) a job with a large chemical manufacturer should demand security clearance.[1] But the fact that a prospective employer has no valid security responsibilities does not eliminate from his consideration the underlying causes for the dismissal. If the employee's failings are grave ones, they may quite reasonably disqualify him from any responsible job. Even if the new employer is satisfied that the dismissal had little foundation, he still may confront a real problem in public relations. The possibility of embarrassment for the prospective employer depends largely on the notoriety of the case. Few cases are notorious; but few contested cases can be entirely covered up. There is too much activity about witnesses and affidavits. So, pursuing further the problems of the hypothetical diplomat, he is going to have a tough time. No university, no corporation has any obligation to hire him. Routine applications will probably get nowhere. It takes some friendly connection, with an employer who discounts the charges and trusts the person, for the diplomat to re-establish himself.

Similarly, what is there for a teacher to do outside teaching? Of course, teachers are not like diplomats in having only one employer for their profession. The scholars who refused to take the University of California loyalty oath got other university appointments. However, few if any of the Fifth Amendment casualties of 1953–54 did. Teachers in public school systems seem to be especially immobile. Certification usually operates on a statewide basis. A dismissed teacher is probably formally barred throughout the state and would have difficulty in getting a certificate elsewhere. Opportunities in private schools are limited. We hear much of teachers who have bettered their miserable incomes by

1. But see Joseph Rauh, in Industrial Rel. Res. Ass'n, *Personnel Security Programs in U. S. Industry* (1955), p. 23, citing *Chemical Week* (April 16, 1955), p. 28, on the imposition of loyalty questionnaires by some chemical companies.

abandoning teaching to run filling stations; but this is small comfort
to the man, and even less to the woman, who wants to be a teacher and
not a filling station operator.

Similarly, what can a physicist do outside physics? Here the question
should not even arise, for there is no dearth of unclassified employment
for a competent man, either in teaching or in industry. But it does arise,
because of the usual qualms about public relations, or about the import
of the charges. Industry, as we have seen, may be particularly concerned
to have all its technical people cleared or clearable. The Scientists' Committee on Loyalty and Security made the following report on the
situation, a few months after their dismissals, of eight men dismissed
from the Army Signal Corps at Fort Monmouth:

> Of the eight dismissed, accurate information is available on
> five. One has opened a small shop and is reported to be doing
> well in business for himself. Three have technical jobs, all obtained
> through the intercession of friends. To the best of our knowledge,
> none of the eight would have been able to obtain technical jobs
> without the assistance of some third party.
>
> Another one of the eight sought employment without success
> from January to April of 1954. From April through August he
> obtained, with the help of a friend, temporary technical employ-
> ment at a salary roughly half of what he had formerly earned at
> Fort Monmouth. His wife also obtained part-time employment in
> this period. In the last several months this former high-ranking
> physicist has opened a small, private, semi-technical business and,
> at last report, had met with very meager success. Thus far he has
> sent out over 100 letters in an effort to obtain technical employ-
> ment commensurate with his background and experience. These
> letters were generally sent to firms which clearly needed technical
> personnel and where opportunities for unclassified work seemed
> to exist. One large company replied to this physicist: ". . . en-
> gineers in our nonclassified areas are more beneficial to us if
> they have clearance, since they may be exposed to classified
> work." [2]

There is not much point in multiplying case histories, for there is no
way of knowing how representative they are. All I can say in summary

2. Scientists' Committee on Loyalty and Security, "Fort Monmouth One
Year Later," BAS (1955), *11*:150. Quoted by permission of the Educational
Foundation for Nuclear Science, Inc.

about the employability of the major casualties of the programs—those who are dismissed—is that it is not good. Some wind up better off than they were before. Some hold their own. The great majority must be worse off. I say "must" without statistical support because a history of dismissal on security or loyalty grounds obviously puts the employee at a great disadvantage in dealing with a prospective employer. Even when an indulgent or an indifferent employer is discovered, the employee is still in bondage to his past. He knows—and his employer knows—that another job will be hard to find. He is on probation, if not perpetually, at least as long as present attitudes persist.

This last point opens up one aspect of the noneconomic injury caused by a dismissal. How are we to appraise a loss of self-confidence and self-respect? If the employee thinks he has been unjustly rejected by the loyalty–security system, will he ever be as effective a member of society again? Will he withdraw into a private world, peopled with delusions of persecution? [3] If his talents included independence and initiative, will they be blunted? If these things happen to demonstrable traitors, one might say "serves them right." But the preceding chapters have shown that the reach of the tests extends far beyond those whose culpability may justify severe hardships.

MORE CASUALTIES—THE WALKING WOUNDED

These same questions, and some of the economic uncertainties too, apply to another large group. I have referred to the dismissal estimates as "casualty rates." There is a much larger and motley group of walking wounded. They are first the people who, in formal programs, are cleared after charges and hearing. Another contingent is composed of those who get in a tangle about clearance for access to classified material and resign. Another consists of those in government service who have their clearances revoked but are neither served with charges nor removed from the payroll—they are in what is sometimes known as the "leper colony." Another, of soldiers who serve out their term and get a less-than-honorable discharge. Still another, of those in private employment who suspect that they are on a "graylist"—under a cloud but not pro-

3. These considerations are opened up by Charlotte A. and Herbert Kaufman, "Some Problems of Treatment Arising from the Federal Loyalty and Security Program," *Am. Jour. of Orthopsychiatry* (1955), *25*:813. See also Paul Chodoff, "Loyalty Programs and Mental Health in the Washington Area," *Psychiatry* (1953), *16*:399.

scribed. Many recruits for this shadow army come from those who have been denounced before or by investigating committees. Some of the committees (state and national) have been ready enough to condemn, but deny themselves the power to acquit. A cloud of suspicion hangs about many people even after they have denied the accusations against them, because no official judgment is ever pronounced.

The common plight of the walking wounded is that their situation is ambiguous. Consider these observations by an engineer in private employment who, eighteen months after "Secret" clearance had been requested, was in the end cleared for "Top Secret":

> Fully cleared, I had finally overcome the problems of delays, inaccuracies, lack of specification of charges, and the numerous other problems related to the hearing, but I could not overcome the question of stigma. My recent boss had not granted me an affidavit for the hearing, although he agreed that I had done nothing suspicious in regard to security. Could I believe that, from his slight knowledge of the hearing, my boss now dismissed the grave doubt which apparently had arisen in his mind due to the denial? Could the doubt ever be completely dismissed from the minds of all those in the company who knew—some of whom knew me only because they knew of the security problem? Echelon on echelon knew about the thing now; could my advancement ever be assured with this shadow of a doubt on my record? [4]

Perhaps this man is a victim not of the programs but of his own fears. Is his advancement really retarded? Of course, we do not know; and the engineer himself does not know either—that is all I am trying to say.

If a man who has been cleared may rightly consider himself handicapped (and there is also the hazard of multiple jeopardy: clearance is never final), surely all the other groups, those without formal clearance, have more trouble. The case history just quoted is one of a group in the *Bulletin of the Atomic Scientists* that illustrates the multiple entanglements of the complex federal programs. The subjects of these case histories are seven scientists. One case, the only one with a clear-cut conclusion, is the chronology of a prolonged denial of clearance after hearing. The others are largely chronicles of frustration. Hearings are delayed or unavailable. Clearances are granted, revoked, and reinstated. Actually, these seven scientists fared rather well. With their clearances

4. Scientists' Committee on Loyalty and Security, "Some Individual Cases," BAS (1955), *11*:158. Quoted by permission; see n. 2 above.

somewhere in limbo, four of the seven got (or retained) university appointments. One, the man quoted above, moved to an unclassified job. Only one, as I said, was formally dismissed. The seventh's situation is unclear but apparently not desperate.

Even if the employee lands on his feet, any contested clearance is an ordeal. First, money costs arise from the expenses of meeting the charges. The cost of legal counsel, of gathering evidence, and of necessary travel can vary from nothing to many thousands of dollars.[5] Sometimes an employee may appear without counsel, and with affidavits or witnesses gathered in the same building. If he has a lawyer and is well advised, he will pile up phone and secretarial charges in garnering affiants who can establish his lifelong anticommunism. The money costs are incurred at a time when, often, the employee has no income. Suspension without pay, which for a long while was standard operating procedure in federal security programs, leaves the employee with no income and with the first of a series of social and psychological difficulties. How does he explain his idleness, either to his children or to his neighbors? How much does he have to explain to those from whom he seeks help? How far does he dare strain friendship by asking help from other employees who are afraid they will get themselves involved? I would say a man who has to prepare for and then go through a security hearing is subject to strains that are quite comparable to those that would accompany a trial for a serious crime. There is less publicity but a good deal more mystery.

However, a bout with security proceedings is not always and entirely a calamity. The man who gets any opportunity to clear himself is certainly better off than one who gets none. Once derogatory information has come into the employer's hands, the employee is in trouble unless he can refute it. If he refutes it decisively enough, he may never be bothered again. But for those who are brushed even lightly with security suspicions, the upshot is often a special kind of personal insecurity. If they have any kind of tenure in a job, they can probably hang onto it; but their ability to move either upward or outward is much lessened. A possible promotion, or a different job, are occasions for a formal review of the employee's record; they revive the old doubts, and require a new decision whether those doubts are a barrier to the new position, though they are not to the old one.

I have little direct evidence about the effect of past clearance troubles on promotion. Information that I have obtained from counsel about

5. For legal costs in contested cases see below, App. B, Table 17.

the later history of clients is indecisive. In some instances the employee
has advanced normally; in others he has expressed a feeling that he is
being bypassed. But there is no way to establish either the fact or its
cause. Certainly there have been many federal employees who believed
that their future would be uncertain after a successful clearance; they
acted on this belief by fighting a case through and then (if they had
somewhere else to go) resigning.

The parenthesis is important, because it is fairly clear that mobility
to other jobs is hindered. We have seen some examples already. One
more will underscore the point, and serve as a reminder of some other
harassing aspects of the situation. Dr. *E,* a physicist, was employed at
a laboratory with classified government contracts. A request to the
Navy Department for clearance lay dormant for three years. When the
head of the laboratory pushed the matter, a tentative denial, based on
alleged communist associations before 1947, resulted. However, a hearing before one of the Industrial Personnel Security Boards led to a reversal. The local security officer did not acquiesce in the Board's certification that *E*'s employment was consistent with the national security, and
withheld clearance further until he was ordered by the Department
to grant it. *E,* not surprisingly, thought he might be better off elsewhere,
and got a job with an aircraft manufacturer. After one week he was
summarily dismissed, on the pretext that there was no place for him
after all. His complaints about the curtness, not to say crudity, of this
action were countered with the fact that he was still a probationary
employee with no rights. He then applied to a dozen or more firms in
the area that were advertising for physicists, with no success. In two instances where he obtained initially favorable interviews, nothing came
of them.

I have no positive knowledge that *E*'s security involvement caused his
employment troubles after he left the laboratory; but there is a strong
inference of a security officers' blacklist in the area; he could hardly
have been worse off if he had stayed put.

I cannot even make a guess at the numbers of the walking wounded;
but enough has been said to demonstrate that they, like the major
casualties, can and do suffer severe economic and emotional hardships.

The Untouched Millions

Thus far we have been considering the probable effects of loyalty and
security tests on the tens of thousands who run directly afoul of them.

On the other hand it can be confidently assumed that there are millions for whom the tests hold no terrors at all, even though they are nominally exposed. I have heard it argued that almost everyone ought to be a little bit uneasy, because it is possible to turn up derogatory information on almost anyone, by linking remote associations and inflating trivial ones. People who make this argument may well have had such associations themselves if they are city dwellers with a wide acquaintance, and they may be justly alarmed to think that only a slight extension of current standards would involve them. But for most of the population no such hazard presents itself. This assertion can be based on Stouffer's opinion survey, in which only 3 per cent of the respondents said that they had ever known an admitted Communist, and only 10 per cent more said that they had ever known anyone whom they suspected of being a Communist. The reasons given by the 10 per cent for their suspicions were often outlandish. Acquaintance with a real or suspected Communist is not presented as a precise index of liability to charges. There are other political hazards, as well as the wide world of nonpolitical misdeeds and aberrations. But Stouffer's survey gives force to conclusions that reflection would make apparent anyway. There are great portions of the population who have never seen a Communist or a fellow traveler, never joined anything to the left of the Elks, never expressed any sympathy with Russia. If their past is free of ordinary crimes, they can easily pass a security test; so far as their background is concerned, they can qualify to be security officers themselves.[6]

There still remains a multitude of unknown dimensions, composed of people to whom the tests do make a difference, even though blemishes on their past do not exist. These are the people who have accepted a pattern of behavior for the future different from what they would have chosen if there were no tests. They have noted that one gets in trouble for political activities at either the extreme right or the extreme left. In the current crisis the left attracts the most unfavorable attention; but extremism of any sort is suspect. These people have also noted that one enters the zone of suspicion as soon as one moves any distance from the most orthodox of political or civic involvements. Indeed, they might reasonably go further and conclude that the safe course is to

6. On acquaintance with supposed Communists see Samuel Stouffer, *Communism, Conformity, and Civil Liberties* (New York, Doubleday and Co., 1955), pp. 175 83; on political orthodoxy, passim. Derogatory information about other traits is obviously much more frequent. Cf. the data in Ch. 2 above, n. 61, showing the percentage of applicants for civil service jobs with criminal records, etc.

avoid any involvement. In the celebrated case of Abraham Chasanow, his diligent efforts to bring about private instead of government ownership of the houses in Greenbelt, Maryland, earned him the epithet "Communist" for his pains on behalf of free enterprise.[7]

The result is an impoverishment of the after-hours public life of government servants and of others who feel that they have to be careful. The American habit of joining in voluntary associations for good, bad, or trivial purposes, celebrated by de Tocqueville and one of our most proudly self-conscious national traits, is said to have suffered. This opinion is borne out by the preliminary study of Jahoda and Cook. In an admittedly small group of civil servants whom they interviewed, a distinct trend was observable, a trend away from joining, away from nonconformist associates, away from unconventional belief and expression.[8]

These effects are social as well as personal in their primary impact.

7. See *Time* (May 10, 1954), pp. 22–3.

8. Marie Jahoda and Stuart Cook, "Security Measures and Freedom of Thought: An Exploratory Study of the Impact of Loyalty and Security Programs," *Yale Law Jour.* (1952), *61*:295. The official impetus to such results is typified by the Navy's "Suggested Counsel to Employees":

> A number of our citizens unwittingly expose themselves to unfavorable or suspicious appraisal which they can and should avoid. This may take the form of an indiscreet remark; an unwise selection of friends or associates; membership in an organization whose true objectives are concealed behind a popular and innocuous title; attendance at and participation in the meetings and functions of such organizations even though not an official member; or numerous other clever means designed to attract support under false colors or serving to impress an individual with his own importance.
>
> It is advisable to study and seek wise and mature counsel prior to association with persons or organizations of any political or civic nature, no matter what their apparent motives may be, in order to determine the true motives and purposes of the organization. . . .
>
> The existence of [rights and liberties under the Constitution] should encourage and inspire each one of us to so conduct ourselves that there cannot be the least concern on the part of our associates as to our adherence to the principles of this government, or as to our reliability . . . This counsel is prompted by the Commanding Officer's sincere interest in the continued well-being of all employees of the activity.

Appendix to Navy Civilian Personnel Instructions, Enclosure 10 (reprinted BNA MANUAL, p. 15/231, and JOHNSTON HEARINGS, p. 836).

In a Navy case where the hearing-board's memorandum of reasons was inadvertently disclosed, the board, in finding the employee to be "impressionable . . . naive," said that a federal employee "must order his life with such positive knowledge as will absolutely negate the risk of guilt by association." A denial of clearance in this case was, however, reversed by the Assistant Secretary of the Navy. ACLU [No. Calif.] *News* (Nov. 1954), p. 3.

When people change their social behavior in order (as they think) to hold on to their jobs, the community is surely a loser. A man who rejects an old friend or gives up a cherished avocation doubtless hurts himself more than he hurts the community; but his action leaves the community less rich, less diverse, less alive.

FREEDOM OF SPEECH AND OPINION

I have relied partly on inference and partly on direct evidence for the conclusion that employment tests have some inhibiting effect on off-the-job associations. The same inhibitions will presumably affect the employee in his private speech and action and may in time alter the structure of his beliefs. There is a little evidence on this too from the Jahoda–Cook study, which is consistent with the random observations of various reporters. These observers say that federal employees whom they have encountered tend to censor their reading and their conversations, and to adopt what they take to be officially prescribed attitudes. There has been more than a little editorial assertion to the point that civil servants, teachers, and other affected groups are afraid to speak their minds. These declarations, made with honest fervor and dismay, have been hard to verify. The only extensive study so far available leaves this issue unsettled. The Stouffer inquiry (which was directed to a sample of the whole adult population and to another sample of selected community leaders), asked first for an opinion whether "people feel as free to say what they think as they used to." Of the community leaders, 41 per cent felt that some people do not feel as free, 7 per cent that "hardly anybody" does. Of the national cross-section, the percentages giving the same replies were 31 and 10. Thus in both samples a substantial group thought that restraints had increased. When asked "What about you personally? Do you or don't you feel as free to speak your mind as you used to?" 13 per cent of both samples replied that they felt less free. However, the reasons that were advanced for this feeling, though they made frequent reference to injury to a job or business, were not specific enough to cast any light on the inhibiting role of loyalty and security tests. Stouffer points out that we need more research, concentrated perhaps on government officials and scientists.[9]

9. Stouffer (n. 6 above), pp. 78–83. See the forthcoming study by Paul Lazarsfeld, *The Academic Mind: Social Scientists in a Time of Crisis* (The Free Press, 1958). Its findings (summarized by Joseph Lyford in *AAUP Bull.* [1957], *43*:636) show a marked degree of "apprehension" among those interviewed. They also indicate a much larger number of dismissals than I have estimated.

Inhibitions on belief, speech, and action ordinarily have a tangle of causes. Even if you have a forthright subject who says, "I denounced communist China at a dinner party because otherwise I would be in trouble with the security gang," neither you nor he can be confident of his motives. This hypothetical official is probably also affected by the opinions of his fellow officials (even if they would not dismiss him for uttering a heresy), by general public hostility to the Chinese regime, and by whatever risk he runs of incurring other sanctions, such as unfavorable exposure.

We take for granted a certain burden of social pressure on private belief and speech, and inquire anxiously only if we think it is applied intolerantly. But the pressures that employment tests bring to bear are, I believe, of a different order from community disapproval. Behind them is a severe sanction: conform or lose your job. Furthermore, the sanction usually has the weight of government behind it. We thus meet head on the deep-rooted repugnance of our people, expressed in the First Amendment, to official control of opinion.

I do not say that thought control is the purpose of employment tests. And there is little *direct* evidence that thought control is their result. But what is known about the operation of the programs makes it clear that most of them press strongly in that direction. To find extensive probing into private views and expressions one has only to recall charges and hearings in the federal programs. The state and private programs of lower intensity may be less sweeping in their inquiries. On the other hand, the private blacklist, with no visible criteria and no feasible avenue of escape, may be the most repressive of all.

To discover that a man has lost his job and has been injured thereby is relatively simple. To discern that he has lost his freedom of mind is most difficult. All I can safely declare is that the programs endanger freedom of mind. I cannot say that they are *known* to have such-and-such repressive effects. But to those who still value the inquiring mind, even above the full dinner-pail, a catalogue of effects would be seriously incomplete if it ignored any attack on freedom of thought. The success of such an attack would be more paralyzing than any amount of lost earnings.

MONEY AND MANPOWER COSTS

Effects that can be measured in money are of three kinds. First is the cost to the employee when he has to defend himself in a formal proceeding. Second and most obvious is the expense of running all the programs. This is a concrete charge on all of us, reflected in taxes or in the prices of goods. Third is the cost to society of losing the services of people who are forced into employment beneath their abilities. In money terms it is the same as the loss to the employee through his decline in earning power. The point of stating the cost in this way is simply to emphasize that underemployment, to use an economist's term, is at once an individual cost and a social cost.

We do not know with any precision how much the federal government has been spending on employment tests, let alone the outlays of other goverments and of private employers. Towering above a thicket of scrubby and rather miscellaneous data on the cost of federal programs stands one seemingly solid oak. In 1955 the Senate Committee on Post Office and Civil Service, through the staff of the Johnston subcommittee, pried out of almost all federal agencies figures on the cost of their personnel security operations for the fiscal year ending June 30, 1955. The major subtotals were these, and they mostly included investigative, administrative, and adjudicative costs:

Military departments—civilian, military, and contractor programs	$18,000,000
Atomic Energy Commission	9,700,000
All others	9,700,000
Total	$37,400,000

These estimates, as one committee staff member said, are surely "on the low side rather than on the high side." For example, the Air Force did not report administrative and adjudicative costs; the Army apparently did not include its share of the industrial security program, which could be substantial.[10] Further, though these estimates doubtless represented a conscientious attempt on the part of the reporting agencies, they do not always fit with other estimates. For example, the AEC Director of Security testified earlier in 1955 before Senator Humphrey's Government Operation subcommittee that the AEC spent on investigations in 1952, 1953, and 1954 fairly stable amounts averaging $12,800,-000 a year. As is so often the case in federal discourse, it does not appear whether the Director was referring to calendar years or fiscal years. The investigative component of the 1955 figure reported to the

10. See JOHNSTON HEARINGS, pp. 959, 963–4. Note that no figures are given for the CIA, and incomplete ones for the National Security Agency.

Johnston subcommittee was $8,700,000. Now it is quite possible that AEC hiring fell off by one-third in 1955. Whatever the explanation (and the AEC figures should be accurate, for they represent amounts charged to AEC by the Civil Service Commission and the FBI) this particular illustration warns against projecting the 1955 figures too readily.[11]

Another datum that gives some sense of costs is the average cost of a full field investigation. Over the years this figure has moved in the range from $200 to $250. A simple national-agency name check, which is all that is required in most nonsensitive cases, costs about $5.

With these unit costs and other data one can estimate the investigative costs of the loyalty program that ended in 1953 at about $40,000,-000. I have no basis for estimating administrative costs. The relatively few full field investigations made this program quite economical in comparison with the security programs.[12]

Of the major security programs, it seems reasonable to suggest a total for the AEC of around $100,000,000 since it started large-scale screening in 1947. The military departments had all their various programs going by 1950. The total spent through 1956 must be at least $150,000,000. The cost of applying E.O. 10450 to all other agencies, plus the security programs of some of them from 1950 to 1953, must be at least $50,000,000.

The grand total for ten years of major federal programs seems to be around 350 million dollars, and may be more. The current annual cost may be stabilized at a figure somewhat lower than the ten-year average. The employees' program has been on a current basis since mid-1955; and there have been other retardations of tempo. But it would be imprudent to assume stability in any phase of this subject, whether it is dollars or doctrines.

For state, local, and private programs I have nothing on which to

11. HUMPHREY HEARINGS, p. 293. While all AEC contractor employment increased in 1955 by 6600, construction employment (where the turnover is largest) decreased by 73 per cent to the lowest point (16,000) in five years. See AEC, Semiannual Report, *Major Activities in the Atomic Energy Programs, July–December 1955* (1956), pp. 108–9. On AEC manpower in all kinds of security work, see Gordon Dean, *Report on the Atom* (1953), p. 241.

12. BONTECOU, p. 149, discusses the costs of investigations under the loyalty program. See HUMPHREY HEARINGS, p. 236, for 1954 cost data on both national agency and full field investigations; p. 189 for Air Force cost of full field investigations; and p. 294 for FBI and CSC full field costs. Cf. Commission on Government Security, *Report* (1957), p. 436, stating that an FBI full field investigation costs almost $600. See also p. 637 on costs of hearings.

base even a guess; but it is fairly certain that the total outlays are in no way comparable to those of the national government. The programs are less intense and appear to cover only about half as many people.

As for the economic loss in excluding people from the exercise of their talents, it was suggested that this loss could theoretically be measured by the decline in earning power of such people. This measurement must remain theoretical for want of data; so we are thrown back on deductions and examples. A modest instance of successive downgrading in the employment of a putative Communist can be found in the case of one Shonick, whose recent history came to light when the municipal authorities of the District of Columbia proposed, because of his politics, to revoke his license as a dealer in second-hand pianos. He had been an economist in the Office of Price Administration, then a business agent for the Federal Workers Union, then a school teacher. When reports of his political reputation reached the school superintendent, he resigned and went into the piano business.[13] I do not suggest that Shonick ought to be restored to government employment. It may be that his history properly disqualifies him from federal service, union leadership, or teaching. But if he was competent at any of these occupations, he presumably was more usefully employed in them than in trading old pianos.

Suppose he was making more money in the piano business than in his genteel but poorly paid professional posts? Do we adhere to an economic approach? If we do, then whichever occupation pays the best is the place for Shonick to be. And so generally, if a chemist barred from government service makes as much money teaching, or more money in industry, a society that rewards services chiefly with dollars cannot, by its own measuring-stick, be the worse off. However, dollars are the chief but not the only way of valuing services. This is notably true in the higher levels of government, where in the name of patriotism or national need talents are commandeered at bargain prices. The advice that the administration got from J. R. Oppenheimer may not always have been palatable, but his brains are certainly worth more than the $50 a day he received as a consultant.

13. Shonick's license difficulty followed his invocation of the Fifth Amendment before the HUAC. See *Washington Post,* Nov. 15, Dec. 9, 1954. The subsequent recommendation of the examiner was to renew the license, on the ground that even if Shonick was a Communist the substantial hardship and possible constitutional aspects of the case outweighed the dangers inherent in his possession of a second-hand piano dealer's license. See ACLU, *Weekly Bulletin,* No. 1703, June 20, 1955 (mimeo.).

EFFECTS ON GOVERNMENT OPERATIONS

These uncertainties about costs bring out a distinction that is often overlooked between losses to the government and losses to the whole community. If employment tests reduce a nuclear physicist to selling aluminum storm windows, we can be fairly confident that everyone is worse off than before. If he is ruled ineligible for classified work, and stays in a university post, the government may be worse off; but that is no indication that the community is. Oppenheimer, now devoting himself to cosmic ray studies, may be spending his time more usefully than in advising on air defense. Observers who think that basic research is being dangerously neglected might well take this view. Unless the government cuts itself off from possessors of some skill which it uniquely requires and the rest of the community does not (for example, a man who can do nothing but design bombs; there have been such cases), the exclusion of any one individual from the classified world is not necessarily a social loss.

It is the multiplication of cases and the creation of an atmosphere of harassment and insecurity that harms government without any possible offsetting gains for other groups. One may argue that too much scientific energy is going into the government development of military equipment and not enough into theoretical research, but practically no one derives any satisfaction from the disruption of an important laboratory working on radar equipment. Yet that is what is responsibly reported to have happened at Fort Monmouth, the center of Army Signal Corps research, as the result of an onslaught by Senator McCarthy combined with a wave of security cases. Thirty-six employees were suspended for periods of many months, of whom eight were finally dismissed. A dozen more were made practically useless by having their access to classified material revoked. Since a number of those suspended were section chiefs, those sections were left headless, at least temporarily. Resignations by others who were not implicated are said to have increased, and replacements have become harder to find.

Fort Monmouth is the outstanding example of a scientific installation the efficiency of which was visibly impaired by exaggerated personnel security activities. The AEC decision against J. R. Oppenheimer, coming in the same year, sharpened the fears of many scientific leaders that intemperate security measures might jeopardize the entire fabric of relations between scientists and government, with especially dire results for military technology. No large-scale breakdown has occurred;

scientists generally have swallowed their resentments and continued to serve.[14]

The most important example of conspicuous damage to a government agency is the State Department, which, as the senior department in the executive branch, has responsibilities more weighty than those of any single laboratory. I cannot at this point even begin to elaborate the background of the Department's troubles. Among the trouble-brewing elements were: first, the great expansion of its staff with survivors of wartime agencies who included a number of vulnerable fellow travelers and party members; second, the Hiss case; third, the failure of our China policy and the resulting recriminations; fourth, the unwillingness of Secretary Acheson to give way to all the demands for scalps that were made upon him. The Department, beset by both Senator McCarthy and Senator McCarran, retreated slowly, and was routed utterly when the new administration installed Scott McLeod as chief security officer with broad powers. McLeod, generally supported by Secretary Dulles except in his attempt to block the confirmation of Charles Bohlen as Ambassador to Russia, laid about with such vigor that five prominent and respected veterans of the Foreign Service were impelled to make a serious protest that the integrity of the Service was being undermined. A remarkable journalistic investigation in *Collier's* magazine strongly confirmed their forebodings. In addition to heavy losses of expert officers (practically all the "old China hands" for example), recruitment into the Foreign Service has been lagging.[15]

14. For descriptions of the effects of the various investigations on Fort Monmouth see the report by the Scientists' Committee on Loyalty and Security, *The Fort Monmouth Security Investigations, August 1953–April 1954* (1954), and the article by the Committee, "Fort Monmouth One Year Later," BAS (1955), *11*:148. For examples of the scientific community's reaction to the Oppenheimer case see BAS (1954), *10*:188–91; and esp. Vannevar Bush, "If We Alienate Our Scientists," NYT Magazine (June 13, 1954), p. 9.

15. For example, not a single Junior Foreign Service Officer was appointed from 1952 to 1954. For the significance of this fact see Secretary of State's Public Committee on Personnel (Wriston Comm.), Report, *Toward a Stronger Foreign Service* (June 1954), pp. 6–7. There seems to be no doubt that the loyalty–security programs have been responsible for severe damage to the morale of the Foreign Service. See Senator Wiley's survey of 200 Foreign Service Officers in European posts, NYT, Jan. 6, 1955; Wriston Report, above, p. 4; Hans Morgenthau, "The Impact of the Loyalty–Security Measures on the State Department," BAS (1955), *11*:139–40; Charlotte Knight, "What Price Security," *Collier's* (July 9, 1954), p. 58; Letter to the Editor, signed by Norman Armour, Robert Woods Bliss, Joseph C. Grew, William Phillips, and G. Howland Shaw, all former holders of ambassadorial or other high diplomatic posts, NYT, Jan. 17, 1954

The most serious charge that is made with respect to the functioning of the Department has to do with the quality of reports and recommendations. Its officials have constantly to weigh alternative courses of action in the light of our conflict with communism. Some alternatives appear to be more anticommunist than others; but the others may in the long run, or even in the short run, strengthen the national interest. Our policy-makers should recommend and decide in accordance with their expert views of what will advance the national interest; but they are constrained—constrained by what the security officers may think is evidence of communist sympathies. Thus they may be led into wrong decisions, because the wrong decision carries the appearance of fervent anticommunism and cannot arouse the suspicions of the security staff. Similarly, the reporting of Foreign Service Officers should reflect only their dispassionate observations. These officers should not feel that their appraisals of communist movements will be judged by the security standards of a later period. Professional criticism by their peers they expect; but the hazard of suspicious analysis by security officers may lead to distorted reporting. Thus another falsifying element comes into decision-making. Our diplomatic missions have before them the example of John Paton Davies, who, after rebutting a series of direct accusations of disloyalty, was dismissed when a security board declared that his reporting and judgment on Chinese affairs were unreliable and indiscreet. The members of the board were all lacking in diplomatic experience.[16]

Similarly, the damaging inferences drawn in security cases from associations with suspected Communists puts diplomats to special hazard, and may incline them to avoid useful sources of information because the contact may later be used against them. This point was well made by Davies in his reply to the hearing board.

Probably every employee in a sensitive position now and again feels obliged to ask himself what the security staff will think of his record. Some people have a degree of fortitude and rectitude (or of pigheadedness and self-righteousness, depending on how you look at it) that makes them proof against such qualms. And there are fortunately many

(cf. John Foster Dulles' comments, NYT, Jan. 20, 1954). On the "China hands" see Ch. 15 below, n. 14.

16. For the texts of the Davies defense, the Dulles ouster statement, and the Davies reply see NYT, Nov. 6, 1954. Useful criticisms of the Davies case include Dean Acheson, *A Democrat Looks at His Party* (1955), pp. 131–4, and Editorial, *Harper's* (Jan. 1955), p. 20. See Ch. 15 below, p. 368, for further consideration of the Davies case.

decisions that do not lend themselves to an appraisal of what the security staff would take to be sufficiently anticommunist positions. But it is probable that the State Department is peculiarly vulnerable. Its officers have to deal with many international intangibles that are capable of later misinterpretation; at the same time they are the objects both of some public suspicion and of intense internal security surveillance.

There seems to be no way of knowing how much judgments have been warped by fear of reprisals. The process may be unconscious as well as unspoken. But unless one takes security standards as universal guides to right action, any distortion of judgment occasioned by them must be considered a detriment to the conduct of government.[17]

Outside these trouble spots in the federal government, general opinions on efficiency are about all we have, and they are contradictory. Critics of the programs often take it for granted that they must result in lowered morale and efficiency, wherever they are applied. Official defenders assert with equal confidence that (in the case of federal employees) morale improved with the knowledge that effective measures were being taken to weed out the unfit and the faithless.[18]

There is practically no evidence on the consequences of state, local, and private tests for the efficiency of the government or firm administering them. As a general observation, it can be noted that the inception and operation of tests must consume a great deal of legislative and executive energy. This is in addition to the manpower specifically allocated to carrying on the various programs; some suggestion of the resources so enlisted was made in the preceding section. What I have in mind here are the labors of legislative committees, and the burden on top executives who have to pass on out-of-the-ordinary cases and policies. In view of the recurrence and importance of employment tests, the

17. Another instance where McCarthy's forays, plus heavy-handed security decisions, certainly impaired the work of an agency is the hectic history of the International Information Administration around 1953. The best description of the havoc wrought is by the former deputy director of the agency, Martin Merson, in *The Private Diary of a Public Servant* (1955). See also James Rorty and Moshe Decter, *McCarthy and the Communists* (1954), pp. 19–38.

18. Weighty judgments that the programs have injured morale are expressed by the Task Force on Personnel and Civil Service of the (Hoover) Commission on Organization of the Executive Branch of the Government, *Report* (Feb. 1955), p. 121; by the American Assembly Report on *The Federal Government Service* (Oct. 10, 1954), p. 184; and by the ASS'N OF THE BAR, REPORT, p. 130. For the contrary view see Seth Richardson, "The Federal Employee Loyalty Program," *Columbia Law Rev.* (1951), *51:553.* Cf. Dillard Stokes, "How Insure Security in Government Service," *Commentary* (Jan. 1954), p. 25; Stouffer (n. 6 above), p. 225 (little public concern with this problem).

out-of-the-ordinary has become commonplace. The Atomic Energy Commission estimated in 1949 that perhaps one-third of all its meeting time had been concerned with personnel security matters.[19] This experience is surely not typical, but it illustrates the point. So does the complaint of a university president to the writer that two Fifth Amendment episodes in his faculty had each taken him away for weeks on end from other pressing duties. However, when public concern with loyalty and security problems runs high, such problems cease to be abnormal preoccupations for leaders with public responsibilities. The wise solution of those problems becomes part of their job. The exercise of leadership then becomes one of the costs of the programs; efficiency suffers only when the job is badly done.

GOALS AND GAINS

This chapter has focused on losses rather than on gains. The effects of employment tests so far considered have been largely unfavorable. This was entirely to be expected, since the chapter began with the impact on the employees whom the tests reject, and on those whom I characterized as the "walking wounded." As the discussion moved on to the effects on others, it was noted that both individuals and the community were injured to the extent that the operation of the programs inhibited lawful associations and discouraged freedom of the mind. Turning from these important but intangible considerations, we noted the available data on the costs of the tests in terms of money and manpower, and in the efficiency of government operations.

Practically all of this chapter, then, has amounted to a review of the social and economic costs of clearing some people and dismissing others. Little has been said about the costs of *not* dismissing them. A listing of undesirable effects, no matter how lengthy, is inconclusive until the desirable effects have been set off against it.

The gains from employment tests can be measured only in terms of their goals. And until we have a coherent view of what we are securing ourselves against, we cannot begin to estimate how successfully the job is being done. The fear that there were actual or potential traitors in our midst, notably in government, teaching, and defense industries, has spawned a vast system, or rather a cluster of systems, to try to

19. Joint Committee on Atomic Energy, Report, *Investigation into the United States Atomic Energy Commission* (1949), p. 85, from Gellhorn, *Security, Loyalty, and Science* (1950), p. 81.

detect those who might be traitors. I think it is fairly clear that this is a blunderbuss operation, that its reach extends to a large part of the labor force, and that its costs are high. Are the costs higher than need be? That depends on some serious problems of national security which Part II will examine. It also depends on the validity of employment tests aimed primarily at repressing disloyalty; these will be scrutinized in Part III.

The Russian-Communist Threat to National Security as a Basis for Employment Tests

8. Security by Achievement

THIS CHAPTER, and the following one, will try to do two things. One will be to show the chinks in our national armor; what an enemy can attempt to do, short of open war, to hinder and nullify efforts to make the country militarily strong and politically effective. The second will be to describe and evaluate the countermeasures, other than employment tests, that are available to prevent such injuries. The last three chapters of this Part will develop the proper role of employment tests, against this background of danger and of alternative responses to the danger.

To proceed in this way requires a sharper distinction between security tests and loyalty tests than some of the discussion so far may seem to warrant. It remains true that questions of loyalty supply most of the content of security cases. For the time being, however, our concern is not with the content of employment tests, but with trying to establish a rationale for them, a rationale based on considerations of national security.

In general, I take security programs to be chiefly concerned with Russia and communism as an external threat, resting ultimately on the military potential of the Soviet Union. In this respect the problem is not much different from that posed by Germany in World Wars I and II. I take loyalty programs to be directed not only against potential spies and traitors, but against communism as an internal, revolutionary, political movement. Here the fear is that a disloyal employee will use his position to advance a cause abhorrent to the majority of the American people. Loyalty programs may also express dislike for the employment in certain fields of people considered disloyal, regardless of their capabilities for harm. In practice it is often hard to tell which reasons explain a particular program; to a large extent the varying demands of security and loyalty overlap and coalesce. For purposes of analysis, however, these varying justifications will be treated separately.

Beyond question, the most compelling argument for some kinds of employment tests is that they are necessary for national survival. In this view, the United States is engaged in a bitter struggle to prevent the Soviet Union from attaining world domination, including eventual conquest of the United States. This is a struggle which may erupt into open war at any time. Thus it is to be expected that Russia, following the pattern of past enemies, will attempt to infiltrate large numbers of spies and saboteurs into the United States. In addition, there is the American Communist party which, at least in its disciplined core, is controlled by the Soviet Union. In the event of war the party could be expected to serve as a domestic fifth column, perhaps even to the extent of guerrilla operations in the manner of the Partisans and the Maquis in World War II. This, of course, is painting the picture darkly. Nevertheless, if this estimate is at all founded in fact, it provides strong justification for security programs designed to frustrate such results.[1]

To the extent that employment tests rest on grounds of national security, however, they ought to be limited to the reasonable needs of that security. This postulate leads to an examination of the components of "national security." To borrow a distinction popularized in discussions of atomic weapons policy, the concept of security can be broken down into two elements: "security by achievement" and "security by concealment." [2] Employment tests are said to introduce a third element —"security by exclusion." Security by achievement is the result of what we ourselves do to maintain a posture of strength against potential aggressors. It rests on such massive elements as a strong economy, a strong military–diplomatic position, and a strong morale. Security by concealment, on the other hand, is negative in purpose. It attempts to hide our plans, our weapons, and our weaknesses from unfriendly eyes. Both aspects of security are important and both can be endangered by an enemy underground. However, security by achievement is primary; without men and weapons in sufficient quantity, any other system of security is helpless to prevent aggression. Therefore threats to security by achievement will be examined first.

In theory at least, enemy agents can frustrate security by achievement in a number of ways. In view of the predominance of technological superiority in modern warfare, which represents what may be called crucial achievement, as distinguished from the mass achievement of high productivity and large armed forces, the most effective technique might be to disrupt and demoralize our research programs. The most extreme way of accomplishing this would be some judicious murders. Without resort to violence public denunciations of prominent scientists might

1. See Nathaniel Weyl, *The Battle against Disloyalty* (1951).
2. These phrases seem to have been first publicly used by Louis Ridenour in "Military Security and the Atom Bomb," *Fortune* (Nov. 1945), p. 170. This essay is still unexcelled in its lucid penetration of the limits of security by concealment.

also be effective by making them mistrusted. Equally desirable from a Communist's point of view would be creation of dissension and factional strife within the laboratories, in order to hinder recruitment, induce resignations, and distract attention from the objects of research. One reason for mentioning these latter possibilities is that employment tests may themselves contribute to the impairment of crucial achievement if they demoralize the scientific community and keep talented people out of weapon development.

In a period closer to actual conflict, interruption of critical industrial production would be the primary target. Here, too, attacks on morale can play a part, but the principal weapons would undoubtedly be physical stoppage through strikes and sabotage. Finally, if actual hostilities began, the underground would strike at such sensitive points as the communications and transportation industries and attempt to destroy production centers and stored supplies by fire and explosion.

The problem, however, is not to determine how much harm a fifth column could do but how much of the danger is attributable to risky employees. Here it is worth remembering that, though Moscow may support the trained agent, the ordinary Communist sympathizer must usually earn his own living. If he should attempt to obstruct national security by poor performance on the job, he faces dismissal and exposure, quite apart from any organized security program. Where there are objective standards of performance, whether in theoretical physics, typing, or ditch-digging, an employee is unlikely to botch his work unless the benefit to the enemy clearly outweighs the adverse consequences to himself. Realistic appraisal of employment tests, therefore, requires us to weigh not the total possibility of harm but the practical likelihood that employees in their employment will threaten security.

Sabotage

Physical sabotage is probably the most obvious technique by which an employee can endanger security by achievement. It can take two forms. Active sabotage destroys goods or facilities by such means as fire or explosives. Passive sabotage involves only intentional failure to perform one's work as expected. Some classic examples are the manufacture of defective ammunition and the failure to lubricate vital bearings. Passive sabotage is more difficult to detect; on the other hand, active sabotage achieves more dramatic results.[3]

3. In both world wars much of the sabotage on both sides was perpetrated by

Fire is probably the most effective method of sabotage from the employee's point of view. Because many plants are constructed from, or contain large quantities of, inflammable material, fire usually causes a maximum amount of destruction. In addition, arson is particularly easy to disguise as an accident. In some cases a well-placed cigarette might be enough to gut an entire building. Another device is the incendiary pencil, first used by the Germans in World War I. This handy gadget looks like a pen or automatic pencil and can be left on a workbench or in a jacket pocket without attracting attention. Inside the "pencil" the incendiary materials are kept separate by a piece of metal. The bomb is exploded by means of acid which eats through the metal divider. To eradicate incriminating clues, the case is made of magnesium which is completely consumed in the resulting blaze.

Employee-saboteurs, of course, may exploit a variety of other techniques. To knock out hard-to-replace facilities such as generators, dams, and bridges, explosives would probably be used. Similarly, time-bombs may be concealed on ships so that they explode at sea. Expensive machinery can be crippled by putting sand or emery in the bearings. In recent years, cutting electric cables has been a favorite device of amateur saboteurs. Of course there are numberless ways of producing defective goods.

While the potential danger from sabotage by insiders is considerable, much of the damage can be avoided by proper plant protection. Even though fire is the most damaging form of sabotage, it is relatively easy to control. Fire-proof construction, sprinkler systems, and dispersion of plants can keep destruction to a minimum. Frequent patrols can catch fires before they are well started. Similarly, fencing and lighting critical facilities can reduce the chance of after-hours tampering. Vigilant gate guards make it hazardous to smuggle in explosives. Finally, by restricting the movement of personnel within the plant, the number of possible culprits can be narrowed sufficiently to create a high probability of catching the saboteur.[4]

The risk of detection is probably the greatest deterrent to sabotage.

---

outsiders rather than employees; nevertheless Fiodore Wozniak successfully set off the Kingsland explosion of 1917 from his workbench; see Weyl (n. 1 above), pp. 119–20.

4. For examples of sabotage see Weyl, n. 1 above. On counter-measures, see bibliography in Univ. of California Bur. of Public Admin., *Sabotage and its Prevention in Wartime,* ed. Dorothy Tompkins (1951). That elaborate precautions may still be of no effect is shown by the destruction of a General Motors Hydra-

In this respect the employee is at a great disadvantage, as compared to the hit-and-run guerrilla. The use of explosives, for example, could hardly be disguised as an accident. In these troubled times, suspicion of sabotage would stir up a maximum of police activity, accompanied by scientific methods of investigation. Moreover, the employee-saboteur would have to sit quietly while the net closed in around him; to flee would immediately arouse suspicion. The result is that the police could use interrogation and narrow the circle of suspects to a degree impossible when the saboteur strikes from the outside.

The saboteur who is caught faces severe criminal sanctions. Under present cold war conditions, the most comprehensive provisions are found in the federal antisabotage laws, 18 U. S. Code Sections 2151–6. The heart of the statute, for present purposes, is in sections 2153 and 2154, which deal with wartime sabotage but which are in effect during the current emergency. Section 2153 prohibits willful injury or destruction of any material or facilities which can reasonably be used in the conduct of a war; section 2154 forbids making such goods or facilities in a defective manner. Under either section it is unnecessary for the government to prove a specific intent to injure the national defense; the prosecution need only show that the defendant had reason to believe his actions would obstruct or interfere with the defense effort. The maximum penalty is thirty years imprisonment, plus a $10,000 fine, and attempts and conspiracies are punishable with the same severity as successful sabotage.

If additional circumstances can be shown, the saboteur may be liable under other legislation as well. There are a number of federal statutes covering willful damage to such specific items as ships, communication lines, and government property. If murder or arson can be proved, the saboteur faces further punishment under state criminal law.

Once hostilities have begun, still further provisions may be brought into play. Fifteen states have the Model Sabotage Prevention Act, which is effective only in wartime. Not only does it furnish coverage similar to that in the federal statute, including attempts and conspiracies, but it provides for detention of suspects pending investigation and for restricting streets which border on vital plants.[5]

Matic plant by fire—see *Fortune* (Nov. 1953), p. 132—and by the embarrassing spectacle of common burglars being able to "crack" a vault and steal $46,500 from the heavily guarded Sandia atomic weapons base in New Mexico (NYT, Oct. 25, 1955).

5. An extensive discussion of the Model Act is Sam B. Warner, "The Model

Another consequence of actual war is that the saboteur may become subject to a treason charge. This is a difficult crime to prove, since the Constitution requires the testimony of two witnesses to the same overt act, or a confession in open court, in order to obtain a conviction. Thus well-established techniques of proving guilt by circumstantial evidence, such as fingerprints or chemical analysis, are useless without the additional testimony of eyewitnesses to some treasonable act. Nevertheless, if a case can be established the maximum penalty is death.[6]

Even though criminal provisions against sabotage are adequate in their coverage and severity, they are probably insufficient in themselves to prevent damage from occurring. The criminal law is no deterrent to an employee with a fanatical disregard of consequences.

Another general weakness of criminal sanctions—that they operate only after the event—is somewhat mitigated by the doctrine of conspiracy. For example, if more than one person is involved in a plan to commit sabotage and if some overt act, such as the purchase of explosives, has been taken in furtherance of the scheme, the plot can be prosecuted as a conspiracy even though the sabotage has never actually been attempted.[7] In theory, therefore, criminal prosecutions can be brought to forestall any designs that are really dangerous. But the difficulty lies in discovering the conspiracy in time. Unless one of the conspirators betrays his comrades, or a chance slip reveals the existence of the plan, the authorities would be forewarned only through the use of planted spies or constant surveillance. Countermeasures of this sort against sabotage are presumably widely practiced; but we know too little

Sabotage Prevention Act," *Harvard Law Rev.* (1941), *54*:602. For an attack on the Act see Pressman, Leider, and Cammer, "Sabotage and National Defense," ibid., p. 632. Statutory references for states that adopted the Act are in FUND DIGEST, pp. 257–65. Its constitutionality was upheld in People v. Gordon, 62 Cal. App. 2d 268, 144 P. 2d 662 (1944), affirming a conviction of sabotage for cutting the wing surface of an Air Force training plane. The Model Act is reproduced in the Warner article and in FUND DIGEST. The federal statutes were broadened in 1954; see 62 Stat. 799 (1948), 68 Stat. 1216 (1954)

6. Compare Cramer v. U.S., 325 U.S. 1 (1945), with Haupt v. U.S., 330 U.S. 631 (1947), on the inferences that can be drawn as to whether an act, to which the two witnesses testify, gave aid and comfort to the enemy. The necessary intent of adhering to the enemy may be established circumstantially. The definitive study (up to the Haupt case) is Willard Hurst, "Treason in the United States," *Harvard Law Rev.* (1945), *58*:226, 395, 806.

7. On the long reach of the federal conspiracy statute, 18 U.S.C. § 2384, see Krulewitch v. U.S., 336 U.S. 440 (1949); Note, "The Conspiracy Dilemma," *Harvard Law Rev.* (1948), *62*:276.

about their effectiveness to assume that they can do the whole preventive job.

The most conspicuously successful use of sabotage in connection with modern warfare was the series of outrages that the Germans committed in this country both before and after our entry into World War I, such as the Black Tom explosion and the destruction of ships by time bombs. At that time all our security arrangements reflected in their modest ineptitude the long period of peace which the country had experienced. In World War II there appears to have been almost no sabotage within the United States of known enemy origin. The amount of destruction accomplished in occupied countries in World War II has little relevance to this inquiry; a hostile population creates a formidable obstacle to prevention and detection.[8]

Now that the surreptitious introduction and assembly of atom bombs is said to be possible, a horrid new dimension has been added; sabotage has come a long way from throwing wooden shoes into machinery. But atom bombs, though more deadly, are easier to detect than incendiary devices. The defenses that were so effective in World War II still seem valid. In summary, these defenses are, first, physical protective measures at key plants and facilities; second, countermeasures by intelligence agencies; third, criminal deterrents; and, fourth, employment tests. The last, I should reiterate, are effective for a limited purpose: thwarting sabotage by insiders. Employment programs are not going to apprehend the man who leaves an exceptionally heavy suitcase in Grand Central terminal which in due course blows up most of midtown New York.

POLITICAL STRIKES

If Communist domination of key unions could be maintained, the resulting danger to security by achievement might exceed the threat of sabotage. Strikes and slowdowns may disrupt production just as effectively, and are less vulnerable to stern countermeasures. What is usually adduced as the classic example of a politically motivated strike is the one in the Allis-Chalmers plant near Milwaukee, Wisconsin, in 1941.

8. "The only reported sabotage case that has been discovered in which there has been a clearly identifiable subversive motive is that of a Nazi saboteur whose conviction was affirmed in Roedel v. United States, 145 F. 2d 819 (9th Cir. 1944)." FUND DIGEST, p. 9. According to Don Whitehead, *The FBI Story* (1956), p. 206, no case of "enemy-directed sabotage" was found by the FBI in World War II.

In this plant the union (which had encountered great management hostility) had been Communist-dominated from its beginning. After the Hitler-Stalin nonaggression pact, when Allis-Chalmers was busy making war materials for Great Britain and the United States, Eugene Dennis allegedly gave orders to Harold Christoffel, union president, to start a strike. The resulting stoppage lasted for 76 days and was marked by considerable violence on the picket line. Even such exhortations as telegrams to each employee, sent by Navy Secretary Knox and General William Knudsen, the Army's production expert, were unable to persuade the workers to return to their jobs. The strike ended only after Germany invaded Russia. Yet it has been estimated that there were only about fifty Communists among the 12,000 workers at the time this strike was engineered.

Despite their small numbers, however, the Communists exercised rigid control within the union. At the time of a Congressional investigation in 1947, all of the officers and most of the shop stewards were alleged to be Communists. In part their support rested on carefully nurtured grievances and on antagonism toward the management. It is not at all unusual for an oligarchy to dominate a union. Christoffel's band, however, relied to an unusual extent on force and fraud. Discipline was maintained through the "flying squadron" or "goon squad," which consisted of about thirty toughs, many of whom were hired for the purpose. Another discouragement to opposition was the "nerve" treatment: anonymous threatening telephone calls, dead rats hidden in lunch boxes, and similar devices. Members who criticized the leadership in public were tried for "conduct unbecoming a union member" and were fined or expelled, thus facing loss of their jobs under the "maintenance of membership" clause in the union contract.

To ensure control of elections, the officers hand-picked the elections committee by postponing selection until late at night when most of the membership had left the meeting. In addition to this well-worn strategem, elections were rigged to such an extent that in the 1941 strike vote the Wisconsin Labor Board found some 2000 fraudulent ballots had been cast—a fact later admitted by the union. Moreover, many members were disfranchised on tenuous technical grounds.[9]

9. For an extended discussion of the Allis-Chalmers strike see House Comm. on Education and Labor, Hearings, *Amendment to the National Labor Relations Act* (1947), pp. 1335–1487, 1973–2142, 3603–23; HUAC, Hearings, *Communism in Labor Unions in the United States* (1947). Max Kampelman, *The Communist Party vs. the CIO* (1957), pp. 25–6, describes other Communist-led strikes of the same period.

There are unhappily other like episodes in trade union history that cannot be blamed on Communists. The point here is the effectiveness, in a political setting, of such tactics. The rank and file at Allis-Chalmers were either intimidated or apathetic. The UAW International wouldn't or couldn't take action. The company could not interfere because of the inhibitions of the Wagner Act. The employees would not have welcomed its intervention in any case. By default the Communists were left in undisturbed control.

Today, of course, the situation is much changed. Many unions, as we know, have purged Communists from leadership positions. By 1956 there were no more than four or five unions in defense industries which were generally considered "Communist-dominated." And all Communist-dominated unions together controlled less than one per cent of the membership in organized labor. The remaining Communist-led unions nevertheless do pose a threat to security by achievement. Communist-dominated unions still represent some workers in such important producers as Westinghouse, General Electric, Anaconda, Kennecott, and Phelps-Dodge.[10] A pessimistic estimate of their capabilities would take the following form. Prolonged and bitter strikes in these plants could shut down substantial portions of American industrial potential. Without an organized anticommunist resistance within the union, there would be very little the individual worker could do to prevent such a strike. Presumably the issue would be framed in economic terms, and in such cases it is customary for the union membership to vote a strike in order to give the officers bargaining power. Once the strike has been called, the worker has little choice but to stay out. Otherwise he suffers the obloquy of being a scab, and risks manhandling on the picket line or attacks at home. While such violence is unquestionably illegal, the Allis-Chalmers strike indicates that a determined communist minority will brave contempt citations and criminal prosecution in order to accomplish its objectives.

Once a strike has started, government countermeasures are not immediately effective. The most promising weapon today is the eighty-day injunction provision of the Taft-Hartley Act. Under this procedure, if the president finds that a strike imperils the national health or safety, he may, after receiving a report from a special fact-finding board, direct the Attorney General to seek an injunction against the strike. If the district court also finds that the strike affects at least a "substantial

10. See *Fortune* (March 1956), pp. 206–8, and, in general, Kampelman, n. 9 above.

part" of an industry engaged in interstate or foreign commerce and that it will "imperil the national health or safety," the court may issue the injunction. If the dispute has not been settled at the end of sixty days, the president's fact-finding board must issue a report summarizing the positions of the parties and publicizing the employer's last offer of settlement. On the basis of this report the NLRB then holds a back-to-work vote within the next fifteen days. However, if this still does not result in a settlement, the injunction must be dissolved on the expiration of eighty days.[11]

If properly handled, this procedure conceivably could prevent a political strike. It seems doubtful whether any union could successfully defy the injunction itself. And while the union would be free to strike at the end of the eighty days, a clear-cut finding by the board of inquiry that the union was Communist-dominated and the strike called for political purposes might easily result in a back-to-work vote by the rank and file. Certainly such a finding would, at least in a time of crisis, turn public opinion strongly against the strikers.

In practice, however, the issues would seldom be so clear-cut. Skillful union leaders could raise economic issues with little difficulty. And conclusive evidence of actual Communist domination may be difficult to obtain. Moreover, workers in the few remaining communist unions are doubtless well aware of the existing charges. The repetition of these charges in the form of findings by a fact-finding board might not disturb them unduly.

Aside from this Taft-Hartley procedure for injunctions in strikes creating a danger to "national safety," there seem to be no other direct legal means for stopping a political strike. Of course, if public opinion is sufficiently inflamed against the strikers, sanctions will be improvised. Incidents of violence can be made the occasion for mobilizing the police or the militia against the strikers. A judge will be found who will issue an injunction, and enforce it with contempt citations. The leaders of the strike can be arrested, for breach of the peace, or, as in 1917–18, for utterances that are said to transgress a section of the Espionage Act discussed in the next section of this chapter. All these devices for breaking an unpopular strike are familiar from trade union history. But they do not keep the political strike from leaving wounds. The atmosphere of public hostility that permits strong measures to be taken may only strengthen the unity of the strikers with their disloyal leaders. Defiance of authority, under such circumstances, may become a badge of soli-

11. 61 Stat. 155–6 (1947), 29 U.S.C. §§ 176–80.

darity. In the Allis-Chalmers strike the Wisconsin Labor Board had procured an injunction against mass picketing; yet the union went ahead with mass picketing. From the standpoint of a communist labor leader, the risks of flouting the law are only skirmishes in the class war. If the workers get their heads cracked by the police, that will just bring them more quickly to a revolutionary mood.

The threat of political strikes envelops the whole issue of control of communism in trade unions. As exemplified by the Allis-Chalmers' episode, it is what chiefly impressed the Supreme Court as a justification for the Taft-Hartley non-Communist oath. And, when the oath proved to be inadequate, Congress chose another untried and dangerous device, the proscriptions of "Communist-infiltrated organizations."

It is worth emphasizing that the political strike is much more a matter of conjectural possibility than of threatened reality. When our productive effort is geared to a long-range augmentation of our military capacity, such strikes can be damaging, but they are not crippling; only when the country is nearly or actually at war do they become intolerable. The difficulties of controlling them, which have been fully canvassed, give the subject an interest beyond its importance. The most direct form of control curtails the right to strike. Except for the cooling-off mechanism of the Taft-Hartley Act, this approach has been wisely avoided. The right to strike for what its members consider legitimate objectives is indispensable to a free labor movement, and, many people would say, to a free society. The measures that have been taken include employment tests—on union leaders through the Taft-Hartley oath, on rank-and-file members if the union is found to be "Communist-infiltrated." These measures may be effective, but it is doubtful if they are necessary or desirable. The straight road to a loyal labor movement has been taken by the unions themselves. They have for the most part, without government coercion, rejected Communist leadership. The pockets that remain do not threaten the national security seriously or immediately enough to warrant government intervention.

PROPAGANDA

In the modern world a nation's military potential may conceivably be undermined as effectively by propaganda as by actual physical damage. One method is to weaken military and civilian morale. In the United States this might be done by playing on the grievances of minority groups, or by attempting to instill a panicky fear of modern weapons such as the hydrogen bomb or bacteriological warfare. Another technique is to use propaganda to influence national policy. A communist propaganda line might attempt to persuade the United States that it should convince the world of its peaceful intentions by relinquishing foreign bases and reducing military preparations without insisting on similar disarmament by the other side.

Assuming that such propaganda, if successful, could be highly damaging to security by achievement, how much danger is there that the American people today would be taken in? Successful propaganda requires a receptive audience already predisposed toward the propagandist's viewpoint. The prevailing mood in the United States today is hardly inclined toward pro-Soviet opinion. Moreover, even propaganda that is not obviously of communist origin can best be neutralized by counterpropaganda or by exposure to the communist motivation of the author. Open communist propaganda activity on the part of an employee is self-defeating, since it normally results in loss of audience or loss of employment or both.

In addition to these informal pressures, there are legal sanctions against the more blatant forms of propaganda. These controls operate in two directions: to force disclosure of the source of certain types of propaganda, and to punish statements which are untrue. Under the Foreign Agents Registration Act, for example, persons who are engaged in publishing, writing, broadcasting, or similar means of communication and are acting as agents of a foreign principal must register with the Attorney General. Any political propaganda put out by such agents must be clearly labeled as to its source. The Internal Security Act of 1950 establishes a similar scheme for registration of "Communist-action" and "Communist-front" organizations and for labeling of their propaganda.

The other approach to the propaganda problem is found in a section of the Espionage Act that punishes the willful making of false statements in time of war where there is a general intent to promote the success of the enemy or to interfere with the operation of the armed forces.

The major limitation on the application of this section is that its operation is apparently restricted to wartime. However, the section is among those war powers which have been extended and are (in 1957) still in effect.[12]

12. The false statements section of the Espionage Act of 1917, 40 Stat. 219, § 3 (1917), was repealed by 62 Stat. 862 (1948), but its substance is retained in 62 Stat. 811 (1948), 18 U.S.C. § 2388; see FUND DIGEST, pp. 188–90. See also the

Strict enforcement of either type of statute might conceivably create grave difficulties for communist propagandists. It would also create grave difficulties for the survival of the First Amendment to the Constitution. Both compulsory registration and punishment of "false" statements encroach deeply on traditional freedom of opinion and expression.

Attempts to force disclosure of source, for example, may seem salutary, and a sincere case can be made for this principle by supporters of free speech and thought. If the strength of a statement depends on who says it, then, they argue, by all means let us know who the speaker is. The self-same statement—for example, "America should pull out of NATO"—may be considered respectable when spoken by a United States Senator, and dangerous when spoken by a communist sympathizer. It does not follow that coercive measures are desirable to label the latter. Among other reasons, it is too easy to work backward and infer communist sympathy from the content of the very statement it is proposed to label. Opinions independently conceived and honestly expressed can be interpreted, depending on who does the interpreting, as fitting squarely within the current communist propaganda line. Then it is an easy step to infer that their author must be a Communist. This sort of hasty or malicious imputation of bad motives is commonplace. Putting legal sanctions behind it is full of danger. The Foreign Agents Registration Act was confined to persons whose relationship to their foreign principal was objectively determinable. The Internal Security Act, however, includes among its criteria the loose test of similarity of "line" just discussed.

The punishment of "false" statements that are considered harmful to the national interest has a similar air of specious plausibility about it. Its attraction disappears when we consider that this provision of the Espionage Act was the foundation for many of the prosecutions in World War I that, at least since Professor Chafee excoriated them in his *Free Speech in the United States,* have been considered a national disgrace. The most trivially disparaging remarks about the war effort were made the basis for jail sentences. This provision was administered much more cautiously in World War II.[13]

Foreign Agents Registration Act of 1938, esp. 22 U.S.C. §§ 611–14, and the Internal Security Act of 1950, 50 U.S.C. § 786 (registration provision) and § 789 (propaganda provision).

13. See Chafee (1941 edition), ch. 2. The only important World War II case relying on the "false statements" provision is U.S. v. Pelley, 132 F. 2d 170 (7th

A brief survey of punitive measures does not suggest that they have much merit as a weapon against propaganda. The use of employment tests for this purpose has the same defect: whatever they do to bolster national security seems strongly offset by their harmful effect on free expression. Employment tests are directed at people who might spread harmful propaganda—teachers, writers, and workers in the media of mass communication. These people undoubtedly have an impact on public attitudes. But they can hardly, *in the present climate of opinion,* inflict any substantial damage to our military potential without being exposed and discredited. Whether there are valid loyalty grounds not immediately related to security for subjecting these groups to some sort of employment test is a question reserved for Part III.

We should never forget that "propaganda" is usually just a disparaging way of describing an opponent's ideas. So, when we talk about punishing propagandists, or when we erect employment tests against potential propagandists, we are saying that the nation's security is imminently threatened by the expression of ideas. It is remarkable that the public can sometimes have so little confidence in its own integrity.

Pro-Soviet Policy Making

A fourth technique by which Communist employees might undermine security by achievement is directly related to employment and to employment tests. It requires the adherence of employees who will use their positions to foster policies disadvantageous to the United States and favorable to Russia. This activity is effectively restricted to those few employees, mostly in the federal government, who are in a position, either through their own decisions or through recommendations to superiors, to establish or alter policy on a large scale.

The possibility that pro-communist policy-making existed on a large scale during the nineteen-thirties and forties has been extensively investigated by congressional committees. It has been variously hypothesized that employees of the NLRB used their strategic position on the Board to entrench communist unions in American industry; that Alger Hiss urged President Roosevelt to make disastrous concessions at Yalta; and that secret agents in the Far Eastern Division of the State Department stymied support for Chiang Kai-shek during the Chinese civil war. The

Cir. 1942). There were a number of successful treason prosecutions after the war of Americans who carried on propaganda activities for Axis powers, e.g. D'Aquino v. U.S., 192 F. 2d 338 (9th Cir. 1951) ("Tokyo Rose").

existing evidence is quite inconclusive that the policy recommendations of suspected or proved Communists differed substantially from those of others whose loyalty is unquestioned. Nevertheless, for purposes of argument it can be conceded that during this period there were Communist agents or sympathizers in policy-making positions and that they did what they could to foster Soviet objectives.

Today, of course, the situation has radically changed, and would be changed even if security programs were nonexistent. A Communist agent could do relatively little policy-making which would be of direct assistance to the Soviet without exposing himself. With a high degree of subtlety and indirection, however, such opportunities conceivably might arise. One technique could take the form of semisabotage. For example, Senator McCarthy once charged (entirely without evidence, as it developed) that engineers in the Voice of America intentionally planned to locate transmitters in places from which it was almost impossible to reach the intended audience. Similarly, an employee of the Defense Department might urge adoption of a weapon which he knew to be ineffective. In a different field, State Department experts conceivably could argue against giving military aid to a country which the Communists intended to take over, perhaps even raising the deceptive objection that the country's government was too soft toward communism. Finally, carrying a nationalistic approach to an extreme, a skillful agent could block advantageous diplomatic or economic negotiations by intransigently taking a position unduly favorable to the United States. Settlement of the Iranian oil dispute, for example, might effectively have been prevented by demanding terms for the American companies which none of the other parties could reasonably be expected to accept. And if such "wrecking" tactics were ever questioned, the employee could claim—probably with success—that at most he was overzealously patriotic.[14]

All this borders on the fantastic, but it may create real fears on the part of security-conscious department heads. In many areas of executive action, the side of national interest in an open question of policy is not immediately apparent. Division chiefs and department heads must rely on the best judgment of informed subordinates. They want

14. Hans Morgenthau in "The Impact of the Loyalty–Security Measures on the State Department," BAS (1955), *11*:134, argues persuasively that the formation of foreign policy is so diffuse that "no one foreign agent, however highly placed, could deflect the foreign policy of the United States." On the Voice of America transmitters see James Rorty and Moshe Decter, *McCarthy and the Communists* (1954), pp. 24–5.

assurance that this judgment is exercised free from any allegiance toward a foreign power or a rejected ideology.

Policy risks of this type are one area, at least, where there seems to be no substitute for some form of employment screening. Although pro-Soviet decision-making would fall in the general realm of treason, there appears to be no criminal sanction available against the type of behavior conjectured here. Moreover criminal prosecutions of this type would be highly undesirable. They could easily open the way to the practice of proscribing the authors of unsuccessful policies, solely on the ground that they were unsuccessful. Finally, criminal action would normally not be available until after the damage had been done.

CONCLUSIONS

The four major areas of danger to security by achievement, before the bombs start falling, are sabotage, political strikes, propaganda, and pro-Soviet policy-making. I find no objection to a thorough barrage of countermeasures against sabotage, including employment tests to the extent that they are fair and effective. No competing values are at stake. The control of political strikes and propaganda, however, is less clear-cut. When is a strike subversive, or when will it be so labeled in order to discredit its supporters? When is propaganda subversive; when is it simply communication of a controversial position? The formulation of either employment tests or of alternative sanctions in these areas challenges freedom of association and freedom of expression. Covert pro-Soviet policy-making is also a slippery charge to make; every mistake of judgment is open to pitiless hindsight and twisted suspicions of treason. It is possible, however, to contemplate the real dangers from treacherous officials without imagining universal conspiracies led by President Roosevelt and General George Marshall. Against the real dangers discreet employment tests are probably the only remedy. Thus we are recalled to the main inquiry: how far can security by exclusion bolster the security of achievement?

One general qualification. I have rested a good deal of argument in this chapter on the temper of the times. An aroused public opinion, I have argued, offers little scope for communist strikes, for communist propaganda, or for communist policy formation. Suppose one confronted these formidable ogres instead: a firm communist grip on the labor movement; the mass media infested with communist journalists; a hundred secret Communists among the top thousand government officials.

There are some people, of course, to whom this is an accurate appraisal
of the situation; I leave them to Westbrook Pegler. If this were a book
about France, one would have to take such possibilities into account.
If it had been written in 1937, with the clairvoyance that only a few
anti-Communists then possessed (as they often remind us), one who
could foresee the cold war might have taken a dark view of the situation
around him. But the time is not 1937, nor the place France. It is the
United States in the 1950's, suspicious and alarmed, but also strong
and alert. The suspicions and alarms generate repression. We are immersed here in the pros and cons of repression for the sake of security.
To ignore the elements of strength and alertness would be to ignore the
real foundations of security.

9. Security by Concealment

UP TO THIS POINT Part II has been concerned with the question of how pro-Communist employees could interfere with our own ability to wage war. In the popular mind, however, the major threat from disloyal employees is the danger that they will turn over official secrets to Soviet intelligence. In part this belief rests on the questionable assumption that an extremely important part of our military-diplomatic strength rests on secret weapons. But of even greater importance is the fact that espionage is the political crime *par excellence* for office-holders. They know the secrets, and transmitting them secretly is consistent with staying in office, while sabotage and other treasonable behavior are more likely to be detected.

Secrecy—security by concealment—is important only as it reduces the enemy's military potential relative to our own; of itself it cannot add one soldier or one gun to our defense. What secrecy does is to prevent an enemy from using his strength to maximum advantage. Not knowing our plans and capabilities, he must prepare for the worst, thus dispersing his forces and curtailing his own ability to strike. Moreover, in the special case of secret weapons, such as long-range missiles, concealment could protect the United States from reprisal by similar weapons—at least until it turned out that the Russians had developed them sooner and better.

There has been a tremendous volume of discussion about the importance of successful concealment and about the dire consequences of failure. Against this is posed a massive body of opinion that concealment may hinder achievement and that basic scientific discoveries cannot be kept secret. Furthermore, since espionage is popularly considered the most glamorous of the hazards to internal security, it is the most productive of shallow and excited journalism. Resisting the temptation to settle down with a good spy story, I shall economize in this chapter and present only a summary appraisal of the concealment issue.

CLASSIFIED INFORMATION

In order to talk meaningfully about the ways in which employees can endanger security by concealment, the system through which information becomes officially secret should first be examined. The authority to create secrets at present stems from two principal sources: President Eisenhower's Executive Order No. 10501, dated November 5, 1953, and the Atomic Energy Act of 1946 as amended in 1954. The executive order covers information concerning the national defense, and sets up uniform procedures by which such information is to be protected by the executive departments. The order establishes three categories of secret information: "Top Secret," "Secret," and "Confidential"; no other classifications are authorized. The category of "Top Secret" is reserved for information requiring the highest degree of protection, where "unauthorized disclosure . . . could result in exceptionally grave danger to the nation." For use of the "Secret" classification the criterion is "serious damage to the nation." All other information, disclosure of which would be "prejudicial to the defense interests of the nation," is to be classified "Confidential." Authority to make any of these classifications is limited to certain designated officials.

What are the consequences of classification? Perhaps the most important is restricted access to the information. No one is allowed to use, handle, or even know about classified documents or objects unless he is specifically authorized. Authorization, in turn, is confined to those who need to know the information to carry out their official duties—this on the common sense theory that the fewer persons who know the secrets, the less chance that they will be revealed. To obtain this authorization, the employee must first have clearance for the highest level of information to which he may have access. In practical terms, this means that security officers investigate his background in a manner similar to that described in the earlier chapters of this book. The extent of the inquiry varies with the level of clearance required—ranging from a simple file check for Confidential to a full field investigation for Top Secret.

To enforce these secrecy regulations, a number of physical precautions must be followed. Classified documents are stamped with the appropriate classification in red letters on the top and bottom of the page. When not in actual use, classified material must be locked up. Custodians of documents must keep a careful record of each copy of classified material and must obtain receipts for all material leaving their hands. Similar precautions are followed in transmission and destruction of classified material.[1]

1. See, in general, E.O. 10501, *Fed. Reg.* (1953), *18*:7049; Commission on Government Security, *Report* (1957), pp. 151–71.

The president's executive order does not apply in the field of atomic energy. Instead the pattern of secrecy is prescribed by the Atomic Energy Act. In general the same type of security precautions prevail. But under the Atomic Energy Act, *all* information concerning "(1) design, manufacture, or utilization of atomic weapons; (2) the production of special nuclear material, or (3) the use of special nuclear material in the production of energy" is "Restricted Data," and thus an official secret, unless the AEC has declassified the information. Furthermore, the AEC like other agencies relies on the principle of "compartmentalization" to ensure that secrets will not be dispersed more than "need to know" requires. Employees of one laboratory may be told nothing of the work going on in other laboratories, or sometimes even in other buildings in the same installation. Similarly, scientists are not supposed to discuss their work with anyone outside their immediate team. Thus it is hoped that even if a disloyal or indiscreet scientist should slip through all the security checks, he could not learn enough by himself to compromise the program seriously.[2]

The elaborate web of secrecy set up by these two authorities is not without its disadvantages. Many prominent scientists have criticized the restrictions surrounding research, particularly the principle of compartmentalization, as preventing the cross-fertilization of ideas and discoveries in different fields which they feel is necessary to scientific progress.[3] Other critics have complained that the power to classify may be, and sometimes is, used to cover up mistakes, inefficiency and even malfeasance within the government departments.[4] Finally, apart from these more serious objections, the mere administrative burden of stamps, clearances, safes, and receipts must inevitably hamper efficiency and increase expenses, both for the government and for private companies

2. The quoted portion of the Atomic Energy Act of 1954 is from 68 Stat. 924 (1954), 42 U.S.C. § 2014(r). See also 68 Stat. 940–3 (1954), 42 U.S.C. §§ 2161–6, and Herbert Marks and George Trowbridge, "Control of Information under the Atomic Energy Act of 1954," BAS (1955), *11*:128. On the secrecy provisions of the Atomic Energy Act of 1946 see Walter Gellhorn, *Security, Loyalty, and Science* (1950), pp. 19–27, and John Palfrey, "The Problem of Secrecy," ANNALS (1953), *290*:90.

3. See Gellhorn (n. 2 above), esp. ch. 2; Edward Shils, *The Torment of Secrecy* (1956), ch. 7; Ralph Lapp, *The New Force* (1953), ch. 11; Lloyd Berkner, "Is Secrecy Effective?" BAS (1955), *11*:62; and L. V. Nordheim, "Fear and Information," BAS (1954), *10*:342.

4. See House Comm. on Government Operations, Subcomm. Hearings, *Availability of Information from Federal Departments and Agencies* (1955–7), esp. Part I; Allen Raymond, *A Report* [to ACLU] *on the Denial to the American Press of Access to Information in the Federal Government* (Oct. 1955).

which hold contracts to build items of a classified nature. Despite these considerable inconveniences, however, both the precarious international situation and the public temper will probably require that a substantial amount of our defense activity be kept under secrecy regulations for some time to come.

LEAKS

Once information has been properly classified, the security officer's most vexing problem is to prevent its unauthorized disclosure. Of course there is always a slight chance that some cloak-and-dagger international spy will slip in during the night and blow open the safe. But the principal danger is from those who already know the secrets. On one side, a trusted employee may turn out to be an espionage agent. On the other, perfectly patriotic Americans, either deliberately or through careless-ness, may "leak" secret information to the public. On one occasion, for example, two Congressmen on the Armed Services Committee emerged from a secret session and told newsmen how many operational B-36's the United States had at that moment—information for which the Krem-lin would doubtless have paid thousands of dollars.

Intentional leaks may stem from a multitude of causes. But probably the most common reason for revealing classified information is dissatis-faction with policies or operations within the employee's department. Thus an employee who felt that the personnel security program was not moving fast enough turned over classified reports to Senator McCarthy. Similarly a Pentagon general, outvoted on a matter of weapons policy, may try to take his case to the people by leaking his objections to a newsman. Analogous situations can be imagined in other military de-partments, or in the State Department and other important policy-making agencies.[5]

Though the intentional leak may be a political device of considerable importance, it is probably not an effective technique for subversive assistance to Russia. In the first place, while the information is com-promised, the authorities know it has been released and how much has been released, so that at least some action can be taken to repair

5. See Elmer Davis, "Security and the News," *Pub. Admin. Rev.* (1952), *12*:85 (B-36 episode, particularly); NYT, Nov. 4, 1952 (McCarthy informant exposed). Examples of leaks motivated by policy differences include the disclosures of Navy Capt. John G. Crommelin in the B-36 controversy (see NYT, Sept. 11 and 16–18, 1949), and, in the service squabbles over the missile programs, those lead-ing to the court-martial of Col. John Nickerson (NYT, June 1957, passim).

the damage through stratagems such as a change of plan. The second point is that the intentional leaker deliberately places his job in jeopardy in order to get a change in policy. For a pro-Communist it would be political and economic suicide if his motives should ever be suspected. And it certainly would end his usefulness as an undercover agent.

The careless leaker is probably more of a threat to national security. Unlike the deliberate leak, which seeks maximum publicity, the careless leak may not be known to security officials, with the result that proper remedial measures are not taken. Furthermore, the intentional leaker will usually calculate the risk to national security involved in his disclosure. On the other hand, the damage from the lost briefcase, the stolen diary, or the unguarded remark at a cocktail party may be disastrous or may be of no consequence at all, depending on who receives the information and how far he spreads it.

The careless leaker may properly be sought out and eliminated through appraisals of reliability, sobriety, and discretion; but I doubt that he is a major threat to security. The fortuitous nature of his disclosures, whatever their value, do not make him a really dependable source for unfriendly intelligence officers. Of course, if carelessness with official secrets was epidemic, then successful espionage would require only an assiduous round of Washington cocktail parties. But present sanctions and condemnation, though not particularly severe, seem to hold in check most loose talkers.[6]

ESPIONAGE

The primary danger to security by concealment is not from leakage to the public, however, but from spies who covertly transmit secret information to Soviet Intelligence. It is also necessary to guard against unauthorized disclosures to friendly nations. At times like the Suez crisis, when there was considerable divergence between our position and that of some of our allies, considerable harm could have resulted if

6. Perhaps the most notorious careless disclosures since the war were those of Maj. Gen. Robert W. Grow, who, while military attaché to Moscow in 1951, confided to his diary not only classified material but also his unkind views about the Russians. The diary, left carelessly in a German hotel room, was filched, photographed, and published in a communist newspaper. Grow received a reprimand from a court-martial and then retired. See NYT, July 18, 1953; 3 Ct. of Military Appeals Reports 77 (1953). Sanctions against intentional or careless leaking are in 62 Stat. 736 (1948), 18 U.S.C. § 793, esp. §§ (d) and (f); and 65 Stat. 619 (1951), 18 U.S.C. § 798.

our plans had reached them prematurely. Again, a great volume of our military secrets are not supposed to be known to any other nation; but even our friends may try to satisfy an illicit curiosity.

There is nothing new and startling about this. Espionage is always going on; and it has been a well-recognized part of warfare since the earliest times: even the American hero Nathan Hale was, after all, a spy. In World War II the Nazis had an elaborate spy network in the United States before it was broken up. Is there anything about communist espionage, therefore, that should impel us to pile employment tests on top of traditional countermeasures, or is it, like the espionage of the past, merely something to be guarded against and punished when it occurs?

Modern communist espionage does appear to differ in intensity from anything that we have encountered before. Unlike the Germans and Japanese, Russia does not have to depend primarily on her own nationals as sources of information. The international Communist party organization has provided the Soviets with a large group of potential agents of domestic origin who are not automatically suspect, as Russian citizens would be. Second, Russian espionage is better organized than the German. Apparently the Germans were quite contemptuous of the capabilities of American counterintelligence. At any rate, they used notorious Bundists as agents, who were easily spotted by the FBI. In addition they took insufficient precautions during the transmission of information, so that surveillance of one agent led the FBI to the others.

Russian intelligence requires its spies to sever all radical connections and instead to appear as normal and innocuous as possible. Similarly, to pass information from an agent to his superiors, the Communists have perfected the use of the go-between or "cut-out"—an apparently solid citizen whose only contact with the agents on either end may be a wordless encounter on the subway. Thus even if one agent should be caught, the activities of the others could continue undetected. This superior discipline makes communist espionage much more difficult to curb than anything Americans have experienced before.[7]

7. Accounts of the World War II Nazi spy rings are in Nathaniel Weyl, *The Battle against Disloyalty* (1951), ch. 11, and Don Whitehead, *The FBI Story* (1956), ch. 21. The best general work on the worldwide Russian espionage system is David Dallin, *Soviet Espionage* (1955). Alexander Foote, *Handbook for Spies* (1949), is the best short account of modern techniques. For indications that even a highly skilled espionage system has frequent failures see Winston Burdett's testimony about his rather footless career with Russian espionage in Europe, ISC, Hearings, *Strategy and Tactics of World Communism* (1955), pp.

Since successful espionage is likely to go completely undetected, it is impossible to know exactly how much the Russians have learned through undercover agents. But the record of known spy rings can give us some inkling of the extent to which disloyal employees may have injured national security. Best known and most important are the defections in the atomic energy program. Klaus Fuchs, a British scientist of German birth, has confessed that he passed information about the production of Uranium 235 to a Communist agent while working in the United States on the Manhattan Project. During the same period David Greenglass, an Army sergeant at Los Alamos, made sketches of the triggering device for the atomic bomb and delivered them to Julius Rosenberg for transmission to the Russians. In Canada and Britain two other scientists have likewise betrayed atomic information. Alan Nunn May was convicted in 1946 of espionage in Canada. In 1950, Bruno Pontecorvo suddenly left England and disappeared behind the Iron Curtain, not to reappear there until 1955.

Sober appraisals have concluded that Russian scientists could undoubtedly have constructed an atomic bomb independently, without relying on information obtained through espionage. Furthermore, it is doubtful that the information supplied by all the atomic spies together could have enabled anyone to construct atomic weapons on the basis of that information alone. Nevertheless, it is generally agreed that Fuchs' and Pontecorvo's knowledge, at least, was sufficient to put Russian research many months ahead. If nothing else, it saved the Soviets from the expensive trial and error methods which the American program had to use, and allowed them to concentrate on the most effective processes.[8]

In other areas the pilfering of secrets has been less dramatic, but nonetheless the information obtained has doubtless been of at least short-run advantage to the Soviet Union. For example, Julius Rosenberg

1324–54. And see Walter Millis, *Individual Freedom and the Common Defense* (Nov. 1957), pp. 63–80, for a severe deflation of the utility of secrecy and espionage.

8. On atomic espionage and its effectiveness see Brown, "Personnel Security," ANNALS, *290*:100 (1953); testimony of General Leslie Groves, AEC, *Oppenheimer . . . Hearing* (1954), pp. 174–6; Lapp (n. 3 above), pp. 213–16; Nordheim, n. 3 above; Shils (n. 3 above), pp. 219–21; Joint Committee on Atomic Energy, Report, *Soviet Atomic Espionage* (1951). For studies of individual spies, consult Rebecca West, *The Meaning of Treason* (1947), pp. 198–207 (Nunn May); Alan Moorehead, *The Traitors* (1952) (Fuchs and Pontecorvo); NYT, March 5, 1955 (reappearance of Pontecorvo); Oliver Pilat, *The Atom Spies* (1952) (Greenglass and the Rosenbergs); Dean Brelis, "The Making of a Spy," *Life* (June 12, 1950), p. 7 (Harry Gold).

stole a proximity fuse from his employer, the Emerson Radio Corporation. Numerous other incidents concerning weapons data have been suspected.

Another target of espionage rings has of course been information on plans and operations within the executive branch of the federal government. Alger Hiss in the State Department, Harry Dexter White in the Treasury, and a number of others in the so-called "Silvermaster" and "Perlo" rings have been strongly implicated as espionage agents during the thirties and forties. Finally, Communist agents have even obtained access to counterintelligence information. Judith Coplon used her position in the Justice Department to pry into FBI reports on communist espionage.[9]

COUNTERESPIONAGE

Granting, then, that there have been serious breaches in our screen of secrecy, what are the available antidotes? Since the major problem in protection against espionage is to discover when and where the espionage is taking place, the first requirement is competent counterintelligence. The duties of counterintelligence include discovering the existence of enemy spies, infiltrating their ranks and feeding the enemy false information, and eventually, when it is certain that the network can be broken, bringing the offenders to trial. Counterintelligence agencies are also concerned with the safeguarding of information by proper physical precautions such as guards and safes, and with the integrity of cryptographic systems. In the United States, these functions are carried out principally by the FBI and the Department of Defense. The counter-

9. U.S. v. Coplon, 185 F. 2d 629 (2d Cir. 1950) and 191 F. 2d 749 (D.C. Cir. 1951). James Burnham, *The Web of Subversion* (1954), summarizes the numerous Congressional investigations and reports on espionage in the Government. See also ISC, Hearings, *Interlocking Subversion in Government Departments* (1953–55); cf. Whittaker Chambers, *Witness* (1952), and Elizabeth Bentley, *Out of Bondage* (1951), with Alger Hiss, *In the Court of Public Opinion* (1957), and Nathan White, *Harry Dexter White: Loyal American* (privately printed, 1956). After reviewing most of the published material on Russian espionage in the United States in the last twenty years, I can find no solid basis for making final judgments in individual cases, except for the few in which criminal convictions have been obtained, or in which there has been a confession. But I have no reason to doubt that there were Russian spies in government positions, even though some of those who have been accused may be innocent. There has been little objective and skeptical examination of the spy stories of this last decade; but see Norman Redlich, "Spies in Government," *The Nation* (Jan. 30, 1954), p. 85; (Feb. 6, 1954), p. 109.

intelligence activities of these agencies, of course, are not public information and little is known about their methods of operation. But enough is known to make possible some analysis of the potential effectiveness of these agencies in checking espionage.[10]

The initial step in any counterespionage operation is to learn that espionage is going on. In some cases the first lead will turn up by chance. In one case, for example, an agent who had been giving information to the Russians left a classified document in the pocket of a coat which he sent to the cleaners. More frequently, however, the original leads in espionage cases come from disaffected agents within the ring. Thus disclosures by Igor Gouzenko, the code clerk from the Russian embassy in Canada, broke the Canadian ring. Similar defections have recently occurred in Australia and Japan.[11]

In rare instances the FBI may even work a double agent into the spy apparatus. This was done in one of the Nazi rings in World War II. Once the counterintelligence agency suspects the existence of espionage, it will attempt to uncover all the members of the apparatus. This must be done without arousing the suspicion of the spies themselves—otherwise the undiscovered members of the plot will break off contact with the suspected agent and reform their lines of communication without him. This unraveling of the espionage web requires constant surveillance of each member of the ring. If possible, double agents work into close contact with the spies. Phones are tapped and, although the counterintelligence agencies may deny it, there is doubtless rifling of mail.

If sufficient admissible evidence can be obtained and the counterintelligence agents are sure that they know the whereabouts of all the spies, their surveillance may result in arrest and prosecution. But this is not the only alternative. It may be more advantageous to infiltrate or

10. The present United States counterintelligence organization is discussed in Commission on the Organization of the Executive Branch of the Government (Hoover Commission), Report, *Intelligence Activities* (June 1955). See also Ladislas Farago, *War of Wits: The Anatomy of Espionage and Counter Espionage* (1954). For an historical survey see James W. Thompson and Saul Padover, *Secret Diplomacy: A Record of Espionage and Double-Dealing, 1500–1815* (1937).

11. The coat-at-the-cleaners episode—see Weyl (n. 7 above), p. 150—was the basis for the prosecution in Gorin v. U.S., 312 U.S. 19 (1941). Official investigations into the Canadian and Australian rings were made by the governments involved, both of which published Royal Commission Reports (Canada, 1946; Australia, 1955). Y. A. Rastovorov defected in Japan and was granted asylum in the U.S. See NYT, Aug. 14, 1954.

take over the apparatus in a way that the enemy headquarters will not detect. For example, in World War II FBI double agents operated a radio station on Long Island which fed false information to the Nazis. Or, if prosecution is impossible because of evidentiary weaknesses such as wiretapped calls, the suspected spy may be transferred away from access to secret information.[12]

Because of the secret nature of our counterintelligence it is naturally impossible to evaluate its present effectiveness in coping with Soviet spies. But some judgment can be made, based on what appears in public records about the past. During World War II, the FBI's performance against the Nazis was apparently good. At least four major rings were apprehended and their members sent to jail. Against the Communists, however, the FBI and other agencies have had more difficulty. The widespread underground of the 1930's, of course, must be disregarded in this appraisal, as we had little organized counterintelligence in that period. But the Gold-Rosenberg apparatus operated right under the nose of those guarding the supersecret Manhattan Project without being discovered until long after the damage had been done. Apart from this group, the abortive trial of Judith Coplon, and the recent exposure of the Abel-Soble apparatus, there have been no reported prosecutions for communist espionage within the United States in the postwar period. Yet Congressional committee reports are full of strong circumstantial evidence of espionage in government agencies at least as late as 1948.[13]

12. The transfer method was finally used to immunize Judith Coplon before her arrest. That some of the intelligence reports produced in the Coplon case appear to have been founded on data obtained by rifling mail is shown by "Report on Certain Alleged Practices of the F.B.I.," *Lawyers Guild Rev.* (1950), *10:*191. For the false radio operation see Whitehead, n. 7 above. On the tactics of breaking off from suspects and regrouping, see Foote, n. 7 above.

13. The failure to detect the wartime activities of the Gold-Rosenberg-Greenglass communist ring was categorized as "inexcusable" by John Lansdale, who had been chief security officer for the Manhattan District. AEC, *Oppenheimer . . . Hearing* (1954), p. 262. Alfred Dean Slack was not a member of the Rosenberg spy ring, but he worked directly under Harry Gold. See Slack v. U.S., 203 F. 2d 152 (6th Cir. 1953). In one postwar prosecution Otto Verber and Kurt Ponger were convicted of espionage for the Russians in Austria; but their activities were said to have been directed from Washington. NYT, April 14 and 15, and June 9, 1953. Jack and Myra Soble pleaded guilty; see NYT, April 11, 1957. Thereafter indictments were brought against George and Jane Zlatovski, who were in Paris (NYT, July 10, 1957); Col. Rudolf Abel of the Russian secret police was apprehended; Alfred and Martha Stern fled to Czechoslovakia; and a remarkable counterespionage agent, Boris Morros, was brought to light. NYT, Aug. 10–20, 1957.

CRIMINAL PROSECUTION OF ESPIONAGE

In fairness to the counterintelligence agencies, however, one should not judge their effectiveness in detecting espionage solely by the record of convictions. There is a vast difference between the amount of evidence necessary to arouse the suspicions of a reasonable man and that sufficient to support a conviction for espionage. Presumably, most of the espionage information brought out by Congressional committees was already well known to the FBI. Nevertheless the paucity of prosecutions emphasizes the extreme difficulty involved in efforts to unearth a well-disciplined spy ring.

The difficulty in obtaining espionage convictions does not stem ordinarily from any inadequacy in the statutes. The basic sanctions are found in the Espionage Act of 1917 and its numerous amendments. These provisions are far too involved to bear detailed discussion here. But the thrust of these acts is to forbid either the transmission or the acquisition of information, documents, or objects, "concerning the national defense" unless one is duly authorized to do so. The punishment will vary, however, depending on whether there is an "intent to injure the United States" and whether the offense is committed in time of war. An amendment in 1954 made the death sentence a regular penalty for peacetime spying. This had the further effect of removing the statute of limitations, since there is no time limit (in the federal courts) on prosecutions for capital crimes.

In the special field of atomic energy there are additional provisions. Provisions similar to those of the Espionage Act prohibit the unauthorized transmission or acquisition of "restricted data."

As long as information is classified and is not a matter of general knowledge, the courts show no hesitation in relating it to "national defense" so as to make the Espionage Act applicable. But what of the Communist in the Commerce Department, for example, who transmits only unclassified economic data? Has he violated the Espionage Act? If there has been no attempt to keep the information secret, or if it is freely available in public sources, one court has said that no violation has occurred, even though the agent compiles the data into a highly useful report on the war readiness of American industry.[14]

14. See U.S. v. Heine, 151 F. 2d 813 (2d Cir. 1945), and *Harvard Law Rev.* (1946), 59:617; cf. Slack v. U.S., 203 F. 2d 152 (6th Cir. 1953). The relevant provisions of the Espionage Act of 1917, as amended, are in 62 Stat. 736 (1950), 65 Stat. 719 (1951), 68 Stat. 1216 (1954), 18 U.S.C. §§ 793–8; of the Atomic

This possible gap in the espionage laws is partially plugged by the Foreign Agents Registration Act. The gist of this legislation is that persons who collect information for, or otherwise act as agents for, a foreign government or political party, or who have had foreign sabotage or espionage training, must register with the Attorney General unless specifically exempted. Thus the agent who deals only in unclassified information is placed in a dilemma. If he registers, his usefulness as an agent is, to say the least, compromised, especially if he had been acquiring his information by virtue of his position in government or industry. If he fails to register, on the other hand, he can be convicted for that offense.[15]

The substantive coverage of the statutes certainly appears adequate. Why then have so many FBI agents and so many years of Congressional inquiry produced so few convictions? Perhaps it is because there has been little espionage in fact, though the evidence points the other way. A more serious obstacle may be that crucial evidence has been obtained by wiretapping. Congress has been urged to make such evidence admissible; but it has not yet done so. The real answer probably lies in the difficulty of obtaining the evidence required to establish the commission of espionage. The ideal solution is to catch the culprit in the act of passing secret information. This was what was attempted in the Coplon case. Sometimes the FBI may have a planted agent in the ring. This was the case in several of the Nazi spy prosecutions. A third solution, and the most common, is to get testimony from someone inside the ring. This may take the form of a confession, or a guilty plea by the suspect himself; or one or more of the conspirators may be persuaded to testify against the others in the hope of leniency. This seems to have been the technique in the *Rosenberg* case. All the successful prosecutions that I know about were based on one or more of these elements.

But if none of the supposed conspirators will confess, and no incriminating papers are found in the suspect's possession, the prosecutor can hardly show that any crime has been committed. Moreover, even if it

---

Energy Act of 1954, 68 Stat. 958 (1954), 42 U.S.C. §§ 2274–7. On the death sentence for peacetime spying see 68 Stat. 1219 (1954), 18 U.S.C. § 794(b); on the removal of the statute of limitations for capital offenses, 62 Stat. 827 (1948), 18 U.S.C. § 3281. Other applicable statutes are discussed in Commission on Government Security, *Report* (1957), pp. 618–19.

15. Foreign Agents Registration Act, 52 Stat. 631 (1938), 22 U.S.C. §§ 611–21. 70 Stat. 899 (1956), 50 U.S.C. §§ 851–7, revised the registration requirements for persons with foreign training in espionage.

could somehow be shown by circumstantial evidence that information had been taken, that the suspect had taken or transmitted it, and that he had reason to believe that it would be used to the advantage of a foreign power (proof that he was a Communist might be relevant on this point), it would still be necessary to link the defendant to the other agents if the whole ring were to be destroyed. Since the parts of a Communist apparatus are usually well-insulated from each other, even a successful prosecution may accomplish little toward breaking up the heart of a spy apparatus.

In sum, the utility of criminal penalties against espionage is uncertain.

CONCLUSION

Some responsible officials that I have talked to have felt that an efficient counterespionage backed up by prosecutions would be sufficient to keep the espionage threat under control. The punishment to be expected in a period of public alarm is formidable. One need only cite the case of the Rosenbergs; they were executed. But there are doubts about the likelihood of catching a spy under circumstances where he can be convicted. This does not suggest that the law can or ought to be changed. We do not put people in jail because an official thinks they might be spies.

The necessary shortcomings of a decent criminal law and those of an imperfect counterespionage system do suggest some scope for employment tests. Can they effectively screen out the probable spies? It is reported that the Russians, despite the Gestapo's ruthlessness, managed to keep a well-located agent in the German General Staff all during World War II.[16] It is necessary to inquire, in the following chapters, whether employment tests can efficiently and at the same time fairly help minimize the espionage hazard.

16. And then paid little attention to his reports. See Foote (n. 7 above), ch. 9.

10. Security by Exclusion: Defining Sensitive Jobs

THE LAST two chapters have described serious threats to national security. To counter those threats we have a formidable array of deterrent and punitive sanctions on the statute books; and we have also the preventive tactics of counterespionage and countersabotage. But it is obvious that these measures do not exhaust the possibilities of defense. At the sensitive points, where the most damage can be done, there are sensitive people, those employees of government and industry who know the secrets and man the controls. The essence of personnel security is to keep risky people off sensitive jobs. In practice our prime defense against breaches of security by employees is to try to screen out the faithless *before* they can do any harm.

But, though it sounds simple and straightforward to say that we will bar risky people from sensitive jobs, it is far from simple to decide what people, and what jobs. A forced simplicity can be achieved by adopting what appears to have been the policy of the federal government: take no chances; resolve all doubts in favor of increased security. Such a policy, however, may actually reduce security by achievement; and in view of what has been said about the indignity and fallibility of screening tests, its ethics are deplorable. It should be possible to set some rational limits on what is sensitive.

IDENTIFYING MAJOR SENSITIVE AREAS

Within the government the first step of those that have been taken to separate sensitive from insensitive jobs has been to name entire departments that presumptively fall in one category or the other. If one begins with the assumption that whole departments must be labeled, the entire defense establishment goes on the sensitive side, taking with it more than half the civilian employees of the federal government and all the armed forces. The Atomic Energy Commission goes here too, and those parts of the presidential establishment, like the Bureau of the Budget, that oversee the operations of the sensitive agencies.

At the other extreme one has no hesitation in labeling as insensitive the next two largest employers after the defense establishment: the Post Office and the Veterans' Administration. Other important agencies that are overwhelmingly concerned with normal government operations other than defense are the new Department of Health, Education, and Welfare, old-line Departments like Agriculture, Interior, and Labor, and the independent regulatory agencies.

This preliminary separation is not vitiated by the fact that almost any major department may have some contacts with critical security areas. Thus a few employees in the Post Office may be privy to the location of unpublicized airfields. The Interior Department's Bureau of Territories and Insular Possessions may be consulted on the location of these fields, if they happen to be in a strategically important area like Alaska. The Civil Aeronautics Board may be asked not to rule openly on the movement of air freight by private carriers to those same fields.

At a time like the present, when prestige and appropriations alike depend somewhat on the agency head's ability to identify his agency with defense needs, such connections are likely to be exaggerated. One can of course argue the indispensability of any link in an interdependent economy. If the Department of Labor promotes policies that worsen labor-management relations so that strikes result, then defense production may suffer. If the Federal Reserve Board constricts credit excessively, plant expansion may be hindered. The multiplication of such examples, however, misses the point of screening tests. The present danger such tests have to meet is not the collapse of the entire agency but the harm that disaffected individuals or small groups can do *in their jobs*. A treacherous (or an indolent) postman can cause some embarrassment by failing to deliver the mail. The immediate question is whether we are justified on that account in considering the Post Office Department, over all, as a sensitive agency. The answer is clearly no.

In between what I consider fairly clear cases of inclusion and exclusion—still proceeding agency by agency—lies a group of governmental agencies of less certain status. Legislation prior to the cold war recognized the sensitive character of the military establishment and the AEC. Between 1946 and 1950 Congress may be said to have conferred similar status on the State Department and the successive foreign-aid programs by such legislation as the summary dismissal power bestowed on the Secretary of State, and the extraordinary loyalty requirements for employment in Mutual Security and other foreign-aid agencies.[1]

1. See BONTECOU, pp. 63–7.

Public Law 733 of 1950 recognized employment in ten agencies as subject to security criteria. Among them, in addition to the military, were the Departments of State, Justice, and Commerce.

Each of these three departments carries on sensitive operations of varying extent, and each of them has certain functions that are entirely open to the public eye. One would surmise (I know of no basis for quantitative estimates) that the degree of sensitivity for the whole of each Department would run about in the order that they are named above—State most, Commerce least.

Unless the Commerce Department has been carrying on clandestine activities, its only major sensitive part would seem to be the defense activities of the Bureau of Standards. Smaller segments of other offices such as Patents and International Trade have some security responsibilities. If that is the case, the Department's policy when it had both loyalty and security jurisdiction in the period 1950–53 was questionable. The Secretary considered it proper to find security risks in, for example, the Bureau of the Census, a policy which, it was explained to me informally, was justified by the possibility that a person in a nonsensitive Bureau might wander around the building and get access to classified material.[2]

For the State Department, in the same era, to treat all its operations as sensitive had more reason. Quite aside from the Congressional and public pressures that forced the Department to purely self-defensive measures, it was impressed on me by persons in the Department that, even in the Voice of America, where the end-product was broadcast to the world, many of the staff would have to be advised of intended policies and actions that were not yet public. And the McCarthy hearings on the Voice of America early in 1953, by way of unverified charges of suppression and distortion of broadcast material, dramatized the rather bizarre possibility that a propaganda line could be sabotaged as well as an assembly line.[3]

Similar observations may doubtless be made about other parts of the State Department. Once it is apparent that sensitive information and

2. Other Bureaus and Offices of the Department of Commerce include Business Economics, Civil Aeronautics, Coast and Geodetic Survey, Maritime Administration, Public Roads, and Weather.

3. See Senate Comm. on Government Operations, Permanent Subcomm. on Investigations, Hearings, *State Department Information Program—Voice of America* (1953). But the evidence of any communist influence in the USIA was flimsy. See James Rorty and Moshe Decter, *McCarthy and the Communists* (1954), pp. 19–31.

materials reach most responsible officials, then a case can be made for protecting that material from clerks, messengers, etc., all over the Department. This situation is markedly different from that of the Commerce Department, large parts of which operate entirely in the public eye.

It is a sterile exercise to go on pigeonholing departments or parts of departments according to their degree of security sensitivity.[4] Two points, I think, readily emerge. The first is that agency heads at present will try to get into the most sensitive pigeonhole available to them. The second is that even an objective selection based on major functions of an agency sweeps into the sensitive category many jobs that are of no security consequence at all. This is especially the case in the enormous military departments. One may not be able to indicate any large areas in the State Department that are a matter of security indifference, because the State Department is not very large anyhow (approximately 11,000 citizen employees). Consider, however, the Army Finance Center. This huge establishment was once thought to be harboring Communists or communist sympathizers. Some of the suspects fought their cases in and out of the courts and won reinstatement, at the cost to the government of substantial back-pay awards for prolonged periods of suspension.[5] It seems unlikely that these clerk-typists could have seriously threatened the national security, even if they botched all the pay accounts in their charge.

A greater degree of refinement is wanted than the simple designation of sensitive and nonsensitive agencies. One widely used way to achieve some refinement is to tie job sensitivity to the system of information classification described in the last chapter. That is, before an employee gets access, either as part of his job or as a matter of physical proximity, to Confidential, Secret, or Top Secret information (or material), he must be cleared. Furthermore, the three levels of the classification system provide a ready guide to the intensity with which a particular applicant must be scrutinized. Is he going to be dealing with Top Secret material, or only with Confidential? "Cleared for Top Secret" is the ultimate stamp of approval from the security officer.

4. As a rough guide to nonsensitive agencies, § 2 of E.O. 10501, Nov. 5, 1953, excluded many agencies from originating classified material (although they might still receive it), and in other cases restricted the classification power to the head of the agency or specifically designated "responsible" officers or employees.
5. See Deak v. Pace, 185 F. 2d 997 (D.C. Cir. 1950); NYT, Jan. 12, 1952.

This approach is fine in theory and well enough in practice, except for one considerable flaw. The same prudential impulses that lead officials to overstate the sensitivity of a job impel them to overclassify information. Almost everyone with experience in the military departments, whether in or out of uniform, has some tale to tell of newspaper clippings stamped Confidential, or of classified bus schedules. Sometimes these odd practices have a rational explanation; and in any event such aberrational episodes would not often be decisive in determining the screening required for a particular job; but they can be decisive. For example, I know of one case where the employee was denied clearance to continue editing training manuals that were classified Confidential. The employee and his counsel felt strongly that the classification was silly; but they had no standing to urge its alteration.

Most errors in classification are the product of honest doubt, but their effect is all in the same direction. Doubts are resolved in favor of the higher classification; nobody ever got into trouble, one hears it said, for making a paper Confidential rather than not. As a result, drifts of classified material invade every office, only slightly kept back by the inconvenience entailed in having to lock them up.[6] Whether information classifications formally control personnel security requirements or whether they indirectly influence the discretion of security officers, the effect is bound to be the same: overclassification of documents leads to overclassification of jobs.

Despite the prevalence of overclassification, access to classified materials is a helpful measure of sensitivity. If those who do not have such access are excused from clearance requirements, dramatic reductions can be made in the number of employees who need to be cleared. This has certainly been the case in the military departments. It was a cause for astonishment when Secretary Wilber Brucker, then General Counsel of the Department of Defense, gave an "educated guess" in 1955 that two-thirds of the civilian employees of the military departments were in nonsensitive work. Later, exact figures required by the Johnston Com-

6. House Comm. on Government Operations, [Moss] Subcomm. Hearings, *Availability of Information from Federal Departments and Agencies* (1955–57), and House Report No. 2947 (July 27, 1956) constitute an extensive but inconclusive study of security classification and other techniques for withholding information from the public. The Report of Nov. 8, 1956, to the Secretary of Defense by his Committee on Classified Information concludes that "overclassification has reached serious proportions" (reprinted Moss Hearings, p. 2133; see **p. 2136**).

mittee confirmed this estimate.[7] It would be interesting to know how closely agencies like the Department of Commerce adhere to a relationship between sensitivity and access to classified material. The Department reported to the Johnston Committee that 21,000 of its 36,000 employees in 1955 were in sensitive jobs, almost twice the proportion found in the military departments.[8] But, even if there is undue elasticity in the discretion of some administrators, access to classified material is still the starting-point for any confining definition of sensitivity.

How Much Refinement in Classifying Jobs?

Information classification, therefore, provides a ready-made basis for a fairly refined system of separating different degrees of employment sensitivity. As a first step, it is possible to put aside many positions as nonsensitive or unclassified, using the terms synonymously for the present. The principal touchstone would be the absence of any need to have authorized access to classified material or of any ready opportunity to gain unauthorized access. One can still recognize that there are also people who can do serious damage even though they never come near formally classified material. A questionable example, suggested by the Taft-Hartley noncommunist oath, is the labor leader with some control over the rank-and-file of a defense industry. A more vivid and direct one is the crew of a power-plant serving a vital installation like the Pentagon. The standards for such employees will be considered later in this chapter.

This initial separation of the classified from the unclassified permits, as has been suggested, the elimination from screening procedures of a great many jobs even in agencies that are predominantly sensitive. Worth-while savings follow in the number of people engaged in screening, and worth-while opportunities are created to use elsewhere the services of individuals who are disqualified from sensitive jobs. These gains may be partly offset by an increased burden of physical protective measures, to ensure that the classified areas are kept inviolate.

Should one go on to a meticulous identification of Confidential, Secret, and Top Secret jobs based primarily on the exact level of access involved? To some extent these distinctions internal to the classified world have been used. For example, some agencies confine the preliminary in-

7. HUMPHREY HEARINGS, p. 158; JOHNSTON HEARINGS, p. 1109. The total for the three departments, as of June 30, 1955, was 388,287 sensitive positions.
8. See JOHNSTON REPORT, p. 433.

vestigation to a national agency file check if only Confidential clearance is needed; a full field investigation is made only for prospective Secret and Top Secret positions.[9] But if the file check turns up derogatory information, the complete investigation is launched, and thereafter the process of determining whether a security risk exists is the same for all classifications.

Side-by-side with the formal procedures for determining whether a man will be retained there flourish the veiled decisions of the security officers, which, so far as one can tell, are often explicitly linked to the level of classification involved. It should be recalled that the applicant for a federal job (except in the Atomic Energy Commission) usually has no right to a hearing or any other formal procedure. The security officer, presumably with an eye on the level of classification involved, passes or rejects the appointment. Further, security officers can sometimes deny an employee access to classified material, even though the hearing board and the agency head have certified his retention as consistent with the needs of national security. I have heard of instances where an employee was cleared but was then denied access to any work higher than the now-discarded bottom classification, Restricted.

These instances of graded clearance do not go very far. What could be done is best brought out by a hypothetical example. Let us take the Office of General Counsel of the Air Force and make the conjectural assumption that all the people in the office are now cleared for Top Secret. Would there be any merit in deciding, hypothetically, that only the General Counsel and some of his staff needed Top Secret clearance, that Secret would do for others, and that there was enough unclassified or low classified material going through the office to warrant having a group of lawyers and secretaries with only Confidential clearance—or none? And, having made these evaluations throughout the Air Force, could not the security people profitably direct close attention to the highly classified people (as they presumably do now) and relatively little to the others?

This kind of precise classification might effect economies in screening and in employability, but I have been assured by administrators that the costs in operational efficiency would be substantial. The chief burden would be the daily nuisance of keeping in mind who was cleared for what—not only in the office itself, but in others with which it frequently deals. The more elaborate the warning apparatus of different-

9. E.g. Treasury, § 1(j); Agriculture, § 2332b. BNA MANUAL, pp. 15/302, 15/362.

colored badges, special telephone circuits, etc., the greater the impediments to communication become. The already hierarchic structure of a government or business office is not likely to be improved by superimposing on it a caste system based on clearance.

These considerations suggest that a practical approach to levels of clearance can do no more than mark out the groups of people who have to communicate freely with each other, and then determine what is the highest classification that the group as a whole needs to be exposed to. In such cases two levels of classified employment might exist. Everyone in an activity (defined for this purpose in terms of its functions *and* its location) would have the same clearance, say Secret. The top people might require a higher clearance if they had occasion to reach out into Top Secret activities. With the required clearance for any job thus broadly established, the assessment of an employee could always be made with reference to the level of clearance attached to his job.

This practical model, as distinguished from the excessively fussy approach that was discussed and rejected, is not just a model. In generalized form I think it describes what some agencies with security responsibilities have been doing. Thus departmental regulations for determining whether a man is a security risk sometimes distinguish between more and less sensitive jobs.[10] Whether or not regulations make this distinction, hearing boards, I have been advised, often take account of the sensitivity of the employee's work. In addition to the over-all question of employability, clearance has to be requested for access to classified material related to the activities of the place where a new employee is going to work. The security officers who make these decisions about clearance have in some instances express rules for their guidance; but to the extent that these formulations differ from the conventional criteria for employability they are not available to the public.

Though these practical distinctions have been part of the internal practice of security clearance, there was not much need, through most of the history of the Civil Service programs, to draw sharp lines around sensitivity. When the Loyalty Program was in effect from 1947 to 1953, it applied to all federal employees, without regard to the sensitivity of their jobs. In this respect, 1953 brought little more than a change of

10. Cf. the military departments' concept of "sensitive–critical," referring to employees with access to war plans and the like, e.g. Army SR 620–220–1, § 9b, BNA MANUAL, pp. 15/135–6. For discussion of the advantage to the AEC of a two-level system see Joint Comm. on Atomic Energy, Hearings, *Amending the Atomic Energy Act* (1952), pp. 77–8.

label. Everyone then had to be reviewed for security rather than loyalty. The demand first for universal loyalty and then for universal security blurred any sensitivity boundaries that developed. Until the Supreme Court, in *Cole v. Young*,[11] decided that P.L. 733 did not authorize the application of security tests to all public employees, the most meaningful experiences in placing firm boundaries between sensitive and nonsensitive jobs occurred in the programs that bore on private employment. There the distinction made the difference between exposure to, and freedom from, political tests.

SENSITIVITY IN PRIVATE EMPLOYMENT

The federal security programs that reach into private employment do not purport to rest on the demand for loyalty, only on the necessity for security. Because these programs pointedly invade private rights, it might be expected that they would be confined to the strict necessities of the situation, and that refinements of sensitivity would be encouraged for the sake of making it possible for doubtful cases to continue with the same employer, or at least in the same occupation.

Actually, only one of the three important federal programs in private employment has any history of significant contribution to the sensitivity problem. That is the Defense Department's Industrial Security program for its contractors. This program brings certain suppliers inside the system for classifying information and material. For a contractor to use or produce such material he must first satisfy the Department that he (usually meaning the officers of a corporation) is trustworthy; and he must take the first steps to ascertain the trustworthiness of those of his employees who will have access. It is at this point that degrees of sensitivity, corresponding to the degrees of classification, get some recognition. If the work is only Confidential, government clearance is not required unless something derogatory is turned up by the contractor. If it is Secret or Top Secret, the Department investigates. Derogatory information in any case leads to a tentative denial of access, resolved by charges and hearing. The review process directs attention to the level of clearance sought, and decisions authorize clearance for access to a specified classification, from Top Secret down.[12]

The Atomic Energy Commission, like the Department of Defense,

11. 351 U.S. 536 (1956).
12. See Secretary Brucker's testimony, HUMPHREY HEARINGS, pp. 208–9, and BNA MANUAL, pp. 21/6–7, 10–11.

supposedly leaves untouched these contractors and contractor employees who do not need access to classified material—"restricted data" in the language of the Atomic Energy Act. But in view of the sensitive character of most AEC undertakings, these innocents are relatively few. For the great majority, the original statute was thought to preclude any initial gradations in sensitivity, and to require full investigation in every instance before access to "restricted data" was allowed (except in emergencies). The 1954 amendments to the statute now permit the Commission to determine the degree of investigation required for different levels of clearance. The Commission, in the case of contractor employees who require only the equivalent of Confidential access ("L" clearance), has substituted the relatively simple file check for the full background investigation. The Commission also makes distinctions among those who have achieved "Q" clearance after full investigation. This is known as "operational clearance"; but little is known about the basis for these distinctions, which presumably rests on the "need-to-know" principle.[13]

Whatever the internal refinements may be, the acid test of formal arrangements that appear to narrow the scope of screened employment is found in their effect on employees who do not pass the screen. Do employers try to find nonsensitive jobs for them? There are widely held opinions, reinforced by evidence from individual cases, that the answer is often no. The practice of one large aircraft company appears in frank testimony by its security officer. Douglas Aircraft dismisses anyone to whom government clearance for Secret or Top Secret is denied, though only 13 per cent of the company's 75,000 employees require these levels of clearance for their work. The principal explanation advanced was that the company is not told the reasons for the denial; since disloyalty may be involved, it does not want to retain the employee. However, Douglas' policy is more lenient when the company discovers derogatory information in discharging its responsibility to initiate Confidential clearance. In such cases Douglas knows the reason for the failure to grant clearance, and may be content, while keeping the employee in unclassified work, to go no further than a reprimand.[14]

13. On "operational clearance" see HUMPHREY HEARINGS, pp. 277–8; Joint Comm. Hearings (n. 10 above), p. 83; also BNA MANUAL, pp. 21/24–5.

14. See testimony of B. F. Fitzsimmons in HUMPHREY HEARINGS, pp. 363–6, 378–9. For a further discussion of this problem see Comment, "The Role of Employer Practices in the Federal Industrial Personnel Security Program—A Field Study," *Stanford Law Rev.* (1956), 8:234, 252. The Director of Security at Republic Aircraft was more blunt: "Fire 'em. That's my answer to anyone who asks me how to handle security risks in his plant." Quoted from Fleischman,

The Douglas example is an illustration—perhaps an unnecessary one —that it is not enough to draw the line between screened and open employment only on paper. There must be a further willingness on the part of the employer not to extend clearance requirements beyond their necessary limits.

The third major federal invasion of private employment has been the Port Security program administered by the Coast Guard, which screens seamen and dock workers. The prevention of sabotage and the control of communist couriers are the aims of this program, which affects most maritime workers, even those who would not know a classified document if they saw one. In its supervision of waterfront workers, the Coast Guard requires clearance only for access to certain docks, presumably those where military cargoes are handled. This is an elementary instance of distinguishing sensitive and nonsensitive jobs. As applied to seamen, however, the program has been of a grab-bag character. The Coast Guard has authority to make exemptions from the sweep of the executive order which plunged it into the personnel security business. When the program was instituted, shortly after the outbreak of the Korean War, "because of limited manpower, the Coast Guard first concentrated on the crews of ships in foreign trade . . . But the Commandant has gradually extended the categories of restricted vessels, so that the Program now covers practically all shipping, even barges on the Great Lakes and the western rivers." There is no refuge for a seaman who is found to be a security risk, unless he can sign on a ship of foreign registry.[15]

The Coast Guard's shotgun approach to maritime security emphasizes both a strength and a weakness of linking personnel programs to the classification system. The strength lies in the availability of a set of independent criteria for distinguishing sensitive jobs. Information classification, though it is still far from being an exact science, has at least an impersonal aspect; the level of classification that the holder of a particular job is exposed to is determined by decisions that are already made when the security officers come to appraise the sensitivity of the job.

On the other hand the weakness of leaning heavily on classified labels

---

Kornbluh, and Segal, *Security, Civil Liberties and Unions* [AFL–CIO, 1956], p. 35. Compare another abuse of the system, that of requiring clearance for employees not in fact on classified work. See Ch. 5 above, n. 27.

15. See generally Brown and Fassett, "Security Tests for Maritime Workers," *Yale Law Jour.* (1953), *62*:1163; the quoted passage is from p. 1173. Restricted waterfront areas have recently been much reduced. See ASS'N OF THE BAR, REPORT, p. 117.

(aside from that of overclassification, already discussed) is that these labels are primarily aimed at keeping secrets, and are not a sufficient guide to other security hazards. Thus the Coast Guard would have been remiss in its mission to guard the security of ports and shipping if it had looked only for formally classified matter to protect, and no further. For example, the threat of war makes invaluable the small fleet of liners capable of high-speed transport service. Yet nothing except some special equipment is classified on these ships, prime targets for sabotage though they might be. Again, some vital military cargoes to Korea doubtless consisted entirely of food and fuel, neither of them "classified" in the conventional sense but still critical at the time.

Nevertheless, the neglect by the Coast Guard of the familiar test— access to classified matter—may have contributed to its failure to develop any coherent equivalent. The Coast Guard does pursue a selective policy in restricting waterfront areas. But the only policy visible in the screening of seamen has been to require clearance for the crew of almost anything that floats. It may be argued that the language of the Executive Order points toward a more thorough coverage of seamen than of dock workers, but thoroughness does not exclude recognition of degrees of sensitivity. For instance, a difference between the clearance required to sail military cargoes to Korea and that for shepherding sand and gravel around New York might have obviated the removal of a 68-year old barge captain, as in one case described to me. He imperiled the national security, it was charged, by reason of former membership in the IWW. One may concede a remote possibility that this venerable Wobblie could lend his barge to a scheme to blow up the Erie Basin. But the possibility is remote indeed. Does the risk warrant depriving him of his modest livelihood?

The rudderless course of the Port Security program is not inevitable. Even though analogies from information classification offer little guidance, other aids are available. What is seriously needed for this security-conscious era is a "general theory" of sensitive employment, a theory that would lean on the experience of information classification, but would have other means of support as well. Such a theory would draw on the shady histories of sabotage and betrayal described in earlier chapters. It would point to the nerve centers and bottlenecks that are not already designated by the presence of classified matter. It would lay a foundation for rational choices between the hardships of employment tests and the necessities of national existence.

Let us look again at the Defense Department's screening of contractor employees. In contrast to the Coast Guard, which has laid its hand on almost the whole maritime industry, the military services have usually stayed within the bounds set by the classification system. Their spokesmen have argued that they lacked authority to insist on screening except by way of conditions in contracts. Without reconnoitering to see how far they could travel along the contract road before encountering serious legal or political obstacles, the services have prudently halted to await orders from Congress. So far, none has been given, except for the prohibition found in the Internal Security Act of 1950. That statute bars members of designated communist organizations from employment in defense facilities, a list of which the Secretary of Defense can promulgate. The compilation of this list has so far been unnecessary because litigation has delayed the effective designation of "Communist-action" and "Communist-front" organizations under the 1950 Act.

Meanwhile, the Department of Defense has been strongly nudging Congress for marching orders in the form of the Butler bill, a measure which, in effect, permits the application of conventional screening practices to *any* employee of a defense facility. The possibility that people could be labeled security risks and barred from whole industries as the result of an uncontrolled administrative process centered in the Defense Department has aroused much opposition to the bill. The Department, on its side, has insisted that it needs broad powers in order to root out a few hundred dangerous characters in unclassified but vital areas.[16]

Suppose that Congress gives the Defense Department power (or that the Department assumes it) to require screening of employees in supposedly critical points where there is no classified matter, and where there need be no direct contract relationship between the Department and the employer. One can start with the familiar easy case—the outside power plant serving a vital munitions works. Presumably some of its employees could do a great deal of harm; therefore they should be screened. Since the steady operation of the power plant is assumed to be vital, no great objection can be made to treating these few employees in the same way as their compatriots inside the munitions factory.

So far, so good. The power plant, however, is only one thread in the complex pattern of interdependence that is all industry. Where does ap-

16. For discussion of the claimed merits and demerits of the Butler bill see Industrial Rel. Res. Ass'n, *Personnel Security Programs in U.S. Industry* (1955), pp. 25–32, and pp. 18–24, 75–7; Brucker testimony in HUMPHREY HEARINGS, pp. 220–25; Rauh testimony in HENNINGS HEARINGS, pp. 548–50; NYT, June 4, 1955. The cited section of the Internal Security Act of 1950, 64 Stat. 987 (1950), is 50 U.S.C. § 784.

prehension of potential dangers stop? With the other public utilities? With raw material suppliers? With the sources of repair parts, of abrasives, of lubricants? With the carriers of all these things?

A GENERAL THEORY OF SENSITIVITY

There are thousands of operations in government, and, for that matter, tens of thousand outside of government, the crippling of which would in due course cripple vital industries. This is certainly true for the short run, although for the long run it may be true that nothing is indispensable and that there is a substitute for everything. However, not even for the short run does security require that employment tests be made universal. This is as true in private employment as in government. The heart of a feasible general theory of sensitive employment, I suggest, can be found in simple propositions something like these: (1) A reasonable classification system adequately designates the areas of employment where there are espionage hazards. (2) In guarding against the other hazards of a cold war, employment tests should be concentrated on positions where one employee, or a few employees, can do great harm. (3) In this country at this time it is unnecessary and impractical to screen masses of people against the remote risk of mass breakdowns.

That is, we do not have to ask what would happen if all the trains stopped running because all the main-line switches were spiked. Neither in railroading nor anywhere else is there in this country such a concentration of Communists as might well be found in France or Italy. To take another example, we do not have to screen all refinery workers the minute it is realized that machines will not run without lubricating oil. We can take time to ask questions about the structure and technology of the industry, about the composition and history of its labor force, about the opportunities for concealed wrecking operations of any character. In the end, we might find a few critical engineers who need to be checked on; or we might decide that it is better to leave them alone. Though everyone is interdependent, everyone does not have to pass a security screen. Our security experts can identify the critical points. How many Sault Ste. Marie Canals are there, through which all the iron ore from the Mesabi must be transported? How many ocean liners or jet transports? How many power plants without any standby source? Along with the arsenals and laboratories that are readily flagged by the presence of classified matter, these are the places to watch.

When using this approach to measure the effectiveness of employment tests as a safeguard against sabotage, it is not enough merely to identify the critical areas. Employment tests screen only employees; if the general public has access to the area, then reliance on employment tests creates a false sense of security, and is an inefficient use of our security forces. There is no point, for example, in screening the trainmen on the New York City subways. Any member of the public has an equal opportunity to sabotage the subways, just by leaving a bomb in a Times Square locker. This possibility was brought home when the so-called "mad bomber" planted bombs—fortunately small ones—all over New York for several years.[17] This does not mean that we are helpless against saboteurs. The mad bomber was hard to catch because he was a lone wolf. There is more chance of apprehending saboteurs who are part of an enemy apparatus. Organized sabotage has lines of communication that can be intercepted, or weak links that can be broken. Countermeasures should focus on these, and on the few areas that can be sealed off without much difficulty. Against the infinite theoretical possibilities of sabotage, the best remedy is a little stoicism.

It might also be well to repeat and emphasize one more simple proposition that has been much discussed in this chapter. *There are degrees of sensitivity.* The barge captain does not require the same examination as does the captain of the *United States*. And though it is not feasible, in administering programs, to distinguish *all* the shadings that lie between the barge captain and the liner captain, efficiency and justice both require some distinctions to be made.

THEORY INTO PRACTICE

I should like to follow this statement of general considerations with some recommendations for action. Their intention is to promote a reexamination of the whole question of sensitive and nonsensitive employment in every program where the distinction is relevant. Once the boundaries are redrawn—much more narrowly than at present—security screening should be eliminated from nonsensitive employment. If an employee is not in a sensitive job or a sensitive area within the terms of the discussion thus far, he is not in a position to do serious damage by

17. See dissenting opinion in Lerner v. Casey, 2 N.Y. 2d 355, 141 N.E. 2d 533, 544 (1957); ASS'N OF THE BAR, REPORT, p. 144. The "mad bomber" did turn out to be a mental case. NYT, April 19, 1957.

reason of his job. Therefore his employment does not create a security risk. This approach makes sensitivity and security risk opposite sides of the same coin.

As a first step, it would exempt from the federal programs all employees whose jobs are already officially described as nonsensitive. This eliminates most employees of most civilian departments, with such exceptions as State, Atomic Energy Commission, the Central Intelligence Agency, etc. It eliminates about two-thirds of the civilian employees of the Department of Defense. I cannot foretell the effect on the armed forces, of which more later.

As a second step, I would take a hard look at the assumption that access to *any* classified information makes a job sensitive. Specifically, I would suggest that screening for access only to Confidential material could be dropped without seriously imperiling the national security. The rather humble host of "secrets" treated as Confidential is familiar to anyone who has ever been exposed to information classification. Someone has suggested that we could cripple Russian intelligence if we delivered to it, by the shipload, everything that we classified Confidential. Conversely, the bits and pieces of Confidential material to which one employee ordinarily has access do not add up to much.

This change would probably require an amendment to the Atomic Energy Act, but could otherwise be accomplished by amending executive orders (or agency regulations). The effect of it would be, obviously, to reduce further the number of employees who have to be screened and kept under surveillance. An authoritative estimate indicates that less than a third of the clearances under the Industrial Security Program are for Top Secret and Secret.[18] That is, at least two-thirds of the present clearances could be eliminated.

Writing off Confidential access as a basis for clearance might help to put screening of military personnel on a rational basis. Apparently the services do not want to investigate and evaluate everybody who passes through their ranks. They now appear to act only when something derogatory turns up in a questionnaire at induction, or later on when a man's qualifications for a sensitive assignment are in question.

18. ASS'N OF THE BAR, REPORT, p. 146. I submitted this proposal to the Special Committee of the Association of the Bar in a memorandum of Oct. 27, 1955, and consequently am pleased to note that the Committee reached the same conclusion (REPORT, p. 141). Cf. Commission on Government Security, *Report* (1957), pp. 174–6, which also recommends that screening be confined to jobs with Secret or Top Secret access, in conjunction with a proposal that the Confidential classification be abandoned altogether.

But glaciers of Confidential material lie heavily on the military establishment. So long as sensitivity is routinely equated with any access to classified material, it is hard for the outsider to see how the services can avoid masses of cases. Therefore, a general policy of ignoring the Confidential classification—for screening purposes—would be one means of permitting the services to concentrate on critical areas.

I do not propose for a moment that Confidential be discarded as part of the classification system. There has to be a bottom classification, if for no other reason than to avoid hopelessly debasing the next level above. Now that Restricted has been abolished, Confidential is the workhorse for all the material that ought to be kept under control; but it is not critical. The category is necessary for purposes of physical security, and as a reminder that negligence or faithlessness in handling the material is punishable. It is a quite different thing to say that no one can see it without having been through the whole screening process.

The question of redefining sensitive jobs where no access to classified material is involved cannot be resolved so cleanly. In government employment, there is a need to develop open criteria for positions where policies are made or influenced, and where penetration for hostile purposes may occur. The Civil Service Commission has, under E.O. 10440 of March 31, 1953, developed a Schedule C of confidential or policy-making positions which are excluded from the competitive requirements for appointments and tenure. It might serve as a starting point for this redefinition. A somewhat broader base, for the armed forces, is found in the policy of treating all officers as holders of sensitive positions.[19]

In both government and private employment we need to look for the vital installations that are peculiarly vulnerable to sabotage by employees. It is hard to make specific recommendations, because there is such a dearth of informed discussion. The main thing to remember is that sabotage by employees is all that employment tests help to avert, so that there is little value in screening employees when any number of other people can do the same damage.

One can certainly predict with confidence that a selective approach would sharply cut back the Port Security program. Here both the harm and the good of universal screening have already been done. For the future, as I have suggested, it should be sufficient to concentrate on

19. On Schedule C, see Commission on Organization of the Executive Branch of the Government (Hoover Commission), Task Force Report, *Personnel and Civil Service* (1955), pp. 35–8. The Armed Forces policy is in Dept. of Defense Directive No. 5210.9, § VIIIB, BNA MANUAL, p. 31/52.

critical ships, cargoes, and waterfront areas. Indeed, the Association of the Bar Committee recommended that the Port Security program be abolished.[20]

The industrial security programs, in making similar designations of critical areas, would—unlike any other—broaden their scope as they reached beyond classified material. How is this extension of authority to be accomplished and safeguarded? The blank check that the Butler bill hands to the Defense Department is inexcusable. If the Department, as its spokesmen insist, is concerned about only a few hundred cases, the bill could be more narrowly drawn. I will concede that a legislative formula using the same words that I have been using—words like "vital," "critical," and "vulnerable"—does not effectively guide (or constrain) the Secretary of Defense. But a legislative committee framing such legislation has unequaled powers to find out just what it is that needs to be protected. With more information, draftsmanship can become meaningful. We have had a great deal of talk about sabotage but very little expert guidance on the value of employment tests in averting it.

There is one objection to making a public catalogue of critical installations, namely, that it is quite helpful to a prospective enemy. President Truman in his veto message made this argument against the list of defense facilities called for by the Internal Security Act.[21] I wonder whether it has any real force. It is too bad to have to pinpoint the open areas that *we* think are especially vulnerable, because it reinforces judgments that enemy intelligence has surely made already; but that, I suggest, is as far as the harm goes. It is equally too bad to have to draw up a list of priority targets for civil defense purposes; but we do it because we need the information as much as the Russians do. If you really want to hide something, you classify the whole project and take deceptive measures, as we did in World War II to hide the entire atom bomb undertaking.

If it is difficult or embarrassing to frame a cautious statute permitting the government to exclude people from unclassified employment, perhaps we can do without it. Nothing insuperable prevents close cooperation between the government and the managers of vulnerable facilities. The Defense Department's apparent frustration is typified if not inspired by the General Electric situation. It appears that some officials would

20. REPORT, p. 143.
21. Truman's veto message is printed in NYT, Sept. 23, 1950. The Internal Security Act requires the list to be published in the *Federal Register*. See 50 U.S.C. § 784(b).

like to see GE take stronger measures to get rid of United Electrical Workers' influence, and also of certain UE members. GE officers, on their side, say that the responsibility should rest with the government.[22] If there are dangerous persons lurking in unclassified but vital parts of GE and other companies, the government, if it has evidence, can indict or expose them. If it has only suspicions, it can watch them. A much stronger case than has yet been made is needed to justify major extensions of the industrial security program.

The programs with a basis in security considerations now reach between seven and eight million employees. I will not burden the reader with more detailed estimates; but the cumulative result of applying the proposals made here would, I believe, reduce the total to not many more than two million.[23] I believe that this cut-back by two thirds or more can be made without seriously endangering the national security. The gains to values other than security of freeing 5,000,000 people from security programs are obvious. There may indeed be a net gain to security. Trained men with some skill in averting security breaches are a scarce resource, and need to be prudently allotted. If the talents and energies of our security forces are concentrated on the truly sensitive areas, their performance is likely to be more effective than if they are spread thin. To borrow a pithy observation, "The moment we start guarding our toothbrushes and our diamond rings with equal zeal, we usually lose fewer toothbrushes but more diamond rings." [24]

22. See Ch. 5 above, p. 136.
23. This estimate is a close approximation to that of the Association of the Bar Committee, with whose recommendations as to the proper coverage of the security programs I am generally in accord. Its REPORT, p. 146, gives a total of about 1,500,000, but the Committee did not consider the program for military personnel. I would make a somewhat lower estimate for civilians, and a pure guess that only about one-third of the armed forces need to be screened carefully.
24. Dean McGeorge Bundy of Harvard, quoting Prof. J. H. Van Vleck, also of Harvard, in HUMPHREY HEARINGS, p. 473.

11. Security by Exclusion: Identifying Risky People

THE LAST chapter undertook to define sensitive employment, on the hypothesis that in the vital parts of our government and our economy employment tests may be necessary. That is, in situations where an employee can seriously jeopardize national security, we should not put all our faith in the criminal law or in counterspies. We should try to make some sort of advance judgment about who is likely to be a spy or a saboteur, so as to keep him away from vital parts of our government and our economy. The problem is, when can we make a reasonable prediction that John Doe cannot be trusted? It is a far more difficult problem than the definition of sensitive jobs. After all, we do not often catch graduates of a sabotage school with instructions for making bombs among their effects. Once one moves beyond the obvious but minute category of persons known to be trained for or engaged in treason, espionage, or sabotage, uncertainties begin to develop.

There are three general types of potential security risks, in addition to the clear-cut one just mentioned; each of them includes both easy and hard cases. These three types may be summarily described as risks of liability to pressure, other reliability risks, and political risks.

LIABILITY TO PRESSURE: HOSTAGES AND HOMOSEXUALS

The people in this category might be called "pressure-prone." They are assumed to be in a vulnerable position, so that if a Communist strikes at their weak point they will become his tool, even though they are quite free of any communist sympathies. The two types most frequently advanced as characteristic of this category, though for quite different reasons, are homosexuals and people with close relatives behind the Iron Curtain.

The "iron-curtain relative" case appears to be a quite special situation. I have no information on the number of cases in which employment was denied for this reason, nor on the frequency with which coercion is in fact attempted by means of hostages. It is not an altogether groundless fear. One pathetic case was publicized in which a Romanian couple in New York, cut off from two young sons in Romania, was approached by a member of the Romanian Embassy staff and urged to "cooperate." They refused, and rightly; for the cruel twist of the knife in these situations is that the hostage remains at the mercy of the extortioner (though in this case the children were later released).[1] A policy of keeping the American victim in unclassified obscurity may be justified on humane grounds, whatever the security risk.

On the other hand, the pertinence of "iron-curtain relatives" was reduced to absurdity in the famous case of Wolf Ladejinsky. This eminent expert on Asian land reform was in process of transfer from the State Department to Agriculture when Secretary Benson, on the advice of his security officer, declared him a security risk. When the security officer, Glen Cassity, was forced by intense public criticism of the decision to justify it, he leaned heavily on the fact that Ladejinsky had three sisters in Russia. Reporters pointed out that Ladejinsky had a conspicuous anti-Communist record. Cassity had a ready rejoinder. "Would you write articles critical of the communist government if close members of your family were living in Russia and you knew the tactics the Communists used? It is doubtful anyone would do it, unless he had reason to believe his family was safe." Director Stassen of the Foreign Operations Administration, who relieved the White House of some of the embarrassment of the case by promptly employing Ladejinsky for a post in Viet Nam, took no notice of this theory. His statement affirming Ladejinsky's reliability and loyalty simply mentioned the existence of the sisters, and observed that "none of them are known to be Communists." This scarcely met Cassity's point, but perhaps it was not worth meeting.[2]

1. After this episode was publicized, President Eisenhower intervened directly with the Romanian government, and the boys were reunited with their parents. *Time* (June 8, 1953), p. 26; (April 26, 1954), p. 22.
2. For a survey of the Ladejinsky case see NYT, Jan. 16, 1955. The source of the Cassity quotation is *Time* (Jan. 10, 1955), p. 12. The Mutual Security Act requires an affirmative finding of loyalty by the Director. See 68 Stat. 859 (1954), 22 U.S.C. § 1791. Only a short time after he was cleared, Ladejinsky got involved in a conflict of financial interests and was required to resign. NYT, Feb. 11, 1956. With the Ladejinsky case, contrast Industrial Security Program Report (n. 6 below), p. 74 (a preposterously easy case of an employee who had worked for the NKVD in Russia, and had left a wife and children there). A Congressional reaction should also be recorded. Congressman Alfred D. Sieminski interrupted a bland explanation of the "iron-curtain relative" concept by the Treasury's General Counsel to declare that it was an affront to Americans of Polish descent,

These cases are not automatic in their solution. A fairly arbitrary rule of exclusion could be rationalized; the employer wants to spare the employee the possible anguish of a severe conflict of loyalties. But such an arbitrary rule would be too sweeping in its reach, for it would close the door on an employee who was in fact estranged from, or indifferent to, his foreign connections. So a judgment has to be made whether a substantial risk results. That judgment may display the usual excessive caution of the security officer, but it also reflects on the trustworthiness of the employee. After all, he is not compelled to submit to threats if they should be made. If it is decided that he might do so, and thus betray the obligations of sensitive employment, that decision is a reflection on his fortitude and patriotism. He is blameless up till now, but his capacity to resist pressure in the future is called into question.

In the case of sexual aberrations, the employee's own deviant behavior supposedly makes him vulnerable. It seems to be taken for granted that political blackmail centers on homosexuals, though as a matter of fact everyday extortion has a number of other targets. Illicit heterosexual encounters—the takeoff for the traditional "badger game"—come first to mind; and such affairs are surely far more numerous than abnormal ones. However, I doubt that security officers regard any other possible liability to extortion in the same uncompromising way that they do homosexuality.

In support of the belief that homosexuals—and other types of sex deviates—are poor security risks, the classic case, as reported by a Senate subcommittee, is that of

> one Captain Raedl who became chief of the Austrian counter-intelligence net in Russia and had done considerable damage to the espionage net which the Russians had set up in Austria. However, Russian agents soon discovered that Raedl was a homosexual and shortly thereafter they managed to catch him in an act of perversion as the result of a trap they had set for that purpose. Under the threat of exposure Raedl agreed to furnish and he did

---

like himself, and indeed to all Americans. Suppose, he inquired, the Germans had overrun England in World War II? Would that cast suspicion on the Anglo-Saxon stock? Indeed, the Congressman concluded, this policy could "depopulate America—give it back to the Indians." See House Comm. on Appropriations, Subcomm. Hearings, *Treasury-Post Office Departments Appropriations 1955* (1954), pp. 688–90.

furnish the Russians with Austrian military secrets. He also doc-
tored or destroyed the intelligence reports which his own Austrian
agents were sending from Russia with the result that the Austrian
and German General Staffs, at the outbreak of World War I in
1914, were completely misinformed as to the Russian's mobilization intentions. On the other hand, the Russians had obtained from
Raedl the war plans of the Austrians and that part of the German
plans which had been made available to the Austrian Government.
Shortly after the outbreak of the war Captain Raedl's traitorous
acts were discovered by his own Government and he committed
suicide.

The subcommittee from whose report this account of the Raedl case is
taken also received testimony from the principal U.S. intelligence agencies. All of them, the subcommittee said, "were in complete agreement
that sex perverts in government constitute security risks." In addition
to the hazard of blackmail, sex deviates were said to be unreliable because they tend to be emotionally unstable.

Another responsible opinion on this subject comes from Gordon
Dean. He reports that, while Chairman of the Atomic Energy Commission, he was told by a homosexual employee who was about to be
dismissed, "Never permit a homosexual in the program. The opportunities for blackmail are too great." [3]

Whether homosexuality should be an automatic bar to government
employment, either on suitability or on security grounds, is an issue
that has had little public discussion. This is not surprising, because the
whole delicate subject was for a long time taboo. But a marked increase
in candor in the last few years is apparent. Whether Dr. Kinsey's work,
or a general decline of prudery, is responsible, it is now possible to
investigate and discuss sex deviations without mumbling about "morals

3. See Gordon Dean, *Report on the Atom* (1953), p. 231. The quotations on
the Raedl case and the unanimity of the intelligence agencies on homosexuals
are from Senate Comm. on Expenditures in the Executive Departments, Subcomm.
on Investigations, Report, *Employment of Homosexuals and Other Sex Perverts
in Government* (1950), p. 5. Cf. L. Farago, *War of Wits* (New York, Funk and
Wagnalls, 1954), p. 186: "In the entire history of espionage, there are only
two renowned spies who were proven homosexuals, and only one whose homosexuality caused him to engage in espionage [Raedl]. The legend is that sexual
deviates are vulnerable to blackmail and so forced into spying activity. In point
of fact, very few homosexuals have been trapped by their sexual aberrations
compared to the charms of the opposite sex acting as decoys."

charges," the standard newspaper euphemism. The subcommittee under Senator Hoey, already cited, made a general investigation of deviates in government employment in 1950. It found that in the armed forces there existed a traditionally aggressive policy of removing homosexuals. Other government agencies, however, had not recognized the problem to any marked extent until the alarms that led to the legislative investigation. If cases came to light, for example because of an arrest, the employee would be removed in a way that would obscure the reason. Since the Hoey investigation, only the Department of State has been the object of any marked public attention. The Director of its Office of Security stated in March 1953 that 425 employees had been separated as a result of "investigation into allegations of homosexuality." All of them were dealt with by the Office of Security, presumably under the authority of the summary dismissal powers which the Secretary then possessed, and not by Loyalty–Security Board action.

The State Department record, which because of its many cases is surely disproportionate to the experience of any other agency, raises qualms about this ground for disqualification. Grant (for the moment) that the expert opinion on homosexuals' liability to pressure is sound. Give full rein to common opinion that the State Department has for some reason attracted colonies of homosexuals. Still, the methods that resulted in 425 "separations" are disquieting. The official who reported this total said that "the very nature of the problem" made it "virtually impossible" to have a group of Board members try the case. "It has to be done," he explained, "on a personal, across-the-table basis, with hours of interrogation and by experts." [4] Interrogation, he might have added, without specific charges and without any review outside security channels; interrogation that necessarily probes into the most intimate details of a person's life. A lawyer who was permitted to attend one such session with a woman client characterized it as "obscene." An employee who was cleared describe the so-called experts as a "bunch of tough cops with a smattering of Freud." Finally, it is in this area that the Department has countenanced the use of the lie-detector—on a

4. The 425 homosexual separations were reported by John William Ford before the House Comm. on Appropriations, Subcomm. Hearings, *Departments of State . . . Commerce Appropriations for 1954* (1953), p. 114. The tabulalations of the Civil Service Commission under 10450 (see Ch. 2 above, n. 58) list a grand total of 837 cases of sex perversions, 147 of them in the State Department, for the period May 1953–June 1955. See JOHNSTON HEARINGS, p. 732.

"voluntary" basis. Perhaps the relative impersonality of a polygraph test, whatever its shortcomings, makes it preferable to across-the-table questioning by laymen about one's sex life.[5]

The trouble is that these procedures, in addition to their inadequacies, suggest the violent aversion that many—perhaps most—Americans feel toward either latent or practicing homosexuals. In such a hostile atmosphere, does suspicion tip the scales, rather than objective proof that the behavior in question would expose the employee to the risk of blackmail or disgrace? State Department folklore has it that unmarried employees over thirty-five are automatically suspect, and it spins tales of marriages of convenience, made in order to present a façade of normality. Like all folklore, these stories may have a core of truth, or they may be malicious fantasy.

One cannot summarily condemn the people who have been given this dirty security job to do. But one can ask, since sex deviations are a psychiatric problem, whether the experts include any psychiatrists? One can wonder whether the hazard is serious enough to require government investigators' asking about applicants after the usual "Have you any reason to doubt his loyalty," a new question: "Have you any reason to doubt his masculinity?" [6]

From the standpoint of pressure risk, the problem in cases of sexual deviation is not simply whether the employee has a blot on his past, or a current vice. It is whether he is so concerned to conceal his shame that he might betray his country rather than face exposure. In cases that have been the subject of hearings rather than of arbitrary dismissal, the employee's fear of being exposed has sometimes been established. In such cases, an unacceptable risk can doubtless be found. But the possibility of the employee's yielding to blackmail is only one element in these cases. As I have suggested, aversion for the aberration may be an

5. The quotations are from interviews. On the use of the polygraph in these cases see NYT, Dec. 20, 1951; JOHNSTON REPORT, pp. 176–8 (State Department reports only 76 instances of polygraph use, 1950–55). The widespread but erratic use of the polygraph in other agencies is described by Dwight MacDonald in "The Lie-Detector Era," *The Reporter* (June 8, 1954), p. 10; (June 22, 1954), p. 23.

6. This is not a common question, but it has been reported to me. A case reported in Dep't of Defense, Industrial Personnel Security Review Program, *First Annual Report* (1956), p. 93, illustrates the thesis that concealment makes the subject vulnerable. Szilard (n. 7 below), has made a whimsical suggestion that exposes the overinflated character of the homosexual security risk. His solution was for the government simply to publish lists of known homosexuals in its employ, thus removing by exposure any possibility of blackmail.

important background element. A third element is the notion that people of loose habits are generally unreliable, and not to be trusted in sensitive employment.

MIDDLE-CLASS MORALITY

The investigation of sensitive jobholders, one gathers, turns up all sorts of sexual misbehavior, especially liaisons and illegitimate offspring. Such episodes are certainly not evidence of perversion, but rather of an abundance of normal impulses. They are deviations from convention that one segment of the community will view with indifference, another with compassion, another with indignation. If they are flaunted so as to outrage dominant opinion, any employer may decide that the misbehaving employee's usefulness to him is fatally impaired. If on the other hand they are concealed, presumably with shame, a security issue does arise: the possibility that an enemy agent who uncovers the secret will use it for blackmail.

But even where an extramarital relationship, for example, involves neither scandal nor shame, it may get into the security mill. One gets the impression that officials concerned with security have succumbed to the temptation to establish themselves as moral censors. The evidence is inconclusive—a few publicized episodes, and some recent instances of security charges based on immorality. The most notable confusion of security and morality occurred in the contest between Senator Mc-Carthy and the administration over the confirmation of Charles Bohlen as ambassador to Russia. The debate on the floor and the committee proceedings emphasized Bohlen's identification with Roosevelt policies, notably Yalta, and the politically suspect associations attributed to him. However, it was widely understood at the time that the real debate— in the Senate cloakroom—centered about charges of loose living in the Foreign Service. After certain damaging innuendoes were made by the Senator from Wisconsin, one item of fact was confirmed by the Under-Secretary of State, Donald Lourie: Bohlen's brother-in-law, the author of two entertaining volumes of memoirs, had resigned from the Foreign Service in the face of charges of immorality.[7]

7. Lourie's reported statement about Bohlen's brother-in-law's removal was, "He was separated on a basis of morals charges—I don't believe that was the wording. I'm groping for the wording—and he resigned." NYT, April 21, 1953. For more general discussions of the Bohlen confirmation fight see NYT, March 24, 1953, and Sen. Morse's speech in *Cong. Rec.* (March 23, 1953), 99:2206–8. For

In one important State Department loyalty case, it is fairly certain that the decision was influenced by evidence that the employee, who was married, had kept a mistress while on a remote foreign station. What is unclear is the extent to which the offense was compounded by allegations that the mistress was a Communist. Note that there were no charges that the employee had been guilty of any security indiscretions with a Communist mistress; it was just a case of moral outrage at his infidelity. Another State Department employee, it is said, was urged by security officers to resign because her first child arrived too soon after her marriage. The Government Printing Office decided that there was a security risk involved in retaining the respondent and the correspondent in a divorce case, and dismissed them both. Another case of marital discord led to a wife's charging her husband with "misconduct off duty," for which he was dismissed. It appeared that the wife was lying, so she was dismissed. Security risks again. It was the latter case in particular that led to the remarkable spectacle of the *American Legion Magazine* editorially attacking the security program. Recent industrial security cases have charged young men with fornication; [8] and in at least one case known to me premarital intercourse of a couple who subsequently married was set down as evidence of the husband's gross immorality (he was cleared). On the basis of Dr. Kinsey's well-known statistics, this sort of thing opens alarming possibilities.

The whole keyhole-peeping business would not be worth raising were it not for the ugly prospects that even a few cases suggest. Full field investigations are bound to keep on turning up reports of family skeletons and of wayward lives. Such information, when laid before a puritanical person, is apt to deflect judgment away from valid security grounds.

What can be done, if it is agreed that private lapses should not be

---

a satire on the security consequences of deviation from conventional behavior see Leo Szilard, "Security Risk," BAS (1954), *10*:384.

8. See ACLU [No. Calif.] *News,* Feb., June, and Sept. 1955, for other morals charges. The story of the State Department employee who had her baby too soon, by Anthony Lewis, is in *Democratic Digest* (March 1954), pp. 83–4. The Government Printing Office case was first reported in the *Washington Post,* May 31, 1954. The man involved, E. R. Dixon, told the entire story during the JOHNSTON HEARINGS, pp. 564–76. It is significant to note that Dixon was an important Legionnaire, the divorce proceedings were public records so that no pressure could be applied, and that the divorce itself was apparently not granted on adultery grounds. For the American Legion's concern over members who were discharged despite the falsity of their wives' accusations see *The American Legion Magazine* (Jan. 1955), p. 36, reprinted in HUMPHREY HEARINGS, p. 625.

drawn unnecessarily into the reach of public officials? These personal affairs, are, after all, *sometimes* relevant to security. They may raise the possibility of liability to pressure. Or the investigators may have to follow the scent of an illicit affair, if they suspect that the employee's paramour is an espionage agent.[9] So probably nothing can be done, beyond urging self-restraint on those who come upon evidence of scandal. The evidence should be examined for direct security implications, and, if none is found, unmistakably put out of consideration. This kind of administrative scrupulousness, which would keep moral questions out of security channels when they do not belong there, may be fostered by regulations that are narrowly drawn.

SECURITY RELIABILITY AND RELIABILITY IN GENERAL

Indeed, it may be argued that some of these problems have been created by the broad sweep of E.O. 10450, the Eisenhower security program's charter. That order directs the attention of investigators and reviewers to "any behavior, activities, or associations which tend to show that the individual is not reliable or trustworthy" (§ 8(a)(i)). Further criteria give this catch-all some content, by referring to such matters as "deliberate misrepresentations . . . of material facts," and "Any criminal, infamous, dishonest, immoral, or notoriously disgraceful conduct, habitual use of intoxicants to excess, drug addiction, or sexual perversion." "Willful violation or disregard of security regulations," though it is found in a different subsection of the Order, also falls into this group.

One has little occasion to quarrel with these criteria in their most direct applications. Any employer may understandably want to use whatever choice he has in the labor market to exclude liars, criminals, drunkards, and maniacs. A security program is indeed not required for that purpose. In a civil service system these are all questions of "suitability." Long-standing regulations make it possible to remove an employee on any of the specific grounds just listed.[10]

In fact, it seems fair to say that there is only one other reliability

9. This was the situation in the Irmgard Schmidt case in Berlin; she compromised several Air Force officers. See *Time* (Jan. 3, 1955), p. 22, and NYT, Dec. 21, 1954.

10. See ASS'N OF THE BAR, REPORT, pp. 54–5, 284, pointing out the identity of Civil Service regulations with this part of E.O. 10450.

factor, in addition to the pressure cases already discussed, that seems peculiarly linked to security needs. That is the case of the "blabbermouth." A person who is careless with classified information is indeed the archetype of a reliability risk. Whether he talks under the relaxation of alcohol, or from a desire to impress others with the importance of his work, or from whatever combination of motives, an employee who is compulsively or carelessly garrulous is not the one to be trusted with classified information. Nor are people who are contemptuous or casual about physical security measures. The blabbermouth or his companion the briefcase-loser are of course no asset to any administrator. Even in nonsensitive offices there is usually work in progress that should not be broadcast; similarly, it is proper to discipline an employee who betrays unclassified confidences. But the whole matter assumes a quite different dimension when classified material is at stake, and it does come rightly under the jurisdiction of security.

Of course, all sorts of questions of general reliability and trustworthiness do arise in sensitive employment—and elsewhere. If a job is so sensitive that only a superman can fill it, then anyone who falls short of that mark incurs some hazard in accepting it. And so on through varying degrees of sensitivity. But this is to say no more than could be said about the appraisal of men for any circumstances of responsibility. If a man's background does not fill you with confidence about his trustworthiness on the job, you will not hire him—provided the job is attractive enough so that someone else with a better record is at hand to fill it. If he is already employed in a subordinate position, you will not promote him. If some previously hidden scandal shakes confidence in a subordinate, his superiors will attempt to remove or demote him. All this is commonplace, and equally applicable to insensitive as to sensitive employment.

In recognition of this fact, some departmental regulations cut back the generality of the reliability provisions of E.O. 10450 by directing the use of regular civil service removal procedures in cases where general reliability is called into question. This is highly desirable. For a security program which combines all these elements of reliability and pressure risk with the dominant issue of political reliability—that is, of loyalty—creates a special hardship for the employee, in addition to the hardship of losing his job. No program of any consequence has provided for specifying and disclosing the actual grounds for dismissal. To say that a man is a security risk, without explanation, leaves open the probabil-

ity that disloyalty is the ground. It is certainly a common belief, fortified
by such evidence as we have, that charges suggesting disloyalty predomi-
nate in security cases.[11]

It can be said, even without a definitive ranking of degrees of infamy,
that disloyalty is more infamous than many everyday vices or shortcomings. On the other hand, there are depths of evil even more repellent than disloyalty. It is unnecessary to decide which is worse than
what. It is certainly fairer to remove altogether from the loyalty–security
context matters that do not belong there.

When questions of reliability do arise in a security setting, imputations
of wrongdoing more severe than the facts warrant can still be avoided.
All that is necessary is a change in operation of formal programs: require the employer, if the employee so requests, to state the specific
grounds for disqualification. If the employee prefers to leave his good
name to the hazards of uninformed speculation, the choice can be his.
But if he feels that the reasons that will be given for his disqualification
are less damaging than the reasons that will be imagined, the option to
force disclosure should also be his. One can speculate that the result
of such an option would be widespread disclosure of venial sins, and
continued concealment of mortal ones. The inferences that would arise
about people who avoided disclosure would be pretty compelling; they
would be assumed to be near the inner circle of infamy. But this cannot be helped, unless one wants to reverse the present line of argument,
and urge that all victims of security programs should share each other's
guilt.

A requirement that the triers of formal cases be able to explain their
decisions is in any event desirable, for reasons that will be discussed in
Chapter 16. It may be putting too fine a point on it to suggest that the
employee should be the judge of whether the findings should be disclosed; the suggestion simply stands between complete disclosure and
the present practice of imperfect concealment. If we have to pillory
people on security grounds, everyone may as well be pilloried for his
own shortcomings.

I now turn from questions of reliability to the special problem of our
time, the determination, in a security context, of unacceptable political
risks.

11. The military regulations make a special point of separating security from
suitability. Their 1957 revisions (Ch. 3 above, n. 35), also provide for some
disclosure of reasons for security discharges.

POLITICAL RISKS

Present membership in the Communist party is an automatic disqualification for sensitive employment. Whatever reservations may be made in other connections about imputing to the member the subversive goals of the party need not be made here. We are concerned at the moment with risks, not with personal guilt. Disqualification also follows clearly when the employee's personal adherence to a policy of violent overthrow can be established. This is usually just another way of saying that he is a Communist. But not always. Do we make an exception if the employee is a Trotskyite or some even more esoteric kind of revolutionary?

For some sophisticated counterintelligence purposes, we might make an exception; members of left-wing splinter groups are said to be veritable bloodhounds at sniffing out orthodox Communists. But for the run of sensitive jobs, the refinements of doctrine and loyalty that separate left-wing extremists from each other need not be considered. Even though some unorthodox Communists declare a hatred for the present Russian regime surpassing that of most conservatives, their subversive ideals, if firmly held, should be firmly respected. We may provide extremists with soapboxes, but we need not install them in sensitive jobs where their capacity for harm is substantial.

Of course, government employment and much private employment are already closed to Communists and other known revolutionaries on loyalty grounds. But I want to keep this discussion as distinct as possible from the critical examination of loyalty programs to follow in Part III. All that is necessary now is to keep in mind that some political disqualifications from sensitive employment are clear cut. As one follows the maze of ambiguous belief, sympathy, participation, affiliation, and association that make up the great bulk of political cases, it may be forgotten that there are Communists and there are spies.

100 CHARGES ANALYZED

Few cases involve charges of clear-cut disqualifications; this assertion can be illustrated by a group of cases that attracted considerable attention in 1953–54. The respondents were nineteen civilian scientists, engineers, and technicians employed by the Army Signal Corps at Fort Monmouth, New Jersey. They had all been engaged in research and

development work, for periods averaging about ten years; a number
of them had previously undergone charges and hearings and had been
cleared. The work was largely sensitive but not entirely so. The cases
became notorious because Senator McCarthy got wind of some trouble
at Monmouth, launched his own investigations and headlines, and provoked a great furor with wholly unsubstantiated outcries about espionage. The pressures built by the Senator do not seem to have had much
effect on the charges about to be reviewed, because most of them had
been brought before he thundered into the arena, and those which were
added later were of no greater substantiality.[12]

I do not want to claim that these cases are a scientific sample. One
could not claim that about any collection of cases that has come to
public attention, because so little is known about the universe from
which these small gleams of light reach us. Most if not all of the Monmouth employees were from the metropolitan New York area. This
enormously increased their possible exposure to communist associations
compared, say, to a group from the rural South.[13] It also affects the
organizational affiliations that are charged; it is the American Labor
party that recurs, not the Progressive party. But after these and other
reservations have been made, the Monmouth cases still look pretty typical of their period. That is, they are like most other security cases that
I have heard about. They contain, if there is any difference, a higher-
than-average proportion of serious charges.

Their special value lies in the fact that the tabulations below represent *all* the charges in nineteen cases that were brought in an important
installation following the Eisenhower administration's review of past
security records there. That review included these elements. According

12. The charges analyzed in this section were collected by the Scientists'
Committee on Loyalty and Security, then affiliated with the Federation of American Scientists. The author (though no scientist) was a member of the committee.
This analysis of the charges, and of their distribution among the criteria of the
Army regulation (SR 620–220–1, § 17) was used (with a slightly different method
of counting) in the principal source for this section, the S.C.L.S. publication,
The Fort Monmouth Security Investigations, August 1953–April 1954 (April 25,
1954), pp. 4/16, 29, 31. This report was supplemented by S.C.L.S., "Fort Mon-
mouth One Year Later," BAS (1955), *11*:148. The McCarthy hearings are Senate
Comm. on Government Operations, Permanent Subcomm. on Investigations,
Hearings, *Army Signal Corps—Subversion and Espionage* (1954).

13. Also, all but two of the Monmouth employees were Jews. On the possibility of anti-Semitic motivations in the Fort Monmouth cases see Arnold
Forster and Benjamin Epstein, *Cross Currents* (1956), pp. 67–121.

to Secretary Stevens, there had been, since 1946, 167 cases at Fort Monmouth (including the present ones) in which there was "some derogatory information." With an average employment of twelve to fourteen thousand, a normal turnover in a seven-year period would mean that the 167 were drawn from a total of perhaps 25,000. That is, "some derogatory information" had turned up on roughly one-half of one per cent of the employees, not an unusual number. Many of these cases presumably never came to hearing; in others the employee may have decided to resign in the face of charges; in others it was doubtless decided that the information did not warrant charges and hearings. Senator McCarthy said that the dismissal of thirty-five employees had been recommended by the First Army Loyalty–Security Board, but that it was overruled in all but two cases by the Department of the Army Appeals Board. Those cleared, as I have said, included some of those charged again in 1953.[14]

Now for the nineteen. The charges against them total approximately 100. Approximation is necessary because sometimes association with two suspected Communists was alleged in two separate charges; more often similar associations were lumped together. So with events. The exact number would not be meaningful. The figure of 100 is a convenient approximation of the charges as listed.

Only eight of these charges are not political. Five charges, involving two employees, raised what I will call "imminent security risks," in that they appear to charge "sympathetic association" with spies. The first employee has a brother, Felix Inslerman, who was named by Whittaker Chambers as the photographer for the ring which Chambers served as courier in 1937; Felix recently confessed to these activities.[15] Connections with the brother made up three separate charges. This employee

14. In addition to the nineteen cases, six more were brought in the following months, eleven employees were suspended and reinstated without charges, and about two dozen employees were denied access to classified material for varying periods; that is, their clearances were suspended and they were put on innocuous work, without charges and without any formal way to challenge the denial of clearance. Six of the nineteen were dismissed, as were two others whose cases came up later. The dismissed employees have commenced lawsuits attacking the legality of their dismissals. Coleman v. Brucker, 156 F. Supp. 126 (D.D.C. 1957) (complaint dismissed). An appeal is pending.

15. For the testimony of Felix Inslerman, see Senate Comm. on Government Operations, Permanent Subcomm. on Investigations, Hearings, *Subversion and Espionage in Defense Establishments and Industry* (1954), pp. 97–110; see Whittaker Chambers, *Witness* (1952), pp. 421–4.

was cleared. The second employee, Aaron Coleman, was charged with an old acquaintanceship with Julius Rosenberg, and with a close acquaintanceship, through 1947, with Morton Sobell, a convicted member of the Rosenberg ring. He was dismissed. Note that here, and throughout this dissection of the Monmouth cases, I am putting the charges in their apparent relationship to one of the Army criteria defining security risks. The associations in these two cases would be imminently dangerous only *if* they were continued under circumstances that suggested complicity by the employee in the espionage activities of his relative or friend, or a risk that the employee might inadvertently disclose classified information. The charges do not necessarily lead to such inferences, and the employees of course denied that the inferences would be correct.

Three charges only, against three employees, raised issues of reliability, on account of improper handling of classified material. One employee (the same one who had known Sobell) took classified material home for study. The other is alleged to have given papers to a fellow worker outside proper channels. The third is charged with attempting to transmit a technical paper to a professor in Czechoslovakia. Since the Czech had requested an unclassified reprint from the *Physical Review,* this charge is silly. However, the explanation appears only from the employee's affidavits; so this charge, like the others, is treated as though it seriously related to some category of security risk. The last two men were cleared.

There was no charge directly raising the issue of liability to pressure. That leaves ninety-two charges that I have classified as political. They include *no* charges of present Communist party membership, nor of individual advocacy of violent overthrow of the government. These would be absolute disqualifications. All other political charges I take as open to explanation, and as subject to evaluation. They range from past membership in the Communist party to having a brother-in-law who was a past member of the American Labor party.

The categories of political charges that follow were devised by taking the seventeen criteria from the Army Security Regulations, rearranging them, and consolidating them. It is often difficult to tell at which of related criteria a charge is directed; maybe the person who drafted it had no clear idea of its significance. The subtotals given here are the averages of scorings by several persons. Their independent assignments of charges to criteria had a good correlation within the groupings shown here.

Number
of Charges

I. *Beliefs and Expressions*
   "Sympathetic interest" in Communist or totalitarian
   movements (usually said to be evidenced by statements in conversation)   8

II. *Activities and Affiliations*
   Past membership in a Communist or other subversive
      group   12
   "Sympathetic association" with such a group, or par-
      ticipation in its activities where one should have
      known of its subversive aims
   Participation in a front organization, with views sympa-
      thetic to its subversive purposes   23
   Participation in, or sympathy with, the subversive infil-
      tration of a group

III. *Associations* (*with individuals*)
   Sympathetic association with Communists or advocates
      of violent overthrow   49
   Close association with a person who falls in any of the
      above categories

These figures represent the cumulated charges, and tell us nothing
about the pattern of charges against individual employees. Taken as a
whole, they emphasize the ambiguous nature of most of the affiliations
and associations that are alleged. Participation of some sort in a front
organization, or in an infiltrated one, accounts for about one-fourth of
the charges. Since a front, by definition, has avowed legal goals and
hidden subversive ones, belonging to a front has no significance even
under the security criteria unless the member was sympathetic to the
subversive purpose of the group. Most of the charges in this category
state only that the employee was an "active member of" or "a member
of" the suspect organization, such as the United Public Workers or
United Electrical Workers unions, the Progressive party or the American Labor party, the Federation of American Scientists or the American
Veterans Committee. That some of these organizations should be
characterized as fronts or as seriously infiltrated by Communists at the
time and place of an employee's membership is of course the security
officers' judgment, not mine.[16] It is quite probable that the government

16. Examples of charges, later retracted, that the American Veteran's Committee was communist infiltrated and dominated are given in JOHNSTON HEAR-

would not and could not make such a showing in every case. But it does not have to. Once the charge is laid, it is up to the employee to show that his affiliation was *not* subversive, first by establishing his own innocence, and then, if he can, that of the organization.

The whole area of associations with individuals (aside from the strict security charges of association with spies, etc.) is equally ambiguous, yet these charges account for half of all those directed at the Monmouth employees. The Army regulations distinguish two types of associations. The first is "sympathetic association" with members or sympathetic associates of a Communist or other subversive organization. The second is "close continuing association" with anyone who falls within almost any of the criteria classified as "imminent security risks," as "absolute political disqualifications," or as general political risks. Association, either sympathetic or close, with reliability risks or pressure risks is apparently not considered significant.

"Sympathetic" is thus the key word in some personal relationships, as it is in relations with groups; and again one would suppose that the sympathy in question is the employee's regard for his acquaintance's subversive character, not for his personal traits. The Monmouth charges assigned to this criterion vary in their wording; most of them are simply a bare statement that "You have associated with *X,* who is reported to be a Communist or a Communist sympathizer." Suppose the employee simply acknowledges (if it is the case) that he has associated with *X.* Would this concession suggest that the association was "sympathetic" to *X* as a Communist? In the security world, the answer seems to be yes. In theory, the employee can make any of these answers: (1) that he did not associate with *X* except casually; (2) that *X* is not a Communist; (3) that if he was, the employee had no reason to know it; (4) that the employee, though he knew *X* was a Communist (or a sympathizer), disapproved of *X*'s politics and associated with him only because he lived next door, say, or played the cello in the same string quartet.

Thus there are four possible innocent replies to the charge of association with *X,* a Communist, though the fourth would probably be coldly received. Just as it stands, the bare charge of association does not convey anything; but I have assumed that a sympathetic association was implied.

INGS, pp. 264–5. On A.V.C.'s defeat of an attempt by the Communists to capture the organization see pp. 268–70. I do not know of an instance of significant communist penetration of the Federation of American Scientists.

The second association category—"close and continuing"—purports to get its strength from proximity and not from sympathy. It therefore has an element that can be determined by observation. That is, a man does have a close and continuing association with his wife, as long as they are living together. Whether the couple is sympathetic is much more a matter of opinion. But whatever solidity comes from the concept of "close and continuing" melts away when we consider the kinds of people whose propinquity raises security doubts. Some examples from the Monmouth charges illustrate this point.

First, associations that are of serious significance should be separated from the general muddle. The status of an imminent security risk has already been ascribed to associations with spies, provided the associations are not too casual or remote. This does not mean that anyone who ever knew Julius Rosenberg *is* a security risk; it does mean that a security issue needs to be resolved.[17] A security issue also arises when a member of one's immediate family is said to be an active Communist party member. That is the substance of two of the Monmouth cases. In one of them, the single charge was the employee's association with his father, a professor about whom a long list of communist connections was recited.[18] The employee in reply denied any sympathy with his father's politics and advanced his own good record. In the other case, the employee was descended (but wholly estranged, he said) from a whole family of Communists of unchallenged notoriety.

"GUILT BY RELATIONSHIP"

The rest of the "close and continuing" cases are quite equivocal in their import. Does it add any weight to a case to charge that an employee's wife, when herself employed, belonged to the same left-wing union that he did? Or to another case, that several members of the employee's family were registered in the American Labor party, when he was not? Or to another that the employee's sister signed Com-

17. The answers of the Monmouth employees in question, if true, do resolve the issues. The man who knew Rosenberg in college said he had not seen him since. The Inslerman answer describes total noninvolvement in the brother's subversive activities, and almost complete estrangement, except in response to a desperate appeal for a loan in 1949. See the S.C.L.S. study (n. 12 above), pp. 4/15, 4/17.

18. The professor, Dr. Louis Weisner, retired after a hearing board recommended his dismissal from Hunter College. See NYT, Oct. 1, 1954, Nov. 24, 1955 (at end of story on Hughes case).

munist party nominating petitions in 1941 and 1943? Such charges say, at most, "You may be a security risk because one or more of your relatives may be a security risk."

Charges of this sort, when they come to public attention, give rise to a good deal of resentful opposition to "guilt by relationship." In 1950 the Air Force attempted to deprive a Detroit Reserve officer, Capt. Charles Hill, of his commission, chiefly because of his father's left-wing activities. The case became a mild public issue; Secretary Finletter intervened, and reversed the proposed action. In 1953 another Michigan reservist, Milo Radulovich, took an almost identical case to the public— a subversive sister was the only added element. Secretary Talbott intervened, and again reversed the proposed action. The Monmouth charges, however, showed that ties of kinship continued to figure heavily in security cases, despite the popular sentiment against visiting the sins of parents on their children.

In 1955 a whole rash of kinship cases broke out in the press, touched off by the success of Midshipman Eugene Landy, a graduate of the Merchant Marine Academy, in effecting a reversal of a Navy Department decision denying him a reserve commission. The case against Landy was based entirely on his mother's former membership in the Communist party and her party activities. Secretary Thomas, overruling a "Special Review Board," found that Landy's "association with his mother was the natural relationship of mother and son and not a sympathetic association with her political beliefs. . . . In fact, he has, since high school age, been unsympathetic with and in disagreement with her apparent political beliefs." Most of the publicized kinship cases involved commissions or discharges of members of the armed forces, and almost all of them resulted in ultimate clearance.[19]

The same resistance appears to "guilt by marriage." Cases turning on the political tendencies of a spouse happen not to have aroused the same

19. Hill, NYT, Jan. 31, Feb. 4, 1951. Radulovich, NYT, Sept. 24, 25, 30, Oct. 14, Nov. 25, 1953; this case became widely known through Edward R. Murrow's television program, "See it Now," Oct. 20, 1953. Landy, NYT, Aug. 5, 6, 7, Sept. 10, Oct. 1, 1955; George Sokolsky, "The Landy Case," *Saturday Review* (Oct. 22, 1955), p. 23.

Other such cases in 1955 were Stephen Branzovich (Air Force), NYT, Aug. 23, Oct. 28, 1955. Joseph Gaberman (dismissed from Navy civilian job, but retained reserve commission), NYT, Aug. 8, 1955, HENNINGS HEARINGS, pp. 579, 590, 675. Pierre Gaston (Coast Guard Academy graduate), NYT, Aug. 18, Sept. 13, 1955. Robert Jones (Air Force), NYT, Sept. 17, 1955. Walter Novak, NYT, Sept. 3, Nov. 2, 1955. Joseph Summers (dismissed from Navy civilian job), NYT, Sept. 1, 1955; JOHNSTON HEARINGS, p. 577.

degree of public concern as did cases just mentioned; but they pose a
similar emotional conflict. "What is a man to do?" one hears asked,
"Divorce a wife who flirts with left-wing movements?" That is not the
question the security officer is trying to answer. He has to decide
whether the employee can keep a sensitive job, not whether he can
keep a radical spouse. Even if it is a dubious inference that Mr. Z shares
Mrs. Z's political views, their close and continuing association creates
some risk that Mrs. Z will worm out classified information, or that she
will wheedle Mr. Z into performing some disloyal act. But before these
risks become substantial, it should be established (1) that Mrs. Z is
really a dangerous character; and (2) as in the pressure cases, that Mr.
Z is too weak to resist whatever importunities she might bring to bear
on him. If Mr. Z knows that the damaging relationship is known to the
authorities, it would seem probable that he would be a zealot for security
measures.

Six of the association charges against as many Monmouth employees
involved their wives. The charges against the wives ranged in gravity
from past Communist party membership to membership in the United
Public Workers union. As it happens, none of these cases presents a
clear instance of "guilt by marriage" alone; in all of them some activity
or voluntary association of the employee himself is present, of as
much significance or greater significance than his wife's doings.

Indeed, after the Monmouth charges have been added and divided
in a variety of ways, still all they show is the heavy predominance of
charges that allege ambiguous organizational affiliations, ambiguous acquaintance with alleged Communists, and ambiguous kinfolk. Statistics,
however, do not decide individual cases. When you have an average
of five charges against each suspended employee, what do they add up
to in the individual case? How many ambiguities create a reasonable
doubt?

One could turn the Monmouth cases into a sinister parlor game, and
invite the reader to play at security officer by giving him a summary of
the charges in each case. How would he decide? Of course the game
would be artificial, because none of these cases was decided on the basis
of the charges alone, without explanation. None of the parties, so far as
I know, dared elect one of the procedural options that would say, in
effect, "So what? I do favor the policies of Max Lerner, which you
describe as 'leftist.' I did list as a reference J.K., who you say was
removed as a security risk in 1951. I do associate with my brother,
against whom you have brought rather mild charges—including asso-

ciation with me." These are all of the charges in one of the weakest of
the Monmouth cases. They do not amount to much, but a very good
reason for trying to explain away even these allegations is that the
Army form letter bringing the charges states that "It is determined that
your retention in employment is not clearly consistent with the interests
of national security by reason of the following reliable information . . ."
With the case thus prejudged, the employee would be ill-advised to try
to test the legal or logical sufficiency of the charges standing alone.

APPRAISING THE WHOLE MAN

Under what circumstances, then, do political cases create significant
security risks? I am assuming that the purposes of a security program do
not include punishing people for radical and unpopular views, affiliations, and associations, and that they are confined to weeding out those
who might commit any of the offenses catalogued in Chapters 8 and 9.

The security officers are looking for people who they think might
be willing to betray the interests of the United States and work for
Russia. They presumably expect that political tests will turn up both
concealed communist tools, and those who, while not yet Communists,
have communist sympathies strong enough so that they could be pressed
or persuaded to violate their trust. Most feared seems to be the "sleeper,"
the person whose loyalties are already committed—to the other side—
and who is lying in wait for the day when he can tell the secret, smash
the controls, or take over the office. It is not surprising that fear of the
undiscovered employee who is a certain source of danger should haunt
the security forces. You have to assume he is there, as General Bedell
Smith once pointed out, even in the guarded mysteries of the CIA.[20]
How to identify him? Presumably a person in this dangerous position
avoids any current missteps. Are you likely to detect him by combing
around in his past? True, a man now underground may once have had
above-ground Communist connections. But the ventilation of FBI reports about radical activities of undergraduates is not likely to expose
the true "sleeper."

Are such reports any better as a clue to the discovery of a wavering
sympathizer? If you are honestly trying to appraise a man's political

20. The fear of the "sleeper" is expressed in Harold Martin, "Those Loyalty
Investigations," *Saturday Evening Post* (June 20, 1953), p. 124. General Smith's
observation assumed unwonted importance because it came in the midst of the
1952 presidential campaign. NYT, Sept. 30, Oct. 1, 2, 1952.

trustworthiness, and he is honestly trying to establish it, then almost any information about him is relevant. The trouble lies in the process of selection and emphasis that inevitably occurs. The charges select and emphasize "derogatory" affiliations and associations. How far afield, and how long ago, is it reasonable to go in weaving this web? What has evidentiary value? The faculty advisor to the undergraduate Physics Club at Brooklyn College was an alleged Communist. Does that association taint all the physics majors at Brooklyn who were eager students and joined the Physics Club? It appears in one of the Monmouth charges.

The scope of derogatory information spreads like ripples from a stone thrown in a pool. The inner circles are composed of party membership and the like, engaged in by the employee himself. Then the circles include his friends and relatives and their affiliations; then fellow members of organizations and their affiliations; and so on as the circles get wider—and fainter.

Against the derogatory information must be balanced the employee's picture of himself, as he develops it in affidavits and testimony, from himself and his friends. Especially at the hearing stage, close attention will be paid to the employee's beliefs and attitudes. These will not figure so much in the charges (only 10 per cent of the Monmouth political charges are directed at beliefs or their expression), partly, I surmise, because even the FBI does not have much opportunity to find out what a private citizen thinks. But political catechisms come into their own at hearings. Again the emphasis will be on the unorthodox elements in the employee's thinking.

Once a case has gone beyond the preliminary screening of the raw files and one begins to have the employee's version of events, there are at least six groups of data to be considered:

(1) The derogatory information.

(2) The employee's denials, explanations, and admissions with respect to the derogatory information.

(3) The over-all record of the employee.

(4) The image one forms of the employee. Does he strike the trier as a responsible, stable personality?

(5) The sensitivity and importance of the job.

(6) The importance of the employee to the employer. How much risk will you accept to keep a genius in the office?

And, though political charges dominate the typical case, there may be other charges to be considered. I have been trying to separate the various categories in order to describe them. Now, at the risk of confusing them, it seems necessary to say that even in a wholly political case the ultimate issue is still one of reliability—*political reliability* against communist threats or blandishments, or against the pangs of conscience, or the tumult of emotion, or whatever moves people to change sides. Also, since we are now considering the whole case and the whole man, conventional elements of reliability will mingle with the political ones. If the employee sees a lot of another suspect person, do they improperly discuss classified materials? Might they? The answer has to depend on judgment, not on the bare fact of the association.

It is hard to imagine a more difficult decision to make conscientiously than the formal finding that X is or is not a security risk. That is, in the typically ambiguous case. It is a decision that any employer in a sensitive area has to make, and always has had to make if the question was raised. But, in calmer times it was not raised in any compelling way; and we did not think that there were doubts about many people. Now the path to decision has become a minor pilgrim's progress, beset with sloughs of doubt and with senatorial dragons. A conscientious estimate of the employee's potential behavior in the light of all his past history is what is called for. Well-drafted regulations make this explicit, and it should be implicit in any event.

But there are strong countervailing forces to the making of an overall appraisal. Foremost is the difficulty of doing it, which leads to a search for rules of thumb. It has been suggested, for example, that anyone who had ten "citations" by the House Committee on Un-American Activities, or other agencies, is an "extremely bad risk." [21] More pervasive, I think, is another retreat from judgment. The slogan of this position, as we have often observed, is "take no chances." If you are looking for security, "take no chances" seems a plausible motto, and it is confirmed by the cautious terminology of statutes and regulations. E.O. 10450 puts on the decision-makers the responsibility of finding that the retention of an employee is "clearly consistent with the national security." It is also strengthened by the obsessive fear of the "sleeper." You can never, as a security officer, be sure of anyone. But if you take no chances, if everyone in your department is (like yourself) "lilywhite," then you have done your best.

Seen in this light, the Monmouth charges take on a baleful aspect. These varied and ambiguous incidents are not easily overbalanced by the harmonious development of the whole personality. They are suspi-

21. Select Comm. to Investigate Foundations, *Final Report* (Jan. 1, 1953), House Report No. 2514, p. 8.

cious circumstances; and the employee must be above suspicion. They suggest the chance that the employee may be faithless; and the authorities may have decided to take no chances. Apply this approach to the ever-widening ripples of derogatory information; it becomes no feat at all to suspect security risks in all the hundreds of thousands of New Yorkers who at one time or another adhered to the American Labor party.

The ALP appeared in charges against five of the Monmouth employees. It was charged against *A* (in a generally feeble case) that his father was registered in the ALP from 1937 to 1941. *B* was himself a member from 1947 to 1949 (when he was in college as a veteran); so were his parents and his brother. *C*'s mother and sister were ALP registrants around 1947. *D* and his wife were both in the ALP from 1938 to 1947, as was his sister from an unstated date until 1947. *E*'s mother was so registered in 1947 and 1948.

Now, what are the principal facts about the American Labor party? It was founded in New York City in 1936, with the support of many labor unions, including the International Ladies' Garment Workers and the Amalgamated Clothing Workers. It also attracted right-wing Socialists. When it supported F. H. LaGuardia for mayor in 1937, it amassed 483,000 votes for him—more than 20 per cent of all the votes cast. Communist infiltration, both directly and through trade unions, became significant in 1938; but right-wing elements remained in control until 1943, when Sidney Hillman (of the Amalgamated) aligned his Political Action Committee with the left group in ALP. Then David Dubinsky (of ILGWU) and other right-wingers withdrew from ALP and formed the Liberal party. In the 1944 presidential election 496,000 New Yorkers voted for Roosevelt on the ALP line, a gain over 1940's 417,000, despite the 330,000 votes that went to the seceded Liberals.

The Amalgamated forces (and the state CIO) left ALP in 1948. It was as an ALP candidate that Henry Wallace ran for president in 1948 in New York, getting 510,000 votes. In 1952, when ALP also supported the Progressive party candidate, Vincent Hallinan, he got only 64,211 votes. Thus there was a swift decline in the ALP fortunes after 1948. Its only organizational support was now from left-wing unions; and communist sympathizers of one sort or another were doubtless in control. It formally dissolved in 1956.[22]

22. NYT, Oct. 8, 1956. This account of the ALP is drawn from the following sources: Hugh Bone, *American Politics and the Party System* (1949), pp. 150–2; Bone, "Political Parties in New York City," *Am. Pol. Sci. Rev.* (1946), *40*:277;

When you find members of a family registered in ALP before 1948, can this be considered derogatory information? The party had 228,668 registrants in 1947. How many of them are thought to have been Communists? When you find registration after 1948, what does that signify about any one of the 176,143 registrants in 1949 (the latest date appearing in the Monmouth charges)? That he was indifferent to the menace of communist infiltration? Possibly. That he was part of the infiltration? Possibly; but note that none of the charges says so. Still, the allegation of registration is another stone thrown into the pool. It is up to the employee to show that the ripples lead nowhere. If the employee himself was not a member, was it only because he was living in New Jersey and could not be? Maybe. What is the significance of the possibility that if he had lived in New York he might have been a member? Does that make him an anti-anti-Communist? Is he indifferent to the menace? It could be, when you throw in (as in one Monmouth case) his alleged failure to "take a positive stand against the infiltration of the Monmouth County Chapter of the American Veterans' Committee." If he is possibly not fervently anticommunist, by the standards of the security officers, is it possible that he will leak, give away, or sell military secrets, if he knows any? Certainly; anything is possible. Well, then, is his employment clearly consistent with the national security? Perhaps not.

Thus taking no chances leads to absurdity and worse. A family history of ALP affiliation, when combined with other facts of like character, may understandably set a little bell ringing in the wary security officer's consciousness; but should it trip the general alarm?

If you have a hearing, and if the employee does not lose his composure, and if his answers are docile, then the harmless whole man may become visible, and the alarm bells can be stilled. But remember, the suspect often has no right to a hearing. In the federal government, he may be an applicant or a temporary employee. In private employment, there may be no formal procedures at all. In such cases, the security officers are the judges; the raw file is the evidence; "lilywhiteness" may be the standard. Then the Monmouth charge that "you gave as a reference in 1947 *M.N.,* who in 1940 was on the active indices of the American Peace Mobilization" may be unrebutted, even though it was in fact dissipated by the reply that *M.N.* is a venerable Baptist minister, that the reference to "active indices" of the American Peace Mobiliza-

Howard Penniman, *Sait's American Parties and Elections* (1948), p. 141; NYT, Dec. 7, 1948, Dec. 9 and 13, 1952.

tion seems to mean its mailing list, and that the sole recollected activity of *M.N.* with regard to the Mobilization was to file its propaganda in the wastebasket.[23]

KEEPING NATIONAL SECURITY AND PERSONNEL
SECURITY ISSUES SEPARATED: THE OPPENHEIMER CASE

One special way in which a security inquiry may be overextended requires attention. There is a possibility that security proceedings may become an arena in which major issues of policy are fought out, with removal as the price of defeat. This possibility is most vividly demonstrated in the Oppenheimer case. That case was more than the trial of J. Robert Oppenheimer, more than "the trial of a security system," as Charles P. Curtis describes it. It was also a trial of certain weighty differences of military policy.

The charges against Oppenheimer undoubtedly raised substantial questions about his affiliations and associations before the war. His wife had been a Communist. A number of other people close to him, including a fiancée and a brother, had been Communists. He had impeded the Army's investigation of an espionage proposal that had been made to him. He had maintained some connections with latter-day security risks —including the intermediary in the abortive espionage incident. All these were items that fell clearly within the purview of the Atomic Energy Commission's security criteria, if, for whatever reason, the Commission chose to blow up such dying embers, in the face of Oppenheimer's almost continuous record, since 1942, of distinguished public service. But the hearing board, while it exhaustively combed over these and more trivial matters, let its attention be diverted to prolonged testimony with respect to Oppenheimer's position on issues of military strategy where he was at odds with the Air Force and, more specifically, with the Strategic Air Command. The nature and motivation of his objections to the development of a thermonuclear weapon inevitably came up because they were part of the letter of charges; but there was nothing in the charges about Oppenheimer's views on the tactical use of atomic weapons, or on continental air defense. Yet both these matters,

23. Without further multiplying examples of equivocal charges, I should mention, as a tribute to the assiduity of the internal security agencies, another type occasionally encountered. It runs like this: A car bearing license plates indicating registration in your name was observed to be parked on [date] in the vicinity of a public meeting sponsored by the *X* organization [not necessarily one on the Attorney General's list].

and still others even more recondite, occupy much of the second half of the transcript. They had little relevance to Oppenheimer's trustworthiness. They had a great deal of relevance to deeply felt differences among officials about the road to national security. The requirements of military security, in this part of the hearings, came to overshadow the criteria of personnel security. It is true that the decision of the Gray Board did not advert to any of these matters, except for Oppenheimer's "lack of enthusiasm" for the H-bomb; and the decision of the Commission itself abandoned the H-bomb imbroglio as well. But conflicts of high policy in and around the Pentagon nevertheless make up a substantial part of the record. This fact, no matter how much or how little it affected the outcome of the case, illustrates the point I am now concerned with, that is, the misuse of employment tests for fighting out differences on policy.

There were two groups of witnesses who had come to suspect Oppenheimer's principles. With a very few exceptions, these witnesses were not malevolent. The leading spokesman for a group of scientists who had strongly opposed Oppenheimer's position on thermonuclear development was Edward Teller. Teller went no further than to confuse national security with personnel security. "I thoroughly disagreed with him in numerous issues and his actions frankly appeared to me confused and complicated. To this extent I feel that I would like to see the vital interests of the country in hands which I understand better, and therefore trust more . . .

"In this very limited sense I would like to express a feeling that I would feel personally more secure if public matters would rest in other hands." [24]

Anyone might make the same observation about any public figure who displeased him—Secretary of State Dulles, for example. The harm comes when such statements are made in a proceeding designed not to decide on a consultant's good judgment but to pass on his loyalty and trustworthiness. A difference in feeling, on the part of a witness with every reason to feel strongly about professional differences, becomes grist for the security mill.

The other witnesses who had deep differences with Oppenheimer consisted of Air Force representatives. Their cherished institution was the Strategic Air Command—the big bombers. General R. C. Wilson

24. AEC, *In the Matter of J. Robert Oppenheimer,* Transcript of Hearing (1954), p. 710.

testified that he felt "unhappy" about Oppenheimer's military proposals in connection with a variety of study projects. "This was a matter of real worry that a general pattern of activity coming from a man of such stature seemed to me to be jeopardizing the national defense." So he discussed his "concern" with the Air Force Director of Intelligence, though he testified that he had no reason to doubt Oppenheimer's loyalty. A former Chief Scientist for the Air Force, Professor David Griggs, combined his distaste for Oppenheimer's views on global strategy with what he had heard about his political past, and came to have "a serious question as to [his] loyalty"—fears which, he testified, were impressed on him by his superiors in the Air Force.[25]

These parts of the published transcript are so lacerated by security deletions that it is difficult to piece together precisely what Oppenheimer's views were that so disturbed the Air Force. It is not necessary to make the effort. The point is that the hearings became a forum in which disputes within the military–scientific community were ventilated, disputes which had relevance to Oppenheimer's reliability only as his opponents began to view them in that context.

This kind of distortion of a security case could not occur unless the employee occupied a significant policy-influencing position. Such cases are exceptional, as compared to those of the numerous middle-level scientists of the Monmouth cases, and the depressed array of cafeteria workers and postal clerks who have made up the wasteful bulk of the cases. But we should not ignore even a unique Oppenheimer case. To the extent that it goes beyond the now familiar tests for trustworthiness, it raises the shadow of proscription—of exclusion from the inner councils of the nation, under ignominious circumstances. A councilor whose views are rejected may resign; or he may not be reappointed; but he does not, in our society, expect to be labeled a security risk. In the Oppenheimer case there was a smell of political proscription. This was most apparent in the testimony of David Lilienthal, chairman of the AEC when Oppenheimer was first cleared for the chairmanship of the General Advisory Committee. Lilienthal had been denied access by the AEC to files of his own chairmanship, which he sought in order to refresh his memory. When pressed about his acts as AEC chairman, Lilienthal became very cautious in his testimony, and spoke of having to "protect" himself.[26] Old differences of opinion were hardening into

25. Wilson, Transcript, pp. 685, 694; Griggs, ibid., 748–9.
26. Transcript, pp. 372–82, 398–425, esp. 410.

differences of principle; and the price of holding the wrong principles was written on the face of the proceedings.[27]

We return from the epic figures of the Oppenheimer case to the everyday job of appraising the everyday man. Judge the whole man, I have insisted, but not the whole world in which he moves. Balance his failings against his virtues; discount remote and equivocal derogatory information; sometimes take a chance. Still to be decided is the kind of process appropriate for this judgment, a matter to which we turn in the next chapter.

27. I have not attempted here to give a general view of the Oppenheimer case, which for adequate treatment would require a book in itself. Charles P. Curtis, *The Oppenheimer Case* (1955), combines large excerpts from the record with acute criticism of the standards and procedures involved in the case. Among the numerous other discussions of the case, Arthur Schlesinger, Jr., "Oppenheimer Case," *Atlantic Monthly* (Oct. 1954), p. 29, and (Dec. 1954), p. 21, best brings out the issues here under discussion. There is also the charge, vigorously pressed but unprovable, that the bringing of the case was considerably motivated by animosity against Dr. Oppenheimer on the part of Chairman Lewis Strauss of the Atomic Energy Commission; see Joseph and Stewart Alsop, *We Accuse!* (1954). The somewhat similar cases of Foreign Service officers caught up in Chinese policy are treated in Ch. 15 below, p. 365, in a loyalty context.

12. What to Do about Personnel Security

KEEPING risky people out of sensitive jobs, one reflects wistfully, should be a routine part of personnel administration. Under the unobtrusive guidance of counterintelligence agencies, the careless and the faithless would be diverted into harmless employment, while the rest of us went about our business untroubled by security measures.

But in the U.S.A. of the cold war, every aspect of security is controversial. Among the chronic issues, which the preceding chapters in this Part have reviewed, are these:

(1) The nature of the threat to security. The evidence of Russian assaults on our military, political, and material position, so far as those assaults come through jobholders, are about what one would expect from a powerful enemy who has a few domestic allies; but they are not paralyzing.

(2) The areas of sensitive employment that need to be protected. Here I urged that we need to watch closely only the areas where crucial damage could be done by a few traitors. This approach is obviously at variance with amorphous notions of total security, such as the position that *any* employee of the U. S. government, no matter what his job, may be a security risk.

(3) The criteria for identifying risky people. The last chapter separated different kinds of risks: the absolute political disqualifications that are easy to decide—but that hardly ever arise; the reliability and pressure cases; and the great mass of ambiguous political cases. On the central issue, how to determine when an individual fits any of these categories, that chapter offered chiefly admonitions against the tendency, in the name of taking no chances, to make decisions on far-fetched inferences from shaky charges.

ARE EMPLOYMENT TESTS NECESSARY?

If one is persuaded that the central issue—who is a security risk—is undefined and perhaps undefinable; that the procedures are cumbersome and burdensome to everyone concerned, and that their outcome is to impose severe deprivations, both in obloquy and unemployability;

that the hot winds of partisan controversy distort and magnify the dimensions of the problem, one must ask if there is not a better way.

Chapters 8 and 9, in the course of assessing the dangers the country faces, also took note of the countermeasures other than personnel screening that are available. Is it possible that these measures, instead of simply complementing personnel screening, might supplant it? In other words, if we gave up administrative security tests as a bad job, what would remain for protection?

First we can, and do, fight fire with fire. Against espionage, for example, the classic weapon is counterespionage, the deadly game of penetrating and turning the enemy's spy rings against him. There are historic examples of brilliant successes at this game, and of disastrous failure, for you have to give the enemy a lot of rope, and he may decline to hang himself. Furthermore, underground countermeasures require that the security police be ready to act ruthlessly, unscrupulously, and without regard for legal niceties. And if we put most of the responsibility on the secret security police, they are going to reach for commensurate power. Especially if they find themselves foiled by what they consider subtle attempts at political sabotage in government or labor unions, they are likely to take on political roles. To the extent that political judgments are required in security matters, the policy should be to keep such judgments out of the hands of the security police, who should stick to their spy rings.

Second, we have a battery of criminal sanctions available against almost every form of attempted security breach. Assuming that criminal sanctions stay within traditional bounds, that is, that they aim at the punishment of identifiable unlawful acts, along with the usual baggage of attempts, conspiracies, solicitations, and accessories to commit those acts, reliance on them has a considerable attraction. For valid criminal laws are in the spirit of due process of law, and their prosecution embodies all the apparatus of due process. But earlier speculations on the effectiveness of criminal punishment as a deterrent leave me dissatisfied with it except as one weapon in the security arsenal.

Third, we have an array of specific physical security measures to safeguard classified information and critical installations. Do they obviate the necessity for personnel screening? The quickest answer, with which I agree, is the professional opinion of a security officer that: "You can have all the guards you like; you can put all the barriers around the plant that you like; but if the people involved in carrying out your programs are not loyal persons, you might as well not bother to put up the alarms, to put up the fences, and to hire the guards." [1]

On reviewing the alternatives, I conclude that it would be reckless to ignore personal histories altogether, *within narrow areas of sensitive employment*. Some kind of security screening seems unavoidable under present circumstances. Beyond the reach of routine personnel evaluation, there are unstable individuals; there are careless ones; there are those who are pressure-prone. More-than-routine efforts are needed to keep such risky people away from critical jobs. I am not saying that present methods detect them with any accuracy; but we have to try.

So it is also with the political tests. They are degrading to the employee and irksome to the employer; they penalize the independent, the imaginative, the obstinate; they reward pliant orthodoxy. They are a powerful indirect curb on freedom of thought, speech, and association. But when two hostile political systems stand opposed, it would be perilous to ignore the political sympathies of those employees who are in a position in which they could do great harm. A few pages back I suggested that the customary results of ordinary investigation would not be of much use in discovering a deeply buried enemy agent. Judith Coplon apparently had no trouble with her initial loyalty check; Harry Gold would doubtless have passed one. But on the other side stand the Hiss case and the Fuchs case. If Whittaker Chambers' spy stories had sounded plausible in 1939, if the British had found Gestapo reports of Fuchs' Communist party membership credible, so the argument runs, there need never have been a Hiss case or a Fuchs case. Both men would have been quietly removed from government service.

Quite aside from the possibilities of personnel screening in protecting against real dangers, the feared dangers of our time are such that it would be unreal to ignore them. Administrators and other employers certainly cannot. They stand exposed to overpowering criticism unless they make a show of compliance with the popular demand for total security. In addition to critics who are honest but ill-informed, demagogues are always ready to pounce on any episode or attitude that can be interpreted or misinterpreted as "coddling" Communists. In the atmosphere of tension and alarm that has prevailed in this country since around 1947, a great display of personnel security arrangements may be needed

1. Tyrone Gillespie, chief security officer, Dow Chemical Co., "Security Maintenance in Industrial Enterprise," in Michigan Summer Institute, *Atomic Energy Industrial and Legal Problems* (Ann Arbor, 1952), p. 200.

also to reassure employees inside the sensitive agencies. People need to feel that their associates are reliable. One may agree with Judge Learned Hand, who said, "I believe that that community is already in the process of dissolution where each man begins to eye his neighbor as a possible enemy . . ." [2] The question remains whether we can check further dissolution by measures of reassurance that one's neighbor is not an enemy.

By what process then, should the necessary measures be taken? Or rather, by what processes? Even within the security-sensitive area it is not desirable that a single code should govern all types of cases. Extremely sensitive operations, like the secret parts of the Central Intelligence Agency, may properly be governed by extremely rigorous and indeed arbitrary employment and removal policies. As the foundation for a general formula, I would say first that the degree of sensitivity gives a tentative measure of the degree of deliberation and consideration to which the employee is entitled. Second, practical administration requires some degree of standardization; you do not start from the beginning with each case. Third, a humane system will take account of the degree of hardship imposed by exclusion. This does not mean that you inquire how poor an employee is and how many children he has, but rather what his occupation is, and the effect of a security rejection on his employability. Hardship also includes something more than economic loss; there is the problem of stigma resulting from unfair or ambiguous decisions.

Before exploring ways of applying such a formula, an outlook should be noted that, in effect, abandons any solution. It regards both loyalty and security programs, whatever rationalizations may be advanced for them, as predominantly outgrowths of an antiradical, antirational fever that has seized the nation. There are no remedies for it except the inherent constitutional vigor of the country. The country has been sick before, and has recovered before. What is going on now in effect is a political pogrom. It is no use trying to call the cops, because they—like the Cossacks in Tsarist Russia—are conducting the pogrom. There is nothing to do but wait it out.

This view combines short-run pessimism and long-run optimism; and I suppose there are also short- and long-run pessimists who would likewise do nothing because they think the society is already mortally ill. I find any "give-it-up" position unacceptable so long as there is still

2. Address before the Regents of the State of New York, Oct. 24, 1952, in NYT, Oct. 25, 1952.

any hope of a cure. Let us see what can be done to make over the present system.

THE JUDICIAL IDEAL AND THE ADMINISTRATIVE IDEAL

There are two directions which change could take, toward two rather differing ideals, one the judicial ideal, the other an ideal system of administrative discretion, which I will call the "administrative ideal."

The case for the judicial ideal, which has many supporters,[3] rests heavily on the premise that the employee is in effect on trial for his loyalty. This is such a grave matter that the least we can do is give him the safeguards of a judicial trial. The pursuit of this ideal would require in general terms that we do three things:

(1) Develop a uniform and discernible standard for all employees.

(2) Narrow and sharpen the issues in a case.

(3) Give the employee all the procedural elements of a fair trial, such as an unbiased trier, confrontation, and the presumption of innocence.

It is not necessary to use traditional courts to approach this ideal. Formal administrative tribunals will do just as well. If it were impractical to start off with an exact code of security risks, the tribunal's reasoned decisions would in time provide guidance.

The opposite movement, toward administrative discretion, rests on the premise that the issues in security cases cannot be presented like an indictment and tried before a judge or jury. The question is essentially the confidence of one man in another. The man whose confidence must be sustained is the employee's responsible superior. He must simultaneously, in public employment, consider whether the employee is worthy of public confidence. The setting for his exercise of judgment should be one that:

(1) Tailors the standards to the needs of the job.

(2) Makes the issue "the whole man."

(3) Simplifies procedures, to make the process of decision less burdensome both for the employer and for the employee.

I have stated the three components of each ideal in such a way that they run counter to each other. A mixed system is of course possible. In a way, that is what we now have. For the sake of coherent discus-

3. See Ch. 16 below, n. 9, for advocates of the judicial approach, and also Phelps, Brown, and Goudsmit, "Toward a Positive Security Program," BAS (1955), 11:165. I have, as will appear, modified the views expressed there.

sion the judicial ideal and the administrative ideal will be contrasted, as though we had to make a choice between them. That choice reflects the age-old cleavage between law and equity. Law (in this restricted sense) aims for certainty and predictability. Equity tries to give each man his due. The two ideals are not opposite, but they are divergent in their application. Both seek justice; both confirm that perfect justice is unattainable.

Let me expand a bit the arguments in favor of the judicial ideal. The first premise underlying it has already been suggested. It is that findings of security risk are more injurious to the employee than other grounds for dismissal, and that they will continue to be so. This is believed to be true because most cases raise (or people think they raise) imputations of disloyalty. The attempt in E.O. 10450 to upset the equation of security risk and disloyalty (by broadening the elements of security risk) was not successful, assuming that it was genuinely intended. In any case, even if partisan misinterpretations were corrected, it would not be possible to diminish the stigma of a security risk very much, because the programs, in their criteria and in their application, *are* concerned with disloyalty.

If this argument is accepted, then the approach to justice is to set an understandable and attainable standard, interpreted by impartial judges. There is no need to invent machinery for this purpose. The models are ready to hand in the Anglo-American rules of due process of law as they apply to the proceedings of impartial tribunals, whether those tribunals are courts, boards, or arbitrators. One should be willing to recognize that an adverse decision of the tribunal, because of its solemnity, would be very damaging to the employee; but the hazard would be one he could afford to take if he had a fair chance to defend himself.

The main arguments against the judicial ideal (which are not the same as the arguments *for* the administrative ideal) may be put as follows, with some rejoinders appended. First, you cannot set a uniform meaningful standard for different degrees of sensitive employment. True, but you can distinguish certain large classes of employment; a higher standard for the more sensitive classes is acceptable. Second, you cannot take control of hiring and firing away from the responsible head of the agency. But you can and do, through the Civil Service Commission, wherever there is a compelling policy reason (as in requiring racial nondiscrimination). Third, you cannot, because of the alleged practical necessities of protecting sources of information, let the employee always confront the witnesses against him. Fourth, he has no right to such safeguards anyway (this on the theory that employment is a "privilege"). Fifth, the cases would drag on, and would cost the government (and the employee) too much time and money. The urgencies of the international situation are such that we must deal summarily with cases that raise any element of risk. The last three arguments might also be rebutted. For the moment it is enough to say that they are widely held.

Even if the judicial ideal could be practically pursued, is it a good choice? What about the virtues of the administrative ideal? They may be put as follows: a man's fitness for sensitive employment can never be more than an exercise of fallible discretion. The best approach is one that apprehends how poor traits may be outweighed by good traits, how suspicious episodes may be canceled out by a generally good record. Questions of character and reliability can be resolved only on the basis of observation and reflection. Especially when the issue is the probable future behavior of the employee, judicial process is inept. It can tell us who killed the cow, but it cannot tell us who *might* spy for the Russians. Furthermore, a proper regard for the public interest will consider the need for the employee's services. Here the principle of calculated risk comes into play. If the employee can make an unusual contribution, we may take unusual chances with him. This means that there can be no uniform standards. There may be some absolute disqualifications, such as current membership in the Communist party. Beyond generally applicable minimum qualifications, the decision for employment or retention, as in most human relationships, is partly intuitive, partly reasoned. To require charges, evidence, findings and so on is to stifle responsible judgment.

This approach puts great responsibilities on a man's peers or on his superiors, who may make grave errors on imperfect information. But rejection by an almost casual process—the argument goes on—is kinder to the employee than rejection by a pretentious sham. If it is understood that the process is arbitrary and fallible, then the stigma is less, and the employee is free to claim that he was the victim of bad judgment.

That, in brief, is the case for the administrative ideal. In arguing against it, one may first denounce as feeble the suggestion that an unjust administrative decision inflicts a lighter wound than a judicial one. The world at large is unaware who made the decision; and its practical effects may be formidable, if other employers give it credence.

The major objections hold the ideal up to what are considered current realities. It is all very well to talk about appraising the whole man.

It may be possible in a compact group like the Foreign Service, with little more than a thousand members. There may be considerable agreement that the senior members of the Foreign Service are better qualified to appraise their colleagues than are the inexperienced agents of the department's security office. But this instance (which would not pass unchallenged) gives us little guidance through the anthills of the Pentagon and of other military installations. How, in the hundreds of thousands of sensitive civilian employees of the Department of Defense (to say nothing of the larger numbers in uniform), do you evaluate the whole man? Of course this overstates the situation. Just as the Foreign Service is only one piece of the State Department, so the military departments are divided into manageable units. In those departments especially the command concept puts power where it can be directly exercised. The commander, the man in charge of the unit, has the facilities for appraising the whole man. But—and this is the test—has he been allowed to make security decisions on his own responsibility? He has not. The regulations of the military departments are a criss-cross of screening boards, review boards, minor commands, and major commands; in the end the lines all go through Washington.

The second aspect of current reality that tends to defeat the administrative ideal is the omnipresence of the security officer. Whether the decision is made on the spot or at the top, the official with the most intense interest in it is the one whose exertions are going to be in the direction of caution, of suspicion, and of exclusion.[4] That is his job. Especially if, as we are now assuming, formal hearings and the like are omitted, there is no effective forum in which to rebut the doubts raised by the security officer. His sprouts of derogatory information, his dimly seen conspiracies, may be well-grounded, or they may not survive one blast of fresh air. Who is going to provide the needed ventilation? This is the most telling argument, as things stand. Decision may well turn not on the whole man but on the incomplete dossier.

The influence of the security officer may go far to explain the widespread reluctance to let security decisions be made down the line of command at a point where the employee is a real person instead of a file folder. There are not yet many people with training or discrimina-

---

4. "The type of people who make the best operatives . . . are incapable of a balanced evaluation of an intelligence or counterespionage report. Such minds tend to believe all the gossip and other 'evidence' . . . They see everything pointing to guilt as true, and disregard all counter-indications." Brig. Gen. Thomas R. Phillips, quoted in John R. Green, Review, *Va. Law Rev.* (1956), *42*:136–7 n.

tion in the detection of security risks. A supervisor, otherwise well-qualified to hire and fire, may be badly advised by his local security officer. Under the present system, the findings of subordinate hearing boards apparently have not inspired much confidence either. If they have, then why the intricate review arrangements in large agencies?

The administrative ideal seems to be clouded by the shadow of the security officer. Does this send us back to the judicial solution? Perhaps it does. An elaborate adversary proceeding before an impartial tribunal may be the only way, under present circumstances, to counterbalance the accumulations of associations, affiliations, and opinions that are heaped up in a security case. Let us not, however, be limited by present circumstances. We are, after all, trying to find a way out of them.

ESSENTIAL CHANGES

I believe that the administrative ideal is approachable and would be preferable in security cases if the following conditions could be satisfied:

(1) The coverage of the programs must be vastly reduced. This is the most important change that is called for. We should, as I proposed in Chapter 10, confine systematic clearance procedures to jobs with the equivalent of access to Secret material. At the same time, we should dispense with the ritual obeisance displayed by cabinet officers in submitting to clearance. If a man's public record will not stand on its own feet, he has no business being Secretary of State.[5]

(2) The standards and criteria should be revised. Current formulations put too much stress on exclusionary factors. Instead of requiring employment to be "clearly consistent with the interests of national security," would it help to state that "employment should tend to advance the national security, taking into account both the risk involved and the contributions that the employee can make"? The AEC regulations include an injunction of this sort.[6] This approach would permit

5. That cabinet officers in the Eisenhower administration had to be cleared I infer from statements like President Eisenhower's press conference remarks about the nomination of Neil McElroy as Secretary of Defense, NYT, Aug. 9, 1957.

6. "The decision as to security clearance is a comprehensive commonsense judgment, made after consideration of all the relevant information, favorable and unfavorable, as to whether or not the granting of security clearance would endanger the common defense and security." AEC, Security Clearance Procedures (*Code Fed. Regs. 10:* § 4.10). Though neither the Hearing Board nor the Review Board is permitted to consider the "possible impact of the loss of the individual's services upon the AEC program" (§§ 4.28 and 4.31), the General Manager, who normally makes the final determination, does give "due recog-

greater recognition of the need for security by achievement, and would subordinate security by exclusion. A revision of specific criteria would go on to minimize the consideration of remote associations or of hypothetical exposure to pressure.

Above and beyond the formal regulations, there needs to be official recognition that public servants, like all of us, have their unavoidable share of original and acquired sin.

(3) If security officers are to be specialists in the collection and interpretation of derogatory information, they should, like all specialists, be kept in an advisory role. Theirs is a necessary job, but there is no need to glorify it. The only specific suggestion that I can make is to place all responsibility for decision in the hands of officials other than security officers. That is, the responsible superior mentioned earlier should be someone up the line of command from the employee or prospective employee, and not a staff functionary whose only responsibility is to watch security. Wherever this duty to decide comes to rest, there should be measures to insure that it will not be delegated. To help ensure that the decision actually will be made by someone in the open line of command and not pushed off on a staff officer, the practice of referring decision to the agency head should be discarded as unrealistic, at least in large agencies. The head will have ultimate responsibility for the maintenance of security; but there is no need to insist on the pretense that he decides the case, if he does not in fact.

(4) The primary avenue for avoiding hardship should be a forceful policy of providing other jobs for those who are excluded from security–sensitive positions. A man's record may, of course, be so bad that the employer will not keep him in any capacity. But most cases that arise nowadays, I suggest, are borderline cases. They are people who *may be* too risky to keep on sensitive work. It is unnecessary and wrong to exclude them from nonsensitive work too. In the federal government there has been little alternative as long as the entire executive establishment was blanketed by a security program. Section 7 of E.O. 10450 creates a re-employment or transfer possibility for security risks; but we learn from Chairman Young of the Civil Service Commission, which must

---

nition" to this factor (§ 4.32). See also ASS'N OF THE BAR, REPORT, pp. 149–51, for a similar proposal, except that "the interest of the United States" is made the touchstone. This phrase has a somewhat unhappy history in that it was used in the statute giving summary dismissal power to the Secretary of State (Ch. 2 above, n. 55).

pass on applications for transfer from one department to another, that only nine were granted from May 1953 to March 1955, and that the departments had reported only five cases of re-employment within the department after an adverse security determination.[7]

If the security programs are cut down to size, the whole problem of individual hardship can be reduced. The vast mechanism of Civil Service should facilitate readjustments within the government service; I assume that present practices are not so ingrained that the same administrators who have now learned to speed the departing security risk cannot adapt themselves to finding him another job in government—provided, always, that he is competent and not disloyal.

This is not to say that relocation is a complete remedy. The employee may have to change his residence; he may find the new job uninteresting; his ineligibility for sensitive work will probably become known, and this will impair his standing. But he will not have been forced into unemployment; and his retention will establish that his failings were not grave ones.

Nor is relocation always an easy remedy. It is sometimes said that we do not have a federal Civil Service; we have a number of departmental services, and within them a number of bureau services. Quite aside from the parochialism suggested by this observation, the process of job analysis has carried the number of occupational specialities into the thousands. But even if there is little mobility for a wind-tunnel design engineer in the Air Force, there are usually other available posts for the trained administrator near the top of the ladder, and there is always a place for a good clerk-typist, no matter what her politics.[8]

7. The five cases were for the period May 1953–Oct. 1954. HUMPHREY HEARINGS, pp. 529–30, 736. Two publicized cases were resolved by transfer to less sensitive work in their department. One was Annie Lee Moss, who was a victim of Senator McCarthy in what was probably a case of mistaken identity; see Ch. 15 below, n. 7. The other was Sidney Hatkin, who while under suspension from the Air Force pending a security hearing, rebuffed an espionage approach and won the support of former Senator Harry Cain. NYT, May 6, 13, 1956; BNA MANUAL, p. 19/537. Contrary to my suggestion that most cases are borderline are some of the flagrant cases in Industrial Personnel Security Review Program, *First Annual Report* (1956); but I daresay that these cases were selected with an eye to their dramatic quality, and to counterbalance the employee-oriented case histories that most people have heard about.

8. See Everett Reimer in Columbia Univ. American Assembly, *The Federal Government Service* (1954), pp. 153, 156, 164–5, 178, on the fragmentation of the career service. But cf. studies showing considerable mobility within the government, Frances Cahn, *Federal Employees in War and Peace* (1949), pp.

How can one approach the more difficult problems of private sensitive employment? Here is a possible route. First, it should be recognized that granting or denying clearance is a governmental function, accepted by the employer as a term of his contract to do sensitive work. The same contract can provide that denial of clearance shall not subject the employee to discriminatory treatment. That is, unless the record disqualifies the employee for nonsensitive work also, because it establishes a failing that violates some reasonable general personnel policy of the employer (for example, prohibitions against retaining acute alcoholics or Communist party members) the employer must try to find another place for him. If there is no such place, because the whole enterprise is sensitive, or because it has no slot for, say, an uncleared engineer, then some government mechanism should be directed to help the man find another job. In cases of special hardship, where another job cannot be proffered, provision for cash grants, in the form of severance pay, could be made by the contracting agency. This is a familiar device that would soften the impact of an unavoidable but unmerited dismissal. These last suggestions would apply equally to government cases where no transfer was feasible.[9]

Finally, if there remain any programs that must cover an entire occupation, and that close it entirely, or practically so, to persons without clearance, then I contend that administrative discretion must give way to full due process. The Port Security program is the outstanding example of one that envelops a common calling, and provides legally insufficient safeguards for the seamen subject to it. I have set out elsewhere the constitutional basis for this view.[10] Further exploration of it can be omitted here, for if scrupulous canons of sensitivity were adhered to, it is unlikely that whole occupations would be closed to risky people. To be sure, the employment opportunities of an electronics engineer, for

203–6; (Hoover) Commission on Organization of the Executive Branch . . . , Task Force Report, *Personnel and Civil Service* (1955), p. 227 (60 per cent of a large sample of top people had served in more than one agency).

9. A proposal for severance grants is made by William Buckley, Jr., and Brent Bozell, *McCarthy and His Enemies* (1954), p. 260. See Perkins v. Lukens Steel Co., 310 U.S. 113, 127 (1940), for a sweeping assertion of the government's power to impose conditions in its contracts (with respect to minimum wages). The Industrial Personnel *Report* (n. 7 above), pp. 11–12, argues that the government should not "intrude" in the personnel policies of private employers but should confine itself to educating them. But the government has already intruded in a substantial way by requiring clearance.

10. Brown and Fassett, "Security Tests for Maritime Workers," *Yale Law Jour.* (1953), 62:1191–1200.

example, would be considerably restricted if he could not get clearance. Relocation rights must have real substance if these constitutional issues are to be avoided.

A reader conversant with this subject will already have recognized that the combination of carefully defining sensitive areas, and relocating those who should not be in them, is exactly what the English have been doing for some years in their government service. The cases have been handled unobtrusively; and though there has been some concern expressed about the absence of any formal safeguards for the employee, careful studies of the system have found no noteworthy unfairness. The defections to Russia of civil servants, notably MacLean and Burgess of the Foreign Office, do not reflect on the matters here under discussion. They were failures of the security police, partly caused by inadequate screening *within* sensitive areas.[11]

In summary, the major changes in present attitudes and practices that appear to be essential before a shift to administrative discretion can be entertained are:

(1) Concentrate on sensitive employment.

(2) Consider the whole man.

(3) Put the responsible superior over the security officer.

(4) Transfer freely; dismiss rarely.[12]

11. The surveys of the English system are BONTECOU, Ch. 8; Hugh Wilson and Harvey Glickman, *The Problem of Internal Security in Great Britain, 1948–1953* (1954). Within sensitive areas, tighter standards were applied after the Fuchs case; they are described by Sir David M. Fyfe in "How Britain Handles Communists," *U. S. News and World Report* (Oct. 15, 1954), p. 86; see also Sir Hartley Shawcross in "Community Security vs. Man's Right to Knowledge," *Columbia Law Rev.* (1954), *54*:734, 745. The belated official concession in 1955 that Donald MacLean and Guy Burgess, Foreign Office officials who defected in 1951, had before their disappearance been committing espionage led to a further examination and intensification of screening, especially with respect to reliability criteria, including homosexuality. See, on MacLean and Burgess, NYT, Sept. 24, 1955. The subsequent "Statement [by the Prime Minister] on the Findings of the Conference of Privy Councillors on Security," Cmd. 7915, is adequately summarized in NYT, March 9, 1956, reporting its presentation to Parliament on March 8, and in ASS'N OF THE BAR, REPORT, pp. 199–202, where a statement by Prime Minister St. Laurent on the informal (and summary) Canadian system is also reprinted. For the Dutch system, resembling the English, see Isaak Kisch in *Columbia Law Rev.* symposium (above), pp. 832–7. Material from ten European countries is collected in Library of Congress, Law Library, *Survey of Legislation on Security Safeguards and Anti-Subversive Measures . . .* (1957, mimeo.).

12. The administrative approach, not necessarily in these same terms, has been supported by Thurman Arnold, JOHNSTON HEARINGS, p. 365; Dean Acheson, *A Democrat Looks at His Party* (1955), p. 148; Buckley and Bozell (n. 9 above),

OUTLINE OF A NEW PROGRAM

A program oriented toward administrative discretion would still be far from simple and would still have set procedures and detailed regulations. Let us see what would happen, in broad outline, to the main stages of the present programs described in Chapter 2; some loose ends can be gathered up along the way.

Investigation. There would probably be little change in the thoroughness of investigations, since they would be focused entirely on sensitive jobs. One could desire improvements in technique, such as confining the agents' inquiries to relevant matters, and requiring more critical appraisal of the accuracy of informants. For the future, screening will be mostly of applicants. Investigations of applicants especially should try to develop a rounded picture for the prospective employer, so as to make available both favorable and unfavorable data. The job should be considered accomplished for those already in sensitive work (though one may be skeptical of this suggestion—think how many times it has been considered done before!).

Evaluation. This stage, more than ever, should be the heart of the process. The preliminary evaluation will assemble all the information needed for a responsible decision, not just a hash of derogatory information. Perhaps it will be necessary to inject in the process, along with the security officer, a personnel officer charged with clarifying the need for the man, and the value of his talents. If preliminary consultation with the employee would be helpful, it should be had; but with strict prohibitions against urging him, at this point, to withdraw. That is something to be decided between the employee and the responsible superior.

Here the evaluation of organizational affiliations should be mentioned. They are certainly going to be considered, and wise evaluation of them would be furthered if there were some authoritative guide to their

---

ch. 12; Abe Krash, Review, *Yale Law Jour.* (1956), *65:*571; Herbert Packer, Review, *Harvard Law Rev.* (1956), *70:*392. Any residual doubts about the infringement of First Amendment freedoms resulting indirectly from this process may be allayed by resort to the "least abridgement" test: that the proposal affects the smallest possible number of people in the mildest possible way. See Comment, *Yale Law Jour.* (1956), *64:*1182, n. 100, for a formulation of this approach. Cf. Eugene Rostow, "Needed: A Rational Security Program," *Harper's* (July 1957), p. 33, which endorses the responsible superior's loss of confidence as a basis for removal, but calls for a hearing, with full due process, to review the reasonableness of the removal.

significance. This function the present Attorney General's list does not fulfill, because it is a list and nothing more. The judgments of the Subversive Activities Control Board will not serve either; they do have content, but they cover too limited an area. Repugnant as the idea is to many people, screening for sensitive jobs requires blacklists and whitelists. But not just bare lists. Is it not possible to prepare reasoned histories of organizations that Communists are said to have penetrated or controlled? The information surely exists in the files of the Department of Justice. There should be no legal significance, and no required inferences, to be drawn from these reports. As a matter of decency, the organization, if it exists, should have a right to make comments, and these should be available to the superior. Finally, the employee should be free to attack the characterizations of the report. Every critic of the present inadequate Attorney General's list, and of the even more miserable compilations that circulate in security quarters, has pointed out that time, place, circumstances, and motive are essential to give meaning to any suspect affiliation. Now the employee is expected to supply all this by way of defense. This is a wasteful and burdensome process. Considerable expertness about these matters is supposed to exist on the government side. To have it compiled and available would permit quick evaluation of most affiliations.

This proposal to develop fairly complete histories, for official use only, is not the same as the attempt to make the Attorney General's list respectable by granting hearings. The present list should be junked. We already have in the Internal Security Act, for better or worse, a statutory plan for labeling Communist organizations that provides as much due process as is possible in an essentially repressive undertaking. The decisions of the Subversive Activities Control Board, though insufficient for guidance to employers, go quite far enough in establishing formal proscriptions. The administration of security measures requires not another list but intelligent information.[13]

Charges and Hearings. The employee would be invited to comment on substantial derogatory information in an informal way. But he would face the same handicaps that he does now, if he needed to know the source and the authorities would not tell him. I accept deficient con-

---

13. The ISC has also called on the Attorney General to prepare a handbook, noting that the list was "widely misunderstood and misapplied." See NYT, June 28, 1955. There is in HENNINGS HEARINGS extensive information on the misuse of the list, e.g. pp. 223–38, 249–96; see also JOHNSTON REPORT, pp. 221–9, esp. recommendations of Harry Cain.

frontation as a probable—not a desirable—fact, in a system of administrative discretion confined to eligibility for sensitive jobs. The insistent demand of investigators to be permitted to conceal their sources is not likely to weaken when the employee is protected by a strong policy of relocation.

If a dismissal is in prospect because of the gravity of the charges, then the employee should be entitled to whatever protections standard civil-service procedures now give him. For government employees with tenure this would mean, at a minimum, specific charges and an opportunity to reply either in writing or in a hearing.[14] The general formula laid down at the beginning of this chapter would still permit more arbitrary proceedings in the case of extremely sensitive agencies. As a legal matter, offices like the CIA and the FBI are not under civil service rules anyhow. People who undertake such careers are forewarned that security considerations may expose them to summary dismissal.

For some observers a policy of administrative discretion would leave that discretion uncontrolled in all cases. Thus C. D. Williams, writing with a background of experience as chief law officer of the Department of Commerce, urged the extension to all government agencies of the power which the Secretaries of State and Commerce held for a few years to "terminate the employment" of any employee in their "absolute discretion" whenever "necessary or desirable in the best interests of the United States." [15] This, it seems to me, as it did to Congress in cutting off this extraordinary authority in 1954, makes mincemeat of any assurances of status to career civil servants. Even if a summary dismissal power were confined to sensitive areas—a limitation which Williams did not suggest—it goes beyond the needs of the situation. Broad power to remove from sensitive work, yes, if its exercise does not close other doors. Uncontrolled power to dismiss, no, except in a few hypersensitive areas.

Review and Coordination. There would be no need for any structure of reviewing boards and the like in the sensitive area, although the decision of the responsible superior would doubtless be subject to some sort of review by *his* responsible superior, because the agency head cannot avoid ultimate responsibility in these matters. Nor would there be a need for formal coordination of results between the different agencies. After all, I am now proposing to give play for individual judg-

14. See Ch. 16 below on due-process requirements in disloyalty dismissals as compared to suitability deficiencies.

15. Letter in NYT, Feb. 10, 1953; see Ch. 2 above, n. 55.

ments in individual cases, and there will be little basis for comparing one decision with another. Where coordination would be necessary would be in relocating a man rejected by one sensitive office. Perhaps another less sensitive agency would take him; more likely nonsensitive work would have to be found. What is wanted is the sort of resolution that was finally achieved in the Ladejinsky case, where the Foreign Operations Administration profited by the Secretary of Agriculture's inept exercise of discretion in rejecting Ladejinsky.

Efficiency and fairness will improve if a central authority takes steps to minimize duplicate investigations, to make available full information on suspect organizations, and to facilitate relocation. Further than these modest measures it seems unnecessary to pursue any semblance of one big program. What I am aiming for is many little decisions.

Eliminating Irritants

There are four minor irritants in the present process that can be minimized. They are not minor to an employee who experiences them.

(1) Withdrawal of clearance without deciding the case. As presently practiced, this is a crude form of relocation. It takes a man away from sensitive work, on the security officer's say-so, and often leaves him fiddling with trivial assignments. Perhaps the hope is that he will get frustrated and go away. A proper relocation system would deal with such a case squarely. Perhaps some relocated employees will leave anyhow; but at least the action will be free of subterfuge.

(2) Multiple jeopardy. The reopening of cases on the appearance of substantial new derogatory information cannot and should not be prevented. Whether the new material is substantial is a question that only good sense can answer. However, the simplification of procedures will make multiple jeopardy cases less burdensome.

(3) Heavy expense for the employee. A quick and summary decision at least spares the employee from costly defense preparations. If this is inadequate relief, perhaps the practice of the armed services, which supply counsel to soldiers who face security charges, could be generally followed, on the theory that it is to the employer's interest to see that *both* sides of the case are properly presented.

(4) Suspension pending decision. This should also be a matter of responsible discretion. If there is evidence of actual security misbehavior, then the sensitive area should be protected. If, as in the usual case, the issue is potential unreliability, then one may ask, "What's the hurry?"

I am inclined to be skeptical about the case for suspension, because of the way the device was abused in the first two years of the Eisenhower program. A standard technique was developed by which, at about 4:45 P.M., the employee was abruptly notified that he was suspended without pay, and ordered to get out and stay out. After he had fretted for some days or weeks, charges would be delivered. After more weeks or months, with the employee's savings melting away, the case would grind to a conclusion. We have graphic descriptions of the effect of this treatment on the employee's morale, in cases that contained not a suggestion of imminent risk.[16] The whole business was so unnecessarily callous that I suspect it must have been intended, in some agencies, to force the employee to resign.

To recapitulate the bare procedural outlines of the new program in comparison with the present one, investigation and evaluation would continue to be the foundations for decision. But they would be reoriented, along lines suggested by the last chapter, toward an appraisal of the whole man, rather than toward a mechanical analysis of derogatory information. Formal charges, hearings, and review would give way to informal negotiation and deliberation. The alternative to clearance would normally be relocation, not dismissal.

PRIVATE EMPLOYMENT

The application of this proposed procedure to security programs in private employment raises some difficulties. I have already urged that clearance is a government responsibility. This means initially that investigation and preliminary evaluation should be undertaken by the contracting departments, as they do now where access to Secret or Top Secret material is required. If, as I have also urged, it is only for these levels of classification that personnel screening is desirable, no innovation is necessary at the beginning of a case. But when preliminary evaluation suggests an undue risk, who is to make the decision? Reliance on the employee's responsible superior is awkward. The responsible superior is in this situation a private person. He may not have any training in the elements of security. Such a handicap can be overcome by giving him training. He may not have access to necessary investigative reports. This also can be overcome by giving him access. The greatest obstacle is the delegation of government responsibility that occurs

16. See, e.g., the case of Beatrice Campbell, JOHNSTON HEARINGS, p. 594. See Ch. 2 above, n. 49, on reforms in suspension practices in 1955.

if a private employer makes the decision. This can be met by having a power of review at a high level in the contracting department. There the judgment of the responsible superior, which balances the man's virtues and his shortcomings, is still available. If a clear misunderstanding of security requirements leads the employer to deny clearance, the contracting department can restore it, thus protecting the employee. If the employer mistakenly grants clearance, the department can overrule him, thus protecting its own security responsibilities.

This proposal may be unfeasible for several reasons, including the reluctance of private employees to get into security decisions, and the reluctance of the security forces to let them in. In that event, perhaps a hearing board should be maintained. It seems to me, however, that a board is unnecessarily cumbersome for the kind of informal balancing of interests now proposed. A panel of substantial citizens around the country, one of whom would serve as a referee when a dispute arose, might be more useful. The Department of Defense and the Atomic Energy Commission could jointly select the nationwide panel, after consultation with representatives of labor and management. The latter groups are accustomed to referring their own differences to impartial umpires. The paramount security interest would still have to be respected by reserving, at the top level of the interested departments, a power to deny clearances. The Security Referee, as we might call him, could not make as rounded a judgment as a responsible superior could, but he would still have the advantage of relative freedom from control by the security office.

Any of these arrangements requires the preparation of fairly systematic memoranda of reasons, because of the necessity of submitting the decision for review by the responsible agency. The formulation of reasons is always a desirable exercise anyhow; even if imponderables enter into the judgment, they may be clarified by exposition.

The assignment of reasons for a denial of clearance would also be necessary for another purpose. If the clearance is denied, I have argued that the government should intervene and press for relocation to avoid unwarranted dismissals. Whether a dismissal following denial of clearance is unwarranted depends on the gravity of the disqualifications. The employee who thinks he has been unfairly dismissed should be free to complain to the industrial relations division of the contracting department, or to initiate a grievance proceeding through his union. He must be able to say something like this: "I was found to be a security risk because of some family connections that have nothing to do with my fitness for nonsensitive work." If that is the case, he should be able to refer to a responsible document that says so. On the other hand, the employee may prefer to drop the whole controversy and seek non-sensitive work elsewhere. If that is his preference, he should not be dogged by what may be at best an imperfect judgment about a specula-tive risk. Here is an appropriate occasion for letting the employee dis-close the reasons if *he* wants to.

There is a residual problem of fairness if the denial of clearance in private employment purports to rest on a grave charge like involve-ment in espionage, or Communist party membership. A government career employee would have some protection from the full impact of a charge of this sort in that his dismissal—as distinguished from disquali-fication for sensitive work—would follow only after appropriate civil service removal procedures. There is no equivalent protection for the private employee who is discharged because his employer accepts the opinion of the Security Referee that such grave offenses were correctly charged. When the government proposes to make a finding that will be seriously damaging to a person in private employment, probably the hearing process should then be broadened so as to satisfy the require-ments of full due process. The contracting departments will often be able to avoid this obligation, if they find it onerous, by framing charges in milder terms.[17]

PROBATIONERS, APPLICANTS, AND DOSSIERS

All of the processes that have been outlined should be available for probationary employees, except the right to relocation. A probationary period, during which the employee understands that his retention is still tentative, is standard practice in any developed personnel system. But it is not sensible to be arbitrary about it. The employee has cut loose from his old job and committed himself to the new one; he has some stake in it. The employer has a stake too, in his investment in selection and training. If possible disqualifications for sensitive work crop up, both parties gain from deliberate assessment. The employer need assume no obligation, however, to find another place for the pro-bationer who does not come up to the mark.

I have left to the last the hard case of the applicant. Let us recognize at the outset that if an employer with security responsibilities puts them

17. See text at n. 14 above. Cf. conclusions of Kenneth Davis, "The Require-ment of a Trial-Type Hearing," *Harvard Law Rev.* (1956), *70:*280.

foremost in choosing among applicants, that is his choice, and it is futile for anyone else to try to force on him an applicant he does not want. Even in a strict competitive system like civil service, the employing agency has some choice among qualified candidates. If there is a security question about Brown, and spotless Jones seems to fill the bill, Jones will get the job.[18] In a tight labor market, the wise employer will try to clear up Brown's availability. Then concessions may be made, like the AEC's opening of its hearing procedure to applicants.

Indeed, there should always be a way to give an applicant's security problems fair consideration. The predominant policy among government agencies of providing no hearing opportunities at all for applicants is both harsh and shortsighted. Derogatory information can so often be explained away that it is hardly rational to forego the services of a promising applicant because of a one-sided decision from the security office. If a responsible superior in government decides that he wants Smith's qualifications to be explored, Smith should have an opportunity to respond to derogatory information, to be interviewed, and to have the decision made by the person who wants to hire him, not by the security office whose mission it is to keep him out. Similarly, if a private employer certifies that he will hire Smith if he can get clearance, the procedures for clearance should go into operation.

But, I repeat, it does not seem feasible to require an unwilling employer to take pains with an unwanted applicant. There are too many ways of preventing the job-seeker from even reaching the threshold of recognition as an applicant. In no discussion that I have seen of the applicant problem has anyone faced the question where this threshold lies. It is a trail that need not be explored here. For the man whose training or interests drive him to seek employment in the classified world, it is not the rebuff from one employer that is decisive. It is the frustrating effect of repeated denials, with no more than perfunctory reasons—"not quite suited to our requirements," "position already filled." What is this man's difficulty, assuming that he is competent to fill the position he seeks? His difficulty is not the refusal of any one employer to sit down with him and lay open his doubts. The trouble, in all probability, is that he is butting his head against an unfavorable dossier. Somewhere a file has been assembled on him. The information in it may be factually wrong. It may be factually correct but easily

18. Scott McLeod's colloquies with the subcommittee in HUMPHREY HEARINGS, pp. 325–39, are frank and illuminating on the applicant problem. Cf. Commission on Government Security, *Report* (1957), pp. 51–2.

explained away. It may require a great deal of explanation. The man on the outside has no way to get a look in this dossier, unless somebody gives him a break. Because he is outside, nobody is obliged to give him a break.

The accumulation of dossiers on anyone and everyone is a traditional badge of the police state with implications that go far beyond the scope of this study. That the practice is growing in this country is surely disquieting. The immediate problem is this: how can a man straighten out his dossier? A solution would be reachable if we really had a centralized political police, so that all the derogatory information on everybody was neatly collected in the FBI's endless rows of file cabinets in Washington. As it is, everybody is in the dossier business. There are eight government files that may be consulted for even the routine name-check described in Chapter 2. There are the files of the various state investigating committees. There are the private peddlers of dossiers. So, even if a man suspects what is in his dossier, he may not know who put it there, or how to get it out. Some sort of administrative procedure should be available for the correction of dossiers, which any citizen could resort to if he showed adequate reason to believe that he was being injured. Maybe there is no place to center such an operation. The FBI files seem to be the logical repository for the citizen's side of the story; but here we run into the alleged refusal of the FBI to circulate any of its material outside the government. Maybe such a proposal gives the compilation of dossiers too much standing. It is disturbing to think of having to petition the police to stop circulating false reports, the very existence of which you can only conjecture. Bishop G. Bromley Oxnam, a leader of the Protestant churches, found out what was in the dossier the House Committee on Un-American Activities had compiled on him. His attempt to get the Committee to correct it is sobering reading. Some members of the Committee were clearly more interested in bolstering up slanted "research," shaky informers, and their own loose statements than they were in the careful winnowing of truth. Unless we could have fairer hearings than Bishop Oxnam got, this trail has a dead end too.[19]

19. On the Oxnam episode see Ch. 6 above, n. 5. The dossier-clearing process might not involve a hearing. Perhaps it can go no further than letting the applicant have a statement of the derogatory information against him, and an opportunity to submit written replies. See ASS'N OF THE BAR, REPORT, pp. 185–8, for such a proposal. Here confrontation problems arise. The security officers would argue with some reason that an unrestricted process would permit every Communist to inquire what the FBI had on him. Who is going to decide the

I therefore end this sketch of a program based on administrative discretion with unconcealed misgivings. But then, if misgivings seem to send us back toward the judicial ideal, consider that the present hearing arrangements reflect, in a distorted way, the judicial approach. The Ladejinsky episode may be enough to scare anyone away from administrative discretion. But if you seek a case where the procedures bore some resemblance to judicial behavior, what do you find? Oppenheimer.

Without a substantial change in attitudes, a shift to over-all administrative discretion, I have to concede, could become a reign of terror. It is not reassuring to find that the supporters of administrative discretion include Senator McCarthy's apologists, Messrs. Buckley and Bozell. And the Senator's name serves to remind us that we have provided no magic that will immunize administrators from legislative and other pressures. I know of none. When a lion is in the streets, the only protection for agency heads, or hearing boards, or impartial referees, is fortitude. It is true that a complexity of procedures permits a certain amount of buck-passing. It may be true that an outside board is less easily intimidated than a senior civil servant. But I am inclined to think that such defensive proposals are expedients.

The time for expedients has passed. We have had almost twenty years of experience with internal security problems, first in a hot war with Fascists, now in a cold war with Communists. Personnel security measures during the hot war were arbitrary, but they were not too far-reaching. The measures of the cold war have an excessive reach, and only purport not to be arbitrary. It is time to decide whether we trust ourselves. If we do not, then we can try to fling up safeguards of law against our mutual suspicions. They may work. They may be elaborate futilities. It seems bolder and wiser to cut the whole problem down to size, to move toward simplification and discretion.

---

good faith of the applicant? Must we have a judicial stage, with a court passing on the validity of the request? This is a difficult point.

As an indication of the accumulation of dossiers, the Civil Service Commission's "Security Investigations Index is the central index established in 1948 of all personnel investigations completed since 1939 or now pending in the federal service. It contains approximately 5¼ million card records." Letter of Philip Young, Nov. 25, 1955, in Comm. on Gov't Operations, Subcomm. Hearings, *Availability of Information from Federal Departments and Agencies* (1956), p. 406. The total of FBI files on all subjects from 1918 to 1956 is 4,742,000. Don Whitehead, *The FBI Story* (1956), p. 353.

PART III

The Rationale and Administration of Loyalty Programs

13. Control of Domestic Communism

MANY OF the questions raised in security programs and loyalty programs overlap substantially. Most security cases, as we have seen, do bear on questions of disloyalty—past, present, or potential. Conversely, a person branded in a disloyalty case—if the label is correct—is potentially dangerous to national security. In this sense, if we ignore the kind of job that is involved and look only at the kind of person, there is little difference between security and loyalty programs, except in the nonpolitical issues of reliability and pressure risk that sometimes come up in security cases, but which are irrelevant in loyalty programs. However, the whole analysis has insisted that the kind of job that is involved cannot be ignored. The security significance of an employment test turns on the threat to security of a particular person in a particular job. Every loyalty case is not a security case. This distinction between job and jobholder is partially reflected in popular and official labels. It is pinpointed by the policy of the federal government toward American employees of international organizations. These people are screened on a loyalty standard, in contrast to the ubiquitous security label in other federal programs. More extensively, some four or five million state and private employees are subject to loyalty programs, but not to security programs. If the recommendations that I urged in Chapters 10 and 12 for cutting back the coverage of security programs were accepted, more millions who escaped the security frying-pan might still find themselves exposed to the loyalty fire.

Back in Chapter 1, I proposed a broad working definition of the kind of disloyalty that current loyalty programs are aimed at, namely a preference for communism.[1] Looking now at employment that is not security-sensitive, the problem is when and why it is appropriate to exclude people because they (1) are known to be Communists, (2) are known to have been Communists, (3) might be or might have been Communists, (4) might become Communists. Some programs create additional categories for exclusion. In addition to proscribing Communist party members and people who speak and act exactly like party mem-

1. For examples of the occasional application of loyalty tests to members of extreme right wing organizations see BONTECOU, pp. 106, 163, 165.

bers, they raise employment barriers against people who speak and act something like party members. Criteria based on words like "affiliate," "support," "contribute," and "sympathetic association" break down the dikes of strict construction and engulf wide areas. Furthermore, these criteria also may be unconfined in time, and may look to the past, the present, or the future.

To locate the main channel, it is necessary to take some soundings in the history and activities of the Communist party U.S.A. and in the public controls that have been exercised to counter its activities. For the time being, I put aside the complicity of the party in some of the security offenses discussed in Part II. We know that the open party has been a recruiting ground for spies and a conduit for money and messages. But we also know, I think it fair to say, that the Soviet intelligence organization has a much broader base than the American party provides, and that its underground activities here are directed by Moscow, not by Earl Browder or his successors. Security problems, as we saw them in Part II, would exist even if the Communist party U.S.A. did not exist.

The existence for almost two generations of a domestic Communist party has brought out other problems. At a time when communist Russia, wracked by its own revolution, could barely survive, the revolutionary message of the party was alarming enough to arouse in this country the fears and repressions of the period immediately following World War I. In the decade since World War II the global threat of a powerful Russia has overshadowed the threat of revolution, but the problem is still there, the subject of spasmodic efforts at public control in all the intervening decades. This challenge to the legal order, and the response to it, form only one episode of a recurrent conflict in our history. How far does a society that values both freedom and order tolerate rebellious minorities? When does repression begin? Before the Communists there were the anarchists; before the anarchists, the abolitionists; and so on. It is comforting to know that as a nation we have passed this way before. But it was not really the same way; Communists are not abolitionists. And though history may teach us to avoid some errors, it is no substitute for the exercise of our own judgment on what is critical for our own time.

THE NATURE OF THE COMMUNIST PARTY

Two ways of characterizing the Communist party U.S.A., both unfriendly but otherwise at odds with each other, are to view it as a futile band of fanatics or as a ruthless, dedicated conspiracy. In the 1919–20 crisis the public image of the Bolshevik depicted him as an insane bomb-thrower, and his party as a desperate crew of foreign ruffians (indeed there were some bombs thrown, and the dominant wing of the American party in one period was not English-speaking). In the 1930's it became popular to regard the Communist party as a small radical faction which might actually help American democracy by directing attention to our shortcomings (this was the picture the party painted of itself during the United Front period, and again in 1942–45). But the disillusionments of 1945–47, and the international peril that has ruled since that time, have brought a renewed popular emphasis on the party's allegiance to a strong and malevolent Russia, and a renewed alarm at the prospects of internal subversion.[2]

It is possible, and quite plausible, to adopt more than one characterization, and to ascribe to the CPUSA a dual character. One of its aspects is that of open agitation for radical goals; the other is that of the agent of Moscow, fomenting revolution and aiding in crimes against security.[3] In the last decade both public and private decision-making have been overwhelmingly based on the position that sees only the malignant conspiracy. I shall chip around the edges of this view; while I think it is true, I also think that it is not the whole truth, at least not when applied to individual cases. The party may be legally and politicically a revolutionary conspiracy; but to infer that every individual who is or has been a member is a hardened conspirator is either a legal fiction or a prejudice. Of this more later.

Since communism is almost the anthithesis of dominant American economic and political values, it is unnecessary to catalogue the many reasons for its moral quarantine. I will mention only four attributes that have led in repelling even those who were once attracted to the austere regimen and utopian goals of American communism. The first is the repeated resort to violence by the Soviet Union either to suppress dissent at home or to achieve conquests abroad. The alacrity with which Communists resort to falsehood and betrayal to further their goals is another disturbing factor, and one which ultimately disillusioned many

2. For a list of standard sources dealing with the history of the Communist party in the United States see Fund for the Republic, *Bibliography on the Communist Problem in the United States* (1955), p. 275. A good short history of world communism is Harold H. Fisher, Hoover Institute Studies, *The Communist Revolution: An Outline of Strategy and Tactics* (1955).

3. See, e.g., statement of Norman Thomas, representing the ACLU, before House Comm. on the Judiciary, Subcomm. on Internal Security Legislation, Hearings (April 5, 1954), pp. 67–70.

who participated in United Front activities with them in the 1930's. A third is the callousness with which Communists, when they are in a position to do so, suppress civil liberties; this has brought some former well-wishers to question whether those who would deny civil rights to others are themselves entitled to freedom of speech and association. A fourth repellent is the totalitarian fist discernible, even in this country, in the disciplined conduct of party affairs. Communist theory requires adherence on pain of expulsion to the principle of "democratic centralism," which means unquestioning obedience to the party line, once it has been handed down by higher authority.[4]

It is this last trait especially that has made glaringly apparent the domination of the American party by the Communist party in the Soviet Union, a domination that accounts for abrupt and absurd flip-flops on the part of domestic Communists, like the reversal of policy in 1939 when Stalin made his treaty with Hitler, or the repudiation of Earl Browder in 1945 after the publication of a letter of criticism by the French Communist Duclos. The report of the Subversive Activities Control Board ordering the Communist party to register as a communist-action organization under the Internal Security Act describes forty-five major instances where domestic Communist policy corresponded to announcements of Soviet policy, and finds no instance of deviation.[5]

STRENGTH OF THE PARTY

But even if this catalogue is extended, as it easily could be, we would still have to ask what its significance is, and how much it contaminates those who have been not at the center of the movement, but somewhere around the edges. Both of these questions relate to the numerical strength of the party. In my opinion it is now so weak as to be insignificant as a politically subversive force; and the numbers of its followers through

4. For discussions of some of these characteristics see Fisher, n. 2 above; Nathan Leites, *A Study of Bolshevism* (1953), chs. 3, 14. On falsehood and betrayal see C. Milosz, *The Captive Mind* (1953), Granville Hicks, *Where We Came Out* (1954), and Arthur Schlesinger, Jr., *The Vital Center* (1949), pp. 134 ff.

5. Testimony of Philip E. Mosely, Director of Columbia University's Russian Institute, before the Subversive Activities Control Board in the case of Brownell v. CPUSA, summarized in Sen. Doc. No. 41 (April 1953), pp. 80–6. There has been considerable criticism of Russia by leading U.S. Communists since the death of Stalin and particularly since the uprisings in Poland and Hungary. Does this represent a permanent loosening of the bonds or only uncertainty and a breakdown of communications during the post-Stalin era?

time has been greatly exaggerated, both in quality and intensity. A few vital statistics should be recalled. The largest number of votes ever achieved by a Communist presidential candidate was around 100,000, in 1932. The largest number of dues-paying members ever claimed by the party was again about 100,000, in 1940. Recent estimates by J. Edgar Hoover have the membership down to 20,000, and communist sources conceded a precipitous further decline in 1956 and 1957.

Hoover has always been quick to remind us, however, that for every party member there are a number of close sympathizers who, for reasons of prudence or of incomplete commitment, do not appear on the party rolls. The ratio given is usually ten to one, which would mean that there were a million hidden henchmen in 1940, and that even in 1956 there were 200,000. This is one of the shakiest statistics in American politics. Its original source seems to be a communist boast by William Z. Foster, surely an insufficient guide for national policy; and though our antisubversive agencies may have adopted it as a cautious rule of thumb, so as not to underestimate their adversary, no substantial evidence of its accuracy, so far as I know, has ever been produced. There is probably a large degree of confusion in these estimates, between the various degrees of fellow travelers and those who are wholly committed to the communist cause but who deliberately abstain from party membership. The latter should certainly be included in estimating communist strength. But when a clergyman, for example, allies himself publicly with Communists in some peace propaganda, it does not follow that he would be found with them on the barricades.[6]

6. On the maximum number of dues-paying members see Alan Barth, *The Loyalty of Free Men* (1951), p. 25. The 20,000 figure is from an interview with J. E. Hoover, *New Haven Register,* Feb. 17, 1956. See NYT, Sept. 10, 1957, for a report of a falling-off to perhaps 10,000. The following colloquy on the ten-to-one ratio is revealing. Hoover was testifying before Senate Comm. on Appropriations, Subcomm. for the Departments of State, Justice, Commerce, and the Judiciary, Hearings, *Appropriations . . . 1952* (1951), pp. 83–4: "Every seasoned member of the party is a potential saboteur and spy. . . . The communist leaders themselves have claimed that for every party member there are 10 others ready, willing, and able to do the party's work.

"*Sen. McCarran:* I have used that statement. What do you think about that?

"*Mr. Hoover:* I think it is generally correct for this reason: It may not be ten today. It may be slightly lower. I would say probably seven or eight, but certainly a year ago before the country became so security-conscious and when it was not considered unpopular to be pro-communist, there were many persons, not members of the party, many persons, in the so-called ultra liberal class— who would carry the torch for the communist cause.

"For that reason, when they said for every member they had ten fellow travelers,

The ranks of fellow travelers have also been inflated by uncritical reliance on the press-agentry of the front organizations that they supported. Promoters' claims are always a frail reed, especially so if one recalls that the effective spokesmen for front organizations often came from communist ranks. Murray Kempton reports that when J. B. Matthews identified the American League for Peace and Democracy as a Communist front, before the Dies committee back in 1938, "The American League claimed to represent four million members, a species of inflation which Matthews passed on to Martin Dies and the House Committee On Un-American Activities as though it were fact. At the time of its dissolution in October, 1939, it had just twenty thousand members." Kempton pointedly adds, "We might all have been better off today if the honest opponents of J. B. Matthews had conceded that the American League for Peace and Democracy was a Communist front and challenged the assumption that it had four million members." [7]

Another misused indicator of the strength of communism in the 1930's and 40's is the number of ex-Communists in our midst today. In addition to those who have made a career of magnifying the power of their former comrades, and whose alarms Kempton has so skillfully cut down to size, there are the thousands who joined the party and then quietly left it. Ernst and Loth, in a bold attempt at a numerical estimate, come up with a total of 700,000. Compared to the maximum claimed party membership of 100,000, this estimate betokens an extraordinary rate of turnover. What some people fail to notice is that this army of ex-Communists is evidence of weakness, not of strength, in the movement. It suggests that the hold of the party on its rank-and-file has been tenuous, and the period of commitment transitory.

A fantastic proposition that enhances the apparent solidity of the party is the theory, diligently cultivated by some experts, that one cannot resign from the party; the only exit is by expulsion. A basis for this notion exists in a supposed party rule. This rule is entitled to no

---

I think it was a sound statement. That is their estimate. They claim it. I would feel today that it is one or two too high because today it is not popular to be espousing the cause of communism. They still have at least six or seven fellow travelers for each one of their members. Their own statement is that they have ten." See Chafee, Review, *Harvard Law Rev.* (1953), 66:551–2, criticizing Nathaniel Weyl, *The Battle against Disloyalty,* for its uncritical acceptance of the ten-to-one figure.

7. Murray Kempton, *Part of Our Time* (New York, Simon and Schuster, 1955), p. 172.

more credence than the civil liberties provisions of the Russian constitution; and in any case it seems to be confused with a popular fallacy that resignation from a voluntary association has to be accepted to be effective. This is not so; by withdrawing all support and adherence, one resigns from the Communist party as decisively as from the Elks or the Methodist Church. Of course, expulsions do occur. In the schism-ridden history of the CPUSA, whole factions have been expelled, whose members formed the left-wing splinter parties that still feebly exist. But the transcripts of the investigating committees contain many more accounts of former Communists who, as they often put it, "just drifted away." [8]

These same rich chronicles, the Congressional hearings, furnish abundant evidence that the party's hold on its members while it had them was by no means so viselike as its pretensions suggest. Though cooperative witnesses may be tempted to slant the truth in order to minimize their own conspiratorial activities, they are tempted even more strongly to help build up the committees'—and the public's—image of the party as monolithic, disciplined, tireless, efficient, and inured to violence. The investigating committees do not help their cause—or their appropriations—by hearing descriptions of party units that were ineffective, discordant, bookish, and peaceable. Yet one meets again and again in the hearings cooperative witnesses whose testimony gives just such an unexciting picture, and who for the life of them cannot recall any illegal activity or any teaching of violence during their careers as revolutionaries. [9]

Justice Douglas aptly characterized the American party, in his dis-

8. On the cumulative total number of party members see Morris Ernst and David Loth, *Report on the American Communist* (1952), pp. 14, 33. For variations on the "can't resign" theme see Brief for Appellant in Gold v. U.S., 237 F. 2d 764 (D.C. Cir. 1956), pp. 10–12, in which government witness Hladun was unable to cite any written evidence of the rule. "He stated that the rule was 'so evident' that 'they would be foolish to put it in writing.'" Judge Bazelon commented, 237 F. 2d 769, that two of the seven witnesses who expounded the "can't resign" policy "stated that they themselves had quit." For an example of a party functionary's quitting unobtrusively see testimony of Stanley B. Hancock, HUAC, Hearings, *Investigation of Activities in the State of California* (1954), p. 4593; see also Ernst and Loth, passim, esp. ch. 13, on the undesirability of making an explicit break for fear of slander and other reprisals. For a summary of the schisms and splinters of the CPUSA see Daniel Bell in *Socialism and American Life,* ed. Egbert and Persons (1952), pp. 334–45, 366–9.

9. See, e.g., HUAC, Hearings, *Communist Activities among Professional Groups in the Los Angeles Area* (1952), pp. 2501–2603, esp. 2535–82.

senting opinion in the *Dennis* case, as "the best known, the most beset, and the least thriving of any fifth column in history." [10] But it is still a fifth column, an enemy within the gates, and it may be argued that as its ranks decrease and its isolation increases, the residue represents a really hard core of conspirators. The present state of public animosity almost forces the party into conformity with what people think it is. Except for a few old-guard fellow travelers who live on memories of battles against social injustice in which the Communists were their allies —and a few young dupes moved by heaven knows what confused impulses—who now stands up for the Communist party? To endure the alienation and the hazards of being a Communist in America in the 1950's, one must be convinced heart and soul that our democratic capitalist creed is rotten, that the Marxist gospel is right, and—hardest to take—that the Russian hierarchy is its only authentic interpreter. The hard core is dangerous, not for what it can accomplish, but for what it is willing to accomplish.

It may be thought that I have not given deserved weight in this quick survey to the argument that Communists have had an influence disproportionate to their total numbers, because of their concentration in certain powerful occupations. Government and organized labor are certainly centers of power. Teachers and other intellectuals are more disputably so. In discussing the heavy incidence of loyalty tests in these occupations, the record of communist success in these fields has not been overlooked. Here it should be said that a few conspicuous examples of Communists in key positions tend to exaggerate the effectiveness of the American party. There have been times and places where Communists got into influential positions. For example, there were some bright young men in the Ware cell in Washington in the early 1930's, and some of them went far—Lee Pressman, for one, who sat next to the throne in the CIO. But the Ware cell was not typical, and it is quite wrong to assume that every cell had a Pressman. When one looks behind the luminaries to the parade of witnesses from the middle and lower levels of party life, it is reassuring, I think, to observe that though almost all of them worked hard, they were no more gifted, more compelling, or more successful than most of us.[11]

10. 341 U.S. 907 (1950). But cf. Justice Jackson's concurring opinion in American Communications Association v. Douds, 339 U.S. 382, 422 (1950).

11. Consult Gabriel Almond, *The Appeals of Communism* (1954), Part 3, "Social and Psychological Characteristics." On the Ware cell see James Burnham, *The Web of Subversion* (1954), p. 36, and testimony of Nathaniel Weyl, ISC, Hearings, *Subversive Influence in the Educational Process* (1953), pp. 711–13.

PUBLIC POLICY TOWARD COMMUNISM

Though revolutionary alarms have stirred the country in several periods of its history, a coherent theory of constitutional limitations with respect to sedition has been slow in emerging. Of course it has never been doubted that an actual attempt to overthrow the government would be punishable, nor that the usual legal apparatus of conspiracies, attempts, and solicitations, if linked directly to a proposed insurrection, could also be. Most of the offenses that fall within the settled law of crimes against public order involve more than talk; they include acts. Where the offense does consist only of speech, the lawmakers may recognize that "Words are not only the keys of persuasion, but the triggers of action," as Judge Learned Hand put it. Thus it is a crime to threaten the life of the president. Such threats seem so closely related to the detestable assassinations which have stunned the country that it is considered reasonable to make the words alone punishable. But though we may agree with Justice Holmes that "Every idea is an incitement. It offers itself for belief and if believed is acted on unless some other belief outweighs it or some failure of energy stifles the movement at birth," we do not, under our Constitution, punish words and ideas indiscriminately. There stands the First Amendment, with its command that Congress shall make no law abridging the freedom of speech or of the press.[12] Under its shelter, a broad scope of political agitation is permissible. How broad? That is the critical question which had no authoritative definition until the Supreme Court began to grapple with free-speech cases during World War I.

The first cases had to do with propaganda in opposition to wartime conscription; the defendants were anarchists or Socialists—the most conspicuous being Eugene Debs, the great Socialist leader. Though the actual obstructive effect on the draft of these pamphlets and speeches may be doubted, the cases did arise in wartime, and the portions of the Espionage Act under which they were brought did aim to protect the morale of the armed forces. The Court refused to find any protection for such speech in the First Amendment; and this attitude carried over when communist cases began to come before the Court, based not on

12. Learned Hand in Masses Publishing Co. v. Patten, 244 F. 535, 540 (S.D.N.Y. 1917). Holmes, J., in Gitlow v. New York, 268 U.S. 652, 673 (1925). 18 U.S.C. § 871 makes it a crime to threaten the life of the president, president-elect or vice-president. For an application of this statute in World War I, see Clark v. U.S., 250 F. 449 (5th Cir. 1918) (the accused said that he wished President Wilson "was in hell, and that if I had the power I would put him there").

statutes like the Espionage Act of 1917, applicable only in wartime, but on laws, which the state legislatures had enacted in profusion, that condemned any advocacy or teaching in favor of violent changes in the government.[13]

The landmark case for the proposition that communist propaganda could be forbidden, even though it was published in peacetime and though the revolution it advocated was to occur in the remote future, was *Gitlow v. New York*. Here Justice Sanford for the Court put aside the contention that no consequences had resulted from the defendant's turgid manifesto. Although the Court held that state legislatures, like the Congress, were required to honor the First Amendment's protection of free speech, it said that the protection disappeared if the legislature decided that words like the defendant's "are so inimical to the general welfare and involve such danger of substantive evil that they may be penalized in the exercise of its police power." This position, that a dangerous tendency is enough to set aside a constitutional guarantee, was persistently countered by Justices Holmes and Brandeis with their famous "clear and present danger" test. Its first enunciation by Holmes (not in dissent, as it happened) was in one of the World War I cases: "The question in every case is whether the words used are used in such circumstances and are of such a nature as to create a clear and present danger that they will bring about the substantive evils that Congress has a right to prevent. It is a question of proximity and degree." Justice Brandeis later fully assimilated the test to the classic argument for free speech by explaining that so long as there was time for the subversive words to be met by the persuasive power of opposing words, there was no danger justifying suppression. Only when talk clearly portended action, so immediately that there was no time for adequate argument, could the prohibition of the First Amendment be overridden.[14]

13. See Debs v. U.S., 249 U.S. 211 (1919), Frohwerk v. U.S., 249 U.S. 204 (1919), and Schenck v. U.S., 249 U.S. 47 (1919). The 1918 amendments to the federal Espionage Act made a great variety of criticism of the government and of its war effort criminal. The first communist case to come before the Supreme Court, Abrams v. U.S., 250 U.S. 616 (1919), arose under this Act. The defendants had attacked our sending troops to Russia in 1918, and the counts of the indictment that were sustained were those that charged interference with the prosecution of the war and with war production. Thus it may be considered a wartime case, even though it involved a discredited and peripheral episode of the war. The 1918 statute was repealed in 1921. Chafee, *Free Speech in the United States* (1941), chs. 2, 3.

14. Gitlow v. New York, 268 U.S. 652 (1925); Schenck v. U.S., 249 U.S. 47 (1919); Whitney v. California, 274 U.S. 357 (1927).

This is not the place to expound further the theory and development of the clear-and-present danger test. We have only to observe that, though its direct application was infrequent, the attitude toward the First Amendment that the test symbolized triumphed in the Supreme Court under the Chief Justiceships of Hughes and Stone. For a period of about fifteen years attempts to suppress the propaganda of the Communist party, to halt its meetings, or to deport its members, broke on the "preferred position," as it came to be called, of the First Amendment, strongly reinforced by the due-process clause of the Fourteenth. Of course the Communists were not the only beneficiaries of the libertarian spirit in the Court. The sect of Jehovah's Witnesses undoubtedly won the most victories. It is also instructive to note that German sympathizers in World War II benefited by the new mood. Thus, in the leading case to come before the Court on writings tending to obstruct the draft or to cause insubordination in the armed forces, the Court directed an acquittal. Yet the facts were certainly as strong for the prosecution as they were in the strongest of the World War I cases, the *Schenck* case, in which Holmes, for a unanimous court, sustained a conviction as meeting the clear-and-present danger test.

For a while the judicial tide ran strongly in favor of toleration. It was aided in communist cases by sentiment in favor of Russia during the World War II alliance. Thus Wendell Willkie, Republican candidate for president in 1940, appeared before the Court in 1943 and argued successfully against the deportation of the secretary of the Communist party in California.[15]

Still there were cross-currents, especially in the legislative branch. Congress may have been carried away by the defense of Stalingrad, but the earlier legislative record shows that it was not impressed by the popular front. Even its isolationist near-majority in 1939–41 found little common ground with the Communists in their opposition to U.S. involvement in the European war. The chief landmarks of Congressional intransigence were these: in 1938 the House Committee on Un-American Activities was established; in 1939 the Hatch Act provision forbidding government employment to members of organizations advocating the

15. On the attitude of the Hughes-Stone Court toward the First Amendment see Louis Lusky, "Minority Rights and the Public Interest," *Yale Law Jour.* (1942), *52*:1; Wallace Mendelson, "Clear and Present Danger—from Schenck to Dennis," *Columbia Law Rev.* (1952), *52*:313. For a situation similar to the World War I sedition cases see Hartzel v. U.S., 322 U.S. 680 (1944). The Communist deportation case was Schneiderman v. U.S., 320 U.S. 118 (1943). Schneiderman is a defendant in the Smith Act case of Yates v. U.S., 354 U.S. 298 (1957).

overthrow of the government was enacted; beginning in 1941, the cognate provision in all appropriation bills made its appearance; legislation in 1938 and 1940 required the registration, as a means of propaganda control, of agents of foreign principals, and of subversive organizations subject to foreign control.

Of the greatest long-range significance was the Alien Registration Act of 1940. Along with deportation penalties for aliens who had in the past belonged to subversive organizations, Congress with little debate put on the books the first general peacetime sedition statute since the execrated Sedition Act of 1798. Advocating or teaching the desirability or necessity of overthrowing the government, assisting in any publication advocating violent overthrow, helping to organize a group to advocate overthrow, membership in or affiliation with such a group, and conspiracies to do any of these things—all became crimes. As the Constitution was then being interpreted, the new provision (which came to have its own identity under the name of the Smith Act) could not be applied unless the clear-and-present danger test was satisfied. But those who remembered the senseless prosecutions of 1918–19 under the World War I law, and who had read about the persecution of editors by the Federalists in 1798–1800, vainly protested this expression of anticommunist zeal by Congress.[16]

Of course neither the Smith Act nor the other measures that have been mentioned were aimed entirely at Communists. Then at large was Adolph Hitler, and some attention was paid to the bumbling activities of his supporters in this country, who were probably no more numerous than the Communists. The Emergency Relief Appropriation Act of 1940, for example, baldly specified that no relief employment was to be given to aliens, Communists, or Bundists. One of the two cases brought under the Smith Act before 1948 indicted a large group of alleged propagandists for the Nazi cause. This case collapsed of its own weight, killing the trial judge, of exhaustion, along the way. The defendants in the other case were a tiny group of militant Trotskyites in Minneapolis. Their convictions were affirmed by the Eighth Circuit Court of Appeals, pretty much on the authority of the supposedly discredited *Gitlow* case; and the Supreme Court declined to review. The executive branch was not disposed to repress orthodox Communists during the palmy days of the

16. See Ch. 2 above, n. 1, on the Hatch Act and appropriations rider. Legislation designed to control foreign agents and propaganda is summarized in FUND DIGEST, pp. 179–87. For an account of the passage of the Smith Act see Chafee, *Free Speech in the United States* (1941), pp. 462–5.

military alliance; and in Congress even the Committee on Un-American Activities was muted.[17]

POLICY SINCE WORLD WAR II: EXIT CLEAR AND PRESENT DANGER

After the war, Congress was quick to scent new dangers from domestic communism. The Labor-Management Relations Act of 1947 included the test oath for union officials. To the general formula denouncing adherence to violent overthrow something new was added: the union official must forswear membership in the Communist party. This was the first significant postwar measure that drew a bead directly on the Communists, without circumlocution and without any other major subversive target in sight.

When the Taft-Hartley oath reached the Supreme Court in 1950, the Court had changed. Of the majority that had exalted the freedoms of the First Amendment, death had removed three (Stone, Murphy, and Rutledge). Time had modified the convictions of two (Frankfurter and Jackson). Only Justices Black and Douglas pursued an unswerving course. Chief Justice Vinson, speaking for the Court, recognized that the oath had the "necessary effect of discouraging the exercise of political rights protected by the First Amendment." But the abridgement of speech was "indirect, conditional, partial," and he found it difficult to apply literally the clear-and-present danger test as Holmes had formulated it. This was not a case where the punishment of speech was squarely before the Court. With a bow to the "high place" of the Bill of Rights, the Chief Justice said that the Court's duty was to decide which of "two conflicting interests demands the greater protection." The interest that conflicted with freedom of speech was a Congressional finding that interstate commerce was menaced by political strikes. There was little to support this finding except the Allis-Chalmers strike discussed in Chapter 8. Nevertheless, the majority thought that the legislative judgment was controlling, and that it was "a permissible one in this case under the Constitution." Justice Jackson backed up the major-

17. The pro-Nazi propagandist trial was U.S. v. McWilliams, 163 F. 2d 695 (D.C. Cir. 1947). See also Weyl (n. 6 above), pp. 162–4. The Trotskyite trial was Dunne v. U.S., 138 F. 2d 137 (8th Cir. 1943), cert. denied 320 U.S. 790 (1943). See also Louis Boudin, "Seditious Doctrines and the Clear and Present Danger Rule," *Va. Law Rev.* (1952), *38:*143 and 315, esp. 174–7. On the relative quiescence of the HUAC during this period cf. FUND DIGEST, pp. 603–5, with pp. 558–603, 605 ff.

ity with his famous essay on the unique and deadly character of the Communist party. But he (and Justice Frankfurter) balked at sustaining another clause of the oath which required abjuration of belief in violent overthrow. This brought about an even division of the Court on the belief clause, and left standing the lower court's decision which had sustained it.[18]

Meanwhile the Department of Justice had tried the national leadership of the Communist party under the Smith Act for conspiring to organize the Communist party as a group to advocate violent overthrow, and for conspiring themselves to advocate revolution. When this case reached the Court in 1951, revaluation of the clear-and-present danger test could not be avoided. The defendants had contended that neither they nor their party taught revolution; the contents of books and speeches were searched by both sides. The latter-day pronouncements of the party had been so mild that the government was forced to develop the theory of "Aesopian" language—that surface fables had a deeper meaning. The jury then found that the defendants intended to overthrow the government, and that they had conspired, as charged, to promote the cause of revolution through the propaganda of the party. The trial judge on his part decided that the danger was sufficient for the statute to be applied, even though it was the speeches and writings of the defendants that were thus condemned. How could this be? There was no evidence in the case, and I suppose little popular belief, that the danger of an insurrection was "present"—i.e. imminent. All that could be said was that the defendants would promote revolt as speedily as circumstances would permit. Was this enough? Yes, said Judge Learned Hand in his influential opinion for the intermediate Court of Appeals. What the Holmes–Brandeis test really meant, he told us, was that courts "must ask whether the gravity of the 'evil,' discounted by its improbability, justifies such invasion of free speech as is necessary to avoid the danger." And, he added, "We have purposely substituted 'improbability' for 'remoteness' because that must be the right interpretation." So (paraphrasing an acute commentator), if the feared evil—a totalitarian revolution —is of almost infinite gravity, then the probability of its occurrence can be almost zero, and still support a conviction for seditious propaganda. To support the proposition that the danger from these defendants was more than zero, the judges resorted to a variety of readings of recent history. The common element in these stressed the precariousness of the international situation. And indeed it was precarious.

18. American Communications Association v. Douds, 339 U.S. 382 (1950).

Under the strain of the cold war and the impact of dominant public sentiment against communism, the clear-and-present danger test crumpled. The importance of the *Dennis* case for this analysis is that the Supreme Court adopted Judge Hand's revision of the test. At any rate, four members of the Court did; they were supported in the result by some hand-wringing from Justice Frankfurter on judicial incapacity to deal with such a question, and by a drastic theory of Justice Jackson's that the element of conspiracy made the First Amendment irrelevant. It is unnecessary to pursue the nice technical question whether the case retreated all the way to the doctrine of the *Gitlow* case—that seditious utterances can be punished if the legislature finds that they would have a bad tendency. The decision certainly went far enough to demonstrate that even in the area guarded by the First Amendment—that of political agitation through speech, press, and assembly—Communists were almost beyond the pale of judicial protection.[19]

CONGRESSIONAL EXPOSURE

Congress did not wait for the *Dennis* decision; it passed, over President Truman's veto, the Internal Security Act of 1950. This elaborate patchwork of antisubversive devices was quite forthright in specifying communism as its target, though it was a little coy in finding that the direction of world communism "is exercised by the communist dictatorship of a foreign country"—unnamed. The main weapon of the Act is exposure, though employment disabilities, already discussed in Chapter 3, are also imposed on the members of the various categories of Communist organizations. Once they have been identified by the Subversive Activities Control Board, "Communist-action" or "Communist-front" organizations must so describe themselves on their publications and broadcasts. They must supply the Attorney General with information about their organization and contributors; and Communist-action organi-

19. Dennis v. U.S., 341 U.S. 494 (1951). L. Hand's opinion is in U.S. v. Dennis, 183 F. 2d 201 (2d Cir. 1950). For conflicting views on the role of the Court in implementing the First Amendment see Boudin (n. 17 above), and Elliot Richardson, "Freedom of Expression and the Function of the Courts," *Harvard Law Rev.* (1951), *65*:1. See also Harold Chase, *Security and Liberty: The Problem of Native Communists, 1947–1955* (1955), pp. 11–23. The infinity-zero figure is Boudin's, p. 330. The Smith Act cases of 1957 (Yates v. U.S., 354 U.S. 298) reaffirmed the correctness of the charge to the jury in the Dennis case that advocacy of action and not mere advocacy of abstract doctrine is required. This and other holdings in the Yates case will make convictions in Smith Act cases more difficult than they had become in the intervening years.

zations must register the names of their members. If the organization fails to register, the members must turn themselves in—with criminal penalties for willful defaults.[20]

This scheme of compulsory registration took a long time to get started. The Internal Security Act was procedurally pretty good, and therefore (from a popular standpoint) pretty slow. The hearings before the Board were elaborate, and there was an appeal to the courts. At the end of 1955 the case of the Communist party itself came before the Supreme Court. The Court of Appeals in the District of Columbia had upheld the validity of the Act, against a persuasive dissent by Judge Bazelon on issues of self-incrimination. In view of the network of offenses that a Communist was possibly caught up in, could he be required to announce his status to the Attorney General? The Act attempted to overcome this severe flaw by providing that the fact of registration could not be introduced as evidence of crime. But the privilege against self-incrimination excuses a culprit from providing any meaningful leads to his prosecution; it is doubtful that excluding the fact of registration from evidence after the registrant has been hauled up for violating the Smith Act is enough to satisfy the privilege. The Court did not then meet the issues. It found that the record before the Board was tainted by possibly perjured testimony, and sent the case back for reconsideration.[21]

While this orderly arrangement for making Communists nail their own hides to the barn door made little progress, the Congressional committees, in their own disorderly way, did a quite thorough job of exposure. Chapter 1 reviewed, in a preliminary way, the effectiveness of committee investigations as a sanction against disloyalty. They may also be seen as a mirror reflecting the rise of anticommunism. The perseverance with which appropriate and sometimes inappropriate committees delved into every aspect of communist activities and influence

20. 64 Stat. 987 (1950), 50 U.S.C. §§ 781–98. The Act also tightens existing legislation against espionage. Title II, the alien exclusion provisions, which deals with the authority of the Attorney General in deportation cases and naturalization and citizenship requirements, has been superseded by Titles II and III of the Immigration and Nationality Act of 1952, 66 Stat. 175, 8 U.S.C. §§ 1151–1503. Title III, now Title II, the Emergency Detention Act (64 Stat. 1019, 50 U.S.C. §§ 811–26) provides a legal framework for concentration camps in time of war or insurrection. See Arthur Sutherland, Jr., "Freedom and Internal Security," *Harvard Law Rev.* (1951), *64*:383; Note, "The Internal Security Act of 1950," *Columbia Law Rev.* (1951), *51*:606, and Chase (n. 19 above), pp. 24–37.

21. See Communist Party v. Subversive Activities Control Board, 223 F. 2d 531 (D.C. Cir. 1955), reversed and remanded, 351 U.S. 115 (1956).

needs no discussion. But I do want to mention a few points that bring out the hardening of opinion and policy.

The work of the Dies Committee (1938–45) was remarkably like that of its successors in the postwar decade. It gave rather more attention to fascist groups, because they were then the avowed enemy; but the reader revisiting its record will be struck by the profusion of familiar names and charges on the communist issue. However, in the prewar hearings Communist party spokesmen (Browder, Foster) testified fully and with some candor about the aims of the party. And there were few, if any, technical claims of privilege; some witnesses simply refused to answer questions. Though they were threatened with contempt proceedings, they were not in fact prosecuted.

The movie hearings of 1947 began the systematic practice of directing witnesses to testify as to their own communist beliefs and associations, past and present. When the courts failed to sustain the contentions of the Hollywood Ten that the Committee had no right to ask the questions, witnesses resorted to the privilege against self-incrimination. Thereafter the various investigating committees settled on a standard operating procedure. After private screening in executive session, suspected Communists or ex-Communists might be called to testify in public. If they invoked the privilege, they earned the epithet "Fifth Amendment Communist," which Senator McCarthy popularized. If on the other hand the witness was willing to testify freely about both himself and others he had believed to be Communists, he was again put forward, thereby earning absolution. The theory that the public naming of names was a badge of sincere repentance and an unavoidable duty to the country was perhaps first formally enunciated by Senator McCarran in opening the hearings on the Institute of Pacific Relations in 1951. Almost without exception, if a witness without validly invoking the Fifth Amendment has since tried to take a position that did not satisfy what we may call the McCarran doctrine, he has been cited for contempt. This shift in attitude toward recalcitrant witnesses, especially that toward reluctant informers, signalized the increased drive for exposure, which brushed aside individual claims of conscience.[22]

22. For general references on the work of committees investigating communism see Ch. 1 above, n. 17. On contempt proceedings against witnesses who refused to answer, without invoking the Fifth Amendment, see Ch. 17 below. The "McCarran Doctrine" is stated in ISC, Hearings, *Institute of Pacific Relations* (1951), p. 3. For references to the prewar testimony of Browder and Foster see

OTHER TRENDS—CENSORSHIP, BANISHMENT,
MISCELLANEOUS DEPRIVATIONS

So far the background of public policy toward communism has been sketched by depicting trends in two of the sanctions discussed in Chapter 1—criminal penalties (in the case of seditious talk), and exposure. Another sanction, censorship, is not of much importance in this era, outside of doubtful cases of security classification. However, one symptomatic practice should be mentioned. The Attorney General had ruled in 1940 that the Foreign Agents Registration Act of 1938 permits the Post Office to stop foreign propaganda not addressed to registered agents. Apparently the ruling was given some application to pro-German material. Around 1952, the Post Office, with the help of the Customs Bureau, commenced large-scale seizure and destruction of printed material of communist origin, unless it was addressed to a very few registered distributors. The seized publications included newspapers, journals—anything that fell within the vague criteria of propaganda developed by the postal authorities. Despite protests from scholars and publicists that they were hampered in their studies, the practice continued, with the Post Office issuing occasional bulletins about its success in stopping floods of propaganda from reaching adult American citizens.[23]

Still another sanction is banishment, which occurs in our law in the form of deportation of resident aliens or of those who, having become citizens by naturalization, are deprived of their citizenship. The severity with which this sanction is used against foreign-born persons of communist taint is another index of public policy. In 1919–20 the mass arrests and subsequent deportations of aliens were among the outstanding excesses of those frightened years. The detention procedures employed by the Department of Justice were undoubtedly illegal; but the determination to deport was in the control of the Secretary of Labor and of the federal courts; calmer counsels reduced the number of actual deportations. The law permitting deportation of seditious persons was then fairly quiescent until 1940, when, in response to a Supreme Court decision that party membership, to justify deportation, must exist at the

FUND DIGEST, pp. 583, 588, 597. Instances of witnesses who have not been cited for contempt after unprivileged refusals to answer are collected by Daniel Pollitt, "Pleading the Fifth Amendment . . . ," *Notre Dame Lawyer* (1956), *43*:47, n. 10.

23. See Note, "Government Exclusion of Foreign Political Propaganda," *Harvard Law Rev.* (1953), *68*:1393. See also George Sokolsky, "Open Letter to the Post Office," *Saturday Review* (April 23, 1955), pp. 9–10.

time the warrant is issued, Congress made past as well as present membership a ground. For a few years the Court continued to set exacting standards, within the statutes, for both deportation and denaturalization. Further legislation in 1950 and 1952 again reversed the judicial trend, which for that matter had reversed itself. The subject is much too complex to explore in detail. Among the current deportation provisions are, on the one hand, explicit condemnations of communist advocacy or membership (it is unnecessary to establish that membership was with knowledge of the party's subversive aims) and, on the other, a broad authorization for the Attorney General to deport on grounds of prejudice to the national security.[24]

Denaturalization (which may be followed by deportation) has also been made easier in cases of alleged subversion. Any of an extensive catalogue of communist or other totalitarian affiliations or beliefs, if held within ten years before citizenship is sought, will bar naturalization, and will therefore authorize later revocation of the naturalization. Two related theories are available, that the citizenship was acquired by fraud, or that the petitioner was not in fact eligible for citizenship in the first place. A citizen facing denaturalization does have the advantage of procedural safeguards not granted to aliens; but the government has been successful in a growing number of contested cases that charged party membership in the 1930's or early 1940's.

The harshness of the laws dealing with the foreign-born, especially in their procedural aspects, is of course not entirely a measure of anticommunist policy. The Supreme Court long ago decided that aliens were entitled only to minimal constitutional rights. Immigration policies have been stiffening toward exclusion for half a century. Even so, the lawbooks today contain some remarkable evidence of current anticommunist feelings. Surely the most remarkable is the provision of the McCarran-Walter Act of 1952 revoking the citizenship of a person who within ten years *after* naturalization is convicted of contempt for refusal to answer investigating committee questions about his subversive activities. This is untested and probably unconstitutional.[25]

Loss of citizenship, with the threat of exile, was carried one step further in 1954. There is a traditional list of grave crimes (treason, in-

24. On the 1919–20 deportations see Chafee (n. 16 above), pp. 196–240. For general analysis of legal sanctions against aliens see Milton Konvitz, *The Alien and the Asiatic in American Law* (1946); Konvitz, *Civil Rights in Immigration* (1953); Note, "Developments in the Law—Immigration and Naturalization," *Harvard Law Rev.* (1953), *66:*643, esp. 687–8.

25. Immigration and Nationality Act of 1952, 66 Stat. 260, 8 U.S.C. § 1451.

surrection, and the like) which entail loss of nationality for either native-born or naturalized citizens. To this list was added the crime of the Smith Act. Thus a conviction for conspiracy to advocate violent overthrow—in other words, a conviction for being a Communist party functionary—results automatically in loss of citizenship.[26]

Still another form of sanction is to withhold government benefits ranging from passports to relief payments. This technique might be dismissed as too eccentric to mark a trend, for its manifestations can hardly be brought into any kind of system; but they are sufficiently widespread to indicate the relentless character of current anticommunism. I will not attempt a catalogue here; but it should be noted that this may be an area where the courts are about to call a halt.[27]

OUTLAWRY AND ITS IMPLICATIONS

The last official expression of anticommunist sentiment that should be mentioned is the legislative device of "outlawing" the Communist party. What those who sponsor this modern form of an ancient doom seem to have in mind are chiefly two things, first to exclude the party from the ballot, and second to strip it of any legal privileges or immunities. Both purposes have been given form on a national scale in the Communist Control Act of 1954. The denial of any legal status to the party (for example, to enforce contracts in the courts) is still quite unclear in scope. But exclusion from the ballot, which has also been decreed by a number of state laws, is an explicit sanction drastic in its implications.[28]

It implies that Communists are not to be allowed an opportunity to bid for power even through orderly means. Such a policy carries the further implication that communism is a criminal conspiracy and nothing else, and that all its aims are so wicked that they cannot be pursued by either foul means or fair. Support for this theory comes from an argument suggested by Justice Jackson in the Taft-Hartley and Smith Act cases, and by the legislative findings in the Internal Security Act. Since

26. Immigration and Nationality Act of 1952, 66 Stat. 163, 268, 8 U.S.C. § 1841(a)(9), amended by the Expatriation Act of 1954, 68 Stat. 1146. See Comment, "The Expatriation Act of 1954," *Yale Law Jour.* (1955), *64*:1164.

27. Lists of denials of incidental benefits appear in FUND DIGEST, pp. 232–8; see also ACLU, *36th Annual Report* (1956), pp. 33, 59, 64–5.

28. See Comment, "The Communist Control Act of 1954," *Yale Law Jour* (1955), *64*:712, esp. 738–44. The Act is in 68 Stat. 775, 50 U.S.C. § 841.

Communists will resort to endless cunning and deceit, the argument runs, the prohibition of force and violence is not enough. We cannot afford the risk that their trickery will succeed, thus making the prevention of violence academic. If this argument is met by the suggestion that cunning can be out-maneuvered, and deceit exposed, then the ultimate implication of the outlawry approach comes into view. It is this: the overwhelming sentiment of the country would not permit a communist regime to exist anywhere in the United States, least of all in the federal government. If we are convinced that communism would mean the end of our most cherished institutions and ideals, why should we tolerate even peaceable attempts to bring it to pass? Why let people vote on something that would be forcibly prevented from happening, so long as sufficient force was available to suppress it? Why let them even talk about its desirability?

The policy of repressing, and indeed of exterminating, people who you know are criminally wrong is of course not new. It makes up much of human history. But it is alien to our constitutional theory, as Justice Holmes made forever clear in his dissent in the *Abrams* case: "Persecution for the expression of opinions seems to me perfectly logical. If you have no doubt of your premises or your power and want a certain result with all your heart you naturally express your wishes in law and sweep away all opposition. . . . But when men have realized that time has upset many fighting faiths, they may come to believe even more than they believe the foundations of their own conduct that the ultimate good desired is better reached by free trade in ideas. . . . That at any rate is the theory of our Constitution. It is an experiment, as all life is an experiment." In our system, the testing-ground of free trade in political ideas is to subject them to the verdict of the polls. If we really mean to say to the Communists that they may not change our form of government even by persuading people to vote for them—which is what exclusion from the ballot must mean—then the communist threat is indeed unique. It has caused us to suspend the great experiment.[29]

29. The statement of Holmes, J., appears in Abrams v. U.S., 250 U.S. 616, 630–1 (1919). For a sophisticated expression of the theory that you might as well suppress what you won't let happen see Ernest Van Der Haag, "Controlling Subversive Groups," ANNALS (1955), *300*:62. See also Carl Auerbach, "The Communist Control Act of 1954: A Proposed Legal-Political Theory of Free Speech," *Univ. of Chicago Law Rev.* (1956), *23*:173, which argues that the Act is constitutional but undesirable. Cf. Walter Berns, *Freedom, Virtue, and the First Amendment* (1957).

WHERE DO WE STAND?

This account has been principally one of legislation, but it has been legislation mostly welcomed by the executive branch and for the most part blessed by the judiciary. Also, it has stuck pretty close to laws passed by Congress. A few years ago state laws would have been the chief indicators of the trend to repress communism. However, beginning with the Internal Security Act of 1950 and culminating with the Communist Control Act of 1954, Congress has caught up with the procession. The flowering of state antisubversive laws, of which some suggestion was given in Chapter 4, is simply one more indicator of the dominant trend.[30]

There is a real question, however, whether it is right to extrapolate from the high fervor reached in the second session of the 83d Congress. Perhaps that session marked the crest of a storm-tide which is now receding. Some of this fearsome legislation, like other antisubversive laws in the past, may simply fall into disuse. Some of it may be "repealed" by the courts. If either of these things—disuse or invalidation—becomes commonplace, it may be assumed that public opinion is changing too. But these possibilities are still uncertain. They are affected by the temperature of the cold war, which is bound to affect our judgment of domestic communism. Therefore, it is hazardous to speculate about them.

One other factor points more strongly toward a relaxation of tension, namely the glaring inconsistency between the undisputed weakness of the American Communist party and the extreme lengths to which repression has gone. Many of the repressive measures followed the party's decline in power, and could not have been the cause of it. If this sequence is appreciated, it seems likely that doubts will begin to arise whether measures so drastic and so alien to our best traditions are necessary.

This increasing difficulty of reconciling the feebleness of the party with demands for additional sanctions against it shows up in the pronouncements of Justice Department officials with direct responsibilities for internal security. On the one hand, they are understandably con-

30. See Pennsylvania v. Nelson, 350 U.S. 497 (1956), which held with respect to a state sedition prosecution that "Congress has occupied the field to the exclusion of parallel state legislation." The scope of federal supersession of state antisubversive legislation is unsettled, and of course subject to Congressional revision. There is no indication that state employment tests are affected by the Nelson decision.

strained to announce great victories over communism, and to parade
with pride its shrunken effigy. On the other, they are even more constrained (especially at appropriation time) to warn that the party is
still incredibly dangerous. We thus find Attorney General Brownell—
in answer to the question "But they (the Communists) are relatively
small in number aren't they?"—stating that in Italy the party had only
15,000 members who later grew to two million and that in Red China
at one time there were fewer than 10,000 members who later grew to
some six million—as if conditions in this country bore any resemblance
whatever to conditions in those countries.[31]

If I am right in thinking that public opinion may already have discarded some of its wilder growths of recent years, just as Senator Mc-
Carthy was left to wither on the vine, what consensus is likely to result
about the propriety of loyalty tests? They are not likely to be abandoned.
It remains apparent that the American public is thoroughly fed up
with communism, with communist methods and communist goals. No
foreseeable changes of Russian policy are likely to affect our deep-seated
opposition to communism. Still less is anything the American Communists say or do likely to win many friends.

A rationale for loyalty tests that bears some analogy to the theory
of security tests is likely to retain wide support. This rationale will stress
the harm that Communists can supposedly do in their jobs. In practice,
it will exclude them from any positions of trust and confidence, from
any positions where they could be said to have special influence, from
any positions where it is believed that they will have a platform to
spread their gospel. The next chapter will consider to what kinds of jobs
this rationale is applied, and whether the impulse to root out Communists can be confined to plausible areas of employment, for it is an
impulse with a strong admixture of vengefulness, and the resulting emotions are heady ones. We also have to see whether it is possible to confine their force to identifiable Communists. Discriminating identification
is not easy, and our anti-Communist crusaders have developed a large
catalogue of other culpable types. Important programs are not directed
narrowly at Communist party members and their undercover confed-
erates. They are also directed at communist sympathizers, followers,

31. Contrast Herbert Brownell, "Shall Doors Be Open to Spies and Subversives?" *U.S. News and World Report* (April 29, 1955), p. 54, with his memorandum to President Eisenhower on the weakness of American Communists, NYT,
Oct. 8, 1956. Cf. Walter Millis, "Are Subversives Really Subversive?" *Saturday
Review* (Sept. 3, 1955), p. 16.

dupes, and thinkers. Now, these terms are all within the legitimate range of political antipathy. But we have to ask if it is not quite another matter to level employment proscriptions at people who, though they may be foolish and unpopular, are not plotting the overthrow of the republic.

14. Occupational Justifications for Loyalty Tests

THE CASE for loyalty tests takes several forms. The most sweeping one simply asserts that disloyal people are enemies of society, that society does not owe them a living, and that if nobody gives them a job they will either repent or starve. For all its simplicity, this approach to the problem does not have much support; most going loyalty tests have more elaborate justifications, varying from occupation to occupation. By developing a special case for one occupation after another, these justifications implicitly reject the all-inclusive "repent or starve" solution.[1] The special cases have a family resemblance to each other, because they all pay some attention to the supposed needs of the job as well as to the politics of the jobholder. But the individual variations among them are marked enough to require separate treatment of each of the major types of programs: those for government employees, for teachers, for writers and show people, and for lawyers and other licensed professions.

GOVERNMENT EMPLOYEES

The question now, putting to one side security standards applicable to sensitive employment, is whether every public servant should pass some kind of loyalty test. At the outset, I might as well dispose of an alleged blockbuster of an argument that is actually pretty much of a dud. That is the assertion that a public employee has no standing to complain about loyalty tests, because public employment is a privilege

1. Cf. Senator William Jenner: "There is no place anywhere in American life for anyone who has ever collaborated with the Soviet fifth column for gain— whether it was Soviet gold, Communist votes, political office, fat business contracts, or moving-picture credits. There is no place even for innocents who scattered the Soviet word mines because the Soviet agents say they aren't loaded. . . . If they are foreigners, let us send them home. If they are American citizens, let us deprive them of the rights they despise. Let them earn their living as dishwashers or ditch diggers, but not in places where they can poison our minds." *Cong. Rec.* (Aug. 14, 1954), *100:*14,469.

and not a right. The same shibboleth is also repeated about the professions.

There is nothing wrong with the "privilege and not a right" slogan except that it does not answer any important questions. Specifically, does the "privilege" label make it possible to deny public employment arbitrarily, so that officials do not have to provide a rational basis for such denials?

This question has been answered for us by the Supreme Court. In *Weiman v. Updegraff* an Oklahoma loyalty oath came up which made no distinction between innocent and knowing membership in subversive organizations. Unanimously, the Court held that here was "an assertion of arbitrary power. . . . The oath offends due process." In reply to the argument that there could be no denial of due process because no *right* to public employment had been invaded, Justice Clark said, "We need not pause to consider whether an abstract right to public employment exists. It is sufficient to say that constitutional protection does extend to the public servant whose exclusion pursuant to a statute is patently arbitrary or discriminatory." [2] Until there is a marked change in membership and sentiment on the Court, this case and its antecedents make it clear that "when 'only a privilege' comes in the door, due process does not fly out the window."

This does not mean that the privilege–right distinction is altogether empty. It may be an important clue to the outcome of judicial proceedings. Due process of law is a pretty flexible concept. If a court says that one's right to life, liberty, or property is threatened, due process comes to the rescue in full force. The Supreme Court has also told us, however, that we don't have to find a right in order to claim due process; a privilege gets some due process too. But the support of due process may not be so powerful in the second case. In a "privilege" case, the courts will not inquire so closely into the rationality of what the government is trying to do (this is "substantive" due process); and they may allow more leeway in the way the operation is carried out ("procedural" due process). And in any case the appeal for due process assures only minimum protection. What the judges say the Constitution *requires* does not

2. Weiman v. Updegraff, 344 U.S. 183, 192 (1952). The conclusion of the Weiman case was foreshadowed in earlier cases. See especially Adler v. Board of Education, 342 U.S. 485 (1952), discussed in Brown and Fassett, "Security Tests for Maritime Workers," *Yale Law Jour.* (1953), *62*:1192, and Note, *Indiana Law Jour.* (1953), *28*:537–44. The last quotation in the paragraph is from Brown and Fassett, "Loyalty Tests for Admission to the Bar," *Univ. of Chicago Law Rev.* (1953), *20*:506.

necessarily tell us what is desirable policy—any more than does the bare invocation of "privilege" or "right." The usefulness of the *Weiman* case is that it knocks on the head the notion that if you call something a privilege you don't have to worry about whether it is being unfairly withheld. However, many lawyers and judges need just a little knock on the head to dislodge this old fallacy; they still talk about "privilege vs. right," as a substitute for thought about what disabilities and conditions can properly be imposed on public employment.[3]

That public employees do have certain employment disabilities not shared by the rest of us is commonplace. Notably, they may not go on strike; and, under the Hatch Act and the brood of little Hatch Acts in the states, most of them may not engage in partisan politics. The main purposes of the Hatch Act are to strengthen the career service by neutralizing individual party workers who enter it and to avert the risk that the great numbers of civil servants might be welded into a partisan bloc. The Supreme Court took these to be reasonable goals and upheld the Act, despite the loss of political freedom suffered by civil servants.[4] This has a considerable bearing on our problem. If a public employee can be required, in the public interest, to abstain from almost any normal political activity except voting, is it too much to ask that he abstain from the abnormal political activity of promoting communism?

Put in this form, the question answers itself. People dedicated to the overthrow of the government have no business working for it. This answer can be enlarged into what appears to be a powerful argument for insisting on loyalty affirmations from civil servants. The preamble of E.O. 9835 began by declaring (I have left out the "whereases"), "Each employee of the government of the United States is endowed with a measure of trusteeship over the democratic processes which are the heart and sinew of the United States . . . it is of vital importance that

3. Much of the "privilege–right" confusion has been wrongly blamed on Justice Holmes for his epigram, "The petitioner may have a constitutional right to talk politics, but he has no constitutional right to be a policeman." In the same paragraph Holmes went on to say, "On the same principle the city may impose any *reasonable* condition upon holding offices within its control." McAuliffe v. Mayor . . . of New Bedford, 155 Mass. 216, 220, 29 N.E. 517 (1892) (emphasis supplied). For detailed criticisms of the doctrine see Arch Dotson, "The Emerging Doctrine of Privilege in Public Employment," *Pub. Admin. Rev.* (1955), *15*:77; Alanson Willcox, "Invasions of the First Amendment through Conditioned Public Spending," *Cornell Law Quar.* (1955), *41*:37–44.

4. Cf. D. H. Nelson, "Public Employees and the Right to Engage in Political Activity," *Vanderbilt Law Rev.* (1955), *9*:27, which is critical of United Public Workers v. Mitchell, 330 U.S. 75 (1947).

persons employed in the federal service be of complete and unswerving loyalty to the United States." To which most of us would agree. The flaw in this particular way of putting the case is that, though it asserts a national preference for loyal public servants, it stops short of demonstrating that the rest of E.O. 9835 was a good idea.

Does a public policy against Communists in government require the extraordinary standards and extraordinary machinery of loyalty tests? Two practical reasons for applying loyalty tests to government employees are frequently put forward. One claims that when there is a group of Communists in a single agency, or even one in a key position, they try to get more in; and then they recommend each other, and promote each other. A great deal of confirmatory evidence of this can be found in the work of the Congressional investigators. There is not much question that in a number of federal agencies, and perhaps in some local government offices—for example, the New York City Department of Welfare —there were enough Communists to pursue such tactics effectively. They are difficult tactics to meet, especially if the people are in fact capable and efficient. This kind of logrolling and back-scratching in an office is troublesome and unfair, whether it is done by Communists, Harvard men, or the softball team. But it is hardly a sufficient reason for extraordinary protective measures.

A second allegation is that Communists are duty bound to be disruptive and inefficient on the job. The evidence for this is quite inadequate. If one considers the large group of former civil servants whose careers have been reviewed by the Internal Security Subcommittee, most of them appear to have performed competently in responsible positions; and they by no means wrote all of each others' fitness reports. Of course, positions near the summit opened such unusual opportunities for espionage or for influencing policy that one might expect their occupants to perform as ably as possible, the better to carry out their hidden criminal designs. But in the lesser ranks, and in nonsensitive positions, one gets no different impression. James Burnham, who paints the infiltration of the federal service in the darkest possible colors, observes that "The normal tactical rule of the Communists is to swim, so far as possible, with the current rather than directly against it. They do not pull policies out of a hat, but put their money on that one already present which they feel to be most nearly in accord with their aims." [5]

5. See ISC, Report, *Interlocking Subversion in Government Departments* (1953), pp. 21–2, and James Burnham, *The Web of Subversion* (New York, John Day, 1954), pp. 72–4. The quotation from Burnham is at p. 218. Herbert Fuchs,

If a Communist is not in a position to influence policy, and has no access to classified materials, his opportunity to do harm is limited. We can imagine that he might be a trouble-maker, that he might try to obstruct other people's work, that he might simply lie down on the job. But, as I have said, there is little indication that such things occur. If he has a warped personality, he may create discord. But that is the result of his neuroses, not of his communism. All of these conjectural misdeeds result in poor performance. They seem much more amenable to removal proceedings for unsuitability than to a loyalty test.

We tend to have an image of the Communist as a powerful and incendiary person, with no preoccupation except the cause. On the contrary, the rank-and-file member is as likely as not to be an insecure, alienated person. If he has an inconspicuous government job that he can fill inconspicuously, he will be slow to jeopardize such a piece of good fortune, especially if he has a family to take care of. The revolution can be promoted after hours.[6]

Another, and perhaps sufficient, explanation for loyalty tests in government is that they are one of the easiest ways of manifesting our national exasperation at domestic communism. After all, it is our government, and its employees are our servants. Along with a view that our servants ought to be saints runs a view (probably more prevalent) that they are in fact loafers. As long as the stereotype persists that most civil servants are the recipients of partly unearned public bounty, there is likely to be a quick impulse to impose conditions on that bounty. Consequently, there was no audible objection when Chairman Bingham of the Loyalty Review Board, starting from the rhetoric of E.O. 9835, developed an exacting definition of loyalty that condemned anyone who would ever put his personal interest before his country's.[7]

It would be helpful, I think, to consider another estimate of public

---

testifying about his communist activities, said, "we told ourselves, and were told that to be good Communists at the N.L.R.B. the better job we did for the Board and for the government, that was it. . . . Now, I know that this doesn't correspond to present-day notions of the Communist party and it does not correspond to my present-day notion of the party, but that is the way it was." HUAC, Hearings, *Investigation of Communist Infiltration of the Government* (1955), p. 2986.

6. See Almond, *The Appeals of Communism* (1954), Part 3; Ernst and Loth, *Report on the American Communist* (1952), p. 7.

7. Hiram Bingham, address before American Bar Association, Section on Criminal Law, Sept. 18, 1951 (mimeo.). On the popular conception of public employees see Carol Agger, "The Government and Its Employees," *Yale Law Jour.* (1938), 47:1110–11; Dotson (n. 3 above), pp. 77–81.

service. As Philip Graham has pointed out, the contention that no one has to work for the government unless he will accept hard terms "has a hollow ring today when a great many people must work for an $80 billion government." [8] A Navy welder, classified work aside, is just another welder. His productive efforts are not markedly different from what they would be if he were doing the same job for a private contractor. For him (and other millions of rank-and-file employees) his pay simply registers value received. It is not at all self-evident that his obligations and constraints should be markedly different from those that he would bear in the private sector of the economy. When he does have a special obligation, it should be reasonably enforced. The Hatch Act ban on partisan activity again is instructive. There is no attempt to exclude people who have been hardened politicians, on the ground that they will probably be unable to maintain the neutrality demanded of the career service. The Act is stringently enforced by the Civil Service Commission, but only by way of punishment (ranging from loss of pay to dismissal) for overt violations of fairly explicit regulations. Similar regulations forbidding harmful acts attributable to disloyalty would be unimpeachable. Further, a general policy against disloyalty is comprehensible when it simply says that people should not work for the government who want to overthrow the government, either by revolution or by aiding its external enemies. If we could hold to that line of exclusion, and enforce it with caution and with some respect for due process, a statutory declaration like Section 9-A of the Hatch Act, which forbids government employees to belong to revolutionary organizations, might be acceptable.

The record of the last decade, however, suggests strongly that the hardest thing to do with loyalty programs is to confine them. The development of the federal programs has left the simple problem of the certified Communist far in the rear. All the arguments for excluding him have been carried along into vast operations that today rarely turn up even a probable Communist. State and local governments are still circling around an almost deserted outpost. By and large, their formal policies seem to be directed at the authentic Communist public servant. But when, as in California and New York, systematic efforts are made to enforce those policies, the same restless search for probable Com-

8. "A Publisher Looks at the Law," *Record of the Ass'n of the Bar* (1952), 7:21. See also Dotson, "A General Theory of Public Employment," *Pub. Admin. Rev.* (1956), *16:*197.

munists and possible Communists begins. A natural preference for loyal civil servants seems destined, in the present era, to grow into a formidable structure of investigation, inquisition and mistrust.[9]

TEACHERS

The fact that most teachers are public employees makes them especially vulnerable to loyalty tests on the grounds already advanced with respect to civil servants. On the other hand, this is a field in which no valid security considerations exist, except in special areas of applied military research that are not primarily part of the business of seeking and transmitting knowledge. We have here, then, a distillation of pure loyalty, produced by the heat and pressure of the community's demand for assurance. Assurance against what? Apparently against subversion of beliefs. Teachers are the transmitters of ideas; as a group they have a massive influence on the plastic minds of the young. Parents and clergy, in this view, play a minor part. It is true that there are contradictions in the popular image of the teacher. For all his feared power over the mind, he is at the same time, and often by the same people, held in low esteem. "Those who can, do; those who can't, teach." Yet in the end the community loads on to the schools, and thus on to the teachers, responsibility for matters that are vital to the child's whole life, such as his outlook on liberty, property, and the nature of man. In the political sphere, teachers are expected to be able to instill a regard for democracy; immediately a fear arises that, if they can teach democracy, they can and might teach communism. Stouffer's study shows that the danger of communist ideas was much more present in his respondents' minds than the dangers of espionage and sabotage.[10]

Chapter 5 described the stages by which, in the postwar decade, there came to be a substantial consensus that membership in the Communist party is in itself sufficient ground for exclusion from the teaching profession. However, the arguments advanced in support of automatic exclusion should be critically examined, because they bear the difficult burden of proving a universal—i.e. that *any* Communist is disqualified,

---

9. The constitutional issues with respect to loyalty tests in public employment are discussed and the principal cases cited in Ch. 16 below, pp. 408–10.

10. Samuel Stouffer, *Communism, Conformity, and Civil Liberties* (1955), pp. 158, 184. On paradoxical images of the teacher see W. Record, "The American Intellectual as Black Sheep and Red Rover," *AAUP Bull.* (1954), *40*:536.

without regard to his record of professional conduct. At what might be
called the theoretical level, the main justifications for total exclusion, in
brief form, are these:

(1) The communist teacher has surrendered his independence of
judgment and is subservient to the party line.

(2) He is committed to the destruction of democratic institutions, including academic freedom, and is therefore not entitled to the privileges
of academic freedom.

(3) He is a member of a criminal conspiracy.

The charge of intellectual subservience rests on an assumption that
at any given time all party members are good party members. Good
party members must and do accept the teachings of the party on any
matter of doctrine. Bad party members, who disagree with the party,
will be expelled, and are thus no longer within the terms of the charge.
The question remains whether there are only goods and bads, or whether
there exist within the party people who accept the core of communist
doctrine because they believe it is the truth, but who also have doubts
and disagreements. The evidence on this point is confused. One encounters many statements from ex-Communists intended to establish
that they retained a degree of freedom while they were members. Others
assert, with greater force and frequency, that they bound themselves to
a rigid orthodoxy.

Debate on this first charge has largely ignored the uncertainties about
how American Communists actually behave, and has fixed on the question of entering and leaving the party. To Alexander Meiklejohn, the
party's high rate of turnover signified that an American Communist
was not a slave to the party, since so many struck off their chains. Sidney
Hook, on the other hand, took the willing acceptance of bondage to be
the critical point. Even if a teacher was free at any time to reclaim his
judgment, for as long as he left it in the keeping of the party he was not
fit to be a member of the academic world of independent minds.

That such a contrast—the Communist with a closed mind against
everyone else with an open one—put most non-Communists in an un-
deservedly favorable light Hook was quite ready to perceive. However,
there were others who, in their effort to disqualify the Communist, prescribed standards for professorial detachment that few could meet. After
all, everyone has attachments and commitments of varying intensities.
It has been particularly pointed out that Roman Catholics take their
faith and morals from an authoritative external source whose dictates
are often as uncompromising as those of the Kremlin. This is all a mat-

ter of degree, Hook rejoined; Catholics do not, in this country, endeavor to subvert temporal authority.[11]

Enough has been said about the subservience charge to suggest that it does not provide a *conclusive* basis for automatic disqualification. It is a sophisticated version of a much more profound prejudice, that no one in his right mind could conscientiously and independently adopt the full dogma of modern communism. I term this position, which has a great deal of appeal, a prejudice, because it ignores a fact—the unpleasant fact that some sane and able people, in our own and other democratic countries, adhere to communism because they have searched their minds and believe it leads to truth. If we decide to exclude such people altogether from academic life, we ought to affirm straightforwardly that their views are taboo, and not try to persuade ourselves that they are under some kind of hypnosis.

The second argument for automatic exclusion may be arrestingly paraphrased in a slogan: "No freedom for the enemies of freedom." The grievance here is that a Communist should dare to raise the banner of academic freedom in his defense, when it is well known that academic freedom is not tolerated under communist regimes. I pass over the problem of proof: do all Communists disbelieve in academic freedom, so that we are justified in using this ground to dismiss a Communist? The more difficult question is the validity of the major premise, that only those who believe in academic freedom are entitled to it.

There are many definitions of academic freedom, but they all contain the following elements. The whole community has an interest in

11. For background on the automatic exclusion argument see Robert MacIver, *Academic Freedom in Our Time* (1955), pp. 158–201; Brown, Review, *Yale Law Jour.* (1956), *65*:578. The classic debate between Alexander Meiklejohn and Sidney Hook, "Should Communists Be Allowed [Permitted] to Teach?," is in NYT, *Magazine,* Feb. 27 and Mar. 27, 1949. See also Carey McWilliams, *Witch Hunt* (1950), pp. 171–89. On the relationship of party membership to a given degree of intellectual subservience contrast Granville Hicks, *Where We Came Out* (1954), pp. 46–7, with Louis Budenz, *This Is My Story* (1947), pp. 234–8. See also Charles Frankel, "The Government of Scholarship," *AAUP Bull.* (1955), *41*:700–10. On open-mindedness compare D. Bolinger, "Who Is Intellectually Free?" *AAUP Bull.* (1955), *41*:13 with the Association of American Universities statement, "The Rights and Responsibilities of Universities and their Faculties," adopted March 24, 1953. The intellectual demands made by the Catholic Church as compared with those of the Communist party are discussed by Norbert Wiener, *The Human Use of Human Beings* (1950), pp. 219–29, and Hook (above). See also Journet Kahn, "The Threat to Academic Freedom," American Catholic Philosophical Ass'n, *Proceedings* (1956), *30*:160 (able presentation of liberal Catholic view).

guaranteeing teachers and scholars, of demonstrated competence and integrity, that they will not be silenced or punished if their teachings are unpopular. Academic freedom, reinforced by the institution of tenure, is an extraordinary concession that will be made only by a society which is willing to expose its institutions to criticism, and which is convinced that limitless discussion—especially within the peaceful atmosphere of the university—is an aid to the endless search for truth. This exemption from one or two of the hazards of competitive existence is not a prize bestowed on teachers for perfect attendance or spotless footnotes; it is a privilege given a whole profession in order to encourage its members to inquire boldly. Bold inquiries necessarily challenge the established order. Is the established order with respect to academic freedom uniquely beyond criticism? It cannot be, for the ideal is constantly under attack, constantly subject to erosion or improvement. It seems odd to bar members of the academic community alone from joining in the attack, if they think that some unfree system is a better way of exploiting the intellect. There is no more reason to make belief in academic freedom a condition of sharing in the privilege (and the attendant responsibilities) than there would be in making belief in the efficacy of aspirin a condition for taking aspirin.

The second charge proves too much. Just as the "subservience" charge gives rise to an unrealistic ideal of total detachment, so this charge enthrones the noble ideal of academic freedom on an unneeded eminence. If the ideal is valid, it can withstand criticism, especially communist criticism. Finally, we should take to heart Professor Machlup's penetrating observation that "if we silence him [the man who advocates totalitarian institutions] *we* have *actually* abrogated freedom of speech, whereas *he* has merely talked about doing so." [12]

The third ground for automatic dismissal—participation in a criminal conspiracy—again requires an assumption that *all* Communists are criminally culpable, under the Smith Act or a state sedition law. It is

12. Fritz Machlup, "On Some Misconceptions Concerning Academic Freedom," *AAUP Bull.* (1955), *41*:781. Cf. Samuel Morrison, *Freedom in Contemporary Society* (1956), p. 136. Examples of unorthodox views about academic freedom are found in the statements of the Very Rev. Hunter Guthrie, S.J., who declared that "the sacred fetish of academic freedom . . . is the soft underbelly of our American way of life, and the sooner it is armor-plated by some sensible limitation the sooner will the future of this nation be secured from fatal consequences"—cited by MacIver (n. 11 above), p. 135—and the Rev. Robert Gannon, President of Fordham University, "Academic freedom gives only the right to teach the truth," NYT, Jan. 26, 1949, quoted by Vern Countryman, *Un-American Activities in the State of Washington* (1951), p. 278.

not necessary to spend much time on this proposition. At least as the laws are now administered, party membership does not infallibly sustain a conviction for conspiracy; that is, there have been acquittals of Smith Act defendants, although there seems to have been little question that they were Communists. The crime consists of knowing participation in a group advocating violent overthrow. In the courts this is a matter of proof of personal guilt,[13] and so it should be also in academic dismissal cases. Academic employers do not have to wait until a man is convicted of a crime of moral turpitude before they dismiss him; but they should hesitate to create presumptions of criminality that outrun the law's sweeping condemnations of sedition.

To say that the three arguments just examined do not cover every case is not to say that they are insubstantial. On the contrary, the charges of intellectual subservience and of criminal conspiracy, when directed at current Communist party members, are very weighty ones and probably sufficient to decide most cases. What I have been suggesting is that they do not decide all cases. The issue, in most of the numerous theoretical discussions, has not been "Should Communists teach?" Most of the time it has been whether Communists should never teach, or just hardly ever. But the shading between "never" and "hardly ever" is important, because it leaves a place for the exercise of judgment on the over-all competence and integrity of the accused teacher. Such a judgment, made by the teacher's colleagues (and not by administrators or lay trustees or public officers), is the essence of an effective tenure system; and effective tenure is the main prop of academic freedom.

This position has been fully maintained, among major educational interest groups, only by the American Association of University Professors. The Association has remained faithful to an understanding of cause for dismissal that requires proof of immoral conduct, or of incompetence, or of perversion of research or teaching.[14] These are admittedly offenses which, even if they have been committed, are difficult to prove, and the last is the hardest of all. In a case charging excessive or dishonest indoctrination in the classroom, which is probably the one

13. See A. L. Wirin and S. Rosenwein, "The Smith Act Score," *The Nation* (Feb. 26, 1955), pp. 177–80, and NYT, April 20 and Aug. 1, 1956; Yates v. U.S., 354 U.S. 298 (1957).

14. Report of a Special Committee of the AAUP, "Academic Freedom and Tenure in the Quest for National Security," *AAUP Bull.* (1956), *42*:49, 59, adopted by the Association at its annual meeting, ibid., *42*:339. See the comment by Sidney Hook and Ralph Fuchs, "A Joint Statement on a Matter of Importance," ibid., *42*:692.

thing the public is really concerned about, the problem of proof reaches a near impasse. Even if the fine lines can be drawn between teaching and indoctrination, and then between right and wrong indoctrination, we run into the ethical problem of using students as informers. In flagrant cases, and with mature students, the difficulties of ascertaining the facts may be slight. But if, as is popularly asserted, communist indoctrination is "subtle" or "concealed," the thought of ferreting it out by cross-examining children has repelled observers as diverse as Professor Hook and Justice Douglas. The totalitarian echoes of such a practice are deafening.[15]

One way around the implications of investigating the classroom has been to suggest another automatic argument: communist teachers will *inevitably* attempt to misuse their position, because they are instructed to do so. A few exhortations to this effect have been dredged from the party literature. But communist preachments are not credible evidence of actual practice, and there is a remarkable dearth of published evidence of attempted indoctrination. One painful effort to illustrate indoctrination was produced by R. E. Combs of the California Un-American Activities Committee; he told of a communist instructor in public speaking who gave himself away by scrapping Masefield and Kipling in favor of a sustained examination of Mill's *Essay on Liberty*.[16]

All these subtleties make it desirable to avoid the issue of performance in the classroom. "The member of a college faculty," President Taylor observes, "who has been known and trusted as a colleague and teacher for five to twenty-five years does not suddenly change into a different

15. Compare Hook, *Heresy, Yes—Conspiracy, No* (1953), pp. 184–6, with Taylor (n. 17 below), pp. 247–50, on the problems of subtle indoctrination. On using students as informers see Hook, pp. 188–91; Justice Douglas, dissenting in Adler v. Board of Education, 342 U.S. 485, 508–11 (1952); James Marshall, "The Defense of Public Education from Subversion," *Columbia Law Rev.* (1951), 51:599.

16. The same bits of party literature containing the exhortations to indoctrinate may be found in Marshall (n. 15 above), pp. 588–9, Hook (n. 15 above), pp. 181–3, and Hamilton Long, "Permit Communist-Conspirators to Be Teachers?" House Document No. 213 (1953), pp. 6–7. The Combs example of alleged indoctrination is from ISC, Hearings, *Subversive Influence in the Educational Process* (1953), pp. 614–15. Some other examples may be found in E. M. Root, *Collectivism on the Campus* (1955), esp. ch. 7. Had there been other significant examples available, it would seem reasonable that Root would have included them. See also Hook, pp. 184–5; statement of the Rev. A. St. Ivanyi, quoted HUAC, *Annual Report for 1951* (1952), p. 16; Lawrence Chamberlain, *Loyalty and Legislative Action* (1951), pp. 122–7 (evaluation of testimony before Rapp-Coudert Committee).

person by reason of the discovery by his university that he has been attached to the Communist party; unless, of course, there is evidence that in concealing his political connection he has also concealed activities of an illegal or subversive kind." Faced with awkward solutions, such as having to assert that a good pathologist was no longer a good pathologist because he was a Communist, administrators have discovered another subtlety: an extraordinary obligation on the part of the teacher to be candid. If a teacher has withheld information about himself, then it does not much matter what the information would have been; the refusal to talk becomes itself a ground for dismissal.

The insistence on professorial candor reached a climax in the 1953 declaration of the major university presidents: "Above all, he owes his colleagues in the university complete candor and perfect integrity, precluding any kind of clandestine or conspiratorial activities. He owes equal candor to the public. If he is called upon to answer for his convictions it is his duty as a citizen to speak out. It is even more definitely his duty as a professor." [17]

Does this statement mean what it says? *Any* kind of clandestine activities? Are even secret fraternity meetings forbidden? Does a professor have to answer for all his convictions? *Any* kind of convictions? As the statement goes on to observe, the teaching profession claims the maximum protection for freedom to speak. Even if a right to speak implies a duty to speak, which is doubtful, the right is claimed only for the teacher's professional functions. Outside his field of teaching and scholarship, the teacher claims exactly the same freedom of speech as any other citizen, no more, no less; and one might deduce that he had the same freedom not to speak as any other citizen. But apparently the university presidents think that every professor has to expose his convictions, no matter how privately they might have been held.

Probably all the statement means, considering its internal and its external context, is that professors have to say whether they are Communists or have been Communists and (in some cases) whether they know of any colleagues who have been Communists. They have to say because their jobs have been made to depend on their willingness to give the right answers. Their convictions about other controversial issues need not in fact be laid before the public. If this is what "complete candor" boils down to, it is a duty which is not peculiar to teachers. It is a major outgrowth of the loyalty problem at large; the jobs of all the

17. AAU (n. 11 above). Harold Taylor's observation is from his essays, *On Education and Freedom* (New York, Abelard-Schuman, 1954), pp. 288–9.

people we are talking about may depend as much on *whether* they answer critical questions as on *how* they answer.

There are thus a number of ways in which a Communist might very probably disqualify himself from the enjoyment of academic freedom and tenure, even in the absence of an automatic rule of exclusion. But the proof of most of these matters is so beset with obstacles that the reader may well begin to simmer with exasperation. "What about general competence?" he may reiterate. "How can a person have such wild politics and still be entrusted with the education of youth, or the expression of learned judgments, in any field?" Or, as Congressman Simpson put the matter to Robert Hutchins, apropos of foundation grants to members of subversive organizations, "Why would you want to deal with a dumbbell like that?" Mr. Hutchins replied, "If you are engaged, as I was, for a very long time in such projects as the atom-bomb projects, you find that there is no necessary correlation between political sagacity and scientific eminence." Despite the pertinence of this observation, many people are likely to distrust profoundly the competence of a teacher who is so eccentric as to favor communism.

They will also distrust his influence on students, and hold that the risk that communist teachers will misbehave is great enough to justify dropping them. The analogy to security risks is at once apparent. Is it a valid one? We avoid the security risk because he can do irreparable damage. So can a teacher, the answer goes: he can mar a student's life by converting him to communism. This recalls the observations at the beginning of this section about the great powers attributed to teachers. It is true that some teachers do mold their student's lives, for good or ill. A gifted teacher could fix a bent toward communism, and (this is less likely) perhaps he could do it surreptitiously. The possibility lights a train of powder that could explode in tragedy, as it did for some parents whose sons went off from college to the Abraham Lincoln Brigade and death in Spain. So, this is what the risk comes down to. Some students may be converted.[18]

There is a clearly expressed community demand to shield the young from *any* risk of communist temptation. That such a demand is impatient with the theories of academic freedom and tenure, that it betrays a lack of faith in the influence of home and church, that it ignores the

18. The Simpson-Hutchins exchange appears in House Select Committee to Investigate Tax Exempt Foundations, Hearings (1952), p. 297. Instances of conversion of students leading to enlistment in the Abraham Lincoln Brigade are reported in Countryman (n. 12 above), p. 132; Root (n. 16 above), pp. 27, 124.

countervailing force of myriads of noncommunist teachers, is irrelevant. The demand is there. I would find it hard to try to persuade the American public in this era that substantial numbers of Communists should be tolerated in our schools and colleges. Their influence and aspirations, unless they were remarkably subdued, would run strongly counter to deeply felt community preferences.

In point of fact, there are not, and have not been, substantial numbers of communist teachers, except in parts of the New York City schools and colleges twenty years ago. Nowadays, if there are any anywhere, they must be quite subdued. One might conclude that little is to be gained by solicitude for whatever remnant is left, except to "let them stand undisturbed as monuments of the safety with which error of opinion may be tolerated where reason is free to combat it." [19] Jefferson, however, counseled a perfection that our people have rarely achieved, and never in moments of crisis. And I do not think there is any substance to the argument that we need some Communists on hand to expound the principles of communism. One might as well contend that we need criminals to teach criminal law. So, one might bow to realities, and argue that, if Communists would quietly identify themselves and go away, their numbers are so small that the loss of trained teachers would be slight.

But Communists do not quietly identify themselves and go away. This is a very wicked animal; when one attacks him, he defends himself. In our national ardor to shield ourselves from his concealed—and much overrated—influence, we have made an unholy mess. We require teachers to take loyalty oaths, which are degrading and which eliminate only non-Communists of stout conscience. We launch investigations that blunder about our universities and schools, breaking reputations. We encourage the compilation of secret dossiers, and the exploitation of those dossiers without fair hearings. We erect presumptions around equivocal associations, and draw inferences from silence, that extend the ban from Communists to people who may be Communists, from people who were Communists to people who may have been Communists. We do not stop to have such people judged by their peers, or to weigh their contributions to knowledge. We only worry about what false doctrine they might spread if the charges against them were true.

Has it been worth the cost, in suspicion and snooping and hardness of heart, to find the last Communist, and after him the last may-be Communist? Aside from the human wreckage that has been created,

19. Thomas Jefferson, First Inaugural Address (1801).

there has been an injury to the academic ideal of the untrammeled search for truth. The Communists have done enough injury to the ideal; but that is no reason for the rest of us to harm it more. The search for truth is carried on by fallible human beings. Our system of academic freedom, while conscious of fallibility, is primarily respectful of integrity. After an exacting professional apprenticeship, it leaves the mature scholar free to follow the trail of truth wherever it leads him. It assumes, until the contrary appears, that the teacher has integrity. Of course it is a betrayal of the ideal for a man to profess one thing and believe another. It is equally a betrayal to forbid the holding of a system of beliefs, even a hated system, or to declare that the holder of such beliefs *must* be dishonest, or to expel him from the company of scholars without any proof that he has falsified his research or teaching. These wounds the academic community has inflicted on itself.

As a postscript, it should be noted that the secondary schools have traditionally extended less hospitality than the colleges to academic freedom. There has been less need for freedom of research, because research (except in educational method) has not been a function of the schools. Freedom to teach (and its correlative, freedom to learn) also have had less scope. The main rationalization for the fact of tighter controls has been the relative immaturity of the students. A related line of argument places on the schools a positive duty of indoctrination in favor of democracy, or the American way of life, or some other community value. Freedom is accordingly deferred until the student is mature enough, and thoroughly enough indoctrinated, to resist contagion from bad ideas.

There has been growing recognition in recent years that a sharp dividing line cannot rationally be drawn between the high school senior and the college freshman. On the teacher's side, the wide extension of tenure principles to the public schools requires at least that their teachers be treated as full citizens and not as censored wards of the community.[20] Nevertheless, the public school stands in a different relationship to the community than does a private school, or an institution of higher education. It has a near-monopoly. The law keeps children in school until a certain age. For most parents there is no practical al-

---

20. See Howard Beale, *Are American Teachers Free?* (1936), esp. ch. 23. Cf. ACLU statement of 1932, Beale, pp. 769–70, with ACLU, *Academic Freedom and Academic Responsibility* (1952). See also Martin Essex, "What Does Academic Freedom Mean for Elementary and Secondary Teachers?" *Educational Leadership* (Jan. 1952), 9:237.

ternative to the public school. They have every reason to be concerned
if they think the schools are promoting extreme deviations from the
values of the community. Their concern may be ill-informed and inept;
it may thwart values cherished by the larger community. But we cannot
say that the teacher and the curriculum are none of the parents' business, and that they should leave everything to the educators. The educators themselves rarely claim omniscience.

WRITERS AND SHOW PEOPLE

There are few plausible reasons for public concern over the recent
threat of communism in the communications industries. A major infiltration would of course have been a matter of moment, if one defines
"major" to mean enough communist influence to affect perceptibly the
content of the mass media. Those media—press, radio, television, films
—are, with the schools, the chief bearers of our culture.

People who were concerned about the susceptibility of other people
to communist propaganda sounded an alarm that we might all become
infected by way of Madison Avenue and Hollywood. They kept crying
"Wolf," but the wolf never did come. Communists were indeed scattered
all through the communications world. But the bits of evidence that
have been produced to show that they influenced content are either
ludicrous or trivial. In making this judgment I put aside the war years.
There was a great disposition then to believe well of the Russians. The
sort of stories that Whittaker Chambers tells about his experiences on
Time magazine may have been the result of direct communist influence,
but they need not have been. Sober noncommunist journalists took the
same positions as those that outraged Chambers, haunted by his underground history. I also put aside the conspiratorial imaginings of the
right-wing radicals who suspect communist influences still at work on
Time, the *New York Times,* and everything to the left of them.[21]

It is not hard to find the probable reasons why Communists, no matter
how ill-disposed, never injected more than slight traces of their propaganda during the cold war. The mass media not only reach the masses,
they are mass-produced. So many people have a hand in everything

21. See Chambers, *Witness* (1952), p. 498. William Ware, vice-commander
of an American Legion post, criticizing the sponsorship by Time Inc. of an exhibition called "Sports in Art," remarked "Certainly, no one has ever called *Time*
magazine an anticommunist publication." Aline Saarinen, "Art Storm Breaks on
Dallas," NYT (Feb. 12, 1956), § 2, p. 15. Cf. William Buckley, Jr., "The 'Times'
Slays a Dragon," *National Review* (Jan. 25, 1956), p. 11.

that it would be difficult to force a deviant opinion into print or on the air. So many people then read it, hear it, or see it that anything untoward would be pounced on. The communist Hollywood writers, who were probably the most powerful single party group in a position of any influence, wrote the same sort of stuff for the screen as their bourgeois confrères. Like other Communists in an exposed position, they expended their Marxist sentiments after hours.[22]

In the absence of any real effects, the prime explanation for the wide-ranging programs in the entertainment industries seems to be what Horowitz called "public relations risk." [23] What we do not know is whether the public relations risk was real; the employers in broadcasting and films moved so fast that no wide-spread public antagonism ever developed. The employers feared the immediate threat of boycotts by pressure groups. Spokesmen for such organizations as the American Legion asserted that the public would not want to spend its own money, or support sponsors who spent their money for them, on entertainers who in turn would support the Communist party and its satellites. The unresolved question is whether the public would have turned so decisively against those of its idols who enriched the public stock of harmless pleasure and at the same time enriched the Communist party.

In the case of actors, singers, and other entertainment artists, it is hard to see how they could have benefited the party except financially, either directly or through their generosity in lending their names and talents to questionable causes. It is also possible that their endorsements may have lent the party glamour if not respectability.

The case of writers dealing with public affairs is somewhat different. They did have the power to slant their opinions and distort their information. As between employer and employee, this raised a further question of confidence. When the *New York Times* first publicly dismissed a reporter who had invoked the Fifth Amendment, want of confidence in his journalistic integrity was the reason assigned, rather than resort to the privilege in itself. Other newspaper proprietors were even more sum-

22. See Murray Kempton, *Part of Our Time* (1955), ch. 6; Dorothy Jones, "Communism and the Movies: A Study of Film Content," in John Cogley, *Report on Blacklisting* (1956), 1:196–233. But cf. Jeanne Harmon, *Such Is Life* (1956), ch. 11, reprinted in ISC, Hearings, *Scope of Soviet Activity in the United States* (1956), pp. 438–44, which makes the point that Communists in the news media had more success in keeping things out of the public eye than they had in putting them there.

23. Harold Horowitz, "Loyalty Tests for Employment in the Motion Picture Industry," *Stanford Law Rev.* (1954), 6:438.

mary in penalizing staffmen who invoked the privilege. They presumably acted out of a mixture of motives, a compound of public relations fears and loss of trust in the individual who they felt had deceived them.

If an employment relationship collapses because of a genuine loss of confidence, firings on this account need little further justification. Once the employer, after reviewing the circumstances of an individual's case, decides that he can no longer rely on the man's facts or interpretations, he can hardly be expected to continue the employment. Similarly, if an employer believes that an employee in a position of responsibility is hiring actors or buying scripts because the actors or writers are procommunist (or for that matter anticommunist), rather than on their merits, this is also a good ground for dismissal. What is to be criticized is the appearance of automatic rules for dismissal that operate without regard to the individual case. There is a resemblance here to the discussion about teachers, even though the concept of tenure may be alien to the communications field.

The communications experience is even stronger than the academic one as an illustration of the failure of loyalty tests to stay within the bounds of clearly disqualifying subversive conduct. The movie industry's standard became "friendliness" before investigating committees; the radio industry abdicated decision to private blacklisters. Both policies were far removed from a sober consideration of the risks entailed in retaining familiar employees who had acquired some taint of communism. They represented, indeed, a flight from sobriety.

LAWYERS AND OTHER LICENSED PROFESSIONS AND TRADES

The lawyer stands in a somewhat different position from the other professions. If he really is working toward an unconstitutional alteration of our form of government, he would appear to be violating his lawyer's oath to uphold the Constitution. One may argue that the lawyer should not have any such obligation; that he can draw wills or procure divorces without caring two pins for the Constitution; that he is only an educated plumber. However, he *does* have to take an oath to support the Constitution; and until somone persuades the courts that this is an unreasonable qualification—a most remote likelihood—the lawyer can be disciplined for failing to observe the professional requirement of adherence to the legal order of which he is a part.[24]

24. Brown and Fassett, "Loyalty Tests for Admission to the Bar," *Univ. of*

However, the logical incompatibility of communism and constitutionalism should not be decisive in the case of a lawyer with an otherwise good record. It is possible for a man to be a thoroughly prosaic conveyancer from nine to five and a Communist only after hours. Certainly mere inferences of communist leanings (derived, for example, from a claim of privilege before an investigating committee) should not be enough to overbalance a career free of professional blemishes. The principal test when disbarment is at issue should be one of performance, not of ideology.[25]

When we consider admission to the bar, as distinct from disbarment, the familiar difficulties of the applicant arise. His claim to professional standing has less support than that of the established practitioner. He may have a good record as a student and as a youthful citizen, which should be weighed against any present revolutionary intentions; but if (and only if) the latter are clearly established, then the examiners can hardly certify such an applicant to a profession dedicated to the rule of law.

In no other licensed profession should freedom from communism be an issue. Neither communist beliefs, nor sympathies, nor for that matter party membership, I will assert, necessarily impair the professional character of an accountant, an engineer, a dentist, or a physician. If one's fervor for subversive activity carries him over the line into serious criminal conduct—Whittaker Chambers says that his dentist was mixed up in espionage[26]—the situation is different. Also, if the Smith

---

Chicago Law Rev. (1953), *20:*502, suggested—rather casually—that the exclusion of a Communist from the bar could also be justified on the ground that he was not "of good moral character." As the discussion of other professions suggests, I do not now think this position is tenable. The narrower grounds of violation of the constitutional oath, or of unprofessional conduct, are preferable. See Gellhorn (n. 28 below), pp. 131–40. See also the views of a member of a character committee, John Starrs, "Considerations on Determination of Good Moral Character," *Univ. of Detroit Law Jour.* (1955), *18:*195; and Royce McKinley, "Lawyers and Loyalty," *St. Louis Bar Jour.* (Oct. 1955), *6:*15.

The plumber analogy is from Vern Countryman, "Loyalty Tests for Lawyers," *Lawyers Guild Rev.* (1953), *13:*156.

25. See Association of the Bar of the City of New York, "Report and Recommendations of the Special Committee on the Matter of Communist Lawyers," Nov. 29, 1955, and the action taken thereon, reported in *The Record of the Association* (1956), *11:*45–7. The Association rejected a recommendation for disciplinary proceedings against knowing members of communist organizations, but approved a finding that disbarment proceedings could be brought against "lawyers engaged in Communist activities contrary to their oaths to uphold the Constitution."

26. Chambers, *Witness* (1952), pp. 307–9.

Act constitutionally permits the conviction of "mere" party members as distinct from leaders, then party membership may legally come to be considered a ground for disqualification. This would follow from the rather rough rule of thumb—not uniformly applied—that the conviction and imprisonment of a felon automatically mark him of unfit character. We are now discussing what licensing boards *may* do without reversal by the courts. What they should do, even in the case of the felon, is not well decided by resort to a rule of thumb. Let me put three cases, and ask the reader to apply them all to a competent physician. Should the doctor be permanently barred from practicing his profession (which, besides being a severe deprivation for him, robs society of his healing skill) if he:

(1) While driving too fast, kills a pedestrian and is convicted of manslaughter?

(2) Unsuccessfully attempts to conceal his income and is convicted of criminal tax evasion serious enough to warrant a prison sentence? [27]

(3) After many years as an active rank-and-file member of the Communist party, is convicted under the Smith Act of conspiring to advocate the violent overthrow of the government at some future time?

The comparison of these three cases raises troubling problems of moral judgment. Anyone who feels strong disapproval of reckless drivers, tax cheats, or Communists, is free not to patronize doctors who have been guilty of these things. When the doctors have been convicted of crime, a variety of social sanctions will doubtless have been added to the punishments of fine or imprisonment. Should organized society go further, and destroy their professional livelihood? I think most of us stop short of this sanction in the first two cases. If so, what reason is there to impose it in the third? Is the doctor who advocates a distant overthrow of the government worse than one who systematically weakens the government now by defrauding it of lawful taxes? Is the one who teaches the necessity of future bloodshed worse than the one who carelessly takes a life today? Is any of them such a moral monster that he is unfit to practice medicine? Some people may be uncompromising toward all three culprits. But if anyone is disposed to single out the Communist, he should pause. His revulsion against a hated philosophy

---

27. The case of a surgeon who served three months in prison for tax evasion and whose denial of reinstatement at his old hospital (he was permitted to operate at another) caused local controversy is reported in *Time* (Jan. 24, 1955), p. 63. Baker v. Miller, 138 N.E. 2d 145 (Ind. 1956) held that a conviction of a lawyer for income tax evasion did not justify disbarment.

is impelling him to condemn dangerous words more severely than dangerous deeds.

We can ignore almost summarily the trades where technical competence alone is the basis for requiring a license. There is no evidence that the most extreme political heresies have any bearing on ability to relieve a plugged-up drain, or to repair a television set, or to compound a prescription. One can conjure up rather fanciful alarms about sabotage, but they have no substance except in sensitive areas. In fact, only minor gestures have been made toward imposing political tests on the technical trades. There is the Texas statute requiring loyalty oaths from pharmacists, and the Indiana regulation covering boxers and wrestlers (if they can be considered technicians rather than performers). The inaction of the licensing authorities elsewhere excuses any further discussion of such foolishness.

Another basis for licensing is found in relationships based on trust and confidence. Real estate brokers, security dealers, insurance agents, and the like need to have some skill in what they are doing; but the chief public demand is presumably for assurances of a degree of honesty and responsibility. Here requirements of "good character" or "good moral character" similar to those of the learned professions come into play, and arguments about the disabilities of Communists begin to have some faint plausibility. If—it can be argued—Communists are untrammeled by standards of conventional morality, how can they be expected to deal honorably with other people's money? Some such considerations apparently underlie political inquiries made by the District of Columbia Insurance Commissioner, who requires insurance agents to disclose their membership in subversive organizations.

The price of such inquiries, in terms of official meddling and penalties for unorthodoxy, seems hardly worth the conjectural benefits to the community. There is no evidence that communist stock-brokers are undermining finance capitalism, or that communist insurance agents are creating false security for widows and orphans. Until we have a real threat, the whole area should be left alone.

To sum up: among the licensed trades and professions, theories of occupational unfitness based solely on communist political activities have no substance except in the special case of the lawyers. In this one licensed profession communist tenets as such may be unprofessional, because they cut across a lawyer's special fealty to the Constitution. But, before we attempt disbarments, we should keep in view the professional records of accused lawyers. A believer in revolution may well be a practitioner of law and order, irrational as that seems. If he is well-behaved, and if we are going to remove him from a profession solely because his expressions of belief are anticonstitutional, let us pause. Do we apply this rule to all cases? Southern lawyers who are trying to circumvent or nullify the segregation decisions of the Supreme Court have expressed a greater sum of defiance of the Constitution since 1954 than have all the communist lawyers since 1917. True, they say they are for the Constitution; and that the Constitution as expounded by the Supreme Court is what they are defying; but that is the only Constitution we have.

One more qualification: in this discussion I have emphasized the irrelevance of communist *political* dogma to occupational licensing. If a communist line develops that deviates grossly from fundamental principles of a trade or profession, the deviation might be censurable. Thus if communist physicians with one voice declared that smoking cured cancer, the medical societies might undertake to have such extreme heretics expelled from the profession. But this kind of expulsion, I take it, would be justified to protect the community from dangerous nonsense. The communist source of the nonsense would still be irrelevant.[28]

CONCLUSION

Some serious arguments have been advanced to show the propriety of excluding Communists from the occupations surveyed in this chapter; and I have taken them seriously. In view of the probable characteristics of communist disloyalty, a basis for discrimination on loyalty grounds exists in government employment, in the legal profession, in teaching, and in the information (but not entertainment) side of the communications industries. But in each case I have argued that another kind of discrimination is called for too. That is, if there is to be discrimination against Communists, in the form of exclusion from employment, it ought to be accompanied by fair and exact discrimination between the few who are Communists, and the larger number who have only confusing similarities to Communists. I have also argued that we should almost

28. The factual material to which this section refers is in Ch. 4 above, pp. 109–18. My conclusions here are much strengthened by the extent to which they are in accord with those of Walter Gellhorn, whose *Individual Freedom and Governmental Restraints* (1956), ch. 3, is a notable discussion of the whole problem of occupational licensing policies. As for the "right-privilege" argument, which comes up again in this context, see James Barnett, "Public Licenses and Private Rights," *Oregon Law Rev.* (1953), *33*:1.

always consider the individual case, so that earned status in a profession, for example, might outweigh a touch of sedition. If these cautions were painstakingly observed, then disloyalty might rationally be considered an impediment to certain kinds of employment, even in the absence of any security risk.

But the cautions have not been observed; the distinctions have not been made; the individual case has been sacrificed to rules of thumb. Consequently the valid but narrow arguments for exclusion fall into doubt. The whole loyalty business, the next chapter will show, has got out of hand. At the end of that discussion I will consider whether and how it is possible to get it under control again.

15. The Voracity of Loyalty Tests

WE HAVE BEEN sticking pretty close to the formal boundaries of loyalty tests. Since the tests purport to be aimed at Communists, or at other people who, without formal communist affiliations, would like to see communism triumphant, Part II examined the security risk created by such people; the preceding chapter considered the case for excluding them on disloyalty grounds from certain occupations. How far employment disabilities should be pressed against confirmed Communists is a difficult enough problem. Even if that problem is settled, others remain, for the formal boundaries of many programs are not confined to identifiable Communists. And the boundaries themselves are loosely drawn. Employment tests press hard against former Communists, conjectural Communists, and potential Communists. These groups, as well as the hard core of current adherents, are especially engulfed by the tide of security; but loyalty programs tend similarly to overflow narrow channels, either because suspicion replaces conviction as the standard of judgment, or because there is no visible standard.

What now have to be explored are the areas of national life penetrated by political employment tests where the connection with the stated purposes of the programs becomes tenuous or spurious, or both. There is no clear dividing line between the swollen mainstream and these backwaters. It is a matter of increasing remoteness and diminishing relevance. On the one hand, loyalty and security measures flow into areas of partisan or political difference where such proceedings are irrelevant. On the other, extraneous issues pour into the framework of employment tests.

The result in either event is injury to the body politic.

LOYALTY TESTS OUT OF BOUNDS

One of the disconcerting aspects of public life in the last decade has been the willingness of all sorts of people to suggest communist influences at work through their opponents. The tendency has been strongest among investigators and superpatriots who were already obsessed with the delusion that Communists were everywhere. However, they share the blame for this kind of invective with political leaders of both

357

major parties, with spokesmen for some business and labor groups—indeed with a host of disputants who could scarcely be catalogued. Even if the facts will not possibly support a plausible suggestion that one's opponent is in sympathy with communist aims, resort can still be had to the threadbare accusation that he is "unwittingly" carrying out the purposes of the Kremlin. This almost unanswerable accusation was naturally carried to its ultimate in absurdity by Senator McCarthy when he denounced the Select Committee of the Senate that recommended his censure as "unwitting handmaidens" of the Communist party. Another recent example of a variant cliché occurred when an Assistant Attorney General of the United States attacked the Cleveland Bar Association as "dupes" of the Communists. This surprising label was affixed to a conservative professional group because the Bar Association had been helpful in recruiting counsel for the defendants in a Smith Act prosecution, and perhaps also because a number of the defendants were acquitted.[1]

All this is not an effect of the loyalty–security system, but rather a parallel manifestation of what Edward Shils calls the "deformation of civility" that has attended the cold war. And, taking a long view, reckless invective is perhaps a chronic feature of American political life. However, the extensive reach of employment tests provides added ammunition for the practitioners of name-calling. For example: Telford Taylor, who, after distinguished government service, as both a civilian and a military lawyer, had turned to private practice, made a speech at West Point attacking Senator McCarthy. The Senator retorted by declaring that Mr. Taylor's name was "flagged" in the Civil Service Commission because of the existence of unresolved derogatory information, so that he was "ineligible" for government employment "at this time." This could be literally correct; if Taylor had planned to re-enter government service, the derogatory information would have to be assessed. But of course we do not know (nor did McCarthy) what the result of that assessment would be. Again, when Major General Miles Reber testified before the Senate Committee investigating the relations between the Army and McCarthy, the Senator suggested that General Reber's brother Samuel, formerly Deputy High Commissioner for Germany, had been dismissed from the State Department as a security risk. This, besides being irrelevant, was not true.[2]

1. For this incident, along with a rather unconvincing denial by the Assistant Attorney General, see NYT, March 16, 1956. McCarthy's characterization is in NYT, Nov. 10, 1954.
2. See Edward Shils, *The Torment of Secrecy* (1956), ch. 6. The Telford

Perhaps McCarthy's twisted references to loyalty–security cases should not be cited as evidence of anything except the tactics of Senator McCarthy. And the usual relation of such charges to the excesses of public debate was only to add fuel to existing fires. But, in at least one instance, accusations of communist affiliations, coming directly from government investigative reports, played a critical part in a Congressional election.

Loyalty–Security Charges Halt a Congressional Career: R. L. Condon

This was the case of Congressman Robert L. Condon. Without benefit of any formal proceedings, damaging investigative reports were used against Condon in the 1954 campaign. The reports so impugned Condon's loyalty that they must have contributed materially to his defeat when he ran for re-election as a Representative from the Sixth District of California.

The Condon case first came to light when the late Bert Andrews of the *New York Herald-Tribune* discovered that Condon had been excluded by the Atomic Energy Commission from a party of Congressmen invited to witness atomic weapon tests in Nevada in May 1953. The AEC declined any comment. Condon, denying that he had ever been a Communist party member or sympathizer, said that the charges against him were based on associations he had had as a labor lawyer and a politician. They had, he said, been used against him in two campaigns for the California legislature in 1948 and 1950, and in his campaign for Congress in 1952, and he had won election all three times. He strenuously protested the competence of the AEC to decide that he was a security risk.

The Commission then made available to the Joint Committee on Atomic Energy the "reports" on which its action was based, and in January 1954 the Committee held hearings for three days at which Condon answered these charges and others that were brought up by members of the Committee. He acknowledged, for example, membership in the National Lawyers' Guild until 1950, and some representation of left-wing unions before their expulsion from the CIO; thereafter he withdrew from a law firm that had represented Harry Bridges' long-

Taylor affair is reported in NYT, Dec. 11, 1953. For the incident concerning Gen. Reber and his brother see NYT, April 23, 1954.

shoremen, and continued to act for the steel workers and the oil workers. He consistently denied that either he or his wife had been Communists. The Joint Committee made no report, and did not even print the hearings.

In April 1954, the Democratic National Chairman, Stephen A. Mitchell, released a letter about the candidacies of Condon and of James Roosevelt (whose marital and extramarital affairs had caused some scandal), in which he said that financial support or any other action by the National Committee suggesting an endorsement of the two candidates would be withheld. "Mr. Condon's misfortune and the question of his innocence or guilt should not be the burden of the Democratic party; they are personal to him."

If it was not enough to lose the support of his own party, Condon was in the end a principal target of Vice-President Nixon. The Vice-President, asserting that the Navy as well as the AEC had barred Condon from access to classified information, quoted from a Naval Intelligence report, derived from the FBI, charges that Condon had been a member of the Communist party, that he "has been a member of; has contributed to; and has associated with, approximately twenty Communist party fronts and infiltrated organizations from 1938 to the present time." For good measure, the report added that Condon had been arrested seven times for intoxication. It did not state how many times he had been convicted.

Condon lost the election.[3]

THE LOYALTY OF LEGISLATORS

The Condon matter left obstinately unresolved the touchy problems of executive inquiry into the loyalty of the legislative branch. From time to time, concern has been expressed over the probability that the FBI and other agencies were assembling dossiers on members of Congress. Since Condon was *not* cleared for the atom-bomb tests, presumably his

3. The story by Bert Andrews and an interview with Rep. Condon appeared in the *New York Herald-Tribune,* July 6, 1953. See NYT, Jan. 27–9, 1954, on the Joint Committee hearings. The Mitchell letter is in NYT, April 5, 1954. Vice-President Nixon's attacks were reported in NYT, Oct. 27 and 28, 1954. See also NYT, Aug. 22, 1952: The scandal attending an Army CIC investigation of Brig. Gen. Elliott Thorpe (ret.), Republican candidate for Congress from Rhode Island, caused the General to withdraw from the campaign. He was cleared of "any suspicion of disloyalty" shortly after his withdrawal. The investigation was apparently initiated because *The Daily Worker* reported a speech by Thorpe.

colleagues who attended classified briefing sessions *were* cleared. The routine of clearance automatically involves the collection of information like Congressman Condon's alleged arrest record. No one has suggested that the information evaporates. On the contrary, it remains in the files, a magazine of potent explosives. The keepers of the magazine say they will never open it; but there is always the temptation to set off a strategic little explosion, as in the Condon case.

There have been several abortive attempts to have some kind of loyalty or security check on Congressional staff members, who number several thousand. Individual congressmen who asked for FBI reports on their office help have been turned away by Director Hoover, who pleaded lack of manpower and of authority. A Senate resolution in 1953 produced no results, and a further attempt at legislation in 1954 died in committee. Meanwhile, there have been working arrangements for the appropriate executive departments to clear staff members of certain committees (e.g. Atomic Energy, Armed Services) for access to classified materials.

There is no compelling reason why employees of the legislative branch could not be screened in the same way as other government employees. On the other hand, there is no strong occasion to do so, except where valid security needs arise, as in the case of access to classified materials. Possibly the reluctance of the FBI to take on the job arises from fear of embarrassing the congressmen who make the appointments. Equally possibly, the congressmen would like to shift responsibility, and to demonstrate their firm adherence to the security system.[4]

The collection and release of derogatory information on elected officials is a more serious matter. If there are hidden flaws in the past of a candidate for national office, theoretically the voters are entitled to know about them. But, as the case of ex-Representative Condon shows, to have these alleged failings dished up in the form of an arbitrary denial of clearance, based on untested investigative reports, rather prejudices the issue. When, in one of the debates on screening employees of the Senate, Senator Wayne Morse proposed that Senators also be screened, there was no second to his possibly ironic motion. The Senators were right. The current course of political name-calling already includes a

4. The attempts at legislation are reviewed in NYT, Aug. 10 and Dec. 26, 1954, and in Commission on Government Security, *Report* (1957), pp. 101–5. On rebuffs of specific requests to the FBI by Connecticut congressmen see the informed dispatches by Stan Allen, formerly administrative assistant to Senator Benton, *New Haven Register*, Feb. 27 and March 14, 1953.

plethora of rumor and suspicion bearing on loyalty. But rumor and suspicion acquire another dimension when they are decked out in the formal trappings of a security investigation. The party in control of the security machinery then has a weapon of political proscription in its power. If partisan differences become embittered, the weapon may be used.

The trouble is—we cannot get away from this point—that it did not really matter whether any Senator voted to have himself investigated or not. Some cautious security officer, somewhere behind the scenes, had probably already voted in his place. Political proscription may have been remote from the official's mind; his job was only to check the dignitaries who would help launch a new minesweeper. But the result is another dossier. With such a vast apparatus, and with such encompassing notions of what needs to be protected and what ought to be collected, the patient assembly of dossiers seems unavoidable. There they are, so many little hand grenades, sitting in the files.

Congressmen, however, are collectively in a better position than the rest of us to prevent the exploitation of their dossiers. Having the power of the purse, they can exercise some restraint over the executive agencies, and in the past have been very touchy about the collection of information on their number. This is one Congressional prerogative that ought to be cherished.[5]

McCarthy Again

Some of the examples here discussed emerge from a setting labeled "security" rather than "loyalty"; but that I believe is chiefly a reflec-

5. For Senator Morse's proposal and its rejection see *Cong. Rec.* (Mar. 6, 1953), *99*:1687–8. During the 1956 campaign J. G. Sourwine, former chief counsel of the ISC and himself a candidate for the Nevada Senatorial nomination, flung some alleged "Justice Department evidence" at Jacob Javits, who was seeking the Republican Senatorial nomination from New York, NYT, Aug. 31, 1956. This caused a minor crisis among New York Republicans, NYT, Sept. 7, 1956. Javits was subsequently nominated and elected.

Chairman Philip Young of the Civil Service Commission reported on Dec. 28, 1956, that as the result of Congressional objections raised in 1947 and 1948 all Congressmen's names had been removed from the CSC security research file, but that members of Congress might appear in the central index and investigation report files of the CSC if they had been employed or considered for employment by the executive branch in recent years. House Comm. on Government Operations, Subcomm. Hearings, *Availability of Information from Federal Departments and Agencies* (1955), pp. 407–9. The composition of the CSC security files is succinctly

tion of the confusing use of these terms in the history of the federal programs. The forays of Senator McCarthy made no distinction between the loyalty program of the Truman administration and the security program of Eisenhower's; either one could be turned to his purposes. So it was also, we shall see, with the forces that bore on the old China hands in the State Department. The requirements of security *can* be separated from demands for loyalty; but the line of separation is continually blurred if not obliterated by the unconfined spread of loyalty tests.

I have already referred to McCarthy's occasional device of recalling real or fancied employment difficulties in order to embarrass his opponents. A related tactic, one that the Senator developed more or less systematically, was to raise loyalty (or security) charges against his targets, and then to attack the administration for laxity in failing to press the charges. In his heyday, McCarthy could and did use his exposure powers unaided to drive people out of public life. His clamor for more sweeping administrative proceedings served, I believe, a deeper purpose—to discredit the White House. The Senator was in opposition to both the Truman and the Eisenhower administrations. During the Truman administration, in addition to his boldly improvised assault on the State Department, he seized several opportunities to attack the President's immediate official family. Leon Keyserling, chairman of the Council of Economic Advisors, was called a communist sympathizer and his wife a party member. These charges were made while loyalty proceedings were pending against Mrs. Keyserling, an economist in the Department of Commerce; the Senator's suggestion was that the case was being mishandled there. Mrs. Keyserling was later cleared. He made a similar accusation about Loyalty Review Board proceedings in the case of David D. Lloyd, one of the President's administrative assistants, and a further direct attack on Philleo Nash, another of the administrative assistants. These episodes occurred in 1952. In 1953, with a committee chairmanship to operate from, McCarthy commenced the wide-ranging investigations that terrorized the administration and appalled the free world. Since the presidency remained one of his main targets, lax security standards in the executive departments remained a favorite theme. The supposed failures of personnel screening were most dramatically asserted in the Senator's war with the Army, where he magni-

---

described ibid., p. 406. The CSC practices do not control those of other investigating agencies.

fied the case of Dr. Peress, the pink dentist, and distorted the situation at Fort Monmouth. These episodes re-echoed through the painful Mc-Carthy–Army hearings in the spring of 1954. Other agencies whose personnel policies came under attack included the State Department, which got little respite though under new management. It was especially attacked through its subordinate agency the International Information Administration, which ran the Voice of America and the overseas libraries. Finally there was a "feint at the CIA," which was not pushed and was smothered. The example which the Senator gave of laxity within the CIA was a son-in-law of former Secretary of State Dean Acheson. His ostensible offense lay in having contributed to a defense fund for Alger Hiss.[6]

McCarthy has not been unique among legislators in using the loyalty–security machinery as a fiery furnace with which to threaten witnesses, and in complaining at the same time that the executive branch was not keeping the fires hot enough. But he was certainly outstanding. If a reckless opportunist can take a concept like loyalty and distort it beyond reason, is this an indictment of the system, or a failure of the Wisconsin electorate? I think it is the former. There are always demagogues on the political stage. When we create employment tests that so readily lend themselves to unscrupulous manipulation, the system is at fault.

The objection may be made that I have not taken account of Mc-Carthy's salutary disclosures. Having followed closely the rise and fall of Senator McCarthy, especially in its bearing on employment tests, I will assert that his useful contributions were minute. His attacks on State Department personnel did come at a time when the Department was more reluctant than others to make loyalty–security dismissals, if that was a fault. That a few of those on the Senator's lists were bad risks I would concede. That many of the people he named were poor risks can be established, it seems to me, only by urging criteria far different from those that were in force. Thus Buckley and Bozell, in their vigorous de-

6. The attack on Mrs. Keyserling was reported in NYT, April 22, 1952, and her clearance in NYT, Jan. 10, 1953. For the attack on Lloyd see NYT, Jan. 16, 1952; on Nash, NYT, Feb. 5, 1952. On McCarthy's methods contrast William Buckley, Jr., and Brent Bozell, *McCarthy and His Enemies* (1954), ch. 13, with Jack Anderson and Ronald May, *McCarthy: The Man, the Senator, the "Ism"* (1952), chs. 52, 54. For episodes illustrating McCarthy's hostility toward the presidency during 1953–54 see James Rorty and Moshe Decter, *McCarthy and the Communists* (1954), ch. 2, esp. pp. 41–50. The incident concerning Acheson's son-in-law is reported in NYT, July 10, 1953. See also Telford Taylor, *Grand Inquest* (1955), p. 112.

fense of McCarthy *vis-à-vis* the State Department, candidly declare their desire to see liberals evicted from government. Most of McCarthy's cases, tested by conventional criteria, were insubstantial; or they were already proceeding through normal channels.[7]

THE CHINA SERVICE

The failure of American efforts to mold an effective government in China after the war, and the emergence of a bitterly hostile communist regime there, naturally provoked recriminations and attempts to fix responsibility for such a debacle. Nor was it surprising that a conspiracy theory should have emerged; many of us suspect hidden forces behind misfortunes that we wish had been avoidable. In this case the supposed conspirators consisted of a portion of the small group of American diplomats, scholars, and publicists who were experts on China. According to their enemies, this coterie abounded with Communists and fellow travelers who were particularly bent on accomplishing the downfall of the Nationalist regime of Chiang Kai-shek; and they succeeded when Chiang retreated to Formosa at the end of 1949. Senator McCarthy's frontal attacks on the State Department in 1950 helped to develop the thesis of a monstrous conspiracy in the Department. He variously denounced Owen Lattimore, who had not for some time been in government service, as the "top Russian spy" in the United States, and as "one of the principal architects of our Far Eastern policy." McCarthy climaxed the whole performance with his extraordinary denunciation of General George C. Marshall as "steeped in falsehood." Senator Pat McCarran then took the stage, in July 1951, when his Internal Security subcommittee launched extended hearings to show that the web of con-

---

7. See Buckley and Bozell (n. 6 above), p. 333, for their attitude toward liberals in government. While the specific statement is in predictive terms, there is little doubt that it also expresses a preference. The best example of McCarthy's turning up someone who probably was a bad security risk was the case of Edward Rothschild of the Government Printing Office; see Senate Comm. on Government Operations, Permanent Subcomm. on Investigations, Hearings, *Security—Government Printing Office* (1953), pp. 79–87, 136–41. The most conspicuous case which McCarthy failed to make was against Mrs. Annie Lee Moss, a clerk in the Pentagon. He accused her of being a member of the Communist party. She denied it. After a long series of investigations and hearings the Defense Department found that the record "does not support a conclusion that she is actually subversive or disloyal to the United States." However, there was "certain derogatory information" prior to 1946. Mrs. Moss was reinstated in an Army job, but transferred from the Pentagon. NYT, Jan. 20, 1955.

spiracy was woven by the Institute of Pacific Relations, a research center with international affiliations. Owen Lattimore was again found at the center of the web—not as a spy but as a skillful propagandist for Soviet interests. Senator McCarran was so stirred by his discoveries that in presenting the subcommittee report to the Senate he declared that "I am convinced, from the evidence developed in this inquiry, but for the machinations of the small group that controlled and activated that organization [the IPR] China today would be free . . ." Here the conspiracy theory reaches another peak of irresponsibility. As for the actual measure of communist influence in the IPR, it is enough to adopt (with one modification) the characterization made by Buckley and Bozell: "The hearings . . . show that the IPR had a Communist 'cell' that succeeded in putting the organization's official organs at the service of Communist imperialism; and that this was done by 'manipulating' the IPR's policy-making officials." [8] My own reading of the McCarran hearings would require the insertion of one word, "sometimes." The cell *sometimes* succeeded in influencing IPR policy and publications. The great bulk of its output seems to have been scholarly, and impartial.

These fantastic accusations reverberating from the Chinese communist revolution furnished the background for the disloyalty charges that were raised against a group of foreign service officers who, though not old in years, were by nurture and training very much old China hands. The reports of these specialists in Chinese affairs were surely influential in the formation of our policy toward the Nationalist government; and there is no doubt that a number of these officers (along with a number of journalists and other observers) came to be sharply critical of Chiang's regime because of its autocracy, its bungling, and its corruption. It is also clear that some of these same officers contributed to what turned out to be a drastically wrong appraisal of the Chinese Communists. "Agrarian reformers" became a popular mis-description, underwritten by Ambassador Patrick Hurley even when he was at odds with the State Department. It was believed that these dedicated agrarian Marxists were sufficiently independent of Moscow to take part in a stable coalition

8. For McCarthy's characterizations of Lattimore see Senate Comm. on Foreign Relations, Subcomm. Hearings, *State Department Employee Loyalty Investigation* (1950), pp. 92, 284–6; of General Marshall, Buckley and Bozell (n. 6 above), p. 388. The quoted passage on IPR is from p. 104. Cf. Owen Lattimore, *Ordeal by Slander* (1950). Senator McCarran's statement appears in *Cong. Rec.* (1952), 98:8859. Cf. isc, Report No. 2050, *Institute of Pacific Relations* (1952), with Inst. of Pacific Relations, *Commentary on the McCarran Report on the IPR* (1953, mimeo.).

government of China—one that never came into being, and would clearly not have been stable.

Both their valid appraisal of the weaknesses of the Nationalist government and their invalid appraisal of the Communists made some of the China hands objects of bitter criticism, in the first case from the "China lobby" supporting Chiang, in the second from a larger group disturbed by the failure of our China policy. Diplomats have been wrong before and have been criticized before; in this instance the upshot was a series of celebrated loyalty cases, specifically those of John Stewart Service, John Carter Vincent, and John Paton Davies. At the center of all these cases was an accusation, open or implicit, that these men had betrayed American interests out of communist sympathies. In none of them, I think it is fair to conclude, was that charge finally sustained. Yet all three men, after prolonged and tortuous proceedings, were forced out of government employment.[9]

Service, in 1945, had been involved in the *Amerasia* case, in which quantities of classified information were improperly disclosed to left-wing editors of *Amerasia* magazine. For this he had been reprimanded, and thereafter cleared both on loyalty and security grounds by the departmental board. The Loyalty Review Board, however, found that his leakage of classified data raised loyalty doubts, though it absolved him of communist sympathies. Secretary of State Acheson acquiesced in this decision. It was nullified on technical grounds in 1957, so that Service was reinstated.[10]

John Carter Vincent, the senior of the three, had held key positions in the State Department on Chinese affairs, and had reached the rank of career minister. He, too, had been repeatedly cleared by the departmental board. In his case the Loyalty Review Board found that his "whole course of conduct in connection with Chinese affairs" created

9. See "The China Lobby," *The Reporter,* April 15 and 29, 1952. For accounts of the role of the China hands and our diplomacy during the debacle cf. Freda Utley, *The China Story* (1951), with Herbert Feis, *The China Tangle* (1953), esp. pp. 257–64. See also Robert North, *Moscow and the Chinese Communists* (1953), ch. 13.

10. The published record of the Service case includes: transcript of proceedings before the State Department Loyalty Security Board (May 26–June 24, 1950), see Senate Foreign Relations Comm. Hearings (n. 8 above), pp. 1958–2509 (this and the Oppenheimer case are I think the only full transcripts of such proceedings in print); opinion of the Loyalty Security Board (Oct. 6, 1950), see BNA MANUAL, p. 19/501; opinion of the Loyalty Review Board (Dec. 12, 1951), p. 19/511. See also Buckley and Bozell (n. 6 above), pp. 147–52. With respect to the legal problems raised by the Service case see Ch. 2 above, nn. 38, 55.

a reasonable doubt about his loyalty. In addition to Vincent's official history, the Board considered ("without expressly accepting or rejecting") testimony of Louis Budenz that Vincent was a Communist, and severe judgments on Vincent that had been expressed in the IPR report of the McCarran subcommittee. Secretary Acheson did not acquiesce in this decision. He established a special review board. Before this board could function, John Foster Dulles became Secretary and undertook to decide the case himself. Noting that he could base his decision either on grounds of security, or loyalty, or on the Secretary's summary dismissal power, Dulles said that he did not find Vincent to be a security risk; he did not find reasonable doubt as to his loyalty; but he did conclude that Vincent's reporting, evaluation, and advice on Chinese affairs showed "a failure to meet the standard which is demanded of a Foreign Service officer of his experience and responsibility." Vincent, apprised of the Secretary's view that he could not usefully continue to serve, applied for retirement, which was granted.[11]

In Davies' case, the McCarran committee raised a charge of perjury growing out of conflicting accounts of a CIA intelligence operation (which the committee had no business meddling with in the first place). Again there was departmental clearance; again the Loyalty Review Board re-heard the case. This time Chairman Bingham made a prudent observation that it was not within the Board's province "to approve or disapprove of the wisdom or judgment of Mr. Davies as a Foreign Service officer," and, after hearing "highly confidential" testimony from his superiors about the CIA episode, the Review Board found no reasonable doubt as to loyalty. However, Davies was finally removed, in November 1954, after proceedings under E.O. 10450, when Secretary Dulles affirmed the findings of a hearing board that he was lacking in "judgment, discretion, and reliability." This censure was softened, but not averted, by a finding that he was not a communist sympathizer and had not attempted to serve the interests of another government. A principal element in the finding—in effect, one of incompetence—appeared to be that Davies "made known his dissents from established policy outside of privileged boundaries." Presumably the board was talking about Davies' practice of communicating freely, to the American correspond-

11. A departmental clearance of Vincent is reported in NYT, Feb. 20, 1952. The finding of the Loyalty Review Board (Dec. 12, 1952) is in BNA MANUAL, p. 19/519. On the handling of the Review Board's decision by Secretaries Acheson and Dulles see Ch. 2 above, n. 36. Dulles' statement on retiring Vincent is in NYT, March 5, 1953.

ents in Chungking, the critical estimates of the Chiang government held by General Stillwell's staff, to which he was attached. Davies insisted that "my comments to them were, I believe, sober, discreet and moderate." [12]

A fourth China case, disposed of more expeditiously, was that of O. Edmund Clubb. The departmental board recommended his removal as a security risk; but Secretary Acheson reversed the finding, and Clubb promptly retired. He thus avoided the attentions of the Loyalty Review Board by withdrawing from government service.[13]

After these publicized cases, it is not surprising that the rest of the China specialists drifted out of the foreign service. First they were transferred to other areas; out of about twenty only two were on Chinese affairs in 1952; by 1955 only two of them were left anywhere in the Department.[14] It may have been appropriate to disperse a group which had thrown its expertness behind unsuccessful policies. There may have been valid grounds for separating some of them from the service. There was definitely a breach of information security in the Service case, and possibly in the Davies case. The records of Vincent and Davies did raise issues of competence—though stout supporters, especially of Davies, were not wanting. My present concern, however, is with the loyalty issues that were pressed against this group, which amounted to nothing less than a charge of betraying American interests in China.

Could or should formal administrative ventilation of these charges have been avoided? The clamor for scalps came mostly from outside the Department; it was pressed by segments of the Congress and of inflamed public opinion. The Department dodged and retreated, but in the end had no choice but to stand or capitulate. Since the loyalty machinery was unavoidably at hand, it probably should have been used with more vigor and finality. The fault lay in the unconfined character of loyalty criteria. An inquest into a national debacle was proper. But a search for scapegoats should not have taken the form of putting civil servants on trial for their careers. If they were really traitors who had betrayed their country, dismissal was an insufficient sanction. If, as I believe the record shows, they had at most made considerable errors of

12. See statements by Davies and Dulles, NYT, Nov. 6, 1954; the text of Davies' clearance by the Loyalty Review Board is in NYT, Dec. 16, 1952. See other references, Ch. 7 above, n. 16.

13. NYT, Feb. 12 and March 6, 1952.

14. On the disappearance of the China hands see *The Reporter* (April 29, 1952), p. 18. The 1955 information is from an interview.

judgment, or had transgressed information security regulations, their advancement in the Foreign Service could have been halted, or they could have been unobtrusively retired. In the cases discussed two men retired and two were dismissed, but all after a formidable ordeal and under a heavy cloud. Though no final finding of disloyalty was made in any of these cases, their confused histories did little to dispel the accusations of disloyalty.[15]

A paradoxical element in these cases is that they involved not just the usual clutter of ambiguous associations and affiliations but a very substantial criterion of the programs, the one that authorizes dismissal of an officer for "performing, or attempting to perform his duties, or otherwise acting, so as to serve the interests of another government in preference to the interests of the United States." On its face, this is a grave dereliction, and certainly justifies dismissal if it can be established. Trouble comes when the loyalty machinery is used to try to settle deep divisions about large issues. Then the temptation arises to reason backward from what seems a disastrous result, and to account for it in terms of personal culpability. Senator McCarthy, in far less plausible circumstances than the China cases, was especially addicted to asserting that someone's actions were just what a devious Stalinist would do to advance the cause; therefore the person must be a Stalinist. He carried this to a pinnacle of hyperbole when he suggested that anticommunist declarations by James Wechsler, editor of the *New York Post,* were probably inspired from Moscow. This particular performance inspired Malcolm Muggeridge, the conservative editor of *Punch,* to compose a brilliant skit demonstrating that McCarthy must be a Communist, because his behavior was so demoralizing to the free world.[16] Buffoonery aside, the loyalty programs have provided a standing invitation for angry men to suggest base motives in public servants, who are then left to struggle free of the net of circumstance if they can.

15. Seymour Lipset calls attention to "the parallelism in the rhetoric employed by liberals when criticizing the State Department's policy toward the Loyalists in the Spanish Civil War of 1936–1939, and that used by extreme rightists toward the policy of the same department a few years later in the Chinese Civil War. . . . Various individuals, some of whom are still in the State Department, such as Robert Murphy, were labeled as pro-Franco." "The Sources of the 'Radical Right,'" in *The New American Right,* ed. Daniel Bell (New York, Criterion Books, 1955), pp. 185–6. The difference between the two experiences is that there was no machinery to make Murphy answer official charges of fascist disloyalty, and that he (and others similarly attacked) continued their careers.

16. See James Wechsler, *The Age of Suspicion* (1953), pp. 266–88; Malcolm Muggeridge, "Senator McCarthy McCarthyized," *Punch* (June 10, 1953), p. 678.

LOYALTY POSTURING IN STRANGE PLACES: THE FCC
DOES ITS BIT

Edward Lamb is a Toledo lawyer and businessman of kaleidoscopic interests and abilities. He was one of the founders of the National Lawyers Guild. He was also one of the pioneers in commercial television, and in 1948 got a license for WICU in Erie, Pennsylvania, where he also owns a newspaper. He owns several other radio and television stations, and has recently engaged in some spectacular corporate operations, including an unsuccessful attempt to get control of the Seiberling Rubber Co. In the 1930's, and during the war, he was on the letterheads of several front organizations. He also, after visiting Russia, produced a careless and laudatory book about the Soviet experiment.

An FCC license, especially for a television station, is more than an opportunity for lucrative employment; it is an exclusive franchise that may become very valuable, and that others would like to possess. Lamb's career has not been one to deprive him of enemies; on several occasions he has had to fight off opposition inside and outside the FCC to get a license. His political associations have inevitably been used against him.

In 1948 he answered FCC interrogatories denying communist affiliations and associations. When WICU's license came up for renewal, the FCC charged, in 1954, that these statements were false and that, moreover, Lamb had been a Communist party member from 1944 to 1948. Lamb made sweeping denials of all the charges. Since false statements are a ground for denying a license, the case went to a hearing, amid loud protests from Lamb and from the general counsel of Lamb Enterprises, former Attorney General J. Howard McGrath, to the effect that Lamb was being persecuted by the FCC.

These protests seem to have had some substance. The FCC's Broadcast Bureau produced in support of its charge as sorry a collection of unreliable and mendacious witnesses as have appeared in any recent political case. Lamb's array of counsel demonstrated the value of cross-examination by discrediting some and refuting others. Finally the case practically blew up when two witnesses recanted and accused FCC representatives of suborning perjury. One of them, an unbalanced woman, was promptly indicted and convicted—not for the substance of her testimony, either for or against Lamb, but for making false statements about the government attorneys. The hearing examiner, in recommending that the license be renewed, charitably absolved the FCC of bad faith in instigating the proceeding, observing that "the picture of

Lamb which emerges is one of uncertain authenticity—that of a shrewd, successful, and aggressive lawyer who was connected in some way with several Communist-dominated matters which, despite his recognized acumen, he failed to recognize." However, he concluded, "There is no proof that Lamb personally engaged in any subversive activity." Nevertheless the Commission waited eighteen months before granting the license, in a very guarded decision which emphasized that the issue was misrepresentation, and concluded that the charges were not supported.[17]

The Lamb case, though extraordinary, was not unique. The FCC, through a proposed regulation reported at about the same time the Lamb case was brought, would require loyalty information from all radio licensees, commercial and amateur. Past membership in Communist-front organizations, the report said, would be considered in evaluating an application for a license. Although this regulation has not been formally adopted, apparently some applicants are being asked about communist affiliations.[18]

The main question, therefore, is this: Why does the FCC have to get into the loyalty business, either for the thousands of commercial broadcasters, or for the hundreds of thousands of amateur licensees? There is a tangential security problem here, with respect to the use of transmitters for espionage purposes. A licensed transmitter would, for point-to-point communication, have advantages over an illicit one. Theoretically, code messages could also be concealed in the emissions of commercial broadcasters. A station-owner, however, would arouse suspicion if he attempted to dictate the exact language of broadcasts. Employees such

17. Lamb's many business activities are described in F. Lincoln, "Ted Lamb, Toledo Riddle," *Fortune* (May 1956), p. 144. On the recantation of Mrs. Marie Natvig, see NYT, Feb. 17 and 18, 1955. An appeal from her perjury conviction was denied, Natvig v. U.S., 236 F. 2d 694 (D.C. Cir. 1956). See also *Time* (March 21, 1955), p. 94, for a summary of the impeachment of other government witnesses. Lamb tried unsuccessfully to enjoin the FCC proceedings against him, see Lamb v. Hyde, 223 F. 2d 646 (D.C. Cir. 1955). The decision in Lamb's favor by examiner Sharfman was in Pike and Fischer, *Radio Regulation* (Dec. 7, 1955), *13*:237–348, but it has been supplanted by the Commission's decision of June 14, 1957.

18. For the proposed rule changes see Pike and Fischer, Vol. *1,* Part 2, p. 63/ix–xvi. In one reported case an application for renewal of a licensee who repaired marine radios was turned down because the applicant refused to answer questions about past or present communist associations. The examiner's decision stressed the importance of communications to national defense and the dangerous nature of the Communist party. Matter of Lafferty, Pike and Fischer, *13*:641 (Feb. 21, 1956). It appears from this decision that similar questions have been put to some but not all applicants. A decision by the Commission on Dec. 18, 1957, substantially supported the examiner's conclusions.

as disk-jockeys would be in a far better position to convey secret messages. If this thought leads to the suggestion that everyone with access to a microphone should be screened, the inappropriateness of wholesale employment tests as protection against a rather special espionage hazard is revealed. This is clearly an area for concentrated counterintelligence work. One can hardly conceive of a less effective counterespionage tactic than wholesale loyalty inquiries by the FCC.

The Commission does have a statutory responsibility to satisfy itself that the holders of the limited number of commercial channels will operate in the public interest. Especially if two or more applicants want the same channel, the public and private character of the individual applicants (ignoring corporate façades) will be weighed and may be found wanting.[19] Presumably it would be proper to deny a license to a present Communist, because of doubts about his qualifications and about his intentions to put on the air just the right blend of commercialism and entertainment that satisfies the public interest standard of the statute. He might instead attempt to broadcast communist propaganda. Commercial broadcasters, however, operate in a goldfish bowl; and opportunities for subversive propaganda by a station owner are confined first by the resistance of his audience and second by FCC procedures that purport to evaluate the quality of the licensee's operation. In any event, what about a former Communist, especially one who has had a record of satisfactory performance as a licensee? What about a person who collected some affiliations in the 1930's or 1940's with organizations now condemned? This last is a familiar type of loyalty case; and it is pretty close to the Lamb case. I do not overlook differences in the Lamb case. First, there is the charge of membership in the Communist party; but that charge was not supported by any trustworthy evidence and is of no more weight than the inference of possible party membership that is built up from lesser charges. Second, there is the formal posture of the case, which was to determine whether Lamb had lied to the FCC; but underlying that determination was an assumption that the true facts were something the Commission needed to know. Third, there is the

19. On comparative hearings by the FCC see Harry Warner, *Radio and Television Law* (1948), § 12e. The character of the applicant as a criterion is discussed in § 22d. For an appraisal of the variety of factors which might be considered in such hearings see Louis Mayo, "The Limited Forum" and "The Free Forum," *George Washington Law Rev.* (1954), 22:261, 387. The leading case on character qualifications is Mester v. U.S., 70 F. Supp. 118 (E.D. N.Y. 1947), affirmed 332 U.S. 749 (1947); see Brown, "Character and Candor Requirements for FCC Licensees," *Law and Contemp. Prob.* (1958) 22: No. 4.

outcome; Lamb was cleared. But so are many other parties to loyalty proceedings; questions about the propriety of such proceedings remain. Indeed, the Lamb case seems to bring all the excesses of loyalty programs into an area where they could well be avoided.

GOVERNMENT AND THE ARTS

The Library of Congress has twice withheld the appointment of consultants because of unsubstantiated derogatory information. Dr. William Carlos Williams, the well-known poet, had a tendered appointment expire before investigation and evaluation of his case were ever completed. In 1955, the Library had suggested to Dr. Albert Sprague Coolidge that he serve on a committee to help administer the fund for the encouragement of chamber music established by his mother. On discovering a number of supposed affiliations with front organizations, the Librarian dropped the proposal. Since there was a salary attached to both posts (though a nominal one in Dr. Coolidge's case) it was probably necessary under existing regulations to effect a clearance. Except for this hurdle, there was no possible security aspect to either position, and no necessary reason for mixing politics with poetry and chamber music.[20]

Somewhat similarly, the gun-shy Information Administration decided not to sponsor a showing at Melbourne, in connection with the 1956 Olympics, of an art exhibition originally assembled by *Sports Illustrated*. It seemed probable that this decision was at least partly the result of a noisy protest made by some citizens of Dallas, Texas, when the show visited there, over the inclusion of work of four artists who had a record of suspect affiliations. Again, after rumors that a few members of the Symphony of the Air, an independent symphony orchestra originally formed by the National Broadcasting Company for Arturo Toscanini, had exhibited communist sympathies during an earlier Asiatic tour, the Information Administration abandoned a projected second tour.[21]

20. On Dr. Williams see NYT, Oct. 12, 1954. Dr. Coolidge's case appears in NYT, Feb. 1, 1956. For the position of the Librarian of Congress see Library of Cong., *Information Bulletin* (Feb. 6, 1956), *15*:73: "The Librarian felt that Dr. Coolidge's past associations and activities, entirely aside from the 'loyalty' or 'security' issue, would impair that objectivity in the fulfillment of his duties that one has a right to expect of a public employee, even in an advisory capacity on cultural matters."

21. On the Dallas Art Show see Ch. 14 above, n. 21; on the Symphony of the Air, NYT, March 24 and 25, 1956; cf. NYT, April 11, 1957 (HUAC hearings). Other stirrings of political tests in the arts include the following: The ubiquitous Judge Musmanno (Ch. 4 above, n. 45) attempted unsuccessfully to thwart a Pitts-

The probable explanation for such actions (the official statements were evasive) is bureaucratic fear of Congressional displeasure. That displeasure, which would doubtless have been expressed in some quarters, would have this basis: members of front organizations may be disloyal. People who may be disloyal should not have employment from the government; no more should they have endorsement, encouragement, or recognition from the government.

It is probably a good thing that government support of the arts is on such a modest scale. If there were more, extensive official blacklisting of artists might well be added to private sanctions.

GOVERNMENT AND THE FOUNDATIONS

In 1952 the House of Representatives authorized a special investigation of "educational and philanthropic foundations . . . which are exempt from federal income taxation" to see whether they were "using their resources for un-American and subversive purposes." In the course of the hearings, foundation officers were repeatedly presented with derogatory information about people to whom they had made grants. Unverified "citations" by the Committee on Un-American Activities were usually proffered. Was it proper to support research carried on by persons with such records, the officers were asked? Some witnesses firmly maintained the irrelevance of political associations to scientific competence; others agreed that they should investigate further, that they should not make grants to "known subversives," and so on.

Though the Special Committee concentrated on information already on record about foundation beneficiaries, it produced, at the end of the hearings, two well-known informers, Maurice Malkin and Louis Budenz, who obliged with some new names of alleged Communist party members from their capacious memories. A second foundation investigation, justified on the claim that the first one did not go far enough, went so far with scurrilous accusations in its opening phases that it was derided out of existence before foundation representatives were ever called to testify.[22]

---

burgh performance of Roy Harris' 5th symphony, because of its 1943 dedication to the "heroic Russian people." *The Nation* (Dec. 13, 1952), p. 548. An Orozco exhibition was canceled at U.C.L.A., NYT, July 9, 1953. Martin Merson, *The Private Diary of a Public Servant* (1955), p. 84, reports a proposal by Roy Cohn to "blacklist" Aaron Copland, and George Sokolsky's opposition to it.

22. The quoted resolution establishing the House Select Committee to Investi-

There is an obvious resemblance here to the former practice of the Department of Health, Education, and Welfare of denying medical research grants to investigators whose loyalty the Department questioned, a practice that was roundly condemned by an eminent committee of the National Academy of Science and then abandoned. In the case of the private foundations, Congressional pressure was exerted to try to bring them into line, partly by means of exposing their past defaults, partly by brandishing a potent sanction, the removal of tax exemption. Loss of tax exemption, in addition to stigmatizing the organization, would mean that gifts to it would not be deductible by the donor, and that other tax-exempt organizations, fearful for their own status, would not transfer funds to it. This was not an empty threat. The Treasury revoked the tax-exempt status of the Institute of Pacific Relations, without waiting for any direct legislative guidance. The legal basis for this action is not clear, nor has the vulnerability of other organizations of less notoriety been established.

The activities of private foundations touch considerable areas of employment. First, there are their own salaried staffs. Then there are the direct recipients of grants. There are also the staffs of subsidiary agencies dependent on foundation bounty. Furthermore, the denial of tax exemption is a sanction that can be extended beyond philanthropic foundations. It reaches private schools and universities, churches, and a host of other community organizations. At the state level, where tax exemption refers chiefly to the removal of local property taxes, one attempt has already been made to exact a loyalty oath as a condition of exemption, through a California statute recently upheld by the state Supreme Court. Until the constitutionality of such statutes is finally settled, and until we have some understanding of the limits (if there are

gate Tax-Exempt Foundations and Comparable Organizations is in its Hearings (Nov.–Dec. 1952), p. 1. On the responses of foundation witnesses, esp. with respect to grants to the Institute of Pacific Relations, see testimony of Charles Dollard, pp. 362–4; Russell Leffingwell, p. 374 (Carnegie Foundation); and Dean Rusk, pp. 519–29 (Rockefeller Foundation). Cf. testimony of Robert Hutchins, esp. pp. 287–8 (Ford Foundation), and Henry Moe, pp. 601 ff. (Guggenheim Foundation). The testimony of Malkin is at p. 689 and of Budenz at p. 716. In spite of all the "evidence" adduced, the Committee report gave the foundations a clean bill of health. House Report No. 2514 (Jan. 1953).

On the second (Reece) Committee see House Special Committee to Investigate Tax-Exempt Foundations and Comparable Organizations, Hearings (1954). See also NYT, July 5, Oct. 1–2, and Dec. 21, 1954. Although no foundation representatives were called, President Pendleton Herring of the Social Science Research Council did testify, p. 794.

any) on the Federal Treasury's power to grant and revoke exemptions, denial of tax exemption is a vague, circuitous, but potent device for forcing public loyalty standards into private spheres.[23]

LIBERALS IN QUICKSAND

The examples used in this chapter almost all touch in one way or another on the activities of the federal government; but I would not want to suggest that it is only through the pull of national policies that loyalty tides flow into strange channels. We have earlier noted some bizarre extensions of state licensing practices—to ensure the loyalty of pharmacists in Texas, of wrestlers in Indiana, of piano dealers in the District of Columbia. Private employers have adopted loyalty oaths, sometimes in ludicrous circumstances. In Los Angeles, a greeting-card manufacturer instituted a loyalty oath, though he later abandoned it.[24] Labor unions have gone beyond the arguable case for keeping Communists out of positions of power, and have imposed loyalty standards for ordinary membership. All this is in addition to the critical blocs of civil servants, teachers, and others whose cases were considered in the last chapter, and to the millions of industrial employees, military men, and related groups subject to security programs though often no valid security need is present.

Along with this expansion in breadth or extent of coverage has come a recurrent pattern of increase in depth, or intensity. As used in Chapter 6, "intensity" denotes the range of inquiry, through time and space, into actions, associations, and beliefs. A security program has the greatest intensity because it digs out remote and slight political associations; and it also exposes failings of character and bad habits. Many loyalty programs are still of low intensity, because they make only superficial inquiries (e.g. by way of a loyalty affidavit) about present seditious advocacy or action. But the results of such superficial inquiries are so consistently negative that there is a strong tendency for them to branch

23. See First Unitarian Church v. County of Los Angeles, 48 Cal. 2d 419, 311 P. 2d 508 (1957), upholding (4–3) Calif. Revenue and Tax Code, § 32. BONTECOU, pp. 176–7, lists organizations which lost tax exemption because they were on the Attorney General's list. I.P.R. was not in this category; see NYT, Oct. 14, 1955. The legal issues of federal tax exemption are briefly stated in "Tax Notes," *Am. Bar Ass'n Jour.* (1956), *42*:773, and at length in testimony of Norman Sugarman, Asst. Commissioner of Internal Revenue, 1954 Hearings (n. 22 above), pp. 418–63. The Supreme Court agreed to review the Unitarian Church case, Oct. 21, 1957.

24. See ACLU [So. Cal.] *Open Forum,* July and Nov. 1955.

out, like their prototype the federal loyalty program. Then loyalty programs—with inquiries into past communism, into affiliations with front organizations, into associations on and off the job, into writings, opinions, and reported conversations—come to be of almost equal intensity with security programs.

Once loyalty criteria lead into these peripheral areas, the vulnerability of the liberals becomes a sore issue. For it was the liberals, however defined or enumerated, who made up the rank-and-file of the front organizations, who were likely to have known Communists or fellow travelers, who championed some causes that the Communists also championed.[25] The liberals in domestic politics found themselves on the same side that Communists took on many issues of economic reform in the 1930's. Similarly, on the international scene, liberal opposition to fascism, notably in the Spanish Civil War, put them on the same side with communism in those periods when the Comintern assumed antifascist attitudes.

Starting from these authentic entanglements, right-wing opponents of liberalism have developed a long calendar of complicity. For example, "liberals" included "Socialists." It is a central article of right-wing faith that socialism is only sugar-coated communism. Liberals were likely to be internationalist in outlook, and to support the United Nations. Since the extreme right includes strong isolationist elements who perceive international organizations as inherently communistic, here was another count against the liberals, and against internationalists generally. Liberals were likely to be concerned with civil rights and liberties, and particularly to be in opposition to discrimination against Negroes. American communism professed a similar concern; this made it convenient for the extreme right, which includes a strong racist element, to describe opposition to segregation as a communist trait. The American intelligentsia, so far as it was identifiable, had been dominated by liberals in recent decades. Since the extreme right included strong anti-intellectual elements, it was easy to infer that the intellectual camp leaned toward communism.

The diverse elements of the extreme right-wing are bound together by fervent anticommunism. Like any extremists, its members believe

25. Aside from freakish individual cases, about the only large-scale involvement with Communists on the part of people who would call themselves conservatives occurred during World War II through such organizations as the National Council of American-Soviet Friendship. The National Council, which at its peak had many eminent conservative sponsors, wound up on the Attorney General's list. BONTECOU, pp. 188–90.

that whoever is not with them is against them. Anyone who is against them must be procommunist. Therefore the whole cloudy constellation of New Dealers, civil libertarians, internationalists, and eggheads are procommunist, or, to be charitable, "soft" on communism.

The radical right appears to be the most sincere and unrelenting source of both plausible and implausible charges of identifications with communism. Some of these charges will ring true with one group of onlookers, some with others. Some of the eruptions of the right gain no credence, as when they denounce public education as Marxist because the 1848 Manifesto supports it: this sort of thing makes most of us Marxists, and will not go down. But as long as the tireless in-and-out-of-season enemies of the liberals stick to relationships with some support in history, they implant doubts.[26]

These doubts are fully expressed in loyalty tests of any marked intensity. Did the employee contribute to the Joint Anti-Fascist Refugee Committee? Did he once argue for nationalizing the railroads? Did he have mixed white and Negro parties in his apartment? Does he favor some form of world government? Does he have many books on Russia? These are representative questions, and they put the liberal (still broadly and loosely defined) at a marked disadvantage. Before a loyalty tribunal, and before other less formal tribunals, he must clear himself. He must establish that a parallel is not always deadly, that *post hoc* is not *propter hoc,* that the times were different, that he got his ideas from *The Saturday Evening Post.*

Is it the fault of loyalty tests that questions like those posed above get asked? Is it not simply a historical necessity to delve into these matters? Take a man who answers "yes" to all the prying questions above. Is it not reasonable to wonder whether he had a flirtation with communism? Did he perhaps go further? If he did, has he broken off the affair? Is he now true to the red, white, and blue?

---

26. On liberal relations with the Communists, especially in the 1930's, from a liberal viewpoint, see Granville Hicks, *Where We Came Out* (1954); Murray Kempton, *Part of Our Time* (1955); cf. Eugene Lyons, *The Red Decade* (1941). On the postwar period, for the extreme conservative point of view consult *The National Review,* 1955– . A valuable collection of essays on the composition and attitudes of the extreme right wing is *The New American Right,* ed. Daniel Bell (1955). The authors in this volume generally stress that the elements of the new right represent a protest based on dissatisfactions with status. That is, certain rising and declining social groups are embittered by their lack of power and respect; antagonisms based on class differences arising out of differences in wealth are less marked in a period of high prosperity like the present. This analysis is more convincing than what may be termed a traditional class warfare one, e.g. Carey McWilliams, *Witch Hunt* (1950).

When, with the gravity and seeming deliberation of an administrative program, a decision of doubtful loyalty is based on this sort of historical inference and innuendo, a lot of people are in trouble. They face the risk of severe sanctions, ostensibly aimed at Communists, though they are not and never were Communists.

The severe impact of intense loyalty tests on the liberals has led to some charges that this was the purpose of the tests. The objective of digging out Communists, the argument runs, is a false front. What we have is a heresy hunt, intended to cripple the unorthodox and the non-conformist. Since conservatism is in the saddle, liberalism is heresy; and loyalty tests are a new Inquisition (at which point some striking parallels between the methods of the real Inquisition and of the supposed new one can undeniably be brought forward).[27]

To agree that the real purposes of the programs are concealed requires one to accept another conspiracy, a conspiracy of the right. Ordinarily, spokesmen for this group complain that *they* are encircled by a liberal conspiracy. Without accepting any kind of conspiracy theory, one may surmise that the extreme right is well represented in the loyalty–security offices. Most liberals lack either the predisposition or the qualifications to be security officers. Also, it is clear that the antisubversive investigating committees have been largely staffed and controlled by conservative anticommunists. However, it is unnecessary to try to guess at the inner motivations of the people who run loyalty programs. Perhaps they are out to proscribe liberals as such, or perhaps they take seriously the structure of inference and suspicion that lies so plainly on the surface of intense tests. Perhaps they tend to get rid of liberals as liberals, or perhaps they tend to get rid of liberals because they think that some liberals must be Communists, and we can take no chances. Whichever explanation is correct does not matter a great deal, because, no matter how many are in the end cleared, either approach to decision is unjust. The punishment—to be branded as disloyal—does not fit the crime. Liberalism, even when attended by obnoxious associations, does not equate with disloyalty.

A PROGRAM FOR LOYALTY PROGRAMS: END THEM

My purpose has been to use the plight of the liberals to illustrate the tendency of the programs to expand. The last chapter examined the

27. See McWilliams, pp. 250–5, 300–20, on the techniques of heresy-hunting by the Inquisition, and generally for the thesis that we are in a period of blind repression. See also BONTECOU, pp. 216–19, on parallels with the Inquisition.

plausible (but not conclusive) arguments that there are substantial areas of employment from which, though they are not vital to the national security, a reasonable public policy would exclude Communists. On the understanding that a hard-core Communist does espouse illegal and revolutionary methods of change, and that he is more devoted to the interests of Russian and international communism than to the interests of American democracy, it is reasonable to say that he cannot stay in public employment, including teaching. But in this chapter we have seen that the drive of administrative machinery and the elaboration of test oaths have gone far beyond the hard-core Communist. Loyalty programs have introduced a disruptive element into party politics and other disputed sectors of public policy. They have injected loyalty standards into kinds of employment where their relevance is slight, and where they appear to inhibit freedom of thought and action without any compensating gains. Worse, they have dangerously relaxed our national standards of what constitutes disloyalty. The real traitors and would-be traitors are thought to be so hard to isolate that we let "reasonable doubts" take the place of proof. Test oaths go further and set up automatic barriers against people who have in the past had subversive connections, without any attempt to decide whether they are still subversive. Resort is had to doubtful inferences and presumptions to get at people whose records indicate that they *might* be subversive. All this is inflamed by those who think that Communists are everywhere. When the public at large reacts to these alarms, it seems to hold that communism, though totally wicked, is nevertheless irresistible, so that one drop of virus produces an infection that the most healthy democratic body cannot throw off.

In the light of this state of affairs, it may be useless to urge that the whole loyalty apparatus, *outside the field of sensitive employment,* does more harm than good, and ought to be swept away. But on balancing the modest need against the major abuses, that is the only conclusion I can reach.

There should be an end to investigations, an end to complex screening arrangements, an end to loyalty oaths and certificates. Doing away with administrative programs and test oaths would not leave employers helpless. There is no objection to either a public or private employer's having a policy against employing or retaining Communists (or any other troublesome characters) where such a person's traits or behavior adversely affect performance of his job. That policy could be given effect whenever the employee's on-the-job conduct demonstrated his unsuitability. Similarly his public record and conduct off the job could be considered when they reasonably bore on his ability or reliability. But exclusions based on doubts, weak presumptions, "controversiality," and other shaky standards should be discarded.

If it is still necessary to express a public policy against public employment of Communists as such—regardless of their conduct—the foundation for such a policy in federal employment already exists in the 1939 law forbidding employment to advocates of violent overthrow, and by the appropriations rider, both of which have now been codified in a single law.[28] Many state governments have similar measures.

A general policy against seditious employees can be enforced by punishing violations when they come to light. There is no need for extraordinary preventive measures. Many other bad traits, besides belief in communism, are undesirable in public servants. But we usually wait for a positive manifestation, for example of thievery, before we act. In areas where the opportunities for harm on the job are limited, we could afford to wait for manifestations of disloyalty too. If relatively mild prohibitions—or no prohibitions at all—should result in a few Communists getting undetected into nonsensitive government employment, I cannot believe that any harm they might do on their jobs weighs as much as the harm that our present policies have done and will continue to do.

28. See Ch. 2 above, n. 1.

16. Adequate Standards and Procedures for Loyalty Programs

AT THE END of the last chapter I recommended that loyalty programs be abolished. This is probably utopian; there will probably be a continuing demand for testing loyalty by way of formal programs. This chapter therefore inquires how a fair and workable program can be devised. The standards and procedures that will emerge are directed to programs for civil servants, but their essentials are equally applicable if government undertakes to test the loyalty of anyone in private employment. The same norm of administrative decency is relevant for the private employer, though his legal obligations are not the same as government's.

THE SEARCH FOR A STANDARD: PRESENT AND PAST DISLOYALTIES

The central problem is to formulate a fair standard for finding disloyalty. Who is disloyal? I have ruled out much speculation about the myriad possible kinds of disloyalty by concentrating on the one kind that is currently important, communist disloyalty. There are fascist disloyalties that were significant and may again become so; there are home-grown enemies of the legal order, like the revolutionary Puerto Rican Nationalists or the renascent Ku Klux Klan; there are splinter Marxist groups.[1] They are of little consequence compared to the fear of communist disloyalty that has bemused the country for the last decade.

1. See Ch. 13 above, n. 1; Bell, Ch. 13 above, n. 8. Existing splinter groups include the Socialist Workers party, whose situation has been kept in the public eye by the loyalty problems of James Kutcher; see his book, *The Case of the Legless Veteran* (1953), and Maurice Goldbloom, "A Study in Due Process," *Commentary* (1956), *21*:250. Another one is the Workers party (now the Independent Socialist League), recently involved in the passport case of its leader, Shachtman v. Dulles, 225 F. 2d 938 (D.C. Cir. 1955), and in hearings with respect to its inclusion on the Attorney General's list, NYT, July 26, 1955. Groups like this are communist, and have a revolutionary ideology; but they exhibit various degrees of opposition to orthodox communism.

A loyalty bar should be imposed only for disloyalty in the present tense. A person is not disloyal, and cannot fairly be so damned, either because he has been disloyal, or because somebody thinks he may become disloyal. An estimate of future loyalty is relevant to a security program, but not to loyalty decisions in nonsensitive areas. A finding of past disloyalty may be relevant to the issue of present disloyalty, but it is not determinative. Someone who was never a Communist is less likely to be a member in 1958 than is someone who was a Communist in 1955; but, especially in view of the party's decline, 1955 membership does not, by itself, establish 1958 disloyalty. The regulations of some programs have indulged in a presumption to the effect that a past course of conduct was presumed to continue until the contrary was shown. This is a poor evaluation of American communism, where the turnover rate has been so rapid that the opposite might better be presumed—i.e. that a past Communist is *not* a present Communist. The official presumption, one may surmise, was intended not to state a probability but rather to increase the burden on the employee to clear himself. Of course, as past conduct gets closer to the present it becomes increasingly relevant. If you have evidence that a man was a party member last week, then the burden is certainly on him to establish his sudden transformation.

If past Communist party membership will not of itself support a finding of present disloyalty, neither will past associations or affiliations that fall short of membership, if they are of the same vintage. Again, however, recency enhances relevance.

On the other hand, convincing evidence of a criminal act such as espionage or sabotage is another matter, even if the crime was committed several years before. The employee should certainly have an opportunity to dispel the strong inference of disloyalty arising from such a crime, but it would not be surprising if he were disbelieved.

Attitudes or actions from the past, in sum, are never wholly irrelevant. But they cannot be decisive until their gravity and recency point convincingly toward a finding that the employee is disloyal to the United States.

The Inescapable Difficulties of Identifying Current Communists

The difficulties of identifying current Communists are so great that there is a strong tendency to sidestep the issue. Is there any possibility of designating different grades of disloyalty, so that some discrimination can be used and public feeling still satisfied? The following might cover the field:

Grade	Z	Now disloyal
Grade	Y	Once disloyal
Grade	X	May have been disloyal
Grade	W	May be disloyal
Grade	V	Loyal now, but potentially disloyal

One step in this process has been tried. The Federal Loyalty Program started out with the standard that "on all the evidence, reasonable grounds exist for belief that the person involved *is disloyal* to the Government of the United States." When President Truman in 1951 changed the standard to "a reasonable doubt as to the loyalty of the person involved," this lightening of his burden made Chairman Bingham, of the Review Board "much happier," he said, about making an adverse finding. But an employee who fell under the new standard was no less unemployed; and there is no indication at all that the community made any distinction between those who were dismissed before or after April 28, 1951.[2]

This was a shift from Grade Z to Grade W on the scale. But experience by now shows that any kind of adverse loyalty decision is considered degrading by the community. The whole area is so charged with confused aversion that any one of the lesser grades is likely to wind up in as bad a plight as a full-blown Z.

Let us get back to necessities. Outside of sensitive employment, government has no need to stigmatize publicly anyone but a few Grade Z traitors. The internal security agencies will want to collect information on the W's, X's, and Y's; but the last thing they should do is publish their findings about who *has been, perhaps* has been, and *may be* disloyal. Their function is to prevent security breaches, not to make headlines. I am proposing a minimum program to bar those who are now disloyal from public employment. Administrative grade labeling of human beings should stop right there.

If proof of disloyalty is difficult to adduce, that is as it should be. The brand should not be casually imposed. Government has the resources, and should have the patience, to put doubts to the test of proof, and either lay them to rest or establish their validity. What is meant by a disloyal man in the current context is one who is a Communist. That,

2. See BONTECOU, pp. 68–72, esp. n. 98.

at least, is the reasonable lay understanding of the concept. The law usually seizes on advocacy of force and violence as the critical fault. Let us consider how either of these accusations can be verified.

The most direct way of establishing that John Doe is a Communist is to have proof of his enrollment in the Communist party. But, as the party is driven deeper underground, enrolled membership becomes harder to find. Only a few open leaders admit that they are Communists. The party, it is said, makes extraordinary efforts to conceal the identity of its other members. This leads to reliance on elaborate equivalents of membership. Carey McWilliams, in an acute passage, lists ten kinds of membership that have been seriously advanced: admitted membership, concealed membership, strategic nonmembership, membership by interest, "subject to the discipline" of the party, membership by assumption, membership by reputation, lapsed membership, fellow travelers, and former members.[3]

The last seven of these may have some relevance toward building a case, but they are no substitute for proof, either direct or circumstantial, of actual membership. Strategic nonmembership, however, is a valid (though much abused) category. A Communist who goes into underground work such as espionage will cut all his party ties, and end any public association with Communists or with open communist causes. He must be more than usually devoted to the ultimate goals of the party, since he is willing to take great risks, and he is more than usually dangerous. For different reasons, a public spokesman for communism may, by arrangement with the party leaders, abstain from enrolled membership and be free of any routine obligations, such as paying dues, the better to pose as an objective herald of the revolution. Similarly, some communist labor leaders resigned from the party in order to be able to take the Taft-Hartley oath, but remained sincere Communists for all of their formal separation.

The common distortion of the concept of strategic nonmembership lies in applying it to fellow travelers. "Fellow traveler" is a convenient though inexact term used to describe people who are not Communists but who willingly support and promote some but not all communist causes, while excusing or denying the malevolence of international communism. A person who takes such positions may be a strategic nonmember, or he may simply be a fellow traveler. His pursuers, in their often understandable zeal to end the fellow traveler's influence, are not

3. *Witch Hunt* (1950), pp. 282–7.

content to make him out as a fool, but tax him with being a Communist. He denies it, and cites instances in which he differs from Communists. The rejoinder is that these instances are simply a camouflage for his strategic nonmembership. The more differences he cites, the more strategic his opponents believe his nonmembership to be, until the result is absurdity. A person sometimes regarded as a fellow traveler may indeed be a Communist, but to prove it one must show that his differences with communism are few, not that they are many.[4]

Indeed, the only really satisfactory way to show membership or the falsity of nonmembership is evidence from party sources. Such evidence can come only from FBI counterintelligence, or from ex-Communist informers. The record for truthfulness of such witnesses is decidedly mixed. Rarely today can we come by documentary evidence; the "party card," even in photostat, is a vanished symbol of complicity.[5]

If, then, the proposition that Doe is a Communist can be supported only by evidence apart from direct proof of formal enrollment or of ties more intimate than enrollment, the confusion and difficulties become really deep. To adduce circumstantial rather than direct proof that Doe is a Communist invariably requires a probing of his beliefs. This is not only offensive to our traditions but a poor way to prove anything. However, it is part of the cost of going into the loyalty test business, because disloyalty *is* a matter of belief. A Communist holds certain doctrines to be true that the rest of us hold to be false. If we are not content to wait until he expresses his conviction in illicit action, we have to probe the intensity of those convictions. The advantage of having evidence of party membership or its equivalent is that it is good evidence of disloyal convictions. McWilliams, who is very critical of these matters, declares that "to say . . . that joining the Communist party is an 'act' which can be determined without an inquiry into the suspect's deepest beliefs and convictions is sheer nonsense." Is it nonsense? In view of the weighty

4. The extreme example of matching published views with communist lines was reached in the Lattimore perjury prosecution, which was finally abandoned. See U.S. v. Lattimore, 112 F. Supp. 507 (D.D.C. 1953), affirmed 215 F. 2d 847 (D.C. Cir. 1954); 127 F. Supp. 405 (D.D.C. 1955), affirmed 232 F. 2d 334 (1955); and NYT, June 29, 1955.
5. See Herbert Philbrick, *I Led 3 Lives* (1952), p. 239. Richard Rovere, "The Kept Witnesses," *Harper's* (May 1955), p. 25, reviews recent dissatisfactions with informers. The Taft-Hartley oath cases illustrate the difficulties encountered in establishing membership without documentary or eye-witness evidence, e.g. Fisher v. U.S., 231 F. 2d 99 (9th Cir. 1956). Even more difficult is the question of "affiliation"; see Justice Burton concurring in Jencks v. U.S., 353 U.S. 657 (1957).

body of public opinion and public policy which condemns the party, it is almost inconceivable that anyone would join it today who did not hold the convictions that lead to the party's condemnation. One may agree with McWilliams that "the real test goes to the intensity of feeling, which is purely subjective," but full affiliation with the party is not subjective; it is a fact.

I return to the difficulty of proving, in the absence of the fact of membership, that Doe is disloyal, because he is a Communist. Mrs. Hede Massing, out of a rich experience in the party, once testified that "A Communist knows when a Communist is a Communist." Maybe; but there are no tame Communists available to make these intuitive determinations for us; and Mrs. Massing, with good reason, did not claim this same degree of perception for ex-Communists. The problem of definition was further illustrated in the same hearings when the committee counsel, J. G. Sourwine, was trying to get Owen Lattimore to say whether he had known a long list of people as Communists. Lattimore said his answers were generally negative because by Communists he meant party members. This was too restrictive for Sourwine, who offered the following: "A person . . . who is or has been willingly cooperative or collaborating with Communists for the furtherance of communist purposes" and Senator Ferguson said that was a good definition. It is a passable definition of a fellow traveler; but it cannot serve as a definition of a Communist without important modification of the phrase "communist purposes." Communist purposes have, from time to time, included support for public housing, pressure for the opening of a second front in Europe, and so on. A person who collaborated for those purposes may have chosen his allies unwisely, but he was not thereby a Communist. What one would have to say is something like, "for the furtherance of purposes that are exclusively and vitally communist." Otherwise we drift off again into the fogs of acrimony and ambiguity about what does or what does not help communism, and whether so-and-so is a communist dupe, a communist sympathizer, or worse.[6]

THE ESSENTIALS OF COMMUNIST DISLOYALTY

What are the aspects of communism that are vital to communism and vital to a finding of disloyalty? I venture to say that there are three

6. McWilliams' observations are from *Witch Hunt* (Boston, Little Brown, 1950), pp. 288–9; Mrs. Massing's from ISC, Hearings, *Institute of Pacific Relations* (1951–52), p. 257; Sourwine's colloquy, ibid., p. 3526.

and only three essential elements, but each of them takes in a good deal of territory. They are:

(1) adherence to illegal and revolutionary means to establish a communist regime (the familiar "force and violence");

(2) support of the totalitarian character of that regime once it is established;

(3) a consistent preference for Russian interests over American interests, when the two are in conflict.

If all three of these elements can be established, then the case for finding disloyalty is fairly clear. Is any one of them sufficient? The first one listed, advocacy or other support of force and violence, commands legal primacy, so much so that it does not have to be hitched to communism to support a variety of severe deprivations. Without reviewing all the talk about the higher loyalties of rebels, one can say that anyone who is so disaffected with the established constitutional order that he is willing to shoot its defenders is disloyal to that order. But because the legal case and the popular feeling against armed dissent are strong, it is not easy to catch anyone even talking about revolution. The Smith Act prosecutions have shown that the most sacred revolutionary epistles of the communist fathers will be explained away, even by defendants who do admit they are Communists. This discussion concerns a hypothetical employee who will not admit that he is a Communist. He has to be pinned down with his own revolutionary utterances, and the chances of proving them are slim.

Many supporters of democracy are most appalled by the second aspect of communism—the totalitarian contempt for the individual and the glorification of the state that has marked every known communist regime. However, the practical difficulty of using totalitarian beliefs as evidence of disloyalty is that no one will admit possessing such beliefs, except an occasional fascist crackpot. Certainly Communists do not; their official dogma proclaims the perfectibility of man and the goal (after a transitory dictatorship of the proletariat) of a stateless society. If we *know* that Doe is a Communist, we can infer that he is antidemocratic. But when we are trying to decide *whether* Doe is a Communist, we are quite unlikely to find much totalitarian baggage that he will admit owning, any more than he will admit to being a revolutionary.

The third vital element, consistent preference for Russian interests over conflicting American interests, has the apparent merit of relation to concrete issues and to concrete positions. Arthur Schlesinger, Jr., has declared that "the only evidence relevant to questions of loyalty is evidence of connections with another government" [7] and, without being quite sure what he means by "connections," I suppose that a steady denial of the claims of one's own country, matched by persistent support of the claims of another, do point to a connection inconsistent with loyalty. When the other country is Soviet Russia, we have a familiar manifestation of the communist mind at work. However, there are pitfalls in this approach also. Not many people publish a newsletter or give lectures or have some other channel through which their views on international affairs are regularly made known. An occasional rejection of an American position may simply signify independence of judgment and does not necessarily imply disloyal acceptance of a contrary Russian position. Thus when the Russians in 1956 complained about our invasion of their airspace by meteorological balloons, and our spokesmen in return made pronouncements about the wholly scientific purposes of the launchings, the Russian position could have been supported by an old-fashioned believer in national sovereignty, and the American position rejected by anyone more than mildly skeptical about diplomatic denials. No disloyalty would be involved. Also, the last chapter pointed out that accusations of aid and comfort to the enemy are an all-too-common staple of political controversy. This avenue of proof has to be carefully mapped, for it is full of false turns.

The disloyal condition of "being a Communist" *can* be approached with evidence either of revolutionary ardor or of slavish devotion to Soviet Russia. But since both states of mind may be concealed by a person who really holds them, and mistakenly imputed to another who does not, one hopefully looks for a magic key that will fit only the right lock. One technique of considerable substance is to make an expert tracing of the communist line for, say the last quarter-century, and see how close a fit one gets from the suspect's known positions. If he has followed every zig and zag right down to the present, then it seems a fair assumption that he has been and still is a Communist. However, this is an arduous undertaking. Again only public figures who are inveterate signers of petitions and makers of statements are likely to be on record with respect to the Finnish War or the murder of Trotsky or some other passage of history that helped to separate the Reds from the pinks. If one turns to recent events, where the vision of most of us is a little blurred by the dust and heat, is it possible to seize on a unique occurrence and declare, *"Only* a Communist would believe or say or

7. *The Vital Center* (Boston, Houghton, Mifflin, 1949), p. 215.

do this. Doe said it, therefore Doe is a Communist?" Declare it, that is, responsibly, as a basis for a finding of disloyalty? There is still enough nonconformity left in our society to make room for people to believe or say almost anything, and with the purest of motives. I would be inclined to think that the germ-warfare charge of the Korean War comes very close to being the magic key. Any American who believes and propagates that particular canard must be—well, he may only be a fuzzy fool.

No matter how one tries, one comes back to an examination of beliefs, of intent, of states of mind. Even if charges in loyalty cases are limited to recitals of verbal or physical acts, the inferences that arise from these acts will rarely be so unambiguous that the employee will not in defense undertake to rebut the inferences by showing loyal motives for whatever he said and did. When he purports to lay bare his mental processes to show that he is well disposed toward the fundamentals to which we demand loyalty, cross-examination will inevitably probe deeper to show that he is disaffected. This is at best a sorry business. Yet, if the programs are confined to a starkly objective standard, such as enrolled membership in the Communist party, they probably satisfy no one who thinks that we have to have loyalty tests. If we take the next step and try to identify the strategic nonmember, we are already in the realm of inference and circumstance. If we try to search out the revolutionary, the communist totalitarian, or the patriot to whom patriotism means helping Russia, we will rarely find a helpful culprit who declares that he is what his accusers say he is.

STANDARDS FOR A CONTINUING LOYALTY PROGRAM

In the light of this discussion, a set of standards, adapted from those of E.O. 9835, might read something like this (the original language of 9835 is set out in the left-hand column for comparison):

1. The standard for the refusal of employment or the removal from employment in an executive department or agency on grounds relating to loyalty shall be that, on all the evidence, reasonable grounds exist for belief that the person involved is disloyal to the Government of the United States.

1. The standard for the refusal of employment or the removal from employment shall be that, on all the evidence, reasonable grounds exist for a determination that the person involved is disloyal to the United States.

2. Activities and associations of an applicant or employee which may be considered in connection with the determination of disloyalty may include one or more of the following:

2. Proof of one or more of the following may be considered as establishing disloyalty:

a. Sabotage, espionage, or attempts or preparations therefor, or knowingly associating with spies or saboteurs;

b. Treason or sedition or advocacy thereof;

a. Commission of acts of treason, sabotage, espionage, or participation in attempts or conspiracies therefor;

(This stays within the boundaries of criminal acts, and omits the "preparations" and "associations" mentioned in E.O. 9835.)

c. Advocacy of revolution or force or violence to alter the constitutional form of government of the United States;

b. Acts or advocacy of revolution or of force and violence to alter the constitutional form of government of the United States, or to deny other persons their rights under the Constitution of the United States; advocacy of treason;

(Here we go into the realm of speech as well as action.)

d. Intentional, unauthorized disclosure to any person, under circumstances which may indicate disloyalty to the United States, of documents or information of a confidential or non-public character obtained by the person making the disclosure as a result of his employment by the Government of the United States;

e. Performing or attempting to perform his duties, or otherwise acting so as to serve the interests of another government in preference to the interests of the United States;

c. Willfully attempting to perform his duties, or otherwise willfully acting, so as to serve the interests of another government in preference to the interests of the United States;

(I include the above one with misgivings, earlier expressed, and only allayed by the inclusion of the word "willfully," which brings in the necessary disloyal intent that distinguishes wrecking from mere blundering. I do not think it is necessary to specify intentional breaches of information security as a separate criterion. This would surely be included in my section *c*.)

f. Membership in, affiliation with, or sympathetic association with any foreign or domestic organization, association, movement, group or combination of persons, designated by the Attorney General as totalitarian, fascist, communist, or subversive, or as having adopted a policy of advocating or approving the commission of acts of force or violence to deny other persons their rights under the Constitution of the United States, or as seeking to alter the form of government of the United States by unconstitutional means.

d. Membership in the Communist party; or such consistent identification with the operations or objectives of the Communist party as to sustain a finding that the absence of enrolled membership is a deception intended to promote the operations or objectives of the Communist party.

(We might as well name the Communist party if that is what we are concerned about. Language to cover a change of the name or apparent identity of the party can be included, but need not be; a statute or regulation can always be amended. I have intentionally excluded front organizations and the whole apparatus of the Attorney General's list. The second part of this clause, designed to catch strategic nonmembers, will also cover the party-directed leaders of front and satellite organizations. I have also omitted any catch-all references to membership in other than communist organizations that espouse violent overthrow or denial of constitutional rights. The individual activities of members of such organizations would expose them to charges under section *b* above.)

This standard can be used by state governments by adding references to the state constitution at appropriate places. I do not think, however, that in paragraph 1 of the proposed standard any obligation of loyalty to the state of, say, Texas, should be added. The basic requirement of loyalty to the United States includes all the states, even Texas.

This is the loyalty standard. Its keystone is insistence on a stern finding of present disloyalty, and nothing less. If the triers are permitted to find something less, to express doubts, to condemn politically harmful or foolish attitudes and behavior, we ought to call the result not a loyalty test but rather a conformity test or a reliability test. Such partial measures seem to wind up with a total stigma, once the proceeding is colored at all by the ultimate nonconformity of disloyalty. In these proposals I have tried to require an all-or-none response.

The response that Doe is disloyal ought to have a factual, objective basis. The proposed standard is not factually objective. I have not made it so, by confining the evidence to unequivocally disloyal behavior, because I feel confident that the results would not satisfy anyone who believes in the necessity of testing loyalty. The standard cannot be made any more narrow, and still have any effect at all, because of the nature of disloyalty. Practically nobody flaunts disloyalty; and when we try to penetrate what we suspect is a false front of loyal behavior, we have no choice but to judge a man's mind. For loyalty and disloyalty are both states of mind. If as a nation we are unwilling to wait for an overt manifestation of a disloyal state of mind, we have to adopt inquisitorial methods, and to probe deeply into beliefs. We have come a long way from Justice Jackson's stirring declaration in the flag-salute case of 1943: "If there is any fixed star in our constitutional constellation, it is that no official, high or petty, can prescribe what shall be orthodox in politics, nationalism, religion, or other matters of opinion or force citizens to confess by word or act their faith therein." [8]

Let us now see what fair procedures can do to ameliorate trials of orthodoxy.

FULL ADMINISTRATIVE DUE PROCESS IS REQUIRED

In Chapter 12 I suggested that the "judicial ideal," in trials for loyalty, would require that we

"(1) Develop a uniform and discernible standard for all employees.

(2) Narrow and sharpen the issues in a case.

(3) Give the employee all the procedural elements of a fair trial . . ." [9]

The content of the first two requirements has now been discussed. Here is what is needed to satisfy the third:

1. *Specific charges; confrontation.* The employee must be clearly told in what respects he has failed to meet the standard of loyalty. If new issues develop during the proceedings, the charges should be amended so that the ultimate findings will relate only to charges that

8. West Virginia State Board of Education v. Barnette, 319 U.S. 624, 642.

9. For general discussion of the desirability of due process in loyalty–security cases see BONTECOU, chs. 6, 7; Lloyd Garrison, "Some Observations on the Loyalty-Security Program," *Univ. of Chicago Law Rev.* (1955), *23*:1; Walter Gellhorn, *Security, Loyalty, and Science* (1950), ch. 8; JOHNSTON REPORT, pp. 179–248, 543–8; ASS'N OF THE BAR, REPORT, pp. 159–88; Harry Cain, "Strong in Their Pride and Free," *Cong. Rec.* (March 18, 1955), *101*:3158–64; David Fellman, "The Loyalty Defendants," *Wisc. Law Rev.* (1957), p. 4; Frank Mankiewicz, John Mangum, and Graham Moody, Jr., "The Federal Loyalty-Security Program: A Proposed Statute," *California Law Rev.* (1956), *44*:72.

the employee had an opportunity to meet. Specifications must include names, dates, and places.

The policy of protecting allegedly confidential sources may impair orderly procedures in three ways. First, charges may be vague or withheld entirely, on the ground that more detail would suggest the source of the information. Second, the employee will not be confronted with the witnesses against him. This incidentally may impede the government's case as much as it does the employee's defense, for a live witness may make a stronger impression than does an anonymous accusation. Third, the decision may be based on material not in the record available to the employee. His counsel has no way of arguing about the import of the information, because he does not know what it is. The decision is not open to healthy criticism, because the trier can always rejoin, "Ah, but if you knew what I know."

A good deal of ingenuity has been spent in devising substitutes for confrontation, like distinguishing between undercover agents and casual informants, or having the board question the witness, or having a properly cleared and reliable lawyer cross-examine on the employee's behalf, without disclosing to the employee the witness' identity. Such devices may be of some use in a security proceeding that does not pretend to full due process. But substitutes for confrontation—using the term "confrontation" to include all the beneficial results of having all the evidence on the record—still are just stopgaps.[10]

There is no effective substitute for confrontation in a proceeding of this sort. Its denial may control the outcome of relatively few cases, but a system that permits its denial cannot be said to afford due process. The use of secret information vitiates the proceeding in too many ways.

Does insistence on this fundamental right "cripple" the counterintelligence agencies? Is it not inconsistent to condone the denial of confrontation in security cases, where the danger is such that the FBI might be willing to expend an informer, and to forbid it in loyalty cases, where the security risk is minimal? The short answer to both these questions is that the responsible officials have discretion not to bring a loyalty case if they think the price is too high. This is a decision that prosecutors have to make all the time in criminal cases. Which is more important,

10. The requirement that findings be based only on charges which the employee had a chance to meet is discussed in Kutcher v. Higley, 235 F. 2d 505 (D.C. Cir. 1956). For some alternative solutions to the confrontation problem see ASS'N OF THE BAR, REPORT, pp. 174–80, and proposals by Senator Hennings, NYT, Nov. 4, 1955, and Judge Samuel Hofstadter, NYT, Dec. 17, 1956.

getting a conviction or ending the usefulness of an undercover informant?

Of course the choice is usually not either-or. If you want to keep your informer and use him too, you take his information as leads to develop other evidence that can be disclosed. If the government is willing to rely on its disclosed evidence, the employee cannot go behind it and demand to know how the government was led to it (unless unauthorized searches and seizures or other illegal means are employed). This is all familiar practice and familiar law.[11]

As for the casual informant—the neighbor, former employer, fellow employee, and the like—there is no good reason for concealment. The federal government has repeatedly taken the position—most explicitly in its brief in the case of *Peters v. Hobby*—that information flows more freely if the informant knows he will be protected, and might dry up if publicity and the trouble of testifying are possible consequences of cooperation with investigators. This is an argument of convenience, and only partially true. It seems to me an unwarranted reflection on the patriotism of the American people to assume that they will withhold material evidence of disloyalty. The recent Fifth Amendment controversies have drummed into everyone's head the citizen's basic obligation to aid in law enforcement by giving testimony. If we are going to have a lawful policy of denying public employment to the disloyal, the public that demands loyalty programs should be willing to cooperate in making them work lawfully. The extra labors of the investigators in extracting evidence from the unwilling can be balanced against the cumbersome expedients that now result from attempting to compensate for denial of confrontation.

The first and last consideration, however, is one not of convenience but of elementary fairness. No one has produced, and I doubt that anyone can produce, an effective refutation of President Eisenhower's famous "Abilene code":

> I was raised in a little town of which most of you have never heard. . . . called Abilene, Kansas . . . Now that town had a code, and I was raised as a boy to prize that code.
>
>   It was: meet anyone face to face with whom you disagree. . . . Today, although none of you has the great fortune, I think, of being from Abilene, Kansas, you live after all by that same code, in

11. Cf. Rovario v. U.S., 353 U.S. 53 (1956), discussing circumstances when the government must disclose the identity of an informer in order to go forward with a criminal case.

your ideals and in the respect you give to certain qualities. In this
country, if someone dislikes you, or accuses you, he must come
up in front. He cannot hide behind the shadow. He cannot assassi-
nate you or your character from behind, without suffering the
penalties an outraged citizenry will impose.[12]

So much for the confrontation issue.

2. *A fair hearing.* This means that the tribunal must not be subject
to pressure or reprisals for its decisions. It can be composed of part-
time panels of private citizens, like some of the loyalty boards; of other
government employees, providing their independent status is scrupulously
prescribed; or of a single hearing examiner, making a tentative determination for a body like the Civil Service Commission. Preferably, the
tribunal should have some continuity, so that it will gain competence.
The government case will be presented by a government attorney, never
by the tribunal. The employee can of course have counsel. It would be
admirable if a successful employee were reimbursed for reasonable
counsel fees, as the Association of the Bar Committee has proposed;
but it is not essential. An employee under loyalty charges should not
be suspended from a nonsensitive position. There is no imminent peril,
and suspension without pay is a severe handicap. A reasonable leave
with pay for preparation and for the hearing would be a generous policy.

The tribunal will have the power to subpoena (and examine) witnesses, and funds to pay their expenses. Either the government or the

12. The "Abilene code," stated by President Eisenhower in a speech on Nov.
23, 1953, is quoted by Justice Frankfurter, dissenting in Jay v. Boyd, 351 U.S. 345,
374–5 (1956). The President later, in a press conference, amended the code to
allow anonymity for undercover agents in employment cases, NYT, March 17,
1955. On the problems of confrontation see Commission on Government Security,
Report (1957), pp. 657–64, esp. quoted statement of J. E. Hoover; Brown and
Fassett, "Security Tests for Maritime Workers," *Yale Law Jour.* (1953), *62:*1198–
1203; Richard Donnelly, "Judicial Control of Informants, Spies, Stool Pigeons,
and Agents Provocateurs," *Yale Law Jour.* (1951), *60:*1091.

The cases so far have not demanded confrontation in noncriminal internal security cases. Bailey v. Richardson, 182 F. 2d 46 (D.C. Cir. 1950), affirmed without opinion by an equally divided court, 341 U.S. 918 (1951). Among strong
minority opinions challenging Bailey v. Richardson on the confrontation point are
those in Joint Anti-Fascist Refugee Comm. v. McGrath, 341 U.S. 123 (1951),
concurrence by Douglas (Attorney General's list); Shaughnessy v. Mezei, 345
U.S. 206 (1953), dissent by Jackson (deportation); Jay v. Boyd, 351 U.S. 345
(1956), dissents by Warren, Black, Frankfurter, and Douglas (deportation); U.S.
v. Nugent, 346 U.S. 1 (1953), dissents by Frankfurter and Douglas (selective
service). See also, on confrontation in the Port Security program, Parker v. Lester,
227 F. 2d 708 (9th Cir. 1955).

employee can ask to have witnesses summoned; each can cross-examine the other's witnesses. The tribunal would set reasonable limits on the calling of witnesses, and on cross-examination. It would accept affidavits and other documentary testimony without regard to technical exclusionary rules of evidence.

Whether the proceedings should be public or private is debatable. I am inclined to think that publicity is a great protection for the employee against rough tactics. There seems to be considerable sentiment for private hearings, however, because of the personal intimacies that get dragged in. The simple solution would be to let the employee choose.

This will be an adversary proceeding, not an "inquiry" or a "discussion" or any other kind of administrative hybrid that will blur the essential controversy; the employer is trying to establish that the employee is disloyal, and has the burden of producing evidence and of persuading the tribunal; the employee declares that he is not disloyal, and has to rebut any fair inferences that arise from the government's case. The time for preliminary explorations will have passed; this is, and should be, a serious and formal proceeding.[13]

3. *A reasoned decision based on the record.* I have already asserted that the tribunal cannot give any weight to unverified reports, or indeed to any material that is not made available to the employee. It is of great importance that the tribunal give reasons for its decision, based only on the record, and make findings of the essential facts. I can think of nothing better calculated to balk the understandable tendency, in a matter of this kind, to slide away from knotty issues. Unsupportable results will also be avoided if the parties are given an opportunity to criticize a tentative decision before it becomes final.

Even if the hearing is private, there seem to be considerable advantages in making these decisions (and their reasons) a matter of public record. The employee cannot really conceal the fact that he has been through a loyalty proceeding. If he is disloyal, his associates, and other prospective employers, ought to know why; if he is not, the only

13. Open hearings at the employee's option are available in the Port Security program, see Brown and Fassett (n. 12 above), p. 1177. See Charles Curtis, "The Way to Be Safe Is Never to Be Secure," *Saturday Review* (Aug. 20, 1955), p. 7, and his testimony in HENNINGS HEARINGS, pp. 239–45.

Legal aid in loyalty–security cases has been made available by a special committee of the American Bar Association. NYT, Jan. 13, 1955. Senator Hennings has urged that the government set up a public defender system for such cases. NYT, Nov. 4, 1955.

harm in publicity is the disclosure of whatever aberrations led to the charges. The embarrassments of publicity, it seems to me, are over-balanced by this consideration: the salutary effect of having to write a reasoned decision is scarcely felt if the decision is not going to be published. Further, if we are going to have a disloyalty code, people are entitled to know how the common law of disloyalty is developing around the regulations, so that they can govern their behavior (and their thoughts) accordingly.[14]

4. *An opportunity for review of arbitrary decisions.* There is no need for the many levels of administrative review that characterize some recent programs. In my opinion, a procedure that is piled up like the layers of a wedding cake suggests that it is being run by second-rate people, who have to be checked and rechecked. Or, less invidiously, it is a recognition that a hearing without confrontation is not really a hearing, so that the chances of error are great. Successive reviews perhaps reduce error. All that due process of law and sound administration require is one full and fair hearing. But there must be some higher authority to review complaints that the hearing was not full or fair. The courts have a pretty good grasp of due process. A statutory appeal, limited to contentions that the hearing was (in a technical sense) arbitrary, is called for. If that appeal is not provided, the courts might well fashion their own remedy, once it became clear that these proceedings were supposed to be under the rule of law.

Even this brief survey of the well-known elements of administrative due process suggests that full and fair procedures can do much to make tolerable the application of searching and rigorous standards. As Justice Jackson observed in his magnificent dissent in the *Mezei* case, "Procedural fairness and regularity are of the indispensable essence of liberty. Severe substantive laws can be endured if they are fairly and impartially applied." [15]

14. The need for making reasoned decisions part of the public record is discussed by Curtis, n. 13 above. Knowledge of the board's reasoning helped employees to show that the board had erred in the Chasanow case, Ch. 2 above, n. 19, and in the William Taylor case, Ch. 3 above, n. 27. For general enlightenment, it might be possible to publish decisions without disclosing the employee's identity.

15. 345 U.S. 206, 224 (1953). Appeal procedures are elaborately dealt with in a bill that was introduced by Rep. Edward Rees. NYT, June 19, 1956. On the scope and effectiveness of judicial review cf. Ralph Fuchs, "Administrative Determinations and Personal Rights in the Present Supreme Court," *Indiana Law Jour.* (1949), *24:*163, and Henry Hart, "The Power of Congress to Limit the Jurisdiction of Federal Courts," *Harvard Law Rev.* (1953), *66:*1386–1402.

ADMINISTERING LOYALTY PROGRAMS IN CIVIL SERVICE SYSTEMS

The foregoing review of the indispensables of a fair administrative procedure was purposely generalized. These elements can, presumably, be fitted into any conventional administrative structure. I want to avoid details, or any specification of exactly who is to do what; but some attention should be paid to the consistency of these proposals with the practices of the federal Civil Service, and with the prevailing patterns of state practice, on dismissal and exclusion of civil servants.

In the federal service the problems that require attention are those of achieving uniformity of decision, of coordination with existing removal procedures, and of the treatment of applicants.

In discussing security procedures I did not call for uniformity among the sensitive agencies, because degrees of sensitivity vary, and because the judgments needed are so individualized. Here the situation is different. Though disloyalty is a matter of individual attitudes, a loyalty program puts those attitudes on trial within a framework of limiting definitions. The resulting judgment of disloyalty carries with it sweeping disqualifications and degradation. It would generally be considered intolerable, I assume, for the many federal agencies to affix the same brand, while holding widely varying notions of what met the standard. Either control or centralization is wanted. The obvious way to achieve control would be to re-establish something like the Loyalty Review Board. I said above that an administrative appeal was not essential; but it is certainly not harmful except as it increases the time and trouble for everyone in a case.

A more direct way of approaching uniformity of decision would be to centralize all hearings, probably in the Civil Service Commission. The operating agencies have no such direct concern or responsibility for loyalty in nonsensitive jobs as they have for security in sensitive ones. To put all loyalty decisions in the Commission would offend a doctrine of public administration that exalts the appointing and removal powers of the employing agency, and regards the Commission simply as a service agency. But this is a chore so special (and so distasteful) that the operating agencies would hardly fight to keep it. The Commission might as well take all the business. The likelihood of numerous cases among incumbents, we can at least suppose, is remote, so that a few panels, or a few hearing examiners geographically distributed, ought to be able to bear the load. If they are conversant with one another's operations, adequate uniformity may result without a superstructure of formal review.

Centralized control is not an unmixed blessing. Concentration on the disloyal may lead to obsession with unfounded fears. Diffusion of decision, and a slight disorder, may introduce more humanity; and then again, they may not. There is nothing inherently unfair—either to the employee or to the government—in a single center of decision. Fair decisions depend finally on the stature of the judges. The way to avoid meanness and sterility in loyalty cases is to have good triers, and then to subject their decisions to publicity.

In attempting to coordinate a system of full administrative due process with existing modes of removal from the federal civil service, the first thing to note is that these modes are plural and not altogether rationally related to each other. The statutory baseline is the Lloyd–LaFollette Act of 1912; it permits removals for cause from the competitive service, which includes 85 per cent of all civilian employees, after the serving of specific charges and an opportunity for the employee to make a written reply. There need be no hearing. From the agency decision, which must be accompanied by reasons, there is a limited appeal to the Civil Service Commission on claims that the statutory procedure was not followed, or that the dismissal was for some improper reason, such as racial or religious discrimination. A finding by the Commission in the employee's favor is said to be advisory only.

This is the alleged norm. Deviations spring from it in all directions. On the summary side, during a probationary period of twelve months after appointment the employee is entitled to a notice giving the reasons for his discharge, and nothing more. For an overlapping period of eighteen months, the Civil Service Commission retains a power of summary removal if its investigations satisfy it that the employee was not qualified for employment in the first place. Summary removal also obtains for the 15 per cent of employees not in the competitive service. They are in the "excepted" service; holders of these positions, who have not entered by way of competitive examination, include attorneys, those in high policy-making positions, uncommon specialists, and so on. These people also have no statutory protection against summary removal, unless—and here we go off in the opposite direction—they are veterans.[16]

16. The Lloyd-LaFollette Act is 37 Stat. 555 (1912), 5 U.S.C. § 652. The Civil Service Commission regulations on exclusion and removal procedures are collected in ASS'N OF THE BAR, REPORT, pp. 283–9, from *Code Fed. Regs.*, Vol. 5. For discussion of the "staff" role of the Civil Service Commission cf. Herbert

Almost exactly half of all federal civil servants are veterans, and the percentage is not likely soon to decrease. The procedural protection of the Veterans Preference Act of 1944 applies to them, once they are past probation. At the agency level, the required steps are essentially the same as under the Lloyd–LaFollette Act—charges, answer, and decision in writing. But a veteran can appeal to the Commission. His "appeal" takes the form of a full-blown hearing, except that there is no subpoena power. The hearing is conducted by a hearing examiner; a full tentative decision is made by a higher official; if it is adverse to the employee, he can get a review of the record by a Board of Appeals, and that Board may in turn let him appeal to the Commission itself. The final decision is binding on the agency. Here is a surfeit of due process, except for the inability to compel appearance of witnesses.[17]

Many agencies provide intradepartmental hearings and appeals that go far beyond the statutory minimum of the Lloyd–LaFollette Act. Indeed, the 1955 Report on Personnel and Civil Service of the second Hoover Commission, defending the Lloyd–LaFollette procedures as wholly adequate, says that "Over the years, agencies have tended to make this simple removal procedure more complex than it need be. They have added elaborate removal requirements and have given employees appeal rights in some cases through every step of the organizational chain."

What is an adequate routine procedure for removal of civil servants with indefinite appointments, loosely identified with "tenure"? There seems to be no rational basis for making the gaping distinction between veterans and nonveterans. However much a grateful country wants to ease the entry of veterans into civil service, no good reason appears for

---

Kaufman, in Columbia University American Assembly, *The Federal Government Service* (1954), pp. 48–50, and Commission on Organization of the Executive Branch of the Government (Hoover Commission) Task Force Report, *Personnel and Civil Service* (1955), pp. 141–8. On the status of employees in the "excepted" service see ibid., pp. 195–7. I have ignored a number of details in this summary of removal procedures, as well as certain refinements in terminology. The "competitive" civil service is often called the "classified" service, but the latter term is confusingly similar to classified information, to which it is *not* related.

17. The Veteran's Preference Act is 58 Stat. 387 (1944) as amended by 61 Stat. 723 (1947), 5 U.S.C. ch. 17, esp. § 863. For brief descriptions of its effect on the mechanics of discharge procedure see ASS'N OF THE BAR, REPORT, pp. 56–9; Note, "Review of Removal of Federal Civil Service Employees," *Columbia Law Rev.* (1952), *52*:789–90; cf. Robert Morgan, "Federal Loyalty–Security Removals, 1946–56," *Neb. Law Rev.* (1957), *36*:412. Its broader implications are discussed by Frederick and Edith Mosher in American Assembly (n. 16 above), pp. 131–9. See also Hoover Commission (n. 16 above), pp. 110–16.

blocking the "open back door" of removal for cause where veterans are concerned. Personnel experts and thwarted supervisors grumble perennially about the practical difficulties of removing the incompetent and the unreliable from federal service, difficulties that are often enlarged, one must add, by pressures from congressmen to temper justice with mercy. Eighty-five per cent of veterans' appeals to the Civil Service Commission in the end result in the agency's being upheld, yet months and years are spent in the appeal process. The gross volume of dismissals is said to be gratifyingly large, yet complaints continue that it is far easier to abolish a position altogether than to remove its occupant.[18]

Assume for the moment that it is desirable, in ordinary cases of incompetence or lack of qualifications, to have an expeditious and fairly summary removal procedure. Does it follow that such a procedure is also sufficient for loyalty cases? For reasons that have been sufficiently reiterated, the answer is no. Disloyalty carries a different aura of obloquy than does dissatisfaction. If I were remodeling the whole patchwork structure of federal removals, I would leave something like the Lloyd–LaFollette procedure for ordinary cases of unsuitability—ineptitude, bad personal habits, concealment of a relevant criminal record, and the like. Then I would borrow the old legal concept of moral turpitude to mark off especially blameworthy causes, which would include disloyalty and serious criminal acts. In these cases I would require full due process. If a criminal conviction has already settled the question of guilt, there is no need to retry the facts. But if an administrator has to find whether or not a man is a traitor, or a thief, or a molester of teenage girls, he should welcome the support of a full and fair hearing.[19]

18. Removal procedures of a number of agencies are described in Senate Doc. No. 33, *Appeals and Grievance Procedure in the Federal Government* (1953). The Hoover Commission reaction appears in its Report to Congress (Feb. 1955), p. 67. For varying views on problems of removal see American Assembly (n. 16 above), pp. 76–137; John Fischer, "Let's Go Back to the Spoils System," *Harper's* (Oct. 1945), p. 362, and Frances Cahn, *Federal Employees in War and Peace* (1949), pp. 164–72. Recent figures on the volume of dismissals from government service are in testimony of Philip Young, JOHNSTON HEARINGS, pp. 407, 706.

19. On the concept of moral turpitude see John Bradway, "Moral Turpitude as the Criterion of Offenses That Justify Disbarment," *California Law Rev.* (1935), 24:9; cf. Edmond Cahn, *The Moral Decision* (1955). The alleged "molester of teenage girls" case is Money v. Anderson, 208 F. 2d 34 (D.C. Cir. 1953). The accused employee, after his dismissal without confrontation, hired a private detective, found out who made the charges, and successfully sued them for conspiracy and libel. It was held that he was entitled to a new hearing, because the charges were insufficient, though the case was in the end dismissed for excessive delay. Another nonloyalty case where full due process was withheld is Angilly v.

If such a distinction could be introduced, the employer should be explicitly required to use ample procedures in loyalty and other appropriate cases; otherwise he may be tempted to short-circuit the full procedure.[20] There is little gain in establishing a method of due process, unless it is by law made exclusive in the grave cases, like disloyalty, for which I have urged it.

As for applicants and probationers, it would be desirable to make the same distinction in their cases between a cause for rejection that involves moral turpitude and one that is put on lesser grounds. Broad discretion in rejecting unqualified applicants and in getting rid of unpromising probationers is a desirable element in a merit system; for the system soon constricts the employer with a species of tenure, and it is important to weed out unfit employees before they become too rooted. On the employee's side, it seems to be accepted as a normal hazard that one may not catch on in a new job. But it should not be a normal hazard of employment to be declared disloyal, especially after only hasty consideration. No more, to repeat a previous example, should government arbitrarily stigmatize a man as a thief. To provide full hearings, within this category of grave offenses, would not be an undue burden. The Truman loyalty program covered new employees as well as incumbents. So do the industrial security programs of the Department of Defense and the AEC.

Applicants can never be fully protected, for the reasons advanced in Chapter 12. A practical personnel officer, if he wants to avoid the trouble of a loyalty hearing, will find another ground for rejection. The man who is frequently rejected because he has a bad dossier is in deep trouble. All I have been able to propose for him is some kind of novel opportunity to rectify his dossier. However, the conclusion that universal

---

U.S., 199 F. 2d 642 (2d Cir. 1952), in which a customs inspector was discharged for "misappropriating" customs duties. The administrative and judicial lumping together of unsatisfactory and dishonorable discharges from government service has been criticized by George Gardner, "Bailey v. Richardson and the Constitution of the United States," *Boston Univ. Law Rev.* (1953), *33:*176.

20. E.g. under present law the Civil Service Commission can and does effect summary removals for a period of eighteen months after employment, on a number of grounds, including disloyalty. Or the employing agency, if its removal procedures for unsuitability are more summary than those provided under P.L. 733, may frame loyalty charges in suitability terms, e.g. that the employee has failed to disclose membership in a subversive organization. See Ch. 17 below, p. 426. For the Civil Service Commission's summary removal power see *Code Fed. Regs. 5:* § 6.107. It was upheld in Kirkpatrick v. Gray, 198 F. 2d 533 (D.C. Cir. 1952) and Kohlberg v. Gray, 207 F. 2d 35 (D.C. Cir. 1953).

hearings for applicants cannot be provided does not mean that none should ever be available. There will be cases where both the government and the prospective employee will want to settle the loyalty question. I repeat that there is only one way to settle it effectively, short of a trial for treasonable acts, and that is by an administrative process that includes all the elements of due process of law.

STATE AND LOCAL GOVERNMENTS

Accurate general statements about removal procedures in state and local employment are not possible, because of the not surprising variations from state to state. Also, merit systems are by no means universal in their coverage; the spoils system still operates around the courthouse and statehouse to a considerably greater extent than it does in the federal government. Public-school teachers are fairly extensively protected by concepts of tenure and by prescribed removal procedures; but even then local school boards often have a great deal of power to dismiss, though the state educational authorities control the issue and revocation of certificates qualifying a person to teach.[21]

Where a civil-service merit system is in effect, it will of necessity lay down some safeguards against arbitrary removal. In Illinois, for example, the removal procedures provide full administrative due process, and an appeal to the courts as well. A helpful description of Illinois practices in the various governmental units operating in and around Chicago says, "It is commonly asserted that the civil service system in Illinois has resulted in keeping the rascals *in* instead of *out* of public employment," but the author concludes that this charge is rather overdrawn. The same commentator found a meticulous observance of procedural requirements, and indeed a too meticulous regard for technical evidentiary rules. New York, as a variant example, until recently had

21. On shortcomings of state merit systems see Murray Seasongood, "The Merit System—An Essential of Good Government," *Vanderbilt Law Rev.* (1955), 8:838. On their prevalence see Norman Powell, *Personnel Administration in Government* (New York, Prentice-Hall, 1956), p. 76: "by the middle of the twentieth century [there were] 20 states with comprehensive civil service programs . . . Of the 808 cities with populations more than 10,000, 303 have all employees under civil service, and 317 have partial coverage. County civil service programs have lagged behind. Of the slightly more than three thousand counties in the country, only 185 have merit systems." On teachers see Ch. 4 above and Newton Edwards, *The Courts and the Public Schools* (1955), chs. 16, 17. Summary loyalty removals of teachers are explored by Lawrence Martin, *Faceless Informers and Our Schools* (pamphlet reprint of *Denver Post* dispatches Sept.–Oct. 1954).

procedures that roughly followed the federal pattern. That is, removal normally called for charges and an answer in writing. An informal hearing was recommended, but not required. A 1955 amendment made hearings available in all cases, and broadened their scope. There is a limited appeal to the Civil Service Commission *or* to the courts. Veterans (and, curiously, volunteer firemen) already had an assured hearing plus a full appeal to the Commission, plus judicial review.[22]

From these two brief illustrations it is obvious that in a state like Illinois there would be no difficulty in adapting adequate procedures in loyalty cases to the existing standard procedure. In New York the 1939 statute barring public employment to advocates of violent overthrow went beyond the then existing civil-service norm and provided for a full judicial review of dismissals under it. However, dissatisfaction with this procedure was in part responsible for the enactment in 1951 of the New York Security Risk law, which, for employees in "security positions" as defined by the Civil Service Commission, withdrew court review, and substituted something more like the standard civil service charges-and-answer arrangement, with an appeal to the Civil Service Commission. For several years the Security Risk law was not used, though it gave the state the opportunity to utilize confidential information. Most cases were more easily handled by charges of unfitness under the regular civil-service statutes.[23]

It is not feasible to attempt any further state-by-state and point-by-point comparison of civil service removal arrangements and those provided in state loyalty laws. Yet nothing less would have much meaning, for the procedural variations among state loyalty statutes are even greater than they are among their civil-service fitness rules. There are loyalty laws with quite adequate procedural provisions (notably some of the Ober-type statutes described in Chapter 4); there are others that are defective in various ways. Finally, there are a large number of legislative thunderclaps forbidding the employment of seditious or subversive persons that include no removal procedures whatever.

22. On the situation in Illinois see Comment, "Civil Service Discharge Procedure in Illinois: Asset or Liability to Good Government?", *Northwestern Univ. Law Rev.* (1952), *47*:660. For a conventional survey see Oliver Field, *Civil Service Law* (1939), chs. 9–11. The New York statute is Civil Service Law, § 22, implemented by N.Y., *Manual of Procedure in Disciplinary Actions* (1952). See also Arthur Olick, *The Removal of Undesirables from the New York State Civil Service* (1954) (unpublished paper on file at the Yale Law School Library).

23. See Ch. 4 above, pp. 106–7; Hughes v. Board of Higher Education, 309 N.Y. 319, 130 N.E. 2d 638 (1955).

The total absence of procedural safeguards from many statutes is quite shocking, if one assumes that the law-makers intended to repose in unnamed officials arbitrary power to dismiss on the basis of unproved charges. Of course, the assumption is not a necessary one. The intention may have been simply to add one more type of good cause to existing grounds for removal, and to have standard procedures apply. Even more simply, the intention may have been to do nothing at all except to demonstrate the fearless anticommunism of the legislators.

THE MERITS OF NO ADMINISTRATION

This last possibility prompts me to say that the absence of any administrative machinery may be a blessing. Inordinate legislative furor is a customary accompaniment of a loyalty crisis; both the Civil War oath legislation and the anticommunist agitation after World War I are cases in point. Legislation is often harder to repeal than it is to enact; but we get along well enough despite obsolete laws cluttering the statute books. The abandonment of unnecessary laws becomes much more difficult, however, when a bureau has been created under their shelter. Bureaucrats, like all of us, are reluctant to think that their jobs are unnecessary, and will fight to preserve them.

Loyalty tests, as we have seen them, are a product of the cold war; and it may be that with the prospect of an indefinite armed truce between ourselves and Russia, we face a demand for loyalty programs of indefinite duration. On the other hand, there is much to be said for the view that the tests are a special burden on the New Deal generation. Alex Elson, a lawyer with wide experience in these matters, writes, "If I were to make a montage of the cases I have handled, there would emerge an individual of middle age, somewhat New-Dealish in political outlook but so inactive politically as to border on apathy. . . . The charges usually relate to a period of idealistic thought and endeavor" [24] —a period in which the employee, sowing his radical wild oats, got more or less entangled with communism.

With the passage of time, old New Dealers will fade away, and so will those who either beguiled or bedeviled them. Stalin and Senator McCarran both proved to be mortal. To be sure, there is always the possibility that new canons of disloyalty, condemning the milk-and-water unorthodoxies of the 1950's, will arise. Another turn to the right, and

24. In "People, Government and Security," *Northwestern Univ. Law Rev.* (1956), *51*:87.

those who praised the smiles of Geneva in 1955, or who visited Russia in 1956, may fall under the same suspicions as those who made the pilgrimage to Moscow in 1934, or who hailed the glorious Red Army in 1944. But this kind of pessimism is not a basis for action. If, as I hopefully believe, the whole subject-matter of this book will decline in significance, let us not be left saddled with a horde of officials whose interest it is to keep the fires glowing. Programs that are really functioning already have officers and clerks and cases; the additional manpower required to make them operate as fairly as possible is a worthwhile investment. But those that exist only on paper should be left in that state. I cannot think of a single area of American life where there is any need to activate a loyalty program. I conclude this discussion of administration by saying that its most important characteristic should be impermanence.

Constitutional Considerations

A reader alert to legal dialect will have noted that in discussing the necessity of due process I have not yet invoked the Constitution. The argument has been intentionally phrased in terms of what is fair and desirable, not in terms of what the Constitution requires. What the Supreme Court will say the Constitution requires in times of tension is difficult to predict and rash to depend upon. In the *Bailey* case in 1950 the precise question whether, in a loyalty program, procedural due process was a constitutional requirement came before the Court. The Court divided evenly, thus affirming a divided court below that had found only a slight constitutional flaw; this was an exclusion from federal employment for three years, which the court held to be a bill of attainder. The same counsel brought the same question back before the Court in 1955 in the *Peters* case, and this time the Court avoided it in a manner that has been mentioned earlier. *Cole v. Young,* the first case to reach the Court under the Eisenhower program, made an important finding about the limitation of E.O. 10450 to sensitive jobs, and did not need to reach constitutional issues. As long as the security program is thus circumscribed, so that it affects only part of government employment, and as long as its standards and administration purport to avoid a judgment of disloyalty, it seems unlikely that the Court will require due process procedures in a case arising under E.O. 10450. Further modifications of the security program along the lines suggested in Chapter 12 would make constitutional issues even less pressing. That leaves the residual Civil Service loyalty regulation, and those state programs that do not afford due process, as sources from which it might be possible to move toward a clear-cut decision.

It seems fairly predictable that, at one extreme, the Court will not take refuge in the "privilege not a right" fallacy and say that constitutional requirements don't apply at all to employment cases. The course of decision is clearly turning away from that chestnut. At the other extreme, it seems to me equally predictable that the Court is not going to require the full panoply of due process for every removal from public service. Such a decision would be hopelessly at war with practicalities. How then to make a niche for a decision that loyalty cases require due process? The tenor of the earlier discussion permits a short answer. The severe collateral sanctions that flow from dismissal for disloyalty put it in a different category from "ordinary" dismissals.

But are these sanctions unique in their intensity? I believe that they are not. I have suggested that a considerable number of grave reasons for dismissal, besides disloyalty, can cause the victim to be shunned and scorned quite disastrously. Of course, the Court decides only one case at a time, but it is not blind to the next case on the horizon. Consequently I see considerable difficulty in the Court's overthrowing the *Bailey* case unless it is prepared to take one of two courses: either to maintain that loyalty cases are truly unique, or to move on and pick out the line of due process protection for other similar cases that will surely be pressed on it. The first course seems to be indefensible; the second may give the Court pause, because it is a line that ought to be drawn with more knowledge of personnel management and community reactions than some of its members will think they possess. Therefore, we may be told that drawing the line is initially an executive or a legislative function that the Court ought not to undertake. A rejoinder to this argument points to the other side of the coin, on which is inscribed "due process of law." On that subject the primary expertness lies with the courts, not with the other branches of government.

All in all, I would not find it surprising if the Court somehow never grasped the opportunity to yoke these loyalty procedures to the rule of law.

We may pass quickly over any probability that the substantive standards of a loyalty program will be rejected. They will not be if their drafters heed these modest requirements: avoid vagueness; do not impose penalties *ex post facto;* do not penalize innocent associations; generally, stay within a broad range of "reasonable qualifications." A program that bars current advocates of revolution or current members of the Communist party from public employment, I venture to assert, will not be found unconstitutional by a majority of the present Supreme Court. I doubt that any state Supreme Court would take a more critical view.

Does this mean that programs of approved substance can run riot in their procedures? Not necessarily. The courts are not the only enforcers of the rule of law. In our national government the basic code of administrative conduct is the Administrative Procedure Act of 1946. Congress knows what due process requires, and has expressed itself in this general charter. The only trouble is that Congress has not seen fit to require due process in internal security matters. Loyalty and security programs, deportation and denaturalization cases, passport denials— these are among the glaring areas of omission from the safeguards of the Administrative Procedure Act. Congress can plug these gaps whenever it ceases to regard "national security" as an absolute, and takes it instead as a valued goal to be harmonized with the equally valued goal of liberty under law.[25]

25. Bailey v. Richardson, n. 12 above; Peters v. Hobby and Cole v. Young, Ch. 2 above, pp. 24, 46–7. Compare Elliot Richardson, "Freedom of Expression and the Function of Courts," *Harvard Law Rev.* (1951), *65:*1, with Eugene Rostow, "The Democratic Character of Judicial Review," *Harvard Law Rev.* (1953), *66:*193, on the role which the court should be expected to play. The privilege–right argument was dealt with in Ch. 14 above. A more affirmative view than mine about the likelihood of judicial intervention is expressed by Nathaniel Nathanson, in "People, Government and Security," *Northwestern Univ. Law Rev.* (1956), *51:*101–3, while a more restrictive one is put forth in Ivor Richardson, "Problems in the Removal of Federal Civil Servants," *Michigan Law Rev.* (1955), *54:*233–48. The First Amendment approach to substantive due-process requirements is to be found in the dissents of Justices Black and Douglas especially; see n. 12 above. For an argument based on the Sixth Amendment's requirement of a fair trial contrast Gardner, n. 19 above, with Ivor Richardson (above), pp. 245–8. On the bill of attainder issues see Comment, "The Constitutional Prohibition of Bills of Attainder: A Waning Guarantee of Judicial Trial," *Yale Law Jour.* (1954), *63:*844. On avoiding *ex post facto* effects, and the penalization of innocent associations, see Brown and Fassett, "Loyalty Tests for Admission to the Bar," *Univ. of Chicago Law Rev.* (1953), *20:*486–7. The failure to apply the standards of the Administrative Procedure Act to internal security affairs is criticized in Walter Gellhorn, *Individual Freedom and Governmental Restraints* (1956), ch. 1. See also Kenneth Davis, "The Requirement of a Trial-Type Hearing," *Harvard Law Rev.* (1956), *70:*193.

17. Three Major Side Issues

THE THREE TOPICS to be discussed in this chapter—unwillingness to inform, pleas of self-incrimination, and falsehoods—frequently arise in loyalty cases, and frequently divert attention from questions of loyalty. But they are not spurious diversions. Each has an independent ethical and practical bearing on employability, and none is uniquely an off-shoot of loyalty programs. For each of these collateral issues some standards are necessary; otherwise they become havens for troubled decision-makers and traps for an employee who presses on to defend a loyalty case. Their relevance both to public and private employment will be considered.

UNWILLINGNESS TO INFORM

Should a former Communist or fellow traveler be required to identify people he knew as Communists? If he will not "name names," what then? Is he following a sound moral code in refusing to become an informer, or is he shirking his duty as a citizen and therefore casting doubt on the sincerity of his present professions of loyalty? These questions have been raised again and again in recent years, most insistently by the legislative investigators. Their stock answer was given classic expression by Senator McCarran: "Fortunately, it is possible to verify the loyalty of an ex-Communist, in large part, by the very extent of his willingness to give full and frank testimony against the Communist party." If a witness objected, as John T. Watkins did, to giving testimony that required the names of people who to his "best knowledge and belief [had] long since removed themselves from the communist movement," he had to challenge the legal power of the Committee to ask the question. Watkins' challenge succeeded in the Supreme Court, not because he was privileged to avoid informing, but because of the Court's refusal to enforce, in contempt proceedings against him, the vague mandate of the House Committee on Un-American Activities. Other witnesses profited from Watkins' case; meanwhile, Professor Furry of Harvard and his former colleague Kamin had similarly escaped punishment because a lower court found that the Senate Committee on Govern-

411

ment Operations had not been authorized to pursue Senator McCarthy's vendetta with Harvard University.[1]

But the ethical considerations that move the unwilling witness have made no impression on the courts. Take a witness in the position of Professor L. B. Arguimbau, then of M.I.T. After explaining that he would not invoke the Fifth Amendment, he said,

> . . . I have decided that the thing I should do is to talk about what I have been doing and at the same time, however, you recognize that a thing of that sort puts a person under strain. I have lost six pounds and may lose my job and it is a difficult situation . . . I should like to take the position that I can give all the information that is pertinent without talking about other people and subjecting them to the same difficulties that I have been subjected to. I realize that doesn't give you fully what you would like and I realize it puts me in jeopardy, but I am doing what I can for you and what I feel I morally can do.

The investigators were not to be turned aside from their lists; so Arguimbau and a number of others who persisted in their refusals were held in contempt. It could hardly be otherwise. Once the court concedes that the questioner is pursuing an authorized and lawful line of inquiry, the sensibilities of the witness cannot be given any legal effect. The questioner may voluntarily desist; but he does not have to.[2]

This conclusion does not, however, determine what view an employer should take. The employer is not obliged to add the sanction of dismissal to the punishment that follows contempt of a committee or a court. Nor does it seem right for him to do so, unless the employee fails in some duty to the employer when, basing his refusal on apparently sincere reasons of principle, he refuses to name his former associates in communist ventures. If the employer is the executive branch of the federal

1. U.S. v. Kamin, 136 F. Supp. 791 (D. Mass. 1956); see Ch. 5 above, n. 9. Senator McCarran's observation is from his remarks opening ISC, Hearings, *Institute of Pacific Relations* (1951), p. 3. Watkins' statement is quoted in Watkins v. U.S., 354 U.S. 178, 185 (1957). Proceedings dismissed in the wake of Watkins are in Nat'l Lawyers Guild, *Civil Liberties Docket,* §§ 271–4, 331–5.

2. The Arguimbau testimony is from HUAC, Hearings, *Communist Methods of Infiltration (Education)* (1954), p. 4014. He was fined $500 and sentenced to a year in prison; but both were suspended. NYT, Nov. 3, 1955. In some other cases still pending when the Watkins case was decided, the trial court refused to dismiss, and appeals were taken, notably in the case of Arthur Miller, the playwright. NYT, June 29, 1957. The argument of conscience was explicitly rejected in U.S. v. Kamin, n. 1 above.

government, and the employee has declined to assist the legislative branch in its self-imposed task of compiling a directory of Communists and ex-Communists, there may be such a breach of duty. But not necessarily. The New York Commissioner of Education had the case of five teachers who refused to say, in the course of inquiries as to their own loyalty, whether they had known any of their colleagues as Communists. The New York City Board of Education had suspended them when they stopped short after accounts of their own communist careers. Since the school authorities are obliged to enforce the Feinberg law and to certify that their ranks are free of Communist party members, the Board's counsel argued before Commissioner Allen that "If these petitioners are sincere in their denunciation of communism, they should demonstrate that sincerity in a concrete way, by cooperating with the board and giving the board the information it needs to carry out its obligation under the law."

Commissioner Allen was not persuaded that the Board needed informers' testimony so badly. He said,

> I do not dispose of this case on the question of the board's legal power. The problem is a much deeper one and affects the administration of our entire educational system. There is near unanimity on the part of teachers throughout the state that indiscriminate use of this type of interrogation immediately engenders an atmosphere of suspicion and uneasiness in the schools and colleges. . . . The allegation by a member or former member of this organization [the Communist party] standing alone could well be untrustworthy, yet it levels a deadly suspicion which is most difficult to disprove. . . . The policy under consideration here would do more harm than good . . . this type of inquisition has no place in the school system . . .

In the case of one appellant who was a school principal the Commissioner pointed out that he had a definite obligation under the Feinberg law "to report to [the Board] the name of any person in his school whom he knows or believes to be a communist . . ." [3]

This decision sanely recognizes the demoralizing effects of compulsory informing. An investigating committee hits and runs, taking with it the praise of part of the community for "ferreting out" possible Communists and for squeezing the last drop of repentant "cooperation" from the

3. NYT, Aug. 9, 1956.

ex-Communist whose pardon is at stake. An employer, public or private, has to live with his employees. They, like the New York state teachers, are likely to feel mistrusted and humiliated if for some of their number the price of employment is exposing others.

A policy of forebearance does not mean that the employer must ignore all refusals to inform. Somewhere between the law's unfeeling demand for total testimony and the individual's reluctance to embroil his friends lies an area where strong social pressures may be expected to fall. Anyone with information about the perpetrator of a serious crime is expected to volunteer it; if he willfully fails to come forward, he may possibly be punished for misprision of felony.[4] This offense, though rarely invoked by prosecutors, suggests the location of the boundary of tolerance. One would not expect either the employer or the community at large to extend much sympathy to a person who refused to tell what he knew about a kidnapping. Consistent with this distinction has been the attitude of some witnesses before committees, who have declared that if they had any information about espionage they would bring it forward, but that they would not testify to Communist party associations that (in their opinion) violated no law. Suppose, to take a close case, that a person in Professor Furry's position was asked by a competent tribunal about his communist fellow workers in radar research in World War II. Would it be defensible for him to interpose his personal belief that the scientists in question had done and would do no harm? I doubt it. Here was a group whose employment almost surely involved deception of security officers at the time. There are still valid security reasons for wanting to know the identity and present employment of its members. An employer might decide to stand aside while the government used its considerable powers to extract this information; or he might with equal reason decide to employ no longer a person who, in his honest judgment, failed in an elementary obligation of citizenship.

This is obviously not an easy place to draw firm lines. The basic trouble is that there is no consensus on the ethics of informing. At one extreme is the schoolboy's (and gangster's) code: tell nothing. At the other is the law's demand (with a few exceptions): tell everything. When the problem intrudes on a loyalty case, one can only ask that the em-

---

4. On misprision of felony see *Corpus Juris Secundum* (1939), *15:*703, cf. *22:*169. In the case of a teacher with tenure, his conscientious refusal to inform is probably not a basis for dismissal unless he has been convicted of contempt or some related offense. Otherwise, his employers are simply substituting their judgment for his in an area where the right course of conduct is far from clear.

ployer (and the community of which both he and the employee are a part) try to make a fair appraisal of the employee's motives, of the importance of having the names, and of the other sanctions that will be applied to extract them. The best test is to ask whether the refusal to talk would be respected in another situation of similar significance. The predecessor of the present New York Commissioner of Education decided, in 1954, a case of a dismissal based in large part on failure to inform. The culprit was the basketball coach at C.C.N.Y., who held the rank of Associate Professor of Hygiene. The world of sport at that time had been torn by revelations of bribery of college basketball players by gamblers. It came to light that Coach Holman had known of a bribery attempt and of another dishonest episode that he had not reported to the president. The Commissioner found that Holman was guilty only of "bad judgment," and ordered his reinstatement. I would venture to say that the corruption of youth involved in this affair shocked the community to a degree that makes it roughly comparable to the threat of communist corruption inherent in the other teachers' cases. But, so far as I know, the City did not protest that the Commissioner's decision undermined its attempts to preserve the integrity of amateur athletics; and it did not, as it did in the teachers' cases, seek to have the decision reversed by the courts.[5] Such analogies are often helpful.

I have said very little in this discussion about the argument that willingness to inform is an essential badge of repentance. That this argument is seriously advanced only emphasizes my contention that we tend to erect unduly severe standards in matters of loyalty. Willingness to inform may be a sign of reformation; it may also be a deceitful hoax wrapped in a tissue of false accusation, the last resort of a desperate scoundrel or an equally desperate neurotic. There are plenty of other ways for an employer to judge whether a person who says that he was a Communist but is one no longer is telling the truth. There is no need inexorably and inflexibly to override sincere claims of conscience. Whether such claims are sincere may be a troublesome point of decision; but it also can be resolved by appraising the employee's demeanor and the plausibility of his claim in the context of the whole case.

A few words should be said about the converse of the problem under

5. See NYT, Aug. 28, 1954; Matter of Holman, N.Y. State, *Department Reports* (1955), 75:82. For the City Corporation Counsel's reaction to the Commissioner's decision in the case of the teachers see NYT, Aug. 18, 1956 ("Education Ruling Bogs Inquiry . . ."). The court held that there was no occasion for judicial interference. NYT, May 22, 1957. The City has appealed.

discussion—that is, the possibility of sanctions against employees who do inform. There have been suggestions that in the entertainment industry some outspoken anti-Communists have been discriminated against. Any such instances in the last few years have probably occurred because anticommunist employment tests boomeranged in an ironic way. That is, the search for Communists has widened the industry's test for employability, the crude standard that rejects anyone who has become "controversial." A few right-wing figures have apparently become as "controversial" as their targets, and have lost employment opportunities.[6]

The case of Professor Herbert Fuchs of American University was thought by some observers to involve punishment for informing. Fuchs, called before the Committee on Un-American Activities, at first refused to name names. Then, on the strong urging and with the apparent support of his superiors, he unfolded a tale of extensive communist penetration of the National Labor Relations Board and related agencies from 1937 to 1948. He was promptly suspended and not re-appointed. The case was clumsily handled by the University authorities and was extraordinarily tortuous. I can find no foundation for the suggestion that Fuchs was penalized for informing. Rather, his disclosures about the extent of his own involvement—see the following section on falsehoods —may have been decisive.[7]

An employee who had made *false* damaging charges might understandably be ostracized by his fellow workers; and the employer might then conclude that the informer was unemployable. Only a person of unusual charity could be expected to work with Harvey Matusow. But in the ordinary case of the ex-Communist who talks, reprisals are unjust. Once such a person gets in the toils either of an investigating committee or of a loyalty program he has very little choice. If the committee

6. See Ch. 5 above, n. 59.

7. For a chronology of the events in the Fuchs case see Ass'n of American Law Schools, *Proceedings: Annual Meeting 1956* (1957), pp. 118–25. Criticism of American University's action in discharging Fuchs, on the assumption that it was motivated by his informing, has been expressed by the American Committee for Cultural Freedom, "The Case of Herbert Fuchs," [March 1956] (mimeo.); Brent Bozell (exchange with Dr. Hurst Anderson, President of American University), *National Review* (Jan. 25, 1956), p. 13; and Congressman Gordon Scherer, in HUAC, Hearings, *Investigation of Communist Infiltration of Government* (1955), p. 3018. Cf. ACLU criticism of the dismissal on academic due-process grounds. ACLU News Release (dated March 13, 1956). Fuchs was subsequently employed by the House Judiciary Anti-Trust subcommittee at the recommendation of Congressman Francis Walter, Chairman of the HUAC. *Washington Star,* Oct. 7, 1956.

demands names, he must either answer, plead self-incrimination, which may be dishonest and will certainly be damaging, or refuse and risk going to jail. If a loyalty tribunal insists on names, he must answer or risk the penalties of being branded as disloyal. Anyone who would vent hostility on people who have named names under such circumstances should first consider what he would do if he were caught in the same web.

PLEAS OF SELF-INCRIMINATION

A person who refuses to give information, either about himself or about others, on the ground that his answers might expose him to criminal prosecution, is in a rather different position from the unwilling talebearer who stands on principle. He has a constitutional privilege behind him, derived from the federal constitution or from equivalent provisions in state constitutions, and if there is any apparent substance to his claim, his answer cannot be coerced. In some cases his motive may be the same —to avoid informing on others—but he neccessarily exposes himself to suspicions of personal wrongdoing.

We do not need to go into all the subtleties of current debate about the meaning and scope of the privilege. The Supreme Court has in recent cases hammered home the proposition that invocation of the Fifth Amendment in itself does not justify an inference of guilt. In reaffirming the principle that the privilege protects the innocent as well as the guilty, the Court recalled that it protects a witness from compulsory disclosures that may tend to incriminate him, that is, expose him to prosecution. Fear of prosecution, as well as fear of punishment, is a sufficient ground for claiming the privilege. From this firm foundation the Court went on in the *Slochower* case to condemn, as a denial of due process, New York City's policy of automatically dismissing teachers who invoked the privilege before any investigating body—in this case the Senate Internal Security subcommittee. This decision cast doubt on the propriety of using dismissals from government employment as a lever for coercing abandonment of the privilege by unwilling witnesses. Equally, it cut back the growing doctrine that any use of the privilege is misconduct, a doctrine which has made it possible to avoid in many cases the hard underlying issues of communism and loyalty.[8]

8. See Ullman v. U.S., 350 U.S. 422 (1956), extolling the privilege while upholding the validity of the Federal Immunity Statute; Slochower v. Board of Education, 350 U.S. 551 (1956); Twining v. New Jersey, 211 U.S. 78 (1908), establishing that fear of prosecution, as well as conviction, is a legitimate ground

So, loyalty issues can no longer be sidestepped, when the Fifth Amendment comes into a case, by seizing an erroneous understanding of the scope of the privilege. However, the private or public employer does not have to ignore a claim of privilege; and the weight that he attaches to such a claim may still effectively dispose of a case.

The requirement of a full hearing followed by a reasoned decision in loyalty cases should help to put the privilege in perspective. If the trier keeps in mind that he is required to find disloyalty, not simple recalcitrance, he will expect to have brought before him a reasonable body of evidence of disloyalty. The effect of the employee's silence will be that the employee deprives himself of the opportunity of rebuttal, and the case against him will stand unchallenged. But a case will still have to be made; it cannot be conjectured entirely from the silences of the employee.

The trier has also to consider what inferences can arise from the use of the privilege, given the circumstances of the individual case. There is one school of thought that would permit no inference; this is similar to the formal admonition in criminal cases when the accused fails to take the stand. The "no-inference" rule is unenforceable. You can forbid explicit inferences, but you cannot forbid trains of thought, and they will surely color the rest of the decision.[9]

What is preferable, it seems to me, is to bring the possibilities out in the open. The employee, let us suppose, is asked if he signed certain checks payable to a known Communist. He invokes the privilege. The trier is inclined to decide that the supposed answer, to be incriminating, would have had to be "yes." He therefore proposes to infer that the signatures are genuine, as one step in a line of proof. Before he so decides he should put himself in the position of the employee. This he can do very imperfectly, because he cannot ask the witness why he invoked the privilege. But, there is at least a possibility that the employee's own situation is innocent. For example, the employee may have a sufficient legal excuse for not saying whether he signed the checks, in that his answers may be drawing him into apparent complicity in a criminal conspiracy. But his motive for refusing may be to

---

for invoking the Fifth Amendment; and Laba v. Board of Education of Newark, 23 N.J. 364, 129 A. 2d 273 (1957) (outstanding state court opinion following Slochower). See also Erwin Griswold, *The Fifth Amendment Today* (1955); cf. Sidney Hook, *Common Sense and the Fifth Amendment* (1957).

9. See the dissent of Judge Frank in U.S. v. Grunewald, 233 F. 2d 556, 571 (2d Cir. 1956).

block off further questioning about the membership of others in the organization to which he contributed. If he admitted his own participation, the doctrine of waiver might operate to compel him to answer questions about others, under threat of contempt, on the ground that the protection of the privilege was no longer of any use to him, and was therefore not available.

It is quite doubtful that a negative answer to the supposed question, "Did you sign the checks?" would be incriminating. On the other hand, the full truthful answer might have been, "Yes, but . . ." followed by some explanation that would help to clear the employee—and that would at the same time implicate others. So, as is true in many exercises of the privilege, we cannot be sure whether it was properly claimed. It is also debatable whether the suggested motive is a commendable one; this goes back to the discussion of the preceding section. In any event, if a reasoned decision is required, these complex considerations will be brought to the trier's attention, and he will have to resolve them as best he can.

As the questions to which the privilege is interposed come closer and closer to the heart of the matter—Communist party membership and the like—an obligation to deal fairly with the employer may in time override the deference owed to a constitutional claim. The familiar analogies are those of a bank teller who refuses to say whether he knows who robbed the bank, or a policeman who stands mute before accusations of receiving bribes. There is a clear line of cases that permits dismissal for refusal to answer questions that relate directly to "official conduct." Similarly, it is said, if we have a valid policy forbidding Communists to be public employees, then an employee cannot refuse to say whether he is a Communist, and still expect to hold his job. Independently of the inferences one may draw from the refusal to answer, the refusal in itself creates, according to this view, an intolerable rupture of confidence between employer and employee. Here we are back in an automatic cause for dismissal. If this reasoning is correct, hearings and all their apparatus become unnecessary. All the employer has to do is ask the question, and then fire anybody who refuses to answer.

One way out of this distasteful impasse is to recognize that if there is a relationship of confidence between the employer and the employee, it should be reciprocal. The employer should not demand candor from the employee and at the same time refuse to hear any special circumstances that may have impelled the employee to fall silent. In a word, the necessity of a hearing has been restored; but the employee now has the burden of trying to convey whatever reasons of conscience or of feared persecution led him to invoke the privilege, either before some competent outside tribunal, like an arbitrator, or before the employer himself.[10]

In short, an employer who is scornful of the privilege against self-incrimination, and of anyone who uses it, may want to let that attitude control his decision, so that he never really reaches the question of disloyalty. But if he is a public employer, he is bound by the Court's interpretation of due process of law. This requires him to grant a hearing before he makes use of the constitutional privilege the ground for dismissal. The hearing can be dispensed with (if ever) only when the employee refuses to answer critical questions about his conduct on the job.

A private employer is probably not bound by the constitutional mandate; but he ought to heed the reasoning behind it. If the employment relationship is one that can legally be terminated at the employer's will, only self-restraint can operate. If, under an individual contract or a collective bargaining agreement, a dismissal must be based on "just cause" or some similar formulation, invocation of the privilege cannot be considered automatically to constitute cause. The employer should have to show the court or the arbitrator or whoever settles disputes under the contract that the employment depended on a relationship of trust and confidence which can be reasonably considered to be undermined by the circumstances of the plea. Alternatively, the employer can show that the reaction of his customers, or his other employees, is in fact so hostile to the silent employee that his retention would cause the employer economic injury. The employer does not have to be heroic. On the other hand, the courts should not entertain conjectures of injury, nor should the employee be sacrificed to an illegal boycott (of which more in the next chapter). For brief example: Newspaper

10. On official misconduct see Note, "Denying the Privilege against Self-Incrimination to Public Officers," *Harvard Law Rev.* (1951), *64:*987; annotation, "Assertion of Immunity as Ground for Removing or Discharging Public Officer or Employee," *Amer. Law Reports 2d* (1955), *44:*789. See also Regan v. New York, 349 U.S. 58 (1955), on advance waiver of immunity by public officers. For an expansive view of the inferences which may be drawn from an invocation see C. Dickerman Williams, "Problems of the Fifth Amendment," *Fordham Law Rev.* (1955), *24:*42–9; cf. Leonard Ratner, "Consequences of Exercising the Privilege against Self-Incrimination," *Univ. of Chicago Law Rev.* (1957), *24:*472 (strong "no-inference" position, and narrow limitation of official conduct exception).

publishers who have dismissed reporters who invoked the privilege as to Communist party membership can reasonably establish a loss of confidence. Again, in one of the movie cases, RKO satisfied the court that it was justified in withholding screen credit from a writer who made the same plea, because of public hostility—and this may have been reasonable, in view of the activities of the American Legion and other pressure groups. General Electric also persuaded a lower court that everybody—customers, stockholders, and other employees—would be angry if it did not promptly fire Fifth Amendment cases. Here skepticism intrudes.[11]

These elements of lost confidence and economic injury, as against the employee's claim to have his record and his good motives respected, work out somewhat differently in academic cases. Professorial tenure can also be ended for cause; but cause does not have the same content as it does for a movie-maker. The purpose of tenure is to reinforce academic freedom in teaching and research. Academic utterances often run at cross-currents to popular views; and a university administration does occasionally have to try to be heroic. Loss of popularity, even when euphemized as "bad public relations," is not a valid element in university cases. The judgment has to be a professional one. On one side is the teacher's record; on the other the evidence of unfitness, including the use of the privilege and whatever inferences may properly be drawn from it in view of all the circumstances. The judgment sought is whether the teacher's peers continue to regard his academic integrity as intact, or whether they think he is a criminal, a perjuror, or a traitor who is unfitted to the pursuit of truth. Fifth Amendment pleas in loyalty inquiries do not, in themselves, decide these grave questions.

It may be objected that, though I have continued to deprecate pleas of self-incrimination as a ground for summary dismissal, I have left the private employer a great deal of leeway. Even if he is contractually bound to dismiss only for cause, his adverse reactions to the employee's silence—reactions that are either subjective or speculative—may be accepted as adequate cause. Such a formula is clearly subject to abuse. But I doubt whether it can be made foolproof. In general, the possible innocence and the possible good motives of the person who invokes

11. For references to episodes referred to in the text see Ch. 5 above. On the question of whether pleading the Fifth Amendment is *per se* "just cause" for discharge under a collectively bargained contract contrast Republic Steel, 8 Amer. Lab. Arb. Awards, par. 70, 341 (1957), and Worthington Corp., 24 Lab. Arb. Rep. 1 (1955), 236 F. 2d 364 (1st Cir. 1956) (not "just cause") with Bethlehem Steel Co., Ch. 5 above, n. 33.

the privilege ought to be explored and respected. But the fact that the privilege is a valued part of the Constitution does not mean that anyone who resorts to it becomes a man of distinction. If we have official or popular policies that exclude Communists from wide areas of employment, the man who swears that it may incriminate him to say whether he is or isn't one is bound to be in trouble.[12]

Two postscripts are required to round off this summary of the Fifth Amendment problem in employment cases. First, as to state-licensed professions and trades, a plea of possible self-incrimination on loyalty subjects cannot justify revocation of a license. The only profession to which loyalty is even relevant is the practice of law; and there, though the plea may prompt investigation, it needs to be supplemented with affirmative evidence of professional failings before disbarment or other discipline can be imposed.

Second, as to labor union membership. Even if a union has a valid policy against Communists as members, a matter to be discussed further in the next chapter, the union would have no business expelling a person solely on the basis of a self-incrimination plea. In the case of a rank-and-file member, the arguments of loss of confidence or of economic injury seem to have no plausibility. Subject to the uncertainties of judicial review of union affairs, a member who had not been given a fair hearing on the underlying disqualification of disloyalty should be able to obtain relief from the courts. A union officer or employee stands in about the same position as a private employee—that is, the circumstances of his invoking the privilege might make his continuance in his union job untenable. However, expulsions from union membership have occasionally followed precipitately on the heels of a plea before an investigating committee. So far as I know, these expulsions were not successfully challenged.[13]

12. Judicial recognition of the employer's privilege to dismiss an employee who has invoked the Fifth Amendment may conceivably be interpreted to involve "state action," so as to make the private employer subject to the constitutional requirements of due process; see Harold Horowitz, "Legal Aspects of 'Political Blacklisting' in the Entertainment Industry," *Southern Calif. Law Rev.* (1956), *29*:272–8, and Ch. 18 below, pp. 457–9. The necessity of an investigation of the merits in each case in the academic field is discussed in Clark Byse, "Teachers and the Fifth Amendment," *Univ. of Pa. Law Rev.* (1954), *102*:871–83. A similar code has been adopted by the Ass'n of Amer. Law Schools; see *1954 Proceedings* (1955), pp. 22, 115–20. See also Zechariah Chafee, Jr., *The Blessings of Liberty* (1956), ch. 7.

13. For examples of summary expulsion from unions for invoking the Fifth Amendment see HUAC, Hearings, *Investigation of Communist Activities in the*

FALSEHOODS

On the face of it, this subject should cause no trouble. There is no open conflict about the ethics of telling the truth, as there is about informing. Nevertheless, in loyalty (and security) cases questions of veracity introduce practical problems of administration, substantive issues of materiality, and ethical questions of justice and mercy.

On the administrative side, if the proceeding is a security case where both loyalty and suitability for sensitive work are in question, the detection of a significant falsehood uttered by the employee can enter directly into the final decision. His reliability is at issue; and the fact that he has lied, especially if the lie was part of his case and intended to deceive his superiors, conveys a strong suggestion of unreliability. However, this raises a risk of error in a formal proceeding where the employee is entitled to know the charges against him, and where the burden of refuting the charges is laid on him. Unless the triers notify the employee that they are making his supposed lie a basis for decision, and give him an opportunity of rebutting this new charge, they are likely to go seriously astray. The Hynning case brings this point to mind.

Clifford J. Hynning, a Treasury lawyer, was charged under E.O. 10450 with a variety of communist associations, all of which he vigorously denied. In a 1954 hearing a conflict developed between Hynning's recollections and those of an FBI agent about the substance of an interview in 1942. From the incomplete material available on the case, it is difficult even to conjecture why the board thought this an important matter. Perhaps they did not. What they did decide was that Hynning had lied, and on that basis alone he was dismissed. Fortunately Hynning discovered the situation. After patiently obtaining affidavits that supported his version of the interview, winning the intercession of some influential figures, getting his case aired before the Hennings subcommittee, and persuading the members of the hearings board to ask that the case be reopened, he finally won a reversal from the Treasury.[14]

This case is such a vivid example both of defective procedures and

---

Pacific Northwest Area (1954), pp. 6732–4. The Executive Committee of the AFL-CIO has declared that union leaders who invoke the Fifth Amendment may be deprived of their offices. NYT, Jan. 29, 1957. See NYT, June 11, 1957 (IAM organizers expelled). Cf. the retention of UAW local officers who invoked the privilege, but denied Communist party membership before union trial boards. The UAW Public Review Board upheld this action. NYT, Dec. 27, 1957.

14. See NYT, Jan. 28, 1956; HENNINGS HEARINGS, pp. 691–714.

of the wrongness of hanging a decision on a seemingly minor point of veracity that further comment on it is unnecessary.

An employee is at an even greater disadvantage than was Hynning when the triers resort to a generalized impression that he was "less than candid." This sort of characterization appears in two famous cases—those of Oppenheimer and Davies. It we take the phrase as a polite way of saying that the employee had not told the whole truth, such a judgment leaves the whole case floating in midair unless there is some specification of the matters on which more candor was wanted. Of course, the triers have to judge the credibility of the employee and of any other witness or document with which they are dealing, and it may be that the employee does indeed create an unfavorable impression. Sometimes he is lying; sometimes he is laboring under the confusion, nervousness, and apprehension of being on trial for his job and his reputation, and of having to recall and explain remote events. When the scope of the proceeding is so broad that want of candor in itself becomes a ground for rejection, one can only hope that the triers have some competence in appraising veracity.

Theoretically, the issues are more confined in a loyalty case, and the triers are not free to give decisive effect to vague dissatisfactions with the employee's bearing. They have to decide whether the employee did belong to the League of Women Shoppers, and, if she did, what inferences that permits about her loyalty. They cannot stop short on concluding that the witness, in denying the membership, told an untruth. But unless the triers are astute and experienced, they may do just that. *Falsus in unus, falsus in omnibus* is a misleading maxim. An English barrister, writing about criminal procedure, says "Juries . . . always draw the inference that the prisoner who tells them lies in his evidence is guilty of the crime with which he is charged. It is a very natural inference, but it is not invariably well founded, and it does not follow that, because a man tells lies about where he was on a particular occasion, he ought to be convicted, say, of a murder which he did not commit. Nor is the disposition to tell lies, though [one is] innocent, very exceptional." [15] Here again we have to depend on the sagacity of the trier; but good procedures are of some help in narrowing the issues and in bringing the findings out into the open.

The employee who tells a lie to his employer, though he does not convict himself as disloyal, does of course cast doubt on his fitness for

15. Quoted by Judge Frank dissenting in U.S. v. Grunewald, 233 F. 2d 556, 584 (2d Cir. 1956).

the job. This is in civil service parlance a matter of ordinary suitability, as distinguished from questions of security and loyalty. Even if the employment relationship is quite impersonal, as between the Civil Service Commission and a clerk-typist, the Commission (like any other employer) has an interest in defending the intregrity of its recruiting and reporting procedures. Thus we find, among the Commission's grounds for disqualification, "Intentional false statements or deception or fraud in examination or appointment." More emphatically, the Commission retains power to remove an employee on this ground for an unlimited time, whereas other qualifications are subject to continued investigation (and thus to Commission jurisdiction) for only eighteen months after appointment.[16]

This regulation has resulted in severe procedural entanglements with loyalty and security programs. One possibility, which got the Commission into security cases through a side door, was to seize on inconsistencies between testimony in a security (or loyalty) proceeding and the employee's statements in his original application for employment. The differing forms in use have at one time called on the employee to state whether he was a member of any communist organizations, at another whether he was a member of any organization advocating violent overthrow. Suppose it appears that the employee had been a member of an organization on the Attorney General's list, before the list was promulgated. He answers, "No" to a question about communist organizations. The Commission can say, and has said, that this was a false answer. We then have a little loyalty case, and one subject to no procedural safeguards. Did the employee know that the organization was communist? Should he have? What about the fact that the Attorney General's list has been shifting in its characterizations, and may have carried the organization as "subversive," but not as "communist"? Take another actual case. If the form asked "have you ever been a member of an organization that advocated the overthrow of the United States government by force?", what are we to say about an employee who in 1937, as a Rhodes scholar, was a member of the British Communist party? He answered "No" to the question in the early 1940's, and then in 1955 he was dismissed. He had no recourse but to try to persuade the Civil Service Commission that the British Communist party in 1937 was not seeking to overthrow the American government.[17]

A litigated case illustrates the pitfalls of veracity tests in a three-way

---

16. See *Code Fed. Regs., 5:* § 2.106–7.
17. See NYT (Feb. 6, 1956), p. 7 (case of Kenneth McClaskey).

system with separate procedures for security, loyalty, and suitability. Evelyn Burrell, a clerk-typist in the Department of the Army, was suspended and had a hearing on security charges, under P.L. 733, in 1952. At the same time the Civil Service Commission's Fourth Regional Loyalty Board independently held a loyalty hearing in her case. It found a reasonable doubt about loyalty, and unsuitability as well, because of "false statements concerning material loyalty matters." On appeal to the Loyalty Review Board, the disloyalty finding was reversed, but the Board said that the Commission had confirmed the unsuitability finding, and ordered the Army to dismiss Mrs. Burrell. This it did, without concluding the security case. She then brought suit, contending that the Commission itself had not made a proper finding of unsuitability. The case stalled until September 1955, when the Commission vacated the removal for unsuitability, and returned the case to the Department of the Army for proceedings under E.O. 10450. The Army promptly restored Mrs. Burrell to her earlier status—that is, she was left suspended. The Court of Appeals ruled that the unsuitability discharge had indeed been improperly accomplished, and left Mrs. Burrell to pursue whatever remedies she might have against the Department of the Army. In passing, the court expressed wonder that Mrs. Burrell could have been cleared for loyalty when her denials of most, if not all, of the charges were found to be false. Viewing the case as an example of the actual operation of the loyalty program, one can share the Court's bafflement. But as a matter of logic, there is no inconsistency. So far as the loyalty proceeding was concerned, the charges, even if they were admitted, might not have raised a reasonable doubt about Mrs. Burrell's loyalty. The fact that she denied them, and was disbelieved, adds no weight to the charges themselves. The disbelief does reflect on her suitability. As for the unsuitability ground, it appeared that Mrs. Burrell, in employment applications in 1951–52, had denied present or past membership in communist organizations. The Loyalty Board held that these denials were fatally inconsistent with the fact that in 1949 (apparently in an earlier loyalty proceeding) she had admitted membership in the Washington Bookshop; the Board found that "she was aware of the communist nature of the Washington Bookshop." If the Civil Service Commission had reached the same conclusion through other channels, I suppose there is little doubt of its legal power to order a dismissal. One might think this a drastic penalty; the Washington Bookshop, though communist-controlled, included many innocent "members" who joined to buy ordinary books and phonograph records at a discount and not because of its "communist nature." But the Attorney General had put it on his list; and thereafter a civil servant had no choice but to confess first and explain afterward.

Snarls like the *Burrell* case, by the way, support arguments for a unified federal program combining security, loyalty, and suitability in one proceeding under a single control. It has been implicit in my discussion that I regard this as unfeasible. Each judgment requires different standards, and, to a large extent, different procedures.[18]

Several of the foregoing examples of alleged falsehoods invite doubts about their materiality. There are inexcusable big lies and excusable little lies. Which is which? We might look to the criminal law for guidance. If the verdicts in a number of perjury cases growing out of employment tests are examined, they confirm the expected: that some people have lied about such central issues as Communist party membership. At the opposite extreme, in a recent prosecution growing out of a naturalization proceeding, it was held that the defendant's misstatement of his place of residence was punishable. The minimum levels of materiality that can be found in prosecutions for perjury (or for the companion crime of making false statements to the government to obtain some benefit), do not supply a particularly helpful guideline for an employer trying to distinguish between mortal and venial lies. The twin crimes of perjury and making false statements are necessary supports to a judicial and an administrative structure that are constantly eroded by the falsifications of interested parties. In both areas, if the question was one that the questioner had some plausible reason to ask and the respondent some reason to answer, a false answer can be punished.[19] On the other hand, it is certainly true that many demonstrably false answers go unpunished.

18. Burrell v. Martin, 232 F. 2d 33 (D.C. Cir. 1955); cf. Garvin v. Gillilland, 141 F. Supp. 394 (D.D.C. 1956). On the role which membership in the Washington Bookshop can play in loyalty–security hearings see BONTECOU, pp. 200–1; In Re Hatkin, BNA MANUAL (1956), pp. 19/535–8; the Beatrice Campbell case, JOHNSTON HEARINGS, p. 594. For a discussion of unification of the various types of hearings see BONTECOU, p. 237.

19. Both the perjury (62 Stat. 773, 18 U.S.C. § 1621) and false statement (62 Stat. 749, 18 U.S.C. § 1001) statutes make punishable the deliberate telling of a material falsehood to the government. The falsehood must have been uttered under oath to come within the ambit of the perjury statute, and perjury convictions traditionally require support by the testimony of two witnesses. See *Harvard Law Rev.* (1956), 70:383. Consequently, the false-statement statute is more widely used. On the question of what constitutes "materiality" cf. Freidus

Where should the line be drawn in employment cases? I do not believe that either the theory or the practice of criminal prosecutions for false swearing or false statements tell an employer with any clarity when he should drop a loyalty inquiry because a falsehood has turned up, and then use the falsehood in itself as a ground for dismissal. About all that I can suggest is that the employer should ask himself whether he really thinks the falsehood is material enough to be decisive, or whether he is, perhaps, being hypercritical in order to avoid the pangs of deciding a loyalty question.

The fact that lying under oath is traditionally a serious crime raises a subsidiary question about proper procedures. If, as I have urged, there should be a distinction between grave reasons for dismissal, like disloyalty, and others that are less degrading, like incompetence, with full due process in the first instance but not in the second, where does lying fit? The possibilities are: (1) calling a man a liar characterizes him as immoral; therefore due process is required; (2) although sending a man to jail for lying requires due process, an employer must be free to say, "I think you are a liar; leave my employment." No great stigma results; no elaborate proceeding is necessary; (3) the substance of the lie is determinative: If X's statement, "I am not a Communist," is denounced as a lie and he is dismissed, the necessary conclusion follows that the employer thinks X is a Communist; X should get due

---

v. U.S., 223 F. 2d 598, 601–2 (D.C. Cir. 1955) and Weinstock v. U.S., 231 F. 2d 699 (D.C. Cir. 1956). The naturalization case in the text is U.S. v. Udani, 141 F. Supp. 30 (S.D. Cal. 1956). False statement prosecutions arising directly from employment tests (exclusive of Taft-Hartley oath cases) include the following, all involving denials of Communist party membership unless otherwise noted: Thomas B. Bennett, NYT, Jan. 21, 1955 (acquittal); Emmett A. Carr, NYT, Oct. 2, 1952 (Ku Klux Klan; indictment); De Rosier v. U.S., 218 F. 2d 420 (5th Cir. 1955) (Klan; indictment); Sidney Gallway, NYT, April 7, 1953 (guilty plea); U.S. v. Kitty, FUND DIGEST, p. 88 (conviction; IWO membership); Marzani v. U.S., 168 F. 2d 133 (D.C. Cir. 1948) (conviction of OSS and State Dep't official); U.S. v. Mamber, 127 F. Supp. 925 (D. Mass. 1955) (indictment); Franklin V. Reno, NYT, Feb. 28, 1952 (atomic scientist; guilty plea); Benjamin Smilg, NYT, June 19, 1955 (espionage connection with Harry Gold; acquittal); Wallace Spradling, NYT, Jan. 6, 1952 (guilty plea); Hirsch Touff, NYT, March 5, 6, 1953 (indictment); Sidney Weinbaum, NYT, June 17 and Sept. 8, 1950 (Caltech scientist; convicted). The case of Val Lorwin, which attracted great attention because he was the only person on Senator McCarthy's list to be prosecuted, blew up when a Department of Justice attorney admitted that he had misrepresented the case to the grand jury. Lorwin, an economist, had been accused of lying about Communist party membership in a State Department loyalty hearing. NYT, May 26, 1954.

process; on the other hand, if X is dismissed for lying about his age, the only inference of fact is that he is older or younger than he said he was; no due process is required. Position 3, though complicated, is probably correct.

The discussion so far suggests that the ethics of truth-telling are not so solid as they appear on the surface. There is enough doubt (and perhaps hypocrisy) underneath so that a wide range of employer behavior can win community approval and violate no rule of law. If the employer wants to take an exceedingly stiff attitude toward falsehoods, he may. If he wants to be forgiving, he can be that too. But the caught liar has to petition for forgiveness; he has no rights. However, he may not lack supporters if the lie was remote in time, or about some remote event, or if it was the product of good motives. Two cases will illustrate these points.

In the Oppenheimer case, the decision described as that of the Atomic Energy Commission (each Commissioner, except Chairman Strauss, also contributed a separate statement) laid great stress on the defect of character said to have been conspicuously illustrated in the Chevalier affair. Chevalier, who was a close friend of Oppenheimer's, made a tentative approach to Oppenheimer in 1942 suggesting a channel through which information about the atomic bomb project could be transmitted to our allies the Russians. Oppenheimer spurned the suggestion but was extremely reluctant to disclose it to the counterintelligence officers, and led them seriously astray with what he later described himself as a "cock-and-bull story" about the incident. Oppenheimer, in the hearings, sincerely repented of this folly. His primary motive was reluctance to inform on a friend. This was one of those serious breaches of security where unwillingness to inform was certainly not justifiable, and where the fault was compounded by falsehoods. Oppenheimer's numerous defenders argued that his subsequent record overcame this dereliction, and that it could have been pardoned. The Commission attempted to bolster its case by bringing up other instances of doubtful veracity; but these were equally explicable as slips of memory or as innocent ambiguities of testimony under severe cross-examination. The Chevalier episode was a dramatic example of a remote but grave untruth which sharply separated the stern from the merciful.[20]

20. For specific references to the triviality of other supposed falsehoods during the hearing see the dissenting opinion of Dr. Ward Evans of the hearing board,

The public controversy about Professor Herbert Fuchs of American University was dominated by the notion that he was being punished because he turned informer. This interpretation slights the fact that in his testimony he admitted, in addition to other deceptions, perjury about his communist affiliations in the course of loyalty proceedings in 1948. The administrators of American University knew nothing of this when they employed him in 1949. In 1955 they had to decide whether to let him go on teaching for another one-year term, and the time was approaching when he would have had to be considered for an appointment carrying tenure. How much weight should they have given this admitted false swearing?

One can press the argument for forgiveness to the point of paradox by suggesting that Fuchs, as a Communist, would obviously lie about his membership; this is said to be a standard communist tactic. Is the question then, not whether he lied, but whether he had fully reformed? The paradox occurs in the suggestion that ex-communist liars should be treated more kindly than noncommunist liars. It becomes even more pointed when one considers that most of Fuchs' false statements were made before he left the Communist party in 1946, but not all: there is the false testimony before the loyalty board in 1948. Fuchs' defenders argued that the University's decision lacked the charity that should flow from a Christian institution controlled by the Methodist church.[21] Perhaps; but note that all they could ask was charity. Suppose the perjury had concealed a crime of violence? Or a corrupt official decision? Would the final decision be any different? Should it be?

I have dwelt at some length on these three side issues, with their far-reaching and hard-to-define moral implications. They have arisen so often in loyalty and security matters that it seemed desirable to try to put them in perspective. All that I have urged, in essence, is that informing on others, avoiding Fifth Amendment pleas, and telling the truth should not be a matter of greater insistence in loyalty cases than in other serious disputes about fitness for employment. As things stand, an unproved charge of disloyalty straight away seems to debase the accused in the eyes of many. To redeem himself he has to go beyond proving that

---

AEC, *In the Matter of J. Robert Oppenheimer . . . Documents and Letters* (1954), p. 22; and the dissenting opinion of Commissioner Henry Smyth, p. 66. The opinions of the majority commissioners begin at p. 49.

21. See references in n. 7 above on the Fuchs case. The point about Christian forgiveness was made by Reinhold Niebuhr in a letter dated March 14, 1956, and circulated by the American Committee for Cultural Freedom.

he is loyal; he has to satisfy us that he is a citizen of the most perfect integrity and scruple. I think this is unfair. If, as I believe to be the case, the community generally condones many instances of refusal to inform, some instances of silence on a plea of self-incrimination, and an unknown number of penitent liars, the same standards of condonation should apply in cases where a question of loyalty has arisen to rasp our nerves.

18. Curbing Arbitrary Employment Tests
by Private Employers and Labor Unions

WHEN is a private loyalty test not arbitrary? This is a fair question that must be met. There have been suggestions that private employers ought not to meddle at all in the delicate business of judging loyalty. They do not have the government's facilities for gathering evidence; they are ill-equipped to make quasijudicial determinations. Of most importance, their need to sift the loyalty of their employees is debatable. If the government occupies the security field, as it should, the prevention of acts of disloyalty can be left to the criminal law, and we would all be better off. These same strictures, as they apply to labor unions, will be discussed later in this chapter.

This plausible line of argument does not meet the traditional freedom of a private employer to hire and fire as he will. It also ignores substantial pressures that may make him feel it is necessary to use that freedom.[1]

GOOD AND BAD GROUNDS FOR PRIVATE ACTION

The discussion of the Fifth Amendment problem in the last chapter suggested two reasons that may justify firing an employee who has pleaded possible self-incrimination. Those same reasons apply to the larger issues of disloyalty that lie behind the plea; they can be briefly recalled. First, an employer may defensibly fire (or refuse to hire) if reasonably and in good faith he decides that the job requires some degree of trust and confidence that the employee's communist beliefs or associations have made unattainable. This justification for the em-

1. See Ch. 5 above, p. 134 (industries and industrial trade unions), p. 146 (communications industries). I am much indebted in this chapter to Comment, "Loyalty and Private Employment: The Right of Employers to Discharge Suspected Subversives," *Yale Law Jour.* (1953), *62*:954 (research supported by the Weiss Fund grant to Yale University), and to Harold Horowitz, "Legal Aspects of 'Political Black Listing' in the Entertainment Industry," *Southern Calif. Law Rev.* (1956), *29*:263.

ployer is one that hinges on elusive and subjective states of mind.[2] Still, in some relationships a loss of confidence may reasonably occur. The second defensible ground for dismissal, which is more capable of objective examination, can be applied to an employee who, despite a subversive reputation, is otherwise competent and reliable. That is the threat of economic loss incurred by retaining the employee, if it appears —reasonably again—that the hostility of customers, suppliers, or other employees is such that they would cease to buy, supply, or produce as before. If the sacrifice of the employee is necessary to avert this hostility, then—to the lions. As I said before, an employer in business for profit is not expected to be heroic and to defy the pressures of those with whom he must deal to make a profit. This situation, however, opens up for inquiry the reasonableness of the other parties who make such demands. If, for example, outsiders insist that he hire only white people, or only Negroes, the law can intervene and forbid the employer to engage in racial discrimination, or it can inhibit the activities of those who seek to coerce the employer to discriminate.

Generally, however, the employer is in the clear if he can make a plausible showing that he will suffer economic injury by retaining an employee who deeply offends the community.[3] The directors of an organization not run for profit can take a similar position by demonstrating that its public effectiveness will be impaired if it tolerates communist staff members. The courage of such employers may not be admired, but their prudence can hardly be called into question. If the organization is one that depends on voluntary contributions, its position is little different from that of the business employer; like him, it will suffer economically if it deviates too grossly from community standards in its employment policies.

Some other reasons for firing are not consistent with fair employment policies. First, the private employer has no occasion to become a vigilante. If the employee is doing anything illegal, there are plenty of sedition laws and the like on the books to take care of it. The employer, like anyone else, should report evidence of crime to the authorities; but he should not take it upon himself to substitute for the policeman, or to use

2. That the employer is a corporation does not affect this point. Corporate decisions are made by people.

3. See Burt Manufacturing Co., 21 Labor Arb. 532 (1953). For hostility of other employees as a ground for discharge see Jackson Industries, 9 Labor Arb. 753 (1948); but cf. Worthington Corp. and Republic Steel, Ch. 17 above, n. 11. The arbitrator in Republic Steel points out that the employer can discipline employees who unreasonably refuse to work with a supposed Communist.

his economic power to carry out what he thinks are community preferences. This sort of thing gets altogether too close to the oppression of
the company town, from which the country has just emerged in some
areas, and which, in a more subtle way, the great corporations seem to
be reviving in others.

I would also criticize the announcement of private loyalty tests solely
for the purpose of creating "good public relations." Here there is some
trouble in drawing the line between a response to community pressures,
which may be unavoidable, and the employer's seizing the initiative,
which is entirely avoidable. As Chapter 5 suggested, it is probable that
labor unions have been more eager than employers to declare their all-
out anticommunism, for the reason that unions do feel the need to erase
some public recollections of previous entanglements. Universities and
colleges also have been rather pushing with their protestations, again in
the face of public misunderstanding about the influence of Communists
in teaching. But for a business employer, who after all *is* the capitalist,
the bourgeois, the hated enemy of communism—for him to make a great
play about the loyalty of his employees simply to demonstrate that he is
what he is; this is distasteful. If any more than noise comes from such a
policy, what follows can only be an intrusion by the employer into the
beliefs and associations of his employees, to see if he can find anyone
whose exposure will demonstrate the employer's fidelity to his class.

Existing Restraints: Defamation Actions

The standards that have just been suggested, it should be remembered, are not legal restraints. Such legal restraints as do exist impose
only a slight restriction on the employer's freedom to hire and fire at
will. One restraint is found in the law of defamation, which partially
protects the employee against the employer's impulse to act upon unverified accusations. If the employer makes or repeats a charge that the
employee is a Communist, a Red, a communist sympathizer, or some
other part of the communist spectrum, courts will generally hold that
such an accusation is defamatory. The employer's only certain legal
defense will be to establish that the statements are true. In view of
the difficulties of proving that anyone is a Communist, which have already been discussed in Chapter 16, one would think that loose name-
calling would be exceedingly perilous. But the plaintiff also has a hard
row to hoe. The defendant will attempt to invoke certain technical barriers to liability, some of which will shortly be mentioned. He will cer-

tainly introduce any evidence that has any relevance to the plaintiff's supposed communism. Even if it does not add up to proof that the defamatory accusation is true, a recital of front connections and the like may leave the jury unfavorably disposed toward the plaintiff, so that it will not agree on a verdict, or will award only nominal damages. Any verdict for the plaintiff supposedly helps his good name, but only money pays the heavy expense of carrying such an action through the courts. A hung jury was the result of the protracted 1950 trial in which Larry Adler and Paul Draper sued Mrs. Hester McCullough, a Connecticut housewife who had called them "pro-Communists" and urged that their joint recitals be boycotted. Screen actor Michael Jeffers lost a suit against the Screen Extras Guild after three lengthy trials. On the other hand, a California schoolteacher got a $50,000 judgment against a commentator and his radio station for calling her a "reported Communist or Communist sympathizer," when it turned out that the defendant had no sound basis whatever for his charge; he had inferred it entirely from the plaintiff's membership in the United World Federalists.[4]

Most of the reported defamation cases in this field are against newspapers and other mass media, rarely against an employer. For this there are several probable reasons. The most important is that, while the press must take some risk in reporting the news, only an incautious or splenetic employer need expose himself to a defamation action. After all, if his aim is to get rid of an employee, all he has to do is fire him. Perhaps he has to establish cause in order to satisfy a contract obligation. If he looks hard enough he can often find a less explosive reason that will not invite a lawsuit. So, one effect of the law of defamation is this: if its perils impel an employer to give no reason, or a synthetic one, for a dismissal, the employee may thus escape the damaging communist label; but of course he is still out of a job.

To steer clear of defamatory words is the effective practical way for an employer to steer clear of defamation lawsuits. If he is sued, he may

4. See *Federalist* (Oct. 1953), p. 7. The Jeffers trial results are reported in the *Los Angeles Times,* Feb. 16–17, 1954, first trial, and NYT, Sept. 12, 1954, second; July 20, 1955, third. For the Draper–Adler suit see Ch. 5 above, n. 60. The plaintiff in a defamation action has the burden of proving that the accusation is "of and concerning" him. See discussion by Horowitz (n. 1 above), pp. 280–5. The defendant's defense of truth is usually absolute; ibid., p. 286, and "Developments in the Law—Defamation," *Harvard Law Rev.* (1956), *69*:932. For the scope of "fair comment" as protecting defamatory innuendo see Horowitz, pp. 287–91; *Harvard Law Rev.,* p. 925; and Julian v. American Business Consultants, 2 N.Y. 2d 1, 137 N.E. 2d 1 (1956) (unsuccessful action against publishers of *Red Networks*).

be able to rely on a qualified privilege to communicate adverse information about the employee to other interested employers. Even if he is mistaken, the qualified privilege protects him from liability. The qualification lies in the requirement that his communication must be free of "malice," which means, in this context, that it must not be reckless or spiteful. An illustrative case is *Foltz v. Moore McCormack Lines Inc.,* in which the plaintiff alleged that FBI reports had led to his dismissal from a government job in Korea, and that these reports had their basis in unfounded adverse information given to the FBI by a former employer. The court said that the FBI agents would not be liable for passing on the information to the ECA, but that the former employer would be liable if the plaintiff could prove his allegation that the information was false *and* malicious. As an interesting sidelight, the same plaintiff was later permitted to maintain an action against a newspaper which, in commenting upon his attempt to sue the FBI, reported incorrectly that the adverse information charged plaintiff with being a Communist. The original adverse report had only said (in effect) that he was incompetent and dishonest.[5]

The employer also gets some advantage, according to the New York courts, if he refrains from putting his suspicions in writing. A flimsy but ancient distinction between a written defamation (libel) and an oral one (slander) makes certain words defamatory *per se* if they are written, but if they are conveyed by the supposedly more ephemeral spoken word the plaintiff must allege and prove special damages, such as loss of income, in addition to general injury to his reputation. When the president of a company holding defense contracts said to the chief engineer, "You are a Communist," the highest New York court reached the rather surprising conclusion that this was not slander *per se* and that the plaintiff would have to allege that he had suffered special damages. The Court of Appeals, which did not fully explain its decision, may have been influenced by the reasoning of a lower-court judge who in a similar case observed, "To hold that calling one a Communist is slander [*per se*] would unwittingly trap the unwary, for nothing would please Communists better than to enable them to institute suits for damages promiscuously, regardless of the ultimate outcome." After taking judicial notice of the cold war and of a communist tactic to use the courts "for propaganda purposes," the learned judge concluded, "It is

5. Foltz v. Moore McCormack Lines, Inc., 189 F. 2d 537 (2d Cir. 1951); Foltz v. News Syndicate, 114 F. Supp. 599 (S.D.N.Y. 1953). For the technical definition of "malice," see *Harvard Law Rev.* (n. 5 above), p. 930.

far better, therefore, to allow free play of our emotions in dealing with persons whom we believe to be Communists rather than seal the lips of people who might be frightened into silence and suppression lest use of the word 'communist' should *per se* force upon them costly litigations." [6]

This judicial indulgence for loose denunciation parallels an ingenious protective tactic of the ex-communist informers. From their inner knowledge of communist methods they declare that Communists delight in harassing good people with defamation suits. If one of their targets brings suit, then the fact that he has chosen the only legal means available to clear his name simply strengthens the suggestion that the defendant was justified in accusing him. A survey of the cases brings little objective support to this tricky argument. About the only clear case is that of William Remington, who sued Elizabeth Bentley and won an out-of-court settlement of $10,000. He was later convicted of perjury, partly on the strength of her testimony.[7] It is of course possible that eager exposers of Communists may be oppressed by fears of costly lawsuits. But, as we have already observed, lawsuits are also costly for plaintiffs to finance.

At their best, defamation actions are an indispensable but clumsy device to curb loose tongues. In practice, they are full of pitfalls for either the employee as plaintiff or the employer as defendant. And of course they do not touch the question whether the charges, if true, are a fair ground for dismissal.

Contract Protection

Modern collective bargaining agreements almost universally protect against arbitrary dismissals. The standard provision recites that dismissals should be made only for "cause" or "just cause"; practice varies in specifying what shall constitute cause. If interpretations were left to the

6. Keefe v. O'Brien, 116 N.Y. Supp. 2d 286 (Sup. Ct. 1952). The Court of Appeals case was Gurtler v. Union Parts Manufacturing Co., 1 N.Y. 2d 5, 132 N.E. 2d 889 (1956). For a contrary view, see Joopanenko v. Gavagan, 67 So. 2d 434 (Fla. 1953). The historical distinction between libel and slander is explained in *Harvard Law Rev.* (n. 5 above), p. 887.

7. U.S. v. Remington, 208 F. 2d 567 (2d Cir. 1953); the defamation action is Remington v. Bentley, 88 F. Supp. 166 (S.D.N.Y. 1949) (motion to dismiss denied); NYT, March 1 and June 9, 1950 (settlement). But cf. Fred Cook, "The Remington Tragedy," *The Nation* (Dec. 28, 1957), p. 486. On the alleged tactic see testimony of Louis Budenz before the Senate Comm. on Foreign Relations, [Tydings] Subcomm., Hearings, *State Department Employee Loyalty Investigation* (1950), pp. 513, 539.

employer, arbitrary action might still result; but the effectiveness of a "cause" provision lies in its referral of dismissal cases to grievance procedures established by the contract; those procedures lead usually to a decision by an impartial arbitrator or umpire.

The arbitration cases bearing on disloyalty that have been reported do not fall into any clear pattern. From some of them can be deduced the principles suggested at the beginning of this chapter, that the employer should establish loss of confidence or economic injury before he can justify a discharge for suspected disloyalty. But there are marked divergences in the results of rather similar cases, as with the Fifth Amendment cases.[8]

Though arbitration assures the employee a fair procedure, it is not likely to protect him against anticommunist sentiments shared by both the employer and the union. As Dean Harry Shulman penetratingly wrote:

> A proper conception of the arbitrator's function is basic. He is not a public tribunal imposed upon the parties by superior authority which the parties are obliged to accept. He has no general charter to administer justice for a community which transcends the parties. He is rather part of a system of self-government created by and confined to the parties. He serves their pleasure only, to administer the rule of law established by their collective agreement. They are entitled to demand that, at least on balance, his performance be satisfactory to them, and they can readily dispense with him if it is not.[9]

Nowadays the anticommunist pronouncements of labor unions, especially in the form of barriers to membership, are likely to be every bit as sweeping as those of employers. In some instances the harmony of employers and unions on this issue results in contract provisions that explicitly make subversive advocacy or activity ground for discharge.[10] In others, the union stands aside while the employer thinks up conventional nonloyalty grounds for firing someone who is having loyalty trouble. In either situation, it is not to be expected that collective con-

8. See Yale Comment (n. 1 above) and Benjamin Roberts, "Arbitration and Security Risk Disputes," *Arbitration Journal* (1955), *10* (n.s.):13.

9. Harry Shulman, "Reason, Contract, and Law in Labor Relations," *Harvard Law Rev.* (1955), *68:*1016.

10. See Yale Comment (n. 1 above), pp. 981–2.

tracts will give much protection to the employee who is far out of line. In all their major terms such agreements represent compromise and adjustment of dominant interests; an interest with no strength gets little recognition.

Arbitration usually precludes resort to the courts. In the few cases, such as those of the motion picture writers, where disputes about permissible grounds for abrogating contracts did reach the courts, the range of results has been about the same as in the arbitration cases. The most authoritative court decision, and the least persuasive, is the California case of *Black v. Cutter Laboratories,* which was affirmed by the United States Supreme Court. In this case there seemed to be no dispute that the employee was a Communist, and that she had practiced a variety of deceptions on her employer, including concealment of the fact that she was a graduate of the University of California Law School and a member of the bar. Employed as a clerk-typist, she had been president of her union's local chapter. When she was fired, the arbitrator decided that, though Cutter Laboratories might have had good cause, they had waived it by taking no action until, long after the events that would have justified dismissal, the employee became too obnoxious in her union activities. Cutter went to the courts to have the arbitration award set aside as contrary to law. The California Supreme Court, in a 4–3 decision, apparently held that in California, Communist party membership was a cause for dismissal that could be considered a term of any collective contract, and that it would violate California public policy to construe a collective agreement in any way that would give relief to a communist employee. The implications of the majority decision come close to communist outlawry by judicial fiat. The U. S. Supreme Court confined itself to a narrower ground: if, as a matter of California law, Communist party membership was cause for dismissal, no federal constitutional right of the employee had been violated.[11]

In this case the intemperate character of the California decision is partly explainable by the rare event that the central figure in the case, the underground woman lawyer, was a full-blown Communist—not, as is usually the case, someone who has been or may be a Communist. And the cautious affirmation by the Supreme Court is explainable by its distaste for meeting constitutional issues if they can be avoided. Nevertheless, the California decision stands in marked contrast to the arbitrators'

11. Black v. Cutter Laboratories, 43 Cal. 2d 788, 278 P. 2d 905 (1955), affirmed 351 U.S. 292 (1956).

decisions that have attempted to relate the charges of disloyalty to the circumstances of the particular employment.[12]

The central fact to remember about procedures under collective bargaining agreements is that whatever protection they give is available, generally speaking, only to members of organized labor. Suppose an employee is not represented by a union, as is after all true of the considerable majority of all employees. It is conceivable that he could negotiate a truly individual contract, as distinguished from collective agreements or contracts on standard forms provided by the employer, one that would explicitly protect him against unverified accusations and hasty dismissal. But unless the employee had powerful and unique talents, I should suppose that his mere demand for special safeguards would put an end to negotiations. The practical scope of the employee's "freedom of contract" seems too slight to merit discussion.

PROTECTION AGAINST BLACKLISTS AND BOYCOTTS

Our law takes some account of the probability that the concerted activity of a number of employers may be so oppressive that it overrides each one's privilege to hire and fire at will. If all, or nearly all, of the employers in a particular locality or industry agree, either tacitly or explicitly, not to employ Joe Jones, we say in popular language that Jones has been blacklisted, and he may have a cause of action. As the legal principle is put in the stately language of the *Restatement of Torts,* "Persons who cause harm to another by a concerted refusal in their business to enter into or to continue business relations with him are liable to him for that harm, even though they would not be liable for similar conduct without concert, if their concerted refusal is not justified under the circumstances." [13]

The key word here is "justified." We have little guidance from other fields to tell us what is justifiable in a loyalty context. Is the economic interest of the members of the employers' group enough? In the setting

12. See, e.g., National Food, 7 Amer. Lab. Arb. Awards, par. 69, 895 (1955), where a Pentagon concessionaire was ordered by the Defense Department to fire an employee as a "security risk" on grounds of possible Communist party membership some nine years before. The arbitrator, noting that the employee was not in government employment and had access only to public areas of the Pentagon, ordered reinstatement.

13. Amer. Law Inst., *Restatement of Torts,* § 765(1). See Horowitz (n. 1 above), pp. 267–70; Note, "Tort Liability of Organizations for Intentionally Impairing Economic Relations," *Indiana Law Jour.* (1953), 28:467.

of the antitrust laws, it is not. Combined refusals to buy or sell presumably improve the market position of the members of the combination; yet it is exactly such methods that the antitrust laws condemn. But if we look at the other mainstream of authority, which deals with the privilege of employees to combine—that is, to form unions and go on strike—the law (in modern times) has been quite ready to find justification.[14]

Professor Horowitz suggests that the economic interest of each individual employer may not create sufficient justification for the harm that a blacklist causes. After all, each employer can protect his own interests by exercising his own privilege to hire and fire without constraint. In the motion-picture industry, for example, the producer who decides not to use a particular "controversial" screen writer faces fewer hazards than the one who does use him. If the producer who takes a chance finds that there is no adverse public reaction to the writer and makes a million dollars, that's the reward of risk-taking. This is an appropriate description of what happened with the successful musical "Guys and Dolls." Paramount dropped an option for which it had paid $75,000, because one of the authors, Abe Burrows, was having loyalty troubles. After Burrows had taken steps to clear himself, Samuel Goldwyn took a chance, and produced an artistic and financial success that encountered no political opposition.[15] It would doubtless have been to the interest of timorous Paramount if the movie blacklist had operated to keep anyone else from plucking the fruit it dared not reach. But what about the injury, in that event, to the owners of "Guys and Dolls"? Would not the destruction of the movie rights in their valuable property clearly overbalance whatever justification the combined producers could plausibly bring forward?

Returning to Horowitz' analysis, there seems to be considerable merit in his tentative conclusion that a group interest distinct from the individual interests of the members of the group should be necessary to justify a blacklist. Thus a showing that consumers would stay away from *all* movies if any producer hired Abe Burrows or produced "Guys and Dolls" might be persuasive. Is there also a group interest in purging the industry of people who might be disloyal, because of the support that such a purge gives to public policies aimed at suppressing communism? It seems to me (as it does to Horowitz) that the argument against employers acting as vigilantes applies here. When the law is corrupt or

14. On the applicability of the antitrust laws to employers' concerted refusal to employ particular persons, see Philip Marcus, "Civil Rights and the Anti-Trust Laws," *Univ. of Chicago Law Rev.* (1951), *18*:171.

15. See Ch. 5 above, n. 49.

impotent, vigilantes are sometimes needed. But there is no lack of legal sanctions against Communists.

This analysis has not prevailed in the few cases where an attempt has been made to check concerted employer action. Even if it were accepted by the courts, there would remain a difficult problem of proof. The 1947 Waldorf agreement of the movie producers, that they would not employ Communists, was I think unique in that it was published. More typically, there was certainly no joint announcement of the policy that came to prevail after the 1951 hearings, that the industry would not employ "un-friendly witnesses." In the antitrust field, where the detection of secret combinations has been pursued for half a century, there recently flowered a doctrine of "conscious parallelism" which did away with the necessity for proving actual agreement. But the status of this doctrine is uncertain, and its judicial introduction on either side of loyalty controversies would be a very doubtful blessing.[16]

In any event, the interjection of outside groups into private employ-ment programs often relieves the industry from taking the initiative in compiling a blacklist. This has been notably true in the entertainment field. Such compilations as *Red Channels,* and the activities of such organizations as the American Legion and AWARE, make it possible for employers simultaneously and perhaps spontaneously to accept guid-ance from outside. But where such guidance is reinforced by threats to withdraw patronage from the employer, or to persuade others to with-draw their patronage, the area of possibly illegal boycotts is opened up.

The employee who has been dismissed because his employer has yielded to the requests or demands of third parties has recourse to the rather peculiar tort of unprivileged interference with business relations. Its peculiarity lies in the fact that if *A* induces *B* to dismiss *C, C* may have no cause of action against *B,* who we assume is exercising his privilege to dismiss at will; but *C* does have a *prima facie* case against *A,* simply on the ground that *A*'s interference with his expectation of continued employment by *B* has injured him. As with concerted refusals,

16. An authoritative exposition of the doctrine of "conscious parallelism" is in The Attorney General's National Committee to Study the Anti-Trust Laws, *Report* (1955), pp. 36–42. The 1947 Waldorf agreement is summarized in Ch. 5 above, p. 151. For lawsuits arising out of this agreement see Marcus (n. 16 above), p. 188, n. 94; and Ch. 5 above, pp. 151–2, which also describes the major case that arose from the 1951 hearings, Wilson v. Loew's, 298 P. 2d 152 (Cal. App. 1956), now before the U. S. Supreme Court. On the ineffectiveness of criminal statutes in controlling employer blacklisting see Yale Comment (n. 1 above), p. 961.

A can readily invoke justification. In general terms, the question is whether *A*'s interest in inducing *B* to cease employing *C* overbalances the injury to *C*. The state of the law on this subject is full of uncertainties, and is heavily freighted with problems special to labor union activities. Its application to the problem at hand has been ably analyzed by Horowitz, so that the highlights can be briefly stated by way of a hypothetical case. Suppose that a radio commentator sues AWARE, Inc., alleging that AWARE has published reports of his connections with a variety of Communist-controlled activities, and that these reports have led to his dismissal. Note that he is not suing for defamation; the reports are true. Suppose further that he can prove that AWARE represented to his employer that its members would not listen to this commentator or other programs of the employer; that it would attempt to persuade the general public to do likewise, and that it would invite the attention of sponsors and advertising agencies to the commentator's record, and ask whether they proposed to help support the commentator or his employer. The commentator as a result has lost his job, has not found another one, and has been substantially damaged.[17]

Here we have a whole tangle of inducements to boycott, all brought to bear on the plaintiff, and all instigated by AWARE. What kind of justification can AWARE make? It can say something like this: AWARE is devoted to eradicating communist influences from the air waves. Its members, and anyone else who feels as they do, are quite free not to patronize the commentator, his station, or his sponsors. There may be those who think that it is undesirable for private employers to act as the instruments of an anticommunist crusade; but AWARE thinks differently. It is not suggesting that the employer breach a contract (which would increase its risk of liability), or that he do anything illegal. Furthermore, the only methods that it is using to bring other outsiders to its point of view are those of peaceful persuasion. It has no coercive power; its communications are not triggers to action, as pickets are to union members. They are simply the exercise of free speech, and as such are protected by the First Amendment.

The defense would be likely to succeed in the courts in an action

---

17. On the tort of unprivileged interference with business relations, see Horowitz (n. 1 above), pp. 292–305, and S. C. Oppenheim, *Unfair Trade Practices: Cases* . . . (1950), chs. 13, 14. AWARE has been sued by John Faulk, radio and television entertainer; see NYT, June 19 and July 7, 1956; but the hypothetical case in the text is *not* the Faulk case, because he charged defamation by untrue statements.

against AWARE alone. Suppose the case is broadened by charging concerted action by AWARE, its members, and others who join with them in inducing the station owner to fire the commentator. The same line of justification would probably still be effective. However, as the tactics departed from "peaceful persuasion" and headed toward an organized boycott, the plaintiff's case would be strengthened. So also if the defendant begins to act recklessly, with decreasing regard for any approved community interest. Suppose a plaintiff can establish that the group that brought about his dismissal is really antisemitic and that anticommunism is a secondary motivation. His case looks better. It should improve also if the charges depend so much on peripheral and innocent communist connections that the defendant begins to look less like a crusader and more like a busybody. However, no such suits, so far as I know, have been successfully carried through. There is a great deal of community tolerance, and therefore of judicial tolerance, for the aims of the proclaimed anticommunist. And, as a more enduring obstacle, the First Amendment argument may be decisive. Freedom of speech belongs to the right as much as to the left, to the attacker as well as to the attacked.[18]

GOVERNMENT RESTRAINTS, ACTUAL OR POTENTIAL

What has been said about existing private remedies for arbitrary loyalty discharges shows that these remedies offer only partial and un-

18. The noneconomic boycott cases involving a claim of First Amendment rights have been a distinct exception to the normal tort doctrine. Thus in Watch Tower Bible and Tract Society v. Dougherty, 337 Pa. 286, 11 A. 2d 147 (1940), the defendants were held not to have committed an actionable wrong by successfully demanding, under threat of patronage withdrawal, that a department store's radio station refuse to permit future broadcasts by Jehovah's Witnesses. And in Lawton v. Murray, 61 N.Y.S. 2d 721 (Sup. Ct. 1946), the NAACP and other groups were allowed to picket *Uncle Tom's Cabin*. The court in American Mercury, Inc. v. Chase, 13 F. 2d 224 (D. Mass. 1926), enjoined the Boston Watch and Ward Society's intimidation of book sellers, but only because of the means which the Society employed to express its views on the merits of the books involved. An injunction was granted also in Council of Defense of New Mexico v. International Magazine Co., 267 F. 390 (8th Cir. 1920), where intense semi-official pressures were applied because of a belief that the Magazine Company's majority stockholder (W. R. Hearst) had expressed pro-German views during World War I. But a "neutral" victim of the picketing, e.g. a theater owner, may be able to enjoin picketing which impairs his business opportunities. See references in n. 17 above. A strong statement of the First Amendment privilege of the anti-Communist is made in the Julian defamation case, n. 4 above.

satisfactory solutions.[19] The current armory of either court-made or statute law offers only one other path worth exploring. About half of the states have statutes which, in one way or another, declare a public policy against employer interference with the political preferences or activities of employees. One of the broadest of these is a California law which was invoked by a group of Lockheed Aircraft employees who were dismissed because the employer suspected their loyalty. The statute said that "No employer shall make, adopt, or enforce any rule, regulation or policy . . . controlling or directing, or tending to control or direct the political activities or affiliations of employees." The California Supreme Court upheld the constitutionality of this statute, while making the now-familiar distinction between advocacy of violent overthrow on the one hand, and, on the other, what it considered legitimate political activity. It held the former not to be protected by the statute. This is what one would expect from a cold-war court asked to characterize communist affiliations as "political activity." Judges would probably say, with some reason, that such statutes are designed to protect the normal electoral process, and the secrecy of the ballot, from employer interference. If the activity in question is a revolutionary one, and therefore illegal, neither employers nor courts are bound to respect it. However, illegal activity could be put to one side, and such a statute would still be applicable to the great mass of trouble cases that rest on suspicion, remote associations, and so on.[20]

Here then is more than a faint path. Statutory sanctions against employer interference with employees' politics seem to open up a promising avenue, already staked out. The *Lockheed* case does leave one roadblock; language in the opinion suggests that loyalty might have to be "established to the satisfaction of the employer." Another obstacle is the remedial inadequacy of most existing statutes. They are penal only, and thus depend on the initiative of prosecuting attorneys. The California

19. Two other possibilities should be mentioned. The Taft-Hartley Act was designed to limit an employer's right to discharge where there is a union security agreement. For an appraisal of the slight effect of this provision, in a loyalty context, see Ch. 5 above, p. 142, quoting Yale Comment (n. 1 above), p. 966–7. A highly theoretical limitation may arise also under the Federal Civil Rights Acts, as pointed out in Yale Comment, pp. 968–9.

20. The California statute (Labor Code § 1101), Lockheed Aircraft Corp. v. Superior Court of Los Angeles County, 28 Cal. 2d 481, 171 P. 2d 21 (1946), and other such statutes are discussed in Yale Comment (n. 1 above), pp. 959–60; see Note, *Calif. Law Rev.* (1947), *35*:310, on the constitutionality of the statute. Labor Code § 1102 explicitly prohibits "Threat of discharge or loss of employment" as a means of political coercion.

court did hold that a civil remedy was to be implied from the statute, but conventional money damages are often an unsatisfactory remedy too.

If we want to know what is needed for effective machinery to control arbitrary or discriminatory employment practices, we should look at the labor relations acts, notably the Wagner Act (and its successor, Taft-Hartley), and at the state fair employment practices legislation.

The Wagner Act, and the little Wagner Acts in the states, created administrative machinery to enforce the new national policy of encouraging labor organizations. It also created a particularly potent remedy for individuals injured by anti-union discrimination in the form of reinstatement orders sweetened with back-pay awards. Back-pay awards bear some kinship to common-law damages; but the vital difference is that the employee does not have the burden of carrying a lawsuit through the courts. The administrative agency, once it has found illegal discrimination, acts as his champion. Reinstatement orders have become routine in the labor-relations field, and the courts, assisting the administrative agency with enforcement orders, have become accustomed to a new remedy. Reinstatement, though not beyond the independent powers of courts of equity, has not in the past been part of their traditional practice. Now there should be less hesitation in using it.[21]

The fair employment practices acts, found in about a fourth of the states, condemn employment discrimination based on race or creed. Perhaps because the policies they seek to advance are more controversial than the fostering of collective bargaining, these statutes are by and large less vigorous in their application of remedies. Persuasion and mediation become the central theme. An order to refrain from future discrimination is conventional, but this sanction does not have the same sharp edge as does an order redressing the injury done to a named individual.

There is another noteworthy difference between the correction of discrimination against union members and discrimination against a race. The NLRB cases usually involve dismissals; the fair employment practice cases are more likely to concern applicants. A prejudiced employer does not fire Negroes, he simply does not hire them. This difference increases the difficulty of proof, and makes the status of the individual complainant ambiguous.

21. Courts also order reinstatement to union membership in cases of improper expulsion; see Clyde Summers, "Legal Limitations on Union Discipline," *Harvard Law Rev.* (1951), *64*:1093. See Comment, "The Statutory Injunction as an Enforcement Weapon of Federal Agencies," *Yale Law Jour.* (1948), *57*:1023. The extent of the NLRB's use of reinstatement and back-pay awards is shown, e.g., in its *Annual Report . . . 1954* (1955), pp. 1–2.

The primary lesson to be learned from a comparison of union-member discrimination, racial or religious discrimination, and political discrimination, is not the importance of sharp remedies. It is rather, I think, the unreality of talking about statutory remedies and administrative machinery at all until there is public support for the policies they are intended to advance. The Wagner Act was bitterly opposed by employers, but it had the support of an immensely popular national administration, and of its beneficiaries, the rising labor movement. Outside groups brought no serious pressures to bear on employers who complied with NLRB orders. As Walter Gellhorn observes, "no order of the NLRB ever ended a going business." [22] The fair employment practice acts met a more sullen resistance, but it was largely passive and unorganized. In the northern states where most of these statutes were enacted, few people defended openly the desirability of discriminating against Negroes, Jews, or Catholics.

In recent years, on the other hand, there has been wide support for the proposition that employers were performing a public service if they refused to employ people associated in varying degrees with communism. This support has been reinforced by threats of boycott against employers who were slow to perceive their patriotic opportunities. We do not know, and need not assume, that these pressures would be maintained if the employer was under a legal duty to resist them. The obvious fact remains, however, that both official and private sentiment has run in the opposite direction from the proposals here under discussion. Moreover, a government that has itself pressed loyalty and security measures to extreme lengths is an unlikely guardian for the interests of private employees.

A more emphatic approach to the problem has, however, been suggested by A. A. Berle in his lectures entitled *The 20th Century Capitalist Revolution*. It deserves attention. Building on the proposition that great corporations exert powers similar in mass and thrust to the powers of government, Berle argues that they should therefore observe some of the limitations of government, notably the obligation to extend due process of law before depriving an employee of liberty and property. The great corporations control such wide areas of employment that exclusion by any one of them, especially on loyalty grounds, is a substantial deprivation, either of the liberty to work or of the ability to earn income. The

22. *Individual Freedom and Governmental Restraints* (Louisiana State Univ. Press, 1956), p. 28. See Note, "The Operation of State Fair Employment Practices Commissions," *Harvard Law Rev.* (1955), *68*:685.

corporation should therefore establish internal tribunals to meet "the essential requirement . . . that the facts justifying proscription be established." Berle boldly expresses a "belief that such finding, when made, can be reviewed in a federal court," and even more boldly calls for the invention of an alternative remedy, a "writ, directing a corporation to show cause why a man has been declared unemployable." [23]

These proposals are directed at procedural due process and scarcely touch the matter of standards. Indeed, it is not clear from Berle's brief essay whether he intends his judicial remedies to be confined to political cases or whether he means to extend them to all denials of employment. If the latter is intended, it would be a remarkable encroachment on the employer's prerogative to hire and fire. Also, Berle takes no account of the grievance procedures for unionized employees that have already been considered. However, by this omission he helps to emphasize the seeming helplessness of the unorganized white-collar people, minor executives, and the like.

One may ask, do the unorganized groups need judicial protection, or do they only need to organize? Collective bargaining agreements make provision against most kinds of arbitrary action, and could equally provide against political dismissals, if the employees felt strongly enough about them. One probable reason why the white-collar echelons, especially in large companies, do not band together for self-help is that they are reasonably satisfied. The prosperous concern does offer them a species of tenure. This tenure has no contract guarantee and no legal status; it is rather an outgrowth of paternalism, public relations, and a short labor supply. But it is real enough so that unobtrusive mediocrity will rarely be disturbed.

Neither unions nor paternalism, however, protect the nonconformist. The man who is way out on a political limb gets no help—from contract, from his fellow servants, or from the public. I do not think his situation is any different whether he works for a mammoth corporation or a mi-

23. A. A. Berle, Jr., *The 20th Century Capitalist Revolution* (New York, Harcourt, Brace, 1954), pp. 102–9. Berle attaches considerable weight to Marsh v. Alabama, 326 U.S. 501 (1945), as supporting his argument for corporate due process. There the Supreme Court held that where a corporation owned a town, the state of Alabama could not, by way of a prosecution for trespass, aid the corporation in restricting the "fundamental liberties" of the town's citizens with respect to religious proselytizing on the sidewalks. Cf. Public Utilities Commission v. Pollak, 343 U.S. 451 (1952), where the Court declined to hold that a bus company which was inflicting commercial broadcasts on its customers was subject to a First Amendment challenge because of its governmental franchise.

nute one. In emphasizing the duty of the large corporation rather than the political rights of the small employee, Berle makes us draw a difficult line, and he leaves too much on the unprotected side of the line.

It seems to me that the problem is best looked at from the employee's standpoint. Rather than mold a novel remedy that has its sole foundation in the special obligations of big corporations, we might revert to the aim of the California statute. With its counterparts in other states, this statute stems from a familiar thesis: there is a public interest in the free operation of the political process, which government can help to advance. If some employers try to use their economic leverage to influence. voting, restraints are appropriate. After all, the secret ballot itself is a safeguard against such coercion. Some states have gone so far in attempting to remove any economic detriment from voting that they require employers to give time off with pay on election day. To my mind this particular device is indefensible; but it shows the reach of state power.[24] It is far milder to say that government may restrain employer discrimination against lawful political activities. This does not open up the whole employment relationship to state control, as the Berle proposals seem to do. Like the prevention of discrimination against union members and racial and religious minorities, it condemns a single type of discrimination that is harmful to a democratic society.

Criminally punishable political activities could not and should not have the protection of such a statute; but all lawful exercise of political freedoms could claim its aid. If fairly enforced, a statute like California's would curb the rank profusion of loyalty dismissals that are not well-rooted in satisfactory evidence of communist or other rebellious wrongdoing. How can fair enforcement be attained? I have already suggested that individual redress, in the form of restitution and reinstatement, is far more effective than the uncertain impact of a penal statute. These new remedies have been developed in the practice of administrative agencies. Does this mean that we have to create another cluster of boards and bureaus, for what may be a minor problem? We do not. It is quite possible to equip courts with the remedial powers that seem desirable. Courts are already well equipped to make the determinations of fact and motive that these cases raise. No special expertness is required here, just a technique for getting toward the bottom of things, which is what courts have been trying to do for several hundred years. There is no

24. In Day-Brite Lighting, Inc. v. Missouri, 342 U.S. 421 (1952), the Supreme Court upheld the constitutionality of a Missouri statute which required employers to pay employees for time taken (up to four hours) in voting.

denying that these would be hard cases for the employee to prove; it might be reasonable to require the employer to come forward with his explanation of the dismissal, while leaving the over-all burden of persuasion on the employee. The employer could still justify a political firing if he showed that the employee's views or activities destroyed a necessary relationship of confidence. That is, a Republican publisher should not have to keep a Democratic editorial writer; but the politics of a typesetter should be none of his business. However, outside pressures would no longer serve as an excuse; for if the employee is privileged to hold extreme (but lawful) political views without suffering discrimination in employment, outsiders would not be privileged to interfere with the employment. Neither the First Amendment nor any other interest palliate a boycott intended to compel an employer to discriminate illegally.[25] The effect of this statute in damping boycotts could be as important as its direct restraint on the employer.

The trouble with these proposals is not in making them workable, but in making them acceptable. Consider the entertainment industries, for example. We need to know whether public disfavor against show people with left-wing records is fact or illusion. If it is more than a froth whipped up by pressure groups, how intense is this feeling? If deep animosities do exist, stiffening the legal remedies against boycotts will not dispel them or their effects. A new law will be futile unless there is some willingness to comply with it. On the other hand, legislatures can and sometimes do rise just a little bit above the emotions of the community, just as they can and do sink beneath them, and sometimes they can stir the community conscience to have done with ill-tempered injustice.[26]

25. Thus, in Giboney v. Empire Storage and Ice Co., 336 U.S. 490 (1949), and subsequent cases the Supreme Court has held that picketing was not protected when used to accomplish an unlawful purpose. See Francis Jones, "Free Speech: Pickets on the Grass, Alas! Amidst Confusion, a Consistent Principle," *Southern Calif. Law Rev.* (1956), *29*:137. A distinction must be drawn here between organized pressure, which may become unlawful, and a simple spontaneous refusal of public acceptance. In the case of an entertainer, public aversion or even indifference are fatal. *If it is a fact* that a performer's rating will decline because he flaunts obnoxious views, or she leaves her husband, then the sponsor does not have to shoulder this burden. Sidney Hook discusses this point perceptively in his review of John Cogley, *Report on Blacklisting*, NYT, *Book Review* (July 22, 1956), p. 6.

26. The proposed statute would be difficult to administer except where the employment relationship already existed. About all that I can suggest in behalf of the applicant for private employment who thinks he is being discriminated against on false loyalty or other political grounds is that he take what steps he can to clear his dossier; see Ch. 12 above, p. 304.

RESTRAINTS ON LABOR UNION PRACTICES

Political restrictions on union membership invite inquiry into the state of democracy within the labor movement, a controversial and engrossing subject, but one far broader in its reach than a concern with discrimination by unions as it affects employment opportunities. These effects, as was pointed out in Chapter 5, are a function of union strength. The prevalence of the closed shop and the union shop determine whether union membership is a condition of employment; and the legitimacy of these institutions is also a battleground, with the lines obscured by smoke and confusion. Without venturing onto it, I will proceed from this innocuous premise: If, either formally or informally, a denial of union membership is a barrier to employment in a given trade and locality, then arbitrary standards and procedures within a union are as harmful as they are within a corporation.[27]

The injuries which a union may suffer from communist members are of a somewhat different order from those to which an employer is exposed. Whatever malign intentions a communist employee may have toward the management of General Electric, he has no immediate expectation of supplanting it. Yet it was only yesterday that persons widely believed to be Communists did control the largest union with which G.E. bargained. We have earlier reviewed the decline of communist influence in unions, and need not recall the low state to which it has fallen. Communists do still aspire to positions of influence in labor unions. But with the exception of those remnants still under some degree of communist control, organized labor in all its branches is now thoroughly hostile to communist trade unionism. In addition to the disillusion fully justified by thirty-five years of internecine strife, unions feel the weight of public policies that now make any toleration of communist leadership almost unthinkable. The Taft-Hartley oath bars unions with such leaders from access to the National Labor Relations Board; the 1954 amendments to the Internal Security Act impose new disabilities on a union found to be "Communist-infiltrated." Less tangible but no less real is the low degree of public esteem and support that await a union which has not rid itself of communist leadership.

27. On union membership and employment opportunities see Philip Taft, *The Structure and Government of Labor Unions* (1954); Joel Seidman, *Union Rights and Union Duties* (1943); Richard Witmer, "Civil Liberties and the Trade Union," *Yale Law Jour.* (1941), 50:621; ACLU, *Democracy in Labor Unions* (1952). On the closed shop and "right to work" laws see Columbia Univ. Academy of Political Science, *Proceedings* (May 1954), No. 1.

These considerations seem sufficient to support union policies that bar identifiable Communists from office or staff positions. It is sometimes argued that union members should be free to defy public policy and opinion if they want a communist officer; but it seems to me that the membership should be equally free to decide in advance, by way of properly adopted bylaws or constitutional provisions, to forego this particular privilege.[28]

But this is not the same as saying that it is proper to bar people on loyalty grounds from membership in the union—particularly if membership is a condition of employment. Of course there is no total cleavage between officers and the rank and file. The officers are not a permanent élite (though they sometimes seem to be). Especially among the minor officers there is considerable replacement by recruits from the membership. This consideration still does not create a compelling reason for blanket exclusion of Communists or other subversive persons from simple union membership. If a member's activity in union affairs turns out to be misdirected toward communist aims rather than toward the proper concerns of the union, the leaders have ample disciplinary powers. In fact complaint is often made, by serious as well as syndicated critics of the labor movement, that opposition to established union policies is too often not tolerated at all, let alone allowed to flourish. When Cecil B. DeMille, as a member of the American Federation of Radio Artists, refused to pay a one-dollar assessment for funds to oppose legislation outlawing the closed shop, he was suspended, and the courts upheld the suspension. When one Pfoh publicly supported Wendell Willkie in 1940 after his brothers in the Railway Trainmen had decided to support Roosevelt, he was expelled; and this action too was upheld. If such deviations as these can be made the basis for severe discipline, surely any communist behavior that went counter to established policies of a labor union could be punished.[29]

28. For a statement justifying the barring of "Communists and other totalitarians" from union office, but not membership, see ACLU, Press Release dated May 24, 1951. See also Dakchoylous v. Ernst, 33 Lab. Rel. Ref. Man. 2301 (1953), and Garcia v. Ernst, 27 Lab. Rel. Ref. Man. 2497 (1951). Communists could also reasonably be barred from responsible staff positions, e.g. as organizers, within the union.

29. For a description of political barriers to membership and union repression of dissidents see Clyde Summers, "Disciplinary Powers of Unions," *Ind. and Lab. Rel. Rev.* (1950), *3*:483, esp. 498–504, and Summers (n. 21 above), pp. 1068–72. See DeMille v. Am. Fed. of Radio Artists, 175 P. 2d 851 (Cal. App. 1946); Pfoh v. Whitney, 62 N.E. 2d 744 (Ohio App. 1945). But cf. Morgan v. Local 1150, 16 Lab. Rel. Ref. Man. 720 (Ill. Sup. Ct., 1945), reversed on other grounds 72

Yet unions with a total membership of 6,000,000 have erected political barriers to membership, mostly directed at Communists, sometimes at right-wing extremists as well. Some of these provisions have been cited in Chapter 5. Another illustrative example is taken from the constitution of the AFL Brotherhood of Painters, Decorators, and Paperhangers. Its present form was adopted in 1941:

> Any member who associates himself with any organization or group that expounds or promotes any doctrine or philosophy inimical or subversive of the fundamental principles and institutions of the government of the United States or the Dominion of Canada, the American Federation of Labor, or of this Brotherhood shall be granted a hearing by the local and, if found guilty, shall be disciplined in the manner provided for in this constitution. The German American Bund, the Nazi party, the Fascist party, the Communist party and organizations which subscribe to the doctrine of the foregoing, shall be conclusively presumed to be organizations within the condemnation of the foregoing section . . .

A many-pronged attack on the validity of the provision just quoted was rebuffed by a New York court in 1950. It is questionable whether any court would reach a different conclusion, unless there was a tremendous shift in the general attitude toward communism. The burden on the member attacking such a provision is increased by the traditional judicial stance that regards unions as voluntary associations, with the same freedom to select their members as is enjoyed by clubs, lodges and churches. Though this nonchalant misdescription is meeting some challenges, notably with respect to racial discrimination and occasionally in recognition of the monopolistic powers of closed unions, it is still a massive cliché for a court to rest on if it wants to deflect troublesome issues.[30]

N.E. 2d 59 (Ill. App. 1946), and Spayd v. Ringing Rock Lodge No. 665, 270 Pa. 67, 113 A. 70 (1921) (dissident members upheld).

30. § 107 of the Painters and Decorators constitution is quoted in the case discussed, Weinstock v. Ladisky, 98 N.Y.S. 2d 85 (1950). The classic "voluntary association" argument was criticized in Zechariah Chafee, "The Internal Affairs of Associations Not for Profit," *Harvard Law Rev.* (1930), *43*:993. Some Fair Employment Practice Acts forbid racial discrimination as a ground for denial of membership; see Morris Forkosch, "Internal Affairs of Unions," *Univ. of Chicago Law Rev.* (1951), *18*:729. There has been very little judicial recognition of the effective monopoly position which a closed shop agreement may give a union; but see Seligman v. Toledo Motion Picture Operators Union, 98 N.E. 2d 54 (Ohio App. 1947).

At present, about all that can be done is to watch the application of these barriers to membership, and to curb their loose extension. Since identifiable Communists have flourished in organized labor, it may be that the facts would support most of the expulsions that have occurred in recent years. The great danger to the political and employment rights of trade unionists lies in the extension of political tests to remote or conjectured communist associations. Union constitutions, like the one just quoted, are often distressingly vague in their proscriptions.

In summary, the prevalence of anti-communist tests for union membership, some of long standing, some an outgrowth of currently fashionable public relations policies, is understandable. Even when they were out of power, Communists have been an exasperating and a divisive force. But these blanket exclusionary policies are not essential for union health, because union powers to discipline members for any overt behavior contrary to union interest are so far-reaching.

LABOR UNION DISCIPLINARY PROCEDURES

Both the power to exclude for bad associations and the power to discipline for bad activity can be kept in bounds by good procedures. The attainment of orderly procedures in union expulsion cases should be easier than the creation of similar procedures for dismissals from private employment. The relationship of employer to employee is still strongly marked in law by the status relationship of master and servant, and by the spurious equality of freedom of contract. Both status and contract march, in this instance, toward the same result: the employer has a freedom to fire, balanced by the employee's freedom to quit. The law views a labor union member, however, as nobody's servant; he is a member of a voluntary association, in which his rights are determined by a fictional contract among all the members to abide by the provisions of the constitution and bylaws. There is a fraternal flavor about the formal structure of a union (do not the members still address one another as "Brother"?); and that survival, reinforced by the economic realities of union membership, makes it important that the union constitution afford a seemly appearance of fair procedure before an erring brother is expelled. Many do; but, inconsistently, some constitutions permit baldly arbitrary procedures; and others are ominously silent. Internal procedures, however, are not the last resort. The expelled member can invoke the contract relationship to obtain review by the courts. With the support of principles of "natural justice" (a term derived from

English cases, and close enough, for present purposes, to due process of law) the courts may require the union to grant a hearing.[31]

A theoretical framework for orderly procedures, then, is already part of the organizational structure of most labor unions, and can perhaps be imposed where it is lacking. There are, however, three flawed areas in the structure. First, there is the chronic problem of the applicant, in this case the person who is denied admission to a labor union. He usually has no access to whatever hearing arrangements are provided, nor to judicial relief. Most of the discussion of exclusion from union membership has derived from economic rather than political restrictions, and on the economic front some concessions have been extracted. Under the Taft-Hartley Act, if the union has the benefits of a union security agreement, it may still refuse to accept an employee as a member; but if the employee is willing to pay dues, the employer cannot dismiss him. Thus, exclusionary union policies may deprive the employee of participation in union affairs, but they cannot prevent his employment. We have already seen, however, that this provision has been ineffective in a loyalty context; for if the employer independently agrees with the union that the man is a bad egg politically, he can fire him (or decline to hire him) without being guilty of an unfair labor practice under the Act.[32]

The second and major flaw is that union internal remedies are often, in practice, inadequate. Critics say that charges are loose and vague; they go on to indict the adequacy and integrity of the hearing tribunals and the review procedures in many unions. In essence the objection seems to be that some union leaders use expulsion procedures as a weapon against their opponents in struggles for power. The bringing of charges means that the leadership has determined to rid itself of a troublesome character, and any formal proceedings that follow are blighted by the prejudgment of those who control the machinery and exercise the reviewing function.

These criticisms go far beyond the narrow realm of political tests, and labor experts are divided about the extent of the evil and the remedies for it. There are proponents of (1) internal reform, (2) voluntary creation by unions of impartial outside tribunals, (3) access to the

31. The pioneering paper on union discipline within the bounds of good procedure is Witmer, n. 27 above. See also Summers (n. 21 above), p. 1054.

32. See Ch. 5 above, p. 142. On the general practice of admission to unions see Summers, "The Right to Join a Union," *Columbia Law Rev.* (1947), 47:33, and Walter Daykin, "Union Security under Taft-Hartley," *Labor Law Jour.* (1951), 2:659.

NLRB or other administrative tribunals, and (4) more decisive judicial intervention.[33]

The third major flaw in the structure of due process in unions is the erratic and indecisive operation of judicial review. It may be that review by the courts should be narrowly limited, as an unfriendly intrusion on union affairs. But most commentators think it should be strengthened and rationalized. Judges are initially reluctant to intervene in the internal affairs of unions; they have learned a lesson from futile attempts to settle religious schisms and squabbles among lodge members. But this caution should be carried no further than to assure that an appeal to the courts is not premature, and that available remedies within the union have been pursued. To go on treating powerful unions as if they were private clubs, as conventional doctrine does, mistakes the character of the modern union. Membership in a union (most pointedly for our purposes) is often a gateway to making a living; through welfare funds, and the like, membership may also confer direct money benefits. Indeed, the union is "a government—an economic government." The courts are of course not oblivious to these realities, and they have already, within the confines of voluntary association doctrines, imposed some rules of order in the name of "natural justice." What the most persuasive students of the labor movement say is that they should go a little further, in striking down vague charges, sniffing out bias, and protecting harried members pending the resolution of a case. The judicial remedies are already adequate once the judges decide to act; reinstatement is supplemented with damages. What is needed is a little firmness.[34]

33. The suggested reforms, in order as they appear in the text, may be found in: (1) Lloyd Reynolds, "Postwar Labor Relations—Discussion," *Am. Econ. Rev.* (1946), *36:* Part 2, p. 383. (2) Philip Taft, "Democracy in Trade Unions," ibid., p. 369; ACLU, *Democracy in Labor Unions* (1952). (3) ACLU, *Democracy in Trade Unions* (1943), pp. 83–4. A middle ground is taken in Jerre Williams, "The Political Liberties of Labor Union Members," *Texas Law Rev.* (1954), *32:*826, which would have the NLRB intervene only when a union has failed to provide adequate procedures. (4) Summers, ibid. (1955), *33:*603, and the sources cited by Williams at p. 835. The Upholsters Union has an independent tribunal; so has the United Automobile Workers.

34. The argument for limiting court review is made in Herbert Thatcher, "Shall We Have More Regulation of the Internal Affairs of Labor Unions?" *Lawyers Guild Rev.* (1947), *7:*14. The characterization of the union as an "economic government" is from Williams (n. 33 above), p. 832. On the adequacy of judicial remedies see Summers, nn. 21 and 33 above. Cf. Comment, "Exhaustion of Remedies in Private, Voluntary Organizations," *Yale Law Jour.* (1956), *65:*369.

Extending Judicial Review:
The "State Action" Concept

This sounds generally plausible, for the improvement of existing institutions is usually easier than the creation of new ones. The question remains, by what standards will the courts decide troubling borderline cases? If the supervision of union procedures were entrusted to the executive branch of the government, or to an administrative commission, legislation would have to set down the standards. Legislative efforts so far have been quite futile.[35] If, alternatively, the courts are to extend their control, how will they define the boundaries of "natural justice"? One approach is to use the constitutional rights of the individual against the government as a persuasive analogy—a sort of checklist—in setting down the members' rights against the lesser government of the union. This has the advantage of flexibility, because an analogy can be abandoned if it becomes oppressive; but for that very reason the use of analogies creates uncertainties.

A more decisive way of laying down constitutional imperatives has recently been given countenance by the Supreme Court. It has long been settled that due process of law and other constitutional limitations (such as those of the First Amendment) are binding only on governments, not on private citizens. But, the Supreme Court has ruled, if the courts are asked to enforce a private agreement that discriminates in a way forbidden to government, then the decree of the court is "state action," and may not be used to enforce such a discrimination. This proposition was applied in *Shelley v. Kraemer* [36] to refuse enforcement of racial restrictions in real estate deeds. But such a rule does not control bad practices where the employer (or the union) can enforce them without resort to litigation. The invocation of state action so far has had the effect of requiring judicial inaction; it does not provide affirmative relief for the injured employee or union member.

However, the Court has begun to grasp another lever for finding "state action" in labor union cases, and for extending the reach of the doctrine. Justice Douglas described this device succinctly in his dissent in *Black v. Cutter:* "Employers can, of course, hire whom they choose, arranging for an all-Democratic labor force if they desire. A union has no such liberty if it operates with the sanction of the state or the federal

35. See Summers (n. 21 above), pp. 1097–9.
36. 334 U.S. 1 (1947).

government behind it. It is then the agency by which governmental policy is expressed and may not make discriminations that the government may not make." [37] A few weeks earlier Justice Douglas, writing for a unanimous Court, had advanced similar ideas in upholding the union-shop provisions of the Railway Labor Act. "The enactment of the federal statute authorizing the union shop agreements," he wrote, "is the governmental action on which the Constitution operates, though it takes a private agreement to invoke the federal sanction." Here Congressional authorization of a union shop was essential to its existence; otherwise the "right-to-work" laws of Nebraska, where the case arose, outlawed both the closed shop and the union shop. However, the Court found no constitutional guarantees violated in the case that was before it, because the only condition of membership involved was the payment of dues. "If other conditions are in fact imposed," the Court warned, "or if the exaction of dues . . . is used as a cover for forcing ideological conformity or other action in contravention of the First Amendment, this judgment will not prejudice the decision in that case." [38]

This new concept of state action is at once inviting and troubling. If one would prefer to see labor unions under a legal obligation to grant due process and to refrain from discrimination that infringes on rights guaranteed by the First Amendment, then a theory that makes unions arms of the state, so far as compliance with constitutional limitations is concerned, looks inviting. It is especially inviting, one might observe, to Justices of the Supreme Court who could otherwise exert little influence over union democracy, because the cases would not raise constitutional issues within their jurisdiction. The disquieting considerations are these. First, how much, or how little, "federal sanction" makes union action state action? Does federal regulation of unions under the National Labor Relations Board compel all unions in interstate commerce to meet constitutional standards of fair dealing? Does the fact that the states through the police power regulate many aspects of union

37. I have blended text and footnote here. The second and third sentences are in a footnote, but I think it is clear that in this instance smaller print does not signify smaller importance. The text goes on to say, citing Shelley v. Kraemer, "But the courts may not be implicated in such a discriminatory scheme. Once the courts put their imprimatur on such a contract, government, speaking through the judicial branch, acts." 351 U.S. 302 (1956).

38. Railway Employees' Department v. Hanson, 351 U.S. 225, 232, 238 (1956). A number of anticommunist provisions from union constitutions are quoted in n. 8 of the opinion.

policy make all other unions also responsive to constitutional prohibitions? Do not corporate business enterprises (which means most firms of consequence) operate with the sanction of the state government, in that without a state charter they would have no legal existence? If not all enterprises, then certainly regulated ones? What about licensed occupations? What is left of the old doctrine that constitutions confine only the government, not the people? [39]

Why should anything be left of the old doctrine, one may ask, so long as we are dealing with such beneficent ideals as due process and equality? It is significant that the "state action" theory has been pressed hardest against unions guilty of racial discrimination.[40] What troubles me is the conceptual identification of the union (or the business firm) with the state, even for good purposes. General Motors and the United Automobile Workers may both be industrial governments far larger than most state governments, but they are not *the* government. They cannot put you in jail or draft you into the army. They can keep you out of a job and ravage your social relations. These powers are weighty enough, but should they bind the company or the union to the exact limitations of conduct prescribed for the old-fashioned sovereign government?

Sometimes the standards imposed on government may be too high, sometimes they may be too low, to meet the needs of union members in either the dominant majority or the complaining minority. Justice Douglas in his *Black v. Cutter* dissent said that a union cannot discriminate against Communists because the government cannot. But that limitation on government is his interpretation of the First Amendment; it does not represent the facts of life. When we compel union adherence to constitutional limitations in the name of "state action," we deny the pluralistic nature of our institutions. Making our theory of government more monolithic is a curious way to achieve the blessings of liberty. To give the courts considerable leeway, letting them pick and choose among useful analogies, might seem, to a man from Mars, an equally curious way to achieve the blessings of liberty. But it is deeply ingrained in our system. I would prefer to let judges experiment with what suits modern conditions of union power and responsibility. They should not be bound to a formula, even the formula of the Bill of Rights.

39. An attempt to apply this view to regulated industries failed in Public Utilities Commission v. Pollak, n. 23 above. Cf. Justice Harlan's dissent in the Civil Rights Cases, 109 U.S. 3 (1883).

40. See Betts v. Easley, 161 Kan. 459, 169 P. 2d 831 (1946), noted *Yale Law Jour.* (1947), *56*:731. But cf. James v. Marinship, 25 Cal. 2d 721, 155 P. 2d 329 (1944).

For, returning to the immediate problem, there is no inclusive formula that solves problems of loyalty for either employers or unions. There should be no hesitation about judicial enforcement of minimal fair procedures in union expulsions. The precedents and analogies are ready at hand, and there seems to be a consensus that a union must be more democratic—or, if you will, less autocratic—than an employer. As for the substantive standards that control the grounds for expulsion or exclusion, the starting point should be broadly the same as the one that evolved for private employers: the union member's political behavior is none of the union's (or the employer's) business. When the member's conflicting loyalties lead him to betray proper union policies, or thwart proper union goals, then the union may discipline him. But what are proper union policies and goals? In comparison with business enterprises, a union, I have said, is more democratic; it is also more political, partly because it is more democratic. How political it can be is still unsettled, and cannot be settled by a simple statute like the one proposed for dealing with arbitrary employers. Is it a proper union policy, justifying disciplinary measures against dissidents, to defeat Wendell Willkie? To protect union leaders from criticism? To defend the closed union? Or the closed shop? To eliminate any trace of communist influence? Of possible communist influence? On these and other problems the guidance of the courts so far has been halting or defective. But the courts in turn need guidance from a coherent and accepted theory of union powers. So far as I can see, there are many theories, but no master plan.

PART IV

Conclusion

19. Observations in Conclusion

A SUMMARY of the recommendations that have been scattered through Parts II and III is now in order, to see if they hang together in any kind of coherent system. Also, there are some programs described in Part I about which no recommendations have yet been made. They still have to be fitted into the proposed system.

SUMMARY OF RECOMMENDATIONS:
SECURITY PROGRAMS

The essential thing to do with security programs is to restrict their coverage. If they affected fewer people, they would be far more tolerable. If we direct attention to the harm that a risky person can do in his job, and do not try to make the programs a means of penalizing people for unpopular politics and sex habits, the number of sensitive positions can be markedly reduced. The most effective single step would be to eliminate screening for access to classified material bearing the "Confidential" stamp. In the industrial security program, the employees requiring access to "Secret" and "Top Secret" data are no more than one-third of the total number now exposed. This is a good illustration of the reduction in coverage that comes from concentrating on really critical positions. The Confidential category would be preserved as part of the mechanics of designating information that is not open to the public. Indeed, some supervision might have to be exercised to assure that the present standards of classification were not debased. There might be pressure to upgrade material from Confidential to Secret for no better reason than to extend once again the reach of personnel screening. Ideally, there should be an overhaul of our information policies designed to reduce the extent of classified material. A reduction in the reach of classification, desirable on its own merits, would further reduce the reach of personnel programs.

In recognition of the fact that the classification system does not take account of all jobs that are security-sensitive, there might be some carefully confined federal authority, perhaps centered in the National Security Council, to identify such positions. This would operate chiefly in

463

two directions: first, to designate those that are significant in policy-making posts in government (though without access to classified material); second, to pinpoint positions, in and possibly out of government, that entail extraordinary risks of sabotage.

With this dominant principle of selective sensitivity in mind, we may review its application to the programs now in being.

1. *Federal civilian employees.* The decision in *Cole v. Young* has checked for the time being the practice of treating all federal employment as subject to security tests. The Court was simply undertaking to interpret an act of Congress, however; another statute or executive order could undo the Court's deft solution. Even if the administration acquiesces in less-than-total coverage, there is still much to be done to assure selectivity along the lines just suggested.

In the administration of the federal employees' program, my central conclusion is that informal administrative discretion is preferable to quasijudicial proceedings. The purpose of a security inquiry is to make a prediction about future reliability. That prediction, it is true, will be based in large measure on the interpretation of the employee's life history, which may involve disputes about facts and the reliability of testimony; formal proceedings are concededly better adapted to resolving such disputes. But the central problem is one of evaluation. Given the employee's whole record (the essential biography will ordinarily not be controverted), is there an inadmissible hazard that he will betray his trust? There seems to be merit in requiring a responsible superior to make this decision, not an independent board, and above all not a security officer.

If security programs are narrowly confined to the special needs of sensitive jobs, a security-risk decision of the sort just described should almost never, in itself, result in the dismissal of a career employee. He should have relocation rights limited only by inability to make any use of his particular skill elsewhere in the government. Of course, if a security investigation turns up a bad criminal record or overt disloyalty or some other substantial disqualification for any place in the Civil Service, then resort could be had to ordinary removal proceedings.

The standards and criteria for retention in sensitive employment need not differ essentially from those currently used, for example by the Atomic Energy Commission. The main changes needed are shifts of emphasis, to make it altogether clear that the criteria, especially those relating to pressure risks and remote associations, are suggestive and not decisive. No mechanical standards are of any use, except for the rare occurrence of such imminent risks as present Communist party membership. The task must be one of over-all appraisal, balancing the derogatory information against the employee's personality, record, and promise.

A responsible superior with any regard for the quality of his staff will give this same balanced attention to security questions when they arise with respect to probationary employees, or to those applicants whom he would like to employ. The only difference should be that the rejected probationer or applicant would have no relocation rights. And a responsible superior with any regard for the morale of his staff would avoid unnecessary suspension, suspension without pay, long delays in decision, and rehashing old charges.

2. *Military personnel.* In Chapter 3 I called the military tests "the most baffling of the federal programs," because of their impact on millions of young men who are involuntarily exposed to them. When one undertakes to prescribe reforms, bafflement does not lessen. Except for the pioneering exploration by Watts, these programs have had the benefit of far less criticism than any other major form of employment test.

As a starting point, the services should review their notions of sensitive military employment. We may agree that the armed forces live intimately with secret weapons, that they hatch secret war plans, that the secret fields of cryptography and cryptanalysis are peculiarly theirs. Moreover, the military mind has long been habituated toward camouflage and concealment. The services had classification systems in being when most of us, in or out of government, were in the position of the late John von Neumann, who observed in the Oppenheimer hearings that "Before 1941, I didn't even know what the word 'classified' meant." [1] Since it would be intolerably difficult to unpeel the protective layers of classification from the military system, I would urge here the same restriction on personnel screening that I have urged elsewhere: keep Confidential as an information classification; screen people only for access to Secret material or above. This one stroke would free much of the military establishment from the chains of sensitivity. It would have these immediate effects on personnel programs: First, a much larger area of usefulness—how large I have no way of knowing—would be opened for uncleared people than now exists. I should surmise that a

1. AEC, *Oppenheimer . . . Hearing* (1954), p. 654.

great many Army conscripts could go through their entire training and service without exposure to anything legitimately classified higher than Confidential.

Second, there would be no necessity for preliminary screening of conscripts, whose basic training is certainly innocent of military secrets. The same observation holds for most volunteers. We should not make too much of the distinction between volunteers and conscripts. Many people enlist under some pressure from the draft. Is there not time after induction to screen those who, after a narrowing of sensitive circles, have to be screened? I realize that the services like to treat men as interchangeable. Here is a company of recruits: so many men for the unclassified infantry, so many for the classified specialties. Even so, only the classified group needs to be investigated; and a file check will pass most of them. Those who are not wanted for sensitive duties should be left alone.

Third, there need be no DD 98 or any other elaborate questionnaire at induction. To be sure, an argument for making such inquiries can be put in these terms: most men entering the services are so young that there are no dossiers on them. If the Army does not ask, how then will it know that the Irving Cohen in its midst is the very one to whom a radical grandfather once gave an IWO insurance policy? And if it does not learn about this blighted gift, how would counterintelligence be led to discover that Irving's older sister had registered in the American Labor party as late as 1946, that his uncle had once held an office in the Furrier's Union, that, in a word, Irving is a potential security risk? All this might pass unnoticed.

The rejoinder is that, unless Irving Cohen is going to be in secret work, these facts need not make one earthly bit of difference.

What about the firm policy of the services not to accept "known Communists"? It seems doubtful that DD 98 or any of its variants helps in enforcing this ban. If by some remote chance Irving Cohen is a Communist, the security agencies should already know it; but if, as sometimes happens, the agencies have slipped up, certainly Irving is not going to expose himself on a DD 98.

The elimination of DD 98 would, in a wonderfully simple way, eliminate the spurious subversive. This person, whom I cannot take seriously, is a military bugbear: the man who hopes to evade military service by condemning himself as disloyal. Here is the simple way to foil him: if the Army does not ask incriminating questions, it will not get Fifth Amendment answers. In all seriousness, no problem in this book has a simpler solution.

If the services insist that all officers must be clearable, provision can be made to screen appointees to the service academies and other officer candidates. A system of open entry would prevail for all others who are carrying out their obligation of short-term service. A large number of men would then proceed through their term unvexed by loyalty inquiries. Those who were put to a security test and found wanting would simply revert to the nonsensitive ranks. If the security questions that had been raised were seriously disquieting, there should be no inhibitions about keeping such risky people under surveillance; one is under surveillance anyhow in the Army. On the other hand, there is no excuse for penalizing doubtful cases by confining them to disagreeable "restricted duty" and to the lowest pay grade, as is done now.

These recommendations do not mean that the security-risk decision should be made secretly. An opportunity to explain and rebut derogatory information, so that one does not become the victim of a dossier compiled entirely by zealous CIC agents, is important. But, as I have recommended for civilian cases, formal proceedings are not essential, if the worst that can happen is retention in nonsensitive duties.

No matter what form security screening takes, one hardship that can and must be eliminated is the less-than-honorable discharge based on security considerations. The argument that the soldier has limited his own usefulness by his associations and affiliations in private life attempts to legitimize a novel assumption of power. In the first place, it is often not factually true; a boy of eighteen cannot choose his relatives, and these are the associations likely to cause him trouble. Second, the argument is backward; it is the Army, not the soldier, that erects exaggerated security standards, and then penalizes behavior that is in no way criminal. The only way for the services to avoid judging events and attitudes that are outside their competence is to measure the quality of a discharge strictly by the man's deportment, diligence, and fidelity during his term of service.

This limitation—which I view as essential to our constitutional subordination of the military to the civilian sphere—applies with equal force to the period after active duty. The uncertain status of a reservist, if it must be retained, should not subject the veteran to continued surveillance, especially with regard to his political activities. If the services don't want someone in the reserves, they can at any time give him a final and honorable discharge. The notion that a man can be required to answer to the military for his beliefs and associations for six years *after* his compulsory service, under pain of a discriminatory discharge, is wholly alien to our traditions. The whole military–civilian relationship will be healthier if the services abandon this further assumption of power.

Of course the forces want all their men to be patriots; we all do; we do not use mercenaries of divided loyalty. If a man commits some disloyal act while he is in uniform, then he can be tried and punished, and he can be given a discharge commensurate with the gravity of the offence. But if the Army wants to dismiss him because it has established a disloyal state of mind (but no disloyal acts), the character of the service the man has rendered must still be the controlling consideration in characterizing that service. None of these short-term soldiers can demand to stay in uniform; the services can reject, or dismiss, pretty much when they choose. The situation of the career soldier is different. Career officers especially (and, nowadays, some reserve officers) achieve an elaborate kind of tenure; part of the price of that status may be the hazard of dishonorable dismissal for a disloyal state of mind. But I gravely doubt that this power should exist with respect to citizens who are only for a time part of the military establishment. The implications of permitting professional military people to pass judgment on the state of mind of civilians are too disquieting, especially when that judgment, in the form of a less-than-honorable discharge, will follow them into civil life.

The Army was severely criticized for giving the notorious Major Peress an honorable discharge, when it appeared that perhaps he was a Communist. The Army did not have to take Dr. Peress in the first place; it did not have to keep him. But if he had not told the Army any punishable lies, if he had not engaged in any forbidden political activity while he was in uniform, if he had faithfully filled teeth at Camp Kilmer and carried out his orders, then he was entitled to an honorable discharge. In the Peress case the Army was right.

3. *Government contractors.* The primary point here is this. While the protection of defense materials from sabotage and espionage is a responsibility both of the government and of the contractor, personnel security decisions ought to be a governmental responsibility. Only government agencies have (or should have) access to counterintelligence information; only through some centralized government screening is any consistency of policy and of decision likely to be found. This puts

government, especially the Defense Department and the Atomic Energy Commission, in the position of controlling access to many areas of private employment. Consequently there is a strong case for giving the employee the protection of a formal proceeding. But the kind of judgment needed is still an over-all prediction of reliability, not well attained in a proceeding organized like a court. Therefore I would carry into the contractor area essentially the same technique that should be used for government employees, coupled firmly with the same safeguard of protecting the employee from outright dismissal. This is harder to administer in the private sphere. You can shift a career civil servant from the Air Force to Interior, but you cannot require General Foods to take on someone who has been let go by General Dynamics. The contracting agencies will have to intrude on the personnel policies of contracting companies, to see that there is no discrimination against security risks in available nonsensitive jobs. This does not mean that the employer has to retain a man somewhere in the enterprise *because* he is a security risk. It means that the facts creating the risk must not lead to dismissal unless dismissal would follow from the same facts in an ordinary nonsensitive case.

There is a difficulty here in applying the concept of decision by a responsible superior. The company executive is hardly equipped to bear the responsibility; and the fiat of security officers should not be the last word. The best suggestion I can make is for the contracting agencies to designate a panel of responsible citizens around the country, after consultation with management and labor representatives in the area. One member of the panel will conduct an informal hearing when the employee so desires. Such persons—call them "security referees"—would have a degree of detachment, and should command respect for their decisions. The head of the contracting agency would retain ultimate control; but the rarity of his intervention would be the index of a successfully operating system.

When a university undertakes classified contract work for the government, it creates special problems for itself. Faculty members have to be cleared to work on such projects; denials of clearance, if they occur, raise embarrassing questions of the man's status in the ordinary work of a department, and of government intervention in the university's selection of its staff. Of greater concern, secret projects which cannot be discussed or published are contrary to the very idea of a university. For these reasons, some observers have urged government to take its

classified research elsewhere,[2] and Harvard University refuses to accept
such contracts. I believe this position is a proper one, but a university
administration may equally decide that it owes this contribution to the
national defense, or that it will lose valued faculty members if the work
has to be done elsewhere. In such cases, great care should be taken to
ensure that security measures do not penetrate the ordinary life of the
place.

4. *The Port Security program and other private employment.* The
Port Security program in its present form should be abolished. If it is
necessary to have a limited group of seafaring men screened because they
handle critical cargoes or are involved in classified military transport
operations, perhaps it would be possible to select them from among
naval reservists who have voluntarily assumed the obligation of obtaining clearance. This leaves all routine maritime employment open, as it
should be.

If any other area of private employment raises extraordinary hazards
of espionage or sabotage, government intervention would be possible by
means of a statute requiring those engaged in the field to obtain a federal
license. The denial of such a license ought to be accomplished only
through proceedings of a formal character, with full due process. However, this kind of intervention in private employment, even with elaborate safeguards, ought to be avoided. The experience of the Port Security
program has been so unsatisfactory, and the only serious legislative
proposal, the Butler bill, was so loosely drawn, that one is entitled to
grave qualms about government action that reaches beyond government's employees or contracts. Whatever danger exists ought to be
guarded against by the old-fashioned methods of counterespionage and
countersabotage.[3]

5. *State and municipal security programs.* There is a theoretical
case that certain groups of nonfederal civil servants, for example po-

2. Dr. Merle A. Tuve, who directed the wartime development of the proximity fuse, has advocated the removal of all secret military research from colleges and universities, primarily because he thinks that federal subsidy inevitably
results in an "enormous distortion in subject matter emphasis." See NYT, July 10,
1953; and Tuve, "Technology and National Research Policy," BAS (1953), 9:290.
A committee of the American Council on Education also fears this "imbalance,"
and has further recommended that classified work be physically isolated. A.C.E.,
Sponsored Research Policy of Colleges and Universities (1955), esp. ch. 3.

3. These observations apply also to a proposal of The Commission on Government Security, *Report* (1957), pp. 499–516, that a civil air transport security
program be established. See Brown, "Regression in the Wright Report," BAS
(1957), *13*:253.

licemen, hold sensitive positions because of their responsibility for public order and their involvement in civil defense planning. Similarly, municipal water supply and other vital services might be prime targets for sabotage. State governments, with cooperation from the federal internal security agencies, could administer programs for some of their employees without creating any new problems of legal power. But they would be creating new security programs, programs we have been getting along very well without. New York state purports to have had a security program for six years; its accomplishments have been unimpressive. It may be argued that this function has been fulfilled in other states by loyalty programs, and that if these programs were abolished, limited security programs would be necessary in their stead. The available information on the operation of state and local loyalty tests does not suggest that they have unearthed many dangerous characters in vital public services. Until a much greater need for such state security programs is demonstrated, one can abstain from further speculation about their proper administration.

6. *Government measures toward labor unions.* The Taft-Hartley non-Communist oath for labor union officers has doubtless made some contribution to the decline of communist influence in trade unions, now that a number of successful perjury prosecutions has demonstrated its effectiveness, in the sense that obvious evasion of the oath is no longer prudent. Whether the imposition of this oath was or is a desirable policy is another matter. Its justification on security grounds has only tenuous support. A majority of the Supreme Court nevertheless upheld the constitutionality of the oath in its ban on membership in the Communist party; the Court was evenly divided on the validity of that part of the oath which requires an abjuration of belief in violent overthrow. The effect of the oath is limited to denying access to the National Labor Relations Board by a union whose officers are not in compliance. However narrow the field of application, and no matter what judicial sanction the measure has obtained, I think it is a dangerous extension of a bad device. With this oath government reached into a private sphere where, as it turned out, self-corrective measures were already in the making. Certainly, now that communist power in the labor movement is minute, Congress should repudiate this assumption of power and repeal the oath provision.

The 1954 amendments to the Internal Security Act represented an even more drastic attempt by the Congress to do for labor unions what they were already doing for themselves. In Chapter 3 it was noted that proceedings to designate two unions as "Communist-infiltrated" have started on their way through the Subversive Activities Control Board and the courts. In view of the constitutional doubts which spring from every cranny of the Internal Security Act, there will be a luxuriant growth of issues to be hacked away before the validity of this measure is clarified. Congress could foreclose a lot of litigation, and correct a major intemperance, by repealing this measure too. It is surprising that the democratic labor unions have not pressed harder to be rid of this ungainly crutch.

7. *The accumulation of dossiers.* Even if personnel security programs were slimmed down to the extent that I have recommended, an inevitable by-product of those that remained would be a vast busy-ness of investigation and of assembling dossiers. Normal employment turnover, and the passage of time, will add more millions of files to the millions already accumulated. The mere existence of unfavorable information often bars an outsider from the whole classified world. How can the thwarted applicant straighten out a distorted dossier, when he does not know what is in it? One solution calls for a new remedy—an administrative or judicial action to open up the file enough for the subject to add his own corrections or excuses. With safeguards against applications that are frivolous or in bad faith, such a proceeding represents a bad-tasting but wholesome medicine against a security measure that reduces the individual to a bundle of police reports.

In this proposed proceeding, and in all the surviving security programs (except where I have specifically called for formal due process) I have reluctantly accepted the practice of protecting investigative sources, so that a partial denial of confrontation will often occur. This is tolerable only if the programs are limited in their scope to truly sensitive areas. This concession of inadequate confrontation is made on the assumption that a man barred from sensitive work after informal proceedings will normally have adequate opportunities to practice his profession or trade elsewhere. But some fields, we must realize, will be almost entirely inside the clearance barrier. A young man who wants to make a career in missile development must recognize this fact and order his life accordingly. At least he can foresee the inevitability of having to obtain clearance; and if he does not like that prospect, he had better choose another calling. The security vise of the last decade squeezed hardest on those who had grown up in an unclassified world, had lived and thought as they pleased, and had then found their talents in demand only if they could satisfy the austere morality and orthodox politics of the new classified society.

SUMMARY OF RECOMMENDATIONS: LOYALTY PROGRAMS

The desirable thing to do with loyalty programs is to get rid of them. I will recapitulate the general arguments that lead to this conclusion at the end of this chapter. But first the more moderate proposals that were made in Part III should be reviewed, so that some loose ends can be tied in along the way. I am now, by definition, talking about nonsensitive employment.

1. *Government employees, including teachers.* As long as there is a widespread and deeply held public feeling against Communists in public employment, that feeling is entitled to some expression. There is no denial of constitutional right in closing government jobs to people who will not support our form of government, or whose primary allegiance is to another government. Whether Communists lack this qualification of minimum loyalty seems a rather pointless dispute at this stage of history. We have enough problems in dealing with the individual case, especially in avoiding unfair identifications, without re-assessing the entire communist movement at every turn. If ever communism ceases to be revolutionary and antidemocratic—that is, if it becomes something different from communism—we can modify our public estimates and policies accordingly.

The problem is one of administration. It seems to me undesirable to take special measures to detect communist disloyalty in nonsensitive employment. By "special measures" I mean anything beyond the routine safeguards that are taken to detect other serious disqualifications for employment. It is proper to advise applicants that Communists are ineligible, and to have them state that they are not Communists, just as they would be expected to state that they had not been dishonorably discharged from the armed forces. It is proper to bring removal proceedings against incumbents who commit acts of disloyalty on or off the job. But to investigate the beliefs and associations of every civil servant or prospective civil servant, because of the remote probability that something might turn up, is unnecessary and repressive. To require periodic loyalty oaths is unnecessary and humiliating.

If a removal proceeding for disloyalty becomes necessary, nothing less than full due process, including confrontation, will suffice. A removal proceeding under these circumstances is not an estimate of future suitability; it is a trial for disloyalty; and the stigma arising from an adverse decision is enough to justify the requirement of due process. I do not suggest that unique arrangements have to be made for loyalty cases. Many civil-service removal procedures already satisfy due process. Those that do not ought to be corrected, not just for loyalty cases, but for any charge of grave misconduct.

2. *Employees of international organizations.* The federal government operates one loyalty program not for its own employees. That is the process of investigating, hearing, and making advisory reports on American employees of international organizations. If special circumstances ever called for such a program, they have been satisfied by the review of all the Americans now employed by the United Nations and its related agencies. We stand alone among democratic nations in taking this nervous attitude about our citizens. The familiar delays of clearance have prejudiced American candidates for positions in international organizations. This program should be abolished.

3. *Licensed trades and professions.* The intrusion of political tests of any character into occupational licensing is pointless. The one exception, where it can be said that revolutionary views or conduct are relevant to professional fitness, is the legal profession. Even here there is no necessity for systematic inquiry into beliefs. Every lawyer takes an oath to defend the Constitution (which is why it is inappropriate for him to advocate its overthrow). If he violates this oath in his professional or public conduct, he can be disciplined.

4. *Private employers.* We have to put up with a certain amount of inequity and caprice in the private employment relationship unless we are prepared to make a major inroad on the traditional freedom of that relationship. No broad support for close government control of private political tests is likely to appear. I do suggest that a type of statute now in existence in about half the states might well be extended and improved. It would condemn discrimination in employment on account of lawful political activities of employees. An aggrieved employee could bring a civil action for lost pay and could demand reinstatement from his employer. Such a statute, either by its terms or by implication, would permit the employer to justify a dismissal if the employee's politics were relevant to his job, or to the maintenance of a reasonable relation of confidence between employer and employee. For example, an importer should not have to put up with a vice-president who campaigns for higher tariffs. The statute would also partially protect the employer and

the employee from outside pressure. A boycott could not be legal if its aim was to make the employer discriminate illegally.

The protection of this statute would end at the uncertain margin of criminal sedition. It would thus not protect the Communist or other radical whose activities were criminally punishable.

Labor unions could if they chose be far more effective on behalf of their members, if they would contest dismissals or exclusions from private employment based on flimsy charges and trumped-up pressures. But they have their own house to put in order first.

5. *Labor union employment and membership.* A simple statute will not fit the complexities of labor union membership. Because the political role of labor unions is not crystallized, I cannot say with any decisiveness what political demands they may properly make on their members. Since there is already a practice of limited judicial intervention to protect the rights of union members (and of union organizations in relation to each other), I have suggested that the step-by-step approach of judicial decision was best fitted to this area.

Meanwhile, the blanket exclusion of Communists or members of any other disfavored group from union membership should be discountenanced. The control over employment opportunities which union membership often entails makes automatic exclusion a powerful sanction, one that should be sparingly used and closely controlled.

Employment within unions, as an officer or staff member, stands on a somewhat different footing. The severe consequences for union prestige and legal status that result from communist domination make it appropriate for unions to protect themselves against this hazard.

6. *Loyalty oaths.* The case against the test oath and its oppressive manifestations in our history have been portrayed so eloquently by others [4] that I have made no systematic attempt to add to the condemnation of this device, nor will I now. The test oath is a form of intellectual coercion that singles out a particular heresy for ritual condemnation without contributing anything to its detection and correction. It seems to be true that some people do not mind periodically raising their right hand and attesting to a variety of things that they are not, have not been, and will not be. That others regard such exercises as humiliating, the willing oath-takers find hard to understand. But our current experience with loyalty oaths shows once again that those who refuse to sub-

---

4. E.g. Justice Black, dissenting in American Communications Ass'n v. Douds, 339 U.S. 382, 445 (1950); Zechariah Chafee, Jr., Foreword to Barth, *The Loyalty of Free Men* (1951), p. xxx.

scribe to them are more often than not people of stout conscience whom we should cherish rather than punish. Test oaths stand in glowering contrast to simple affirmations of fidelity, like the oath to support the Constitution that we expect of officer-holders. Oaths that require a series of denials and abjurations are a symptom of disunity and distrust.

7. *Evading real issues of loyalty.* A suggestion that we are not altogether clear in conscience or purpose on all these issues arises from the frequent resort in loyalty and security cases to what I described as major side issues: unwillingness to inform, pleas of self-incrimination, and falsehoods. All these traits of behavior may be relevant, and sometimes they may be decisive. In a touchy security case, even doubts about reliability may be disqualifying. But there is, I think, a tendency to evade the hard problem of judging loyalty by setting up immoderately high standards of cooperation, candor, and veracity. There is such a thing as too much virtue; its face is hypocrisy. What I chiefly urge is that we should not hold the individuals implicated in loyalty tests to higher standards of conduct than we ordinarily expect in human affairs. It is hard enough for a man to have to defend his loyalty without having to make himself out a saint as well. This same observation applies to the standards of personal morality that figure in security cases. Finally, those of us who think we are free of intolerance and hypocrisy should look inward to see if we honestly judge the competence and skill of employees or colleagues whose politics we mistrust. A suspicion of political heresy, like the suspicion of religious heresy in another age, may cloud the clearest judgment. A man is not entitled, except in charity, to have his peers altogether forget his political follies. But his aberrations, if such they are, should be weighed scrupulously when we drop them into a determination of his capacity, whether as a mechanic or as a professor. A man may hold quite unpopular views about peace petitions, reincarnation, or vivisection, and still be a competent mechanic or professor.

A Last Word on Security Tests

Security programs, within their proper sphere, are essentially an application of strict standards for employment, standards that are justified by the needs of a particular job. The harm that the job-holder can do, through such gross crimes as espionage and sabotage, or more subtly by deflecting policy and public opinion in directions harmful to the national interest, are proper considerations in weighing a man's fitness for the job.

The more responsible and critical the job, the more we can demand in the way of a good record, good judgment, and general trustworthiness. And the kind of security that we are seeking, security against betrayal, necessarily requires an appraisal of political reliability. I have already suggested how these appraisals should be made, so as to give a reasonable assurance against betrayal. This kind of security, like all human desires, can never be made absolute. It is not even desirable to aim for absolute security, because the cost is too high. No matter what substitute openings we make for those who cannot pass the clearance barrier, we do them some injury; and we injure ourselves in failing to make use of the special talents and inventiveness that some unorthodox persons possess to a high degree. Further, so long as the population of the classified world is numbered in the millions, the barriers that surround it surely cast a shadow on the thoughts and associations of other millions, including everyone from college students to machinists. Hardly anyone can be comfortably certain that he will never need to pass the clearance barriers.

Personnel security programs, like an expensive military establishment, are a necessity that few of us would be bold enough to forego. But just as we economize (I hope) in our military outlays, so we should also economize in our internal security measures. Their cost is measured not cheaply in dollars but in the more precious coin of liberty and dignity. The greatest wrong that is committed in the name of security is to glorify its name. We are repeatedly reminded that security is the primary value in an insecure world, because all the other values we prize, even life itself, depend on America's ability to maintain its defenses and those of the rest of the free world. Therefore, we are told, if security demands that we give up this or that portion of individual freedom, we have no effective choice but to comply.[5]

This is false reasoning. Security does not demand anything. Security is an abstraction. It is people, mostly officials, who say what security demands, in terms of air wings, missile programs, and employment tests. The rest of us do not have to accept these demands unquestioningly. If the spokesmen for security want too many dollars, we protest; but we have acquiesced in extravagant demands to invade the pasts, the privacy,

5. See, e.g., Paul Sweeney, Review, *Northwestern Univ. Law Rev.* (1956), *51*:81: "There seems to be no dispute as to the necessity for some kind of a security program. On that all agree. It necessarily follows that national security must be the prime objective and that the right of the individual—fair play if you will—must give way where it conflicts with the national interest."

and the minds of millions of our fellows. We can see the dollars going from every pay-check; it is harder to see the freedoms going.

To state every problem in terms of what security demands is wrong; it would be equally wrong to counter with abstractions about what freedom demands. Indeed, the issues do not always have to be posed, as they so often are, in terms of security against freedom. The two values may often conflict, but they are not antithetical. Sometimes they correspond. The security of achievement, for example, rests on bold and inventive minds, on free minds.

The great analytical difficulty is that there are no accurate measuring sticks for either security or freedom, let alone one commensurate unit that will fit both.[6] Consequently, we blunder along, trying to maximize security and, I would urge, trying to maximize freedom as well. As with most public issues that can't be expressed in dollars, we have to rely on rhetoric and intuition and a little logic to express our preferences. What we need, since no precise accounting is possible, is agreement among those who deal with the personnel security problem that claims in the name of security are not to be automatically honored. They may have to compete with claims on whose behalf other weighty symbols are invoked, such as freedom, dignity, and privacy. I have seen little to suggest that security needs are likely to be undervalued. Lest they be overvalued, we should keep in mind the aphorism used by Franklin, "They that can give up essential liberty to obtain a little temporary safety deserve neither liberty nor safety." [7]

FEAR AND ANGER GENERATE LOYALTY TESTS

Loyalty tests are supported by no valid arguments of necessity. The accuracy of this judgment depends, to be sure, on how loyalty tests are defined. The lines between security needs and loyalty demands are not in practice drawn as sharply as I have drawn them, nor are they drawn through the same points. Defenders of many loyalty tests say that security needs justify them too. The reaction to the Supreme Court's interpretation of "national security" in *Cole v. Young* illustrates the area of controversy. The Court said that Congress in enacting P.L. 733 had

6. See Morris Solomon, "A Statistician Looks at the Employee Security Problem," *Personnel Administration* (July 1955), p. 30, for an approach to this problem by way of the techniques of quality control.

7. Burton Stevenson, *Home Book of Quotations* (1934 ed.), p. 1106. See also ASS'N OF THE BAR, REPORT, pp. 43–5, on this theme.

in mind only considerations of military security and defense. Representative Walter promptly proposed that Congress declare its intention to equate security with the national welfare. He wanted Congress to underwrite the proposition that any federal jobholder of doubtful loyalty would probably try to injure the country, and should therefore be excluded from any opportunity to do so.[8] This proposition, sometimes confined in its application to jobholders of established disloyalty, sometimes extended to cases of mere suspicion and conjecture, is a main prop for loyalty tests.

When one examines the capacity for harm of the principal groups of employees to whom this argument has been applied, even the strongest cases boil down to the following. Aside from the opportunity simply to bungle the job, a form of sabotage which could be detected and penalized when it occurred, the disloyal jobholder—let us get back to our prime example, the Communist—could, in a nonsensitive position:

(1) use his job as a propaganda platform;

(2) use the prestige of his position to add weight to communist causes;

(3) use the income from his job to support communist causes.

The first possibility is particularly open to teachers and writers of all sorts; the second to idols of the entertainment world; the third is generalized, and, if I may say so, trivial. If American communist enterprises, lacking money, could do anything effective if they had more money, support would doubtless be forthcoming from Moscow. In any event, cutting off a man's income in order to cut off his donations is too drastic a remedy. The second possibility, the use of big names to magnify small causes, is an open operation vulnerable to exposure. Though one could speculate about the effectiveness of a movie star's endorsements of communism, the question is really absorbed in the larger issue of communist propaganda. What steps should we take to counteract either overt or covert indoctrination? Are employment programs a legitimate way to counter what we consider subversive influence?

The current solution, that we remove from their jobs people who *might* advocate communist doctrine, aims to deprive those people of

8. See NYT, June 13–15, 1956, on the immediate reactions to Cole v. Young, 351 U.S. 536 (1956). A letter of July 5, 1956 (mimeo.), from Chairman Young of the CSC to the House Committee on Post Office and Civil Service endorsed the Walter bill, H.R. 11721, and suggested quite incorrectly that the government had no other means of protecting itself from disloyal persons in nonsensitive jobs. Commission on Government Security, *Report* (1957), p. 37, has only excerpts from this letter.

any platform for propaganda. This is an appalling confession of weakness. Are many of us afraid of communist ideas? "The Russians," one observer has said, "act on the assumption that nearly all Soviet citizens are so weak-minded that their belief in Communism and loyalty to their country would be corrupted by any first-hand contact with the non-Communist west." [9] Do we act on a similar assumption that American citizens will be corrupted by exposure to communist teachings?

It is a never-ending cause of wonder that doctrines so discredited, so unsuccessful, so alien should at the same time be so feared. We are right to fear Russian aggression. But communist propaganda! We might as well fear Mohammedan propaganda, for all the effect it is likely to have. Nevertheless, the fear exists. It probably stems in large part from exaggeration of the power of any propaganda, derived from a misconception of the effects of advertising and the influence of the mass media. Our own publications, and our own advertisers, appeal to existing desires and values. Because most of us are predisposed to a comfortable life, we are willing to listen to the proponents of bigger and better things to buy. A national editorial campaign for austerity would have very little effect. Similarly, when communist propaganda achieved limited successes in this country, it did so at times, especially during the war, when many had an image of Soviet Russia that was not a hostile one. Now our attitude is one of almost universal hostility and suspicion. The notion that apologists for communism could make any significant impression, in the face of these attitudes and of the overpowering volume of counterargument that our spokesmen make, must stem from the special feeling, which I have mentioned before, that communism is uniquely virulent. A healthy mind that can throw off campaign oratory and television commercials with equal ease sickens at the slightest injection of Marxism.[10]

If we needed a rebuttal to these neurotic alarms, the experience of the Korean prisoners of war provides an overpowering one. Here were thousands of Americans, half-starved and apparently forsaken, who were

9. Lord Lindsey, quoted in ISC, Hearings, *Institute of Pacific Relations* (1952), p. 5386.
10. Edward Shils, *The Torment of Secrecy* (1956), ch. 4, has a more complex analysis of the roots of our recent alarms, which includes such elements as xenophobia and populism. On the fear of indoctrination see Stouffer's findings that most people are more alarmed about communist propaganda than they are about espionage. *Communism, Conformity, and Civil Liberties* (1955), pp. 157–65. On the limitations of propaganda see any text on psychological warfare, and Joseph Klapper, *The Effects of Mass Media* (1950).

subjected to such concentrated propaganda that we had to have a new word for it—brainwashing. True, the source was a hated captor, not a friendly teacher; but the captor had a monopoly position, with all known techniques of persuasion at his disposal—including force. The lesson of that grim episode is not that so many broke but that so few did, and that only twenty-one actually embraced the communist way of life and chose to stay behind.

There is a more palatable explanation than fear for our orgy of loyalty tests. Much of the support for them has stemmed from indignation— or annoyance, or hatred, depending on the extent to which the individual's emotions were engaged. There is nothing discreditable about honest anger, so long as it is kept within bounds. The problem is to delimit the ways in which a civilized democratic society may properly vent its indignation. Specifically, how far should we use deprivations of employment as a way of expressing our anger at communist disloyalty?

One extreme position regards the disloyal as outlaws; they have no rights. As we saw in Chapter 13, there have been formal expressions of this position in legislation. I have no use for a theory that seeks to expel a group of Americans from the human race. It denies the possibility of redemption; and it grossly overstates the guilt of many if not most of those who have been penalized by employment tests.

The abiding elements in our law do not make such a drastic condemnation. Communist disloyalty, I have argued, is essentially political, in that it grows out of a struggle for power; and the law naturally distinguishes between lawful and unlawful means of pursuing political goals. Thus bribery, stuffing ballot boxes, threats of force, and incitements to force are criminally punishable. On the other hand speech, even disloyal speech, unless it is directed to carrying out one of these forbidden means, is not criminally punishable.

The line between legality and criminality is one at which employment tests may reasonably come into play. One may argue that the criminal punishment exacts the full "debt to society." On the other hand, there are fields of employment from which a record of political crime is reasonably disqualifying. Even if the state has failed to act against the supposed offender, the rest of the community is not required to treat him as a member in good standing. The presumption of innocence can be dispelled by other processes than a criminal trial. Here the importance of decent procedures becomes evident. If an employer is reasonably convinced that the employee has joined an illegal conspiracy, he does not have to wait for a jury verdict of guilty. But he ought not to act on rumor or prejudice, and he ought not to run ahead of the field and establish new standards of conduct.

These cases deriving from criminal conduct are fairly easy; it is essentially a matter of individual choice whether an employer adds employment deprivations to those of fine and imprisonment. He may not want to have anything further to do with a man whose offense implies disloyalty. On the other hand, the employer may disagree with the verdict, or decide that the offense was trivial, or that it has been atoned.

But the cases where criminal punishment would be constitutional and appropriate are not the ones that are troubling. The true test of our civilized behavior is found in our treatment of people who are guilty of no crime that can be punished constitutionally, but who are still our opponents in a struggle for power, or have been opponents, or sympathize in varying ways with our opponents. This is the chronic problem— loyalty tests that, having started with real Communists, ricochet into ex-Communists, near Communists, possible Communists, and relatives and acquaintances of Communists.

THE SEVERITY OF EMPLOYMENT PROSCRIPTIONS

Before generalizing about the use of tests in these borderline circumstances, a final estimate of their severity should be attempted. The "right to work," as an abstract value, has a high place in modern constitutions and catalogs of human rights. Thus we have General George C. Marshall, when Secretary of State, declaring that "To us, a society is not free if law-abiding citizens live in fear of being denied the right to work or deprived of life, liberty, and the pursuit of happiness." [11] Such a statement is attuned to our expectations of economic security. Moreover, the "right to work" implies some freedom of choice of occupation and of employer, with the self-respect that such a freedom creates.

Recognition of the right to work as one index of a free society carries us a little way toward measuring the inhumanity of recent barriers to employment. If the loyalty barriers were more extensive than they have been, we might seriously assert that employment tests were worse than jail. Alan Barth quotes J. S. Mill that "Men might as well be imprisoned as excluded from the means of earning their bread"; and in jail you at

11. Quoted in Zechariah Chafee, Jr., *The Blessings of Liberty* (1956), p. 63. See Amos Peaslee, *Constitutions of Nations* (1956), 1:7.

least get your bread.[12] Furthermore, prison sentences even for Communist leaders have been fairly short, while no one yet knows how long the displaced persons of the last decade will be kept out of their chosen professions. However, the deprivations of employment tests, by and large, have been rather less than total. On most victims loyalty tests have imposed a degree of economic hardship, a degree of psychic injury, a degree of wasted talents, a degree of misfortune for wife and children. The deprivations vary from occupation to occupation, and from individual to individual. But if we keep in mind that we are now talking about sanctions against people whom we would not think it decent to imprison, we should ask ourselves whether the imposition of any of these hardships is defensible. We are angry at such people, and punish them because they express beliefs and preferences that the majority repudiates. But so long as the minority seeks to advance its beliefs through lawful forms of expression and political agitation, cannot the majority confine itself to similar weapons?

Fear or anger—either motivation for loyalty tests is a common human trait, but neither emotion excuses a retreat from first principles. Loyalty tests for employment, for passports, for pensions, all these devices betray our unwillingness, for one reason or another, to fight propaganda with better propaganda, and ideas with better ideas.

Yet it is not enough to denounce the loyalty programs of the last decade as un-American, and to speak respectfully of the right to work. The employer has some rights too. Solicitude for free discussion does not require us to ignore either incompetence or the asperities of human relations. "I do not like thee, Dr. Fell . . ." is often as near as the parties can come to explaining a discordant relationship. But if Dr. Fell is disliked because he was born black, or has joined a union, or—I would say—because he holds unpopular political views—then there should be *some* restraints on the privilege of the government, or of a private employer, to dismiss him. The need for some measure of control is enhanced when the dismissal is accompanied by the stigma of disloyalty.

THE SEARCH FOR GUIDING PRINCIPLES

We have found, however, that neither law nor custom gives us many settled answers for the techniques and limits of desirable restraints in

12. Barth, *The Loyalty of Free Men* (1951), p. 124; cf. p. 9.

loyalty cases. Where shall we find guidance? In a way, the uncertainty of our answers is a testimony to novel stirrings of the national conscience. The reason why history provides little guidance may be that in the past we have been more ruthless about such matters than we aspire to be in the future.

The lawyer inclines to put his trust in the courts and the Constitution. But we should not expect the courts to carry the whole burden, and in the last decade, lacking leadership from the Supreme Court, the courts have done very little. Even in demanding the elements of procedural due process, an issue on which the judges should be most decisive, their role has been timorous. This is deplorable; but it is not surprising, when the executive, the legislature, and the people have all been hell-bent for repression. Now, as we learn to live with the cold war, there has been some reduction of internal tension, and the judiciary will perhaps take a modest lead. Its capacity for reform is, however, limited. There are few constitutional imperatives in the field of employment tests, and the evolution of new imperatives is a cautious process; witness the twenty-year gestation of the principle that racial segregation in public education cannot lawfully exist. Whether our guidance is to come from the spirit or the letter of the Constitution, the other branches of government have a responsibility equal to the courts'. If statutes and executive orders were properly conceived and executed, the courts would have little to do.[13]

The ultimate responsibility patently lies on all of us. First and last this is a problem of democratic self-restraint. I assume that our democratic theory does not rest on the naked power of majorities. Through the Constitution, the majorities of any given moment have undertaken to withhold some of their power to repress minorities. But when unstable world politics threaten the survival of a life of abundance and promise, we throw off self-restraint. Those who are not for us are against us. Radicals, once tolerated, become disloyal subversives. The ancient weapons of repression are unsheathed. The Bill of Rights, we are told, would probably fail of re-enactment today. No single manifestation of this spirit, whether employment tests, or prosecutions for sedition, or

13. See Alan Westin, "A Critique of Civil Libertarian Reactions to the 'Communist Problem,'" *Northwestern Univ. Law Rev.* (1955), *50*:58, criticizing the "court-seeking psychology." On the obligation of all branches of government to provide leadership see John Lord O'Brian, *National Security and Individual Freedom* (1955), p. 83.

banishment, is likely to be checked in its course until responsible opinion calls a halt all along the line.[14]

It would, however, be naive to suppose that "all of us," even though we are responsible as citizens, are going to experience a spontaneous impulse to reform. Many are, and always will be, indifferent to these problems. Others consciously or unconsciously reject toleration. Confident of their own absolutes, they find virtue in imposing conformity. There remain the large numbers who, though they have a strong concern for individual freedom and dignity, have been overawed. Chilled by the insecurity of the atomic age, they have not questioned the demands that have been made in the name of security. Valuing loyalty, they have not challenged specious definitions of disloyalty. Detesting communism, they have swallowed the excesses of anticommunism. On these people I urge the two dominant conclusions of this book. First, that loyalty and security tests have been practiced with too much rigor and too little humanity. Second, that these tests needlessly impair the great freedoms of belief, of speech, and of association enshrined in the First Amendment.

14. On the large themes of this paragraph see Francis Coker, "Some Present-Day Critics of Liberalism," *Am. Pol. Sci. Rev.* (1953), *47*:1; Robert Dahl, *A Preface to Democratic Theory* (1956), ch. 5 (doubts about the exercise of "majority tyranny"); Learned Hand, "A Plea for the Freedom of Dissent," NYT, *Magazine* (Feb. 6, 1955), p. 12.

Appendix A

DETAILED ESTIMATES OF THE VOLUME OF DISMISSALS

The following tabulations form the basis for the estimated total dismissals discussed at the end of Chapter 6. Some of these figures, and their sources, were given in Chapters 2 to 5. Some other sources are indicated here. Some estimates cannot be documented at all. The available data make the end of 1956 a convenient stopping-place. All totals are rounded.

1. FEDERAL EMPLOYEES

U.S. Civilian Employees to May 1953

Employees' Loyalty Program (1947–53):	560	
Military Departments' civilian security program prior to P.L. 733. The figures in Ch. 2 above, at n. 54, reach back into World War II; as a guess for 1946–50:	150	
State Department alleged homosexuals (1947–53) (see Ch. 11, n. 4):	425	
Dismissals by military and other departments under P.L. 733 (1950–53), combined with summary dismissal powers of State and Commerce Departments (this is a guess; only fragmentary data are available):	500	
Estimated total (all dismissals):		1650

U.S. Civilian Employees 1953–56

Though we know that there were only 343 dismissals under the *procedures* of E.O. 10450 through June 30, 1955 (Ch. 2, at n. 59), many of the other reported separations could have been security cases. As a guess, I will include about half of the reported total of dismissals. That is:		1500

Military Personnel

Army (Nov. 1948–March 1954)	286	
Navy (Jan. 1949–March 1954)	27	
Marines (Jan. 1949–March 1954)	6	
Air Force (May 1949–March 1954)	50	
	369	

The figures given are for discharges from active duty on loyalty grounds, and do not include inactive reservists, "retention in controlled duties," or denials of commissions to doctors and dentists. Of the latter, there were about 50 cases, 1950–54. See Senate Comm. on Armed Services, Hearings, *Doctor Draft Act Amendments* (1954), pp. 14–18, 65, 91, 98–100, 111. Cf. Ch. 3 above, n. 41.

Additional Army cases, July 1, 1954–June 30, 1955 (HENNINGS HEARINGS, pp. 532–3):	207		
Extrapolation through 1956, all branches:	175		
Estimated total, all military personnel:		750	
Estimated total, all federal personnel:			3900

2. FEDERAL PROGRAMS IN PRIVATE EMPLOYMENT

Industrial Personnel Security Program
  Final denials of clearance (July 1949–April 1955) were 960 (HENNINGS HEARINGS, pp. 554, 617). The result here is not necessarily dismissal; as a rough offset to this factor, there were cases back to 1947; and then, through July 1956, there were 75 more denials. Industrial Personnel Security Review Program, *First Annual Report* (1956), p. 29. Take the total as: 1000

Atomic Energy Commission Program
  Dismissals and denials of clearance Jan. 1, 1947 to March 1955 (HUMPHREY HEARINGS, p. 294), were 494. Again, with some allowance for applicants who, having been denied clearance, remained in their previous employment, and with extrapolations through 1956, take the total as: 500

Port Security Program
  Denials of clearance through Dec. 31, 1956, totaled 3783. See ASS'N OF THE BAR, REPORT, p. 221. These were nullified by court action late in 1956, but they had been and perhaps continued to be effective in practice. See Ch. 3 above: 3800

Miscellaneous Federal Programs
  International Organization employees, Public Health Service contracts, Taft-Hartley oath, etc. As a guess: 100

  Estimated total, all federal programs in private employment: 5400

3. STATE AND LOCAL GOVERNMENT PROGRAMS (SINCE ABOUT 1948)

Teachers (school and college) dismissed, mostly for refusals to answer questions or to take loyalty oaths, probably in the neighborhood of: 500

Other public employees dismissed, on similar grounds, or under New York security program, as a guess: 500

  Estimated total, state and local government employees: 1000

4. PRIVATE PROGRAMS (SINCE ABOUT 1948)

(Here my guesses become even more uncertain than in the government programs)

Dismissals of professional people by private employers, or exclusions from the practice of professions (teachers in private institutions, writers, lawyers, doctors), mostly for refusals to answer questions or to take oaths: 200

Operation of blacklists in radio-TV-movies: 300

Dismissals under private industrial security and loyalty programs, estimated at about half the rate of government clearance denials in the Defense Dept. and AEC programs: 700

  Estimated total, all private programs: 1200

  Estimated Grand Total   11,500

Appendix B

TABULATION OF DATA FROM CASE STUDIES
COLLECTED BY THE FUND FOR THE REPUBLIC

AT THE END OF 1954 the Fund for the Republic commissioned Adam Yarmolinsky, Esq. to undertake a collection of cases arising under the various personnel security programs of the United States government. Mr. Yarmolinsky and his associates during 1955 gathered information on 326 cases, the results of which were made available to the Special Committee on the Federal Loyalty-Security Program of the Association of the Bar of the City of New York, and later to the Commission on Government Security. A selection of 50 cases was published in August 1955, by the Bureau of National Affairs, Inc., entitled *Case Studies in Personnel Security*. Data from the entire collection were tabulated statistically by the Bureau of Social Science Research, Inc. of Washington, D.C. under the direction of Robert T. Bower.

At the suggestion of Mr. Yarmolinsky, Mr. Bower and I made a selection of the most significant of these tabulations, which are here presented. They deserve close attention. Since the studies were prepared from information obtained through counsel for the employee, they may not be entirely representative of all contemporary cases, for the reason that a substantial number of employees involved in security cases do not retain counsel. Also, as Mr. Yarmolinsky pointed out in his introduction to the *Case Studies,* "The government file, which was not released to the employee, was also not available to [the] interviewers." Apart from these qualifications, the following tables speak for themselves.

1. PROGRAM UNDER WHICH MAIN PROCEEDING WAS BROUGHT

	No.	Percentage
Public Law 733	10	3
Executive Order 10450	156	48
Military security program	23	7
Industrial security program	88	27
Port security program	27	8
AEC security program	12	4
International Organizations Employees Loyalty Board	9	3
Other	1	*
TOTAL	326	100

* Less than ½ of 1 per cent.

489

2. Occupation of Employee Immediately Before Start of Case

	No.	Percentage
Professional *	141	43
Administrative	38	12
White-collar	79	24
Laborer	51	16
Other	8	2
DK, NA, not applicable †	9	3
TOTAL	326	100

* "Professional" includes doctor, dentist, physician (*not* medical administrator, technician, or nurse); lawyer; teacher, professor; engineer (*not* technician)—mechanical, civil, electrical, etc.; physical or natural scientist; social scientist; professional (unspecified).

† "Employee" unemployed, or not in labor force. DK = Don't Know; NA = No Answer.

3. Salary of Employee Immediately Before Start of Case

	No.	Percentage
Under $3,000 a year	11	3
$3,000– 3,999	19	6
$4,000– 5,999	49	15
$6,000– 7,999	38	12
$8,000– 9,999	27	8
$10,000–11,999	16	5
$12,000–14,999	3	1
$15,000 or over	3	1
Part-time	4	1
DK, NA	151	47
Not applicable	5	1
TOTAL	326	100

4. Employer *

	No.	Percentage
Department of Defense, civilian emp.	61	19
Military service	23	7
Other agencies of U. S. Government	115	35
Private business, industry, shipping	107	33
Academic or nonprofit nonacademic	11	3
International organizations	9	3
TOTAL	326	100

* Project for which clearance was needed, as of start of case.

5. PREVIOUS LOYALTY-SECURITY PROCEEDINGS
BROUGHT AGAINST EMPLOYEE

	No.	Percentage
Interrogatory	46	14
Charges, hearing or both	72	27
No previous proceedings	172	53
Other	26	8
NA	21	7
TOTAL	337	109 *

* More than one proceeding brought against some employees.

6. MOST RECENT YEAR OF ACTIVITY OF EMPLOYEE
REFERRED TO IN ANY CHARGE *
(*excluding allegations of false statements*)

Year	No.	Percentage
1955 or 1954	17	5
1953 or 1952	35	11
1951 or 1950	58	18
1949–1945	117	36
1944–1940	38	12
1939–1935	5	1
1934 or before	—	—
DK, NA	56	17
TOTAL	326	100

* No case in the collection was begun earlier than 1953.

7. STAGE AT WHICH MAIN PROCEEDING BEGAN

Stage	No. of Employees Whose Proceeding Began at Each Stage	Percentage
1. Security interview	42	13
2. Written interrogatory	40	12
3. Formal charges submitted to employee	240	74
4. Hearing	3	1
5. Other	1	*
TOTAL	326	100

8. WITNESSES FOR GOVERNMENT AT FIRST OR ONLY HEARING

	No.	Percentage
One or two	17	5
Three or four	3	1
None	227	70
DK, NA	12	3
No hearing held	67	21
TOTAL	326	100

9. Questions Asked of Employee by Government at Hearing

	No.	Percentage
Employee's views on:		
Socio-economic policies, theories, ideologies other than Marxism or Communism	45	14
Loyalty-Security program in general; criteria of loyalty-security	28	9
Religion, piety, church attendance, atheism	24	7
Perjury, false or inconsistent statements, omissions	23	7
"Cold War" topics (e.g. Korean War, NATO, germ warfare, Marshall Plan, etc.)	18	5
Trade unionism, labor movement in general	18	5
Intergroup relations, race relations, civil rights	15	5
Procedures in employee's case	13	4
Public figures involved in security proceedings (Alger Hiss, Lattimore, the Rosenbergs, etc.)	9	3
Internationalism (interest in the U.N., world government, etc.)	8	2
Pacifism, conscientious objection	3	1
Sexual morality, chastity, continence, etc.	3	1
Civil liberties	2	1
Employee's reading, collection, or subscription to literature	41	13
Employee's family background, education, general interests	37	11
Employee's counteraffirmative case	9	3
Other	37	11
DK, NA	43	13
TOTAL	377	115 *

* Some employees were asked questions in more than one category. No hearing was held in 67 of the 326 cases.

10. Length of First or Only Hearing in Hours

	No.	Percentage
Less than 4 hours	40	12
4–7 hours	40	12
8–15 hours	75	24
16–23 hours	24	8
24 or more	14	4
DK, NA	66	20
No hearing held	67	20
TOTAL	326	100

11. Notice to Employee or Counsel of Result Reached on First Adjudication After Charges

	No.	Percentage
Notice without statement of reasons, except formal	298	91
Notice with statement of reasons, other than formal	11	3
No notice given	5	2
Not applicable	6	2
DK, NA	6	2
TOTAL	326	100

12. Result of First Adjudication After Charges

	No.	Percentage
No decision at last report	3	1
Clearance as full as desired	144	44
Clearance less full than desired	8	3
Denial of clearance	166	51
Decision not given because of employee's resignation or dismissal before first adjudication	3	1
Other	1	*
NA	1	*
TOTAL	326	100

13. Final Result Reached

	No.	Percentage
No decision at last report	14	4
Clearance as full as desired	205	63
Clearance less full than desired	6	2
Denial of clearance	95	29
Decision not given because mooted by employee's resignation or dismissal before final determination	3	1
DK, NA	3	1
TOTAL	326	100

14. Job Status of Employee Between Receipt of Charges in Main Proceeding and End of Case

	No.	Percentage
Not previously employed in job under security program	15	5
Continued on work of same classification	45	14
Given work of lower classification, but not suspended	23	7
Suspended but not discharged *	197	60
Discharged or dismissed	21	6
Other, including resignation	12	4
DK, NA	13	4
TOTAL	326	100

* Suspension was without pay in 194 cases.

15. Months Between Earliest Suspension or Receipt of Charges and Final Decision

	No.	Percentage
Less than 6	125	38
More than 6, less than 12	129	40
More than 12, less than 18	23	17
18 or more	31	10
Not applicable	4	1
DK, NA	14	4
TOTAL	326	100

16. Hours of Counsel's Time

	No.	Percentage
Under 20 hours	42	13
20–49	96	30
50–99	63	19
100–199	38	11
200 or more	15	5
Other and unspecified	16	5
Not applicable	9	3
DK, NA	47	14
TOTAL	326	100

17. Total Fee of Counsel Collected Since Start of Main Proceeding

	No.	Percentage
Free or net loss to lawyer	51	16
Under $100 but not free	9	3
$100–199	36	11
$200–499	80	25
$500–749	36	11
$750–999	19	6
$1,000–1,499	23	7
$1,500 or more	14	4
Fee, or fee and share of restitution, amount unspecified	5	1
Other	1	*
Not applicable	11	3
DK, NA	41	13
TOTAL	326	100

18. Alleged Activities of Employee
(No. of employees against whom allegations were made)

Activity	No.	Percentage of 326 Cases
Communist party and Young Communist League	132	40
Organizations on Attorney General's list, other than C.P. or Y.C.L.	119	36
Organizations on H.U.A.C. list	44	14
Organizations on State U.A.C. list	19	6
Other political activity	227	70
Nonpolitical activity	31	10
Associations	243	75

19. NATURE OF PARTICIPATION OF EMPLOYEE
(against whom Communist party and Young Communist League allegations were made)

Activity	No. of Allegations	Percentage of Total (326)
a. Officer	1	*
b. Member, but not a	71	22
c. Attended meetings, but not a or b	23	7
d. Sponsor or contributor, but not a, b, or c	1	*
e. Other connection and unspecified, not a, b, c, or d	36	11
TOTAL ALLEGATIONS AND CASES	132	40

20. NATURE OF PARTICIPATION OF EMPLOYEE
(against whom allegations were made concerning organizations on Attorney General's list, other than C.P. or Y.C.L.)

Activity	No. of Allegations	Percentage of Total (326)
a. Officer	7	2
b. Member, but not a	77	24
c. Attended meetings, but not a or b	11	3
d. Sponsor or contributor, but not a, b, or c	4	1
e. Other connection and unspecified, not a, b, c, or d	20	6
TOTAL ALLEGATIONS AND CASES	119	36

21. NATURE OF PARTICIPATION OF EMPLOYEE
(against whom allegations were made concerning other political activity)

Activity	No. of Allegations
Signing petitions (e.g. C.P. or A.L.P. electoral or nominating petitions, Stockholm Peace Petition)	20
Membership in or connection with Progressive party or Wallace movement	14
Membership in or connection with "left-wing" organization, subversive status not specified	122
Reading, subscribing to, or collecting literature	87
Political expressions, opinions; reputation as "pink" etc.; alleged political activities, nature unspecified	134
TOTAL ALLEGATIONS	377
TOTAL CASES	227

22. Nature of Participation of Employee
(*against whom allegations were made concerning nonpolitical activities*)

Activity	No. of Allegations
Alcoholism	5
Sexual irregularities	10
Emotional instability, unreliability	23
Incompetence or dereliction of duty	3
Criminal record	13
Perjury, falsity, conflicting statements or omission in formal statements	78
Residence, travel behind Iron Curtain	3
Other unspecified activity	7
TOTAL ALLEGATIONS	142
TOTAL CASES	31

23. Nature of Participation of Employee
(*against whom allegations were made concerning associations*)

	No. of Cases
No personal activity except association	24
Association plus other charges	219
TOTAL CASES	243

24. Alleged Activities of Employee's Associates
(*No. of associates about whom allegations were made*)

Activity	No.
Communist party and Young Communist League	182
Organizations on Attorney General's list, other than C.P. or Y.C.L.	67
Organizations on H.U.A.C. list	19
Organizations on State U.A.C. list	10
Other political activity	134
Nonpolitical activity	16

25. Nature of Participation of Employee's Associates
(*about whom Communist party and Young Communist League allegations were made*)

Activity	No. of Allegations
a. Officer	8
b. Member, but not a	138
c. Attended meetings, but not a or b	6
d. Sponsor or contributor, but not a, b, or c	—
e. Other connection and unspecified, but not a, b, c, or d	30
TOTAL ALLEGATIONS	182

26. Nature of Participation of Employee's Associates
(about whom allegations were made concerning organizations on Attorney General's list, other than C.P. or Y.C.L.)

Activity	No. of Allegations
a. Officer	16
b. Member, but not a	43
c. Attended meetings, but not a or b	1
d. Sponsor or contributor, but not a, b, or c	2
e. Other connection and unspecified, but not a, b, c, or d	5
TOTAL ALLEGATIONS	67

27. Nature of Participation of Employee's Associates
(about whom allegations were made concerning other political activity)

Activity	No. of Allegations
Signing petitions (e.g. C.P. or A.L.P. electoral or nominating petitions, Stockholm Peace Petition)	19
Membership in or connection with Progressive party or Wallace movement	10
Membership in or connection with "left-wing" organizations, subversive status not specified	65
Reading, subscribing to, or collecting literature	32
Political expressions, opinions; reputation as "pink" etc.; alleged political activities, nature unspecified	72
TOTAL ALLEGATIONS	198 *

* Made with respect to 134 associates; see Table 24.

28. Nature of Participation of Employee's Associates
(about whom allegations were made concerning nonpolitical activities)

Activity	No. of Allegations
Alcoholism	—
Sexual irregularities	3
Emotional instability, unreliability	—
Incompetence or dereliction of duty	—
Criminal record	1
Perjury, falsity, conflicting statements or omission in formal statements	1
Residence, travel behind Iron Curtain	5
Other unspecified activity, not political	7
TOTAL ALLEGATIONS	17

Index